THE KIDS WHO GET IN:

A NEW AUTHENTIC APPROACH TO COLLEGE ADMISSIONS

DAAVI GAZELLE

EDITED BY JACK JUNDANIAN

Featuring Real, Successful Applications to Brown, Cal Tech, Columbia, Cornell, Dartmouth, Duke, Harvard, Johns Hopkins, MIT, Northwestern, Notre Dame, Penn, Princeton, Rice, Stanford, U Chicago, UCLA, Vanderbilt, Washington University in St. Louis, and Yale

Contents

What this Book Is 1

Why I wrote this book: 1

Part 1 – A New Approach to College Admissions: 5

What Colleges Actually Want 7

The Old Approach 9

The New Approach: Changing Our Perspective on Admissions 11

The New Approach in Action 13

A Summary of the Two Approaches 17

The Golden Wager 21

Authentic Expression - Using the 20 Entries: 27

The Kids Who Get In: Methodology 29

Part 2 – The Kids Who Get In: 33

Brown University 35

California Institute of Technology 47

Columbia University 63

Cornell University 75

Dartmouth College 89

Duke University 107

Harvard College 117

Johns Hopkins 127

Massachusetts Institute of Technology 137

Northwestern University 153

University of Notre Dame. 163

Princeton University. 177

Rice University 195

Stanford University. 209

University of California Los Angeles 223

University of Chicago. 237

University of Pennsylvania. 251

Vanderbilt University 261

Vanderbilt University - Bonus entry 271

Washington University in St. Louis 285

Yale University 295

Selected Reflections on the Application Process 309

Afterword 317

Copyright

The Kids Who Get In copyright © 2020 by Daavi Gazelle

All rights reserved. No part of this book may be used or reproduced in any manner whatsoever without written permission of the publisher, except in the case of brief quotations embodied in critical articles or reviews.

Dedication:

This book would not have been possible without the help of Dwitt (the Mathwizurd, Mr. Hawaii, Poke Bro #2). Dwitt, you're the man.

Jack Jundanian - one of the coolest dudes I've met. My editor and a beautiful viewpoint into the post grad life aka my life in a couple of years. Thank you for your vision, your help, and a bunch of laughs.

My mom - Gail Gazelle, the real author of the family. For always believing in me and pushing me to get this out there. I love you!

The twenty students who participated in this book. It was a blast getting a window into your lives, and after reading your responses, I feel like I know you. Your openness in sharing your stories helps future generations of students immensely. Thank you.

What this Book Is

There are all kinds of theories about why colleges choose to admit students. There's the idea that colleges want you to be well-rounded ("holistic approach"), and the idea that you should be pointy (being really really good or impressive in one area). Some people argue that colleges want students who will eventually be smashing successes, and bring lots of notoriety to the school (and alumni dollars).

These models presented to us are often contradictory and confusing, and make the admissions process out to be an elusive, unfair game, won by those familiar with its intricacies.

It doesn't help that the only information that exists is partial - stats videos on Youtube, Naviance graphs with absurd outliers, and vague PR statements from elite colleges (half-attempting to ameliorate the mystique, half amplifying it).

This book presents a simpler, more authentic model. And the proof is in the pudding: you'll see exactly what got 20 real life students into 20 of the most prestigious colleges in the United States.

Why I wrote this book:

I wrote this book because I wanted to figure out what actually gets kids into elite colleges. It began as a "cracking the code." I fervently emailed hundreds of students, and spent over a year immersed in admissions. While my college friends moved forward with graduation, and adult plans, I regressed.

I scrolled on r/ApplyingtoCollege, and College Confidential, I reread my own college apps, and I revisited the craze only felt during the fall of an overachiever's senior year of high school.

I remembered how toxic and stressful many aspects of the process were - the competition, the cold, calculated movements of classmates, and the unshakeable feeling that no matter what we're doing, it's not enough. If you're reading this book, you know exactly what I'm talking about.

The years leading up to applying to college can be the worst of your life. It can be easy to get sucked placing an inordinate amount of self-worth on getting into a prestigious college. Life becomes a stressful grind of doing everything that we think these colleges want us to do. And this outward focus prevents us from exploring our own interests and doing what we actually want to do.

But reading through successful applications, and speaking with the kids who got in, I realized that this didn't have to be the case.

Some of the students that I interviewed were stressed throughout high school, and clearly worried a lot about getting into a top college. But other students seemed to have had a healthy, happy high school experience. They did things that interested them, got good grades, and also spent time with friends, watching TV, and getting enough sleep.

It was radical to see - but plenty of the kids who got in weren't world-class overachievers, geniuses, or incredible entrepreneurs. They also (mostly) weren't cookie-cutter variants of the overinvolved college admissions persona. They were memorable, unique individuals - who did high school *their* way, wrote essays that reflected *their* personalities, and got in.

The whole admissions process was flipped on its head. High school didn't have to be cutthroat and toxic - it could actually be centered around personal growth and a heightened sense of self. Time could be spent doing things that we actually care about, and college could be looked forward to as a real chapter of life, not just a name to get into.

I wanted to offer an approach, rooted in the real results of real students, that showed that treating the process this way could actually make it *more* likely that we get in.

That's this book.

This book will show you that you don't have to spend your whole high school experience trying to get into an elite college - that you can actually spend it focusing on what makes you happy.

This book will teach you to focus on yourself, and let go of the stress and competition of the college admissions process.

You'll stress less, and have more time, and paradoxically, you'll have a better shot at getting in.

And you don't have to just take my word for it - you'll see through 20 real, successful applications, exactly what I'm talking about.

If you picked up this book just to read the 20 successful apps, you can turn ahead to the Brown entry and start there. If you're a senior, and it's the night before a deadline, that's probably going to be of the most use. But if you're earlier in your high school career, and have some significant choices about how to spend your high school time ahead of you, keep reading here.

Part 1 – A New Approach to College Admissions:

What Colleges Actually Want

In 2020, the college admissions frenzy has reached a peak. A group of actresses, business leaders, and socialites were caught in an elaborate bribery-scheme to get their children into top colleges; going rate for a private college counselor often exceeds $200 an hour; and several schools have reached a sub 6% acceptance rate.

Applications to each elite college rise annually, as does the fervent competition at America's high schools.

It has become a game of choice - Harvard, Princeton, Stanford, and all of the most selective colleges can fill their first-year class many times over with qualified students.

Elite colleges have their choice of tons of great students, wealthy students, top 1% in the country at [fill in the blank] students. They read applications that are well-rounded, applications that are "pointy," applications that were carefully groomed over dozens of drafts, and applications that were tossed together on midnight of January 1st.

So who do they choose? And why?

In part, elite colleges want future successes, and well-rounded achievers, and single-subject stars. And of course, all of these admits have to be viewed in the context of a class. None of these applications (or human beings) exist in a vacuum - colleges are looking to create a real, thriving community.

Besides being a fuzzy term made to be flaunted on brochures and websites, community is what college is all about. Take away the buildings, the statues, the midterms, the dining halls, the sweatshirts - a college is really just a big group of people.

And colleges have a vested interest in making that as special of a group as possible. They want to admit students that are going to contribute to that group, and make the other people in the group better because of it.

When people say that colleges are creating a class (usually followed by "they want a tuba player from Arizona, and a chess master from Chicago..."), they're half-right. Colleges are looking to build out a dynamic community, and they admit students based on this fact. But college admissions officers aren't playing Animal Crossing or the Sims. They aren't looking to craft some mythical, statistically perfect representation of the different hobbies and passions that a young adult could have. They're looking to assemble a real group of great people.

This means that it's our job to stand out as a special individual worth including in that group - and make sure that our application reflects that.

When reading applications, admissions officers *might* be asking themselves "How much money is this student going to make one day?" "Will this student donate to our school?" "Does this student check the specific mastery box we need checked?"

But they're also people who care about people.

More than the above questions, they're asking "Is this student going to bring a lot to our community?" "Would this be a dynamic, interesting person to room with for a year?" "Will this person make a difference at our school?" "Do I like this person?"

The "special sauce" of college, ask anyone who's been, is the people you meet and the friends you make. Colleges know this, nostalgic admissions officers know this, and smart applicants know this as well.

Because colleges are looking for special, memorable individuals - we need to change the entire way we look at college admissions. It's not about us doing what we think colleges want us to do.

It's about doing what *we* want, and becoming the most interesting, successful versions of our authentic selves as possible. It's about being ourselves.

The Old Approach

In highlighting the qualities that elite colleges desire, it's helpful to first focus on what colleges *are not* looking for.

Contrary to popular belief, colleges are not looking for students who take a bunch of tough classes, do standard "get into college" activities, and get a 4.0. That actually sounds like a pretty boring applicant. Remember, colleges have their choice of literally tens of thousands of qualified applicants.

Imagine being an admissions officer. You work 8-12 hours a day, and your whole job is reading over college applications. If you work for an elite school, you're reading through countless applications with high test scores and GPA's. After a week on the job (let alone years), all of them start to blend together.

Admissions officers quickly develop a 6th sense for applicants who clearly did everything just to get into college. Reading application after application, it becomes clear who did things in high school out of a genuine sense of exploration, and who did things because they thought that admissions officers would want to see them. Of course, the latter is not a unique or interesting path to take in high school.

Think about it this way: If the college of your dreams knew that you were orienting all of your decisions around getting into a top school, would they be thrilled? Would they want you there? Or would they want a student who had done everything out of their own interest and exploration?

Colleges can smell inauthenticity from miles away (just like we can tell when people are being fake, when our favorite artists drop bad projects just to make money, when our favorite YouTuber starts making trash content just to get more views).

If, in our application, we seem like we just did everything to get into a good college, we come across as desperate. Admissions Officers (AOs) (rightly) view this sort of manufactured approach to high school as a preview of who we will be in college (toxic, overly-competitive, not a positive contributor to the community).

It turns out that admissions is one of those things that works backwards.

The more we focus on trying to get into a top college, and orient all of our choices around that metric, the more uninteresting and predictable we become, and in turn, the less likely we are to get in. Paradoxically, the more we focus on our own growth and well-being, the more self-aware and unique we become - the more likely we are to get in.

It all seems backwards - if we aren't supposed to do everything we're told to do to get into a top college, what should we do?

The New Approach: Changing Our Perspective on Admissions

This authentic approach to college admissions requires a complete paradigm shift. Here are some of the shifts in thought that come with focusing on being ourselves, and not who we think we need to be to get into college.

The Old Approach: Focus on appearance	The New Approach: Focus on Authenticity
There are a limited number of spots at elite colleges so I have to outperform everyone around me	I just need to be the best applicant I can be
I have to choose activities that will impress AOs	I want to choose activities that will help me grow and learn more about myself
Community service is great for college apps	Community service is great for the community
I need to take all of the hardest classes	I'm going to take classes that challenge me and interest me
I want to get into a high ranked school because if I don't high school was a failure	I want to go to a great college where I'll keep learning and growing
My essays need to be perfect	My essays need to tell my unique story
College is something to tell people I got into	College is a real place where I will spend some of the most important years of my life

The goal of this book is to move you from the left side of the above chart to the right side (The New Approach). **The New Approach is a happier, more fulfilling path to take - and it's ultimately more successful.**

How we view college:

A big part of the New Approach is changing our relationship with the idea of college. With the Old Approach, a college is a badge of affirmation to be worn, a status symbol that indicates value and worth. But with the New Approach, college is an actual place to be.

When we let go of college just being a name that we tell friends and family so they think we're special, we start thinking about it as an actual place that we will call home. This makes the process much more fun.

In turn, we stop thinking about just getting into the most prestigious college possible, and think more about which colleges we would actually want to attend. Going to a rigorous university might be one of our priorities. But because we've focused on getting to know ourselves, we care about more than just this catch-all external marker of success. We've thought carefully about what matters to us, and we're able to identify a large range of schools where we'll be happy and successful.

Wherever we go, we'll meet amazing people, form life-long memories, and be set up to have a great life.

And we're excited about it!

Accordingly, we stop thinking of where we get into college as a definitive measure of our self-worth, or a test that we have to pass. We have the perspective to recognize how flippant and random the process is, and that all we can really do is focus on being our best self and telling our story honestly.

This makes the process much less stressful - and when we remove that stress and pressure, we're more able to write powerful essays, live a healthy, happy high school career, and - we're more likely to get in.

The New Approach in Action

The logical thought is that when we shift our focus to our own interests and desires over what will get into college, we won't stand a chance at getting in. But again, this goes backwards.

When we focus on our own growth, some interesting things start to happen.

We start choosing activities that genuinely make us excited. We realize how many cool things there are to do with our time besides scrolling on r/A2C, watching stats videos, and competing for the same boring extracurriculars as everyone else.

We might start our own journal, or side project, or get involved with an organization that excites us. If we do, it's because we want to - not because we feel like we have to. Even if part of the motivation is getting into a good school, we're smart enough to know that it's not worth stressing about the same activities everyone else is doing. We're better off doing things our own way.

Framing an Application Around a Unique Pursuit:

These pursuits can end up being core parts of an application. Here are a couple examples from students in this book:

- Instead of vying for the typical coveted positions, Madison (Vanderbilt) emailed a local clothing company and created an internship for herself. She crushed the role, gained responsibility, and eventually pitched a fashion line to Bloomingdales (successfully!)
- Jessica (Rice) volunteered with an organization called "Teen Line," where teens staff a hotline for other teenagers to call in about crises and difficulties in their lives. She wrote a powerful essay about how her experience shaped her perspective on her own problems.

- After getting cut from his high school tennis team, Alex (Duke) worked with tennis clubs and nursing homes to create a program that recycles used tennis balls to pad the bottom of seniors' walkers.

These activities are all unique and memorable, and they all take about as much time as leading any other club in high school (but are much more impressive). Additionally, these involvements led to considerably more growth than any traditional resume-boosting activity.

When Doing Your Own Thing Doesn't Magically Become The World's Best Essay Topic:

You're probably thinking "That's all great, but what if me just doing my own thing doesn't magically stumble into an incredible story for a college application?"

The good news is, that's the case for plenty of The Kids Who Get In.

Several of the students featured didn't do anything like the activities listed above that are sure to stick out.

Brian, a current U Chicago Junior, spent high school playing soccer, skiing, and volunteering with kids. It was a healthy high school experience, for sure, but not an extraordinary one. Lewis, the WashU student feature, spent his summers watching TV, and powerwashing friends and families stuff for money. Shaun, a Junior at the Wharton school at Penn, was captain of the hockey team and a member of the National Honor Society.

Focusing on your own desires and goals doesn't mean that you *have* to choose activities that no one else is doing. Our end goal is to showcase what makes us unique, and stand out from the horde of qualified applicants. But we have plenty of ways to do so - and for these three students, it was their essays.

Brian wrote an unforgettable piece on his love for old school CDs. Lewis' essay focused on a unique family tradition. And Shaun's centered around the growth mindset instilled in him from playing hockey.

These students had healthy, balanced high school experiences - and got into some of the most prestigious universities in the country by being themselves!

In other words, they didn't have to spend all of high school stressing about getting into an elite college. They lived their lives how they wanted to, created an honest, intentional application, and the results speak for themselves.

Ironically, if these students had spent all of high school trying to claw over other students and garner the most impressive accolades and positions, they probably wouldn't have fared as well. By making their own choices and telling their stories in their own way, these students stood out, and got in.

Highlighting a Unique Aspect of Your Identity:

Using our essay to highlight what makes us unique is a great way to stand out, and several students featured wrote essays about unique aspects of their identity. Like Brielle (Columbia), who wrote an essay comparing her multiracial identity to "Szechuanese Gefilte Fish." Or Felix (Northwestern), whose essay began with a nod to his four moms. Bernie (Stanford) and Jake (Brown) also focused on conditions and experiences that make them unique.

But even if we don't have 4 moms or some other unconventional lived experience, we can stand out just by sharing how we look at the world.

Miranda (Princeton) writes about her fervent desire for money, Danai (UCLA) about her drive for independence and her love of learning. Christiane (Harvard) explores the joy she gets from a good book, and Parker (Johns Hopkins) writes about getting over lying to himself.

In short - there are so many different ways to stand out in the admissions process. When we focus on doing high school the way we want to, and telling our story in a way that reflects our genuine personality, we invite colleges to reject or admit us for who we are. This vulnerability makes us more attractive applicants.

Other benefits of moving to the right side:

We have more time. We're able to cut out a lot of the junk in our schedules that would normally be spent on activities and classes that we don't really care about. This can lead to getting better grades, more sleep, and a greater sense of calm around the areas where we do spend our time.

We care less what everyone else is doing. Once we decide that getting into college is just about us being the best version of ourselves, we let go of where everyone else is applying and what they're doing to get in. This cuts out nearly all of the stress of the process.

We stop comparing ourselves to other people. Our application (and life) isn't ranked on some invisible spectrum, charted against all of the lives around us. The process is flippant, and relies on so much more than just a linear ranking of achievement. And when we internalize that, there's no reason to compare our accomplishments to those of other people or compete with everyone else.

Moving in this direction, we become more and more of ourselves - which of course, makes us more appealing to the colleges that we apply to.

The college admissions process becomes fun. This might seem about as far away from reality as possible. But the process can be enjoyable. Just taking the time to get close with ourselves, identify what makes us happy, and get better at telling our story can be gratifying.

A Summary of the Two Approaches

At this point, we're arguing between:

Trying to orient your high school experience around getting into a top school and then trying to trick them into thinking you did it all on your own accord, and then basing all of our self-worth around whether they believe us or not.

This path is **more effort**, more stress, much more detrimental for your growth and happiness, and less effective for actually garnering admission.

Or:

Being honest with ourselves about our goals and desires, crushing high school and growing a lot, creating a college application that accurately represents our lived experiences, and letting the chips fall where they may.

This path is happier, **less effort**, more fulfilled, more confident, and more effective for actually getting in.

Doing Your Own Thing and Getting Good Grades and Test Scores:

Around this point, you're probably thinking "This is all good and well, but don't I still need sick grades and test scores to get into an elite college?"

I want to answer that with three main points.

1. You should do what's in your power to get good grades and test scores

   Getting good grades and competitive test scores are a solid foundation for any college application, and that shouldn't be breaking news.

   For the 20 students sampled in this book, the GPA range is 3.6 - 4.0, the SAT range is 1390 - 1600, and the ACT range is 33 - 36. As a baseline, elite colleges are looking for high achievers. Plenty of students outside of this range get in every year, but we want to do what's in our power to get our numbers within the competitive range for the schools we want to go to.

   There are countless great resources out there for high school students, and "how to excel academically" is within the scope of those outlets, and not this one. I would recommend "How to Be a High School Superstar" by Cal Newport (or anything by Cal Newport, to be honest).

   For standardized tests, take plenty of full, timed tests until you're regularly scoring in the range you want to be scoring in on test day. I took a full SAT every saturday, and another one in chunks over the week, for the 2-3 months before the test. That approach served me well.

2. If you don't have the grades or test scores, standing out is your only option

   Not having perfect, 95th percentile + GPA or SAT isn't a deal-breaker - it just means you need to use the rest of your application to show admissions officers why you're awesome. And that places more emphasis on everything highlighted in this book!

   Look at the 25th-75th range for any of these schools published - if your scores or GPA are below the 25th percentile, then you *need* to tell a compelling, authentic story that convinces admissions officers that admitting you is worth it. This means you need to *have* a compelling, authentic story to tell.

   If your academics are far out of the range of most accepted students, the onus is on you to show that you spent your time outside of the classroom in interesting, fruitful ways - you have less leeway to be one of TKWGI who spent their summers watching TV.

3. All we can do is our best

The message that I keep hammering home is that we want to live high school authentically, do our best, and accept whatever outcome comes from that.

In many ways, we have to treat our academics the same way. All we can do is our best.

You don't need to take *every* AP offered, or get a 4.0, but you should work hard and take classes that challenge and interest you. And after that, the chips will fall where they may.

If you end up getting a high SAT and GPA, then that's great. And if not, there's nothing wrong with that either. By definition, only a tiny proportion of the country winds up with a top percentile standardized test and GPA. It's not a measure of your worth, or the value of your high school experience, or of you.

"Where You Go Is Not Who You'll Be" by Frank Bruni is another essential read that explores our obsession with elite education. Most CEO's, Senators, Governors, and successful people in this country didn't go to elite colleges - and there are infinitely many paths to success besides going to a top school.

So if you do high school your way, and you don't end up with a perfect academic resume, that's ok.

The Golden Wager

The Golden Wager is my favorite concept in this book, and I'll likely expand this idea into a book of its own. It's a distillation of everything you've read thus far into a matrix that measures our approach to college admissions against the actual outcome, and where this leaves us as people.

Here's a visual:

Do things out of our own interest, get in	Do things to get into a top college, get in
Do things out of our own interest, don't get in	Do things to get into a top college, don't get in

Quadrant 1: Focus on your own growth, get into an elite college

You live high school in a happy, self-integrated way. You don't spend a lot of time comparing yourself to others, you focus on your own interests and achievements, and in 4 years, you do some interesting things. You get good grades, and focus on exploring and achieving in a couple areas that are important to you.

After high school you have:

- A couple real ideas of what you might want to study in college and do with your life

- A relatively high-level of self-knowledge, and awareness of what fulfills you and makes you happy
- A strong ability to tell your own story honestly

You apply to colleges where you can continue to grow and hone your interests, and you know that all we can do is our best with applications - the results are out of our control.

You apply to a good mix of schools where you think you can be successful, and don't stress too much, because you know that you'll be ok wherever you end up.

It's ok to still *prefer* some of the schools on your list, but you know that you'll be alright either way.

And voila[1]! You get into an elite college. You're thrilled - you know where you go doesn't define you, but there will be some great opportunities for more growth at that school.

You show up to college and you're happy, and grateful. You live your college life in the same way - making intentional choices, focusing on yourself and what makes you happy. You meet people who fulfill you and help you grow, you get involved with organizations that you like, and you make an impact. You're well on your way to becoming a fully-formed person.

Quadrant 2: Focus on your own growth, don't get in to an elite college

You have a healthy, complete, self-directed high school experience. You live it your way, and you learn a lot about yourself, and what you enjoy.

Senior spring rolls around, and as the news rolls in, you didn't get into the elite school you hoped to get into.

It stings in the moment, and you're pretty bummed (especially as you see other kids in your high school celebrating prestigious acceptances.) But you

---
1   I originally wrote this as "Wallah!"

know that your time in high school wasn't wasted. You enjoyed yourself, you explored genuine interests, and you learned a lot about yourself. And that gives you so much to build on in college.

Getting into an elite college is a nice bonus, but our goal is to become an interesting, fully-formed human being - and if we did that in high school, we're going to be alright wherever we end up.

You don't treat not getting in as a make or break evaluation of your character, or your high school experience. You recognize that it's a pretty random process, and you know you did what was in your power to have an authentic high school experience and send out great applications.

You might end up at a slightly less prestigious school than some peers, or a less expensive public option. But at this school, you're the same awesome person who makes the most of the opportunities around them and makes their community better.

You crush it at your new school, make a bunch of great friends, and have an incredible college experience.

While at your school there may be less exposure to certain prestigious jobs, there's also less competition. You rack up impressive achievements as an undergraduate, and you're in a great position to get your career started.

You seek out opportunities to grow and challenge yourself, and just like high school, choose areas to spend your time that you genuinely enjoy. This gives you a great energy that people want to be around!

In summary, even though it wasn't the path your high-school-self scripted, you lived a great college career, and wind up happy, fulfilled, and successful.

Quadrant 3: Focus on what you think AOs will want, get into an elite college

Despite everything outlined in the New, Authentic Approach to college admissions, there will always be a slew of unhappy students who get in through doing the exact opposite. They spend all of high school cramming in an unbearable load of APs, activities they don't really care about, carefully groom a narrative and essay to make it seem like they did it all on their own accord, and "play the game" into an elite acceptance.

If our only goal is to get into a top college, then they've checked that box. But if our goal is to become a fulfilled, happy, interesting young human being - they've completely missed. How can you be self-fulfilled when you've spent four years doing what you think other people want to do?

Let's say you *did* spend all of high school doing everything I spend this entire book telling you not to do. You do clubs you don't really like, take classes you aren't really interested in, and compete with your classmates for awards and positions that you hope colleges will admire.

If you spent four years with that kind of attitude and life approach, firstly, you probably weren't that happy. You probably didn't get as much sleep as you could have (a pretty big biologic prerequisite for teenage happiness), and you probably didn't feel super confident and energetic about your extracurricular time.

The really sad part about the people who get lost in playing this game is that the game continues in college.

In college, and especially at smaller, elite colleges (pretty much all of the top 20), the same toxic competition comes up again. Instead of honor societies and leadership positions, it's organizations, internships and research opportunities.

The lingo switches; SAT to GRE, Princeton and Harvard to Goldman and McKinsey, Greek organizations and societies replacing high school markers of prestige, but the reality remains the same. It's students doing what they think some external body will like (an elite college, a prestigious job, their parents, their peers), and prioritizing that over their own genuine interests.

Pretty soon, you get sucked into the same mode you were in in high school. Chasing external validators of success. Competing with your classmates. Doing everything that you think you *should* be doing, and little of what you actually *want* to be doing. Everything becomes a box to check - classes to ace, clubs to lead (on paper), sophomore internships to roll over into junior internships to roll into full-time jobs.

At a certain point, college (like high school), can become stressful and miserable. There's a reason why so many top colleges have mental health crises (you'll see this mentioned in the second half).

As someone who took a gap year, took a semester off in college, and is probably going to take some extra time to graduate, I want you to understand that there's no huge rush to get to where you hope to go.

Because the problem with treating getting into a top college as a final destination is that as soon as we get there, there's a next final destination. And whether it's med or law school, or a prestigious job, or fellowship, as soon as we get there, there's a next destination. And getting caught up in the next, and the next, and the next, prevents us from enjoying the life that's in front of us.

Quadrant 4: Focus on what you think AOs will want, don't get into an elite college

You spend all of high school trying to get into an elite school, and you don't.

Firstly, you're going to feel like you wasted all of your time in high school. If you orient all of your choices around an external measure of success, you're going to be pretty bummed if that doesn't happen. The long nights of studying for exams, the meetings after meetings, the hours on Reddit and College Confidential - all of that is going to feel like time wasted.

Secondly, you're probably going to take the actual school you end up at for granted. Because you spent all of high school orienting your success around getting into an elite college, you might treat the actual college you attend as a consolation prize. You might spend the whole year trying to transfer (opening up the same set of quadrants for a new process), or you might just generally have the attitude that your school is beneath you.

It might not come as a massive surprise to hear that the other students at the school (for many of whom the school is their dream school) aren't going to be attracted to that energy. If you walk around acting like the place you're at is beneath you, the other people there probably aren't going to be super excited to spend time with you - people want to meet and interact with other people excited about college!

Additionally, in the midst of sulking and thinking you're better than the school, you'll probably miss out on awesome opportunities. Some of the best things in college happen when you least expect them. Random road trips, new friendships, and fun nights are experienced that are stumbled into - and can't happen if we're spending all of college worried about transferring, or proving that we're still special even though we didn't get into Penn.

This quadrant can be one of the biggest blessings if you let it - it can show you that prestige is overrated, and can jolt you into following your own passions and interests over what you think you *should* be doing. An overworked, unhappy high school student can turn into a happy, fun-loving, college superstar if they let this admissions process be a teaching moment.

But you have to go make the most of where you're at - and not spend all day thinking about where you could have been.

The Golden Wager - a Summary:

Do things out of our own interest, get in	Do things to get into a top college, get in
Do things out of our own interest, don't get in	Do things to get into a top college, don't get in

These are the four outcomes, and they all branch from what's under our control: living and expressing ourselves authentically. As you can see, getting into a top college becomes a secondary goal - one that we are more likely to attain if we prioritize ourselves.

All we have control over is our own high school experience and achievements, and those matter independent of the admissions process.

Furthermore, the value of our college experience is directly tied to our ability to let go of all of the external markers of success and really do what makes us happy.

Now that we've established how to move to the left two quadrants, how can we best increase our chances to end up in the top left? This next section will provide guidance on authentic expression - and putting your unique story to paper. And you'll have the model of 20 real, successful applications.

Authentic Expression – Using the 20 Entries:

After this chapter, you'll get a chance to read 20 complete college applications that worked. My goal in including these applications is for you to see what this idea of "authenticity" and "focusing on yourself" actually looks like in action. Also, these twenty applications are probably what got you to pick up this book!

I have made my case for the New, Authentic Approach - shedding our desire to impress admissions officers and focusing on developing ourselves. Of course, not every successful elite college applicant followed this approach. I have included a wide variety of students, who lived high school in very different ways.

In viewing their applications in this format, you'll see exactly how each of these approaches looks from the admissions officers perspectives. See if you can tell who followed the authentic approach! Not every application featured is a perfect representation of this framework. These are a fairly random sampling of twenty applications that got into elite colleges (see my methodology in the next section).

I want you to use these applications and entries for 3 main purposes:

1. Think critically about what you want in a college

Each featured applicant reflects on their experience at their college so far, and provides a complete breakdown on the school's culture. While these are one-off, subjective takes that shouldn't be taken as fact, they help us think about what we want from our college experience. As you meet these 20 individuals, and hear about their life stories and their experiences in college, you'll get better at knowing what you want to experience. And that's a huge part of the New Approach.

- Some questions to ask yourself as you read along:
- Does this sound like a college where I would be happy?
- Do I want to go to school with students like this?
- Does reading about this college experience excite me?
- How do I want to spend my time in college?

2. Get a real feel for what traits in applicants you admire

In reading this book, you get a chance to step into the seat of the admissions officer. You read complete applications, and you're able to judge them for what works and what doesn't. From this perspective, you can begin to think about how admissions officers make their decisions. Think about which students you would want to be friends with, which students you would be proud to go to college with. Additionally, think about if there's anything that applicants do that you find offputting. This will be immensely valuable as you craft your application.

See if you can tell which students adopted the New Approach!

3. Internalize that you can get in by being yourself

After reading through these twenty applications, I want you to have internalized that the admissions process rewards authenticity, and that you can get in by being yourself. You'll see how twenty real people told their stories and did high school, and you'll see that smart kids living the life they wanted to live in high school was enough, time and time again.

Not every student in this book followed the New Approach - some stressed their way through high school, grinded, competed, and still got into a top school. And that's a real option. But these twenty students will show you that you don't have to go through high school that way, and that stressing less and being yourself can make you a more compelling applicant.

The Kids Who Get In: Methodology

The next 500 words or so are relatively boring but answer a pertinent question: where did these 20 applications come from?

Through a barrage of LinkedIn DMs, cold emails, phone calls, and texts with friends of friends, *The Kids Who Get In* were recruited. Generally, I reached out to several students from each school. I gave a general pitch of the book vision, and what it entailed on their end (an hour-long written interview and the submission of all of their application materials). In exchange for participation, I paid each student $50.

Here is a breakdown of where the 20 entries in this book were sourced:

College contacts sheet: 2

- A Google Sheet was created featuring students at various colleges who offered to give their perspective on their college to high school students who were unable to make college visits because of the Coronavirus. I utilized this contact information for two of the entries in this book.

Personal friend: 2

- Two of the respondents are friends of mine, one from Vanderbilt and one from a summer trip two years ago.

LinkedIn Messaging/Cold email: 8

- I applied a "People" search on LinkedIn, used Google to identify the email format for the school, and emailed students from each school.

THE KIDS WHO GET IN

> It generally took 10-20 cold emails to get a couple responses, and usually one out of 3 or 4 responses were willing to have their application published in this format.

Loose personal connection: 8

- This is primarily people connected to people that I know at Vanderbilt. Because of the wide range of students that attend Vanderbilt, I was able to utilize very diverse networks to pool together a variety of students. Admittedly, this may factor in some network bias, but I was very deliberate to find a wide array of students.

Here are some concrete rules that I followed for assembling a diverse group of 20 students:

- No more than 10 Male- or Female- identifying students

- At least two students from the following main ethnic groups (Hispanic/Latino, Asian, Black)

- At least one international student

- At least one first-generation student

- At least one student from each of the following income brackets (Under 20,000/year, 20,000-40,000/year, 40,000-80,000/year, 80,000-160,000/year, 160,000-250,000/year, 250,000-500,000/year, 500,000+/year)

- At least one collegiate athlete

- A wide variety of intended majors

- Students from many different parts of the US, including rural, suburban, and urban areas

- Students from private, public, religious and non-religious, competitive and less-competitive high schools

All of the above criteria were met. Some additional unintended diverse outcomes were:

- Two non-binary students
- One homeschooled student
- Two legacy applicants
- Several biracial students, including one Native American student
- Several students with atypical families
- Students who applied through the Posse and Questbridge programs

A couple of important things to note about this sampling:

- No student featured was rejected or removed from the book because I felt like their responses or application didn't back my thesis.[2] Occasionally I would push a student to write more on a certain reflection question, but I never pushed a student to take a specific stance. Additionally, I didn't go into the writing of this book with anything specific that I wanted to prove. The book was written as 20 entries, and then "Main Findings," and the other relevant sections were added.

- The most common reason why a student would decide not to participate was "I'm not comfortable sharing my essays." This may skew the participants in this book toward less personal essays (or a higher comfortability sharing essays).

---

[2] Believe me, it was enough work finding these 20.

Part 2 – The Kids Who Get In:

Brown University

JAKE TRAUB

APPLICATION:

Major I applied under / School I applied to: Public Policy

Ethnicity: White/Caucasian

Gender: Male

Family Income Bracket: 250,000-500,000/year

Year of College Graduation: 2022

High School Unweighted GPA (to nearest hundredth): 3.92

High School Weighted GPA: 4.69

Class Rank/Percentile: N/A (not calculated at my high school)

SAT I Score (By Section): 770 Math, 730 Reading (1500 Total)

ACT Score (By Section): 36 Math, 36 Reading, 35 English, 33 Science (35 Composite)

SAT Subject Test Scores: 800 Math II, 750 Biology

AP Test Results: 5: Government, Computer Science, Biology, Calculus AB, 4: Language & Composition, Literature, Psychology, Statistics, World History

Senior Year Course Load: All Year - AP Literature, AP Psychology, Online Newspaper, Advanced Weight Training 1st Semester - Senior Research Project, Organic Chemistry, Astronomy, Political Statistic 2nd Semester - Sports Statistics, Entomology, Immunology, Philosophy[3]

Awards Won in High School: National Merit Scholarship Semifinalist, AP Scholar, Eagle Scout, Wrestling Team Captain, Winner of Children's Research Institute's Annual Research and Education Week Poster Presentation - College/High School Division, Online Newspaper Opinions Editor, National Honor Society Member, Math Honor Society Member, Arthritis Foundation Youth Honoree

Extracurriculars in High School (Put leadership in parentheses): Varsity Wrestling (Team Captain), Online Newspaper (Opinions Editor), Boy Scouts (Assistant Senior Patrol Leader, Patrol Leader), Arthritis Foundation Volunteer, Math Honor Society, National Honor Society, Temple Choir

Job/Work Experience in High School: Summer 2016 - Unpaid Internship at Medical Center in Washington, DC Summer 2017 - Paid internship at Medical Center, Washington, DC participated in research study

Volunteer/Community Service: Boy Scouts, Arthritis Foundation, Temple Choir, National Honor Society

What did you do in the summer after freshman year of high school?

Boy Scouts

What did you do in the summer after sophomore year?

Unpaid Internship at Medical Center in Washington, DC

What did you do in the summer after junior year?

Paid internship at Medical Center in Washington, DC participated in research study

---

[3] Quite the senior year!

ABOUT YOUR HIGH SCHOOL:

State of High School: Maryland

School Type (i.e. rural, suburban, city, public vs. private, etc): Urban, Public

# of Students in Graduating Class: About 800

What was your high school like? Demographics? How many other students went to elite universities?

Many other students at my high school went to elite universities, but most of these students were in a STEM Magnet Program within the high school. About 20 students went to Ivy League schools and several other students went to other top universities (Stanford, MIT, Vanderbilt, Rice, etc.). Racially and socioeconomically the school was very diverse, with about 80% of students being racial minorities and about 30-40% of students receiving Free or Reduced Priced Meals. Due to multiple magnet programs students in the high school came from all over the county with some students from more affluent areas and some from poorer urban areas.

REFLECTION ON APPLICATION PROCESS:

I applied: Regular Decision

What do you think your hooks were?

> My common app essay - compelling story that contextualized my application by showing the obstacles I had overcome.
> - Eagle Scout - a rare achievement that is well-respected by top colleges due to the leadership and community service required.
> - Participated in my school's STEM Magnet Program - a top high school known throughout the country as a challenging school that produces strong students.

What do you think the strengths of your application were?

- Top test scores (especially ACT), very challenging course load
- Many different forms of leadership and community service
- Several impressive achievements such as Eagle Scout, National Merit Scholar Semifinalist, etc.
- Strong work/internship background and clear, defined interest in continuing education
- Well-written and creative essays that revealed important aspects of my person
- Being a triple legacy applicant

What do you think the weaknesses of your application were? Where might other applicants have had an advantage over you?

- Grades - were solid but a difficult course load caused a handful of Bs
- Demographics - came from a very competitive area of the country where academic standards are higher, this was likely taken into account by colleges
- Applied to only out-of-state schools
- Impersonal/Generic recommendations from teacher and counselor

Where else you were admitted:

Georgia, Florida, Wake Forest, William & Mary

Where you were waitlisted:

Rice, Vanderbilt

Where you were rejected:

North Carolina, Yale

Did you get a private college counselor?

No

When did you start preparing for college admissions? How did your family prepare?

Getting into a top college was very important to me and my family and was considered from the time I entered high school. I structured my course schedule to include some classes I was interested in and some meant mainly to bolster my application. Similarly I took up many extracurricular activities, some out of interest like wrestling and journalism, and others mainly to bolster my application such as honor societies. I began visiting several colleges in my junior year and started my application process earlier than most students.

ABOUT YOUR COLLEGE:

Why did you choose this school?

I primarily chose Brown for its open curriculum. The lack of core requirements allowed me to pursue my interests in several academic areas. In addition, its reputation as a laid back school with a good social scene attracted me. Also, as a legacy student I continued the family trend of attending the school.

What is your school known for? What is its reputation?

Brown is known as a school that is difficult and prestigious to get into, but easy once you are there. It is known to have a lot of parties and low workload, aided by the open curriculum. It is also known to be one of the most liberal schools in the country with many students participating in social activism.

Is this reputation accurate?

No, the reputation of Brown as an easy school with grade inflation is not accurate. Several classes are extremely difficult with a greatly time-consuming workload. Although the social scene is still good, students must make a strong effort to get their work done and make time for leisure. Brown's reputation as a very liberal school is true, however, and students and faculty on campus tend to lean strongly to the left.

What are you involved with on campus?

Powerlifting Team, Brown Daily Herald (newspaper), College Republicans, volunteering at local hospital

What do you think your school offers that no other top 20 school does?

The open curriculum is a unique aspect of Brown that no other top 20 school offers. It cannot be understated how important the open curriculum is. Not having to take difficult classes that you are not at all interested in is greatly beneficial to your college experience.

What kinds of people do you think would love your school?

Students with multiple different academic interests fit in best at Brown. Students that can balance work and social life well also fit in, as Brown is not an easy school but also not as restricting as a school with the reputation of Princeton or MIT. More laid-back students would fit in as Brown is not really a crazy party school in comparison to others. Students who don't care about strong college sports teams would like Brown because its teams are almost entirely terrible. Students interested in social activism or outside-the-box extracurriculars would love Brown as there are many opportunities for these around campus.

What kinds of people do you think would hate your school?

Students who cannot handle a difficult workload would struggle at Brown. Also those who dislike the quirky atmosphere of the campus would not fit in either. Since Brown is a very liberal campus, students who are very conservative might not like the political atmosphere, even with the presence of a few conservative student groups. People who love exciting sports games and high school spirit would miss out on those things at Brown. Also, those with low academic and career motivation would certainly not fit in with other students.

Do you like your school? Why or why not?

Yes, the open curriculum is such an amazing academic benefit I would not get anywhere else. Also, the variety of available activities has allowed me to make many different friends in several areas. I am able to take classes I am interested in while spending my free time doing what I enjoy, which is all you can really ask for.

Your college's biggest strengths. What do students appreciate about their school/take for granted?

- Open Curriculum
- Housing situation and social life
- Strong and qualified professors
- Modern campus and facilities
- Countless extracurricular opportunities

Your college's biggest weaknesses. What do students complain about the most? What would an admissions counselor never tell you?

- Divide between students who choose completely different academic paths due to the open curriculum
- Terrible weather (almost always cold and rainy)
- Lack of political diversity
- Terrible sports teams/ low school spirit
- Few large parties/low presence of Greek life

ESSAYS:

Common App Essay:

Take one look at me, and you might not take a second one. An average person at first glance, at least physically, you probably wouldn't bat an eye as I crossed your line of sight. But, of course, you won't know everything about a person just by looking at them. You won't know what they've accomplished, and the challenges that they have overcome. And, you definitely won't know whether or not they have a debilitating disease.

THE KIDS WHO GET IN

Juvenile rheumatoid arthritis, a disease that is almost completely invisible, has affected nearly every aspect of my teenage life and shaped the person I am today. I was diagnosed when I was 13, and at the time I was in too much pain to cross my legs and could hardly muster the energy to stay awake through the school day. Still, I made the mistake of telling none of my peers and teachers.[4] My droopy eyelids in class garnered harsh remarks from teachers, and my hobbling gait throughout the halls earned many strange looks from classmates.[5] Even my parents often failed to sympathize with me, as there was nothing visibly wrong with me. As I coped through this period, I struggled to find the right balance of medication, and my constant shuttling back and forth to the hospital for doctor's appointments made it difficult for me to keep up in school.[6]

As freshman year approached, I finally found the combination of medicines that worked for me. Although taking 70 pills and an injection every week was not ideal, and my pain was not completely gone, I was able to become active again and function relatively normally. I continued to excel academically by making adjustments to my life to adapt to my medical problems.[7] My time management skills improved out of necessity, as I now needed ten hours of sleep to function. Still, the most challenging aspect of living with arthritis remained: I had no one to turn to when times got tough. I persisted in keeping my struggles to myself and attempted to take on the disease on my own.

Once in high school, I decided to make some changes and step into the light.[8] First, I worked hard to get into better physical shape, and made the varsity wrestling team despite the pain that I experienced on a daily basis. I also became more involved in activities I had put on hold due to my health

---

4   Jake does a great job of adding nuance to this major component of his life. We come to understand not just the physically debilitating side to Jake's ailment, but also the human struggle that comes with relating to others.

5   Good imagery here.

6   Not much artistry - Jake tells his story in a straight-forward, linear fashion. I would revise this and frame the "hobbling gait" in the present moment (showing and not telling).

7   Good tie towards academics and how his disease has shaped him.

8   This is the key paragraph that demonstrates Jake's ability to overcome diversity and take advantage of the options afforded to him by his newfound health.

issues, such as Boy Scouts, earning the rank of Eagle Scout. More importantly, I resolved to become more open about my disease, including writing a personal column for the school newspaper about the challenges of wrestling while having arthritis. This turned out to be one of the best choices I have ever made. Opening up about the pain and exhaustion to my friends made it easier to cope with the symptoms, and letting my teachers know what I was dealing with allowed my academic skills to shine more brightly.

The most rewarding part of opening up was that it enabled me to help others. I became involved with the Arthritis Foundation, first speaking to teens and young adults about my disease, and then serving as the Walk to Cure Arthritis Youth Honoree. As the honoree I raised thousands of dollars for arthritis research and appeared on television to share my story. This spring I had the exceptional opportunity to go to Capitol Hill and speak with congressmen about funding for arthritis research and the proposed healthcare legislation's effect on people like myself.

I chose to spend my early years with arthritis hiding behind the invisibility of the disease, which made it impossible for anyone to know who I really am. When I stepped out of the shadows and revealed the obstacles that I faced to others, it allowed my resilience and determination to truly shine through.[9]

Please briefly elaborate on one of your extracurricular activities or work experiences. (150 word limit)

This past summer I had the unique opportunity to conduct research at (name redacted) in Washington D.C. under the supervision of physicians and researchers. I received the Summer Intern Stipend Award, granting me financial support for my research. For my project, I performed a statistical analysis of the clinical differences between pediatric sickle cell anemia patients with and without high pain levels. The aim of the research was to identify factors such as comorbidities and social concerns, associated with pain in sickle cell patients and to use this knowledge to tailor sickle cell anemia treatment based on pain levels. My duties included collecting patient data from the hospital's medical database, creating formulas to determine the significance of clinical differences between high and low pain patients, and writing a paper on my research that I hope to get published in the near future.

---

9   Ending falls a bit short. It's vague and lofty, I would focus more on how opening up has allowed him to help others. If you're going to go broad on the conclusion, it's better to lean on the impact outside of yourself.

Why are you drawn to the area(s) of study you indicated earlier in this application? If you are "undecided" or not sure which Brown concentrations match your interests, consider describing more generally the academic topics or modes of thought that engage you currently. (150 word limit)

Although the two areas of study I have selected, Science and Society and Political Science, may seem somewhat unrelated, they are in fact deeply intertwined. My experiences working at a medical center in Washington, DC and with the Arthritis Foundation have emboldened me to further my education in the area of medicine and public health. Examining the relationship between science and society will give me a better understanding of both the objective and the social side of medicine. Politics historically has played and continues to play a major role in the medical arena, and thus I am also motivated to learn about the driving forces behind political change. Studying both of these areas while at Brown will give me the tools to inspire my own advances in medicine.

Why Brown, and why the Brown Curriculum? (200 word limit)

From a young age I have been exposed to Brown and its bustling campus life. My mother, grandfather, and uncle are all Brown alumni, and I have visited with them countless times. Tailgating at Brown Stadium, strolling down Thayer Street, and reading the BDH are images that have been ingrained in my mind for well over a decade. Because of this, Brown has always felt like home to me. Brown is certainly a place where I would love to live for the next four years, but its open curriculum sets it apart and makes it the best place for me to learn as well. I would like to study a wide variety of subjects, ranging from politics to biology, and from ethics to statistics. This would not be possible at most universities, but at Brown it is completely feasible. The ability to develop my own concentration also appeals to me, as it allows me to define my own standards rather than being boxed in by predefined subjects.[10] Coming up in the spring are the 25th and 50th reunions for my

---

10   Jake touches on some of the specifics of the Brown experience (Thayer Street, the open curriculum, the Brown Newspaper) - but his read on the overall campus culture is relatively generic. Besides the "bustling campus life," I would have touched on how those details fit into Brown's greater values (academic exploration, freedom of expression, a commitment to social justice).

mother and grandfather, respectively, and I hope to look back upon my experience at Brown as fondly as they do.

Tell us where you have lived - and for how long - since you were born; whether you've always lived in the same place, or perhaps in a variety of places. (100 word limit)

While I have lived in my house in Maryland for all 18 years of my life, where I have made my home is in the outdoors. As a young child, the woods behind my house were an outlet for my curiosities, where I would catch small fish in the creek and search the paths for undiscovered treasure. As a teenager, the outdoors became both a source of my ambitions and an escape; camping and orienteering allowed me to release my stress, while mobilizing others in outdoor activities through Boy Scouts helped me to develop as a leader.[11]

We all exist within communities or groups of various sizes, origins, and purposes; pick one and tell us why it is important to you, and how it has shaped you. (100 word limit)

As someone with juvenile arthritis, I belong to a unique community of young people with this disease. Although it seems unfortunate that I belong to such a community, I have made the most of it, devoting much time and effort into finding a cure and inspiring others with arthritis to overcome the challenges they face. My determination to overcome this debilitating disease has led me to success I may have not otherwise experienced, including becoming a varsity wrestling captain. Although arthritis continues to provide a significant challenge, it has made me the mentally strong person I am today.[12]

MY TAKE:

As a triple legacy, Eagle Scout with near perfect stats and a compelling story, Jake was a sure-fire admit. Let's talk a bit more about what worked:

Jake shows us the art to the "adversity essay." The goal of essays that focus on

---

[11] Overall this is a fine essay. It doesn't stand out, but we see another aspect of Jake's personality. These 100 word-ers aren't make or break pieces of the application.

[12] Good connection to his Common App.

hardship shouldn't be to garner sympathy, or exemplify how much trauma or suffering one has been through. The goal is to show how going through a difficult and unique life circumstance impacted you and made you a better person.

This doesn't mean that you have to underplay your struggles or the impact they've had on you, it means these essays should focus on your struggles within the context of how you responded to them.

Jake balances this well; early in the piece, he writes "[juvenile rheumatoid arthritis] has affected nearly every aspect of my teenage life and shaped the person I am today." He's honest about the negative impact it had on his life, and mentions specifics like barely being able to cross his legs and needing to take 70 pills a week that stick with the reader. Because Jake writes concisely using powerful details, he is able to make the difficulties he faced clear in about 200 words (the second paragraph of the piece, and a bit of the third), and in a 640 word piece, that's a completely reasonable portion to take to highlight his struggle.

Jake utilizes the remainder of the piece to showcase how he responded to his disease (350 words). He names concrete actions that he took (joining the wrestling team and being named a captain, becoming an Eagle Scout, working with the Arthritis Foundation, meeting with congressmen). These actions showcase self-improvement and supporting others, and responding to the challenges that life throws our way in this fashion is a hallmark of being a good person. Jake continues to focus on this growth in his final supplement.

Jake had all the on-paper qualifications to attend an elite school, and matched it with a well-written essay that showcased his response to a challenging illness. He's a well-rounded, intelligent, resilient kid, and that combined with his legacy status was more than enough to earn him admission to Brown University.

Jake in a sentence: Resilient rheumatoid arthritis diagnosee turned speaker, triple legacy Brunoian.

California Institute of Technology

ANDREW SCHECTER

APPLICATION:

Major I applied under / School I applied to: Applied and Computational Mathematics

Ethnicity: White

Gender: Male

Family Income Bracket: 80,000-160,000/year

Year of College Graduation: 2023

High School Unweighted GPA (to nearest hundredth): 3.98

High School Weighted GPA: N/A

Class Rank/Percentile: N/A

SAT I Score (By Section): 770 Reading, 790 Math (1560 Total)

ACT Score (By Section): 36 (all sections)

SAT Subject Test Scores: 800 Math II, 790 Physics, 710 Spanish

AP Test Results: 5: Bio, Chem, Physics C (Mech and E&M), Calc BC (and AB subscore), Stats, English Lit; 4: Psychology, Government

Senior Year Course Load: AP Lit, Graph Theory, Probability, AP Government, University CS, Intro to Logic/Proofs

Awards Won in High School: N/A

Extracurriculars in High School (Put leadership in parentheses): Swimming (HS Captain senior year)

Job/Work Experience in High School: I was a private academic tutor

Volunteer/Community Service: Guide Dogs for the Blind puppy raiser[13], swim instructor, math tutor

What did you do in the summer after freshman year of high school?

I worked as a volunteer swim instructor and math tutor the summer after all three years.

What did you do in the summer after sophomore year?

See above.

What did you do in the summer after junior year?

See above. I also toured a bunch of colleges on the East Coast - Princeton, University of Rochester, Rochester Institute of Technology, Case Western, University of Waterloo, and Ohio State, to name a few.

ABOUT YOUR HIGH SCHOOL:

State of High School: Nevada

School Type (i.e. rural, suburban, city, public vs. private, etc): City charter school

# of Students in Graduating Class: ~25

---

[13] The most wholesome EC of all-time

What was your high school like? Demographics? How many other students went to elite universities?

My high school was predominantly white and Asian, and it prided itself on being a school for the "profoundly gifted." It was a combined middle and high school, and we were allowed to take courses at our local university if we had finished the curriculum at our high school. For example, I was taking differential equations and linear algebra there my sophomore year. Despite our low number of students, we had 2 people at Harvey-Mudd, 2 people at Rice, 2 people at UC Berkeley, someone at MIT, someone at Columbia, and someone at Swarthmore.

REFLECTION ON APPLICATION PROCESS:

I applied: Early Action

What do you think your hooks were? (Things that made me stand out in the college application process) (3-5 sentences)

I think my biggest hook was probably my volunteering. Through Guide Dogs, swim instruction, and math tutoring, I had amassed more than 200 volunteer hours per year. I think that really showed admissions officers that I was doing things not just for the purpose of applications or money, but because I wanted to help my community.

What do you think the strengths of your application were? (3-5 sentences)

My biggest strength was probably my passion for math from an early age. Unfortunately, I didn't capitalize on it much in my EA application, which is the primary reason I got deferred (I know this because I was in contact with the Caltech swim coach and the admissions office). When I added this information in my deferral letter, though, it helped me make a convincing case as to why I belonged somewhere like Caltech.

What do you think the weaknesses of your application were? Where might other applicants have had an advantage over you? (3-5 sentences)

My biggest weakness in my application was definitely that it lacked focus. I had all of these qualifications that I could list on my Common App, but I threw most of them out of the window when I was writing my essays. Thus, when admissions officers first read my application, they were wondering whether I was really passionate about all of my strengths.

Where else you were admitted:

University of Rochester, Stevens Institute of Technology, Arizona State University, Colorado School of Mines, UT Dallas, Rochester Institute of Technology, University of Waterloo, Worcester Polytechnic Institute, University of Nevada Reno, University of Puget Sound

Where you were waitlisted:

Harvey Mudd, Swarthmore

Where you were rejected:

Princeton, USC

Did you get a private college counselor?

No

When did you start preparing for college admissions? How did your family prepare?

I started preparing near the end of my junior year. At the end of my summer before senior year, my parents and I took a road trip up and down the East Coast to see some of the schools I was thinking about applying to; this helped me figure out what I wanted in my college experience. I also spent a lot of time beforehand trying to figure out how I was going to write my Common App essay - it ended up being on my journey with autism growing up.

ABOUT YOUR COLLEGE:

Why did you choose this school?

I chose Caltech for quite a few reasons. First and foremost, I knew I wanted to be challenged, and I knew Caltech would provide that. Second, I had met quite a few committed students and upperclassmen before committing, and I knew that I would be happy spending the next four years with them. Finally, even though I told myself that location wasn't a big deal during the process, it's really nice being in SoCal.

What is your school known for? What is its reputation?

Caltech's known as a stereotypical "nerd school." Everyone I've talked to either thinks it's Cal Poly (which gets confusing since my brother went there...) or that everyone who goes there is an absolute geek. However, Caltech is also extremely prestigious to the outside world. Those who don't think it's Cal Poly generally know how incredibly difficult and rigorous the education here is. Also - fun fact - Caltech has the greatest ratio of Nobel Prizes per alumnus in the world.

Is this reputation accurate?

The reputation of being tough is definitely accurate. I've been extremely challenged, even as a freshman, during my time here, and I have to say Caltech classes are *way* more difficult than anything I ever took in high school (including my university courses). However, not everyone here is such a nerd. As weird as it sounds, there are jock subcultures here, and a lot of us have many varying interests outside of academics. For instance, one of the best Guitar Hero players in the world is a senior here, and we also have a Dance Dance Revolution club if you're into that.

What are you involved with on campus?

I'm on the swim team here, and I'm even a school record holder in the 400 IM! Swimming means a lot to me because it helps me get my mind off of academics or social drama (not that I've been in much) when I really don't want to worry about it. It provides that space where I can zone out and escape whatever difficulties I may be having in the outside world.

What do you think your school offers that no other top 20 school does?

The House system. If you don't know what it is, seriously, look it up. Every house has its own unique subculture, which means that when someone decides where they want to live, it's almost guaranteed that they'll be surrounded by people with similar interests and personalities. This is honestly one of my favorite parts of this campus because it's provided such a good platform for making friends, even those who aren't in the same classes.

What kinds of people do you think would love your school?

The people who would love Caltech most are definitely those who subscribe to the "work hard play hard" mentality. This place is, as I've said many times before this, extremely challenging, but there are definitely people here who thrive off of that. However, despite how hard this place is, most people here don't take themselves too seriously. Within two weeks of being here, I got to freeze a stress toy using liquid nitrogen and smash it with a sledgehammer for no reason other than the fact that I wanted to.

What kinds of people do you think would hate your school?

If you are deathly afraid of failure, don't come here. Everyone here struggles, and everyone here has failed at least once, if not several times. I got a 64% on my chemistry final last term, which freaked me out a bit since I was legitimately scared that I failed the class, and I definitely know a couple of people from my high school who would have really had a hard time if that happened to them. You also shouldn't come here if you're convinced you're better than anyone around you; most of the people I know here are very unwilling to put up with overinflated egos, and there's almost definitely someone smarter than you here to put you in your place.

Do you like your school? Why or why not?

I love Caltech. It has become a home away from home for me, and the people here really feel like family. My grandma died this year, and even as I'm sitting down and typing this out, I have a handwritten note from one of my friends telling me that I'm loved and listing out some different ways I should take care of myself. It was an extremely kind gesture, but I know she's definitely not the only one who would do something like this for me - almost everyone here is like this.

Your college's biggest strengths. What do students appreciate about

their school/take for granted?

By far the best thing about Caltech is the collaborative environment. Everyone works really hard here, but ultimately we all want to see each other succeed. If someone asks me how I did on an assignment, I know they're not going to throw it back at my face and tell me that they got a higher grade because chances are we worked together on that set anyway. On top of being collaborative, Caltech is also an incredibly supportive place. Everyone is encouraged to explore their identity, so long as it doesn't harm others.

Your college's biggest weaknesses. What do students complain about the most? What would an admissions counselor never tell you?

Sometimes our administration can be a little uncooperative when trying to work with the undergraduate population. Caltech tends to preach that it's a very high-trust environment, where generally the administration lets the students do what they want as long as it's not illegal, but there have definitely been some instances where students and administration have been petty towards each other. Furthermore, not all of the professors are amazing teachers. I've definitely had a lot of really good professors, but some of them tend to either mumble everything and teach way too fast or just teach things that are entirely unrelated to the homework.

ESSAYS:

Common App Essay:

Growing up, I envied the people who could effortlessly contribute to a conversation without getting interrupted or disregarded. I wanted to be the popular kid like them, but that wasn't who I was, and it isn't who I am. I don't need the luxury of taking my social skills for granted because my childhood struggles have given me a sense of strength.[14]

---

14   It's a strong, compact first paragraph. Andrew forgoes a traditional hook or opener, and instead gives us a preview of his essay, and begins with vulnerability - admitting that he was envious of others social skills. After reading this, we want to read more - the intro works.

THE KIDS WHO GET IN

From a very young age, my parents knew I was developmentally different from other children. I was always in my own little world, never really paying attention to or interacting with other people. My parents would try to get me to socialize, but I was never really interested. I only wanted to play with the puzzles that filled up the shelves in my bedroom. When I was six, my parents found out I have high-functioning autism. According to researchers, I was likely to grow into someone who couldn't socialize, regulate emotions, or recognize body language.[15] I was supposed to be the person who would throw a tantrum at any remote change in my strict schedule. My parents were even told I might not reach total independence. I would have to change significantly to make it on my own.

When I was first diagnosed, I didn't let my autism affect me much. I could just carry on with my day without a care in the world, just being myself and not worrying over what other people thought. In middle school, however, I had an irrepressible urge to fit in with the crowd, and my autism suddenly felt like a huge roadblock that kept me from being socially adept. I was always on the outside of the friend group; my contributions to the conversation were often disregarded. I felt empty and unnoticed. People who I was close with in elementary school suddenly felt distant.[16]

However, over the next couple of years, I started learning more about other people's senses of humor. I realized that if I added more sarcasm, sass, and self-deprecation to my attitude, I could get people to laugh. Throughout high school, I began to develop my ability to entertain, and eventually people would not only pay attention to me, but value my presence. Obviously humor isn't the only thing that is needed to create a social connection, but it helped me pave a path to legitimate social connection. However, my new persona never changed who I was deep in my core; it just allowed other people to see my worth as a person. I don't need to fundamentally change who I am as a person to fit in, there will always be people out there who love and accept me not in spite of, but *because* of my differences.

Despite some of the hardships that autism has given me, I'm thankful for

---

15   We can see Andrew setting up contrast between researcher predictions, and his own life. This contrast hooks the reader - and we end up rooting for Andrew, as an underdog, and someone who overcame these predictions.

16   Vulnerability. Andrew then meets this with gratitude and growth - the best ways to pivot past the challenge in adversity essays.

the fact that I have it.[17] Autism has not only brought me academic talent and a good memory, but it's led to some amazing opportunities. I became involved in both piano playing and swimming as physical therapy, and I fell in love with both and still participate in them to this day. Finally, I've learned how to be a good friend. I know what it's like to be an outsider, and I go out of my way to make sure none of my friends have to feel that way.[18] If I were given the opportunity to restart my life without having to deal with autism, I wouldn't take it because I know that my autism has shaped me into the person I am today: a driven, resilient person who knows not to take anything for granted. I accept that my success will not just be handed to me; there will always be obstacles in my way, but I am resilient enough to survive and conquer almost anything.[19]

List 3 STEM activities that helped spark your interest in the field (Responses should vary between 10 and 120 words per bullet point):

1. In middle school, I, along with three other middle schoolers, competed in MathCounts. Although I definitely had been interested in math before I learned about it, competition math exposed me to a world of mathematics and STEM that I had never experienced before. MathCounts taught me math is more than a set of concrete functions with only one path from a problem to a solution, but rather an elegant set of numbers that have different fascinating properties that allow for mind-blowing phenomena.

2. Advanced Physics, sophomore year. Before my sophomore year, I had never really been exposed to physics. I wasn't sure what to ex-

---

17   Very inspiring attitude. It's one thing to mark how a struggle has helped you grow, Andrew takes it a step further and is actually thankful for it.

18   This is such an inspiring story. It's hard not to smile and root for Andrew after reading this.

19   The one real critique I have of this essay is that the ending is broad. It's not a bad ending, but I would love to see Andrew tie this back to what he's gained from autism. I would have cut it a sentence earlier, and written "...I wouldn't take it because I know that my autism has shaped me into the person I am today: a driven, resilient person, a tenacious student, and above all, a good friend." We want the last line to really leave the AO feeling something, and often that comes from touching back to something powerful we've written earlier.

pect, and I was honestly scared of the prospect of the class; everyone I had talked to said that it was one of the hardest classes of the entire Davidson curriculum. However, the class made me quickly fall in love with physics as a whole, specifically electromagnetism. It showed me not everything works the way I might think, and the opportunity to explore the unknown fascinates me.

3. I'm competitive by nature, which may stem from the fact that I swim and had early exposure to MathCounts, so Science Bowl was a perfect way to combine both my love for STEM and my desire for competition. As a fast-paced competition that rapidly tests scientific knowledge in every subject from physics to earth science, Science Bowl doesn't completely cover everything I need to know about science, but it sparks an interest nonetheless.[20]

Much like the life of a professional scientist or engineer, the life of a "Techer" relies heavily on collaboration. Knowing this, what do you hope to explore, innovate, or create with your Caltech peers? (Your response should range between 250-400 words.)

I'd love to have the opportunity to help alleviate the issue of climate change with the skills I'll learn at Caltech. My junior year, I was in a class called Advanced Geosystems; the class only had three people[21]. The entire class was dedicated to looking at the political issue of climate change from several different perspectives, but the one part that really stood out to me was the ethical implications of geoengineering. I ended up writing a report about stratospheric aerosol injection (SAI), a process where humans release sulfates into the atmosphere to raise the overall albedo of the Earth and cool the surface temperature.[22] SAI is one of the most popular geoengineering options that people look at because it's already been pseudo-tested by the eruption of Mount Pinatubo in 1991. My finding, however, was that SAI causes a very serious ethical dilemma. There's the possibility that it could

---

20   These 3 are standard answers. Especially for CalTech applicants, there are run-of-the-mill STEM activities. These answers probably didn't set Andrew apart.

21   Socrates vibes

22   It's impressive that Andrew was able to contribute a real report on this geoengineering topic as a teenager, even though (as he notes) it wasn't published.

ruin agricultural development in Africa, potentially killing around 500,000 people; in other words, geoengineering could be a real-life trolley problem. I felt like I was able to contribute my voice to academia even though I didn't get published.

While ethics won't be my major in college, Geosystems taught me about another way I can contribute to alleviate the climate change issue: modeling. Climate modeling is very intense and convoluted; there is an incredibly large amount of parameters and variables that go into each model, whether that's the albedo of a certain spot on the Earth, the presence of clouds, an urban heat island effect, air pressure and CO_2 concentration, wind speed, ocean currents, ice caps, Milankovitch cycles, or even the state of the economy. Climate change issues generally cast a very large net that make it extremely difficult to capture exactly what is the underlying issue that causes climate change, even despite the presence of clear associations between carbon emission and global temperature increase. However, even though the issue of climate change is convoluted, it's a direct application of the (non)linear algebra, partial differential equations, and even graph theory that I'll learn at Caltech, and an area I'm extremely passionate about, mainly because I don't want future generations to have to bear the burden of an issue started by our ancestors that we worsened.[23]

Caltech students are often known for their sense of humor and creative pranks. What do you like to do for fun? (Your response should range between 250-400 words.)

"By a vote of 7-6, Steve, you have been evicted from the Big Brother household." I'm sitting on the couch, hugging a pillow, and my jaw is dropped to the floor. Adrenaline is rushing from my body, and I need to take a few moments to process what had just happened. This is only the first episode, and half of the house is already succumbing to blindsides left and right. For the rest of the summer, I tuned in every Sunday, Wednesday, and Thursday to see what would happen next. The twentieth season of Big Brother was so unpredictable that I pretty much never knew what would happen next, and it was absolutely thrilling. It gave me an outlet to temporarily ignore my own difficulties and obligations and take a breather from the craziness of the real world.

---

23   Good, straightforward conscientiousness.

I didn't miss a single episode over the entire summer, as I generally have a guilty pleasure for reality game shows like that. In fact, I probably got a little *too* invested in that season. The social experiment-esque nature of watching a bunch of people deal with issues in real time, whether a player is pulling off an extremely intricate strategy or crying because they feel completely lost in the game, is extremely fascinating to me. When put under pressure, we get to see each other's true colors; some people remain strong and push through, while other people crack and break down.

There's also something about seeing real humans deal with outrageous issues on-screen that relaxes me. By paying attention to other people's problems, I give myself a break from my own stresses, even if it's only for 30 minutes to an hour at a time. Most people will reward themselves for their own hard work, and these shows are a way of letting me do just that. I get to forget about the world around me and experience the thrill of reality TV.

The process of discovery best advances when people from various backgrounds, experiences, and perspectives come together. How do you see yourself contributing to the diversity of Caltech's community? (Your response should range between 250-400 words.)

It was a warm, sunny July day, and I had just finished swim practice. Northern Nevada Pride was downtown at Wingfield Park that day, one that I've wanted to go to for the last three years, and this was the first year I'd finally be able to go. I put on my orange shirt, exercise shorts, and plastic sunglasses that I had worn throughout most of the summer. I then opened my drawer, and sitting there were a pair of rainbow socks[24] that I hadn't worn very often, but that symbolized my identity. I was still closeted to some of my friends, so I had restricted my own self-expression, but when I put on my socks, I felt proud. I was finally being unapologetically myself and holding up a giant banner to the world that told them exactly who I was.

I decided to walk to the event because I didn't want to bother with parking. It was a thirty-minute walk in about eighty-degree heat, and even though I was sweating a lot, I didn't mind. When I finally got to the park, I felt like a

---

24 It's all about the specifics! The rainbow socks! I can see a nervous, excited Andrew in his room, ready to put on the socks for everyone to see.

six-year-old walking into Disneyland for the first time.[25] I met a few of my other LGBT+ friends there, and we had an amazing time. I got myself a bisexual pride flag, met a few new people, and got a ride home from a friend. When I got home, I took out my flag, draped it over my shoulders, and looked in the mirror. I almost cried because it was the first time that I had shown my true self in front of the entire world instead of just a few friends.

Coming to Caltech would allow me to keep showing my true colors. I'd be able to discuss several pertinent LGBT-related issues at PRISM, promote advocacy in the Pasadena area and nationwide, and have access to several help centers should I need them. Furthermore, I would be in the middle of California and thus have several support resources off-campus as well. It's nerve-wracking being out to everyone I know, but I know that I can continue to be myself at Caltech.[26]

Letter that Andrew sent after deferral:[27]

Even though it was almost three years ago, the visit still feels like yesterday. Caltech is a rather small school, but it still feels like several different worlds stitched together in a very impressive manner. From the turtle pond in the center of campus to the futuristic aeronautics lab that looks like an old stone building from the outside to the athletic facilities to the surrounding area in general, Caltech had everything it needed to create a lasting positive impression in my mind, even several years later.

Caltech is obviously known for its STEM departments, and I've been interested in math for as long as I can remember, back to when I was five and my mom bought me a game where the whole point was to add fractions together. Looking back, it's certainly a bit nerdy for one of my favorite childhood toys to be *that*, but it also helps me remember that I've been this way my whole life and my passion for STEM doesn't just come from a favorite teacher or professor. At Caltech, my opportunities would be much greater in everything ranging from research surrounding quantum and electromagnetic

---

25   Great simile.

26   Smooth transition from the moment, to reflection, to his potential future at CalTech. Well done.

27   The deferral update does what it should. Andrew reaffirms his interest in CalTech,

physics to helping revolutionize computer science as we know it to proving or disproving Goldbach's conjecture.

However, STEM to me isn't just about research or technology or numbers. Math, much like the liberal arts, is a living, breathing subject filled with nuances and room for interpretation, and there's no better place to find that than in competitions. My journey with competition math started when I was in sixth grade and some friends invited me to participate in MATHCOUNTS. I didn't know much about math competitions, but I knew I really loved the subject, so I decided to try it. It was the kickstart to one of the most life-changing extracurriculars of my life. Being both autistic and STEM-oriented, I was always somewhat of a rigid thinker. That's why I liked math: there was usually one rigid way to get from point A to point B. However, competition math flipped that entire idea on its head. Suddenly there were a bunch of new tips and tricks that I could put in my arsenal to not only complete math quicker, but have more fun in doing so. These tricks introduced an unfamiliar aspect of flexibility to math that I wasn't familiar with. Every time I start practicing my competition math skills, it seems like I learn a new method of solving a problem that I had never seen before.

I may have been deferred admission, but that doesn't mean I've given up. I am filled with more determination than ever to be a better student and to prove my worth as not only a student, but as a human being. Ultimately, the goal of my college search isn't just to go to the most prestigious college with the best facilities, though that certainly isn't a bad thing. I want to go somewhere where I'll be happy and where I can be unapologetically myself. Caltech provides an environment for me to do that and bond with people like me, whether that's over discussing gravitational waves or whether it was a good idea to include the Piranha Plant in Super Smash Bros. Ultimate.

MY TAKE:

It speaks to the unpredictability of elite college admissions that even a semi-recruited athlete with a 36 on his ACT, a 3.98 GPA at a hyper-competitive high school, 2 years of college math under his belt, hundreds of volunteer hours, and a compelling story was deferred by his school of choice!

Andrew is a fascinating applicant - let's take a deeper dive into what made his application successful:

Outstanding academic background: In addition to having near perfect grades and test scores, at the time of his application Andrew had taken several years of college math and science courses. Because CalTech is such a selective school (one of the best STEM universities in the world, with just 235 spots for first-years), this probably didn't set Andrew apart, but it's a prerequisite for consideration that he satisfied.

Compelling story: Andrew touches on the difficulties that he's experienced in his life because of autism, but also highlights the positives and the areas in which having autism has made him grow.

Makes a strong case for "fit": Andrew uses his supplemental essays extremely well to showcase how he would fit in to the CalTech community.

In terms of his academic and professional goals, Andrew shows a clear love for science and mathematics, and connects potential areas of study at CalTech to ameliorating Climate Change, a future goal. For a school like CalTech with a clear curricular focus, it's especially important to show why you fit in with that aim. In his deferral update, Andrew strengthens this case, connecting his passion for mathematics to his childhood and to his autism.

Additionally, Andrew makes a strong case for cultural fit at CalTech. Andrew is able to touch upon some of the strengths of the school (it's incredibly small, tight-knit community) indirectly by mentioning some of the things that make him unique (having autism and being part of the LGBTQ community, as well as interests like Super Smash Bros and Big Brother), and affirming that CalTech is a place where he will be accepted and embraced for who he is.

Andrew writes "I want to go somewhere where I'll be happy and where I can be unapologetically myself," where his STEM focus and more unique personality traits will be celebrated. This articulation of fit lines up perfectly with his Common App essay, where Andrew talks about his experience being excluded.

Andrew is an outstanding student with a strong story who argued fit well and didn't give up after being deferred! For those reasons, he was able to gain admission to CalTech, one of the most selective and challenging schools in the country.

Andrew in a sentence: Super smart mathematician dedicated to inclusivity because of his sexuality and experience with autism.

Columbia University

BRIELLE CHASAN

APPLICATION:

Major I applied under / School I applied to: Double degree program with Jewish Theological Seminary

Ethnicity: Asian

Gender: Female

Family Income Bracket: 40,000-80,000/year

Year of College Graduation: 2021

High School Unweighted GPA (to nearest hundredth): 3.6

High School Weighted GPA: 4.2

Class Rank/Percentile: 13th/160

SAT I Score (By Section): 800 Writing, 750 Critical Reading, 680 Math (2230 Total)

ACT Score (By Section): N/A

SAT Subject Test Scores: 770 Literature, 700 U.S. History

AP Test Results: 5: World History, US History, Psychology, Literature, Language and Culture, 4: Spanish, 3: Government

Senior Year Course Load: AP Lit, AP Gov, AP Stats, Orchestra

Awards Won in High School: Best sense of humor, Most witty, Most tardy, National Honors Society

Extracurriculars in High School (Put leadership in parentheses): Honors Country Orchestra (Section leader in orchestra), Mock Trial (team captain), Varsity swim team

Job/Work Experience in High School: I worked at my local synagogue as a teacher assistant for little kids preparing for their bar and bat mitzvahs.

Volunteer/Community Service: N/A

What did you do in the summer after freshman year of high school?

I took classes at the local community college and prepared for the SAT

What did you do in the summer after sophomore year?

I read "the fountainhead" by Ayn Rand because my AP Lang teacher forced us to read it over the summer and discuss it for an entire semester

What did you do in the summer after junior year?

I went to Israel on a teen tour type group organized by the Israeli Defense Force

ABOUT YOUR HIGH SCHOOL:

State of High School: California

School Type (i.e. rural, suburban, city, public vs. private, etc): Public high school

# of Students in Graduating Class: ~150

What was your high school like? Demographics? How many other students went to elite universities? (4-5 sentences)

My high school was tiny and very mediocre in every respect, especially my fellow students. Typically only valedictorian and salutatorian make it to a school worth mention, like UC Berkeley or UCLA or something along those lines. However, my year and the year after, several people made it to other prestigious universities such as Yale, another person at Columbia, Georgetown, Harvard, etc.

REFLECTION ON APPLICATION PROCESS:

I applied: Early Decision

What do you think your hooks were?

Being Asian and Jewish and having actual experience with both poles of my identity, understanding the dissonance and limitations in identity-based thinking while recognizing Columbia as a campus that was invested in talking about diversity, but also about the shortcomings of identity politics. I think that I felt a certain willingness on Columbia's part to engage with types of thought that I didn't have access to in high school. I related this to my racial identity because at the time that was the only language I had to talk about all the ways I didn't feel like I ... fit into space that weren't willing to *go there* intellectually (not that Columbia isn't still a bloody corporation on stolen land but alas it tries.)

What do you think the strengths of your application were?

I am a good writer and can make a compelling narrative out of the incoherence of lived experience. I also was consistent about my extracurriculars in high school, like I only did two main things (orchestra and mock trial) and demonstrated that these were formative to me as I stuck with them for years.

What do you think the weaknesses of your application were? Where might other applicants have had an advantage over you?

My report card was not as excellent as it could have been. I got several Cs (2 or 3) in high school that were major detractors in my application. I also had a clear dearth of community service that I didn't realize until this survey. I also don't think actually talking about being a minority/your race is a super compelling way to get into school.

Where else you were admitted:

UC Berkeley, UC Davis, UC San Diego

Where you were waitlisted:

I don't know because I had to rescind many of my applications

Where you were rejected:

nowhere ;)

Did you get a private college counselor? No

When did you start preparing for college admissions? How did your family prepare?

It all began when I turned 11 and my mother deemed me ready to begin SAT training. I was trying to qualify for the Johns Hopkins CTY Summer program, which requires students to take the SAT at a young age. This is when it all began.

ABOUT YOUR COLLEGE:

Why did you choose this school?

It was a fantasy of mine for many years, beginning with when I toured it as a mere child, and bolstered by my listening to Vampire Weekend all throughout high school and fantasizing about going to Columbia with them. I wanted to construct a fantasy of myself (like I said everyone at Columbia does, at least in the beginning) and the fantasy of Columbia felt like the right place to do that.

What is your school known for? What is its reputation?

It is known for being a rich center of Western thought and tradition that has a vibrant student body dedicated to social justice and change.

Is this reputation accurate?

For the most part, yes, but there are also many many niches in student bodies that these reputations do not represent, and that's why they can't be trusted too fully. Columbia has many people who are dumb and uninteresting, but they would never have you think that from the way they market and exploit their prestige.

What do you think your school offers that no other top 20 school does?

New York City, its faculty, its history of civil disobedience.

What kinds of people do you think would love your school?

Columbia has such a mythos owing to its media portrayals and location in NYC and Ivy League prestige. I think every single person who chose to go here has at least a little bit of the "my life is a movie and I'm the main character" mentality. I think people who aren't scared to throw themselves into a really intense environment would eventually love it, or see the great value in doing that.

What kinds of people do you think would hate your school?

People who really want that state school vibe of ra ra athletics and relevant greek life. Sports and Frats do exist on campus, but barely; you have to make a concerted effort to interact with them.

Do you like your school? Why or why not?

I love Columbia, but I'm not sure that I like it. I see the things it has done to my own mental health and that of my friends. I see the way that academic excellence is very often placed in front of our health and sanity and happiness. There is also a very robust culture of unhappiness here, where complaining about one's struggle is almost moralized? All of this percolates into a general distaste for the administration, though, which is fun and the closest thing we have to a school spirit.

Your college's biggest strengths. What do students appreciate about their school/take for granted?

I would say just the concentration of brain power in every department, and the opportunity to forge relationships with professors, since there aren't that many massive lectures (at least in my experience with the humanities). I find that there are incredible opportunities to learn tacked onto every bulletin board; so much that I am overwhelmed.

Your college's biggest weaknesses. What do students complain about the most? What would an admissions counselor never tell you?

The huge mental health crisis that is going on here. There is an inordinate amount of deaths in the student body many semesters, due to suicides or overdoses or, like last night, a girl was stabbed to death. There is very little "school spirit," I would say the main thing that binds people together here is relentless dissatisfaction with the administration. There is definitely a super cutthroat culture here and it is EXHAUSTING.

ESSAYS:

Common App Essay:

It's 2007, roughly 11:00 PM, and I'm practicing a rendition of *Silent Night* on the piano with the muffler pedal down[28]. My piano teacher assigned me to play it at that year's annual Christmas recital, and me, being her star pupil, was expected to play the most beautiful *Silent Night* any of the Chinese mothers sitting anxiously in the audience had ever heard. My mother sits by my side, unfaltering. "Crescendo. Louder. With more *feeling*. Three more times." These commands, along with the stifled sound of my piano playing (for our neighbors' sakes), were all too familiar to me-- practicing piano for hours on end with my mother was as natural a part of my day as eating, or going to school. Sitting at the piano, exhausted, I anticipated my father's inevitable descent from the upstairs bedroom. "Li, please. It's almost midnight. The children have school tomorrow. It's time for them to sleep" he would say, to which my mother would retort, "she could have gone to sleep hours ago if she had played it perfectly then."[29]

Growing up, mostly in San Francisco, such conflicts between my parents

---

[28]   Right off the bat, Brielle works in great specifics that take us right into her childhood home.

[29]   Powerful, concise dialogue that immediately introduces us into their family dynamic. Reading this, I feel like I'm in Brielle's home with her.

seemed natural to me. My mother's unbending, characteristically Chinese determination to see her children succeed so often clashed with my father's more European, Westernized cultural approach, that my brother and I became acclimated to living in a house with two such incredibly different cultures seemingly in constant dissension. As a result, a typical day in my life would be to go straight from my bilingual Chinese school, get dropped off at Hebrew school in the afternoon, and then to come home to an eclectic fusion of Szechuanese spices and Gefilte fish that I am confident existed nowhere outside of our home.[30]

Experiencing both sides of my culture in one day was nothing new, but finding a common ground between them was something that didn't occur to me until later in my teenage years. When I was 12, my family moved from San Francisco to Monterey Bay. Constantly being asked "wait, you're *Jewish*?" made me realize that I could no longer rely on my community to maintain my unique identity. This became especially true in 2013, when my father passed away due to a sudden heart attack.

Losing my father in such an unannounced, jarring way impacted my life in ways far beyond anything my fifteen-year-old self could have anticipated. Initially, my feelings toward Judaism shifted-- seeing my mother and brother suffer in a way that was so unspeakably painful to me made it very difficult for me to focus my attention on a G-d that I felt betrayed by. I had lost not only my father, but also a stronghold of Judaism in my life, someone who constantly read books on Jewish philosophy, who cried before my bat mitzvah, who couldn't walk twenty feet in San Francisco without pointing out what famous building was designed by which Jewish architect.

Confronted by such a colossal change in my life, the world changed for me, and one of the most profound differences I felt was one I never would have expected.[31] My cultural identity, which I felt was fractured, began to fuse in

---

30   After zooming into one moment, Brielle takes a step back to speak in more generality about her childhood, and how it shaped her. This is a great way to pivot. Brielle moves from 1. Specific instance, 2. A broader description of her upbringing, 3. How these experiences shaped her.

31   "one I never would have expected" - the contrast between the expected and the actual inherently hooks the reader! Of course, we want to know what actually happened.

unexpected ways. Watching my mother work tirelessly at her acupuncture clinic reminded me of my father's desperate attempts to re-learn the Hebrew he lost as a child, and made me realize that perseverance, a defining characteristic of both Chinese and Jewish cultures, is an area of common ground between the two. I realized that my two cultures converged once again in my mother's unfaltering devotion toward my academics, and my father's immense pride in my Jewish education. Finding and relishing in these similarities has become ingrained within my character as I have developed from my experiences, and has shaped my identity, as a Chinese Jewish person, into one as unique as the bizarre fusion foods my parents once made together.[32]

If you are applying to Columbia College, tell us what from your current and past experiences (either academic or personal) attracts you specifically to the field or fields of study that you noted in the Member Questions section. If you are currently undecided, please write about any field or fields in which you may have an interest at this time.

I am the first person in my family born into a childhood with no compromise. I was able to do all the things that mattered to me fully and without sacrifice, regardless of how random or obscure they were. Picking up the clunky bass, learning Spanish, these were choices I had the privilege of making and following to the fullest extent. For that invaluable gift, I am immensely grateful to my parents, who could never tout the same privilege. My father, born in Jerusalem but forced to spend his childhood in Communist Romania, and my mother, growing up in China during the Cultural Revolution, were compromised in all aspects of their lives, and as a result, worked tirelessly as immigrants in the United States to make sure I never was.[33]

---

32   This ending works! Amazing way to wrap things up, including a dose of humor and a glance back at her food-based metaphor. Notice how the take-home point isn't monumentous. Her identity struggle culminates in self-appreciation and relishing the unique synchronicities of her life - and it doesn't have to be more than that. This level of self-awareness and storytelling is more than enough to show Brielle as intelligent, thoughtful, and likable - and a much more assuming trait linked to her struggle would probably come off as over the top.

33   In this essay, Brielle forgoes the moment of introduction of the previous piece, but still works in specific details that bring her to life.

I would like to honor that trend in my life, and the place that would best allow me to do so in my educational experience is the Joint Degree Program between List College and Columbia. The renowned Core Curriculum at Columbia would allow me to explore all areas of the spectrum of human knowledge—enabling me to potentially foster new appreciations for subjects I once struggled with or thought I could never pursue. All this, along with the opportunity to explore the faith that has bound my family together, is unparalleled in any other institution.[34] Memories of my father playing Rosetta Stone Hebrew CDs, repeating *slicha* to himself in an attempt to re-learn his childhood Hebrew fostered an appreciation for the opportunity to thrive in a small community of Jewish students in the greatest city in the world.

At Columbia, I would have the opportunity to learn about Israel, my father's homeland, from the most qualified authorities on the Middle East. At List College, I would receive a refined Jewish education in subjects like Women in the Bible, that are unavailable anywhere else.[35] When I visited List and Columbia during Prospective Student Weekend and saw the Alma Mater with her arms splayed out on the steps, and saw the Moadon where List students came together in their shared Jewishness, I saw opportunity.[36]

MY TAKE:

Brielle's academic qualifications (3.6 GPA, 2230 SAT) and extracurricular involvement (a varsity athlete, captain of mock trial, section leader in orchestra) are impressive objectively, but not in the context of an application to Columbia. Where Brielle shines is her writing and her ability to "make a compelling narrative out of the incoherence of lived experience."

Her essay follows a strong framework of hooking the reader in a specific, regular moment in her childhood, setting up an identity conflict, and

---

[34]   Good higher-level connection between her values and the program she's applying to.

[35]   Referencing specific offerings is an important part of the "Why this school" essay, and Brielle nails them.

[36]   The ending falls a little short here, but there's definitely not as high of a bar for the ending of supplements.

gradually moving from action to reflection, culminating in the resolution of that internal conflict. It's a beautiful setup because it *makes a compelling narrative out of the incoherence of lived experience* (often the key to writing a great essay!)

Brielle is able to piece together her Chinese-Jewish background, a move to a new city, the death of her father, and her religious beliefs. She weaves a tying thread through these themes (biculturalism) and bookends the essay beautifully with anecdotes that showcase this theme (a typical night in her household, and the meals her family ate).

I'm going to highlight a couple of specific things that Brielle did well:

1. Opener: Brielle's initial dialogue between parents, in three lines, *shows* the admissions officer exactly what her household was like, and what her cultural conflict actually looked like. By zooming in on this typical night, Brielle encapsulates her parents personalities and the dynamic that she is a part of - her mother as the firm commander, her father as a warmer advocate. This use of dialogue is one of the best we've read - use it as a model.

2. Crafting the narrative: One of the most impressive parts of this essay is it's structure. After the first paragraph, read the first sentence of each paragraph. Notice how Brielle guides us through her self-reflection. Each sentence is succinct and powerful, and they set her up beautifully for a paragraph of thoughtful analysis. These sentences provide **scaffolding** for her narrative.

    a. "Growing up, mostly in San Francisco, such conflicts between my parents seemed natural to me."

    b. "Experiencing both sides of my culture in one day was nothing new to me, but finding a common ground between the two was something that did not occur to me until later in my teenage years."

    c. "Losing my father in such an unannounced, jarring way impacted my life in ways far beyond anything my fifteen-year-old self could have anticipated."

      d. "Confronted by such a colossal change in my life, the world changed for me, and one of the most profound differences I felt was one I never would have expected."

3. Last sentence: The way you close a piece is as important as how you open it - the opener determines how interested the admissions officer will be in reading it, and the ending is the last taste in their mouth as they mentally evaluate the essay and application. Brielle wraps up her bicultural conflict by labeling herself a Chinese Jewish person.

    Again, crafting a narrative - identity struggles are rarely resolved by the time one turns 18 and writes their college essay. She adds a nice touch of comparing her unique identity to the foods her parents once combined - a dose of humor that leaves the reader proud of Brielle for her internal struggle, and rooting for her.

Her academics and extracurriculars were strong, but not elite. But Brielle told her story in a way that stood out - which earned her a spot at Columbia.

Brielle in a sentence: Unique Chinese-Jewish identity, incredible writer, thoughtful, endearing eccentricity.

Cornell University

TALENE LI

APPLICATION:

Major I applied under / School I applied to: Computer Science, College of Engineering

Ethnicity: Asian

Gender: Female

Family Income Bracket: 250,000-500,000/year

Year of College Graduation: 2021

High School Unweighted GPA (to nearest hundredth): 4.00

High School Weighted GPA: 4.73

Class Rank/Percentile: 1%

SAT I Score (By Section): 770 Math, 780 Writing, 710 Critical Reading (2260 Total)

ACT Score (By Section): 35 Reading, 35 Math, 34 Science, 36 Writing (35 Composite)

SAT Subject Test Scores: 800 Math II, 750 US History, 780 Physics

AP Test Results: 5: Statistics, Biology, Calculus AB, Calculus BC, US History, Englishing Language, English Literature, Computer Science A 4: European History, Physics C: Mechanics, Psychology

Senior Year Course Load: AP Calculus BC, AP Psychology, AP Chemistry, AP English Literature, AP Computer Science A, AP Government/Honors Economics

Awards Won in High School: Salutatorian (12th), top 10 AMC score (10th-12th),

Extracurriculars in High School (Put leadership in parentheses): Piano, Violin, Youth Symphony, Students to Students guide, Dance

Job/Work Experience in High School: N/A

Volunteer/Community Service: Board member of local nonprofit organization against drunk driving

What did you do in the summer after freshman year of high school?

Practiced piano, summer camp for youth symphony

What did you do in the summer after sophomore year?

SAT Prep

What did you do in the summer after junior year?

Women's Technology Program at MIT

ABOUT YOUR HIGH SCHOOL:

State of High School: California

School Type (i.e. rural, suburban, city, public vs. private, etc): Suburban, Public

# of Students in Graduating Class: 450

What was your high school like? Demographics? How many other students went to elite universities?

It was ~80% caucasian, wealthy area, about 5-10 people per year went to Ivy Leagues/Stanford/MIT/other elite institutions, about 20-30 people per year went to UC Berkeley/UCLA.

REFLECTION ON APPLICATION PROCESS:

I applied: Regular Decision

What do you think your hooks were? (Things that made me stand out in the college application process)

I think my hook was mostly being a female in STEM. In other aspects, I'm not really a minority especially in my area, but I think being a girl in CS was definitely a hook. Though computer science is becoming way more popular now, the industry is still very much male-dominated. A lot of schools, especially Cornell, are trying to shift that perspective and aim to build a 50:50 ratio in their student body.

What do you think the strengths of your application were? (3-5 sentences)

I showed that I am really passionate about both my field and the potential impacts I saw myself making through it. I was applying to Cornell's College of Engineering with an intended major of Computer Science. It's one of the most popular majors in the nation, and it's one of Cornell's biggest majors as well, so it's incredibly competitive. But I demonstrated my passion for computer science by talking about how my interest in it developed over time.

I also did research on Cornell-specific projects and programs and talked about some that I connected to. At the time, I believed that using computer science for medical analysis and imaging could be a huge advancement, so I looked into Cornell's projects relating to CS and neuroscience. I showed them that it wasn't just the major that I wanted, but specifically Cornell's computer science that I wanted to pursue.

What do you think the weaknesses of your application were? Where might other applicants have had an advantage over you? (3-5 sentences)

I think that a lot of my experiences were "average," at least with respect to other applicants. I participated in a lot in high school, but nothing out of the ordinary. I played piano and violin, was on the dance team, and did some volunteering. I loved my activities, but I wasn't serious enough about any of them to win any major awards or titles with them. While my experiences were genuine, I found them to be somewhat of a weakness considering how many other kids do the same things and how easy it would be for me to fall into the majority when applying to such prestigious and competitive universities.

Where else you were admitted:

UC Berkeley, UCLA, UC Santa Barbara, UC San Diego, UC Davis, UC Irvine[37]

Where you were waitlisted:

Carnegie Mellon Arts

Where you were rejected:

Harvard, Princeton, Yale, Columbia, Dartmouth, Stanford, MIT, Carnegie Mellon CS

Did you get a private college counselor?

Yes

When did you start preparing for college admissions? How did your family prepare?

I started studying for SATs and standardized exams before junior year. I started working on essays around the summer before senior year. My family got me in SAT courses and got me a college counselor.

---

[37] A brief aside - with Talene's academic stats, it's almost impossible to get rejected from an in-state public school

ABOUT YOUR COLLEGE:

Why did you choose this school?

I chose Cornell because I wanted to be on the east coast for my college experience, and because they are well known for their computer science department. I wanted a school that could help me learn as much as possible and help me grow professionally, academically, and personally.

What is your school known for? What is its reputation? (3-5 sentences)

Cornell is known for being extremely competitive and high-stress, as well as having some prestigious programs (engineering, hotel, economics, etc). Unfortunately, Cornell is also known for having some of the most anxious/depressed students, especially due to a history of suicides.

Is this reputation accurate? (3-5 sentences)

The reputation is somewhat accurate, because the workload is intense and difficult. Students definitely put pressure on themselves to live up to the expectations of themselves and the school. However, students are not very competitive against each other and are actually often willing to work together. Additionally, aside from the anomalies, Cornell does not have more suicides than other top 20 schools, so that part of the reputation is not true.

What do you think your school offers that no other top 20 school does? (3-5 sentences)

I think that we offer the best balance of environments. We have a large campus, a student population that is large in comparison to smaller elite schools but is half the size of schools like Berkeley. We also have a wide range of weather and season, as well as incredible outdoor life that a lot of other schools do not have due to their locations. We also have some very special programs that few other schools do like our Operations Research major, the Hotel School, the ILR college, and an Architecture program. Also, we have our own ice cream made from our dairy bar and our own hotel on campus.

What kinds of people do you think would love your school? (5+ sentences)

I think anybody seeking intellectual challenge would love Cornell. The intensity of our work can be intimidating, but I think a lot of people have found that the intensity has pushed them to learn more and learn faster. I found that most Cornellians found internships or full-time work to be easier because of the difficulty of the schoolwork.

Additionally, Cornell has an incredibly large number of majors and programs. While you may be an expert in one major, you can easily find a class or a group that focuses on something you know absolutely nothing about. Additionally, people who love outdoor or physical activities and scenery would love the campus. We are surrounded by nature, and offer an insane number of PE classes from yoga to handgun safety to jogging to sailboating.

I also think people who aren't really sure of what they want would love Cornell. There are hundreds of clubs, hundreds of courses, and thousands of students at Cornell. Most majors have flexibility in electives that you can take to your advantage and take courses that you might have never considered before. Most freshmen are expected to be undeclared, so there's no pressure to come in and start right away with one major. It's nearly impossible not to find your place at Cornell, because there's so many places that you could fit into. Cornell gives a good balance of not being too small where you feel like you're seeing the same people all the time like in high school, but also not being too big where you feel like you're always lost and you're always flooded with strangers.

What kinds of people do you think would hate your school? (5+ sentences)

Somebody who wants a college experience as seen on tv or movies would probably hate Cornell. We are not located in a central area, leaving most of our social life to be on-campus. Because most of our social events are hosted by Cornell organizations, there are stricter policies and regulations. Additionally, anybody who does not like walking or the cold would hate Cornell, as our campus is located on a hill, and we are more north than many other top schools, making our winters harsher.

Do you like your school? Why or why not? ((3-5 sentences)

I have loved Cornell because it has forced me to grow a lot personally and academically. I had a very strict perfectionist mindset in high school that I have learned to let go of a bit at Cornell. I have been more focused on learning and having the experience that I will be proud of later on rather than spending all my time worried about being the perfect student. Cornell has given me so many opportunities and some of my favorite people that I would not have met otherwise.

Your college's biggest strengths. What do students appreciate about their school/take for granted? (5 sentences)

I think Cornell does an amazing job with providing professional resources for students. We have information sessions events hosted by companies all the time, and it is incredibly easy to find a place on campus to ask about jobs and internships. We have two career fairs for engineers, and I know that some other colleges have their own career fairs as well, making it easier to meet recruiters. Additionally, meeting alumni is easy and encouraged, and alumni are always so happy to help current students.

Your college's biggest weaknesses. What do students complain about the most? What would an admissions counselor never tell you? (5 sentences)

Cornell's biggest weakness is that it has very limited resources for student's personal needs. We have over 20,000 students on campus, many of whom, like me, are extremely far from home. There are times when students struggle, but our resources at Cornell Health are fairly limited. They are constantly working to improve this, but it is definitely one of the biggest issues that Cornell faces.

ESSAYS:

Common App Essay:

Three things people told me when I mentioned my depression.[38]

---

38   Great hook. Starts right with some power, and gets the reader invested in learning more.

THE KIDS WHO GET IN

1. "What do you have to be depressed about?"
2. "Oh, it's nothing, compared to something like brain cancer."
3. "You're probably just making it up in your own mind."

30 pairs of eyes rested on me as I shakily finished my speech.[39]

It was nearing the end of junior year, and my AP English final project was to present a speech on the topic of my choice. I pondered heavily on what to write about for my speech. Corgis? Adorable, but not serious enough. Food? Delicious, but not interesting enough. Piano? Maybe, but still doesn't seem right.[40] Depression? At first I laughed. I knew that talking about depression in public was like saying "Voldemort" at Hogwarts -- there's an unwritten law never to speak of it.

But then, I remembered 8th grade. The darkness of my days back then with the times my depression was trivialized and misjudged played in my mind, and a fire lit up within me.[41] I had the chance to be heard now, to speak against those who once labeled me "over-dramatic" and "attention-seeking." So with depression as my centerpiece, I crafted my speech, scrutinizing every word until I felt it was perfect. In the end, however, it wasn't the words I said that mattered. No, what mattered most was the moment of silence between the end of my speech and the applause. In that moment, I found my calling. Facing the inspired looks of my classmates, I knew that I wanted to change the way people everywhere perceived depression.

I have had made hopeful (and hopeless) dreams in the past -- be a lawyer, cure cancer, win a Nobel Prize, write a best-selling novel, establish my own successful startup[42] -- but this goal is different. My yearning to change the

---

39   Also great transition teasing a specific moment, before zooming out a bit.

40   I like this brainstorming because it shows us other aspects of her personality that she might not have had the space to expand upon. These specifics remind the AO that she's a real person.

41   This is a pretty convoluted sentence and could be simplified to "Remembering the darkness of those days lit a fire in me."

42   Ditto with the brainstorming.

way we perceive mental illnesses is not about money or fame or prestige, it's about a chance for happiness. It's about impacting the world for those who cannot stand up for themselves.

I think of the anonymous teens on online forums, hiding their identities in hopes that nobody familiar will recognize them.[43] As they feel ashamed to speak up about their depression, anxiety, or other issues, I find a part of my former self in them. I remember how depression consumed me, replacing the once bubbly, outgoing me with a lifeless, pessimistic girl whom I could barely recognize. I remember struggling to find the words to describe my pain, and failing to speak up after hearing the voices of the skeptics. It is for the people who feel this pain that I find this passion.

I prepare for war, as I did once before. However, depression is no longer my enemy. I no longer feel the burden of its weight, and I no longer grasp for air as it tries to wash away my voice. This time, I combat far mightier opponents: the stigma and stereotypes of the depression. Weapon of choice? I arm myself with my voice.

The greatest triumph I ever felt from overcoming my depression was turning it into my motivation. The misconceptions of depression dominates society, as the illness is intangible, invisible, and incomprehensible, but I am inspired by my past to fight the status quo. Depression reminds me of the change I am capable of -- within myself and within others. I once worried that my past with depression would make me a less desirable candidate for college, but to cower away in fear of what a school may think of me is to surrender my battle. My past is what makes my passion burn so strong, and from it, I have found the warrior within myself. I'm ready for battle, voice is locked and loaded.[44]

Supplement: Why Cornell?

_____

43   I really like this. It's so real - and it's a good touch point where Talene reminds us that other people struggle as well. I would have loved to see her reach back here in the conclusion - more on that in a bit.

44   The conclusion doesn't hit the way it should. It becomes lofty and a bit intense. Talene's message is clouded by the introduction of a new metaphor of war. Conclusions are a great point to revisit earlier themes and metaphors (see Columbia, on food); introducing war here leaves the essay with a disjointed tone.

"I want to be an engineer," little 7-year-old-me told my parents. At the time, all I knew about engineering were the complex codes and circuits on my dad's computer screen.[45]

They appeared to me a foreign language, but all I could think was "how cool is that!" Although I knew nothing about engineering, I wanted to be just like my dad. 11 years later, I say again "I want to be an engineer," and now, I finally know what that means.

At the Women's Technology Program at MIT, I learned how engineering -- especially computer science -- can be applied to fields including art, psychology, and medicine. Hearing guest speakers who used engineering to make art or build prosthetic feet or research a cure for the Zika virus inspired me. I realized that engineering can apply to anything.[46]

Engineering is my key to helping others. I have a passion to build but also a passion to change lives, and the ability to use computer science for both is the main reason I want to enter engineering. Ultimately, I hope to enter Cornell Engineering so I can change the way society treats depression.

For now, treatment for depression consists of prescribed medication and counseling that are not always effective. Although antidepressants and various forms of therapy are available, they are not enough to help everybody. Depression is an illness that is unique to each person it affects, so I believe that treatment should be just as individual.

Studying computer science at Cornell means branching out to a variety of other fields using computer science as my basis. At Cornell, I have the chance to learn about biological mechanisms, cognitive science, and branches of mathematics and relate them all to computer science. Cornell will empower me to take on my goal of finding a better treatment for depression in almost any direction I want. For example, the research of computational biology under the computer science program could give me the chance to study

[45] This comes across as manufactured dialogue. A better way to structure it would be to begin with the object of fascination (her dad's computer screen), and jump to why she was so drawn to it, and how that sparked a lifelong interest. There are plenty of essays out there about wanting to be (career field x) since childhood; it's important to explain *why*.

[46] Great blurb that shows Talene has some understanding of the lesser-known applications of engineering.

functions of genes and connections between genes that link to depression.

Neurotech is another opportunity tied to Cornell engineering that makes me believe Cornell will give me an education I couldn't receive anywhere else. Neurotech's efforts to develop technology to further understand the brain and the connections within the brain is the kind of effort needed to understand the complex disorder that is depression. I believe that Neurotech's expanding knowledge about the brain could unlock doors for students like me. Medical technology such as brain scans can be redesigned through newfound information. Computer science, with many useful applications such as data processing or image processing, could be the field necessary to handle such advanced technology. Cornell provides limitless opportunities outside the classroom that pushes students to become working professionals.[47]

When I first claimed I wanted to be an engineer, I didn't know the hard work or endless possibilities it meant for me. Now, I understand that engineering is one part breaking-apart, one part putting-together, and all innovation. Passion and dedication are necessary for engineering, and I am thrilled by the future I have with it. My goal to change the way we treat depression is lofty, but I believe Cornell's world-renowned engineering program will propel me to conquer my dream.[48]

MY TAKE:

On paper, Talene is a strong college applicant. She has a 4.0, a 2260/35, 12 AP tests and nine 5's, and performed well on the AMC (American Mathematics Competition). This is a phenomenally impressive academic background! Talene also played in the school symphony and was on the board of a local non-profit - she checks all the right boxes for elite college admissions.

Let's start with her essay. Massive amounts of potential here! Mental health

---

[47] In the previous 2 paragraphs, Talene does a phenomenal job of connecting her career interests, her personal passion, and what Cornell has to offer.

[48] Again, goes a little bit too lofty in the conclusion, but this time on a more positive note. I would have worded it "Cornell's world-renowned engineering program will put me in the best position to accomplish this task."

is a bit of a taboo subject (which Talene has the self-awareness to address) and that inherently lends itself to standing out and taking a risk. I admire the courage and tone of the piece.

Talene starts her essay well. Even though her intro is a little bit choppy, we like it because it lends itself well to the college essay (brainstorming speech topics works because it shows us other aspects of her personality). She moves forward and tells the story of giving the speech pretty well (although that section would benefit from additional imagery and detail). The line "what mattered most was the moment of silence between the end of my speech and the applause" is very powerful. I would have ended the paragraph with it or considered making it it's own paragraph.

The last third of her essay (which is the most important) is where Talene slips on execution; the essay doesn't land the way it should. Talene moves to lofty, abstract statements and introduces a new metaphor of weaponry/war which comes across as intense and overly general. Ending any piece of writing is hard, and many students make the mistake of going too broad with their conclusions - it's an easy way to wrap up a piece. Talene brings up the fire instilled in her through her struggle with mental illness, which is an important trait to highlight. **But it's important to be specific with conclusions**.

Talene's best lines in this piece are precise. She laments the struggle of anonymous teens on message boards, and points to the moment after completing her speech preceding applause as a pivotal moment in her growth. These specific pictures help the reader understand who Talene is, and they come across as earnest. At the end of her piece, Talene creates the perfect opportunity to loop back to these specifics and bookend her essay.

She brings up her former inability to find the words to speak about her pain. This is a perfect opportunity to return to that opening moment in her AP English class where she spoke proudly and publicly. This would work with a line like:

"After so many years of feeling voiceless, speaking in front of my English class that day, I never felt more sure of what I had to say."

Talene could also use this section to focus on how moving it was for her to give a voice to the issue faced by those anonymous teens, or how impacted the other members of her class were after her speech. Focusing more on the impact her growth had on others would be a more flattering way of framing this reflection. Alternatively, Talene could hone in on the strength and fire that fighting this battle has instilled in her, and talk about translating that passion to her academics and community service. She says that she is "ready for battle," but it's important to clarify what those battles may be (and show that those battles are ones that impact others).

Besides that feedback on her writing, Talene's flawless academic background and competitive extracurriculars were enough to gain her admission to Cornell. Her essay may have alienated AOs at some of the other schools that she applied to - schools that receive many applications as qualified as Talene's. Tweaking the tone and conclusion of her personal statement and supplement may have made the difference at some of the other elite schools that she applied to.

Talene in a sentence: Super high-achieving, interested in intersections of coding and mental illness, fierce.

Dartmouth College

LOVE TSAI

APPLICATION:

Major I applied under / School I applied to: Undeclared

Ethnicity: East Asian

Gender: Female

Family Income Bracket: 20,000-40,000/year

Year of College Graduation: 2023

SAT I Score (By Section): 800 Math, 790 Reading (1590 Total)

ACT Score (By Section): N/A

SAT Subject Test Scores: 790 Math II, 750 Biology, 710 Physics

High School Unweighted GPA (to nearest hundredth): 3.96

High School Weighted GPA: 4.62 / 5.00

Class Rank/Percentile: N/A (homeschooled)

AP Test Results: 5: English Language, Calculus BC, Computer Science A, English Literature, 4: US History, Calculus AB, 3: Biology, Chemistry

Senior Year Course Load: World Literature*, Science of Cooking (Chemistry + Physics), Statistics*, Calculus 3*, AP Latin, Intermediate French III*, AP Psychology, AP Microeconomics, Personal Finance[49]

Awards Won in High School: AP Scholar w/ Distinction, Joyce Ivy Summer Scholar, National Merit Finalist, Gold and Silver medals (National Latin Exam), Corona Laurea (Medusa Mythology Exam), Honorable Mentions and Silver Key (Scholastic Art and Writing), Varsity letter, Bronze, Silver Medal (music organization), Dale Carnegie Leadership Training Outstanding Performance Award, multiple scholarships and dance certificates

Extracurriculars in High School (Put leadership in parentheses): Classical ballet and dance (senior company member), Concert choir (section leader), Regional youth orchestra - violin I, Junior Academy (team leader), District literature and art magazine (editor-in-chief, co-founder), Joyce Ivy Foundation general student fellow

Job/Work Experience in High School: Hospital Cytopathology internship (unpaid). Babysitting for families with children who have special needs.

Volunteer/Community Service: Hospital ER, reception, surgery recover volunteer. Hospital music therapy volunteer. Org. for those with special-needs volunteer.

What did you do in the summer after freshman year of high school?

Family trip: traveled to Taiwan to visit extended family (my parents were the only ones to immigrate). During this summer, I attended the Dale Carnegie Leadership Seminar, where I learned various aspects of leadership and collaboration. Otherwise, most of it was spent looking after baby cousins and spending time with family.

What did you do in the summer after sophomore year?

Ballet summer intensive and volunteering as camp counselor/advisor:

Spent 4 wks (40 hr/wk) dancing ballet on scholarship.

Spent 1 wk (25 hr total) volunteering as a counselor for a camp servicing teenagers with special needs.

---

49   * are all dual-enrollment

What did you do in the summer after junior year?

Harvard SSP on full scholarship with Joyce Ivy Foundation:

7 wk program where students take two college classes and earn them as credits which can be applied to other degrees later down the road. I took Deductive Logic and Introduction to Neuroscience and went as a Summer Scholar with the Joyce Ivy Foundation.

ABOUT YOUR HIGH SCHOOL:

State of High School: Michigan

School Type (i.e. rural, suburban, city, public vs. private, etc): Homeschooled

# of Students in Graduating Class: 2 (twins, explained more later)

What was your high school like? Demographics? How many other students went to elite universities?

Homeschooled, with two students in a "graduating class" because I had an identical twin sister. Demographics obviously mirror family demographics: low-income, no connections/history with elite schools as both my parents are immigrants, no great resources available, etc.

My parents (mostly my mom) chose to homeschool so that we could spend more time together as a family unit during this transformative period of me and my twin sister's lives (i.e. growing up). We had undergone some family ordeals when I was younger that forced my mother to resign from her job, and this experience really emphasized to my parents how important it was to spend time with those we love, sometimes even at the cost of other things such as prestige, money, or academics. In other words, without love and our relationships, we have nothing. My mom also wanted me to develop a strong work ethic, sense of personal responsibility, and robust worldview and understanding that she felt like wasn't as possible in a public school setting.

In middle school, which is when I started homeschooling, I primarily did online schooling and also went to a lot of co-ops. Homeschool co-ops were often run by retired teachers and families with backgrounds in education with meetings once or twice a week to provide more structure for students and families. Once I started high school, I stopped going to co-ops and started dual-enrollment at the local community college alongside online schooling. Unlike many other families, we operated September-June because I was still in "institutions" that required it: such as taking finals for college courses and AP exams in May. Every day consisted of me doing my work either online or going to class, and then leaving the house to do various extracurricular activities.

Homeschooling is definitely not for everyone. Personally, homeschooling has given me things I find very rarely in my friends and other students my age: an absurdly strong familial bond, equally strong personal convictions, a path/calling, and deeper understanding of myself as a student, a member of my society, and a human being. In addition, I've always had friends from all age groups and walks of life, and just believe that my life was way more colorful because I was homeschooled. Because my parents really didn't care where I ended up in terms of college, this was all that mattered. For those who strongly prioritize their education, homeschooling in general makes things more difficult and uncertain (especially if you're from a lower-income background like me). Also it just requires a lot of self-discipline!

Local high school: 27% of students qualified for free/reduced-price lunch.

Pretty diverse: 50% white and 34% African-American.

Maybe 1 person a year goes to West Point but almost nobody ever goes to elite universities and very few students ever leave the state. Most above average students go to Michigan; a huge number of students go to Michigan State.

REFLECTION ON APPLICATION PROCESS:

I applied: Regular Decision

What do you think your hooks were? (Things that made me stand out in the college application process)

I'm not really sure! I think being homeschooled was definitely something that was interesting about me, but I find it more of a weakness than a strength just because I lacked other things like modes of comparison, substantial LORs, resources to do as well as other students, etc. Otherwise, my application showed that I was a really self-disciplined and driven person. None of my activities, extracurriculars, or awards were provided in the way that other students can join clubs or go to their guidance counselors. Everything my application showed I had to find myself, and this self-starter attitude is what I think really set me apart from others.

What do you think the strengths of your application were?

Test scores (particularly SAT I) were probably good in reaffirming my competency (demonstrated by grades). I was also heavily involved with my community and did many extracurricular activities that required self-discipline and being a self-starter. All my activities really centered around one main narrative that I went back to again and again, so AOs could really see my interests and how they tied together--I didn't do things just because they looked good. Lastly, I am a relatively good writer and probably did a good job in arguing and presenting my case.

What do you think the weaknesses of your application were? Where might other applicants have had an advantage over you?

Being homeschooled just means that a lot of my application could not be easily compared with others. What does an A mean on my transcript? What could be expected of me, and when did I go above-and-beyond? Those were questions that AOs couldn't answer because there was no information for them to go off of.

Being homeschooled also meant that I didn't have the same access to resources and I don't think I reached my full potential in that sense. For example, I taught myself a lot of the material that I learned. I didn't have close relationships with teachers for LORs. I didn't have clubs to go to, established leadership positions to run for, mentors to guide me. Everything was harder in that I had to support myself through school and couldn't lean on anybody else: counselors, school programs, etc. I never knew how I stood in comparison to others and I could have probably done better *concretely* (like in terms of accomplishments, grades, etc.) if I had gone to public school.

Where else you were admitted:

Colorado School of Mines, Michigan State, University of Alabama, Florida, Southern College, University of Michigan - Ann Arbor, Northeastern, Macalester, Colorado College, Grinnell, Notre Dame, Emory, Hamilton, Amherst, UNC Chapel Hill, Boston University, Vanderbilt, Wayne

Where you were waitlisted:

Colby, University of Chicago, Haverford, Williams, Davidson, Carleton, Washington and Lee, Wesleyan, Tulane

Where you were rejected:

MIT, Washington University @ St Louis, Johns Hopkins, Swarthmore, Pomona, Bowdoin, Oberlin, USC, Rice, Harvard, Princeton, Yale, Brown, Penn, Columbia, Tufts, Duke, Tulane, Stanford, Cornell

Did you get a private college counselor?

Yes

When did you start preparing for college admissions? How did your family prepare?

I started preparing for the actual application towards the end of the summer. I got two private college counselors through full scholarships from Collegewise and the College Essay Guy, and these counselors helped me in researching colleges and seeing what was expected of me. My mom had to help with a lot of the homeschool documentation (we had to provide reading lists, course descriptions, contact info, etc. that other students don't have to). My dad stayed out of it pretty much.

For SAT testing and such, I did all my testing in my junior year: I self-studied for the PSAT, took that in October for NMQST, and took the SAT in Nov that year as well. I only took the SAT once.

ABOUT YOUR COLLEGE:

Why did you choose this school?

I chose Dartmouth because I wanted to use my undergraduate years to explore, grow, and be challenged in ways that I haven't before. I thought the location was ideal for this time of my life, when things are simpler and I can just be a college student, spending weekends on-campus instead of running into the city. The size was a little small but good for ensuring that I would have access to resources and not get lost in a sea of 40,000 faces. The people here are kind, outgoing, and fun to be around. I've met a few duds here and there, but it's been mostly good things. I had the option to stay closer to home, but I just wanted to get out and throw myself into this next phase of my life. I didn't want to play it safe!

Sometimes I wonder what life would have been like had I gone to xyz school, but pondering counterfactuals is never an efficient way to spend your time. If I could give any one piece of advice to you, it would be to really sit down and think about the essence of what you want out of your college education. Yes, think logistics about pre-med stuff and grade curves and research, but also think about what kind of person you want to be when you graduate, what things you want to explore, and what places you'll never get a chance to otherwise live in. You can get a good education almost anywhere, so it is going to be these other things that really make a place home.

What is your school known for? What is its reputation?

I actually hadn't really heard of Dartmouth until I was a senior and applying to colleges so I'm not 100% of its general reputation. However, I would say that among students, Dartmouth is usually known as the party school of the Ivy League, not necessarily as "laid-back" or "hippy-ish" like Brown, but more "ragey," although of course this is in comparison to other Ivies. In comparison with other state schools, we are still lacking in that department. In general, think Animal House for social life.

As for the stuff that would appear on ranking lists and more respectable college profiles, Dartmouth is known as having great undergraduate focus, being a small school with many opportunities, and having happy students. It is also known for its outdoor life and rural location, as well as excellent placement for consulting, government, investment banking, etc.

Is this reputation accurate?

I believe so! Dartmouth students benefit from it being a small school connected with a lot of resources and great professors. As for being "crunchy" and outdoorsy, almost 96% of students participate in First-Year trips, a lot of sophomores do STRIPS (which is the 2nd year equivalent that people go on before sophomore summer), and generally everyone goes hiking, skiing, dancing at formal at some point in their Dartmouth career. Even people who have no association with the outdoors will come out a little greener than before.

As for social life, there are pockets of communities where you don't have to go out, drink, etc. to have fun. However, a large portion of the undergraduate population *is* involved with Greek life and most people do associate "nightlife" with drinking, tails, formals, fretting, etc. I have had friends visit other Ivies and say that their student life feels stale or empty by comparison, even though we are by far the smallest school. It is more controlled than Animal House, I think, and each incoming class does place more emphasis on safety and looking out for each other.

What are you involved with on campus?

I've gotten very involved in my freshman year! Here is a list of my major commitments on-campus (not including off-campus jobs):

- dance with two student dance groups (one open, one closed)
- executive board of pre-health society
- involved with Center for Social Impact (non-profit consulting programs, pilot programs, etc.)
- involved with Tucker Center for Spiritual Life (spring break trips, programs, etc.)
- volunteer with elderly afflicted with dementia/Alzheimer's living in the UV

- writer for DUJS (Dartmouth Undergraduate Journal of Science)
- work with the admissions office, student accessibility services
- work as a research intern at DHMC in immunology
- student spiritual life (Christian Union, Agape)

What do you think your school offers that no other top 20 school does?

To be quite honest, I don't think that any one school can offer something *completely unique*. Great education, opportunities to get to know professors, research opportunities, etc. can be found at a lot of places, to varying degrees of success.

However, I do believe that Dartmouth offers an intimate learning environment that allows students to be competitive for the world post-graduation while still being collaborative and not cut-throat. It really is the best of both worlds where you can be accomplished and still cut loose, even with professors!

What kinds of people do you think would love your school?

Students who enjoy having fun, as cliche and slightly childish as that sounds. Students who don't take themselves too seriously, who enjoy midnight snowball fights on the Green, who love to prank prospies or freshmen.

To apply this to academics, students who are truly passionate about what they do--people who can actually find *fun* and do their coursework and their responsibilities, and sometimes even see them as one and the same. The same person you see partying on Friday night you will see on Monday in a suit and tie, getting ready for their presentation or interview. I've seen athletes arguing about math/econ/CS after practice, pre-med students tack on music class after music class because they enjoy it, and TAs teach a course 10 times throughout their Dartmouth career because they love it so much. The distinction between typical party people and academics isn't as strict here, and you can really have it all. Additionally, I've had friends help others with projects when they themselves have work to do; I've seen professors at Homecoming, at snowball fights, at grocery stores--one of my friends took his professor out to dinner through our school program and they ended up talking about dating during college. Everyone has a story that is so different from what you'd expect and people who enjoy being part of a community and finding out those individual stories will love it at Dartmouth!

What kinds of people do you think would hate your school?

People who find the aforementioned activities childish, juvenile, or time-wasting. There are some people who take themselves more seriously, who maybe think that climbing the academic/corporate/"prestige" ladder is the most efficient use of their time. Being a part of Dartmouth may make them feel like they're surrounded by hedonists chasing momentary pleasures, especially when the library empties out on Friday nights.

Also, people who don't enjoy being super busy or who can't operate with the "duck syndrome"[50] mindset floating around. Most students at Dartmouth are both accomplished academically and super involved socially, and this on top of the quarter system means that once week 1 hits, it feels like you're in a marathon until the very end. Everyone will say that they were up playing pong until 4AM and yet they still somehow manage to get As.

Do you like your school? Why or why not?

Yes! I am a pretty optimistic person and probably would have liked any school I ended up going to, but I am overall pretty happy with my choice. I have great opportunities for academic advancement, a lot of support with professors and deans, and so many ways to get involved with the Dartmouth community and our greater UV. Most people I've met are incredibly kind and easy-to-get along with, and though Dartmouth itself isn't perfect, I've always been able to get through it with my friends and staff support. Also, being in quarantine may be making me more sentimental than usual, but I just generally have a lot of love for my school and the potential we have to become an even better institution. People care a lot about others, and I think that as long as we have that, anything is possible.

---

50   From Love: **Duck syndrome** is a term that describes people who look like they have it all together but are actually working in overdrive to get things done. It can be dangerous because if you don't understand the impact of duck syndrome on your campus, you can feel like the only one who is struggling. The term itself comes from the image that you see when you visit a lake and there are ducks paddling around: on the surface, they seem rather peaceful. Only underwater do you notice how fast and hard they're kicking!

Your college's biggest strengths. What do students appreciate about their school/take for granted?

- Funding: there are pockets of money everywhere! As long as you learn how to apply for them, you should have no trouble financing internships, research, etc.

- Study-abroad: many pre-meds forgo this quintessential part of The Dartmouth experience, but I think that most students (if they can fit it in) should still go!

- Access to professors: I've never had a class taught by a TA, have often just sat and talked with professors during office hours about stuff not discussed in class, and have been able to continue a relationship with professors I met during my fall term! Having only 10 weeks for a class often makes it harder to develop a relationship, but I've found that profs are super accommodating and excited to help you

- Overall support: lots of people care a lot about your wellbeing. Use them to your advantage!

Your college's biggest weaknesses. What do students complain about the most? What would an admissions counselor never tell you?

- The Quarter System: everything just moves so fast! You learn something new every day and there is just no time to breathe during the term. Imagine-- after 1 week, you're 10% done with the term!

- "Commitment to academic rigor": the problem is that this manifests itself in departments curving courses down or otherwise doing things no other school does (such as putting medians on transcripts). Econ and chem, for example, have artificial medians set at B. If everyone does well and the median is a 91, that becomes a B. Other professors just enjoy having difficult classes for the sake of difficult classes (orgo this term was supposed to have 6 hour midterms)... While I can understand an argument for academic rigor, if other institutions of similar rank/prestige aren't doing it, I don't really see why we have to.

- The "whiteness" standard: many racial groups tend to self-segregate and white people tend to control many social spaces (think frats or sororities), with frats/srats with URM majorities being considered "B-side" and A-side fraternities/sororities[51] having diversity quotas and using URMs as diversity tokens. In policy/gov/literature/philosophy type classes, the stereotypical pretentious white male takes up many a period with his own thoughts as the girls just sit and watch them blabber on about something no one else cares about. I think girls learn to stand up for themselves more as they become sophomores, but my first writing course was the absolute worst because of these people.

- Introductory math courses: just generally horrible across the board.

ESSAYS:

Common App Essay:

In Taiwan, names are prophecies.

My parents named me Love.

As a baby, I craved emotional connection and fell asleep easily in my mother's arms, only to sob the instant I was left alone. Growing up, this developed into healthier attachment. I never cried at daycare, was always a treat for the babysitter, and ran around town with my twin sister, waving to ecstatic mothers who gushed over our matching outfits. I was an eager toddler: as long as there were people to meet and things to discover, I was happy.[52]

---

51   From Love: **A/b-side** is a way to divide Greek houses into ones that are more "preferable" vs. ones that aren't during rush. In truth, it is quite an adolescent thing to ascribe to and is like distinguishing the "popular" kids in a hypothetical high school. The "best" Greek houses are "a-side" and many people want to rush into them (girls moreso than guys because of differences in the rush process). B-side houses don't have such an "acclaimed" reputation and are often seen as lesser-than. Campus image shifts over the years and houses that once were b-side can become a-side with changing preferences, new members, and differences in the way that the house conducts itself. However, "a-side" houses are usually overwhelmingly white, rich, and "ragey".

52   I like this. It's warm, and sets the essay up perfectly for an abrupt switch.

My mother was diagnosed with cancer when I was five. Ever the loving parents, my twin sister and I were shielded from this devastating news and shipped off to relatives in Taiwan. I didn't find out about my mother's illness until I was thirteen, and when I returned from this spontaneous vacation, things seemed different. There were now strange things hidden around the house, items such as wigs and rows of prescriptions. More than material changes, my whole family dynamic changed.[53]

I was greeted by transformed parents who had remembered what was most important: a true zeal for life. Namely, my parents grew to value a genuine excitement for learning, creativity, and a compassionate heart for others.

Instead of creating a mindless drone, my parents cultivated a curious spirit. As friends did math drills at the tender age of seven, I started piano. During the terrors of middle school, I began homeschooling, eating breakfast with my mom while discussing the ancient philosophers.[54] Today, these philosophers have welcomed numerous other companions-- I don't memorize material for a test and study only for grades; learning happens everywhere, all the time. I've grown into a student of life. Piles upon piles of books fill the shelves in my house, ranging from a Latin text of "The Aeneid" to textbooks of neuroscience and organic chemistry. Each is loved and intensely studied; I particularly enjoy it when my concentrations intersect, such as when a translation of Latin includes Pliny the Elder's "Naturalis Historia" or my neuroscience textbook explains why Van Gogh's stars seem to shimmer and glisten.

After my mother's illness, my family treasured creativity and artistry because life is too beautiful and fragile not to.[55] Before, we moved too quickly for us to ever slow down and appreciate simply existing. This instantly changed

---

53   Love creates a stark contrast between the sunny stroller rides of her infancy and the new household of her teenage years. Think of this as a "record screech" - it jolts the reader into paying attention. Contrast is a good thing!

54   More contrast (the terrors of middle school and dining with her mom)! I expand more on this below.

55   I write something similar in the Vanderbilt entry - it's impressive when applicants draw upon their life experience to make a broader claim about life and what's important. Love draws upon her life and her mother's battle with cancer to show us what's important to her, and we see a fully formed young adult who knows who she is, and why.

following my mother's recovery: me and my twin sister began going to art fairs, concerts, and even the park, trying to recreate a flower using pen and paper. As I grew older and started carving my own path, I discovered an affinity for poetry, ballet, and painting. My love for piano and music manifested itself in two new, yet familiar forms: singing and the violin. Today, sheet music, ballet exam booklets, and enormous art anthologies are stuffed alongside my textbooks at home. I practice my violin in a room housing oil paints, cookbooks, and a sewing machine. The very same art fairs I visited as a child became the ones I would volunteer at ten years later.

I am known as many things: artist, scholar, daughter, friend. Above all, I am Love, and I strive to be worthy of my namesake.[56] Cancer made my parents see what truly matters in life when one's physical, mental, and emotional power is destroyed by illness. What remains except for one's character? During my mother's disease, compassion emerged as the driving force of everything: it gave her the will to survive for her family, brought her comfort, and revealed the true meaning of life. Love is my name: I believe that my purpose is to give myself to others. Whether it's at the hospital, an open mic, or even on the homeschool prom committee, I always enjoy serving others and never see it as work. My parents taught me to place my heart not on my sleeve, but in my hands. I didn't discover what I wanted to do until high school, but I believe that the kindness and empathy my mother so valued from her doctors, perhaps even above their medical knowledge, unconsciously shaped me-- I hope to become such a doctor, sensitive and skilled. Though I know the road is arduous and the heartache incomprehensible, my mission is to change the world, not have it change me.

In the end, I don't know if prophetic names are just Taiwanese superstition, but I do know I make a pretty good case for its validity. At the beginning, my name was simply a hopeful wish. Along the way, life worked in its own, trademarked mysterious ways. Today, I am my name's perfect personification: admirer of beauty, seeker of knowledge, and devotee of compassion.

My name is Love. How could it be anything else?

---

56   Love is humble. Better to understate her relationship with her name (striving to live up to it) than overstate it (saying something like "a trait that I embody everywhere that I go.") She ramps this up a bit with her conclusion, but it works.

DAAVI GAZELLE

1. Please respond in 100 words or less:

While arguing a Dartmouth-related case before the U.S. Supreme Court in 1818, Daniel Webster, Class of 1801, delivered this memorable line: "It is, Sir...a small college. And yet, there are those who love it!" As you seek admission to the Class of 2023, what aspects of the College's program, community or campus environment attract your interest?

When I talk about my peculiar draw to Dartmouth, many a friend or well-meaning adult has withdrawn in horror, proclaiming Dartmouth as the woebegotten college stuck in the middle of nowhere[57]. As for me, I've always loved Dartmouth's quirks, where a special brand of learners take delight in getting to know each other, and through this, themselves.[58] Whether I am exploring with the DOC or sheltering myself from the cold inside Baker-Berry Library, I look forward to being surrounded by fellow passionate, curious, and spirited students.[59]

It is, Sir... a small college. But it means the world to me.[60]

2. Please choose one of the following prompts and respond in 250-300 words:

E. In The Bingo Palace, author Louise Erdrich, Class of 1976, writes, "...no one gets wise enough to really understand the heart of another, though it is the task of our life to try." Discuss.

As a young child, I used to play online games for as long as my parents would let me. I stopped playing when I was ten as I abruptly realized that it was a significantly absurd waste of time. I repeated actions over and over again to get nicer furniture for a house that didn't exist, completed pre-programmed quests just to start on another one, and lived my virtual life by a meaningless, man-made system.

---

57   I'm sure the AO smiled reading this
58   It blows my mind that Love applied to 20+ schools and was still able to nail the "Why Dartmouth" piece.
59   See the "Why Northwestern" essay as well--great balance of specifics and a read of the overall vibe of the school.
60   Cheeky ending but it lands.

It wasn't too long ago when I realized that "actual" life operates in the same way.[61] The modern American lives too focused on things we deem important in a system we've devised ourselves.

We all die at some point. The various ways someone can succeed, evidenced by monetary wealth or the greatest of reputation and power, won't operate as some kind of payment or lucky token in the afterlife (unless you know something I don't). And now, I've realized that games aren't what I want to focus on, virtual or not.

Games aren't real: they're manufactured entities that tell people what is important, what to believe, and how to live. What is effortlessly real is compassion.[62] It will exist through the ages and until the end of time. Though I may never be wise enough, sufficiently competent, or even humble enough to understand the hearts of those around me, it is my duty to try. The meaning of life—the tasks of the human life—isn't to find "success" for ourselves, but for others. Tasks to find a smile in a crowd, provide peace when there is worry, and discern the hearts of humanity. Only then can we grow together and create a culture of sincerity. And only then will we step out of virtual reality and heed the driving force of a brighter future: compassion.[63]

MY TAKE:

As I stated earlier, a lot of elite college admissions is standing out. It's important to not only highlight what makes you unique, but to explain how those life experiences have shaped you and why they will make you a valuable member of that college's undergraduate community.

---

61   Woah.

62   This supplement works really well because it ties into themes that Love brings up in her personal statement (compassion, questioning human priorities), and shows more depth around Love's values and beliefs. Congruent, and drills deeper - a great supplement.

63   Reading Love's essays inspired me to be a better person which is a ridiculously good indicator of the strength of this application.

When I applied to college, I had taken a gap year, and I leveraged that as much as I could - I wrote about the life experience and maturity that I gained during my year of service/work experience, and emphasized how much my growth would enable me to contribute in college.

In this application, Love does a phenomenal job of juxtaposing her educational experience being homeschooled with the typical school experience. As we read, Love shows us what she gained from her atypical experience - a genuine appreciation for the small moments of life and a love of learning. In one of her Dartmouth supplements, Love builds on this with her beliefs about money and compassion. Her essays piece together well to show us a special individual who not only lived through some pretty unique experiences (having a mother with cancer, being homeschooled) but also understands how those experiences molded her into the person she is today.

Love's Why Dartmouth essay is one of the best "Why this college" essays I've ever read. In only 100 words this is more or less a litmus test to see if you understand the essence of the school you're applying to - there's not as much time to cram in course names or clubs of interest. She hits a couple of hallmarks of the Dartmouth experience: its rurality, its focus on self-growth and discovery, and its strong undergraduate community. Love weaves in a couple obligatory specifics to show she's done her homework, and the result is an essay that works.

One more strength of Love's application that I want to touch on is her ability to unassumingly drop little bits of wisdom. This has to be done tastefully because AOs are skeptical about 18 year olds being experts on life. But being able to use one's lived experience to learn and make theories about the world and life is a compelling display of curiosity and self-awareness.

Love seems to understand what is important, and addresses the inherent mystery of life and the inevitability of death. These (especially the latter) could easily be misdelivered, but Love states them with a calm directness that works. This landing is easier to stick when you have a unique background or life experience that would lead to honed maturity and wisdom.

Overall, Love is an intriguing applicant. She's self-aware, passionate, and wrote 3 compelling essays. Her application resulted in a slew of impressive acceptances, including Dartmouth, where Love is enjoying her first-year.

Love in a sentence: Fascinating, compassionate, intentional woman shaped by homeschool, her mother's illness, and the apt-alias 'Love.'

Duke University

ALEX KESEM

APPLICATION:

Major I applied under / School I applied to: Economics

Ethnicity: Caucasian

Gender: Male

Family Income Bracket: 500,000+/year

Year of College Graduation: 2021

High School Unweighted GPA (to nearest hundredth): 3.93 maybe (I got three Bs in middle school for high school credit, no Bs from 9th grade until Graduation)

High School Weighted GPA: 4.62

Class Rank/Percentile: 11/~1000

SAT I Score (By Section): 800 Critical Reading, 720 Math, 680 Writing (2200)

ACT Score (By Section): 33 Science, 35 Math, 35 Reading, 36 English (35 Composite)

SAT Subject Test Scores: 740 Math I, 750 World History

AP Test Results: 5: English Language, Psychology, Government, 4: English Literature, Environment Science, World History, US History, European History, Calculus AB, Macroeconomics, Microeconomics, Statistics, 3: Spanish, Biology, Geography, 2: Chemistry

Senior Year Course Load: AP Spanish, AP English Lit, AP Psychology, AP Euro, AP Environmental, AP Macro/AP US Gov, AP Calc AB

Awards Won in High School: Top ten percent 4 times, Republican Scholar award senior year

Extracurriculars in High School (Put leadership in parentheses): Academic Games President and founder (3 time top three team in Current Events and Presidents National Competition across the country), National Honor Society, Student Government Treasurer and Parliamentarian, Mu Alpha Theta Treasurer

Job/Work Experience in High School: The Tides busser and intern with District legislator

Volunteer/Community Service: Habitat for Humanity Reading mentor Crossover Mission NHS

What did you do in the summer after freshman year of high school?

Nothing

What did you do in the summer after sophomore year?

Nothing

What did you do in the summer after junior year?

Nothing

ABOUT YOUR HIGH SCHOOL:

State of High School: Florida

School Type (i.e. rural, suburban, city, public vs. private, etc): Rural

# of Students in Graduating Class: ~1000

What was your high school like? Demographics? How many other students went to elite universities?

My high school was pretty diverse, about half white and half students of color. About 10-12 of us went to Ivy League schools or Duke or Vandy. Most kids usually ended up going in-state like UCF or UF or FSU. Besides that though, it was like one U-Chi, two Vandy, one Duke, one MIT, one Georgetown, I can't remember where everyone else ended up going. My school was huge.

REFLECTION ON APPLICATION PROCESS:

I applied: **Early Decision**

What do you think your hooks were?

Well, I was very goal oriented in the long term sense. Academic games was huge for my application because I did it during middle school at first. Academic games weren't offered at my high school so I decided to start it for the first two years. By the last two years we were traveling around the country to national competition, winning top three team, and three of us placed individually in the top ten for two straight years. So it went from nothing to National level and it took a while so I looked like a strong leader and used that as a centerpiece of the application.

What do you think the strengths of your application were?

I struggled grades-wise in middle school, so getting straight As in high school helped a lot. I know most kids that go to my school get straight As but for me, it looked like I kinda cleaned myself up and went hard. The second thing was my volunteer hours. I didn't do a ton of orgs, just the few mentioned above, but I got over 1000 hours volunteering through high school.

What do you think the weaknesses of your application were? Where might other applicants have had an advantage over you?

My grades initially didn't help, in middle school I had to repeat geometry on

FLVS and it went from a C to an A, but colleges could still see it. Other than that, on paper at least, I was a pretty strong applicant.

Where else you were admitted:

Miami, UNC, FSU, UF, Georgia Tech, BC

Where you were waitlisted:

Northwestern

Where you were rejected:

Nowhere

Did you get a private college counselor?

No

When did you start preparing for college admissions? How did your family prepare?

Since I was born![64] My mom is very type A and made me do everything super early and super well. Even the slightest grammar error would set her off, so I was very tedious. I was done with all applications by August 23rd and started the Common App the day after it dropped. My mom was on my ass at all times about it for months on end and would constantly remind me about the process.

ABOUT YOUR COLLEGE:

Why did you choose this school?

My dad went to Duke so I was very familiar and comfortable with it by the time I was applying.

What is your school known for? What is its reputation?

Duke is a rich and preppy school. The Harvard of the south (although the author would disagree with that). I learned pretty fast that seeing 800 dollar clothes and expensive cars is so normal. For example, one friend broke my

---

64   I'm sure plenty of readers can relate.

laptop once and not only replaced it, but because it was only a few extra dollars, got me a fucking iPhone 10 additionally.

Is this reputation accurate?

Yes yes yes, the rich and wealthy are felt at all times, another example is that we have a reading period before exams and kids will fly home for four days, study there, fly back and take exams, then fly back again. Imagine the cost and you'll get it.

What are you involved with on campus?

Student Government, AIPAC, Polis

What do you think your school offers that no other top 20 school does?

Connections I guess. honestly I can't say for sure. The alumni are crazy so knowing someone can get you a job but besides that, nothing really different from other elite schools. Our athletics and especially the Basketball team are probably the best of any elite school.

What kinds of people do you think would love your school?

People who like connected learning environments. It's the perfect size. 6,500 undergrads is big enough so you don't feel stifled, but small enough to provide tons of seminar-scale class sizes and lots of familiarity with lots of people. Starting right off in Orientation Week, you feel like you could get to know anyone if you tried. Even the physical campus itself reflects this happy medium, feeling homey but grandiose.

What kinds of people do you think would hate your school?

The people who are the opposite of networkers. If you don't like talking and I mean a lot, Duke is not for you. It's a sink or swim environment.

Do you like your school? Why or why not?

Yes, I love it. It's really hard and has tested my mental health at times. That being said though, it's made me so much tougher and also adapted me to like a very intense situation before the real world.

THE KIDS WHO GET IN

Your college's biggest strengths. What do students appreciate about their school/take for granted?

It's a flexible social scene. If you want to drink and socialize via the traditional partying, there's plenty of that. If you want to live in a tent for a month or more to score sweet seats at basketball games, there are hundreds of others who are thinking the exact same thing. If you just want to unwind and watch a movie in the common room, I guarantee someone else will be too tired to go out, too.

Your college's biggest weaknesses. What do students complain about the most? What would an admissions counselor never tell you?

There is definitely a divide socially between those that have grown up in prep schools, and have been groomed for this opportunity and those who went to public schools. While I don't think the split is 50:50, it must be in the 30:70 range, which can be off-putting if you're not...rich or from the socially elite in any way.

ESSAYS:

Common App Essay:

My parents have said that I was born with a tennis racquet in my hand.[65] When I was 6 years old, I went to the tennis club by my house and started hitting tennis balls, honing my shot. Tennis is not just a game it has been an outlet for my emotion for a large portion of my life. When I failed a test, when I was in trouble, or when someone called me names at school, I went outside to play tennis. In middle school, I met many friends through tennis. You may know how tennis is played but did you know that a tennis ball is made out of a rubber shell filled with nylon and wool, all of which are recyclable materials?[66] Yet every day, hundreds of dead tennis balls are wasted, thrown out, or tossed over fences. While I have never played on an

---

65   This is a bit of a cliche opener. I gave similar feedback to one of the Cornell supplements - if you're going to use the "I've liked this thing since I was a little kid," it's helpful to explain why.

66   A funny transition if only because it's so informal.

organized team, I have taken lessons and played at tennis clubs throughout my home town. I tried for a while to figure out how to become involved in tennis again. An opportunity finally presented itself in eleventh grade, when my friend came to me and told me about an idea he had. This idea was nicknamed Bouncing Back.

Every year, 300 million tennis balls are manufactured and 125 million are used in the US specifically. Consequently, there are millions of tennis balls wasted which leads to overfilling landfills. Tennis balls produce methane gas and are a danger to the environment if wasted. Bouncing Back is an organization that was established in order to make use of dead tennis balls rather than wasting them. The premise is that we take dead tennis balls and recycle them to nursing homes and rehab facilities to use for canes and walkers. The dead balls are placed on the ends of the canes/walkers to provide traction which allows the elderly to walk for longer distances in a safer fashion. The whole reason I became involved with this organization isn't just to be involved with tennis again. Environmental change is a huge issue and 300 million tennis balls is no laughing matter.

In order to do this, my partner and I contacted as many clubs as possible in our local area. Tennis clubs throughout my county compile hundreds of dead tennis balls per day that we could use for our cause. Then, we arranged tennis ball pick up and proceeded to contact local nursing homes and rehab centers. Finally, we dropped off the dead tennis balls to these facilities so they could begin to use them to cushion the walkers and canes.[67] With this process, Bouncing Back has found a use for dead tennis balls and in turn has stopped hurtful methane gas from entering the atmosphere. Bouncing Back is just a microcosm in comparison to the national and global issue of environmental waste.[68] My partners and I want to make this organization national and truly make a difference. My goal is to broaden the organization to wherever I go to college and then expand further throughout that

---

67   This is a nice, albeit simple recounting of the steps Alex and his friends took to make a difference. I would have liked to see more of a focus on what Alex learned from this process (how there are little things in front of all of us that we can do to make a big difference in our community, that different problems (climate change, senior mobility) can be combated at once.

68   Good perspective.

THE KIDS WHO GET IN

area. The only way to make a difference is through continued growth and increased involvement. Dead tennis ball use is just a start. My future plan is to continue to visit the nursing homes and rehab facilities and ask them what other commonly used items they need and increase our efforts to help gather those as well. Environmental damage can have a lasting impact on the Earth. I don't want a damaged Earth, which is why I believe it's my responsibility to make a difference in any way I can.[69]

Duke Supplement #1:

Florida Boys State was something that helped me expand my horizons in economics, politics, and history. The election process was tough but I eventually won a spot in the House of Representatives. While there, experiencing what it is like to create and run a working government was invigorating and educational. At Boys State, I learned the rights and responsibilities of an American citizen. Being elected to positions at the city, county, and state governmental level taught me the rules and responsibilities of a politician.[70] On the first day at the Capitol, I took in my surroundings. As I saw the room open up before me, I was absolutely amazed. As I sat down in my House seat for a Boys State legislative session, I saw the pictures of former speakers and the speaker chair and realized that I want to be part of something like this when I grow up.

If I am accepted to Duke University, I will bring my strong passion for government and my belief that politics should benefit the electors more than it benefits the electorate. I would take advantage of opportunities to participate in programs such as Interns Go to Washington or discuss and debate current issues at the Duke Office of Government Relations. Duke offers spectacular opportunities to learn about government and the way that it functions to serve the community. I know without a doubt Duke is the best place for me.[71]

Duke Supplement #2:

Camping out in front of Cameron Indoor Stadium for 6 weeks. This type of experience is unique to one school and that is Duke University. Ever since I

---

69   Ending falls a bit flat, I would have used this space to highlight lessons learned, or link back to his 6 year old self.
70   A laundry list of an intro, here Alex does more telling than showing.
71   Ends with a bit of a platitude. Alex touches on some good specifics but would do well to hit more of the benefits of the broader Duke community.

was a small child, I have devoured as many sports books, magazines, and statistics as possible. I can only imagine what it would be like to see players such as Harry Giles and Grayson Allen play for the Devils. Duke offers me the athletic achievement and the academic freedom that I want from my university. At Duke, I could be an economics and statistics major and study the ideas behind payrolls in baseball through the Bass Connections Program. Interconnecting my two passions, sports and economics, at one of the best schools in the country is a spectacular situation. I would look forward to studying hard during the week and then watching Duke annihilate other ACC schools during my off time.

MY TAKE:

Alex's application shows us that one can win acceptance to an elite school despite having some weaknesses. Alex boasts strong academic credentials - his 2200 SAT, 35 ACT, 3.93 GPA, and ranking of 11 out of 963 tell admissions officers that he will definitely be able to handle Duke coursework. His extracurricular activities are unique and make him seem likable - Alex had previously participated in Academic Games, saw that his high school didn't have a team, made one, and brought them to top three in the country as President of the team.

That's awesome - and colleges love to see initiative like that because it's a trait that makes students successful in college and beyond. Additionally, Alex noticed that tennis balls were being wasted, saw a need for them at local homes for the elderly, and created a program to bring the old balls to those homes, and cut them open for the bottom of walkers. Alex might not have cured any infectious diseases, but he demonstrated proactivity and care for his community - two fantastic traits[72].

As for weaknesses, Alex's essays may have detracted from the strength of his application. His writing is clear enough and communicates the ideas that he intends to - but definitely isn't at the same level as most of the other essays

---

[72] Independent of college admissions, anyone would love to be friends with/ hire/ associate with people who start programs that address real human needs and solve problems in their community. Alex is an example of a teenager who was a good student and a good person - which, in a nutshell, is a great place to start for being a competitive applicant to an elite college.

featured in this book. His writing comes across as underdeveloped (admissions officers come across phrases like "annihilate the competition," "spectacular situation," and "my strong passion for government" all day.) Using a transitional phrase like "You may know how tennis is played but did you know that a tennis ball is made out of a rubber shell filled with nylon and wool, all of which are recyclable materials?" is a bit juvenile for an application to an elite academic institution.

Alex is a likeable, enthusiastic member of his community, and an application slightly hampered by his essays was still successful at Duke, one of the most selective schools in the country.

Alex in a sentence: Kind-hearted tennis-ball recycler and Duke fanatic (and legacy).

Harvard College

CHRISTIANE WOMACK

APPLICATION:

Major I applied under / School I applied to: Neuroscience

Ethnicity: Black, White

Gender: Female

Family Income Bracket: 80,000-160,000/year

Year of College Graduation: 2021

High School Unweighted GPA (to nearest hundredth): N/A

High School Weighted GPA: 4.15

Class Rank/Percentile: 4

SAT I Score (By Section): 800 Critical Reading, 720 Math, 780 Writing (2300 Total)

ACT Score (By Section): N/A

SAT Subject Test Scores: 700 Literature, 770 Math II, 740 Chemistry, 680 US History, 680 Math I

AP Test Results: 5: English Literature, English Language, 4: Calculus BC, 3: Chemistry, US History, 2: Physics C: Mechanics

Senior Year Course Load: French 4, AP English Lit, AP Bio, AP Physics C, AP Calc BC, Handbells[73], Poetry

Awards Won in High School: National Merit Scholar, Cum Laude Society, President's Education Award for Outstanding Academic Excellence Recipient, High Honor Roll, Johns Hopkins Talent Search College Class Award Recipient, Several other school-specific awards

Extracurriculars in High School (Put leadership in parentheses):

Girls Varsity Tennis, Ringers/ Handbell Ensemble, School Ambassadors (tour guide, Pride Mentor), Peer Tutor, Quiz Bowl (team captain), Robotics Team (drive team), Model Congress, Debate Team (team captain), Science Olympiad, Student Advancement Board, PA Junior Academy of Science, Girls Varsity Track and Field

Job/Work Experience in High School: Summer Camp Counselor

Volunteer/Community Service: Girl Scout, County Youth Council, Public Library Volunteer, Church Youth Volunteer

What did you do in the summer after freshman year of high school?

I attended a science, math, and technology camp at a local college

What did you do in the summer after sophomore year?

I completed a study abroad program in Scotland

What did you do in the summer after junior year?

I attended PGSS, the Pennsylvania Governor's School for the Sciences Summer Program

ABOUT YOUR HIGH SCHOOL:

State of High School: Pennsylvania

School Type (i.e. rural, suburban, city, public vs. private, etc): Suburban, private

---

[73] I had to google this - it's an instrument.

# of Students in Graduating Class: ~75

What was your high school like? Demographics? How many other students went to elite universities?

My high school was a very small private school in Pennsylvania. We were at the time, relatively diverse in terms of East and South Asian students, but far less so in terms of Black or Latinx students. While my school has a near 100% rate of students matriculating to college, there is a wide span of schools people attend. This ranges anywhere from large public institutions to smaller liberal arts schools, as well as some Ivies.

REFLECTION ON APPLICATION PROCESS:

I applied: Regular Decision

What do you think your hooks were?

I was definitely very dedicated to all the things I was doing, especially considering I was involved in so much. Additionally, I think as someone who is really outgoing, I interviewed quite well and also made sure to let my personality come out in my essays. Finally, I think as someone who is biracial, I had done a lot of reflecting about how that affects my life and what that means to me, which was also special.

What do you think the strengths of your application were?

I think while my grades and scores were definitely good enough to not be any cause for concern, my true strengths lied in my essays. I worked really hard to try to bring consistency of my values, personality, and interests into my essays - I believe that this really enhanced the cohesiveness. This is crucial for being able to create an honest and realistic narrative of yourself.

What do you think the weaknesses of your application were? Where might other applicants have had an advantage over you?

I think a weakness could have been some of my AP scores - I didn't submit any of the ones that were 3s or below, as I felt it wasn't necessary. Additionally, I didn't have an outside college counselor (just my school counselor, who was wonderful) or tutor for my SATs/ subject tests, so I think that that is definitely something people do that I couldn't compete with for financial reasons. I also remember my college counselor telling me to potentially prepare myself for some disappointment, because my school list was relatively top heavy. Thankfully, I was lucky enough that it all worked out in my favor, and I did have some "safety" school applications prepared that I didn't have to end up sending.

Where else you were admitted:

Early Action: University of Chicago, Massachusetts Institute of Technology. Regular Decision: Bowdoin College, Yale, Columbia (likely letter received), Dartmouth, Princeton, University of Pennsylvania, Swarthmore

Where you were waitlisted:

Stanford

Where you were rejected:

n/a

Did you get a private college counselor?

No

When did you start preparing for college admissions? How did your family prepare?

In earnest, probably the summer before. That was when I started brainstorming topics for my Common App Essay. After that, I was on the grind to finish my supplemental essays as soon as possible, both for my early action and regular decision schools. My mom was also instrumental in that respect, she made sure I was finished with all my applications before the end of October!

ABOUT YOUR COLLEGE:

Why did you choose this school?

I chose Harvard because ultimately, I felt really comfortable on campus and could see myself there. I think I also partially chose it because I knew I didn't want to alienate any of my contrasting interests as some schools might have, like still being involved in english and science, for example. I also found that I really liked the people I had met there, and I had a lot of fun at visit weekend!

What is your school known for? What is its reputation?

As the oldest school in the US, I think generally Harvard is known for a lot of academic excellence and prestige. This is probably especially true of our liberal arts curriculum. Along with this, I think the reputation can tend towards having a lot of wealthy students, and a lot of high achievers.

Is this reputation accurate?

I would say I was pleasantly surprised by the socioeconomic diversity at Harvard. While there definitely are students on the higher income side, there is also a fair amount of diversity in this respect. In terms of personal tendencies, I've definitely met a lot more people, myself included, who tend to be more goal oriented or "type A". However, I think it's important to note that that doesn't mean everyone is cold or super competitive - most people I know actually don't fall into that particular category at all.

What are you involved with on campus?

Harvard Cheer Team, Project Sunshine, Flyby Blog, Harvard Undergraduate Interdisciplinary Immunology Club, on campus research, Harvard Admissions Tour Guides, Student Employee in the FAS Registrar's Office

What do you think your school offers that no other top 20 school does?

I definitely think that once you get to a certain caliber of school, you can't make a bad choice. That being said, I think that Harvard tends to foster a community of students who are just very, very dedicated to the things that they do. For example, extracurriculars are huge on campus, with most people in 2-4, and you can really see how much time, effort, and joy people put into their activities, sometimes rivaling academics for time commitment.

What kinds of people do you think would love your school?

I think the people who love Harvard the most are those who are willing to go after their passions and create space for themselves. Whether this be through academics or extracurriculars, finding the things you care most about and dedicating time to these things is important. Also, I think you have to be willing to try new things to find the things on campus you're most excited about.

What kinds of people do you think would hate your school?

I think it could be tough to be a really laid back type of person at Harvard. This isn't to say they don't exist, but it's definitely true that most people tend to make themselves very busy and like to live life at a fast pace. I think that could be hard if you're not the type or person who likes to get involved.

Do you like your school? Why or why not?

Definitely! I think that my time at Harvard has both helped me to grow a lot as well as to expand how I think about many things, both in an academic and non-academic setting. I've definitely loved so many of the people I've met and am very grateful for my Harvard experience.

Your college's biggest strengths. What do students appreciate about their school/take for granted?

I think some of Harvard's greatest strengths lie in our academics and our house life. It can be easy to forget that not only do we have access to so many high level courses and niche opportunities, but also that we have the chance to explore academically as well. Your concentration will only take up ~10 -14 of the courses you take during your time at Harvard, so you have a huge chance to explore any academic disciplines you're interested in. Additionally, upperclassmen houses are a huge part of student life, and I think definitely something we sometimes take for granted given how much we love them!

You live in your house for 3 years, so you really get the opportunity to form a tight community with a subset of Harvard.

Your college's biggest weaknesses. What do students complain about the most? What would an admissions counselor never tell you?

I think the things students complain about the most is probably food, and the lack of diversity in some academic departments. On the food front, while there are definitely menu items that are fan favorites and overall it's not too bad (and sometimes is pretty good), it can sometimes be tough if you have any dining restrictions to find something you want in the dhall on a given day. Turning to the other piece, students on campus have definitely become increasingly aware of the lack of diversity within many academic departments on campus, something that manifests in a few different ways. Obviously, there are many ways to represent diversity in faculty and staff, such as race, socioeconomic background, LGBTQ+ identities, gender identity, and more. Sometimes it can be hard to see yourself succeeding in a department or academic field if you never have a professor or instructor who holds some of the identities that you do, and this is something I think that overall, Harvard is becoming more aware of and working towards changing.

ESSAYS:

Common App Essay:

I jolted awake to the squeal of tires and the distinct feeling of spinning. Outside the window, the world was a white blur as the snow and ice whipped by.[74]

It was 6 am, and I was in the midst of a road trip from my house to Montreal, where my cousin lives. I had been napping in the car, but movement woke me. As I looked up, I realized our car wasn't going forward, but spinning, across a lane of traffic, after which we slammed into the guardrail. Everyone looked around. Shaken up and slightly disappointed but otherwise safe, we turned the car around to head home.

---

74   This is a standard opener. It fits the bill of what we're taught in high school English class - starting in the action - and it works well here.

THE KIDS WHO GET IN

On the long drive home, I began to ponder- we were all okay, luckily, but what if we hadn't been? I realized I could have been seriously hurt, and then I realized that I wasn't prepared for that eventuality. I know now that I was probably being a bit melodramatic, but I remember thinking, "I almost just died, and I would have done nothing with my life." Maybe this line of thought was a bit morbid, but I couldn't help myself. I'm not saying that maybe I was going about life the wrong way, but what if I was going about life the wrong way?![75]

Bear with me here. When I say that I thought I was approaching my life the wrong way, I don't mean "Oh there is so much I haven't done." Yes, technically this was true, but I meant it in a much more fundamental way: what if I was literally approaching every single day *in the wrong way, with the wrong attitude?* That is to say, I've always been a hard worker, and usually it has paid off. And like a lot of kids out there, I was never content with decent: I usually pushed myself for excellence, especially when it came to school. In fact, I woke up every day and went to sleep every night thinking about whatever test, quiz, project, assignment, or even sports match faced me in the following days. And that, that is what worried me as I reflected on myself- I didn't want to go through life focused on the wrong goals, when I could emphasize what would be far more meaningful to me later in life than schoolwork. Of course, I don't mean wrong as in bad, I simply mean somewhat less important to my happiness in the long run. I felt like I was so absorbed in the details that I was completely oblivious to the big picture, and it honestly worried me. Suddenly, it seemed like the stuff I had often pushed aside mattered a lot more: I wanted to focus on enjoying tennis, seeing my friends, getting better at piano, and learning things just for the heck of it! For example, my mom reminded me recently that I used to read a book a day, for no reason other than I wanted to, but that I no longer seemed to find time to do what had once made me so happy. I felt like the parts of my life I had once enjoyed most needed to once again take precedence.

Now, I can't tell you that when I finally made it home, I completely changed my ways and lived life to the fullest and took chances and so on and so forth.[76]

---

75   This is an awesome line because the way it's written shows us so much about Christiane. It's a funny declaration that doesn't entirely make sense, but engages the reader and shows us some personality. Here, Christiane is unafraid to take a risk.

76   "So on and so forth" another great injection of personality. It's subtle, but Christiane makes fun of her own response to the experience. It's a tongue-in-cheek admission that she doesn't take herself too seriously.

But I can tell you that every once in a while, I catch myself worrying over something that isn't quite worth it, or that probably won't matter much in the end, and I'm reminded of that unfinished trip to Montreal. Despite how much I might want to linger in the details, I think about what felt like the longest car ride ever, relax a little, and pick up a good book.[77]

Harvard Supplement:

While I was at the Pennsylvania Governor's School for Sciences this summer, one of our guest lecturers was a computer science professor from Carnegie Mellon University named David Kosbie. At first, I was apprehensive because I hadn't been exposed to a lot of computer science, but almost immediately after he started talking, I knew I was in for a good lecture. While the longer than four-hour marathon of a talk proved interesting in myriad ways, one of the things in particular that truly astonished me was a seemingly simple proof he showed us while he was talking about a certain mathematician. Since computer science is heavily math based, we somehow ended up on the quadratic formula, something anyone who has taken high school math is intimately familiar with. However, as Kosbie was talking, he showed us a proof of the formula that I had never seen before, involving equivalent rectangles broken down. As he completed the proof on the board, my friends next to me laughed, because I was quite literally staring agape[78] at this man who had managed to take something I thought I knew insanely well, and twist it inside out. Additionally, he had not lost me in the process, and I completely understood where he was coming from. I will always remember not only that proof, but also that experience, and that feeling of being in awe of what I had learned. That day was my take on the ideal learning experience- being totally surprised, astounded, and excited about a discovery.[79]

---

77   This essay works in large part because of how understated it is. Christiane doesn't try to convince us that the near-accident completely changed her life. She's honest that her growth is still a work in progress! We get a good glimpse of who Christiane is - an energetic overachiever who recognizes the importance of slowing down and soaking up the small stuff, and doesn't take herself too seriously. In your essays, know that it's ok to acknowledge that you're not a finished product- and doing so conveys self-awareness and perspective that colleges admire.

78   Here we see a bit more of Christiane's dramatism. In your essays, you should feel free to inject your personality where you can!

79   This is a nice, simple essay. We see Christiane's love of learning in action, and it's a nice picture of a bit more of her personality. Her last sentence works well, wrapping up the piece with the main lesson that she learned about herself. Consider using this structure for your supplements.

MY TAKE:

Christiane has the academic prerequisites for competition at any school in America. Her 4.15 GPA and 2300 SAT are strong compliments to a *full* extracurricular schedule; Christiane appears to fit the Harvard mold as a high school student.

She's a high achiever with varied interests (debate, science olympiad, robotics, multiple varsity sports) and Christiane seems exactly like the type of college student who would become a tour guide, join the Cheer team, do research, and join several clubs.

Her personal statement is unique, and stands out. I like the way she takes a small life experience and uses it to show us a lot about herself. It's almost the teenage version of a midlife crisis - we see an overinvolved high school student have a near-death experience, and decide to focus on learning and growing "just for the heck of it!" Christiane's self-awareness and questioning of her own priorities at a young age is inspiring - and it's a good reminder, that we're all going to die one day and there isn't enough time for all of the junk that we seem to make time for!

In the essay, we also see Christiane's excitable voice. She talks to the reader:

"I'm not saying that maybe I was going about life the wrong way, but what if I was going about life the wrong way?!...Bear with me here."

The whole piece carries this fun energy, and it matches the picture of a dynamic, overinvolved, tour guiding Christiane! And we see this same energy in her joy of discovery at the summer science course. I think in her reflection, Christiane hits the nail on the head. Her essays work very well with the rest of the piece, and we see a consistent picture of a bright, enthusiastic woman - who got into and now attends Harvard College.

Christiane in a sentence: Dramatic overachiever with a lot of personality and a love of learning.

Johns Hopkins

PARKER ROBERTS

APPLICATION:

Major I applied under / School I applied to: International Studies & Chemistry/Krieger School of Arts and Sciences

Ethnicity: Caucasian

Gender: Male

Family Income Bracket: 160,000-250,000/year

Year of College Graduation: 2022

High School Unweighted GPA (to nearest hundredth): 4.0

High School Weighted GPA: 4.3

Class Rank/Percentile: 1 (Valedictorian)

SAT I Score (By Section): N/A

ACT Score (By Section): 36 English, 35 Science, 34 Reading, 33 Math (35 Composite)

SAT Subject Test Scores: N/A

AP Test Results: 5: Chemistry, Statistics, 4: Human Geography, English Language, US History, Calculus BC, Physics C: Mechanics, 3: Biology

Senior Year Course Load: AP English Literature, AP Psychology (didn't take exam), Peer Tutoring, Honors Chemistry II, AP Statistics, Spanish Teacher Assistant, AP Chemistry, Communications

Awards Won in High School: AP Scholar with Distinction, Highest GPA Award, Governor's Scholar Award, Highest US History GPA, Highest Spanish II GPA, Highest Spanish III GPA, 1st Place in State Spanish Competition, Scholar of the Week for Local News Station

Extracurriculars in High School (Put leadership in parentheses): Future Business Leaders of America (Treasurer x 2, Vice President), Beta Club (Treasurer), Spanish Honor Society (President), Science Club; Student Council (Class Representative, Vice-President), National Honor Society, JV Football, Sand Volleyball

Job/Work Experience in High School: Spanish Tutoring, Scorekeeping for local little league sporting events

Volunteer/Community Service: Mostly through clubs and organizations at my school: translating for refugee health fairs, donating supplies, walking dogs, donating blood, delivering meals to homeless, knitting blankets for homeless, sculpting bowls for homeless, serving the elderly in my community.

What did you do in the summer after freshman year of high school?

Scorekeeping for local little league sporting events

What did you do in the summer after sophomore year?

Scorekeeping for local little league sporting events

What did you do in the summer after junior year?

Community service

ABOUT YOUR HIGH SCHOOL:

State of High School: Kentucky

School Type (i.e. rural, suburban, city, public vs. private, etc): Public Rural

# of Students in Graduating Class: ~300

What was your high school like? Demographics? How many other students went to elite universities?

The school was mostly white and pretty rural. Around half of the school was pretty wealthy, but the other half was low-middle class. Many students came from rural communities or farms. There was little to no diversity in the school.

REFLECTION ON APPLICATION PROCESS:

I applied: Regular Decision

What do you think your hooks were?

I think one of the biggest hooks of my application was the fact that I was applying from Kentucky. There were not many students that had attended Hopkins before I applied. At Hopkins, I might know 5 other students from Kentucky total.

What do you think the strengths of your application were?

I think that my essay was quite strong. Additionally, I think that the depth of my extracurricular activities aided in my admission to Hopkins. Hopkins places value on a large depth and diversity of its students.

What do you think the weaknesses of your application were? Where might other applicants have had an advantage over you?

I believe that the fact that I had little to no research experience before applying was a weakness. Additionally, the fact that I was applying under a STEM major is very common for Hopkins students, which could've been a weakness as well.

Where else you were admitted:

University of Kentucky, University of Louisville

Where you were waitlisted:

Vanderbilt

Where you were rejected:

N/A

Did you get a private college counselor?

No

When did you start preparing for college admissions? How did your family prepare?

I began preparing in October of my senior year. My family did not really have an impact on my college admission process. My teachers, however, read almost every essay that I wrote.

ABOUT YOUR COLLEGE:

Why did you choose this school?

I chose this school because it has an outstanding pre-med program, and I knew that I wanted to go into medicine before I applied. Research is the backbone of the institution, so I knew the opportunities at Hopkins were not rivaled by many other institutions in the US.

What is your school known for? What is its reputation?

The school is known for its pre med program. Additionally, it is known for its strong undergraduate research program. It has a reputation as a cut-throat and depressing environment.

Is this reputation accurate?

Yes, I would say that this reputation is accurate. People try and cover up the fact that Hopkins is cut-throat, but that does not detract from the fact that it is. Students are constantly worried about their GPA and will do almost anything to ensure success.

What are you involved with on campus?

I am involved in Outdoor Pursuits, Biophysics Research, a club that promotes mental health in the Latinx community in Baltimore, and an organization that leads outdoor trips for underprivileged Baltimore youth.

What do you think your school offers that no other top 20 school does?

The access to undergraduate research is quite unrivaled by any other school. We have the largest endowment for research of any university in the US, so it is quite easy to find a lab or group that is doing ground-breaking research that would be interesting to you.

What kinds of people do you think would love your school?

Students who are STEM focused or those that want to do international relations. As I have mentioned, we have an amazing pre-med program and advising office. All STEM at Hopkins is great. If you want to come for IS, that is also a good choice. There is a great relationship with the School of Advanced International Studies in DC, which provides opportunities for IS majors as well. Additionally, those who want freedom of study should attend Hopkins, as there are no core requirements aside from 9 credits in humanities, quantitative, social science, and natural science, which is easily filled by most major requirements.

What kinds of people do you think would hate your school?

People that crave a deep social life would probably not find Hopkins enjoyable. Additionally, students who are looking for a well-rounded liberal arts education should stay away. Most of our humanities programs outside of International Studies are pretty weak, so it would be a waste of time getting a degree in them from Hopkins.

Do you like your school? Why or why not?

I like the school because it is a perfect fit for me and for what I want to do in the future. Aside from being pre-med or STEM focused, Hopkins would not be an ideal place to attend. I additionally do not enjoy the city of Baltimore, but the proximity to DC is very nice.

Your college's biggest strengths. What do students appreciate about their school/take for granted?

Students appreciate the freedom of study and lack of requirements. Also, the faculty are great and always willing to help, as the school is quite small (undergrad of around 1200/class). The access to research is unparalleled. It is an amazing place to be premed. The resources offered by the advising offices are great.

Your college's biggest weaknesses. What do students complain about the most? What would an admissions counselor never tell you?

The climate is quite cut throat and at times depressing. Students are almost always studying because Hopkins is quite difficult for its ranking. There is a social atmosphere, but you'll have to search for it. The food here sucks! The area around campus can be dangerous.

ESSAYS:

Common App Essay:

I am a pathological liar—not in the sense that I lie in order to manipulate those around me or that I lie selfishly to get my way but in the sense that I have continuously lied to myself for eighteen years. I have tried to convince myself over and over again that the world is a good place and that I am a good person. Both are lies. The world is definitely not a good place, and I am definitely not a good person because a good world would not be filled with hatred, racism, war, famine, or poverty, and a good person would definitely not allow the world to be this way. But it is, and I do. As I mature, I am more constantly aware of the utter brokenness and despair that many face on a daily basis. Some instances are minute, while others are outright cruel. This cycle of pain and destruction cannot be as endless as it is vicious; there must be a way to overcome it. How though? How can one—how can I— transform a world that seems to thrive on evil and abhor good? In the same way that a doctor cures an illness or an exterminator eliminates pests: by fixing the source. I am the source. You are the source. We are all the source. All of these problems faced by the world did not materialize out of a cosmic boom or appear by an unlucky chance. They were created. The vicious cycle continues because its creators permit it to do so because we prefer to maintain our states of comfort and deceit in place of enacting change for the betterment of the world. I am tired of staying within our boundaries for the sake of comfort and fear, and I am ready, as well as determined, to end the cycle of despair. In the same manner that a rudder controls the motion of an entire ship, I will transform an entire world. I am not afraid to cross boundaries, but rather I am filled with excitement as I near them. Anything that was created can also be destroyed, and I am set on the path of destruction. Evil things like war, poverty, hatred, and racism can be eradicated just as they were crafted. In order to change the world, however, I must first change myself. Changing myself does not merely mean having an opinion that something needs to occur; it means actively working to prevent it. Limited by the boundaries of high school and youth, which will not bind me for much longer, I have not actively worked to prevent the aforementioned evils; however, in the future, I will strive to enact actual change in everything that I do. Every action that I take will move the rudder of the boat one degree closer toward good and one degree away from evil. My passion and drive WILL affect actual, real change in the world. I will work toward my goal until I am no longer a pathological liar telling myself that I am a good person and that the world is a good place until I AM a good person because I made the world a better place.[80]

Johns Hopkins Supplement:

This summer, 378 strangers and I stepped onto a college campus over 250 miles from home for The Governor's Scholars Program, and we were tasked with the impossible: untying The Human Knot. The Human Knot has been a go to icebreaker since elementary school, bringing people together through close physical contact--one of my least favorite things[81]--and through solving a puzzle of twists and turns. When I was asked to grab two others' hands to begin to form the knot, I was anything but happy. I mean, how was performing twister-like moves with strangers in the hot summer sun supposed to bring us closer? My naive outlook on the task was soon diminished, however, as we began to not only unravel the knot but the barriers

---

80 This is an intense essay. It might be an honest reflection of how Parker views the world - but there are some tweaks I recommend below to make it a bit more polished.

81 I like this small admission. Great vulnerability.

of awkwardness that surrounded us as well.[82] "You go under!" "Move to the left!" "Step over me!"--commands rang out in all directions. Some of us were leaders yelling the commands; others obediently listened. As time passed and as the knot became less tangled, I became amazed at how this supposedly simple task had brought us together. Very quickly, this game transformed 378 strangers into a gigantic family. Yes, it sounds cliché and cheesy, but it's true, nonetheless. Because of this experience, I gained some of my lifelong best friends--most of whom I would have never talked to if I had not have been forced to untangle myself from a web of unfamiliarity. The challenge more so affirmed something that I already knew, rather than enlightening me with some philosophical inspiration: family comes in all shapes, colors, and sizes. Blood is not the only thing that forms a family; experiences do as well. After an hour of stumbling, twisting, and sweating, the knot was finally set free. Each of the friendships that I made while untying myself continued to grow throughout the summer, and each has had a lasting impact on me. They are the people that I talk to daily, the ones that I call when I'm in trouble, and the ones around whom I can be myself. Upon reflection after untying the knot, I realized that I had not just undone something; I had formed something as well: a community and a family.[83]

MY TAKE:

Parker is a solid elite college applicant. He has a flawless academic record (4.0 GPA, Valedictorian, 35 ACT composite) and an expansive (albeit scattered) extracurricular resume. His essay is probably the riskiest essay we've seen - and I'll talk about which aspects we liked and didn't - but having great grades/test scores, a lot of volunteering under his belt and being from an underrepresented community (rural Kentucky) more than made up for it.

Parker's college essay is interesting - it's a broadscale critique of how society encourages complacency and how we can overlook injustice. It begins with a strong hook - starting a college essay with "I am a pathological liar" is a phenomenal way to get your essay read. Additionally, the essay shows us how

---

82   Again, Parker does well admitting his own naivety here.

83   Great ending that summarizes main lessons learned and ends with a nice play on words.

Parker thinks - he is critical of his own motivations, ambitious, and thoughtful about life. He offers his take on human nature and takes a vow to change the world through his righteousness.

Partly because of the format and partly because of content, his essay can come across as intense and lofty. By writing the whole piece as a singular paragraph and making largely aspirational statements, it can feel impersonal and harsh. The piece would benefit from more touches to his personal life and goals - saying that you will affect actual, real change in the world becomes a more sympathetic claim when you nod to *how* you'll change the world. Touching on a potential future career or life path would help the AO connect with Parker here. The lesson here is to be as concrete as possible. Use narrative with relatable details to make a memorable *personal statement*, rather than pitch a lofty manifesto. Frankly, I'm surprised that this essay worked with Hopkins (that said, this student had a small sample size of applications, so it's hard to draw conclusions).

Additionally, the piece could use a bit of self-awareness. The piece needed a one sentence addition of "although I'm a teenager, and don't have it all figured out yet, I firmly believe that we all kid ourselves a bit too much about the reality of the world, and to change the world we have to start with changing ourselves." It's important to qualify your beliefs, especially in broad strokes essays about the nature of humanity. You may draw some eye rolls from AOs if you make it seem like you think you have the universe figured out. In his supplement, Parker does a good job at bringing this humility when he talks about his own naivety around the human-knot exercise. Still, it would be good to see this trait featured within his Common App.

Parker's flawless academic background and extensive volunteer experience outpaced an intense, impersonal essay. He earned a spot at Johns Hopkins, where he is learning more about how he'll change the world.

Parker in a sentence: "Pathological liar" driven to be a better person for his community.

Massachusetts Institute of Technology

JADE ARDEN

APPLICATION:

Major I applied under / School I applied to: Course 20/Bioengineering, switched to Course 2 Mechanical Engineering and Course 6 EECS

Ethnicity: Mixed Asian/Islander

Gender: Non-binary

Family Income Bracket: 80,000-160,000/year

Year of College Graduation: 2023

SAT I Score (By Section): 770 Reading, 740 Math (1510 Total)

ACT Score (By Section): 36 Math, 35 Science, 35 English, 36 Reading (36 Composite)

SAT Subject Test Scores: 800 Math II, 750 Biology - M

High School Unweighted GPA (to nearest hundredth): 3.95/4.0

High School Weighted GPA: 4.61/4.0

Class Rank/Percentile: N/A but not near top 20

AP Test Results: 5: Computer Science A, English Language, US History, 4: Statistics, English Literature, Psychology, 3: Calculus BC, 2: Latin

Senior Year Course Load: AP Lit, AP Psych, AP Calc BC, AP Physics C, AP Latin, Honors Advanced Research, Intro to Organic Chemistry

Awards Won in High School: Nothing until second semester senior year: Regeneron STS Top 300, ISEF Finalist, a bunch of science fair awards

Extracurriculars in High School (Put leadership in parentheses): Yearbook (all 4 years, Editor-In-Chief last 2.5 years), High School Research Journal (Founder/Editor last 2 years), Student Archivist, Student Government (Class president sophomore year, Student Advisory Board member senior year), School Newspaper (Editor, sophomore/junior year), Science Olympiad

Job/Work Experience in High School: N/A

Volunteer/Community Service: Volunteered at my local library for National Honor Society hours

What did you do in the summer after freshman year of high school? I took an archery class and a fencing class, but mostly stayed at home. I also traveled a little bit on weekend trips around my state and fell in love with soft shell crab in Cape May.

What did you do in the summer after sophomore year? I traveled to Paris with my mom and sister for a few weeks, but otherwise stayed home and tinkered with projects.

What did you do in the summer after junior year? I was an NYU Pre-College program, took an intro engineering course and a writing course as a commuter student. I spent my free time roaming around NYC and getting a sense of direction and self-sufficiency.

ABOUT YOUR HIGH SCHOOL:

State of High School: New Jersey

School Type (i.e. rural, suburban, city, public vs. private, etc): Suburban

# of Students in Graduating Class: 250

What was your high school like? Demographics? How many other students went to elite universities?

My school was very upper middle class and had a gap between academic high achievers (mostly Asian) and the general town population, with about 15-20 students per year going to top 20 universities, maybe 5 per year going to any Ivy+MIT. Makeup of the student body was around 65% white, 30% Asian, 15% other. It was possible to get completely straight A's, and clubs were very clique-y as the town itself was. Parent groups had a lot of influence in the town and dominated the culture, often shunning or ostracizing anyone not in the in-group who got too successful. Lots of behind-the-scenes backstabbing. A lot of the high-achieving kids from our town also went to a nearby highly-nationally-ranked technology vocational school following an entrance exam taken in middle school, which left a lot of the people who didn't get in to be resentful and have an inferiority complex in my school.

REFLECTION ON APPLICATION PROCESS:

I applied: Early Action

What do you think your hooks were?

I was very genuine and passionate about the technical side projects I pursued outside of schoolwork. MIT's application process let me show this through their maker portfolio, unlike many other schools, and I think they valued this self-starter creative spirit. I also had a commitment to seeing something through, despite it not being necessarily STEM (yearbook, taking videos/photos of concerts and school events for archive purposes) which probably made me a good contributor to the community. I always went the extra mile even when not asked and made the most of my circumstances.

What do you think the strengths of your application were?

My Maker Portfolio was crucial to showing who I was beyond the scores and numbers, which were honestly fairly average and even considered low among high-achieving students from my school. I like to think that they saw that the technical skills I was lacking in (having never taken a formal engineering class) could be learned, and I would readily absorb new ideas and pursue them in my free time like I had learned "maker" skills online. The "unfocused" way I went about high school was also interesting, pursuing classes and projects that interested me rather than things that stuck firmly to an engineering track. This probably showed that I was open to interdisciplinary ideas and influences, something that's really valued in MIT's fluidity. (ease of ability to change majors, break away from what you were good at in high school if you so choose, very late drop dates without credit restrictions on most terms after the first year, not applying into a major and declaring at the end of freshman year, etc)

What do you think the weaknesses of your application were? Where might other applicants have had an advantage over you?

My scores and lack of awards. While my SAT scores were fairly high, they were considered to be on the low end for my school's high-achieving population. I also applied without any major awards or having attended academic competitions, unlike many of my current peers who are international Olympiad winners and science fair celebrities and all those really impressive kids. I found it really ironic that I only started getting major awards through the science fair after I had already been accepted to MIT. I'm also not very good at math/physics, like better than the average person but much worse than most MIT students.

Where else you were admitted:

USC, Wellesley College, Johns Hopkins University (Biomedical Engineering), Rutgers University, Cornell University, Boston University, Northeastern University

Where you were waitlisted:

Where you were rejected:

Harvard, Yale, Princeton, Stanford

Did you get a private college counselor?

No

When did you start preparing for college admissions? How did your family prepare?

I was honestly pretty blind going into college admissions, since my immigrant parents had gone to college internationally, which put me in a really weird place as a kind-of first-generation student. I learned a lot through my own research on the internet and kept a very organized spreadsheet to keep myself accountable and figure out when I needed to register to take tests (mostly junior year and senior year). I made my parents, teachers, and guidance counselor keep their hands off of the whole process and only directed them when I needed something signed, application fees paid, or dissuading me from making a decision I was doubting (like applying to go to Edinburgh, which was definitely not the move for me personally). I applied for a few fly-in programs that really helped me get a better perspective on some of my dream schools.

ABOUT YOUR COLLEGE:

Why did you choose this school?

MIT's student culture was the biggest draw for me. Coming from a high school where it seemed like everyone was all for themselves, seeing a place where everyone cared about something at MIT and generally felt invested in the generations of students to come made me feel at home. It felt so easy to belong while standing out. There was just a sense of casual excellence I felt I could thrive in. My strengths complemented others weaknesses and vice-versa, and I always had something to learn from others.

What is your school known for? What is its reputation?

MIT is mostly known for its strong STEM programs, particularly engineering. As a budding Institute historian, I've been studying references to MIT in media and why exactly this place seems to be tagged with smart, crafty characters and innovations. Dropping the name MIT holds a lot of weight, so we're part of the crowd that says "I go to school in Boston" even if we're technically in Cambridge. Lots of recruiters think MIT is just full of computer science people, much to the annoyance of many non-CS students.

Is this reputation accurate?

A lot of the MIT mythos is close in spirit, as our motto "mens et manus" mind and hand really does encompass an approach to theory and practice towards making an impact on the world. Lots of MechE students take Tony Stark as an inspiration for creative spirit, myself included. But it's not to say that everyone here is automatically some hacker genius, as students are very diverse in academic interests, with a very strong and overlooked humanities department (with a top economics program). But everyone is here on their merits: they wouldn't be admitted if they couldn't survive the curriculum here, and they probably wouldn't want to be. MIT is a very academically challenging place full of brilliant people to learn from, especially peers.

What are you involved with on campus?

I'm a non-binary member of a sorority, do a lot of publicity for several clubs on campus, am a keyholder for the student-run computing club, help run movies every weekend in a lecture hall, help restock the bananas in our famous Banana Lounge, keep tabs on student government, do a fantasy sport, teach short classes to high school kids, frequently comment on my school's confessions page, I'm all over the place. I also do a little hacking in my free time, as many MIT students do, ssshhh.

What do you think your school offers that no other top 20 school does?

Amazing easy access to research opportunities. It is stupid easy to start doing research at MIT through UROP (Undergraduate Research Opportunities Program), which is well-funded and greatly emphasizes getting students into labs and doing real research work. Opportunities are plentiful and focus on developing student skills with meaningful contributions, even for those with no prior experience. Also, MIT has a strong student culture with a focus on being fairly equal. You can't buy your way into MIT, and honestly who would want to? It's a very hardworking place to be, inspired by peers of a similar level who generally care about their community on campus.

What kinds of people do you think would love your school?

People who know there's more to life than psets (problem sets) and know there's so much learning to be done outside the classroom. The true value of MIT is in the people you meet, in people who want to be part of a class, who really care about something, and want to go beyond requirements. I've learned so much from taking roles in clubs and projects done outside of class. People who will be there for others and use their strengths to complement others' weaknesses really make MIT a great place to be.

What kinds of people do you think would hate your school?

If anyone's looking into MIT just for prestige: don't. You can't expect to cruise off of others, you will be put through a meat grinder of rigorous requirements (required calculus, physics, core sciences). Personally, one of my friends is very pre-professional and was disillusioned by student culture because she prioritized a lot of time spent on professional endeavors rather than on campus. If you choose not to engage with campus and student life, you might feel like you're missing out on what MIT "really" is. On the other end, people who only want to just go through classes and get a degree would probably not enjoy the highly collaborative environment and belief that learning outside the classroom by taking advantage of opportunities and resources.

Do you like your school? Why or why not?

I really love MIT and have rolled right into it. My high school was really lacking in school spirit/culture and I was glad to be somewhere that I could find my people, with a bit of nerdy flair. There's no stigma against first years unlike a lot of other places, as upperclassmen make great efforts to show the pride in their communities and see them carried on by the next generation. I'm continually in awe of my peers, as my weaknesses are complemented by others' strengths (and vice versa). Even if they might be high-achieving winners of international competitions or created amazing projects, everyone is fairly approachable and willing to teach you something, just as I'm so willing to learn from my peers. Very early on you can get invested with a lot of responsibility and initiative, whether it's involvement with student government, research, or spearheading projects, regardless of class year. I love

THE KIDS WHO GET IN

the ability to go out into Boston and go out on weekends, but also stay in on-campus if I choose.

Your college's biggest strengths. What do students appreciate about their school/take for granted?

The MIT name definitely holds a lot of weight wherever you go, for better or worse. In general, we do have pretty decent funding for student activities if you know where to look/ask, which allows for a lot of side projects and small organizations to be started by passionate individuals. Very strong student community cultures, especially around dorms/living groups are very unique and prominent. MIT has a lot of focus put into easy access to opportunities, by not only heavily funding UROP programs for research, student-faculty lunches, global impact programs, and other programs, but normalizing this practice among students. MIT's fluidity is also near unheard of in other schools: ease of ability to change majors, break away from what you were good at in high school if you so choose, very late drop dates, no restrictions on how many classes you can take most terms after the first year, not applying into a major and declaring at the end of freshman year, cross-registration classes, etc.

Also as a queer student, I'd say that the LGBTQ+ community is very normalized on campus. While some places on campus have a reputation to be especially concentrated, the student body as a whole is very accepting and students stand up for their peers to be respected, as well as strong figures in their academic fields. It's been refreshing to not have to sacrifice any part of my identity to be an engineer as well and to be in a supportive environment to learn, grow, and experiment with new fields. I'd say it's also one of the T20 schools with most awareness about its class issues and feels skewed heavily middle class and hardworking in contrast to many other schools with a wider range of studies.

Your college's biggest weaknesses. What do students complain about the most? What would an admissions counselor never tell you?

Conflicts with administration regarding student life are always present. Even with easy close access to administration, they're known to solicit student feedback but mostly ignore it in favor of their own plans, especially in regards to residential life. The stress culture and impostor syndrome are also very prominent. The MIT name often overshadows students, making some people feel like they don't deserve to be at a "genius school" because their accomplishments aren't up to genius level (which is false, everyone who is here deserves to be). Classes are also very high in difficulty, so it becomes a manner of time management and seeking out resources when you struggle. This is often called being "hosed" after the phrase "an education at MIT is like drinking out of a firehose." There's a lot to do in little time, so your time is very valuable.

ESSAYS:

We know you lead a busy life, full of activities, many of which are required of you. Tell us about something you do simply for the pleasure of it. (100 words or fewer)

When I spin my lightsabers, eyes aren't on me anymore but on what I'm doing, where I channel my energy into moving light. In the Senseless Spin, I become immersed in the meditative rhythm of rotations. It's a consequence-free space; the worst thing that can happen is an aching forearm, hitting my leg, or dropping that ornate flashlight of aluminum and polycarbonate.

Although you may not yet know what you want to major in, which department or program at MIT appeals to you and why? (100 words or fewer)

I've been captivated by the projects of the MIT Media Lab. I first loved the Glass video some years ago as I set up my 3D printer and learned about layers. My curiosity dove into the Media Lab's history of experimental projects.[84] With focus on making technologies that make a beautifully presented difference, there is the potential to capture public imagination and change the world, from personal food computers to urban planning LEGOs. The first year Media Arts and Sciences program appeals to me as an opportunity to become part of the bold and beautiful interdisciplinary research I admire.[85]

84   Nice job conveying that they've been interested in MIT for a long time.

85   Here Jade uses the specific program to touch upon the greater value of MIT's that she shares (bold and beautiful interdisciplinary research).

At MIT, we bring people together to better the lives of others. MIT students work to improve their communities in different ways, from tackling the world's biggest challenges to being a good friend. Describe one way in which you have contributed to your community, whether in your family, the classroom, your neighborhood, etc. (200-250 words)

I contribute to my community through publication, with my capstone being when I brought a high school research journal to publication from an idea I had two years ago.[86] The (name redacted) Academic Review features digests of formal research papers from the Honors Advanced Research class. I was disgruntled by my inability to build off of previous students' research projects just because the only thing they left behind was a poster. With the Review, the authors themselves are able to explain their projects to preserve their findings and inspire generations of high school researchers to come.[87] After careful long nights of making templates and careful editing, 27 papers were each abridged to two pages or less. What were once daunting 20-page papers became more accessible to the casual reader. With the help of a friend who jumped on the project, the print journal had an online edition with a blog component. Sales of the Review proved successful in engaging teachers, parents, and other students in understanding projects conducted by students in the program; their pupils, offspring, and fellow classmates were scientists too!

There's so much anti-science rhetoric floating around at the moment. This publication helped to link the work of burgeoning researchers to their peers and relations, making these projects not just a token for competing in a science fair or getting into college but something that makes an impact on positive science affiliations in my community and leaves a legacy.[88]

---

86   Pretty impressive as a high school student to take a project like that all the way from idea to reality.

87   Jade's dedication to preserving this work for future generations is awesome.

88   Jade is able to identify exactly why her journal is so valuable - because it combats misinformation and preserves the work of her classmates, allowing it to be built upon. Making this understanding clear showcases self-awareness.

Describe the world you come from; for example, your family, clubs, school, community, city, or town. How has that world shaped your dreams and aspirations? (200-250 words)

Growing up, I always felt like I had taken bits and pieces of cultures without being fully immersed in any one. Both of my parents were born in Mauritius, a tiny island known for the dodo, tea, textiles, sugarcane, an underwater waterfall, and a melting pot of Indian, African, Arabic/Muslim, and the other native cultures. I grew up eating spicy curries and vindayes, tomato-based rougailles, napolitaines, dhol puris, and alouda glace. In every ethnic grocery store I stood out: Mandarin, Arabic, and Telegu were miles away from my native Kreol Morisien.

Despite being genetically half ambiguously Asian, the town I lived in until middle school had few Asian people, let alone anyone of the just-over-a-million Mauritians in the world. My physical features and pungent lunches stereotyped me into a culture I never was.[89] I was driven to distinguish myself in a better way. I learned to support and motivate myself academically in lieu of community. I picked up skills through YouTube tutorials, ranging from knitting and crocheting to coding, 3D modeling, and papercraft. When introduced to research in a new town, I found a place that valued combining different fields and techniques. I could see how crocheting lent itself to a new stretch sensor for wearables or lines of code translated to polar coordinates in a drawing robot. I finally embraced my identity and insight; I would never quite fit in, but I could see how components could mesh and interact like the cultures that made up me.[90]

Tell us about the most significant challenge you've faced or something important that didn't go according to plan. How did you manage the situation? (200-250 words)

---

89   That's a really powerful sentence. Simple and clear writing that explains the exact box that Jade was put in.

90   This is a cool essay and I wouldn't be surprised if this swung admission for Jade. The parallel she draws between interdisciplinary research and her own patchwork culture is unexpected. Reading this you almost have to smile; "I see what you did there!"

THE KIDS WHO GET IN

"[High school name], we have a problem."

It was in January of my sophomore year that the yearbook editor-in-chiefs just quit. They disappeared without so much as an email. Every frantic "where are you?" message was left on read.

Really, I had joined the yearbook in freshman year because I wanted to get the spelling of my name right.[91] But I found love in designing page layouts and having influence on a physical publication everyone got to see. Holding that satisfying glossy blue book in my hands sealed my commitment.

Despite only a year of experience, it was time for me to step up in the absence of current leadership. My fellow assistant editor Kathryn and I took over a vision that wasn't ours. With no documentation left behind, we were left to find our own way.

I sat down over a weekend and worked through our backlogged deadline, typing out tutorials for every editing process. I borrowed previous editions of the yearbook and reverse-engineered its traditions. I managed our confused staff, delegating roles and small tasks towards page layouts and deadlines. I picked up a camera and taught myself how to be a photographer. At every school event that year, I was the boots on the ground.[92]

Two years later, I'm still the editor-in chief and directing my vision of the yearbook at last. I wrote this version from the ground up, with a printed copy of my manual preserved like the yearbook itself: for years to come.[93]

Maker profile (An optional piece of the MIT application where applicants can share up to 2-minutes of video and some accompanying slides, documents, and pictures to show projects that they are working on or have completed.)

You can view their video here.

A polargraph (robotic drawing machine) made of recycled materials

---

91   Great self-deprecating humor.

92   Queue the 80's montage music. This is a fun paragraph - and we can see Jade locking in and building this plane while they fly it. Not every high schooler would be able to figure this out and it's awesome that they did.

93   Perfect ending.

Crocheted stuffed animals, some of which they invented and wrote patterns for, and a crocheted hyperbolic plane

Designed and 3D printed a modular lightsaber hilt system, and a halo for a cosplay, and Bulbasaur-shaped "planters" for succulents

An (in progress) wearable jewelry typing glove. They hope to make it more intuitive and easily accessible than current wearable keyboards.

Common App Essay (Not submitted to MIT)

There are many powers in the universe. Gravity, heat, mass, love, heart, soul, rock-and-roll. Other omnipotent beings if you believe in them. But it was the power of base ten that allowed me to pull myself together and achieve.[94]

"Who would ever need to estimate the number of blades of grass in Central Park?" my newfound partner Alice asked, dipping a chicken tender in honey mustard.[95] It was the state finals of Science Olympiad and we were sitting in a community college cafe, memorizing unit conversions and quantities. We had just met as a last minute substitute for an inquiry event no one else wanted to take on. Fermi Questions posed dimensional analysis problems to its competitors, relying on estimates and worldly knowledge to find order of magnitude answers.

For a great part of my life, I hid behind useless facts and statistics.

(Did you know that a poronkusema is the unit of distance which a reindeer can travel without stopping to urinate? It's 7.5 kilometers.)

My defense mechanism was to spit bits of trivia as a distraction to uncomfortable situations, and then some.[96] My parents nicknamed me a "walking Wikipedia" for all the time I spent crawling the internet for random knowledge. Then again, not many kids had to defend their ethnic ambiguity by memorizing a script describing where their parents came from.

---

94   Quirky intro that definitely hooks the reader. This is a risky introduction and they pull it off to perfection.

95   Specifics!

96   This is real vulnerability - Jade is sharing a deeply personal aspect of themselves with us. Admitting that this is a defense mechanism takes self-awareness and confidence, and Jade showcases both here.

THE KIDS WHO GET IN

(The island of Mauritius, famous for the extinct dodo, sugarcane, tea, textiles, sega dancers, and that one part of the ocean that looks like an underwater waterfall.)

When we moved towns, I finally understood what an underfunded school district was in comparison. When I no longer had to be the smartest nor weirdest person in the room, I dropped the act. I suppressed the urge to sprout information, not wanting to appear too prideful among my comfortably intelligent peers.

(I spent time with a friend calculating the cost of repainting a 40-foot room until entirely filled with layers of paint. It's only slightly less than four years of sticker price tuition at Princeton.)[97]

But something was missing, as I swallowed an aspect that used to define me. I had to find a new channel for all the facts still rattling around in my brain.[98] When the Science Olympiad team scrambled to find a competitor, I shot up immediately. Fermi questions were preposterous, but Perfect.

Alice and I memorized quantities like the number of hairs on a human head (10^6 hairs) or the mass of Jupiter (10^{27} kg) over lunch. We laughed through the event itself, forming inside jokes as we memorized unit conversions and quantities. There was always "at least 7" of some quantity, whether it be orders of magnitude or poronkusemas. We suggested dropping a zero here or there, casting off massive quantities in calculations. Here, my scatterbrained knowledge was valued, accepted even, and delightedly shared.[99]

Come awards, I promised to bake a cake if we won first. You should have heard the roar when we were last to be announced. My first victory celebration was filled with red velvet cake, covered with 10^2 frosting stars.

A few months later, as we were preparing for prom I examined the medal hanging on Alice's dresser. Sure, hers was scattered amongst dozens of other

---

97   I laughed out loud, this is great.
98   Even moving past her factoid phase, Jade honors this part of her identity and finds the right forum to use it.
99   This banter sounds fun.

ribbons and awards, but it was sweet to know that the matching medal had a place of honor on my bedside table. Our win brought us closer together and found a use for a useless skill, all thanks to the power of tens.[100]

MY TAKE:

Jade has a near flawless academic background (1510 SAT/36 ACT/3.95 GPA), and some interesting involvements and projects. Their 3 on the AP physics exam and 4 on BC Calc are, by their own measure, a weakness in an MIT application, but Jade articulates a strong fit with MIT that extends further than Physics and Math test scores.

The traits that Jade appreciates about MIT's culture (interdisciplinary studies, strong community, collaborative nature, investment in future generations of students) are all traits that they expressed in their application. Jade showcases devotion to the next generation of students at their high school by creating a research journal to ensure that projects did not die after completion, and pours themselves into the school yearbook year after year to memorialize and honor the students who graduate. This care for future generations indicates maturity and is a trait that MIT clearly values.

Jade's maker projects show curiosity without a clear drive for achievement - crocheting, and 3D printing cosplay pieces and light saber handles isn't lining up for an IPO or a large grant. Some of the colleges Jade was rejected from that are more focused on prestige probably viewed this as an application flaw and MIT, more oriented around intellectual curiosity and discovery, saw it as a strength.

In short, just because Jade didn't score perfectly on advanced Math and Physics exams doesn't mean that they weren't a strong fit at MIT - and they did a good job of showing this in their application!

Something else I want readers to take from Jade's application is that you don't need to compete with the rest of your peers for the small number of coveted "prestigious" leadership positions at your high school. One of the

---

100   Good ending - they tie it back to the power of tens reference, and the reader is left grateful to be taken on such a personal journey with Jade.

most impressive things Jade did in high school was found a research journal. This leveraged a passion of theirs and created a ton of value for classmates for years to come, and *set them apart* from the slew of applicants who are stuffing their resume with the same clubs and activities as everyone else applying.

In high school, think about problems in your community and think about how you can solve them! Creating and completing projects like the one Jade completed showcases initiative, responsibility, and confidence - and are refreshing contrasts to oversought positions like "NHS President."

Additionally, Jade utilizes their application well to show their quirks. Jade is a talented student and a curious individual who also likes twirling lightsabers, cosplaying, knitting stuffed animals, and 3D-printing pokemon themed plant-accessories. Sharing what makes you you helps the admissions officer really get to know you and feel a connection towards you as they decide who to advocate for - after reading this application I felt like I really knew and understood Jade.

Jade in a sentence: Quirky, nerdy, thoughtful person with many interests (crochet, coding, lightsabers) focused on preserving knowledge for the future.

Northwestern University

FELIX STOCKTON-KAHN

APPLICATION:

Major I applied under / School I applied to: Journalism/Medill School of Journalism and Integrated Marketing Communications

Ethnicity: Hispanic

Gender: Male

Family Income Bracket: 160,000-250,000/year

Year of College Graduation: 2023

High School Unweighted GPA (to nearest hundredth): 3.96

High School Weighted GPA: 4.81

Class Rank/Percentile: 2nd in class/1st percentile

SAT I Score (By Section:) 790 Reading, 800 Math (1590 Total)

ACT Score (By Section): N/A

SAT Subject Test Scores: 790 Literature

AP Test Results: 5: World History, Statistics, English Language, English Literature, Microeconomics, Government; 3: Calculus BC, Chemistry, Spanish Literature

Senior Year Course Load: AP English Literature, AP Spanish Literature, AP Statistics, Film Production, Choir 5-6, Choir 7-8

Awards Won in High School: National Merit Scholar, Hispanic National Merit Scholar, National School Choral Award, All-State Choir, All-State Jazz, AP Scholar with Distinction x2, National Honors Society

Extracurriculars in High School (Put leadership in parentheses): Choir (Co-President), Baseball (Captain 2 years), Model UN (Vice President), Theatre, National Honors Society, Teen Court, Freshmen Orientation Facilitator

Job/Work Experience in High School: Music Minister at local church, senior year

Volunteer/Community Service: Monthly volunteer at local kitchen for the homeless

What did you do in the summer after freshman year of high school?

Leisure

What did you do in the summer after sophomore year?

Leisure

What did you do in the summer after junior year?

Medill-Northwestern Journalism Institute - 5 week journalism program

ABOUT YOUR HIGH SCHOOL:

State of High School: Arizona

School Type (i.e. rural, suburban, city, public vs. private, etc): Public, suburban

# of Students in Graduating Class: ~400

What was your high school like? Demographics? How many other students went to elite universities?

Primarily hispanic-- over 65% students of color. Graduation rate was mediocre, only about 6 students went to elite universities, most didn't go on to a university.

REFLECTION ON APPLICATION PROCESS:

I applied: Early Decision

What do you think your hooks were? (Things that made me stand out in the college application process)

My SAT score was certainly one thing that made me stand out, and I think my unique background also was a hook.

What do you think the strengths of your application were?

Test scores, my essay, and my extracurriculars.

What do you think the weaknesses of your application were? Where might other applicants have had an advantage over you?

My grades were pretty good, but I think there were certainly some applicants with 4.0 gpa's, which I didn't have.

Where else you were admitted:

Nowhere, since I couldn't apply anywhere else because I applied ED.

Where you were waitlisted:

Also nowhere, only applied to NU.

Where you were rejected:

Also nowhere, only applied to NU.

Did you get a private college counselor?

No

THE KIDS WHO GET IN

When did you start preparing for college admissions? How did your family prepare?

I practiced a little bit for the SAT on Khan Academy, and my mom had me talk to some of her friends from work about how to navigate the college admissions process, but overall my family didn't prepare all that much

ABOUT YOUR COLLEGE:

Why did you choose this school?

After doing the journalism program in the summer, I realized how much I liked the campus and the people, and I was really impressed with the journalism program, so I decided this was where I wanted to be.

What is your school known for? What is its reputation?

Northwestern is known as a school on the cusp of being a top university, but not quite on par with the top Iivies. It excels in some areas, such as journalism and theatre, and falls a bit short in others. It's recently been known for a series of student suicides, which some associate with the high level of academic rigor and pressure at the university.

Is this reputation accurate?

I'd say the reputation is pretty much spot-on. The school is challenging academically, and that often takes a toll on students' mental health. There's a wealth of things to complain about, but overall the university does a good job of living up to its academic reputation.

What do you think your school offers that no other top 20 school does?

For me, it's the journalism program. Almost all top 20 schools don't even have a journalism school, so Northwestern is unique in that it's a great university overall and it has the major I want. In addition, it's somewhat unique in that it offers BiIg 10 athletics and free admission to all school sporting events. In general, though, it doesn't differ much from other top universities.

What kinds of people do you think would love your school?

Someone who is well-connected, preferably from the Chicago area, who values good academics but also wants a vibrant social scene.

What kinds of people do you think would hate your school?

Lower-class students from rural communities would likely struggle in Northwestern's environment. In addition, students uncomfortable with high academic rigor would feel out of place.

Do you like your school? Why or why not?

I generally like it. The generational wealth is new to me and something that's sometimes difficult to be around, and I sometimes feel a bit like an outsider. I like the location, and the classes so far have been interesting. I think most of my challenges just involve getting adjusted to the college environment, but I've mostly found my niche at this point and I'm happy to be here.

Your college's biggest strengths. What do students appreciate about their school/take for granted?

Being so close to Chicago is a huge benefit that people usually don't take advantage of. The city offers tons of opportunities that wouldn't be available at rural colleges, but most students rarely venture into the city. The alumni network is also impressive, and they offer lots of opportunities as well, both during and after college.

Your college's biggest weaknesses. What do students complain about the most? What would an admissions counselor never tell you?

University leadership gets a lot of hate from the student body, whether it be because of their investment in fossil fuels of discipline of student protesters. Greek life is also huge here, and it's something that I didn't understand until I started school. A lot of students who generally wouldn't be in a frat or sorority end up rushing because it's honestly the easiest and best way to have a social life, even for people who hate the Greek life environment.

ESSAYS:

Common App Essay:

An important part of my identity is my life with two houses and four moms.[101] My life started when Judy and Rena decided to have a child. They picked an anonymous sperm donor— a 5'11 Cuban whose name we still don't know — and 9 months later Judy gave birth to me. Fast forward three years or so, and Judy and Rena split up right around the time my brother, Mario, was born. Soon after, my parents both found new partners and my life with four moms began: Judy and Marnie living in one house and Rena and Melissa living in another. My brother and I switch houses every two days (three on weekends) with the exception of holidays and vacations.

My families rarely fight, but the situation presents unique challenges on a daily basis. For one, I've always heard four (often differing) perspectives on everything. This is great on one hand because it allows me to have a more well-rounded mindset and understand many different viewpoints; however, it's also difficult when trying to make important decisions (i.e. college) and asking to go out with friends or stay out late. Since expectations are different at each house, it's sometimes tough to differentiate and both sets require a lot of family time, which can be fun unless I'm really busy.

My family makeup is not only a big part of my identity, but also one of the first topics that comes up when people get to know me. I often have to explain that I have four moms, prompting questions like "how is that possible?", "how can four moms have a kid?", and "where's your dad?" I'm pretty unbothered by answering questions (it's actually often amusing), and most people are genuinely interested and supportive, although I used to be concerned that people would reject me based on my familial situation.

My racial situation is also an interesting topic to address with others. When people first see me they usually think I'm white, possibly with a dash of Hispanic thrown in. Although I'm technically half Cuban, none of my family is Cuban and I don't identify with that culture. Rather, I identify mostly with Mexican culture, as Rena's family is predominantly Mexican and Judy's extended family is as well, so most of my relatives on both sides are Mexican

---

101   Hook of the century!

and practice Mexican traditions. We make tamales every December, call each other Spanish names (nana/tata, tio/tia, etc.) and eat an unhealthy amount of homemade beans and tortillas. However, I hesitate to tell people I'm Mexican because technically it's not true, and then I have to go into the whole family explanation again. In addition, Marnie and my stepbrother Jay are Native American, and their culture and history is also a large part of my life. From the family and traditional values of Mexican culture to the honor and respect of Native culture, I love having lots of cultural influences and values in my life even though my racial and cultural identity is complex and often difficult to explain.

In summary, I now view what some see as problematic in a positive way and I embrace my situation as an important part of who I am.[102] Being a part of different cultures gives me a global perspective and better understanding of different groups; getting four perspectives on everything can be great because I can understand multiple sides of issues; having two families allows me to appreciate a massive, loving extended family (and allows me to get twice the gifts on holidays); and living with people that accept everyone and preach positive values helps me grow as a person and appreciate people's differences. The diversity of my family and community is something I can now say I'm proud of, and I hope to become an adult who carries on my family's values and who loves everyone for who they are.[103]

Northwestern Supplement:

I originally became interested in Northwestern during my sophomore year when I decided I wanted to pursue journalism in college. I looked up what the best college journalism programs were, and Northwestern consistently was at the top of the list. That, along with Northwestern's general academic excellence, sparked my interest and I asked to visit the summer before my junior year. That summer, my family took me on an extensive trip to visit colleges along the east coast. Northwestern was my top interest and the

---

102   This line is a great marker of Felix's growth. Don't be afraid to tell it like it is in your writing; this blunt depiction of his trajectory works.

103   Warm, humble conclusion. Again, the lesson learned doesn't have to be earth-shattering - just being a good, self-aware person is ingratiating and enough to mark a great essay.

THE KIDS WHO GET IN

first school we visited. I loved the campus environment and the people there were very welcoming - in addition, I loved Chicago and the Evanston city life surrounding the university. While at Northwestern, I spoke with several students and alumnus Adam Rittenberg.[104] I loved the idea of the quarter system, the journalism residency, and the career preparation offered through Medill. I also was very interested in the A Capella groups at NU and athletic excellence. Rittenberg then encouraged me to apply for the Cherubs program, which I readily did. I attended the Cherubs program last summer, and it completely affirmed my love for Northwestern.[105] The students and faculty were incredible, the campus environment was welcoming and felt like home, and the city was vibrant and accessible. After calling Northwestern home for five weeks, I feel confident that I will love calling it home for four years, which is why I've decided to apply early decision. I'm excited for the opportunity to learn from top-notch professors at Medill and receive the best journalism education there is. I'm also excited to find a new community of passionate and intelligent people and to be involved in a variety of the activities around campus, from A Capella to intramural athletics.[106] I would be ecstatic to call Northwestern home.

MY TAKE:

Felix's college essay is strong and simple. Written as a thoughtful reflection, Felix includes the reader on his internal thoughts about his lived experience. The essay lacks the frills and details of some of the other successful essays that we highlight (there is no dialogue or action/specific stories), but in the context and structure of his essay, it works. It's an interesting enough back-

---

104   A somewhat famous alum namedrop - Rittenberg is a college football writer for ESPN. This didn't sway AOs in the slightest, probably only reminding them that NU Football has seen better days.

105   Attending two summer programs at the school and applying ED is about as much interest as you can show. If you do this, have the academic qualifications, and tell a nice story, you're pretty much a definite admit.

106   Good balance of touching on his academic interests as well as the broader community.

story that it doesn't take much to hold the reader's interest[107]. It's well-written because the message is clear and concise. Felix cleanly lays out where he's come from, and how it's impacted him, which is a great setup for an essay, especially if you have an interesting or atypical background.

It's a small part of the essay, but Felix threads an interesting motif throughout the piece - his growth in how he communicates his unique background to others. Felix used to be afraid of rejection for sharing his family story but now answers questions with amusement. He's reluctant to share ("I hesitate to tell people I'm Mexican because technically it's not true, and then I have to go into the whole family explanation again"), but out of a sense of chore, not a lack of pride. Indeed, Felix finishes his essay with a lot of pride in his identity. Without walking us through his entire journey, we see growth into ownership of his unique identity - an important step in becoming a fully-fledged person and an attractive trait in a college applicant.

Next, Felix's why Northwestern essay is compelling. Firstly, Felix had clearly done his homework on Northwestern. Mentioning a campus visit, interacting with an alumnus, and spending a summer at Northwestern show that you know what you're talking about when you say you want to go to Northwestern. The "Why this school" essay is especially important for schools like Northwestern that are often treated as a backup to the Ivies (although as an Early Decision applicant that wasn't as important for Felix's application.)

These schools want to discern that you really want to attend the school, and that if they admit you, you will. The higher percentage of admits that accept, the fewer students they have to admit, and the more selective they appear - while I don't think that colleges are *solely* focused on improving their ranking, it is definitely important to them, and if we apply we're playing by their rules.

Felix makes a compelling case for himself as a person and as a potential student at Northwestern. Backed by a strong academic background (3.96 GPA, 1590 SAT), an ED application, and coming from a unique, underrepresented background, admitting Felix was a no-brainer.

Felix in a sentence: Son of 4 moms - loves journalism & NU.

---

107   A hook mentioning having four moms usually does the trick.

University of Notre Dame

JOHN BASILE

APPLICATION:

Major I applied under / School I applied to: Physics / College of Science

Ethnicity: White

Gender: Male

Family Income Bracket: 250,000-500,000/year

Year of College Graduation: 2021

High School Unweighted GPA (to nearest hundredth): 3.81

High School Weighted GPA: N/A

Class Rank/Percentile: N/A

SAT I Score (By Section): N/A

ACT Score (By Section): 35

SAT Subject Test Scores: 800 Math II, 750 Chemistry

AP Test Results: N/A

Senior Year Course Load: Five classes in each of the first two trimesters. Worked at a nonprofit in the last trimester.

THE KIDS WHO GET IN

Awards Won in High School: Dean's List (3.8+ in all classes) after Junior and Senior years

Extracurriculars in High School (Put leadership in parentheses): Varsity Crew, Rec Basketball, CYO Basketball, Various Volunteer Opportunities, Catalyst - community service club, Retreat Leader

Job/Work Experience in High School: N/A

Volunteer/Community Service: Hope Community Services - soup kitchen/food pantry, volunteered at preschool for kids with special needs, Search and Care - run errands for/ assist senior citizens in tasks they no longer can do

What did you do in the summer after freshman year?

Rowed for my local crew team, Community Rowing Association

What did you do in the summer after sophomore year?

Rowed for my local crew team, Community Rowing Association

What did you do in the summer after junior year?

Rowed for my local crew team, Community Rowing Association

ABOUT YOUR HIGH SCHOOL:

State of High School: New York

School Type (i.e. rural, suburban, city, public vs. private, etc): Catholic/Jesuit/City/Private

# of Students in Graduating Class: ~130

What was your high school like? Demographics? How many other students went to elite universities?

My high school is the only tuition-free private/catholic school in the US (maybe the world). Because it's free, it draws from students all over the tri-state area, pulling from Connecticut, New Jersey, New York City and the suburbs. The student body is relatively diverse as a result. Just a ballpark, but I think out of the 130 graduating in each class, anywhere from 45-60 may go to top 25 schools. Many others also go to schools where they've received large scholarships.

REFLECTION ON APPLICATION PROCESS:

I applied: Regular Decision

What do you think your hooks were?

I captained a varsity crew team in my senior year that I had been a part of since the 8th grade. It showed that I was, as a college counselor used to say, "pointed" -- really being able to commit to something. I had a story to tell about my experience, and my passion for it really showed in my supplements.

What do you think the strengths of your application were?

I think certain colleges put a lot of weight on varsity sports, so that definitely helped. I also had a ton of community service on my application demonstrated over four years with a number of different agencies. It showed that even as a 14-year old kid I was looking to give back. I think a lot of kids attempt to cram a bunch of activities in when the process rolls around, but I had my activities spread out over four years. It showed that I had been committed for a while.

What do you think the weaknesses of your application were? Where might other applicants have had an advantage over you?

The biggest weakness in my opinion is that I didn't do anything extraordinary/unique in high school. I had some friends do physics research at Columbia, or win the speech and debate national championships, or something else along those lines. I played a varsity sport, and sure I thought I did well, but that pales in comparison to some of the activities previously mentioned.

Where else you were admitted:

Cornell, Georgetown, Boston College

Where you were waitlisted:

Dartmouth, Bowdoin

Where you were rejected:

Yale, Williams

Did you get a private college counselor?

No

When did you start preparing for college admissions? How did your family prepare?

I started preparing for college admissions around the winter/spring of my Junior year. I had a number of practice tests/review books. I had a number of people read my essays for both corrections and just advice.

ABOUT YOUR COLLEGE:

Why did you choose this school?

I narrowed my choice down to Georgetown and ND. I loved how ND had this consolidated campus feel. I felt that it was much more "up and coming" academically than Georgetown might have been. But really, a major selling point was that I loved the Catholic identity. Notre Dame was the only "Catholic" school I visited where I could genuinely feel the Catholic identity on campus.

What is your school known for? What is its reputation?

ND is known for being a great school academically, with a top tier undergraduate business school. It's known for being a very Irish Catholic school. And of course, it's known for college football.

Is this reputation accurate?

For the most part, this is pretty accurate. Not to knock my school, but it's arguably the most homogeneous place I have ever been. Also, I really have only enjoyed a select few of my business classes so far, but I'm sure they will pick up once I'm taking my electives and really delving into what interests me in finance.

What are you involved with on campus?

Student International Business Counsel, Investment Club, Robinson Community Learning Center, Hall Government

What do you think your school offers that no other top 20 school does?

I think my school offers a fantastic sense of community. Each student is randomly placed into one of the 30 same-sex dorms. With its own tradition, atmosphere, and culture, each dorm provides a unique foundation for each student in completely different ways. The way the dorms are set up creates a slight rivalry between different students, who often attempt to convince or prove to others that his or her dorm is the best. This rivalry not only reinforces a greater sense of community within the individual dorms but also across campus as a whole.

What kinds of people do you think would love your school?

Not say you have to have one, but I think people who have a strong religious identity would like Notre Dame. It's very collaborative, so I also believe people who lean more so on the side of learning rather than competing in the classroom would also like it. It's a pretty sporty school, and the student body is relatively active, so people who really enjoy sports would also have a great time here. People who have a good time going out and meeting other people would also like it. If you're incredibly reserved, you may be stuck in your dorm and cut yourself off from many other people. If you're outgoing, though, you have your dorm as a backbone and you get to meet tons of other great people.

What kinds of people do you think would hate your school?

I don't think there's any typical kid who would completely hate Notre Dame. Even if you aren't into sports, most students just learn to love the atmosphere that encompasses the different sports games. At times it can feel like school itself isn't super academic, so some students could definitely take objection to that. In a similar vein, at times it feels like Notre Dame is super professional in nature. Instead of actually trying to teach material and educate its students, Notre Dame tried to funnel people into top tier entry level jobs. Everything is very career-oriented, which has its pluses and minuses. Some people don't look at college solely as a means to a job, and the people who are more focused on the academic side might object to Notre Dame's career oriented atmosphere.

Do you like your school? Why or why not?

I like my school. It has its ups and downs, but I'm incredibly happy with the Catholic identity, the sense of community, and most of my education so far. Like I've said, I think the school can be too career oriented at times, but it still has that academic side.

Your college's biggest strengths. What do students appreciate about their school/take for granted?

There are a number of strengths, but I would definitely highlight the sense of community. I genuinely feel like it is unmatched. There's a reason why Notre Dame's alumni have such a high rate of giving back, and there's also a reason why it's such a family oriented school: parents want their kids to experience the same things they did. This might be superficial, but Notre Dame also has incredible facilities. Whether it's on campus dining, study spaces, gyms, or just places to hangout, Notre Dame has invested a ton of money into its students, and it shows all around campus. Lastly, I think that Notre Dame has tremendous opportunities to learn outside the classroom. People definitely take the various clubs for granted at times.

Your college's biggest weaknesses. What do students complain about the most? What would an admissions counselor never tell you?

The biggest weakness, in my opinion, is that Notre Dame is the most homogeneous place I've ever been. I think this bleeds into people being more risk-averse and less likely to think outside the box. There's still a ton of opportunity to grow culturally and interpersonally, but the demographics of the school definitely hinder your initial growth. It's just easier to talk to people who are like you, so it might take that extra push to get to know other kinds of people. In addition, I am not a very big fan of the career-oriented mindset. I know some people look at college as a means to a job, but I never looked at it that way. There are way too many people who say, "oh, who cares about grades at this point, you have a job." There's value in an education beyond just setting up your first job. I think with such a strong professional dynamic, Notre Dame fails some students who genuinely went to college to pursue a passion, not their career.

ESSAYS:

Common App Essay:

I didn't move.

An actress from the Royal Shakespeare Company stood in front of my English class. Eccentric and melodramatic, she jumped right into an activity. She lined us up on either side of the classroom and asked a series of questions. If we answered yes to a question, we were asked to walk across the room. This exercise was meant to help us empathize with one of Shakespeare's characters.

"Have you ever been envious of someone?" I walked across the room.

"Have you ever felt like an outsider?" I walked across the room.

A few months earlier, my Aunt Therese had passed away. I wasn't crushed but wasn't fine either. When my mom told me, I felt sick. But minutes later, I continued on with my day. There was no grieving process: no denial, no anger, no bargaining, no depression. In that moment, just apathy. Complete apathy.[108]

"Have you ever lost someone you loved?" the actress asked.

I watched as some of my classmates took the journey across the room.

---

108   At this point, we've seen John's English class, and we've heard about his Aunt passing (that he wasn't very close with). Of course, now we wonder how these two elements are connected! It's a great hook because it makes us curious about what comes next.

I didn't move.

In truth, I didn't even think of Aunt Therese; I just stood there. As a nine-year-old, she had been diagnosed with a malignant brain tumor. The doctors couldn't fully remove the tumor because it was too close to her brain. My only memories of her are inconsequential, like playing 5-card poker at her house with my dad, brother, Therese and her aide. At the poker table, even though I could see Aunt Therese sitting right across from me, it felt as though she wasn't even there. I glanced at her from time to time looking for a reaction—a grin, a nod—but she never did much more than stare blankly at the cards.[109]

While I stood against the wall, none of that even crossed my mind. A moment later, however, something made me think of my aunt. Maybe it was the actress's blank stare as she waited for us to walk. Maybe it was the realization that I was the only person still left standing against the wall. Regardless of why, a rush of emotions washed over me. My mind was racing. Why didn't I walk across the room? Didn't I love Aunt Therese? Why didn't I spend more time with her?

In that brief moment, I forgot someone. It wasn't just someone but a family member, one who was deserving of as much love as the rest of us. Almost as quickly as the flurry of emotion overtook me, it was gone. I began to understand how I had wronged her.[110]

It wasn't a lack of love that kept me from moving. I knew I loved her; she was family. I didn't form a relationship when I should have. I had never needed to take the lead on an emotional level, so I didn't know how. I was a kid, and that's typically what adults do. She may not have had the ability to interact with me, but I still should have tried to connect with her. I should have tried to forge an emotional bond. I couldn't right my past wrongs, but I could act like an adult going forward.

As the questions from the actress continued, I was brought back into the classroom and out of my head. I recognized that in that brief moment, I for-

---

109   This is a chilling image. John does a good job of giving us a picture of his relationship with Aunt Therese, and what she looked like towards the end of her life.
110   Here, John shares a moment where he disappointed himself. This is a vulnerable essay, which is what makes it so powerful.

got a family member, not because I didn't love her, not because I didn't care, but because I didn't know how to foster a relationship with someone who couldn't foster it herself. I wasn't ready to give Aunt Therese what she needed.

I learned what it meant to not be a kid. Life is too short: too short to stay out of touch, too short to keep to oneself, too short to stay on one side of the poker table.[111]

"Have you ever made a mistake you sincerely regret?" the actress asked.

I walked across the room.[112]

Notre Dame is an adventure that will develop more than just your intellect. Blessed Basil Moreau, founder of the Congregation of Holy Cross, believed that to provide a true education "the mind will not be cultivated at the expense of the heart." What excites you about attending Notre Dame? (required response, 150-200 words)

My high school has instilled in me the Jesuit philosophy of striving to be "a man for others."[113] Throughout high school, this philosophy has guided my intellectual, emotional, and personal development. I believe that Notre Dame's strong Catholic values will further this development and aid me in continuing to be a "man for others."

Similarly, Notre Dame's adherence to a core curriculum will promote my growth as an academic and a person. My high school also had a core requirement, for which I am extremely grateful because it led to my growth in all subject areas and, in turn, has made me a well-rounded student. Notre Dame's curriculum supports my top goal in college: personal development.[114]

---

111   John's maturity stands out. John marks his transition to adulthood as taking responsibility for the relationships in his life. There's no longer an excuse to sit back and accept whatever others throw at us. John moves through this reflection without an ounce of self-promotion, but a genuine dissatisfaction with his own response. His sincere will to be a better person as he grows up is inspiring. You can utilize your essay as an opportunity to address an area of growth - and this humility and frankness will appeal to AOs.

112   Absolutely phenomenal ending.

113   A mantra that fits perfectly with the John we see in his first essay.

114   Colleges love what a line like this conveys: a young person who knows what they want to get out of college.

To balance my academic pursuits, I am excited to be a part of Notre Dame's incredible spirit, which ties together a large student body, something that I relish but did not experience at my small Catholic high school. Notre Dame provides one of the largest and strongest ties of any college. I cannot wait. The Catholic values, the core curriculum and the robust school spirit at Notre Dame will help me build on development of both the mind and the heart.[115]

This is your chance to take a risk.

"Take a risk," my rowing coach commands in the final minutes of our season ending tests. These tests will distinguish those who get seats in the priority boats from those who watch from the coach's launch.

When my coach screams "take a risk," he means only one thing: push yourself beyond your perceived limit. Doing so requires trust in yourself. When I first started to row, that trust wasn't there. I wasn't willing to take the extra pain. Now I know that mental grit isn't learned or gained: it is chosen. Once I chose to push myself just a little bit more, I found a reassuring trust in myself. Every time I broke through one barrier, I knew the next one could be knocked down as well.

The risks I've taken on the rowing machine now extend into other aspects of my personality. By passing through milestones that once seemed unattainable, I've learned to trust more in myself. This is what makes rowing so special to me. It has forced me out of my comfort zone and forced me to take a risk. The accompanying trust has instilled in me a mindset that I know will last my lifetime.[116]

---

115   This is a phenomenal "Why this school" essay. John addresses how his core values align with those of the school. He touches on *why* Notre Dame's core curriculum appeals to him (his greater value of personal development), *why* Notre Dame's large, tight-knit community appeals to him (because he went to a close but small high school), and *why* Notre Dame's Catholic identity appeals to him (because of the Jesuit philosophy that he lives by). These *why's* elevate the essay and show that John has put a lot of thought into his application to ND.

116   This is a good supplement that adds grit to our picture of John. In 200 words, it does what it needs to do. The "Take a risk" line from his coach is a little corny given the prompt, but it works and at this point in the app, John has built up enough likeability and fit that this essay was probably a non-factor.

Think about when you first meet people. What is a common first impression they might have of you? Is it a perception you want to change or what else do you want them to know about you?

When people first meet me, they often see me as lighthearted and worry-free. They're not wrong. But first impressions aren't everything, and there is a much more profound part to my character that they'll miss if that's all they see. At my core, I am tirelessly in pursuit of my goals, and those who only see my lightheartedness miss out on my passionate side. I pride myself in being both the person who can lighten a tense situation with a well-timed joke and the person who goes on 10k runs before school, agonizes over physics problem sets into the late hours of the night, and pushes myself on the rowing machine until my hands are completely calloused just to become one second faster.

For the people who know me well, the lightheartedness never diminishes; if anything, it becomes even more prevalent. Over time, however, they come to see my industriousness as its equal. The two seemingly opposite aspects of my character manage to complement one another in a way that allows me to lighten the mood or increase the intensity based on what the moment needs. My personality comprises my industriousness and lightheartedness equally.[117]

MY TAKE:

A quick breakdown on John: he's a competitive applicant, and his 3.81 GPA and 35 ACT are good enough to be in the running anywhere. His extracurriculars are average for elite admissions - he played a varsity sport and did a good amount of community service, but wasn't performing high level research or doing anything extraordinary from a leadership perspective. That being said, John's essays and in particular his Common App set him apart. Let's take a look at what made them so successful.

---

117   I like the balance that this essay brings to his application. At this point, the AO has a clear picture of John as a contemplative, serious individual - and adding this touch of levity helps humanize John.

THE KIDS WHO GET IN

His personal statement is a unique, powerful essay. John captures a distinct emotion - guilt for not feeling as bad as we feel like should. We inherently aren't that close with a majority of the people in our lives, and when one of these people passes, it's hard to know how to react. John reflects on this experience with maturity and poise: he expresses earnest guilt, he recognizes that at that stage in his emotional development he wasn't prepared to lead forming a connection, and he vows to do more in the future. It's inspiring to read such an honest self-critique - college essays don't have to be braggadocious.

John frames this compelling piece in a high school English class - which works really well for a number of reasons:

1. Firstly, the essay goes in a completely different direction than the reader anticipates. Is the piece going to be about acting? English? Being an outsider? It's almost a reverse hook - it's not a particularly drawing first couple lines, but then John mentions his Aunt Therese, and the reader is left wondering "how are these two elements connected?" which makes for a remarkably engaging essay when he answers that question! Keeping the reader guessing can be captivating.

2. John weaves in a great motif of motion. It's subtle, but the entire essay centers around "stepping up," metaphorically, to be the first one to form connections and lead emotionally, and physically, in front of his classmates. This kind of veiled double entendre is such an impressive undercurrent; matching physical movement with psychological movement helps the reader feel what John felt in that classroom. And obviously, being a good writer never hurts in college admissions!

   And what an ending! John wraps up this motif beautifully by countering his initial stagnation with a large step forward.

3. This essay could have easily just been a reflection on his Aunt Therese passing, which probably would have been a decent essay. By adding a setting and action, John brings this reflection to life. In writing your college essay, think about what specific moments and environments you can attach to the larger experiences and themes of your life.

The rest of John's essays are great. I like how he takes some time to highlight his strengths, tenacity and levity, and reflect on how they compliment each other - it adds a layer to his personality that we don't see in his personal statement. His 'Why Notre Dame' essay works well because it focuses on the high-level things that the school takes pride in (Encouraging Catholic values, fostering personal development, having a close-knit undergraduate community).

John stands out by not just demonstrating fit, but establishing what he wants from his college experience and affirming that ND is the place to make that happen: "Notre Dame's curriculum supports my top goal in college: personal development." In this way, John presents himself as self-aware and confident. This articulation of fit, combined with a strong academic background and some great essays, earned John a spot at ND.

John in a sentence: Principled, hard-working kid who wrote an incredible essay about losing the Aunt he barely knew.

Princeton University

MIRANDA ALVARO

APPLICATION:

Major I applied under / School I applied to: Bachelor of Science & Engineering - Operations Research and Financial Engineering

Ethnicity: Latina

Gender: Female

Family Income Bracket: 80,000-160,000/year

Year of College Graduation: 2022

SAT I Score (By Section): 800 Math, 750 Reading (1550 Total)

ACT Score (By Section): N/A

SAT Subject Test Scores: 800 Math II, 750 Chemistry

High School Unweighted GPA (to nearest hundredth): 4.12 (+ to - scale), 4.0 otherwise

High School Weighted GPA: 5.84

Class Rank/Percentile: Co-Salutatorian

AP Test Results: 5: Chemistry, Psychology, Calculus AB, Statistics, Spanish Language and Culture, English Language, Government, Physics 1, En glish Lit, Physics C: Mechanics, Studio Art: Drawing Portfolio, Calculus BC, Macroeconomics, Microeconomics, 4: Physics 2, US History, 3: Computer Science A

Senior Year Course Load:

Computer Science A AP, Eng Lit Comp AP [Wld], Calculus BC AP, Physics C AP (Mechanics), Economics Macro AP, Economics Micro AP, Stud Art Draw Port AP 2

Awards Won in High School: Top 10: Sophomore, Junior, Senior Year; 2 Class Awards Sophomore Year; First Platinum Scholar in Gulliver History (6 class awards, Junior Year - previous highest had been 4); Cornell Book Award Junior Year; I believe 2 more class awards my Senior Year, English Department Award (Senior), $1000 Scholarship my school gave out (nominally for Community Service, but from what my teachers told me, the decision was made by a group of faculty who considered who deserved it); National Merit Recipient

Extracurriculars in High School:

National Art Honor Society (VP Junior Year, President Senior Year)

Spanish Honor Society (Treasurer Junior Year, President Senior Year)

- Started Independently: Food & Medicine Drive for Venezuela, Senior Year I turned it into a project under the Spanish Honor Society

Mu Alpha Theta (President Junior Year, VP Senior Year)

Computer Science Club (President Senior Year)

Students In Action - Local Parks and Recreation Volunteer

Art!!

Job/Work Experience in High School: Private Tutoring in Math up to AP Calc BC, in Physics up to Physics C; Mechanics, in both English and Spanish; Summers as an Office Assistant at a family business; Internship at Finance firm Summer 2017

Volunteer/Community Service: Mainly Community Service Projects through clubs: volunteering with NAHS (National Art Honor Society) working face painting for events, raising supplies or money through drives, hosting events/fundraisers in Computer Science; refurbishing computers to donate in Computer Science

What did you do in the summer after freshman year?

Office Assistant where my father worked.

What did you do in the summer after sophomore year?

Office Assistant where my father worked, and did first successful collection of supplies for Nicaragua and shipped them there

What did you do in the summer after junior year?

Interned at a law firm.

ABOUT YOUR HIGH SCHOOL:

State of High School: California

School Type (i.e. rural, suburban, city, public vs. private, etc): Private Secular

# of Students in Graduating Class: ~270

What was your high school like? Demographics? How many other students went to elite universities?

Very Wealthy, Privileged, Mainly Immigrant Population, Largely Latino, not particularly diverse racially, although there were a substantial number of international students, parents were largely businessmen, it was a preparatory school so besides a few exceptions every student went to university, all students got into good universities (range from UM and FIU to Ivies), in my year as I recall, maybe 4 or 5 people went to NYU (mostly Stern), 1 person Dartmouth, 2 Yale (1 Athlete, other not), 1 Harvard (Athlete), 1 UChicago, 1 MIT, 2 Princeton (1 Athlete, Other Me), 2 or so Columbia University (Both Athletes? Can't Remember), 1 Amherst College, 2 Vanderbilt University, 2 Duke University, 1 Johns Hopkins (did not attend), 1 Georgetown, 2 WashU, ... everyone else went to schools like Boston College, Boston University, Tufts, Loyola, American, GW, etc.

REFLECTION ON APPLICATION PROCESS:

I applied: Early Action

What do you think your hooks were?

Art, for sure. My pieces were very high-quality, detailed, pieces which I had won awards for. My portfolio was full of work that really demonstrated my dedication and skill in portrait art.

What do you think the strengths of your application were?

My grades and AP Scores were really impressive. I think my essays were really well-done and I probably came off as very passionate and intellectually curious in them, and I think my personal statement was a really strong piece of writing that may have made me stand out. My teachers let me read their recommendation letters after I was done with the college process, and I think they must have really strengthened my application, they were really beautiful and personal and really genuine, passionate statements about me as a student and an individual (I had incredibly close bonds with my teachers, they were the best thing I got out of that high school).

What do you think the weaknesses of your application were? Where might other applicants have had an advantage over you?

My extracurriculars in terms of clubs felt relatively wishy-washy: I was a leader of many of them which of course required a lot of juggling and work, but it didn't appear like I was working towards anything in particular, more like I was just taking on arbitrary responsibilities. I had friends who had their biomedical research published, or whose primary extracurricular was robotics and they were applying as an engineer, and I imagine it must have looked great for those interests to line up with their career goals, although I assume I could be wrong about what colleges are looking for.

Where else you were admitted:

I didn't apply anywhere else except for UCLA, where I was accepted before Princeton.

Where you were waitlisted:

N/A

Where you were rejected:

N/A

Did you get a private college counselor?

No

When did you start preparing for college admissions? How did your family prepare?

In terms of SAT and testing, I studied for the PSAT/NMSQT I took Junior Year because I wanted National Merit, and then I took several practice tests in preparation for the actual SAT, which I took twice, once in Junior year, once at the beginning of senior year. I started my application for Princeton probably around mid-September (due at the beginning of November). My family did not make any preparations.

ABOUT YOUR COLLEGE:

Why did you choose this school?

To be honest, I was shooting for the best school I could possibly get. I knew I wanted to do Engineering, and out of the Ivies, this was one of the best choices for that. I also really loved that the class sizes were small and that professors were really there to work with undergraduate students. I liked that it was a college town at the time (though I know now that I would've preferred a school closer to the city), and what really solidified my choice was ORFE, a major they offered which is relatively new. Funnily enough, I'm actually switching from that major to Computer Science now.

What is your school known for? What is its reputation?

It is the highest-ranked school in the United States. It is known for having the largest endowment per capita in the United States, and for having really bright students, famous alums, incredible professors conducting groundbreaking research, and for being the birthplace of much of the world's knowledge about math and science. It is seen as preppy, wealthy, and elitist, which is less true in demographics than it was before, though certain aspects of the school still carry that unfortunate energy with it.

Is this reputation accurate?

See above, and also, it depends what circles you find yourself in. Absolutely none of the people I surround myself with are preppy or elitist, and I actually don't encounter many people like that at all. That said, there are memes about eating clubs[118] with the kinds of members that really (REALLY) embody that reputation, and every once in a while you meet the kind of person that makes you remember what the history of the school is.

What are you involved with on campus?

I'm a Writer, Artist, and Editor for The Princeton Tiger (the humor publication on campus) and I am a stylist for a fashion club called TigerTrends. I'm also part of Princeton Women in Computer Science and Princeton Latinos y Amigos.

What do you think your school offers that no other top 20 school does?

Opportunities to have good relationships with professors: the graduate population is so much smaller than the undergrad population and it is completely true that it makes a huge difference. My classes are small and taught by award-winning professors. Literally, where else are you gonna hang out

---

[118] From our lovely editor and Princeton-grade, Jack: 1) Many liken Princeton's eating clubs to Greek life at other schools, which is largely a half truth. The eating clubs are a row of 12 (number check?) houses alongside campus where ~70% of upperclassmen join to eat their meals and party. That said, they differ from classic Greek life in that they are all co-ed, half can be joined without an exclusionary admissions process, there is no hazing, and membership typically hovers around 200.

one-on-one with Joyce Carol Oates because she's your creative writing professor and she gave you her office hours to come and chat. Everything feels more personal than it would at another school. It's mind-blowing to realize who the people around you are and the incredible things that they've done, and that they're talking to you as an equal.

What kinds of people do you think would love your school?

Students who are intellectually curious and really ambitious. The resources at this school are unparalleled, and like I said before, the kinds of people you meet are as well. If you are willing to take on the challenge, you can get a lot out of the school.

What kinds of people do you think would hate your school?

That said, it is incredibly challenging. More than I could have imagined. And although I wouldn't at all describe the student population as competitive (seriously, at all - unless you're pre-med), literally just being at the school puts this enormous pressure on you to try to do it all and to accomplish incredible things under a whole different kind of stress. This is not the kind of place to go if you just want to have a chill college experience. And that's not to say that the school has a culture of work and only work - more so it's a work-hard, play-hard culture, but in a really extreme way. It can feel really heavy sometimes.

Do you like your school? Why or why not?

I go back and forth. I love the intimate size and the campus is absolutely beautiful. I love that it's small enough to walk everywhere and my friends are right by me. My professors are geniuses, and wonderful and kind and inspiring, and learning from them is a gift. I really love the endowment and how wonderful the financial aid is - I'm so grateful to be able to attend the school and study or intern abroad when the school is taking the financial stress off. I really like the friends I've made and the way that the student population as a whole is actually really humble in personality despite expectation.

But still, the high-achieving nature of all the students can still make it feel like a pressure cooker sometimes and it is difficult to get through. It also is really isolated from the city which is difficult for me considering I grew up in a huge one - I thought it was something I would enjoy but I try to go to New York every opportunity I get to breathe some life into me. Eating clubs can also be exclusive in a really gross way at times, which is just not at all fun. No one should be putting that much effort into attending a social event. Unfortunately, in such a small town there's not much else to do except go to the eating clubs or chill in a dorm with your friends.

Your college's biggest strengths. What do students appreciate about their school/take for granted?

- The Endowment! These Resources are Crazy and we will never have access to them again!

- Research Opportunities. Every professor on this campus is doing incredible things apart from teaching. Reach out to them.

- Study Abroad. Such incredible choices and great financial support. Once-in-a-lifetime experiences. This includes Bridge-Year[119], a program I sort of wish I would've done.

- There are talented people in anything you can think of. You can explore your hobbies and really have them become a huge part of your life if you so choose.

Your college's biggest weaknesses. What do students complain about the most? What would an admissions counselor never tell you?

- Grade deflation.

- Mental Health is pretty bad overall, though I don't know that I can say it's any worse than at other top schools. But the mental health resources are awful, and any student will tell you that.

- It's so hard that sometimes it seems like the people being departments are deliberately malicious. What is a Holiday PSet, ORGO? Explain.

- Humanities professors are earth-shatteringly intelligent. STEM professors, especially tenured ones, can honestly be pretty horrific at teaching. Many bad experiences.

---

119   The Bridge Year program extends the opportunity for a small group of students to live an immersive international gap year experience for 9 months.

ESSAYS:

Common App Essay:

I want to be *filthy* rich.[120]

I crave it the way others crave attention and affection and belonging: with a dizzying desire - the kind that manifests itself in a tug-of-war between admiration and jealousy. I watch my classmates with an unsettling kind of vicarious living, and thrive off of the relaxed look in my friend's eyes after she misplaces a $100 bill, her greatest anxiety that she has to request her allowance a day early. I've stepped into their new sports cars, the smell traveling to my senses and overwhelming them with the scent of luxury, wishing it could be mine, soothing myself: "someday."[121]

Every time I'm a witness, it feels like falling in love over and over again.[122] It feels unhealthy, like the toxic relationship everyone warns you to stay away from. "Money is the root of all evil," they say. But I've realized I'm not a privileged greedy monster: I'm just an intelligent being making associations.

Money tastes like safety.

The careless swipe of a credit card sounds comforting to me. It drowns out the memories of conversations in my living room where I'm questioned why I can't be proactive, and asked why I couldn't have gotten my AP review book a few days earlier, when I could've ordered a used one online instead of the $20 platinum edition in store.[123]

And I know perfectly well my kind of whining only reflects how comfortably I really live, with so much to be thankful for and a life exponentially bet-

---

120   Great hook.
121   We feel like we're peering over Miranda's shoulder into her world.
122   The "dizzying desire" and "toxic" love that Miranda describes introduce the theme of love. It's funny, it's self-depreciative, and it helps the reader understand just how infatuated with money Miranda is (and she gets into why).
123   Once again, powerful specifics that bring us into her world.

ter than my relatives back in Venezuela.[124] But I can't help but be affected by the stress in my dad's eyes when he reviews the bills at the end of the month, the tension in the room as we all sit silently and regret the purchases we made that we know we could have done without, as I feel the permanence of the guilt I acquired 10 years ago, when it dawned on me that I was a burden to my family.

I worry about money not because I don't have it, but because I desperately ache for a life where I have enough to stop thinking about it. The truth is that much of my ambition stems from my fear of instability. However, I am not ashamed.[125]

Despite it all, I'm happy my parents were honest with me about their struggle to be where they are today, and the struggle that continues as we find ourselves in the reality of a country founded on hard work. I am proud that I know the value of money, that I go to a private school with the deepest appreciation for the opportunities my parents provided for me, and a resulting insatiable drive to succeed.[126] I am who I am because I know where I come from. But I also know I have the power to lead a life where money is no object, where instead of being a weight on my parents' work-exhausted shoulders, I can take care of others without concern for a dwindling savings account.

One day, I will feel the smooth leather on an offensively overpriced purse, with a genuine smile and a peaceful mind. I'll know I could afford it if it was what I wanted, but I'll be experienced and grounded enough to instead use the fruit of my and my family's labor for something worthwhile.[127] I'll use it to take care of my parents, my siblings if they'll need it, and the family I wish to have. But most ambitiously, and therefore most probably, I'll invest it into

124   Fantastic note that showcases humility and self-awareness. Miranda ingratiates herself with AOs by reminding them that she knows there are people who have it worse. The author of the Yale application in this book does something similar that works perfectly.

125   This is a wonderful transitional paragraph. It bridges Miranda's financial insecurities with pride, which she elaborates on in the next paragraph.

126   Again, gratitude and humility - Miranda is likable because she's painfully honest about something that bothers her and balances this vulnerability with appreciation for everything she has.

127   Miranda recognizes that her infatuation with nice things is flawed - and conveys her desire to look and touch, but not buy. It's about psychological security, and education not Gucci handbags - and this twist brings the essay to the next level.

the education of kids who will know the meaning of opportunity and will fuel themselves with the same understanding that has pushed me.

Because, no, I'm not in love with the bright red color of the Jaguar in my school's parking lot - I'm in love with the potential it holds for bigger and better things.[128]

Major Supplement (Using a favorite quotation from an essay or book you have read in the last three years as a starting point, tell us about an event or experience that helped you define one of your values or changed how you approach the world. Please write the quotation, title and author at the beginning of your essay.)

"This ice is not made of such stuff as your hearts may be; it is mutable and cannot withstand you if you say that it shall not." *Frankenstein*, Mary Shelley.

I sit at my desk, staring purposefully at my paper and rubbing my thumb repeatedly against the eraser of my pencil, a test-taking habit I acquired to absorb my impatience. A good 20 minutes before, I began to hear the slams of pencils against a wooden surface: the sound of hopelessness, of desperate surrender. It didn't take long for the others to notice as well, suddenly feeling licensed to give up too, because failure with companionship felt slightly less shameful. One by one, whether by half-stifled groans or by burying the corpse of their brain in the casket of their arms, my classmates indicated Question #4 had won the fight. It was understandable: AP Physics tests were notorious for the destruction of student morale. Less than four years ago, I would've been them.

An incoming freshman at an important new school, the version of myself that started my high school journey was insecure to a degree remarkable even for my age (and everyone knows pre-teens are characterized by gaping holes where self-esteem should be.)[129] I had a genius older brother who had already marked the territory, and a severe resulting inferiority complex.[130] Middle

---

128   Perfect ending.
129   This line is great because it's almost like Miranda stepping out of the essay and into a conversation with the reader. Asides like this work really well to build rapport with the AO.
130   An instance where one sentence tells us more than 3 paragraphs could.

school being social anarchy, I had never given much thought to the value of my mind - I had a flawless academic record, but was driven by an ambition I hadn't yet recognized. I was unaware of my ability. The day I created my 9th grade schedule, with freedom to choose the difficulty of my classes, my own confidence failed to guide me in the right direction. My mother, concerned for my stress levels, unknowingly solidified the safe choices I was making. I recalled my mediocre writing in 7th grade and concluded that English wasn't my strength. Although Spanish was my first language, I hadn't studied it in years: I was afraid of failure. I found myself in classes that didn't challenge me, doing work I couldn't grow from.

But that year, I finally discovered myself. I found her in the A+'s that I strived for when the A's were too easy, and also in the mistakes that plagued me in a Chemistry Class full of 10th graders, the only challenge I hadn't backed down from. I found her[131] in the success of my work, and the compliments of my teachers. I found her in the comments of my friends: "You're so smart," not said because they wanted me to do their homework, but because it actually meant something. I realized not only that I was intelligent, and that I was capable of accomplishing amazing things, but that to my core, it was what I wanted: to learn. Since then, I've challenged myself in any way I can, because I've found the secret to success: believing that you are capable of anything you make the effort to do. I reject limits to my potential, and am not ashamed of failure: I make room from my mistakes, and room to grow from them. Slowly, through my acceptance that I didn't have to be the best to be worth something, I climbed my way up high.

So sitting in that desk, surrounded by others who gave up because they felt they'd reached their limit, I defy my own tired brain telling me the same thing - I learned to. With determination and with confidence - real, passionate faith in myself - I analyze the problem in front of me, as long as it takes, until it cannot break me. The solution is in my mind; I have the tools, I have the power, and I have the drive.[132]

---

131   This motif of "finding her" is powerful - Miranda is encountering a new person.

132   Here we see the ambition that Miranda references in her first essay applied to her academics. Again, supplements are great places to continue drilling into a theme introduced in the personal statement.

I try, and I try, and I try, and I do not fail. I do not fail, because I say that I shall not.

If you are interested in pursuing a B.S.E. (Bachelor of Science in Engineering) degree, please write a 300-500 word essay describing why you are interested in studying engineering, any experiences in or exposure to engineering you have had, and how you think the programs in engineering offered at Princeton suit your particular interests.

The day I took my advanced mathematics entrance exam in 6th grade, I was expecting nothing out of it. I had always liked math and done reasonably well in the subject, but as a creative young girl, I had dreams of being an actress, or a singer, or an artist. When I made it to Algebra 1 the following year, it changed my perspective. I was seeing the first steps to what I would eventually view as a tool to solve the world's problems - to understand, to analyze, to change, to create. I was enchanted with the way math could make sense of anything, with the image of a tangible solution. I even found doing math homework *fun*, hiding my nerdy secret from my friends because at the time, I thought the vicious 12-year olds would eat me alive. But it quickly became my favorite subject and my favorite game, and I even ventured out of the classroom to join other pre-teen mathletes.

The difference in high school was that math developed into just one part of the story. I took my first Computer Science class and found the creative aspect of STEM that I'd been craving.[133] I took AP Statistics in my junior year, and knew from the first day it would be my favorite class I'd ever taken. I had never seen so clearly the application of a subject matter, but suddenly I could visualize the connection between numbers and human behavior, and realized the power and purity of statistics in understanding the world.

Funnily enough, that year I fell in love with Princeton. As is only appropriate in a situation of interest, I had been stalking it on the internet. I already knew its academics were second to none, but it was everything: the beautiful campus, the diversity, the creativity and spirit, the professors, and most importantly, the undergraduate focus. All that was left to see was if they offered

---

133   Fits into the way Miranda presents herself throughout the application as a highly creative and highly analytical student.

a program that was right for me. I didn't know what I was looking for until I found it: Operations Research and Financial Engineering.[134]

I still remember that day. Sitting in the middle seat of my dining room table, still in my school uniform, I went over the typical course schedule and departmental electives, my heart growing a little larger as key words delivered jolts of excitement: "stochastic optimization," "statistical design," "risk analysis."[135] I read about the customization and flexibility of Princeton's ORFE program and the variety of fields that students used their education in. I pictured myself in teaching studios, doing undergraduate research and working with the school's distinguished professors, and doing a senior thesis as fascinating as those of previous students. Squealing on the inside until I couldn't hold it, I screeched to the closest person I could find:[136] "Mom!! They literally made this just for me!!" and I knew it to be true. Princeton was where I needed to be.

Please tell us how you have spent the last two summers (or vacations between school years), including any jobs you have held. (About 150 words)

This last summer, I managed to geek out even beyond my own expectations.[137] Throughout both June and July, I interned at a financial advisory firm. Understandably, with my level of knowledge, I couldn't work extensively with the stock analysts, but as I learned about the independent professional experience, and the meaning of documents I had never seen (Investopedia was my best friend), I watched my fellow employees with an avid curiosity. There was another college intern who was working there, who showed me a computer program that he had created to use different filters to sort stocks the company was interested in looking at. While he only saw bright eyes and rapidfire questions, I was confirming my love for comput-

---

134   Miranda turns the "Why this school" essay, normally a laundry list, into a story that the reader is invested in. It's awesome.
135   Again, great balance of specifics and wider cultural values the school holds (undergraduate focus, creativity and intellectual vitality).
136   This is such a real moment - it's hard not to root for Miranda after reading these essays.
137   Another great aside to the reader.

er science. The rest of the summer was slightly less nerdy: I worked on art pieces for my portfolio, spent time with family, volunteered, and slept for alarming lengths only suitable for a teenager.

The summer before 11th grade, I worked at a tax firm full-time for a month doing administrative work. I also worked on the first few art pieces for my portfolio and volunteered in my community. This was the summer that I became inspired to start a food and medicine drive for Venezuela, planned how I would collect supplies, contacted Venezuelan cargo companies, and found who would receive and transport the shipment there.

Please briefly elaborate on one of your extracurricular activities or work experiences that was particularly meaningful to you. (About 150 words)

The day I drew my first complete portrait on a manila folder in the 3rd grade (despite explicit instruction against it), I discovered a unique lens to unlocking the beauty of existence. Of course, I never thought my teenage self would be spending an enormous proportion of my waking hours producing and studying art, in the blurry late/early 3-4-5 AMs before a deadline or the weekends and summers in between, working harder than I ever have. But I do it, because of the same reason I love learning: to make the most out of my world. Without art, there's an upper bound to understanding, but with it, life transcends objective ideas.[138] It is the window, through emotion and feeling, to the depths of the human condition. It's more than a class, even more than an extracurricular activity. It's a passion for life exemplified in a painting, drawing, journal, notebook paper, or sketchbook. Whether for fun, for school, for charity, or for loved ones, the challenging hours I dedicate to producing work I'm proud of never fails to be rewarding. As president of NAHS, guiding students, sharing art with underprivileged children, and creating collaborative pieces, I get to expand what it means to be an artist. But at the same time, I love when my creations are just my own. Sitting in my bedroom, sketching my ideas and fears and dreams, I know art is also a passion for finding myself.

---

138   Similar to the Dartmouth entry, Miranda sprinkles in these beautiful notes about life that highlight her values and the way she sees the world.

THE KIDS WHO GET IN

MY TAKE:

Miranda stands out as an extremely intelligent, self-aware, industrious person with varied interests and talents. Her academic credentials are nearly flawless (18 AP exams, 1550 SAT, 4.0 Unweighted GPA, several academic awards from her school,) and her personal qualities, accomplishments outside of the classroom, and writing are all equally compelling.

Miranda uses her essays to present herself as a dynamic, thoughtful individual. Her common app essay has an incredible hook[139] that orients her fear of financial instability around a drive for success. Miranda craves wealth not for Gucci purses or Jaguars, but for security and opportunity for future children like her.

These neuroses fit the larger picture that Miranda crafts of herself: a leader of several student organizations, a 4.0 student, a hungry intern spending hours on investopedia, and a nonprofit founder. We see a near-addiction to achievement and learning, and it is impressive. As other entries will show, you don't *have* to be this involved to get into an elite school, but for Miranda, it fit the picture that she crafts of herself.

Each supplemental essay that she writes matches this image while also adding more color around her personality. In her main supplement, we see her relentless drive in action and learn a little bit more about it's roots (a sibling rivalry/battles with low self-esteem). In her next piece, we see a teenager squealing for joy at the discovery of a fitting major, and we see how Miranda's ambition translates to her studies. Writing about art, we see a more personal side of her, and a greater account for the sleepless nights and overinvolvement: "to make the most out of my world."

Miranda's accomplishments in disparate fields like art, service, computer science, and leadership reflect a keen desire to maximize her potential - which she pairs with a powerful argument why Princeton is the right place for her

---

[139] "I want to be *filthy* rich" is one of the best first sentences we've read

to do so. Miranda presents herself as a person with varied interests, with an ability to think critically about herself and her place in the world, and a strong picture of what she wants to do (and why!). This, combined with her stellar academic record, is why she got into Princeton, one of the most prestigious schools in the country.[140]

Miranda in a sentence: Incredibly driven lover of learning, art, and money - for the right reasons.

---

140   I'm running out of ways to end these!

Rice University

JESSICA KIM

APPLICATION:

Major I applied under / School I applied to: School of Social Sciences, I applied as Cognitive Science, but I am now a Psychology major with a business minor and am planning on pursuing the Masters of Accounting program at Rice.

Ethnicity: East Asian

Gender: Female

Family Income Bracket: Under 20,000/year

Year of College Graduation: 2022

SAT I Score (By Section): 770 Reading, 760 Math, (1530 Total)

ACT Score (By Section): N/A

SAT Subject Test Scores: 750 Biology-M, 790 Korean, 720 Math II

High School Unweighted GPA (to nearest hundredth): 4.00

High School Weighted GPA: 4.33

Class Rank/Percentile: 1

AP Test Results: 5: English Language, Calculus AB, Psychology, 4: Psychology, 3: World History

Senior Year Course Load: AP Literature, Probability and Statistics, AP Government/Economics, Spanish 4, Vocal Ensemble, Gospel Choir, Musical Theater, Orchestration, Vocal Jazz Ensemble

Awards Won in High School: YoungArts Popular Voice Merit (2016, 2017) Jazz Voice Merit (2017), Jazz Voice Honorable Mention (2018), Academic Achievement in Spanish 1 and 2, President's Gold Volunteer Service Award, Questbridge College Prep Scholar, Questbridge College Match Finalist, Next Generation Jazz Festival Soloist 3rd place, Next Generation Jazz Festival Vocal Ensemble 1st place (2015-2017)

Extracurriculars in High School (Put leadership in parentheses): Asian American Alliance (president 2017-2018), Vocal Jazz Ensemble (student director 2017-2018), Gospel Choir (business director 2016-2018)

Job/Work Experience in High School: N/A

Volunteer/Community Service: Teen Line Listener: teen-to-teen national hotline, California Scholarship Federation (vice president 2018), Youth Orchestra of Los Angeles (mentor for kids 6-14)

What did you do in the summer after freshman year of high school?

I went to Canada and also trained for Teen Line, a five-week intensive on active listener training. I performed at the Hollywood Bowl for the Playboy Jazz Festival.

What did you do in the summer after sophomore year?

I continued volunteering at Teen Line throughout and SAT prep.

What did you do in the summer after junior year?

I continued volunteering at Teen Line. My summers were not really that productive.

ABOUT YOUR HIGH SCHOOL:

State of High School: California

School Type (i.e. rural, suburban, city, public vs. private, etc): Public arts high school (audition required to get admitted)

# of Students in Graduating Class: 150

What was your high school like? Demographics? How many other students went to elite universities?

Since I went to an arts school that accepted students from all around Los Angeles county, it was a fairly diverse school and I had a diverse group of friends. Income-wise, though, it wasn't that diverse since the majority of students came from upper middle-class families. The departments were split up into dance, visual arts, film, music (vocal and instrumental), and theater. Many students were pursuing the arts track so a lot of them attend very notable arts universities like Berklee College of Music, SUNY Purchase, USC, Manhattan School of Music, etc. A few, however, are more academically inclined like I was and some went to Harvard, UC Berkeley, Columbia, and others.

REFLECTION ON APPLICATION PROCESS:

I applied: Early Decision

What do you think your hooks were?

I think that I was a very diverse candidate since I did well in school but I was an arts major (vocal jazz, specifically). I also came from a low-income background, which was why I applied through Questbridge. I didn't grow up in the ideal family— my parents got divorced when I was 4 and I never saw my dad again. He died of cancer when I was in 8th grade, but I didn't find out until my uncle told me during my junior year of high school. Pretty crazy. Also, most of my extracurriculars were musical but I had Teen Line, which I talked about in my essay as being a very eye-opening experience that not many students my age get to have.

What do you think the strengths of your application were?

My grades were pretty much perfect because I was very academically inclined compared to my peers. I feel like my essay was strong in evoking emotion and showing different parts of myself. I also had a unique perspective coming from an arts high school while pursuing an academic career.

What do you think the weaknesses of your application were? Where might other applicants have had an advantage over you?

I was most nervous about the fact that I did not have many extracurriculars that were not musical. Since I was applying as a Cognitive science major, I felt like I might not have had many activities that backed up my academic interests. My school also didn't have many AP classes (only 7 total of which I took 6) so I didn't have as many AP scores to show. My SAT subject test scores weren't amazing either.

Where else you were admitted:

I got my decision from Rice very early so I had to withdraw all of my other applications (which were just UC's) but I didn't properly withdraw from UCLA and was admitted.

Where you were waitlisted:

N/A

Where you were rejected:

N/A

Did you get a private college counselor?

No

When did you start preparing for college admissions? How did your family prepare?

I've basically been preparing since 6th grade. My mom started me up with a tutor at C2 education very early on in which I did some basic SAT practice throughout middle school and high school. My family is just me and my mom, who is an immigrant from Korea. She stressed the fact that college was extremely important from when I was a child. Going to college was not an option for me, it was a requirement. While I didn't start prepping intensively for tests and all that until sophomore year, my mom has always held me to the highest standards in terms of keeping my grades up and never getting a B. So it was pretty intense.

ABOUT YOUR COLLEGE:

Why did you choose this school?

I chose Rice because I felt like it was where I belonged when I visited. It is a fairly small school so it's a close-knit environment, it is located in a huge city that won't limit what you can do, and it is an academically challenging, but low-pressure environment. We have what we call a "culture of care" that is highly stressed from day one, in which we all uphold a certain standard in caring for our peers, whether that is supporting each other through classes or taking care of your peers when they aren't doing well. We also have the residential college system that basically determines your identity at Rice. It is a smaller community that you can bond with, ensuring that you have a group to fit into as soon as you step on campus. Not only that, I have never even heard of a school that cares about its students as much as Rice. Our orientation week is highly coordinated and almost completely run by Rice students. You have an O-week group from the beginning that you get to know really well and keep tabs with during your entire first year at Rice. And because the school is so diverse, everyone basically finds a group of people they fit in with pretty easily. I would not change my decision for the world.

What is your school known for? What is its reputation?

Our school is ranked #1 in happiest student life. It is also well-known for its music school, engineering school, and architecture school. I think that there's also a perception that the students are extremely studious and not very social. Rice is a highly recognized university in the south/middle of the United States, but not at all on the coasts. If you ask someone in California about Rice, they probably won't even recognize the name, but if you ask someone in Texas, they would say all the smartest kids attend.

Is this reputation accurate?

For the most part, all of this is accurate. The academics here are very challenging and can range from manageable to extremely difficult depending on your major. If you are in the architecture or engineering school, you most likely are studying or working the majority of your time at Rice. Socially, a lot of the students are fairly quiet and may stick to themselves, but I have found that you can find someone who matches your personality and preferences very easily. I do agree that student life is pretty positive compared to other schools. I have never met someone who regrets their decision to attend Rice, and the student body is very active in keeping traditions and student culture alive.

What are you involved with on campus?

I was an advisor for O-week, meaning I am a mentor to a set group of students in my residential college and support them throughout their first year of Rice. I am also a Peer Academic Advisor, so I help students with their academic decisions. I am currently a TA for Business Communications as well, and a peer communications coach for engineering students. I also am a member of the Students Demand Actions chapter at Rice (gun-control club).

What do you think your school offers that no other top 20 school does?

I think we offer a very personalized environment. The residential college system makes it so that you have a community around you at all times, and the school is so small that you know the majority of your graduating class. It's a much smaller school than other top 20 schools, so it's so much easier to feel closer to not just the people around you, but the school itself. Also, Rice gives much more power to its students than other schools. Each residential college is run by its own government with over a $40,000 budget for its own committees, initiatives, and traditions, and students run the whole thing! This makes it much easier for students to feel that they have a voice and can speak up when they feel it is necessary.

What kinds of people do you think would love your school?

I think that all kinds of people can find their own community at Rice. If you're a super studious person and just want to study, that's fine. If you want to be very social and go to parties, you can find your people. However, one thing about our school that is pretty impactful is its political leanings. Students at Rice tend to be very liberal and outspoken about social issues, so people who are passionate about these things would be able to fit in very well. Of course, not everyone is like that at Rice, but generally, most students are. Also, people who really want to find their own niche in college would like the way our school is structured.

What kinds of people do you think would hate your school?

Like I mentioned before, our school is very liberal so if you have conservative beliefs, it may be difficult to speak up about it. Also, our school is very involved in making sure each student feels welcomed, so if you're the type of person that doesn't really want to be bothered by group activities and just want to stay in your lane, you might be annoyed sometimes. On the flip side, if you are really into partying hardcore and want to find thriving social scenes like that, Rice may not be able to offer that to you. It isn't really a school well-known for its party culture. Other than that, Rice is extremely diverse and most everyone will find what they like about the school.

Do you like your school? Why or why not?

If it isn't clear by now, I really love my school. My residential college has a very strong floor culture, so I bonded very well with my floormates and my roommate pretty soon after arriving. I love that I have my own community in my dorms and that I also can interact with students in other residential colleges who may have very different experiences. I also love that it is academically challenging but the students are collaborative and support each other. In many other top 25 universities, there is always pressure to compete with your peers but there is none of that here. You're free to explore whatever you want to do whenever you want to do it.

Your college's biggest strengths. What do students appreciate about their school/take for granted?

There are so many resources to help students in their classes, their career, and their social life. Any kind of support you need, Rice will have some kind of resource to help you out. They are very financially giving and there is always someone to reach out to if you want to just talk or get specific help. Also, we

THE KIDS WHO GET IN

are located in a major city where there is so much to explore off-campus. We get to go to museums, zoos, concerts all for free and take the Metro free of cost as well. Not many students take advantage of this as much as they can.

Your college's biggest weaknesses. What do students complain about the most? What would an admissions counselor never tell you?

Our school is small, which I enjoy in some aspects but don't in others. Because everyone knows each other or knows someone who knows each other, there is sometimes a lot of gossip that spreads and it can be toxic at times. Overall, people are very friendly and everything, but I feel like there are a lot of people so ready to attack each other for making a political mistake or something that doesn't fit with the super liberal mentality. Also, our dining is not very great at all. If good food is important to you, then Rice may not be your school. Our athletics department is also pretty weak and the majority of the school does not care about it, so sporting event attendance is usually very low.

ESSAYS:

Common App Essay:

I revel in an eccentric painting of a curled up, blue-haired woman; I overhear a girl rehearsing a classical monologue, perhaps Shakespeare; I soak in the haunting sound of a violinist playing a Tchaikovsky concerto in a nearby classroom. Walking down the green and orange hallways, I catch sight of students filming a group of dancers en pointe.[141] And when I reach my classroom, I prepare to sing with my Vocal Jazz Ensemble, ready to enjoy one more avenue of artistic exploration.

I attend the [name of arts school redacted], in which every inch of the campus is seen as a space to freely demonstrate creativity. For three years now, I have been able to create and express not only within my art form, but through every discipline, whether it be theater, dance, or even composition. There are never any limitations, no outer voice suppressing the most outlandish artistic thought that may emerge. At my school, I am able to connect with everyone because we all share a passion for the arts.

---

141   Good imagery that takes us into her world.

But not only is there artistic diversity, there is also diversity within race, sexuality, gender, and religion. Having come from a more conservative, parochial community, I immediately fell in love with and embraced the open, inclusive nature of my school community, amazed by the diverse makeup of the student body. Every day, I can immerse myself in a different culture and learn something new by listening to Black Student Union presentations and participating in the club Representation Matters, or even just talking with my group of friends, in which each person possesses some unique background to share.

However, this social diversity starkly contrasts the lack of economic diversity here. Considering that only eleven percent of students are socioeconomically disadvantaged, my school tends to fall short when it comes to providing for students who may not be able to attend fellow peers' performances due to high ticket prices, pay for many senior year staples like senior portraits and prom, or even afford to take AP exams. Although there is some aid for students in the free/reduced lunch program, the accommodations are minimal, simply because there are not enough students for it to be a prominent issue, and the inevitable shame of students who may be less affluent prevents them from speaking out. Having experienced this struggle first-hand, I always try to stress the importance of this disregarded issue to student council and administration, in light of the high financial costs that come with attending an arts high school.[142]

Even so, my school has provided me with a plethora of invaluable and utterly unique experiences and resources. Ultimately, I have gained not only a community but also a family and a sense of belonging that would not have been so easily attainable elsewhere. Each memory, each encounter, each connection will long outlast the four years I will have spent in this community—my community.[143]

---

142   Here we move from a tour of her school to Jessica's experience having less money than her peers. Jessica expands on this theme in her subsequent essay, and for now focuses on gratitude for her community and perspective.

143   It's a meandering essay, but the last 2 paragraphs center it and it ends up landing quite well. Jessica is honest and thoughtful. Through the good and the bad, Jessica provides a genuine evaluation of her world. Ending with gratitude is a great touch that showcases perspective and nuance.

THE KIDS WHO GET IN

We are interested in learning more about you and the context in which you have grown up, formed your aspirations, and accomplished your academic successes. Please describe the factors and challenges that have most shaped your personal life and aspirations. How have these factors helped you to grow?

"Mom, it's too expensive," I said, gazing at a mahogany ukulele set aside at a nearby yard sale.

"You love music, Yunna. You should have it."

"No. It's okay. It's not worth it, Mom," I assured her, walking away after running my fingers over the instrument one last time.

A couple of years ago, I would have said yes in a heartbeat. I wouldn't have noticed the doubt on my mom's face, or the way she pursed her lips when she saw the price. But as I got older, the fact that we were poor became increasingly apparent.

I attend a school at which most of my peers are upper-middle class, so they have the privilege of spending money flexibly. When I first started going over to my friends' houses after school, I couldn't help but compare my small apartment to their two-story houses with pools in the spacious backyards.[144] All throughout freshman year, I wanted to mask the "poor" part of me, ashamed and worried that my friends would pity or look down on me.

As a result, I tried to replace appearing affluent with doing well in school. I felt that not having as much money meant I had to work twice as hard for any potential opportunities. I maintained straight-A's, became the business director in both my Vocal Jazz Ensemble and Gospel Choir, and auditioned for a national competition called YoungArts, earning merit in the Popular Voice category. But while this succeeded in drawing attention away from my economic status, the fact that I was motivated solely by external pressures to fit in prevented me from taking any sort of personal gratification in these achievements.[145]

144   The concrete moments that she provides (buying a ukulele, visiting friends houses) helps the reader understand exactly how Jessica experiences financial stress.

145   This arch is eerily reminiscent of the Princeton essay. It's touching in the same ways, and helps form an arch around how Jessica reacts to her financial situation.

Then, in spring of sophomore year, I applied for Teen Line, a crisis telephone hotline that allows teenagers to reach out to other teens and share their own struggles. I underwent an interview process and an intensive thirteen-week training program over the summer. At the time, I naively considered this but a volunteer opportunity like any other. During this experience, however, Teen Line woke me up to a new outlook, one that sparked an unforeseen change.

After nine months of answering the phones and hearing some of the tragic stories of other teens—a girl who was taken away from her family because her father impregnated her, or a boy who was too afraid to leave a gang that murdered his brother—I realized that any teenager could be dealing with unbelievable hardships without anyone to talk to. I soon saw how much I had magnified my own insecurity, which now seemed minor in comparison to these struggles.[146]

Now, I always enter the hotline room with a clear mindset: one that allows me to forget my own worries and just listen to each caller's story. After every shift, I leave the room knowing that I helped a teen somewhere feel just a little bit better that night, and that knowledge always makes me feel better as well.

Through my work at Teen Line, I gained a newfound confidence.[147] I learned how to strengthen my connections with my friends and family by utilizing my active listening skills beyond the confines of the hotline room. Soon enough, it didn't seem to matter how other people saw me because I was much more grounded in myself, as well as in my relationships with others. Once I became more self-assured, I could maintain my grades, conduct songs in choir, audition for competitions—all without carrying the extra burden of appearing successful by other people's standards.[148] I still may not be able to buy every musical instrument I desire, or live in the nicest home, but now I am not ashamed of it; rather, it is only one part of my life, one that shouldn't and doesn't impact my self-esteem. Of course, I still arrive

---

146   Jessica's perspective here is inspiring. This is mirrored in the Yale application, and I touch on it more below.

147   Effective way to transition to reflection and growth.

148   I really like how Jessica uses her experience at Teen Life, and the perspective developed through those calls, to frame her increase in confidence and sense of self.

at barriers, both financial and otherwise, but I feel confident enough not to let those barriers affect how I think about myself. Now, instead of pursuing great opportunities because of some sense of obligation, I do it because I truly want to see for myself what I am capable of.

MY TAKE:

Jessica is a 4.0/1530 applicant with interesting involvements and an *incredible* voice. I really like her essay on her experience with the Teen Life hotline, and I'm going to highlight some reasons why the essay works especially well:

Firstly, Jessica showcases remarkable perspective for a teenager. Being able to put aside one's own problems and insecurities to be fully present with others isn't easy at any age, and it is impressive to Jessica do so with her peers.

We hear the story of someone with a real struggle (being the poor kid at a relatively wealthy high school) who, through serving other teens in crisis, recognizes that other people have it much worse. Jessica is able to put her own issues into perspective - she doesn't minimize her family's financial difficulties and the insecurity they cause, but chooses to not let that define her or prevent her from being there for the teens that she counsels, and her friends and family. On the contrary, she uses this experience as a base for confidence and strength in her identity.

It's so easy to focus on the things about ourselves that bother us, becoming self-absorbed and creating an internal wall between us and the rest of the world. Jessica role models the opposite - minimizing her own struggle in the face of being there for others - and it is inspiring. This trait is also modeled by Edward, the Yale student featured in this book.

Secondly, Jessica's level of introspection is impressive. A compelling motif, which Jessica weaves seamlessly, is understanding why she pursues the activities that she does. Jessica notes that her achievements initially lacked corresponding gain in self-worth because "the fact that I was motivated solely by external pressures to fit in prevented me from taking any sort of personal gratification in these achievements."

As Jessica gains perspective and confidence, she moves from doing things to gain approval or replace seeming wealthy, to pushing her perception of herself. "Now, instead of pursuing great opportunities because of some sense of obligation, I do it because I truly want to see for myself what I am capable of." In your essays, think about ways that you can frame your conclusions in similar ways - focusing on your growth and juxtaposing your initial motivations and beliefs to your current ones.

Jessica's application is another example of how being a great person and being a great college applicant overlap. Her attitude and self-awareness is impressive and mark that of someone on the path to being a fully-formed person (don't panic if you feel like this doesn't apply to you - it certainly didn't apply to me and I made it through admissions alive!)

Jessica's strong writing, unique background, and high-level academic achievement earned her a spot at Rice, a community that it sounds like she is incredibly grateful to be a part of.

Jessica in a sentence: Smart, caring, artistic woman - Teen Life caller and talented singer.

Stanford University

BERNIE ALCOTT

APPLICATION:

Major I applied under / School I applied to: Biology

Ethnicity: Native American, Latinx

Gender: Non-binary/Trans

Family Income Bracket: 20,000-40,000/year

Year of College Graduation: 2020

SAT I Score (By Section): 800 Math, 800 Writing, 780 Reading (2380 Total)

ACT Score (By Section): 36 Math, 36 Reading, 36 English, 36 Science (36 Composite)

SAT Subject Test Scores: 800 Math II, 800 Latin, 780 Biology E

High School Unweighted GPA (to nearest hundredth): 4.0

High School Weighted GPA: 4.5

Class Rank/Percentile: 1/500

AP Test Results: 5: Biology, English Literature, Calculus AB, Calculus BC, Government, US History

Senior Year Course Load: AP Lit, AP Latin, AP Gov, student government, two dual enrollment classes at community college

Awards Won in High School: Debate (won first in state, went to tournament of champions and got numerous individual speaker awards); dean's list/honor roll; lions club student of the year; elks lodge student of the year

Extracurriculars in High School (Put leadership in parentheses): (Debate President/Captain, Student Government, California Scholarship Federation President, National Honor Society VP) Matheletes member, Research Assistant at UC Davis Alzheimer's Disease Center, Volunteer for the Alzheimer's Association

Job/Work Experience in High School: Working at Family Restaurant

Volunteer/Community Service: Corporate Board Member for the Sacramento Public Library

What did you do in the summer after freshman year of high school?

Went to debate camp (5 weeks) at Gonzaga University

What did you do in the summer after sophomore year?

Went to debate camp at University of Michigan (7 weeks)

What did you do in the summer after junior year?

Went to debate camp at University of Michigan (7 weeks)

ABOUT YOUR HIGH SCHOOL:

State of High School: California

School Type (i.e. rural, suburban, city, public vs. private, etc): Public, Urban

# of Students in Graduating Class: 500

What was your high school like? Demographics? How many other students went to elite universities?

Low income, mostly POC who were and who didn't go to college

REFLECTION ON APPLICATION PROCESS:

I applied: Regular Decision

What do you think your hooks were?

I think I stood out because I had a catchy narrative surrounding my grandfather's death from Alzheimer's and my related work in the scientific field. I also was a star debater and I had a whole section of my common app essay dedicated to the importance of advocacy, rhetoric, and storytelling. I am also first generation and low income.

What do you think the strengths of your application were?

I am a skilled writer and I took some risks, especially on the Stanford 5 words prompt where mine were "I ask so many questions." I was authentic and myself and I wasn't afraid to mention where I thought I was strongest and where I had room to grow. My test scores were immaculate and definitely atypical for my high school. I was involved in a lot and I think a lot of people were surprised by my dedication despite somewhat humble upbringing.

What do you think the weaknesses of your application were? Where might other applicants have had an advantage over you?

I think I may have been read as over-zealous or a try hard, to be honest. I did a lot of the activities they tell you to do to get into college and the amount that I did may have made it seem disingenuous. Also, anyone that REALLY knew me would have immediately pegged me for a social science person, not a STEM applicant, as I was for most of my schools.

Where else you were admitted:

Harvard, Yale, Princeton, Dartmouth, Columbia, Brown, Cornell, Cal Poly SLO, UC Berkeley, UCLA, UCSD, University of Washington

Where you were waitlisted:

N/A

Where you were rejected:

N/A

Did you get a private college counselor?

No

When did you start preparing for college admissions? How did your family prepare?

I started preparing around August by drafting essays and getting a timeline together. I wrote essays consistently and applied EA to Harvard and got in. Being First Gen, my family did not help at all with the process as they had never done it themselves.

ABOUT YOUR COLLEGE:

Why did you choose this school?

Weather, Prestige, Financial Aid, Proximity to Home

What is your school known for? What is its reputation?

Stanford is known mostly as a computer science hub, as it is nestled right in the heart of silicon valley. It's known for being the land of tech start-ups, innovation, and integration with technology into the learning environment. It's (non-ironically) the Harvard of the West.

Is this reputation accurate?

Stanford is great for those interested in engineering, but that's not all it's good for. I've found Stanford to be a home for those interested in all of the humanities and sciences, though the student body definitely is geared more toward STEM and computer science more specifically. A lot of Stanford grads do end up working for tech companies and start ups in the area, though some move to nonprofits and social justice work in San Francisco and the Greater Bay Area.

What are you involved with on campus?

Stanford Debate Society (Executive Board), Research @ Center for the Advanced Study of the Behavioral Sciences, Research @ Stanford Humanities Center, Residential Computer Consultant, Anthropology Department Peer Advisor, Editor in Chief of the Undergraduate Research Journal

What do you think your school offers that no other top 20 school does?

Stanford is an incubator for liberal activism and social justice work, though this often happens behind the scenes. Where I felt that Harvard and some of the Ivies had a kind of pretentious air to them, Stanford doesn't, and it purports itself to be incredibly laid back and hands off. I think to an extent, this is new for a lot of the kids that go there, who have been trained to be future-Stanford students for their whole lives, it seems.

What kinds of people do you think would love your school?

People who are interested in the world and studying all of its curiosities, not just for a diploma. Stanford students are the type to go above and beyond, even when grades aren't in the picture. Stanford students take classes from all different schools and fields of study, and it's encouraged that one do so. The introductory seminar system sets one up for dipping their toes into any variety of subjects — without the fear that you'll flunk the term or get a failing grade. The only thing you need is willpower and a drive to try new things. This motivation is necessary to access other on campus resources as well, like the BEAM CareerCenter, which aren't advertised as well as they should be.

What kinds of people do you think would hate your school?

People who are hardcore humanities and detest those who work in the hard sciences would probably dislike Stanford for its STEM emphasis. People who are conservative (or right leaning) might dislike how outright leftist (lol) a lot of the campus is, and some of the actions that administrators take that have been criticized as "too political." The campus is huge, which can also be a challenge for some. Though the greatest barrier to me is location — it's in a rich, bourgeois little enclave with no nightlife and a NIMBY attitude, making it difficult to get off campus and uncomfortable to be in the surrounding neighborhoods.

Do you like your school? Why or why not?

I love Stanford, for what it's worth. It has given me some of the best opportunities in the world, allowed me to meet new people, and gifted me an education like no other. The areas for improvement aren't really unique to Stanford — better mental health services, for instance, are a problem before many campuses today. The struggles I've had at Stanford have led me to be the person I am today. and without a doubt, the mentorship I've received has gotten me through the most difficult times. If I could do it all over again, I'd make the same choice.

Your college's biggest strengths. What do students appreciate about their school/take for granted?

Weather — Stanford is BEAUTIFUL basically year round and gets no snow. The grounds are BEAUTIFUL and MASSIVE and have a lot to explore, see, and do. The housing system is interesting, though they're changing this substantially in the coming years, despite my recommendations on the Residential Education (ResX) board. The school has a lot of money which makes it possible for you to do summer research on topics of interest, even abroad, with it being fully funded by the university. We also have an immensely rich campus culture — see the Stanford University Marching Band — that is really unparalleled across the coasts. Study abroad is a great opportunity for those cosmopolitan students as well!

Your college's biggest weaknesses. What do students complain about the most? What would an admissions counselor never tell you?

Stanford is rigorous, difficult, and (at its worst) unsupportive. It can feel at times like the campus is too big and you're too small, like everyone is paddling furiously to keep their head above water but no one admits it. Being around geniuses all the time can get incredibly tiresome and the expectations imposed upon you for being one can be even more tiring. The Stanford "bubble" is real and it's difficult when you have to leave it. An admissions counselor would never tell you about CAPS (Counseling and Psychological Services) failures and the high rate of student suicide.

ESSAYS:

Common App Essay:

The memories I have of my grandfather aren't the traditional sitting-on-the-knee, storytelling, carousel-riding type of memories.[149] What I do remember are the opaque amber bottles lining the kitchen sink and their familiar pop when opened, the pages of doctors' notes scrawled on clipboards strewn about the dining room table, and the faint, wafting odor of antiseptic wipes. That soft, metallic smell lingered long after we departed his bedside and still reminds me of his absence.

Though I had only met him a handful of times before my tenth birthday, the call from my step-grandmother informing my family of his diagnosis immediately made him the centerpiece of my life. "Stage Four," my dad relayed, his ear pressed tightly against the phone, "It's in his lungs now, and doesn't appear to have spread."

And so my father and I became couriers, bringing both good and bad news, medicines that would make him feel both better and worse, and the occasional butterscotch candy that never failed to light up his face. During those countless hours we spent together, I learned more of him, but he forgot more of me. Each time that I was forced to reintroduce myself as his grandson got harder and harder. My identity shifted from a loved one, to a boy who came to take care of him, to a complete stranger.

As I looked into his quarantined room and couldn't help grimacing as he struggled to form words on his lips, his eyes scanning the room hopelessly and emptily. I began to feel a Lethean[150] rift between us opening wider and wider, even though it seemed that we were just recently united.

---

149   Again, we like the contrast between the typical and the real, lived experience.

150   Greek Mythology, Lethe is "a river in Hades whose water caused forgetfulness of the past in those who drank of it. It's a flex, but fits in with the intellectual identity that Bernie clearly embodies.

Questioning the nature of my grandfather's forgetting, I entered a state of vertigo that was rooted in my feeling of utter helplessness and confusion and became consumed by a ravenous desire to understand what was happening. Why didn't he remember my name, my age, or when we had arrived that night? What role did his cancer play? And most important, what could I do?

Years after his passing, I found myself returning to the same questions, but this time with the determination to find answers. Studying maps of the brain and fastidiously examining its intricacies in the coffee-stained, dog-eared tomes of the public library led me to email the administrator of the University of California Alzheimer's Disease Center. I asked him the questions I had tinkered with for hours upon end, in hopes that he would resolve my qualms over the replication process of neurotransmitters and the viability of an acetylcholine substitute. In reading his response, I found that I could pursue a role in my quest to satisfy my insatiable thirst for answers.[151]

He offered me a position in his lab to research the disease. While I always found solace behind a microscope, I could never have imagined the sense of comfort I would find examining the translucent copies of human brain sections or listening to the discordant hum of an unbalanced centrifuge. Preparing agarose gels alongside accredited scientists allows me to feel as though I[152], too, am working to solve the great physiological puzzles that had caused my family and so many others such immense trauma, contributing my knowledge to the collective game of jigsaw that so many scientists around the world are also playing in their dedicated search to find answers about the mysterious malady.

And so, as I don the same starched white coat as my comrades, I remember the pain of being torn away from someone I loved. Micropipette in hand, though, I remind myself that I am contributing to a greater good, and that this time the faint, lemony smell that once belonged to the antiseptic wipes is the industrial-strength soap in the scrub room encouraging me to procure the puzzle piece that so long evaded my hopeful grasp.

---

151   This is a killer transitional paragraph. Bernie's interest moves from hypothetical to an engaged reality, thanks to their initiative. Readers - this is how you go out and get involved with what you're interested in.

152   This line works well because Bernie has the self-awareness to acknowledge their limited role in the process.

Important to Intellectual Development:

The phrase "curiosity killed the cat" has always frustrated me. Beyond that fact, when the second line of the quote, "but satisfaction brought it back," is almost always omitted, it entirely changes the meaning of the proverb. It's utterly disenchanting to think that something so intrinsic to human nature necessitates a warning.[153] Curiosity, and the innate desire to discover the unknown, remains an unyielding aspect of my educational pursuits. Intellectual vitality is neither the mindless regurgitation of facts after an hour-long lecture, nor is it relegated to the confines of a single classroom. Instead, it exists in my frequent trips to the library, scientific research, and community college classes.[154] Among these extraordinary experiences has been my ability to take an Environmental Philosophy class at my local community college – an opportunity not afforded to typical high school students.[155] It was here that the classroom transformed from an obligation to an absolute necessity, as polar opposites were brought together before my own eyes – Kantian ethics versus Emissions Caps or perhaps second-wave feminism against hydraulic fracturing. It was through my questioning of these new and peculiar areas of study that I learned that so much of the world is undiscovered, and answers to so many of life's dearest quandaries lack solutions or clearly-defined answers. Intellectual vitality isn't always about finding the answers, but about having the courage to take risks and pose provocative questions in the first place.[156]

Note to Future Roommate:

Hey Roomie!

My name is Bernard, but the only person that calls me that is my dad when he's angry, so feel free to just call me Bernie[157].

---

153 Bernie takes a strong stance here, and it's endearing in a very eccentric, Stanford way.
154 In a brief line we see intellectual vitality in action in different parts of Bernie's life. Bernie exudes a true love of learning - and neatly packages it in a familiar idiom, in this piece.
155 Gratitude and self-awareness.
156 Nice way to wrap up the piece with the larger lesson learned.
157 This detail is specific, personal, endearing, and memorable. And fittingly, that's

I also really hope you're an entomology major. It's certainly fine if you're not, but I hope you like dealing with bugs, because I physically cannot.[158] If you ever see me wave my arms and begin shrieking, I'm actually not trying to embody my seagull, I probably just saw a spider. If you're afraid of spiders too, we might have to alert the dorm staff to expect some yelling and to construct a militia of strong-willed souls for arthropod extermination.

Something that might provide some relief is that whether it be late night cravings or "Pre-8a.m.-lecture breakfast," you can pretty much count on me to have food to share. Around mid-way through last year, I found these little disks of heaven called Almond Thins. I don't know if you've ever tried them before, but they're probably the only thing I've ever found that's more versatile than the potato. After rigorous experimentation, I've concocted a few "dorm-ready" recipes that I make, depending on my mood. Recalling carefree times while writing that 15-page term paper? Try some with Almond Thins with peanut butter and jelly. Feeling ritzy while reclining on your lumpy loft bed? I'd be more than happy to whip up an Almond Thin topped with gouda and an apple slice. I can't wait for you to try them!

Bernie[159]

What matters to you, and why?

The first time I asked my grandma her biggest regret, she responded that she always wished she had had a better relationship with her parents when she had the chance. With that thought in mind, I have become increasingly grateful as I recount periods of my adolescence when I never had the spurt of "typical teen" rebellion that I had witnessed first-hand in my peers.[160]

Maybe it was because I grew up in my father's hamburger stand, watching my parents jockeying about the cramped workspace, their movements like a

---

how the reader will think of Bernie as an applicant.
158   A little flair for the dramatic, but it fits their personality and works.
159   This essay does it's job. It fills out the rest of Bernie's application, adding a bit of personality and warmth. Some of the specifics (Almond Thins, fear of spiders) are friendly touches - they feel a bit obligatory, but it's an admittedly awkward prompt and Bernie's take does just fine.
160   I like this self-awareness, and this comparison between their trajectory and the typical tumultuous teen years.

dance they had long been rehearsing. As I grew up, increased responsibility was expected, and I graduated from sweeping floors to making milkshakes and waiting on customers. The ability to rely on my mom and dad inside and outside of traditional family ties transformed our familial relationship into a team working toward a common goal. When one cog in the machine failed, the rest of the machine strained to compensate.

Or perhaps it was the knack for storytelling that travelled along my father's bloodline. Swapping old memories and stories at family get-togethers became commonplace. The constant dialogue between family members recollecting past events made me become acutely aware of the rich history that our family had shared – forced off of reservations, westward bound due to The Dust Bowl, and in constant search of a good laugh.[161]

MY TAKE:

Bernie is one of the most unique and most qualified applicants that I've read, and it's not surprising that they were admitted to every school that they applied to. Having a 4.0 GPA, a 1/500 class rank, and a perfect ACT and near-perfect SAT are as competitive an academic background as an applicant could have. Bernie's unique cultural background (first generation college student, Native American/Latinx, non-binary gender expression) was also appealing to the universities that they applied to - there is definitely only one Bernie Alcott in this world.

Still, Bernie is memorable because they leave the reader with a sense that we know the real Bernie. I want to utilize their application to showcase some powerful rhetorical devices you can use in your writing:

Firstly, Bernie utilizes comparison well. They begin their Common App essay with "The memories I have of my grandfather aren't the traditional sitting-on-the-knee, storytelling, carousel-riding type of memories." Setting up a lived experience as atypical is a great way to hook the reader - of course, after reading that, we want to know what memories Bernie does have of their grandfather.

---

161 This essay is great, and I expand upon it more below.

This is a great way to emphasize uniqueness when telling one's story; juxtaposing the norm with one's actual lived experience inherently draws interest. Again, Bernie writes "I never had the spurt of "typical teen" rebellion that I had witnessed first-hand in my peers" - emphasizing their own uniqueness and self-awareness. When detailing his interaction with his cancer-ridden Grandfather, Bernie writes "I learned more of him, but he forgot more of me." Here we see Bernie's coming of age coincide with his Grandfather's death, and the irony of the situation is made apparent.

In writing about tradition, Bernie notes that their father's family was "forced off of reservations, westward bound due to The Dust Bowl, and in constant search of a good laugh," and we see adversity alongside humanity. A powerful image is created of a wounded bloodline able to find joy in their struggle. Oftentimes less is more in writing, and this brief tease into Bernie's Native American heritage is as valuable as the entire essay might have been.[162] These juxtapositions are valuable because they help transform a life into a story, and they show that Bernie is aware of the contradictions and ironies of their life; having that level of self-awareness and being able to express it fluidly in writing showcases intelligence!

In addition to juxtaposition, Bernie's writing is chock-full of powerful metaphors and similes that add depth to their writing. Bernie describes his parents' movements crammed behind the counter of their hamburger stand as "a dance they had long been rehearsing" - condensing the sweat of years of restaurant co-ownership and marriage into a singular image, a dance. And we see everything. In depicting them and their father as hospital "couriers," we *see* them visiting a bed-ridden grandfather with news and sweets.

Lastly, Bernie utilizes alliteration to blend sounds and create rhythm throughout their writing. Bernie mentions the "mysterious maladies" and "physiological puzzles" of cancer research and the "typical teen" conflicts and growing pains - nice touches that remind me of the miniscule movements that Kobe would make to accent a patented turnaround fadeaway.

---

162   If you have multiple aspects of your identity that you'd like to highlight, or have an important aspect that isn't the subject of a main essay, consider weaving in a 3 sentence anecdote like this one. Bernie does it again, to a smaller degree, in his letter to a roommate when he casually mentions his seagull. You have a seagull??

When you get really good at something, you start to notice the smallest areas of additional expression and fine tuning - and Bernie is a really good writer.

Don't feel like you have to take as much stylistic liberty with your writing as Bernie did! It's important for your writing to match your voice, and take these notes as potential ways for you to explore/deepen the ways that you express yourself. For Bernie's application, it reinforces an identity rooted in intellectual vitality and showcases an applicant who has fun writing, and comes across as authentic - no need to force complex motifs and similes into your writing if that's not how you comfortably express yourself.

As someone from various underrepresented backgrounds with a flawless academic record and a true love for learning, Bernie was a no-brainer admit to Stanford.

Bernie in a sentence: Incredibly intelligent, curious, interesting high achiever with a unique background.

University of California Los Angeles

DANAI MATEI

APPLICATION:

Major I applied under / School I applied to: Pre-Mathematics/College of Letters & Science

Ethnicity: White

Gender: Female

Family Income Bracket: 250,000-500,000/year

Year of College Graduation: 2020

SAT I Score (By Section) N/A

ACT Score (By Section): 34 Math, 32 Reading, 34 Science, 33 English (33 Composite)

SAT Subject Test Scores: 720 Math II, 800 French

High School Unweighted GPA (to nearest hundredth):

This doesn't really apply to me. My school didn't have weighted vs. unweighted. The grades were based on a scale from 1-6, with 4 being the average. Additionally, this does not account for final exam grades.

THE KIDS WHO GET IN

High School Weighted GPA: My overall GPA was 5.2/6

Class Rank/Percentile: 3rd in the class

AP Test Results: N/A

Senior Year Course Load: Mathematics, English, French, German, Philosophy, Biology, Chemistry + a Thesis

Awards Won in High School: My school only had awards if you had a GPA above 5/6 which I did every year of high school.

Extracurriculars in High School (Put leadership in parentheses):

Piano and Music lessons and babysitting. I had school every day from 8-5pm which didn't give me a lot of time for extra curricular + in Switzerland extra curricular aren't offered at your school so you have to do them in other places, which made it more difficult especially since my parents worked a lot and were not always able to drive me.

Job/Work Experience in High School: N/A

Volunteer/Community Service: Red Cross Volunteer, Terre des Hommes (an NGO) volunteer at various events

What did you do in the summer after freshman year of high school?

Travelled or stayed home

What did you do in the summer after sophomore year?

Travelled or stayed home

What did you do in the summer after junior year?

Studied, our exams took place in September so the Summers after Junior and Senior Year I was always studying.

ABOUT YOUR HIGH SCHOOL:

State of High School: Vaud, Switzerland

School Type (i.e. rural, suburban, city, public vs. private, etc): Private School

# of Students in Graduating Class: 37

What was your high school like? Demographics? How many other students went to elite universities?

My school was mainly wealthier children, or children who couldn't keep up in the public system so they had to come to private school. Mainly, Swiss kids who were of middle-upper classes and who didn't want to/couldn't go to public school. My school had a reputation for being hard but you were given a lot of help. My teachers were very pushy but in a good way because you were pushed to always do your best. Most kids stayed in Switzerland after graduation and went to university there. One person went to Babson College, one to Colby College, then two went to the UK, and I went to UCLA. Everyone else stayed.

REFLECTION ON APPLICATION PROCESS:

I applied: Regular Decision

What do you think your hooks were?

I think one thing that made me stand out was that I had an "angle". What I mean by that is, I centered everything around Math, and how I was really passionate about it and how it's all I wanted to do. I used it as a way to explain my lack of extracurriculars. I got a perfect score on my Math exam, applied as Pre-Math and wrote my essay about Math. I think if you find something unique about yourself, something you're really passionate about, and center your application around that, it can make you stand out.

What do you think the strengths of your application were?

I think my essays and my ACT score stood out.

What do you think the weaknesses of your application were? Where might other applicants have had an advantage over you?

I didn't have many extracurriculars or any job experience to speak of, so that was definitely a weak point in my application.

Where else you were admitted:

UCSB, UCSC, Syracuse, UVA and Colgate

Where you were waitlisted:

NYU

Where you were rejected:

Columbia University, Bowdoin and UC Berkeley

Did you get a private college counselor?

No

When did you start preparing for college admissions? How did your family prepare?

I started my sophomore year when my school organized a trip to Southern California to tour a few schools (including UCLA). Then I didn't think about it again until the Fall of my Junior year where I started to take the SAT and do my applications. I was so overwhelmed with the amount of school work I had, however, that I abandoned it. I wanted it to be something I dedicated my full time to, not something I half-assed. Therefore, I decided to take a gap year and devoted the first 4 months (September-January) to working on my college applications. My dad was very reluctant to have me go to school in the US, so he wasn't really preparing. My mom was always very supportive and helped me with tours, my applications, and SAT/ACT study prep.

ABOUT YOUR COLLEGE:

Why did you choose this school?

As I mentioned above, I didn't really intend on going to UCLA at all. But then once I was accepted, it was very hard to say no to. I was really deciding between UVA and UCLA but a little voice in my head kept telling me that I couldn't pass up an opportunity like UCLA. Then I went to Bruin Day (the day for accepted freshmen) and I was sold.

What is your school known for? What is its reputation?

Good in Sciences, particularly Climate Sciences, and Film. I think it's known as a school that is quite difficult, intense, competitive. It is also well known for its athletics, particularly its basketball legacy.

Is this reputation accurate?

The classes are quite difficult, and mostly graded on a curve so you're always competing against everyone else. It's also a Quarter system school, so it's very fast paced, you don't get much breathing room. Therefore, I would say it is quite an intense school. But people also know how to have a good time. In terms of athletics, I would say we're pretty good, I know not as good as in the past. I have stopped following it closely though as I have gotten busy with other things.

What are you involved with on campus?

I'm involved in Eurobruins, the European culture club on campus, and Clean Consulting, a green consulting club that helps campus in reaching its goals to become more sustainable.

What do you think your school offers that no other top 20 school does?

365 days of SUNSHINE! On a more serious note though, I would say there is actually a very good faculty to student ratio, which I think a lot of big universities don't have. I also think because it's such a diverse and multi-faceted school, within such a big city, there are a lot of opportunities. There are always things to do, and offers to take and if you're looking for something, the chances are that you will find it. If you don't find it, then it's really easy to make it yourself!

What kinds of people do you think would love your school?

I think people that really appreciate school pride and spirit, that love to learn while also appreciating the need to have fun and relax every so often, and that like living in a small community within a burgeoning metropolis would love UCLA. I think it has a really good balance between good academics but also focusing on things other than school, and also feeling like you belong to a small community even within a city as big as Los Angeles.

That being said, I do think there is a niche at UCLA for everyone. There are so many different types of people that you are sure to find a place where you fit in.

What kinds of people do you think would hate your school?

Westwood, and LA in general, can be quite loud, so if you prefer the quiet, UCLA is not the place for you. Additionally, if you prefer being given personalized attention rather than carving out your own path within the system, then UCLA would not be a good fit because it is a lot about finding your way on your own.

Do you like your school? Why or why not?

I have a love/hate relationship with UCLA (mostly love though). The campus is beautiful, I've met so many different people from all over the world - and some are now my closest friends - and there are always endless opportunities. On the other hand, because it's so big, it's difficult to get a lot of one-on-one attention, and enrolling for classes is always a nightmare. It's also easy to get that "little fish in a big pond" feeling, but as long as you remind yourself that you're there to focus on your future, and that everyone else is just doing the same, that feeling isn't too overwhelming.

Your college's biggest strengths. What do students appreciate about their school/take for granted?

I think that people (myself included) definitely don't take advantage of everything UCLA offers. I love that even as a senior, I am still finding out little hidden tricks and things that aren't necessarily talked about. This may sound very vague, but I mean along the lines of different places to print for free, places to get free feminine hygiene products and other health necessities or simply just discovering new places to study. We don't have the biggest campus but it still constantly surprises me to this day. Another thing I think people really appreciate at UCLA is the fact that you have so much freedom.

If something doesn't exist, you can create it (be it a club, a resource or a research project). If you want to double major in Physics and Theater, you can. You can even create your own major. The rules are very pliable and it is easy to make your own mold within UCLA.

Your college's biggest weaknesses. What do students complain about the most? What would an admissions counselor never tell you?

Students mostly complain about how (spatially) small the school is for the number of people. There are definitely enough professors, but the dorms, dining halls and campus in general are very crowded. During finals, it's difficult to find space in the libraries (not impossible though) and classes fill up really quickly. I would say another big thing that students complain about is the Quarter system, and how that makes everything so much more fast paced. Classes are only 10 weeks long, and so the material is very much condensed. You don't get much room to breathe. I don't think an admissions counselor would tell you either of these things.

ESSAYS:

Common App Essay:

I wish my parents had put me in dance lessons. When I was a child, my father always thought it was important that I learn how to defend myself, so my sister and I attended Martial Arts classes. While it seemed that every other little girl I knew attended weekly dance classes in sparkly tutus, I wore my kimono.[163] I often felt different from those who went to my school. I was a Third Culture Kid (my father is from Bulgaria, my mother is American and I have spent my whole life in Switzerland), I didn't take ballet, and my accent was hard to place. As a little girl, these things mattered to me.[164]

I was nine years old when my parents got divorced.[165] After that, things like after-school activities and where I was from no longer seemed all that im-

---

163   Specifics and contrast!
164   I love this very matter of fact last sentence. Sometimes the best thing to do when writing our essays is to cut the crap and say what we want to say. Well done, Danai.
165   Abrupt (but ultimately relevant) introduction of new details makes for a nice narrative choice.

THE KIDS WHO GET IN

portant. Once again, I felt different, but not in the same way. Even when I stopped attending my martial arts classes, it wasn't with the sense of relief I had [166]expected because my parents' divorce had become so time consuming.

At the time I don't think I realized how much I was impacted by my parents' decision, but now I realize that it changed the way I perceived and felt about "fitting in". What became important to me was to be someone who could make my own decisions. This change in my feelings toward accountability and decision-making are what really defined my transition from childhood to adulthood.

I was no longer able to trust my parents' judgment, which meant I would have to make my choices without their help. I found writing in a journal and cleaning my room to be comforting: writing in my journal to help me express myself, and organizing to help me have some control over my life.[167]

A year after the divorce, I changed schools to one where no one paid much attention to extracurricular activities and no one based their opinions of others on where they were from. I was at a school that focused solely on academics, and where hard work and classroom success was valued above all else. By applying myself to my schoolwork I was able to fit in better, which in turn motivated me to concentrate even more on my studies. I didn't think about my parents divorce as much and I learned to rely on myself.

My father had always imposed upon me what he felt was the right thing for me to do. He is affectionate, in his own way, but when he told me that he was not letting me enroll in a school with the International Baccalaureate program, it was over the phone. I wished to change schools because I believed doing the IB would give me a better chance at getting into an American University; he insisted I remain in the Swiss system. It made me feel as though my own voice had no value and even though I could tell he knew how upset it made me, he still thought his opinion of my education mattered more than my own.

---

166   This is a great way to acknowledge an ostensible weakness of her application without necessarily pointing fingers or drawing too much attention to it. She's providing ammo to AOs who want to make a case for her in spite of lackluster extracurriculars.

167   Seeing a 9 year old Danai start to journal and clean for some semblance of control is heartbreaking. We see a kid pickup the pieces in the midst of a divorce and begin to lean on herself, and it makes us admire and root for her.

Later, when he told me that he wished for me to stay in Switzerland for university, he again expressed his own desires: he wished me to stay closer to home.

I feel as if I need experience and independence in order to grow and become someone who is responsible for their own actions. I have finally realised that not everything is up to my father. This time I did not let him decide, and keep me from applying to the U.S. for college. I feel that going to an American university will give me a new-found autonomy. I hope to study history and go on to a graduate program in the United States and I imagine myself achieving all that and more. And who knows? I might even sign up for a dance class.[168]

Describe the world you come from — for example, your family, community or school — and tell us how your world has shaped your dreams and aspirations.

My mami is a very sensible person with that so-called eastern European practicality. She always knows how to get the best bargain, she urges the importance of education and she condemns wasteful behavior. She was forced to journey from Sofia to Tunisia because of the political circumstances in Bulgaria in 1969. She has influenced me with her toughness and has taught me the importance of one's family. I remember the times when she would take my sister and I to the park. She would hold tightly to our hands and always feared us wandering off, even under safe circumstances.[169]

My other grandmother's history is quite different.[170] Being the wife of an American diplomat, she circled the globe: her journey was one of pleasure. Consequently, she has a plethora of experiences, living in places ranging from London to Karachi. I admire her open-minded attitude as well as the way that she appreciates and cares for the world she lives in, from raising money for Palestine with olive oil sales to helping college students at her church with their papers.[171]

---

168   Perfect conclusion. Ties back into the beginning, wraps everything up well, and hits with just a little humor to leave the AO smiling.
169   6 sentences and I feel like I know her mami. Concise, powerful, to the point language.
170   Again, contrast - the best way to draw interest.
171   Great specifics here that help us get to know both grandmothers.

Their pasts differ greatly, which has only enriched my background and consequently me as a person. The fact that they both led professional lives, one a doctor, one an editor, has shown me that the value of hard work is immeasurable. Thanks to them, I am very ambitious with regards to achieving my goals.[172]

Both my grandmothers have influenced my interest in human rights. Living in Geneva, has furthered this interest. I have grown up surrounded by people who really define the idea of the "global citizen" and have been fortunate enough to have friends of several different nationalities. Because of this, I am naturally open-minded, understanding from an early age that there is always more than one way of looking at things.

My background has also led me to recognize the beauty of learning[173]; I am grateful for the education I have received until now. I read Albert Camus' La Peste (The Plague) in class this year. It brought to my attention a new philosophy of life, one where we must not cower in the face of injustice, rather confront it. There are economic, social and racially motivated injustices across the globe. Camus' work has made me realize that my generation is too passive and does not oppose it enough. I think that we feel scared because the world can be an ugly place. I hope that I will be brave enough to challenge this passivity.[174]

As I embark on my path to higher education, I aspire to my grandmothers' fierce senses of community and their abilities to, through perseverance and hard work, find ways to ameliorate the lives of others, and hope to one day do the same.

---

172   Notice how Danai doesn't fully answer the prompt - that's ok! You can take these questions wherever you want. She chose to use her two grandmothers to talk about her world, and goes deep. Better to delve into this theme then sprinkle a bunch of tidbits about different aspects of her life.

173   Danai connects to her personal statement and her next supplement here, focusing on her love of learning. She forms a great arch with this theme across her essays.

174   These three preceding lines are great. She makes a larger observation about our generation and the world (showing AOs how she thinks), and humbly asserts her aim to overcome this fear. I think Danai could even be a little stronger here, but better to lean humble than braggadocious.

Tell us about a personal quality, talent, accomplishment, contribution or experience that is important to you. What about this quality or accomplishment makes you proud, and how does it relate to the person you are?

I am sitting in the cafeteria, watching the raindrops slip down the window and trying to cancel out the surrounding commotion. My pencil and math textbook lay forgotten on the table in front of me. It is the fifteenth day of my Swiss Federal Maturity exams, and I am preparing for my second oral of the day. Knowing that I will have completed my secondary school education around 5pm and will receive my results brings me relief.

I am used to orals where I stand in front of the teacher and write things on the blackboard. In this case, however, the examiner is seated beside me and I do my work on a sheet of paper for him to see. My examiner is a portly, middle-aged man in a cerulean polo, with kind eyes and graying hair. He asks me to pick a number between one and four and I hesitate before letting my mouth decide for me: three. Spatial geometry. I am relieved.[175]

I am asked to define the triple product and the cross product, both of which I am able to tell him satisfactorily. He then asks me to demonstrate several formulas, where I get slightly stuck. At this moment I ask myself "What happens if I can't do it?" I try and focus and remind myself to think clearly, I have all of the answers, I just need to find them. No problem ever only uses one element of your knowledge. It's always a web of several separate pieces in your repertoire of equations and mathematical truths. So, I have to extract elements from all corners of my brain and put them together to solve the problem. The question being asked is to demonstrate an equation: why is the area of a parallelogram the cross product between any two vectors?

I am finally able to make the link. This formula is one expression of the cross product and the area of a parallelogram is the height times the base where the base is replaceable by the length of the v vector. The height is replaceable by...

These thoughts may seem scattered and warbled right now, but in an oral where thinking on your feet is essential, each thought is usually overrun by

---

[175] Part of the fun of the essay is that we get to see what exams are like in Danai's world. I've never taken a final like this but it honestly sounds pretty epic.

another before it has the time to be completed.

Solving these kinds of problems is very nerve-wracking, but it is also exhilarating. Even though I have learned so much the past three years, there is still so much I don't know, a prospect that is even more compelling.[176]

At the end of the exam, he asks, "What are you thinking of doing in the future?"

I tell him that I envisage studying in the United States, and honestly add that I wish to focus on mathematics, because it is something that I am passionate about.

"It shows," he says, and I smile.

I receive my results an hour later, and, to my overwhelming shock, I have received the highest grade. I am not expecting this because, even though it is among my favorite subjects, it has also been the most challenging course I have had to take.

I am proud of this accomplishment especially because it is a testament to my hard work. It is not something that I achieved without effort, which makes it all the more rewarding.

My school is one where we focus solely on grades. That is to say that it does not offer any extra curricular activities or clubs. There are no sports teams either. We had classes from 8am to 5pm every day except Wednesday.

MY TAKE:

Danai is a smart, interesting student with a great voice. You can read her entry for a little bit more on her academic background/grading system; I want to dig a bit deeper on how she told her story, and why it was so effective.

What stood out about Danai's writing was her ability to convey strong emotions in a straight-forward, concise manner. Her writing doesn't take the art-

---

[176] Danai has a genuine love of learning and it's exciting seeing her write about the joy she gets from solving problems and mastering new concepts.

istry of some of the other essays featured (Stanford, Columbia), but Danai writes with powerful directness. Danai shares with us her thoughts about her life and her journey towards independence - and it feels like we are entering her world.

She charts her growth toward autonomy:

"As a little girl, these things mattered to me" (fitting in and doing the same activities as her peers). →

"What became important to me was to be someone who could make my own decisions...I was no longer able to trust my parents' judgment, which meant I would have to make my choices without their help" (responding to the divorce with a desire to become self-reliant). →

"By applying myself to my schoolwork I was able to fit in better, which in turn motivated me to concentrate even more on my studies. I didn't think about my parents divorce as much and I learned to rely on myself" (using academics as a basis for confidence, leaning more on her own achievements) →

"It made me feel as though my own voice had no value and even though I could tell he knew how upset it made me, he still thought his opinion of my education mattered more than my own" (battling for educational autonomy with her father) →

"I have finally realised that not everything is up to my father. I feel that going to an American university will give me a new-found autonomy" (speaking up for her own needs, understanding her place in deciding her future, making a decision that will lead to increased autonomy).

It's inspiring to see Danai's growth and her increased self-dependence - and her matter-of-fact style of writing helps her tell this story. While some of the essays featured in this book hone in on specific moments, Danai charts her growth over time - which is a strategy that fits her voice and helps us understand her journey.

In addition to becoming more self-reliant, Danai's essays showcase a love for learning. Using academics as the foundation for her personal statement pairs well with her supplements, where Danai takes pride in her mathematics performance, and notes the "beauty of learning." In her last essay, Danai writes "Solving these kinds of problems is very nerve-wracking, but it is also exhilarating. Even though I have learned so much the past three years, there is still so much I don't know, a prospect that is even more compelling."

We see a hard-working kid who likes challenging herself and pushing herself to learn more - awesome characteristics to show a college you're trying to get into. Additionally, weaving this motif through her three essays shows the reader that learning is a core part of Danai's identity.

One important thing to note is that as an international student, it's unlikely that Danai was given any need-based aid at the American schools she got into (especially not large public schools like UVA or UCLA). The other international student featured, Archie, at Yale, came from a lower-income family, and was able to gain admission to Yale, a school that does provide need-based aid for international students. For all students (and international students especially) it's important to consider the financial implications of your college choice - before the admissions process in making your college list, and after receiving decisions in making a choice.

At 18, Danai has a strong sense of self and understanding of what she values. She now attends UCLA, where she is pursuing her dream of studying at an American University.

Danai in one sentence: Independent learner and thinker with a dream of studying in the US.

University of Chicago

BRIAN TORRES

APPLICATION:

Major I applied under / School I applied to: Political Science (all schools)

Ethnicity: White/Hispanic

Gender: Male

Family Income Bracket: 250,000-500,000/year

Year of College Graduation: 2022

High School Unweighted GPA (to nearest hundredth): 3.72

High School Weighted GPA: 4.17

Class Rank/Percentile: N/A

SAT I Score (By Section): N/A

ACT Score (By Section): 33 Math, 33 Science, 35 Reading, 35 English (34 Composite)

SAT Subject Test Scores: N/A

AP Test Results: 5: English Language, US History, Macroeconomics, 4: English Literature, Microeconomics, Calculus AB, 3: Computer Science A, Physics I

Senior Year Course Load: AP Micro/Macroeconomics, AP Physics I, AP English Lit, AP Calculus AB, Biblical studies.

Awards Won in High School: Freshman/Sophomore Year: Magna Cum Laude, Junior/Senior: Summa Cum Laude, Junior year All State Academic Honors for soccer

Extracurriculars in High School (Put leadership in parentheses):

JV Soccer (Freshman/Sophomore)

Varsity Soccer (Junior)

National Honors Society

Student Council Delegate (Junior)

Job/Work Experience in High School: Full-time babysitting (Junior/Senior summers)

Volunteer/Community Service: National Sports Center for the Disabled (Oct. 2017 - Apr. 2018): Taught sit-skiing to participants with disabilities; Soccer Camp Coach (2015 - 2017): volunteer coaching for a one-week camp throughout high-school

What did you do in the summer after freshman year of high school?

Soccer training

What did you do in the summer after sophomore year?

Soccer training

What did you do in the summer after junior year?

Soccer training, full-time babysitting

ABOUT YOUR HIGH SCHOOL:

State of High School: Colorado

School Type (i.e. rural, suburban, city, public vs. private, etc): Suburban Private Christian High School

# of Students in Graduating Class: ~250

What was your high school like? Demographics? How many other students went to elite universities?

My high school was a mid-size private Christian school, mostly white and located in a relatively affluent suburb of Denver. Due to the fact that it was private, it attracted students from all around the Denver area. There was quite little diversity, I'd estimate that about 20% of students were non-white. Around 15 other students went to other elite schools, with only one student attending an Ivy League institution.

REFLECTION ON APPLICATION PROCESS:

I applied: Early Decision

What do you think your hooks were?

I focused on the way that my hobbies shaped my lifestyle and outlook, and believe that elaborating on this made me appear to fit a unique role in any campus community. I spoke extensively to my love of skiing and the sense of progression it grants me in an effort to show determination and resolve in a non-academic setting. In my supplements, especially for UChicago, I talked about my passion for learning music history through physical media, and the emotional significance of associating it with memories.

What do you think the strengths of your application were?

Since my high school had few clubs that I found myself interested in, I chose to elaborate on what I was doing outside of the classroom to better myself. This resulted in extensive talk about my involvement in the skiing community and passion for the outdoors, something that my admissions counselor later noted in my acceptance letter. In my effort to dissuade attention from relatively little involvement in my school community, I think I successfully managed to convey myself as a well-rounded person with a range of commitments.

What do you think the weaknesses of your application were? Where might other applicants have had an advantage over you?

I had very little leadership experience relative to other applicants, which I was aware of but had little way to remedy by the time the application cycle came around. I not only lacked leadership, but never participated in typical extracurricular academic activities such as debate, Model UN, etc. I was also never a straight A type student, and certainly didn't get 5s on every AP test I took.

Where else you were admitted:

University of Michigan, University of Puget Sound, Miami University Oxford

Where you were waitlisted:

None

Where you were rejected:

None

Did you get a private college counselor?

No

When did you start preparing for college admissions? How did your family prepare?

During my freshman year my family and I went to a required meeting with my school counselor to discuss the way that the process would unfold over the course of high school. From then on I began to take interest in different schools with assistance from my family. Although my parents were relatively hands-off during the process, they did plenty of research to help me decide which schools we'd go tour and made sure to familiarize themselves with the admissions process.

ABOUT YOUR COLLEGE:

Why did you choose this school?

I chose UChicago because I was looking for a sense of academic rigor that I didn't experience in high school. I was specifically looking for people who were willing to engage with their learning in new ways, and UChicago seemed unflinchingly committed to promoting this outlook.

The main thing that differentiated the school was the beauty of the campus and the city of Chicago. I'd never visited the city, and was surprised by how interested I was in learning more about the urban environment and the many people that inhabited it.

Academically, I was almost certain that I wanted to study the social sciences, and UChicago's reputation for economics, political science and sociology made it stand out among other schools I planned on applying to at the time.

What is your school known for? What is its reputation?

UChicago is commonly seen as an odd place with odd people and too much work, summed up by the phrase "where fun comes to die." The combination of nerdy people and a restrictively difficult academic life creates this reputation, and students are always open to complaining about how difficult their days have been. Other than the odd social life, it's also characterized by pioneering work in the hard and social sciences by famous professors.

Is this reputation accurate?

I've never liked the "where fun comes to die" phrase, but it can be true for some students. It's a good representation of the self pity mentality of many students, where hard work and a lack of self care are cause for celebration. This is clearly unhealthy, and although there's no need for students to fall into this it's common to take unrealistically hard classes with too much confidence and little preparation. Many people here are awkward and have unique interests, but those interests create a community diverse enough to find the right people and there's never pressure to be friends with everyone.

Professors are always hit or miss, but I'm always surprised by their accomplishments. They're usually more than willing to discuss ideas with you, and there's always something interesting to take away from their mindsets.

What are you involved with on campus?

I'm mainly involved with community service outlets on campus. I spend a few hours each week tutoring with a student-run club, and participate in other service activities through a community service fraternity. Aside from this, I'm involved with a social fraternity, which helps me separate my academic life from my time spent building friendships and meeting new people.

What do you think your school offers that no other top 20 school does?

I think the city of Chicago is an amazing asset that is often underutilized by students. The diversity of the city is paralleled only by New York, and the friendliness of most people in the city makes for an easy time exploring and learning about the history of its inhabitants. I can't speak for all top 20 schools, but UChicago never feels cutthroat and any sense of competition is usually regarded as pointless. Everyone here acknowledges that adding to each other's stress would be unhelpful and most people are more than willing to help explain concepts other students are struggling with.

What kinds of people do you think would love your school?

If you find yourself content with spending the majority of your time working, you'll be more than comfortable devoting yourself to your studies and staying caught up with various classes. The most successful people here are the ones who truly love what they're studying, and the passion they exude is admirable. If you're willing to spend the time on your work, you'll be rewarded with opportunities and new paths of study.

It also helps to be comfortable with people who you may find little in common with. The housing system groups people with almost no common interests, and people's unique interests can sometimes be overwhelming. Many students chose this school because they wanted a unique community not characterized by single stereotypes, and it shows.

In a cautionary way, it's also good to have solid mental fortitude. This factors into dealing with the long winters, sometimes insular social life and stressful workload. You have to be confident in your abilities and learn to take care of yourself, and if you're already sufficiently skilled at these things you'll have a much easier time adjusting to the rigorous environment.

What kinds of people do you think would hate your school?

If you're coming into college overjoyed about the prospect of a social life characterized by parties every weekend, you'll certainly be underwhelmed and struggle to balance this ideology with a successful and healthy academic life. There's nothing wrong with letting loose, but it's never fun to realize how much work you put off on Sunday mornings - and usually it only leads to further stress. It's taken me nearly two years to determine how much I should be going out each week and developing the foresight to manage it is a weekly process on its own.

If you find yourself much more interested in consuming your time with hobbies and extracurriculars, UChicago will present a challenge in managing your time to balance this with the academic load. Extracurriculars are beyond useful as outlets to manage stress, but during midterms and finals, commitments can feel burdensome and appear as additional stress. Dealing with work-life balance is a struggle across the whole student body, and it's a terrible feeling when your hobbies seem like sources of guilt instead of relief.

Do you like your school? Why or why not?

Although I don't believe UChicago is the best place for me, I definitely enjoy it and feel as though I've been able to find resources and activities to help me enjoy my time here. Classes are often unnecessarily hard, but peer collaboration is useful and helps to build bonds that I would never have found by taking easy classes all the time. The main issue I have with UChicago stem from the social implications of academic rigor. When everyone is fully engaged by their work, it's near impossible to spend time with friends and coordinate schedules. I struggle with this every quarter, and the fact that most of the quarter is defined by midterms and finals causes this to be an issue for about 7 weeks each quarter. All things about the school aside, this city is an amazing place to study and integrate oneself into, and for me the setting of Chicago is what makes my day to day rewarding and exciting.

Your college's biggest strengths. What do students appreciate about their school/take for granted?

The amount of connections this school has is ridiculous, and if you work hard and engage with the community you'll find yourself among countless interesting students and faculty to help you navigate career and academic interests. The location of the south side is often perceived as a negative aspect of the school, and while it presents some challenges it also creates a unique community and allows students to become part of a diverse and often underappreciated area of Chicago. This city is a dynamic and exciting place to be a college student, and it's not difficult to build connections and friendships with students from other schools. The amount of diversity across Chicago gives quick access to different cultural groups, and it's always easy to find new restaurants and hear plenty of languages throughout your day.

Your college's biggest weaknesses. What do students complain about the most? What would an admissions counselor never tell you?

One big concern around campus is the lack of mental health resources. Students have to wait multiple weeks, if not months, for an intake appointment without a referral. This means that students experiencing any sort of crises often have to resort to peer resources, which can be useful but often lack the professional expertise some students may require.

The excessive workload is a major issue for most students, as it's hard to adjust to spending the majority of your time outside of class during the weekdays working and studying. Oftentimes the amount of work can be completely overwhelming and only allows students to put minimal effort into their many assignments, which leads to difficulty retaining concepts. Time management is extremely useful, and with a lot of work it can feel unrealistic to maintain a healthy social life.

Other than academic issues, UChicago students are often very academically focused and not socially skilled. This doesn't mean it's impossible to find good friends, but it isn't as common to hold a comfortable conversation with someone.

ESSAYS:

Common App Essay:

Inversion

Snow swirled on the light wind and quickly awoke my senses. Ski season had finally arrived. I enjoyed the placid morning and breathed in the thin air. The T-bar lift made its rounds, the long bars swinging as the breeze whistled through the valley. Tourists began to arrive, distinguishable by their 1980's style ski jackets and their fearful countenances while they dug their edges into the groomed snow. Apart from them I noticed two kids dressed as the average park-skier might, with long jackets and baggy pants that bunched around the shins. Instantly striking up conversation, we decided to build a jump on the small hillside adjacent to the park.[177]

We finished clumping the snow and began to test our creation. Once we were comfortable, we all knew it was time to define our goals for the day.[178] To my surprise, one of them threw a seamless backflip on his second jump, his head whipping back and his hand tightly grasping his knees. I soon realized that this was the perfect place to attempt one for myself. A backflip is representative of a transition in the world of skiing. It's a niche culture that judges by danger and technique, and landing the backflip is a symbolic preamble[179] to a whole new level of potential. I'd seen the tutorials online and watched countless ski movies. The bend of the knees, the swing of the arms, the shrug of the shoulders and the tightening of the core. When the time came and I was prompted to attempt one that day, I mentally froze.[180] My body did the opposite. My fingers twitched and my arms shook; the sun suddenly became absent as the heat left my body. The wind rushed over me as I gained speed down the hill.

---

177   This is a good opening paragraph. We're welcomed into a specific scene, and Brian teases a storyline - the jump being built with a couple of strangers. Of course, we want to see what happens next.

178   It's a small stylistic choice, but Brian's use of 'we' and 'our' here shows us his closeness with his newfound accomplices. I like this intentionality.

179   I like this wording a lot.

180   Good vulnerability.

THE KIDS WHO GET IN

First I saw the sky, then the snowy ground. My whole body wrapped around the tip of the hard-packed jump we had created only minutes ago. The world spinning, my goggles were displaced from my tightly shut eyes. A cold yet gentle rush of powder engulfed my face. To think I previously assumed I had the skill to land on my first attempt quickly became comical after only one failed attempt.[181] I was dazed yet simultaneously inundated with laughter while I realized my determination rise. I couldn't help but rejoice in vanquishing my fear as I walked back up to the top of the hill and performed the ritualistic high fives with my new friends. I tried around twenty more times that day, but I could not land correctly and went home frustrated but determined.

On the next day, I was ready. My friends had returned to the city and I was alone. I threw my head back and obeyed the technique I had memorized. I failed three times, finally succeeding on the fourth attempt. I spotted the landing and put the tips down, my skis sliding along the snow under me as my body established a sense of balance. I had accomplished my goal and the possibilities for future achievements now seemed limitless as I skied away triumphantly.[182]

Landing the backflip influenced the way I thought and lived. I was quickly surprised at the amount of change a simple ski trick brought to my lifestyle. I soon realized that pouring oneself into daily tasks was rewarding. If I envision a ski trick that I've never thought of, I now attempt it instead of allowing fear to overcome the confidence I place in my abilities. Before that backflip, I had never achieved the same level of focus on any task in my life. School was always a facet of my life I devoted myself to, but I had reached a new sphere of perseverance that shaped the endurance I put into various academic endeavours. Instead of accepting fatigue I now strive to redefine my own endurance.[183]

---

181   Brian is able to laugh at his own arrogance. He quickly realizes that landing the backflip won't be anywhere near as easy as he thought, and he shows self-awareness and levity by freely admitting that.
182   Here is the climax of the story. It's told in Brian's understated style, which works, but he definitely could have added some more emotion here.
183   Brian uses this final paragraph to apply the lessons learned from landing the backflip to the rest of his life. It's a brief reflection, and again, it's understated, but it fits with his voice. The conclusion isn't perfect, but the entire piece is so calm and memorable I'm not sure it matters.

Fans of the movie Sharknado say that they enjoy it because "it's so bad, it's good." Certain automobile owners prefer classic cars because they "have more character." And recently, vinyl record sales have skyrocketed because it is perceived that they have a warmer, fuller sound. Discuss something that you love not in spite of but rather due to its quirks or imperfections:

In a pragmatic sense, Compact Discs are completely obsolete in the age of digital streaming. I'm an avid user of Spotify and often spend upwards of five hours a week making playlists, but still purchase CDs on a fairly regular basis. It could be to hold them in my hands, oddly combining material with the amorphous idea of music. Maybe it's something more, an appreciation for a project instead of a component. When you can create a new age mixtape in five minutes by dragging a few songs into a folder and arranging them in a certain order, you create a tone and set a mood simply by listening to a grouping of songs. It's amazing, and as someone who never learned to play an instrument as a child,[184] I am constantly astounded by the emotion that a minute of music is able to encapsulate.[185]

As I drive home from the mountains or head home after hours in the library, my phone often hangs onto that precious one percent of battery. I let the auxiliary cord hang there as I turn the key, unattached and slowly slipping into the crevice between my seat and the center console.[186] With the push of one button, I switch the receiver from AUX to Disc, selecting the album and listening through. This is what has been forgotten, the art of the album itself. In modern rap and hip-hop, artists are often praised for linking their songs together in certain ways and surprising the listener. This is nothing new, simply a style that has been forgotten in an era of hit singles and plati-

---

184 Great self-depreciation.
185 Here we see an idiosyncrasy and an appreciation of something small that most of us take for granted. This opener is a cool window into how Brian sees music and the world.
186 This is great imagery. We see his phone slip away into the infamous blackhole crevice, and Brian shrugs and turns on a CD. Very old school, and probably ingratiated him with a late 20's/early 30's AO.

num features. I'm able to select a quiver[187] of sorts, comprised of six precious albums that return my mind to different eras of my life.

In the time I've been driving, one of these has remained constant as a reminder of times past. Wild Onion, a 2014 album from young Chicago garage rockers Twin Peaks, has sixteen songs of varying emotions. Each song is powerful in it's own way, some with simple lyrics and others with deeper meanings. The first two songs are unashamedly exciting with a punk rock flair, while the third is tinged with nostalgia and regret. Before I stopped relying on my phone battery, I failed to realize what people meant when they said an album was "great." Of course, certain albums have redefined genres and changed the trajectory of musical eras. But I could only recognize a couple songs from these, and assumed that people viewed records as a container for a few great songs with others serving as interludes between hits. When I slow to a stop, foot on the brake as a song comes to a close, I notice myself drumming the beat of the next song on the wheel before it starts, as if I'm setting the beat for the band to pick up at a concert. Recognizing a lengthy musical process instead of an instance that occurs and fades within a few minutes is unfailingly powerful to me, as each emotion that has been stirred accumulates to a perception of an art piece as a whole. CDs are dying, even as vinyls face a new wave resurgence. If I didn't have a mobile, material form of music to appreciate as I drove, I would lose sight of precious moments, from inner strife to unadulterated joy and absolute confusion.[188]

Why U Chicago?:

When I visited UChicago in March, the admissions presenter, Mason Heller, was quick to note the university isn't looking solely for the student body presidents and class valedictorians for the Class of 2022. Mason's statement resonated with me as I spent the morning on campus keenly aware of the unlimited diversity and unique perspectives of my future peers. I'm truly drawn to UChicago's mission to foster "the life of the mind." Specifically, the Core Curriculum will drive me to openly express and receive view-

---

187   Awesome metaphor.
188   I like this essay because it feels intimate. We get a close look at something that matters a lot to Brian. Underneath the motif of CDs, we see what Brian values: presence and artistry.

points that contribute to a collaborative learning environment. In contrast to the limiting nature of the high school experience, that genuinely excites me. The small class sizes of the Core will not only allow me to gain new perspectives, but to focus on specific topics and relate them to the world around me through lively discussion. I'm not seeking to simply be educated; this may be achieved at any university. UChicago goes far beyond these basic aspirations.[189] Course offerings such as Media Aesthetics and Power, Identity, Resistance are immediately appealing to me as a means to analyze and understand the complex society we live in today. Being a member of society hinges on simply taking part, yet I intend to contribute and eagerly dive into the workings of the modern world. UChicago's Core curriculum and active environment of engaged learners and scholars appeals to me as the optimal environment for the cultivation of my mind- a critical stepping stone for greater purpose in the world.[190]

MY TAKE:

Brian's application offers a great lesson in authenticity. His academic qualifications (34 ACT Composite, 3.72 Unweighted GPA) are in the ballpark to compete in elite college admissions, although his GPA is on the lower end of that range, especially for U Chicago. Brian's extracurricular involvement, as he notes, is relatively scant. Volunteering with kids with disabilities, playing a sport, doing student council for a year, and skiing a ton constitutes a healthy high school experience - but a below average resume for elite college admissions.

Beside his involvements, Brian's maturity and sense of self stand out. His writing is direct and thoughtful; it's full of punchy phrases like "This is what has been forgotten, the art of the album itself," and "My friends had returned to the city and I was alone" (standing alone, these lines read like poetry). His essays aren't tearjerkers, but they are unique and memorable.

---

189   A little bit of buttering the school up never hurts :).

190   Like many of the other successful "Why this school" essays in this book, Brian touches upon specifics at U Chicago that match his goals, and the greater school mission/culture. Name dropping the presenter isn't a bad move here either.

We meet a kid who goes to the mountain alone, makes some new friends, and spends the weekend getting knocked on his ass trying to match their backflip[191]. We meet an 18 year old kid who values the continuity and concreteness of CDs. Brian talks about U Chicago as the optimal place for the "cultivation" of his mind, and his writing shows admissions officers an intelligent, self-aware kid that would make the most of that opportunity. In his "Why Chicago" Essay, Brian pokes at the fact that he isn't a class president or valedictorian (or the type of kid who would want those roles), he's the kind of kid who skis, cherishes his music, and plays sports - a valuable member of a college community!

A lot of times, elite college admissions isn't about stacking up activity and activity, academic achievement after academic achievement, and being the most "competitive" applicant. This truth drives overachievers crazy! It's like the person who showers their significant other with gifts, drops everything on a dime to spend time with them, and wonders why they aren't falling in love. Elite college admissions, like dating, isn't a math problem. A school like the University of Chicago gets countless applicants that are class presidents, valedictorians, elite researchers, and the like. In their quest to craft a dynamic, diverse community, they have to admit some smart, mature kids that like teaching kids how to play soccer, listening to niché CDs, and getting the shit kicked out of them on a mountain.

Many high school students, my former self included, can be intimidated by the prospect of applying to an elite school, and feel like they have to have changed the world by the age of 18 to stand a chance at admission. Being a unique, self-reflective, intelligent 18 year old is oftentimes enough, and it was for Brian, who earned admission to one of the most selective universities in the country by being himself.

Brian in a sentence: Mindful skier, CD-lover, calm, cool individual.

---

191   Showing his ability to make friends is a nice addition to the essay and is juxtaposed well with solo car rides and wars with the powder

University of Pennsylvania

SHAUN MCDONOUGH

APPLICATION:

Major I applied under / School I applied to: Actuarial Science/Business

Ethnicity: White

Gender: Male

Family Income Bracket: 80,000-160,000/year

Year of College Graduation: 2022

SAT I Score (By Section): 780 Math, 700 Reading (1480 Total)

ACT Score (By Section): N/A

SAT Subject Test Scores: N/A

High School Unweighted GPA (to nearest hundredth): 4.0

High School Weighted GPA: 4.3

Class Rank/Percentile: 11/200

AP Test Results: 3: US History, 2: English Literature, Calculus AB

Senior Year Course Load: AP English Literature, AP Calc AB, AP Physics, Religion,

THE KIDS WHO GET IN

Awards Won in High School: Highest math GPA

Extracurriculars in High School (Put leadership in parentheses):

Varsity Ice Hockey (captain), National Honor Society, Mathletes (Captain), Club Ice Hockey

Job/Work Experience in High School: Part time customer service rep, intern at local University Engineering school

Volunteer/Community Service: Salvation Army fundraiser through hockey

What did you do in the summer after freshman year of high school?

I spent my time going to hockey camps throughout the whole summer.

What did you do in the summer after sophomore year?

I took part in an internship at a university in my area. The internship was in the I.T. department at the Temple University Engineering school.

What did you do in the summer after junior year?

In the beginning of the summer after junior year, I went to a camp for aspiring actuaries at a local college. After that camp, I began to explore colleges that I would like to attend.

ABOUT YOUR HIGH SCHOOL:

State of High School: Pennsylvania

School Type (i.e. rural, suburban, city, public vs. private, etc): Private city

# of Students in Graduating Class: ~200

What was your high school like? Demographics? How many other students went to elite universities?

Primarily white catholic students, approximately 4 went to elite universities. 1 student went to Penn, 1 student went to Hopkins, 1 student went to Princeton, and I think one student went to Northwestern. I would say the students at my high school are a part of the lower middle class. A great majority of the students are from the local area, where I did not know of any foreign exchange students. Out of my graduating class, I think about 20% of the class went straight into the workforce, only about 5% went into the military, 5-8% were unsure of what they wanted to after high school, and the other 70% went to a college or university.

REFLECTION ON APPLICATION PROCESS:

I applied: Regular Decision

What do you think your hooks were?

I am a first generation and low income student applying for a niche concentration. I applied to a Philadelphia school and I am a resident of Philadelphia. I think one of my strongest hooks was being the captain of a sports team while also being top 10% of my class.

What do you think the strengths of your application were?

I showed strong leadership qualities and strong academic abilities. I managed to play on two ice hockey teams throughout high school, be the captain of one of those teams, while retaining strong academic integrity. I was also pretty involved with my school, which a university may want to see, because that means I would be involved at their university.

What do you think the weaknesses of your application were? Where might other applicants have had an advantage over you?

I think other applicants might have had more work experience and higher standardized test scores. I only had a small internship at an engineering school, where I was applying to a business school.

What do you think your hooks were?

I am a first generation and low income student applying for a niche concentration. I applied to a Philadelphia school and I am a resident of Philadelphia. I think one of my strongest hooks was being the captain of a sports team while also being top 10% of my class.

What do you think the strengths of your application were?

I showed strong leadership qualities and strong academic abilities. I managed to play on two ice hockey teams throughout high school, be the captain of one of those teams, while retaining strong academic integrity. I was also pretty involved with my school, which a university may want to see, because that means I would be involved at their university.

What do you think the weaknesses of your application were? Where might other applicants have had an advantage over you?

I think other applicants might have had more work experience and higher standardized test scores. I only had a small internship at an engineering school, where I was applying to a business school. An engineering internship may not have been appealing to a university. My standardized test scores were just below average for Penn, so I was convinced many students had higher scores than me.

Where else you were admitted:

Lebanon Valley College, Penn State University (main campus), Temple University, St Joe's University, University of Connecticut, Robert Morris University, University of Pittsburgh

Where you were waitlisted:

None

Where you were rejected:

None

Did you get a private college counselor?

No

When did you start preparing for college admissions? How did your family prepare?

I started preparing for college admissions my junior year when I joined NHS and mathletes. My family became more mentally prepared to pay for my applications and take me to different colleges. My family had never been exposed to the college admissions process, so we all had to learn about the process as we went through it.

ESSAYS:

Common App Essay:

Ever since I can remember, I have been playing hockey, whether it was foot, roller, or ice. I have been on skates since I was three years old, playing in as many as three leagues at a time, as well as attending school as a young child. As my skills in hockey developed, so did my love for the sport. Hockey, in a way, takes me away from the worries of ordinary life for a few hours each time I play.[192]

There was a time when I was in third grade and I was participating in cub scouts as well as ice hockey; along with all of this, I had school projects to complete, nightly homework, and activities for cub scouts such as pinewood derby, a race for hand-made wooden cars. I had come to the conclusion after several months that I wanted to give the majority of my time outside of school to hockey, rather than cub scouts and hockey. It was around this time in my life that I realized my passion for the sport. No matter what the situation was in my life at the time, hockey would take me away from the stresses outside of the rink, and cause me to lose track of time.

Throughout my thirteen years of playing hockey, the sport has become a part of my everyday life, the essence of who I am. While playing the various forms of hockey, I easily lose track of time and surroundings because I am so engulfed in the game.[193] While I am either on the ice or on the roller rink,

---

192   This is a relatively simple opener. I would have opted for bringing the reader into some action on the ice, and then backing up and explaining that hockey has been a life-long activity for Shaun.

193   I would love to see more showing and less telling here. Working in a specific hockey moment, with imagery, would bring this to life.

all other aspects of my life fall away, focusing all of my physical and mental energy on the game at hand. The drive of scoring is such a natural adrenaline-inducing moment that I get lost in time. My mind enters a different dimension whenever I play hockey, and when the buzzer sounds at the end of each period, it pulls me back into the reality of where I am.

Hockey has molded me into an outgoing, challenge seeking, and self-motivated person. I am always seeking to learn new things in each opportunity that arises in my life.[194] This especially pertains to being engaged on the rink. I constantly look to my father and my coaches for guidance to better myself and my skills in the game. I know I can always better myself in my talents when I look to those who already have played the sport for many years, and are aware of how to utilize different strategies.[195][196]

How will you explore your intellectual and academic interests at the University of Pennsylvania? Please answer this question given the specific undergraduate school to which you are applying. (400-650 words)

At the Wharton Business School, I would be focusing on my love for math by studying actuarial sciences. While attending the business school at the

---

[194] In this last paragraph, Shaun makes the important leap of bringing the lessons he's learned in hockey to the rest of his life. This growth-mindset and drive to improve in all areas is a valuable trait, especially for a career in Business, Shaun's intended major. I would have expanded upon this reflection and pushed another paragraph about future goals and potential specific applications for this drive.

[195] This is a subtle personality trait that Shaun reveals - a deep respect for those who have already put in their time and hard work in a given field.

[196] At first glance, this might appear to be an unimpressive essay. It's not going to win a Pulitzer, and centers around a tried college essay topic. But it's a topic authentic to Shaun's life, and he shares valuable wisdom and growth that came from the many hours he's spent on the rink.

This essay fits well into the larger theme of this book - that the most important thing in college admissions is to be yourself. Shaun's not an all-star writer, or an overzealous, president of 6 clubs, prototypical applicant. He's a hard-nosed hockey and math kid with a deep respect for hard-work, who made the most of the opportunities available to him - and that was enough for Penn!

University of Pennsylvania, I will explore my intellectual and academic interests by taking my love of math and applying it to all areas of academics.[197]

When I toured University of Pennsylvania earlier this year, I was given the opportunity to explore the Wharton building. I was fascinated by the dynamics of the entire school. Everywhere I turned, I could envision myself being engaged in student life. I was truly captivated by the architecture, the photos on the walls, the amazing staircase and the rounded balcony where my group congregated.[198] In that moment of listening to the student speak about the different programs and opportunities of the school, I had a revelation. I truly could see myself attending the Wharton School and flourishing as an actuary because of the education I will receive here.

While I was walking the halls of the Wharton school, I was brought back to the memories of where my obsession of numbers and math began. My love for math began when I was younger, around sixth grade. It has only boomed since then, especially within the past few years of high school. Math is not just an academic interest for me. I am interested, engaged, and curious about new math problems formulas and equations. Numbers are my calling and I have always been drawn to the intellectual aspects of figuring out all forms of math.

Throughout my high school career, I have participated in robotics, JV mathletes, and I currently am a part of varsity mathletes. Inside and outside of the classroom, I love working with numbers. While I am out with friends, I always find myself relating the situations around me to numerical values and equations. Even when I go out to eat with my friends and family, I am literally trying to be the first one to figure out the tip. It is always a fun challenge for me.

There are such diverse ways in which to apply math in everyday life, and the Wharton school will educate me on those ways. In high school, the math curriculum taught to the students is just the tip of the iceberg to what can really be learned. At the Wharton School, I would be able to explore the underbelly of that iceberg, and then apply those concepts to my concentration in actuarial sciences. Through the National Honor Society, I have

---

197   Better not to reword the question in the answer.
198   I like this emotional approach that shows Shaun's connection to Wharton.

enhanced my ability to work in groups, just as I have learned how to tutor other students. It brings me great joy and pleasure to be a mentor to those who struggle in certain areas.[199]

Being given the opportunity to tour the Wharton School with a student that actively attends University of Pennsylvania has changed the way I view other schools. Whenever I am doing college research, I compare it to University of Pennsylvania because I was so captivated by the school and all the fundamentals it has to offer me in my future career. My standards, inside and out of the classroom, have been raised ever since I toured the school.[200]

MY TAKE:

Shaun is an interesting applicant. On one hand, he sports a 4.0, 97th percentile SAT scores, and good leadership and involvement on his campus. On the other, his essays are middling, and his extracurricular involvements are varied, but (as he notes) don't line up with a career in business as much as other applicants' may have.

Let's take a closer look. The weaknesses of his application were buoyed by a perfect GPA, first-generation status, proximity to the university (Penn), and application to a niche concentration. Another contribution was probably his direct experience at an actuarial camp. Colleges reward those with prior experience in the fields they intend to study, and demonstrating this domain experience forecasts a continued interest and a likelihood of postgraduate success in the field.

Having a powerful alumni network is in many respects an elite university's greatest vested interest, which means that in admissions they look to select

---

199   This line is out of place - it's missing a connection to Penn. Here, referencing a collaborative academic community would work well to bring his appreciation of helping others to his "Why Penn?" essay.

200   This essay meanders a bit - but Shaun brings it together at the end. Wharton has become his gold standard! His elevated standards for himself fit into the picture he crafts in his first essay - as someone dedicated to consistent improvement. This is a great way to finish the piece.

those who will go on to be successful in their respective field. While Penn might have a greater interest in their future bankers and consultants than actuaries (a less prestigious industry), this experience still probably helped Shaun.

Another note - AOs at Penn understand that as a first-generation applicant from a middle-class background and a middle-class Catholic school, Shaun probably didn't have access to the same resources in preparing for admissions as many other applicants. This grants Shaun some leeway on organizing his extracurriculars around a potential career, and on having perfectly crafted, 11-draft essays.

One last point on Shaun's application: while he wasn't rejected anywhere, had he missed the boat at Penn, his next choice would have been Penn State or Pitt, two schools significantly less selective than Penn (with much less financial aid available, albeit in-state). I recommend that students like Shaun apply to a couple of schools like BC, Michigan, Wake Forest, Rochester - prestigious schools where he would have been a more likely admit than Penn. Having a balanced list is a cliche piece of college admissions advice that holds true.

Shaun in a sentence: Hard-nosed hockey and math kid with a deep respect for hard-work.

Vanderbilt University

MADISON CARTER

APPLICATION:

Major I applied under / School I applied to: History; College of Arts and Sciences (I ended up majoring in Political Science)

Ethnicity: Black

Gender: Female

Family Income Bracket: 250,000-500,000/year

Year of College Graduation: 2020

High School Unweighted GPA (to nearest hundredth): 94.69/100

High School Weighted GPA: 99.98/105

Class Rank/Percentile: 11/1000

SAT I Score (By Section): 800 Reading, 690 Math, 800 Writing (2290 Total)

ACT Score (By Section): 36 English, 35 Reading, 33 Math, 33 Science (34 Composite)

SAT Subject Test Scores: 700 World History, 700 US History, 700 English

AP Test Results: 5: US History, World History, Psychology, English Language, 4: Government

Senior Year Course Load: AP Government, Honors Spanish 4, English 4, Cinema Production, Gym

Awards Won in High School: National Honor Society; Posse Foundation Full-Tuition Scholarship; Phyllis Wheatley Orator Award; Brooklyn Historical Society Teen Innovator Award; Melinda Katz Black Excellence Scholarship; NYC Council Citation

Extracurriculars in High School: Black Student Union (Founder, President); Political Awareness Club (President); Spanish Honor Society (Member); We The People Constitutional Debate Team (Team Captain); Shakespeare Drama Club (Lead Actor); 4-H Club (Member)

Job/Work Experience in High School: YMCA (After School Counselor; Junior & Senior year); Streetwear Company (Marketing and Advertising Intern; Junior & Senior year)

Volunteer/Community Service: Nursing Home (Patient Care Volunteer; 9-12th grade); Local elementary school (reading volunteer; 10-12th grade)

What did you do in the summer after freshman year of high school?

Volunteered at a Nursing Home

What did you do in the summer after sophomore year?

Camp Counselor at local Summer Camp

What did you do in the summer after junior year?

Classes at local College; internship at NYC streetwear company

ABOUT YOUR HIGH SCHOOL:

State of High School: New York

School Type (i.e. rural, suburban, city, public vs. private, etc): Urban

# of Students in Graduating Class: ~1000

What was your high school like? Demographics? How many other students went to elite universities?

It was one of the better public high schools in NYC. Predominately white and hispanic (approximately 150 Black kids at the peak out) of 4000. I'd say most kids went to city or state schools. A few went to other elite schools - Another to Vandy, our valedictorian to Princeton, and a few at NYU.

REFLECTION ON APPLICATION PROCESS:

I applied: Early Decision

What do you think your hooks were?

I applied via the Posse Foundation, so I was able to interview and show my personality directly to admissions counselors.

What do you think the strengths of your application were?

My essay was definitely the strength of my app. It showed that I was a leader and willing to make social change when I got to campus. If anything, it was the perfect predictor for who I would be at Vandy.[201]

What do you think the weaknesses of your application were? Where might other applicants have had an advantage over you?

My unweighted GPA was a little lower than other applicants from my school. I also didn't take many STEM classes in high school and pigeonholed myself into the humanities, so there were definitely more well-rounded applicants.

Where else you were admitted:

Yale, Harvard, St. John's, Stony Brook University, Princeton, Dartmouth, Rice, USC, Howard, Syracuse, Spelman, NYU (all of which were applications I never rescinded after the Posse admission)

---

201   Madison was a classmate of mine at Vanderbilt and undoubtedly lived up to this

Where you were waitlisted:

N/A

Where you were rejected:

N/A

Did you get a private college counselor?

No

When did you start preparing for college admissions? How did your family prepare?

The summer after sophomore year. My mom got me an SAT tutor and I took my first SAT in the fall of my junior year. I kept getting the same score, so she got me a new tutor and I took the ACT. I also had academic tutors for math because it was the only class I would get Bs in. I also have family who work in college admissions, so they reviewed my apps and essays.

ABOUT YOUR COLLEGE:

Why did you choose this school?

It was tuition-free (I got a full-scholarship).

What is your school known for? What is its reputation?

The city. The degree. The SEC. Vanderbilt's known for being one of the best schools in the country (#14). Vanderbilt is also known as a fun, but hardworking school in a fun city. Students are known to get rowdy but also buckle down and focus on their studies. Vandy is billed as a place where anyone can find their niche.

Is this reputation accurate?

I agree that Vandy is academically an amazing school. I don't personally think Nashville is very fun (but that is primarily a function of being from NYC). I do think anyone can find their niche at Vandy if you try, but there is a large racial division on campus that affects that.

What are you involved with on campus?

I was in a sorority, HeForShe, Vanderbilt Student Government, Caribbean Students Association, Vanderbilt Hustler

What do you think your school offers that no other top 20 school does?

I think Vandy's uniqueness comes with having a campus in a city that people actually go to. Also, having the ability to gain close relationships with professors is a major plus. I was able to become great friends with some of my professors, to the point where they supervised my thesis.

What kinds of people do you think would love your school?

The kind of person who would love Vanderbilt would be someone who is upper middle class or upper class.[202] This person was probably popular in high school and is used to navigating predominantly white spaces. A huge part of the Vanderbilt experience is the social climate, and unfortunately the social climate was built on the elitism that whiteness and wealth provide.

What kinds of people do you think would hate your school?

Black and Latinx students probably would not like Vanderbilt. The environment is slightly cutthroat and psychological care is hard to come by. There is a large racial division, where students either pick minority Vanderbilt or white Vanderbilt. That division forces minorities to either pick a side or never truly be able to toe that line. This division exists at many other elite institutions and Vanderbilt is by far not the worst one. However, this division should not exist. Many Black students recall their Vanderbilt experience as slightly traumatic, whereas most white students do not feel the same way.

Do you like your school? Why or why not?

Overall, I liked Vanderbilt. I learned a lot and made friends I'll have for a lifetime. But, I won't act like Vanderbilt did not negatively impact my mental

---

202   I don't disagree. I provide an entry on my experience at Vandy as well at the end that you can check out

health. Additionally, one of my best friends committed suicide at the school, and for that, I can't rate it extremely positively. However, I value my education and am thankful for it.

Your college's biggest strengths. What do students appreciate about their school/take for granted?

The endowment is huge and literally everything I've ever wanted to do has been funded. Study abroad is amazing and half the juniors do it. The alumni network is insane and contributed to me getting my full-time job.

Your college's biggest weaknesses. What do students complain about the most? What would an admissions counselor never tell you?

Access to psychological care is hard to come by. Racism is excused. The largely white student body is generally oblivious to how their actions affect BIPOC. Administration is non-respondent. An admissions counselor would never tell you that Vanderbilt will probably break you before it lifts you up.

ESSAYS:

Common App Essay:

Room 375 was abnormally busy for a Wednesday afternoon; 72 people filled the room and anxiously waited for me to say something, but I couldn't. I couldn't form thoughts or words. It was as if I was trapped in my own body and my vocal cords stopped working. All I had to do was read the PowerPoint slides, but as I opened my mouth, tears streamed down my face. As I looked into the crowd, my mind began to wander; I was taken back seven months earlier.[203]

I walked into the Club Coordinator's office with a proposal for the Black Student Union in my hand. I was 100% positive that when I left his office, BSU would be approved. I was wrong. As I put the proposal on his desk and pitched the idea, I saw his face began to deform and his brow furrowed. He

---

[203] Fantastic hook. The specifics (Room 375, 72 people), the emotions (I couldn't form thoughts or words), the visual (tears streaming down her face), the snapback to 7 months earlier. It's perfect.

looked up at me with disdainful eyes and said: *Why do the Black kids need a separate club? Why isn't there a White Student Union?* and the best of all, *I don't understand why you people can't just be happy with what you have.* He tore apart our proposal, rejected our faculty advisor, and asserted that BSU was not a necessity. I left his office feeling as if BSU would be an unattainable dream.

Contrary to his belief, I knew the Black Student Union was a necessity. Borne from a struggle of being bullied during my sophomore year, I wanted to uplift the small amount of minority students my school had. Rather than give in to naysayers, I went back to school with the goal of creating racial unity in Forest Hills. I knew it wouldn't be easy because even the Black kids sneered at the idea.[204] *Why do we need a Black Student Union? We meet in the lobby to hang out.* The same people who bullied me were against the idea of having a Black Student Union. Instead of letting my dream die, I pushed harder. I went back into the Club Coordinator's office with a new proposal, a new advisor, and 274 signatures that demonstrated student interest. There was no way he could say no, and on that day BSU was born. Although the struggle to get approved was over, our issues had just begun.

Clubs in Forest Hills are allotted 15 posters to gain student interest, so BSU decided we would follow in the steps of other clubs by putting up posters. Our poster was a Black Power fist on a white canvas that read "**Black Student Union. Wednesday's, Ninth Period, Room 375**."[205] It was harmless. However, many students complained to administration, saying they felt alienated, and likened it to a swastika. So our posters, as quickly as they went up, came down. It seemed as if we would never have a successful club. Despite the posters being destroyed, our buzz was too big, and we had a great turnout for our first meeting.

In our first meeting, we posed a question - "What does being Black mean to you?" That question set the stage for the greatness we would achieve. A simple question elicited various responses, from the poetic to the emotional: *Being Black is persevering against all odds to be great* and *my blackness is a*

---

204   Madison tells us the story of an uphill battle. She paints the picture of facing opposition from both sides, and remains persistent.

205   Great specific detail here.

robe of shame, yet I wear it with pride. Students thanked us because they were finally given a completely inclusive space. BSU made a long overdue connection with the students.

When I leave Forest Hills, I leave my legacy. BSU became a staple of the Forest Hills identity, but also of myself; it is the rose that grew from concrete. Against all odds, we succeeded in creating something that completely and irrevocably changed the dynamic of Forest Hills – and that's why I cried in front of 72 people.[206]

Vanderbilt Supplement:

Growing up, I always wanted to be a lawyer. Fueled by my obsession with Law and Order: SVU and Casey Novak, I wanted to be the Assistant District Attorney for New York. As I grew up, however, my career prospects expanded into the marketing and advertising field. I was a big fan of Sprayground, an urban streetwear accessories brand. During the spring of my junior year in high school, I was offered the opportunity to intern with them.

I had no marketing experience, so I was surprised when on my first day, I was handed a big binder with every store in New York that distributed Sprayground bags. After a week, the Vice President of Marketing came to me with a project. Sprayground was gaining more appeal in the luxury market, so he wanted to expand into stores like Bloomingdale's. My job was to make that happen.

I needed to perfect my presentation if I wanted to be taken seriously; my internship depended on this project. I had to convince one of the world's most posh stores that they needed to sell a brand that was traditionally "streetwear." I spent an immense amount of time researching market trends and brand influence as well as conducting statistical analysis. After two weeks of non-stop work, I knew I was ready.

I trekked up Third Avenue hyperventilating with samples from the new season. All I could think was "what if they don't take me seriously." When I arrived at the flagship store, I was directed to the boardroom. There, I made

---

[206]   I love this essay, and Madison wraps it up perfectly, linking back to that initial moment in Room 375. It's a powerful story and Madison tells it succinctly, and directly, which works.

a thirty-minute presentation to the head buyers of Men's and Children's Accessories. My heart was beating so fast it felt like it would pop out my chest, but by the end of the presentation, I felt confident. The head buyer for Men's Accessories was so impressed by my age and ability that he offered me a job as a Marketing Director.[207]

Sprayground bags and accessories are now available at various Bloomingdale's stores nationwide. In the four months I spent there, I developed a new strategy for pitching ideas to buyers, which the company still uses. Sprayground was an outlet for me to explore alternative career paths. Despite its challenges, I realized that my internship was a blessing in disguise. I was taught the cardinal rule of being a working woman - It's all about how you present yourself.[208]

MY TAKE:

Madison is an exceptionally talented, tenacious woman who impressed a slew of admissions officers, including those at Vanderbilt. She boasts impressive stats (1490/2290 SAT, 34 ACT, ~95/100 GPA, 11/1000 class ranking), and her essays show her as someone with a strong moral compass, and an *inability* to give up!

We see a young woman with a lot of heart and determination, who founded her school's Black Student Union despite facing opposition from administration and fellow students and who successfully pitched a streetwear brand to Bloomingdales as a teenager. Both of these accomplishments are incredibly compelling, and they show admissions officers that Madison is someone who will make a difference at their college, and beyond. Colleges are looking for just that - future innovators, leaders, and successful people, and Madison radiates those traits.

I write about this in the Penn entry as well - colleges, and especially elite colleges like the one featured in this book, are looking to produce a genera

---

[207] It's a flex, but works within the context of her admitted anxiety around the pitch. I'll call it a tasteful flex.
[208] This is a sleek ending. Madison wraps up her essay with a larger aphorism that she learns through experience. It's a phenomenal display of self-awareness.

tion of future achievers that will bring additional fame to their alma maters (and hopefully donate!) You definitely don't have to orient your application around your future ability to earn, but anecdotes like the ones that Madison provided that showcase a knack for persistence and accomplishment will never hurt.

Madison's application was packaged around featuring tenacity and confidence, and her essays and activities fit well to create a holistic picture of a driven, ambitious young woman - and earned her a full-scholarship to Vanderbilt.

Madison in a sentence: Unbelievably tenacious woman with bulletproof conviction, a future business leader.

Vanderbilt University - Bonus Entry from your loving author

DAAVI GAZELLE

APPLICATION:

Major I applied under / School I applied to: Secondary Education and Math - Peabody College

Ethnicity: White/Middle Eastern

Gender: Male

Family Income Bracket: 160,000-250,000/year

Year of College Graduation: 2020.5

High School Unweighted GPA (to nearest hundredth): 3.75

High School Weighted GPA: 3.75

Class Rank/Percentile: We didn't rank, I probably would have been around top 15%. I went to a very competitive high school.

SAT I Score (By Section): 800 Math, 800 Critical Reading, 730 Writing

ACT Score (By Section): N/A

SAT Subject Test Scores: 800 Math II, 750 Physics

AP Test Results: 5: AB Calculus, Physics 1, Spanish Language and Culture, 4: Physics 2

Senior Year Course Load: AB Calculus, Physics 1 & 2, Engineering Design, AP Spanish, Honors English Elective

Awards Won in High School: AP Scholar, Volleyball Most Improved Player

Extracurriculars in High School (Put leadership in parentheses): Volleyball team (Captain), Chess team (President), Camp Counselor, Board Member of Town Teen Center,

Job/Work Experience in High School: Intern for local candidate for City Councilor, Camp Counselor

Volunteer/Community Service: Read to inner-city kids, Habitat for Humanity, peer tutoring

What did you do in the summer after freshman year of high school?

Basketball camp, visited family in Canada, that's about it

What did you do in the summer after sophomore year?

Service/leadership in training program at my sleepaway camp

What did you do in the summer after junior year?

Counselor at all-boys sleepaway camp in western Massachusetts

ABOUT YOUR HIGH SCHOOL:

State of High School: Massachusetts

School Type (i.e. rural, suburban, city, public vs. private, etc): Public school in a wealthy suburb of Boston.

# of Students in Graduating Class: 450

What was your high school like? Demographics? How many other students went to elite universities?

Mostly white and asian, high percentage Jewish, moderate percentage of hispanic and black students, about half of whom were Boston residents who went to my school through METCO (a school integration program). I grew up in Boston and my mom and I moved to this town specifically so I could go to the high school.

The town that I went to high school in can be super academically snobby - it has the highest percentage of adults with master's degrees of any zip code in America, and students were very hyper focused on college admissions. We usually send around a dozen kids to Harvard, a couple to each of the other Ivies, a good amount to Michigan, the UCs, ~10 to WashU, and one or two each year to Duke or Stanford. I was the only student in a year or two to go to Vanderbilt and since I've been at Vandy it's been about one a year.

REFLECTION ON APPLICATION PROCESS:

I applied: Regular Decision

What do you think your hooks were?

Male interested in the field of education helped me a lot. I took a gap year after high school and volunteered in a Boston public school for a year - having this level of experience in one field was definitely something that helped me stand out.

What do you think the strengths of your application were?

Good enough grades, strong test scores, very strong recommendations and essays, very well-rounded with a lot of experience in one field (education). Both of my recommenders thought very highly of me and were also phenomenal writers, which I think matters more than people give credit to. Extracurriculars weren't out of this world but I think as captain of a varsity sport and the chess team, I probably checked the "leadership" boxes.

What do you think the weaknesses of your application were? Where might other applicants have had an advantage over you?

Lower grades and less rigorous course load than others from my high school who were admitted to other elite schools. Didn't take BC calculus, didn't take AP Biology or Chem, took Physics 1 and 2 instead of Physics C, and in general, didn't orient my academic or extracurricular life around getting into a good college (which probably helped me stand out, in a way).

Where else you were admitted:

Before my gap year, I got into USC, Middlebury, McGill, Case Western, UMass, Northeastern, UMiami. Afterwards BC, Tufts, and Vanderbilt were the only new acceptances.

Where you were waitlisted:

Before gap year: Harvard, WashU. After gap year: Northwestern, Michigan, Brown, Dartmouth, Harvard again, Bowdoin, Washington University in St. Louis again, Carleton. I was waitlisted at Harvard and WashU applying after high school and after my gap year.

Where you were rejected:

Before my gap year: USC Iovine and Young, UNC Chapel Hill. Cornell. After my gap year: Cornell, Wesleyan.

Did you get a private college counselor?

Yes[209]

When did you start preparing for college admissions? How did your family prepare?

We probably started touring schools my sophomore year, just when visiting family. I wasn't really into the whole applying to college thing (ironic that I ended up writing a book about it), and I remember my friends and other kids at school talking a lot about it sophomore and junior year, before I had

---

209   My college counselor helped me pick a couple schools and read my essays once or twice. Overall it was a pretty big waste of money and I didn't use a counselor the second time I applied.

really thought about it. My mom hired a private admissions counselor and he was good about dragging me along and meeting deadlines, but I wasn't very invested in the process until November/December Senior year.

My senior year of high school I was very sick with Crohn's disease, and ended up taking a gap year to be at home and manage my health. When I finished high school, I paid the deposit at USC and told them I was taking a gap year.

For my gap year, I served as a City Year AmeriCorps member in a high-needs Boston Public School as an academic and behavioral coach, which I touch on in my essays below.

During the gap year, I decided to apply to colleges again - I think I would have been happy at USC but getting waitlisted at Harvard made me want to try again and shoot higher, and I also wanted some options that were more affordable than USC.

ABOUT YOUR COLLEGE:

Why did you choose this school?

It was the best and cheapest school that I got into. I didn't have an amazing visit, I was a little apprehensive about greek life and living in the South (I'm from Boston). But I kinda knew that I had to suck that up or spend a lot of money to go somewhere else.

What is your school known for? What is its reputation?

Vanderbilt is known for its work hard-play hard mentality, for being an elite school in the South with strong academics, athletics (we just won the baseball National Championship), greek life, and for having a very wealthy student body.

Is this reputation accurate?

Everything I wrote above is accurate. I don't think Vanderbilt is quite the party school that it's reputation makes it out to be, especially as the administration takes strides to water down Greek life. In terms of wealth, Vandy has the highest percentage of students from the top 1% of any college in America. Our baseball team is filthy but our football team is one of the worst in the SEC.

What are you involved with on campus?

I'm in a fraternity, I play club baseball, I coach a little league basketball team in Nashville, and I was a VUceptor (mentor for first-year students).

What do you think your school offers that no other school does?

A strong greek life presence combined with the personalization and resources of a small liberal arts college, incredible location in the heart of Nashville. Probably one of the most career-focused top 20 schools, although I'm sure people at a lot of schools would say that.

What kinds of people do you think would love your school?

People motivated by status, people that were popular in high school or care about popularity, people who like being well known. Because Vanderbilt is so small, it can feel like everyone in greek life knows everyone else in greek life, which can make Vandy feel a little bit like high school 2.0. It's pretty easy to amass a large network at Vanderbilt, and outgoing people usually have large and vibrant social lives at Vandy.

Also, people who have a strong knowledge of what they want to pursue after college (Vanderbilt offers incredible resources and mentorship for students, and Vandy is small enough that these resources are accessible to the students who actively seek them out).

Lastly, people who want to be successful! Vanderbilt grads are leaders in every industry and tend to do very well financially. A lot of my peers are graduating with 6 figure jobs, which is a ton of money at 22 years old.

What kinds of people do you think would hate your school?

People who dislike conformity, or who highly value individual expression. People that care a lot about social justice or political activism or academics - not that Vanderbilt culture counters any of these things, but they don't get the conversational air time of greek life or professional recruiting. You can probably find it/create a space for it, but the average Vandy student isn't staying up until 2am discussing the meaning of life or debating philosophy. A lot of people who are at Vanderbilt that hate it really belonged at a small liberal arts college in the Northeast.

People who get bothered by bubbliness or "superficial" happiness, people who are "artsy" or "hipster" probably won't like the amount of Canada Goose worn on our campus.

Also, people who were looking for SEC-level athletics and fandom are disappointed after attending Vanderbilt. Students usually tailgate and party and skip the game, and our home football games are regularly out-attended by the visiting crowd.

Do you like your school? Why or why not?

I love Vanderbilt. I have 7-8 people from college I love and really care about, and a bunch of casual friends on top of that.

It's a super socially competitive school (probably the most "social" of any top 20 school) and at times that can be exhausting. Vanderbilt is definitely an Instagram-heavy school, and it can seem like people are trying to show that they're having a better time than everyone else. But taking a step back from the imposter syndrome and fatigue that all of that causes, Vanderbilt is pretty amazing.

90% of my professors were great, I had a lot of adults believe in me and push me to be more successful, I had a ton of opportunities to try and fail and learn, and I met a lot of cool people.

Especially when it's warm out, our campus has a buzz to it that makes you feel like you're a part of something special. Vandy, for all its flaws, is great.

Your college's biggest strengths. What do students appreciate about their school/take for granted?

- Super high concentration of intelligent and socially competent people
- Phenomenal alumni network
- Mostly great undergraduate professors

- Lot's of orgs/opportunities to lead

- Small enough that you will bump into the same people often enough to maintain a friendship, large enough that you will always have new people to meet and new things on campus to be exposed to

- I felt like it was the perfect balance of being exposed to Southern culture but attending a progressive university

Your college's biggest weaknesses. What do students complain about the most? What would an admissions counselor never tell you?

- High concentration of very very large egos

- Definitely an overprogramming/overinvolvement issue

- People choose courses/extracurriculars for career ramifications and less from genuine interest

- Culture leans white and wealthy, seems like this is trending down though

- Administration has to balance pleasing convervative board members, alumni, and constituents in Tennessee with liberal student body, largely leans toward student body here but of course students want more

- Incredibly bureaucratic institution for only 6600 undergrads

- Some majors are 2-3x as much work as others (probably true of many colleges)

- Going through a serious identity crisis as greek life plays a smaller role and school recruits more talented, diverse students from outside the South

- Not a ton of school pride and little to no shared cultural events/traditions the whole school looks forward to

ESSAYS:

I sobbed between throws, pausing to wind up and hurl the ball with as much force as my twelve-year-old body could muster. I wondered what I had done to deserve such a fate. It was my twelfth Father's Day, an experience that did not get easier with practice.

Why does everyone else have one?

While some people have mysterious missing fathers known only from stories or photos, my unknown is certain. I am the product of artificial insemination, and from a young age I've known that my father was an anonymous donor. And although I prayed for it, I knew he would never show up one day and claim me as his son.

Wanting to expose me to some sense of masculinity, my mom bribed me into playing baseball. With the promise of pizza and thirty extra minutes of computer time per practice,[210] I was officially a member of the Jamaica Plain Autobody All-Stars. My first at-bats were awful. I finally made contact during the seventh game of the season. I stared at my hands, shocked by the dull aluminum clink I was hearing for the first time. I bolted to first base.

"Safe!"

It was incredible. I had done the impossible, and I had done it without a dad. It was a step into a new world, a world where a chubby kid could fuddle[211] his way to first base and receive a chorus of cheers. My teammates yelled and screamed, and I truly felt like I belonged.[212]

The feeling of success was addicting.[213] Baseball became an obsession and I was consumed with improving my game. Every day I threw against my Pitchback, a netted screen that propels the ball back at the thrower.[214] I took

---

210   Nice endearing specifics.
211   Creative and memorable use of the word "fuddle."
212   This to me comes across as a bit heavy handed. But hey, emotions hit hard for
213   Deliberate tone shift and expansion of scope. Still, a natural transition that links the story together well.
214   Clarifying the Pitchback with a dictionary definition is fairly anticlimactic and

practice swings in my room, nearly destroying the trophies I had earned in the process (awarded for participation, but cherished nevertheless[215]). I played baseball with my friends and teammates every weekend. I craved the satisfaction of achievement and the sense of community that followed. Even if I didn't have a dad, I would always have my team.[216]

On my twelfth Father's Day, the Red Sox hosted a Father's Day Catch. My teammates went to throw with their dads, overjoyed by the prospect of playing on the fabled Fenway Park green. I stayed behind. The day was difficult for me. It was a reminder of all the injustice and inadequacy I had felt.

But I knew that I didn't need a dad to practice. So I put on my glove, grabbed a ball, and threw against my Pitchback. As I threw, tears began to flow. I whipped the ball harder and harder against the net.

That day was painful, but it marked the fire and determination that not having a father instilled in me. That grit has carried to my education, my athletics, and my struggle with Crohn's disease. Today, I bring that drive to the school that I serve. I strive to introduce that flame to my students, who need it to overcome far more than an incoming fastball. I dedicate every day to teaching my students that be it mastering long division, writing haikus, or fielding ground balls, they can achieve whatever they dedicate themselves to. Their[217] academic confidence will powerfully translate to the challenges they face outside of the classroom, and that fierceness is the greatest thing I can pass on this year.[218]

After a difficult lesson, or day, or week in the classroom, I remember that teary-eyed me practicing well after dark. And I keep on pitching.

---

breaks up the narrative flow. What if instead, Daavi told the story in a way that naturally clarified how he would whip baseballs at a spring-loaded target that bounced them back with the equal intensity.

215   This detail provides some comic relief and self-deprecation.
216   Solid wrap up sentence to this paragraph. Expands, rather than reiterates.
217   Daavi skillfully transitions from an essay about him to one about his broader community.
218   From Daavi: Reading this essay now, it feels a bit melodramatic - I probably could have toned down the emotions 20-30% and the essay would have been stronger.

400 Word Extracurricular Supplement

Flirting with Failure

My sweaty hands shook, slowly giving in to the cord's tug on the receiver. I placed the phone back on the dock and dropped my head. It was not my first rejection, but it still stung.

I picked up the phone again, worried about what the next call would bring, and dialed the next number.

"Hi, I'm calling on behalf of the Jeff Ross campaign for Boston City Councilor..."

Click.

Jeff Ross was a fantastic candidate, but my calls rarely endorsed him successfully, usually ending with a hurried excuse, grumbled reprimand, or as above, the hollow ring of a dial tone. In a room full of other callers constantly making connections with voters, I felt alone with my failures. *What did all the other callers do that I did not?*

"They flirted their butts off," my supervisor Jesse explained. "You've got 10 seconds to make voters like you enough to listen. Butter 'em up, become their best friend: if they like you, they'll listen."

Occasionally, I would put down the phone and listen in on other calls. I noticed that the calls often left the subject of the upcoming election, and were reminiscent of conversations between friends. I realized that the key to a successful call wasn't speaking assertively, or making Ross out to be perfect, but forming a temporary connection with the voter. It was, in effect, flirting.

Flirting over the phone required confidence. It was difficult befriending strangers, and for many weeks, I anxiously awaited 8 p.m., when I would be cast away to pick up pizza for the office.[219] But over time, calling became easier. I talked sports, laughed at bad jokes, and remained friendly in the face

---

219   Candid acknowledgement of imperfection.

of protests for interrupting the sanctity of suppertime. Flirting bought me the window I needed to pitch my candidate.

On Election Day, without the comfort or separation of a telephone, I worked a local polling station for fourteen hours, and flirted without reservation. Although Jeff did not win a seat, I developed a tremendous set of skills that pertain to all I do. My ability to communicate[220] aids me as an advocate for social justice.[221] The confidence I developed helped me as an athlete. And my newfound spontaneity makes it easier for me to form connections[222] with the children whom I teach and mentor—connections that last far longer than a 30 second phone call.

MY TAKE (A WORD FROM YOUR FRIENDLY EDITOR):

Dr. Daavi has come in for a second opinion, so here I am. By way of brief introduction, my name is Jack Jundanian and I know Daavi as my silent roommate during a ten-day Vipassana meditation retreat. After sparks flew in quietude, Daavi and I have stayed in touch and I've quickly become a big fan of the work he's doing to help young adults come into themselves with some of the grace we may have lacked in the early days of our journeys. As a result, Daavi has brought me on to help edit *The Kids Who Get In*, including this analysis of his own application. And though Daavi and I are close, don't worry--the 4,334 miles of social distancing currently between us in Nashville and Oahu will keep me honest in my praise and critique.

In Daavi's Common App essay, pitching becomes a powerful metaphor for

---

220   "Communication skills" often come across of the softest and least compelling offering that someone brings to an organization. However, Daavi's nuanced likening of selling to flirting shows an insightful new angle and makes me think he is actually on to something.

221   The social justice addendum seems a bit underdeveloped. Tossing in this kind of buzzword when it isn't a core part of your application opens the risk of coming across as disingenuous.

222   As opposed to the social justice claim, this is concrete and compelling, and in line with the application as a whole.

rising above one's circumstances through hard work and determination. While claiming possession over these traits directly might be a bit too on the nose, Daavi is able to lay claim to them while maintaining humility and genuineness. This essay is most memorable for its stringing together of two seemingly disparate experiences: practicing baseball and growing up without a father. This structure equips Daavi to impress readers by demonstrating how a series of experiences has formed who he is and what he cares about. He comes across as tenacious, sensitive, and community oriented. He infuses a sense of intrigue by dropping us into the story in medias res, then quickly opens the scope to demonstrate how this experience proved formative in his development. The essay is refreshing in that it does not draw on lofty sounding "resume builder" experiences in order to demonstrate passion and potential. Rather, Daavi demonstrates that even regular experiences are an opportunity for hard work, introspection, and service to others.

If the takeaway traits from Daavi's Common App essay are resilience and selflessness, he rounds out his profile in the supplement by self-describing as a savvy socializer and salesperson. Much of the same mechanics that work well in the Common App essay are employed again here. Again, Daavi merges two otherwise disparate concepts into a unified narrative--this time, it's campaigning and flirting. He also opens this story in the middle of a moment of despair, and from there relies on self awareness, humor, and self deprecation to convince the reader why this experience matters and why it makes him matter. Though the ending came a bit abruptly and painted in somewhat broad strokes, he came up 4 words short of the word limit, and there's no particular area within this essay that I would cut down.

I was surprised to see scant mention of Daavi's academic or quantitative accolades. That said, his standardized test scores and grades largely speak for themselves, so developing his personality as much as possible was likely the best use of space for these applications.

Daavi in a sentence: Interpersonally curious and adept, confident yet humble athlete, selfless community server

Washington University in St. Louis

LEWIS RENNICK

APPLICATION:

Major I applied under / School I applied to: Olin Business School

Ethnicity: White

Gender: Male

Family Income Bracket: 250,000-500,000/year

Year of College Graduation: 2023

High School Unweighted GPA (to nearest hundredth): 94.0

High School Weighted GPA: 96.5

Class Rank/Percentile: N/A

SAT I Score (By Section): N/A

ACT Score (By Section): 34 Math, 34 Science, 34 Reading, 34 Writing (34 Composite)

SAT Subject Test Scores: N/A

AP Test Results:

4: Computer Science Principles, English Language, Statistics,

3: AB Calculus, Computer Science A, US History, English Literature

Senior Year Course Load: AP AB Calculus, AP Computer Science Principles, APUSH, AP Statistics, AP English Language, Microeconomics (1st semester), Microeconomics (2nd semester)

Awards Won in High School: National Honors Society, AP Scholar, Honor Roll

Extracurriculars in High School (Put leadership in parentheses): Varsity Basketball (Captain Junior and Senior years)

Job/Work Experience in High School: Part time job at Cyclebar East Cobb, started power washing business

Volunteer/Community Service: N/A

What did you do in the summer after freshman year of high school?

I worked as a counselor in training (CIT) at YMCA Camp Thunderbird. I spent 4 weeks there, and then spent the rest of the summer playing travel basketball.

What did you do in the summer after sophomore year?

Played travel basketball for the during May and early June, but then underwent shoulder surgery in mid June which sidelined me for most of the summer. Spent most of my time at home watching TV and doing some ACT practice work.

What did you do in the summer after junior year?

I had another shoulder surgery early in the summer which again kept me sidelined most of the summer. Spent time watching TV and spending time with friends most of the summer and towards the end of it I started to work on college apps.

ABOUT YOUR COLLEGE:

State of High School: Georgia

School Type (i.e. rural, suburban, city, public vs. private, etc): Private

# of Students in Graduating Class: 210

What was your high school like? Demographics? How many other students went to elite universities?

I went to a very elite, very competitive high school. While the student body was white by majority, there was still a lot of diversity. I believe we sent over 30 students to Ivies this past year. I would argue that it is the best school in the Southeast and possibly the whole country.

REFLECTION ON APPLICATION PROCESS:

I applied: Regular Decision

What do you think your hooks were?

I think my college essay was a strong point for me. It is an experience that is really unique which I think sets me apart from others. Because I had a pretty average/below average GPA for the schools I was applying for, I worked extremely hard on my essays in order to stand out.

What do you think the strengths of your application were?

As mentioned before, I think my essays were very strong. However I still stand by that the only reason I got into WashU was due to my relentless demonstrated interest. After I got waitlisted, I was constantly sending updates to the admissions team here and letting them know that this is the place that I wanted to be. I went to every event that they hosted in Atlanta and made sure I was engaged and asking questions.

What do you think the weaknesses of your application were? Where might other applicants have had an advantage over you?

I had little to no extracurriculars, which is probably one of my biggest regrets from high school. I was so one dimensional with basketball, and I always thought that if I just got all As then that would be good enough. But there were other kids that had better grades with more extracurriculars and I would say that had a huge leg up on me.

Where else you were admitted:

University of Georgia (UGA)

Where you were waitlisted:

Georgia Tech

Where you were rejected:

MIT, Emory, UChicago, Johns Hopkins

Did you get a private college counselor?

Yes

When did you start preparing for college admissions? How did your family prepare?

Around the start of senior year. My family didn't do much to prepare me, it was mostly myself and my designated college counselor that my school provided.

ABOUT YOUR COLLEGE:

Why did you choose this school?

This place is amazing. The school is prestigious, everyone here is so collaborative, and the campus is absolutely beautiful.

What is your school known for? What is its reputation?

I think our school is known for being prestigious, but not impossible like the rep UChicago and MIT get. It's a really great place and I think the Olin Business School especially has an esteemed reputation.

Is this reputation accurate?

I believe so. The school is definitely manageable and invites students to get involved in activities they are interested in.

What are you involved with on campus?

I work Athletic Events, I am the manager for the Women's Basketball Team, I am a member of the eSports club, and I am on the club spikeball team.

What do you think your school offers that no other top 20 school does?

A wide array of options. There is literally a club for everyone here, and even if there isn't, it only takes you and 7 of your friends to start a new club.

What kinds of people do you think would love your school?

People who are open-minded, collaborative, and hard working.

What kinds of people do you think would hate your school?

Super competitive people who like to keep to themselves. A lot of classes (especially in the business school) require you to work in groups for most assignments in order to teach you how to work in teams.

Do you like your school? Why or why not?

I love this school. It is the perfect amount of school work, social life, and time to yourself that really allows me to be the best version of myself.

Your college's biggest strengths. What do students appreciate about their school/take for granted?

I think the biggest strength here is the wealth of resources for students to take advantage of. We have access to so many counselors and all of our professors are easily reachable which allows us to really push ourselves and get whatever kind of assistance we require.

Your college's biggest weaknesses. What do students complain about the most? What would an admissions counselor never tell you?

Some people complain about the change of teaching styles that you experience from high school. For example, my computer science class this semester was almost entirely run by TAs and we rarely saw our professors. A lot of people didn't like losing the lecture style class structure from high school.

ESSAYS:

I awake to the sound of my 70-year-old grandfather singing Psalm 118:24 as he strolls through the "boys bunkroom" to ensure that my cousins and I crawl out of bed. Papa pulls back the curtains, flooding[223] the room with sunlight. The words, "This is the day that the Lord has made, let us rejoice and be glad in it", echo off the walls of the basement as Papa leaves our room to go check on the girls. I throw on the crumpled-up t-shirt on the ground next to me and head upstairs, elated to find Mimi's famous French toast waiting there for me.[224]

Mornings like this have become a fundamental part of my summer for the past 14 years. At four years old, I was "inducted" into Mimi and Papa's Cousins Camp: one week, 19 of my cousins, no parents, my wise, ex-Navy grandfather, and the masterful chef and seamstress that is my grandmother[225]. Whether it was constructing a swinging bench by hand, learning the basics of cross stitching, or hiking outside, my grandparents have used this week to show our rag-tag band of cousins the significance of life skills, the power of faith, and, most importantly, the need for family. This past summer marked the 23rd annual Cousins Camp, a tradition that has molded me into a man that can sew and crochet as good as he can hammer and saw.[226]

---

223   Great word choice.
224   This hook is fantastic. We're given access to a unique, special moment in Lewis' life - and of course, we're curious what significance this sunny, fun moment has for him. Lewis hits the senses of taste, sight, and sound in succession which help bring this moment to life.
225   How about that for succinct and memorable character introductions!
226   This contrast is awesome.

In 2004, I attended my very first Cousins Camp. There, I underwent the same initiation as those before me had: my grandfather gave me a toolbox, a spirit animal, and a bible verse to memorize. My toolbox would eventually contain everything from a tire gauge to a power saw and has proven to come in handy more times than one, however; to this day, what I value most is the coupling of my animal, a bear, and my bible verse, Philippians 1:28. This passage reminds me to never be afraid of my enemies and to always be courageous, just like a bear. No matter where I am or what I am doing in life, that notion has been branded in my mind, a constant, guiding light in all I do. I could be guarding a 6'11, 260lb big man from my rival high school or studying all night for a math test that I need to get a good grade on.[227] No matter the challenge, I will not back down.

And I certainly don't back down from the crafts Mimi has in store each year. These activities have become life-long skills of mine that I will forever be thankful for. Thanks to Mimi's sewing lessons, the nasty tear in my picture day slacks was sewn up in 10 minutes flat. The birthday request in my household is Lewis' famous pineapple upside down cake (that Mimi gave me the recipe to). You need any help refurbishing old furniture and staging a house with it? I'm your man. My grandmother has opened my eyes to a world that most guys my age scoff at, yet the skills that she possesses is something I would never make light of. Through Mimi's household tasks and working in the workshop with Papa, both of my grandparents have demonstrated to me that through common sense, hard work, and unfaltering determination, anything is possible.[228]

As I begin my final year of high school, I look back on myself at age 4 in the backseat of our 1999 Chevy Suburban, eagerly off to experience the wonders of Cousins Camp. With all the ups and downs that the following 14 years

---

227   Lewis takes this paragraph to highlight the lessons learned from his grandfather, and how he applies them in his life. I love the last line because it shows just how integrated this toughness is in his life - he leans on it in situations as divergent as a Varsity basketball game and a math test.

228   Lewis mirrors the previous paragraph and focuses here on what his grandmother taught him. In a subtle way, he creates contrast and shows us the roots of two sides of his identity. He wraps up this second paragraph nicely with an overall summary of what his grandparents taught him.

brought me, knowing that I always had a place to go home to has given me a strength and maturity most people never find:[229] through Cousins Camp I am proud to say that I truly do possess the resilience of my grandfather, the work ethic of my grandmother and the fighting spirit of a bear.[230]

MY TAKE:

Lewis checks the academic boxes, has a couple extracurricular activities, and one of the most memorable application essays I've read. That, combined with some tenacity, earned Lewis a waitlist acceptance at Washington University in St. Louis.

By his own admission, Lewis' extracurricular involvement isn't extraordinary. He was a captain of a sport and good enough at it to be recruited at the Division 3 level, and started his own business senior year powerwashing people's homes. Neither of these activities are unique or life-changing, but they fit well into the picture that Lewis crafts as an industrious, hard-nosed kid.

The biggest strength of Lewis' application is his essay - and let's take a closer look why: Firstly, Lewis' story is unique - not many kids go to a week-long 'Cousins Camp' run by their ex-Navy grandfather and seamstress grandmother. In crafting a college admissions essay, it's important to think about ways to set yourself apart - not everyone has a unique family tradition or core life experience they can touch upon, but Lewis did, and he told his story beautifully.

Secondly, Lewis uses powerful *specific* details to bring his story to life. Little things like "Philippians 1:28," "1999 Chevy Suburban," "23rd annual Cousins Camp," make his essay seem real. Lewis brings us into the world of

---

229   This leans a *little* braggadocious, but it works within the context of an experience like this. It comes across as a genuine recognition of how valuable and rare places like his Cousins Camp are, rather than an implication that he's better than anyone else because of it.

230   Lewis concludes the piece perfectly. He touches on his growth since his first Cousins Camp, summarizes the main things he took from this unique experience, and ends revisiting a couple specifics. Well done.

the camp, and we can't help but feel the energy of that bustling bunk room full of cousins.

Thirdly, Lewis does a great job of connecting this unique experience with the life lessons that it imparted in him. Closing a paragraph with a sentence like "Through Mimi's household tasks and working in the workshop with Papa, both of my grandparents have demonstrated to me that through common sense, hard work, and unfaltering determination, anything is possible" gives admissions officers exactly what they need - and Lewis takes the crucial step beyond talking about a unique experience, and explaining how it shaped him.

Lewis wraps his self-reflection up with a bow and ribbon by showing how he applies these lessons in his life: "I could be guarding a 6'11, 260lb big man from my rival high school or studying all night for a math test that I need to get a good grade on. No matter the challenge, I will not back down."[231]

Incidentally, Lewis' continued demonstrated interest (no small thing at a perennial Ivy-league backup school like WashU) showcased the traits evidenced in his application and essay - persistence and a strong work ethic. Admissions officers saw a kid who started his own power-washing business, who captained two basketball teams, who spent his childhood summers building furniture and sewing, and who attended every WashU event in his city and relentlessly updated the admissions office after being waitlisted - who wouldn't root for a kid like that? Lewis earned a spot in the Washington University first-year class, and we have no doubt he's making the most of it.

Lewis in a sentence: Tenacious "Cousins Camp" alum.

---

231 If you know what you plan on studying in college, this kind of reflection is a great chance to connect your life to that (Example: The tenacity and persistence that Cousin Camp instilled in me will translate powerfully to my career as a teacher in underserved communities).

Yale University

EDWARD ASARE

APPLICATION.

Major I applied under / School I applied to: Biomedical Engineering

Ethnicity: Ghanaian

Gender: Male

Family Income Bracket: Under 20,000/year

Year of College Graduation: 2020

SAT I Score (By Section): 660 Reading, 690 Math, 730 Writing (2080 Total)

ACT Score (By Section): N/A

SAT Subject Test Scores: 800 Chemistry, 760 Math II

High School Unweighted GPA (to nearest hundredth): 4.0

High School Weighted GPA: 4.0

Class Rank/Percentile: Valedictorian

AP Test Results: Didn't have APs

IB Test Results: Didn't take the IBs

Senior Year Course Load: Calculus I & II, Organic Chemistry, Physics with Calculus, Advanced Writing, Biology

Awards Won in High School: Best Student in Biology (Thrice- Freshman, Sophomore, Senior) (Public high schools in Ghana is only 3 years long). Winner of the National Science and Math Quiz Competition. 3rd Overall best student in Ghana in the West African Senior High School Exam. 3rd Overall Best Student in West Africa in the West African Senior High School Exam

Extracurriculars in High School (Put leadership in parentheses): Science Club (Secretary, Senior Year) Science Quiz Team (President, Senior Year), Entrepreneurship Club Member

Job/Work Experience in High School: N/A

Volunteer/Community Service: Volunteered on service trips to small towns and villages around my school almost every break- helping the kids with their school work and fund-raising

What did you do in the summer after freshman year of high school?

Private tutoring other students

What did you do in the summer after sophomore year?

Didn't do much that summer

What did you do in the summer after junior year?

We only had two summers in high school.

ABOUT YOUR HIGH SCHOOL:

State of High School: Central Region, Ghana

School Type (i.e. rural, suburban, city, public vs. private, etc): Public, government-run

# of Students in Graduating Class: ~500

What was your high school like? Demographics? How many other students went to elite universities?

My school would be considered an elite public school because it is one of the very first high schools in Ghana. Majority of the kids came from wealthy backgrounds.

A little background about high schools in Ghana - there are tier 1 to tier 3 public schools and then there are international schools (expensive private schools which have IB, A-levels etc) so my school would be considered elite in the public school setting but not ranked as high compared to the international schools. Most of the kids went on to the University of Ghana. A couple went to school in the US - MIT, Columbia, Duke, Vanderbilt

REFLECTION ON APPLICATION PROCESS:

I applied: Regular Decision

What do you think your hooks were?

I think the hook was probably my academics, the award I won in the West African Senior High School exam.

What do you think the strengths of your application were?

I think I had really strong letters of recommendations from my teachers which I believe were helpful because they were not very familiar with the process of applying to colleges in the US, I had to emphasize the importance of the letters and thus they wrote glowing letters for me. My high school grades were also quite impressive. I think although I was quite nerdy in high school, I tried to shed off the nerdy vibe and come across as a chill person in the application.

What do you think the weaknesses of your application were? Where might other applicants have had an advantage over you?

Other applicants probably had AP scores, IB scores which I didn't have because they were not offered in my school. I bet they had other strong extracurricular activities - lab research experience, maybe a publication or winning an Olympiad.

Where else you were admitted:

NYU

Where you were waitlisted:

Columbia

Where you were rejected:

Harvard, Duke, Vanderbilt, Penn, there's probably more

Did you get a private college counselor?

No

When did you start preparing for college admissions? How did your family prepare?

I started after I was done with high school, so essentially I took a gap year after high school preparing for the college admissions. That was when I took the SAT, Subject tests and got my letters of recommendation. My family wasn't very familiar with the process but were generally very supportive and willing to help or seek help from other people they knew who may have attended college in the US.

ABOUT YOUR COLLEGE:

Why did you choose this school?

I chose Yale because I was accepted to only Yale and NYU and Yale seemed to be the obvious choice because NYU didn't want to give me enough financial aid. But that aside, I loved the general vibe of the school - small class sizes and a strong sense of community. A friend from my high school was a junior at Yale so he easily convinced me to come because he really loved it here and I do too.

What is your school known for? What is its reputation?

Yale is known for its liberal arts approach - that's the main selling point as well as the residential college system. There are also many SCOTUS judges from Yale, numerous Nobel laureates, world-class professors, presidents, politicians, wealthy alums, huge endowment and great financial aid, secret societies etc. Yale is also known for its research and strong economics program and being excellent in the hard sciences (physics, chemistry, bio).

Is this reputation accurate?

I'd say it's pretty accurate. I love that I can take many different classes outside my major and also have to complete a language requirement which seems burdensome but enjoyable. Most of the students I have met are super friendly and chill, although everyone is competitive you don't feel the cut-throat competition that exists in other schools.

What are you involved with on campus?

Yale African Students Association, Biomedical Engineering Society, Lab research and the Young Achievers Foundation

What do you think your school offers that no other top 20 school does?

A very supportive and caring environment. I'm pretty sure most top 20 schools have good aid, great professors etc, but the warmth of the administration and the support they give the students is overwhelming. I feel the professors genuinely want you to succeed and are very supportive and generally very flexible. Most try to learn your names and know you as a person, not only a random student taking their class. The residential college system is also unparalleled.

What kinds of people do you think would love your school?

Students who would want to challenge themselves academically, legacies etc. Students looking for a rigorous yet enriching college curriculum plus the perks of an Ivy League connection etc. I'd say students who love community would like Yale very much, same goes for students who are very into the humanities.

THE KIDS WHO GET IN

What kinds of people do you think would hate your school?

Sometimes the pressure is intense- to get a high paying finance internship, work in consulting with BCG, McKinsey etc. because that's what most students end up doing. I'd say some students hate the weather because it gets pretty cold up here. Students who probably wouldn't want to work hard won't love it here because you have no other choice - classes are hard, everyone is smart so you have to work hard even if you were a valedictorian or something in high school.

Do you like your school? Why or why not?

I absolutely love Yale and was glad I didn't have to make a tough decision choosing between Yale and other schools. The professors are incredible and generally the best part is the strong sense of community. Yale is also very generous to low-income students in terms of financial aid so that's a huge plus. Lots of funding for study abroad programs etc.

Your college's biggest strengths. What do students appreciate about their school/take for granted?

Most students love the generous financial aid package and fellowships, funding etc. The sense of community that exists here. The opportunity to have lunch with deans, even the president sometimes. Plus there's a ton of academic and social support - first year counsellors, peer liaisons, big sibs, a lot of such support.

You can also study abroad and Yale would pay for it! And also if you're premed it's a top choice.

Your college's biggest weaknesses. What do students complain about the most? What would an admissions counselor never tell you?

I'd say it's probably mental health - sometimes people have breakdowns because the workload is quite heavy. Also since everyone is very smart, you don't wanna feel like that one student who is failing or doesn't understand something in class, so there's this pressure to keep these 'fake persona'. Another way to put it is to fake it till you make it. Some professors also suck - very inconsiderate with rigid grading policies. STEM at Yale isn't as good as maybe Harvard or MIT, but then again, Yale is not really known for being a powerhouse in STEM.

ESSAYS:

Common App Essay:

From childhood, I had always dreamed not only to don the much adored crimson and black colours of my high school, but also to sit on the grand stage of the National Science and Math Quiz, as a contestant. The National Science and Math Quiz, a highly anticipated annual quiz festival is organized for the crème de la crème of high schools in Ghana and aired on national TV.[232]

Getting into my school was a highlight of my life, and having been chosen to participate in an Interclass Quiz Competition seemed to be a reverie. But it was reality, and what more, I was the brainbox![233]

The Interclass Quiz was an integral part of the selection process for the ultimate pair to represent (Name redacted) School in the National Quiz. My class, Science One came up against Science Two in the final after trashing four other classes in the preliminary stages. As a contestant I could feel the pressure mounting as it had been the tradition for Science One to win. Nevertheless, in my mind's eye I could picture my team lifting the trophy up high, brimming with smiles for the cameras.

The quiz had just entered its last round and tied at 41 points apiece. The whole of the assembly hall was electric with an atmosphere of excitement.[234] The previous rounds had proven to be true tests not only of our academic prowess but also of our mental astuteness. There had to be a single champi-

---

232   Edward begins to build some excitement around the event. As you'll see in the rest of his writing, he leans towards the dramatic - which makes the app fun to read.

233   The Brainbox is the leader of the quiz team (I think!). A playful and genuine tone here allows him to brag about his accomplishments unpretentiously.

234   In this section, Edward leans towards telling and not showing. It works and fits his voice; in general I recommend describing what the atmosphere looks like vs. just saying it's full of excitement.

on, thus it called for a tie-breaking riddle. The team to ring the bell first and answer correctly would win the competition.

The quiz moderator proceeded to read out the clues. I could feel the rush of adrenaline through my body. "I'm a unit you obtain from the university", he read. Before any idea could flash through my mind, our opponents rang the bell with lightning speed and answered correctly-degree! The rapturous applause from the cheering audience was deafening. I felt my pulse suddenly vanish and my palms immediately became sweaty. We had broken tradition, we had lost!

Recounting the effort and toil put in the quiz, I felt so downhearted. With the help of my teacher who believed in me, I found my feet again. I took a cue from what Winston Churchill, the charismatic wartime leader of the Brits once said, "Success is not final, failure is not fatal: it is the courage to continue that counts." I was propelled on to work harder and eventually made the cut for my school's National Science and Math Quiz team.

The National Quiz was a much larger platform compared to the Interclass quiz. It was synonymous to being translated from a small puddle into Lake Victoria! Wow! Just the feeling of contesting for my school was overwhelming. After three preliminary contests we came up against St. Francis Xavier and GSTS, two giants in academia in Ghana in the final. It had been fifteen long years since my school won the National Science and Math Quiz and we were bent on ending this 'drought'. I was determined not to relive the experience of the Interclass quiz. Like Babe Ruth on the home run, we took an early lead in the first round and never looked back.[235] In the end, we won the quiz by a comfortable 14 point margin.

This came as a great achievement, but no surprise to me, because I had built my capacity to yield results even at the highest level. This did not only come from listening to the greatest motivational speakers or watching TED talks, but the inner drive that stemmed from a defeat I suffered in my early years of high school.

As Winston Churchill said "Success consists of going from failure to failure without loss of enthusiasm." No matter how tragic losing the quiz seemed, I

---

235   This is a big swing and a miss on the sports analogy, but there is something endearing about the attempt.

learned that failure, when dealt with properly, may become a stepping stone to much greater success.[236]

Yale Supplement: List your academic interests. Why do these areas appeal to you?

Engineering Sciences - Environmental, Electrical Engineering, Global Affairs

Globally, the issue of developing sustainable energy sources has been confronting mankind for years. With the advancements in science and the development of novel technologies, efficient energy sources must be created to meet demands. I am particularly interested in creating energy sources that would not adversely affect the environment. By studying Engineering sciences and majoring in Environment, I can develop systems that would harness energy from natural sources, possibly man himself, rather than the conventional crude oil and coal.[237] Since, energy crises have global repercussions, knowledge in Global Affairs would help me tackle issues on a global front.

Yale Supplement: Why Yale:

As an international student looking forward to experiencing the American liberal arts education, Yale is the best place to be. Yale's curriculum affords me the opportunity to learn from the arts and humanities together with my major in engineering. At Yale, I wouldn't have a skewed view of the world especially with the opportunities to study abroad and appreciate the cultural diversity. With students from diverse cultural and socio-economic backgrounds, Yale is an excellent opportunity to relate with and understand individuals from different cultural backgrounds. With all these said, what else would I want to be but a Yalie.[238]

Yale Quick Questions:

The two qualities I most admire in other people are honesty and genuineness

---

236   I like the double Churchill quote. Nice ending that conveys the larger lesson learned by Edward.
237   This idea is a little bit out there.
238   This a vague "Why Yale" essay - it fits with Edward's idyllic, broad-strokes style of writing, but he could do a better job of addressing specific things that Yale would offer. Study abroad and diversity are hallmarks of many colleges in America.

I am most proud of Being able to be of help to other people

I couldn't live without Having time off to relax and reminisce about life

Who or what inspires you? Nature-the peace and beauty nature offers inspires me

What do you wish you were better at being or doing? Being more outspoken and assertive

Most Yale freshmen live in suites of four to six students. What would you contribute to the dynamic of your suite? I would incorporate a sense of belonging as well as humor

Supplemental Essay:

Service to people has always been my passion. As such, in my second year in high school, I gladly took part in an outreach to a deprived community called Katakyiase. The outreach was scheduled for the Christmas break and though I was happy with the thought of putting smiles on people's faces, an inner confusion surged within me to either stay for the outreach or to rush home in preparation for the yuletide.[239] Upon second thought, I decided to stay.

Prior to the outreach, it was my duty to collect items for the trip. I had to move from dormitory to dormitory with my big empty bag collecting as many items as students were willing to donate. In the end, I was able to collect a lot of items like canned foods, old clothes, and numerous toys for which I was very proud.

Two days to Christmas in 2013, the journey to Katakyiase began. We crammed ourselves, into our jalopy, excited about the prospects of reaching out to people.[240] The 75-mile journey was tiring and the ride, very bumpy.

The community of Katakyiase gave 'deprived' a whole new meaning to me.

---

239   This sentence aptly invites us to partake in an inner turmoil that proved to be a defining experience in Edward's personal growth.

240   There's an errant comma in this sentence (and in plenty of the essays in this book, and probably in my writing as well). You don't need perfect grammar and schools aren't going to reject you over one or two small missteps.

The houses were built of mud and thatch, and the children freely roamed the streets in tatters, kicking empty tins in place of footballs.

Upon our arrival, the little children quickly gathered around our bus, peering through the windows of our dustbathed bus with expectancy written on their faces.[241] Since it was uncommon to see a bus in the village at that time of the year, they knew we had something to offer. As we alighted, we offered the children biscuits and toffees for which they seemed very content.

An elder of the community led us to our lodge quarters, which was to be our home for the next two days. After taking a stroll around the town and having a feel of the virgin aromas nature could offer, we retired to bed for the night. As part of the activity line-up, we shared the gospel with the village folk and taught the children basic arithmetic and English. It was quite a funny sight, as the little children whose front row teeth were evidently absent, struggled to make the sounds of the alphabets.

I found it particularly interesting how the old people could recollect so much about the legend surrounding the origin of the village. We climaxed our outreach with the donation of our items to the chief of the village for further distribution to the rest of the people.

The people of Katakyiase really loved the time we spent with them and it was sad for them to see us leave. I still remember the priceless smiles they wore throughout our two-day stay. What particularly struck me was the positive attitude of the people of Katakyiase amidst such poverty. Looking back, this experience left an indelible mark on me and made me rethink what the prerequisites for happiness in life really are.[242]

Engineering Essay:

Power outages or 'dumsor' as we call them are common in my part of the country. On one such occasion, our dimly-lit room turned pitch-black when the torchlight, our only light source then, went off because its batteries were dead. My inquisitive mind would just not allow me to sit quietly in the darkness, so I decided to open up the batteries to see what could possibly

241   What an image!
242   Like his first essay, a great conclusion that highlights the lesson learned. This is an inspiring essay that I touch more upon in the "My Take" section.

make them light a torch. I was bent on unravelling its secrets despite mum's numerous warnings to dispose of the batteries. To my utmost surprise, it contained only a black powdery substance and a rod. This triggered my fascination about the whole concept of energy.

I believe energy has always been the backbone of development. Ancient civilizations thrived on energy and as the fabric of energy was woven, numerous energy sources were born. It wasn't long before Alessandro Volta invented the voltaic pile and opened us up to a dynamic world of efficient energy. Soon, numerous energy sources were employed. The dry cell manipulated simple chemical reactions and yielded electrical energy, hydrostatic and thermal energy also surfaced in subsequent years, showing us that uncharted territories still existed in the world of energy. It is against this background that I dream of developing an efficient energy source that would be cheap, environment-friendly and readily harnessed.

Studying Engineering would be an excellent opportunity to do something extra. With technology advancing greatly, efficient power sources must be developed to power the technological 'dreams' of tomorrow. Yale's Engineering is undoubtedly one of the best in the world. With an unparalleled Faculty, a curriculum that supports research and comprehension rather than rote learning, and an emphasis on developing the fundamentals of engineering, Yale produces top-class engineers with broad knowledge in all engineering disciplines. The Science, Technology and Research Scholars (STARS) program provides undergraduates an opportunity to combine course-based study, research, mentorship, networking, and career planning in the fields of science and technology.

As a prospective engineer, with a keen interest in research, Yale's world-class labs and the Energy Studies Undergraduate Scholars Program would afford me the chance to bring theoretical concepts to life even as we crave for sustainable energy sources.

In pursuance of my interest in engineering, I have aided my cousin who is a Materials Engineer in completing his projects. I helped in the design of a system that stores and converts solar energy to be used to power homes. Also, during my time in my school, I helped the Robotics Team in the designing of a computational robot which eventually won the school awards.

My love story with batteries at age eight, coupled with the world-class engineering at Yale University, would spur me on to pioneer the power sources of tomorrow. Who knows? Maybe, Luigi Galvani theory of 'animal electricity' could be proven right and in the near future we may end up charging our gadgets with our bodies![243]

MY TAKE:

Edward comes across as one of the most idealistic, cheerful students of the applicants I've read. His academic background is strong - Edward clearly made the most of every academic opportunity available to him, sporting a 4.0 GPA and strong performance as a leader of the National Championship quiz team. His SAT score is low for a school like Yale, but coming from a low-income public school student in a developing nation justifies that. Edward's writing is highlighted by a sense of optimism and humor - a tone that was probably endearing to some admissions officers and off-putting to others.

His Common App essay is fun - it's written simply and linearly, without a lot of in-depth reflection, but it shows you the kind of kid that Edward is: a hardworking, nerdy, positive kid. Thinking of Edward competing on national television in Ghana is exciting and goofy. It makes you root for him. The tale centers around a simple lesson and a tip of the hat to his hero Churchill: Failure is often the path to success. This kind of optimism and resilience are traits that colleges value.

Edward's first supplement is a twist on an overplayed college essay trope: visiting an impoverished area, doing service, and coming back inspired. It's a cliché, but because Edward is writing it, it comes across as honorable and humbling. It's one thing to attend a private high school in Westchester or Beverly Hills and reflect upon gratitude and perspective after visiting a poor village in a developing country. It's another to come from a family making under $20,000 a year, living in a developing country, to dedicate your Christmas break to helping a local impoverished village and draw those same

---

[243] This is the second mention of this theory - it comes across as a little strange both times.

conclusions.

In his subsequent essays, Edward at times seems naive. This can feel idealistic - aspiring to develop a new energy source as an undergraduate engineering student is unlikely, but an Admissions Officer would probably appreciate the optimism. At other times it can be all but childlike - joking about providing electric current from our bodies jumped out as a strange way to end his last supplement.

Edward's innocence was probably endearing to some AO's and may have miffed others. That being said, being yourself can often be polarizing, and you may have to take risks and authentically express yourself to really win over one college, even if it means you might alienate another. Edward applied to a handful of the schools that we feature, and got rejected by most (Core principle - it's a crapshoot). That being said, you only need one yes, and Edward earned one from Yale.

Edward in a sentence: Goofy, grateful, ingenuous international student excited about life and studying energy.

Selected Reflections on the Application Process:

Besides the above questions, all of TKWGI were asked several questions on the application process. Their responses are here, sorted and selected for clarity and value.

What's your advice for high school seniors about the college process? What do you wish you knew about the college admissions process as a senior?

One thing I wish I knew about the college admissions process is, it is a crapshoot. It will surprise you which students get into top colleges and which do not and you can't take the ups and downs of the application process too hard on yourself - Jake, Brown

Although it is very helpful to make detailed plans about your top choice schools, the actual experience of attending that school and the ways it's going to challenge your self-perception and make it so that you can't really trust your own plans. The college you would've thought was perfect for you could just as easily be the worst fit possible, and vice versa. - Brielle, Columbia

The outcome of this process will not be the defining factor of your life, and if it is, you're living in the wrong way. - Love, Dartmouth

Start early. - Alex, Duke

I wish I could tell myself back then that as long as I ended up somewhere I was happy, it would all be okay. I think it can also be really easy to forget that there's a real person in the Admissions Office of any given school pulling for you! Though it may seem like this is the whole world right now, it's really going to be okay no matter what happens and how it goes. - Christiane, Harvard

Overall, be someone you want to be classmates with. It's so easy to fall into a toxic competitive mindset, but I'd really like to see people relax and focus on being a genuinely good person who helps others. You're joining a class in college, and you can't do everything alone! - Jade, MIT

Be honest and real in your applications. In the essay, make it about you, and don't spend too much time worrying about what the universities want; rather, write honestly about yourself and your experience, whatever that may be. - Felix, Northwestern

Start early and go hard. For every application you complete, lean really heavy into that school, remind yourself why you are applying to that school, picture yourself there, convince yourself it is the place you want to go to, and get really passionate about answering their questions and completing your supplements. For the next application, rinse and repeat.

Also, it feels really embarrassing to brag about all of your accomplishments, but this is not the time to hold back - play up your strengths, and if you feel like you sound obnoxious, ask someone to read over what you've written. There's definitely a way to talk about the things you're great at without coming off badly. Just be genuine - when you read something, you can tell the difference between someone who is writing something stiff that sounds impressive content-wise, and someone who is really proud of their talents and believes they're a great candidate and wants to share that with you. Explore the parts of yourself that you think are incredible and work on letting colleges know what those are. - Miranda, Princeton

The best way to tell the universities who you are is by writing it in your essay. Use this opportunity to make the reader truly understand where you come from, what you have learned, and what you'll be able to offer because of it. Your grades don't mean anything if your personality isn't in your application. Of course, your stats do matter and play a big role, but what matters even more is your ability to convince these universities that accepting you will make their school better both academically and socially. - Jessica, Rice

Although I don't at all regret applying early decision, I think anyone considering choosing to apply ED at a "dream school" should be convinced that they're ready to make the commitment. In the same way, just because a school is considered "elite" doesn't mean it's the right fit for you, so don't waste your time focusing on applications for places you aren't totally interested in. Admissions sees thousands of applications, so putting little focus and variety into applications for many schools will probably be less rewarding than providing well thought out responses on a select few applications. - Brian, U Chicago

If anywhere offers early action just do it. I waited to apply everywhere regular decision and waiting until March to hear about college was kind of nerve racking. Even if it is a school you aren't that interested in, having something in your back pocket is a huge sigh of relief. - Lewis, Wash U

What do you wish you had done differently?

I personally wish I had taken more time simply to enjoy the high school experience. It is not worth stressing about the college application process; you will almost certainly end up at a college that suits you. I also wish I had built up a better relationship with my high school teachers and counselors. - Jake, Brown

I wish I had been more disciplined during the application process. I had a lot of places I was applying, and sometimes I was a bit too scatterbrained about everything - I even ended up missing a few deadlines because of it, much to the dismay of my parents. I also wish I had spent more time researching scholarships because I didn't get to apply for as many of them as I would like. - Andrew, Cal Tech

I wish I was less concerned about the prestige attached to the name of the university. This is something that was inculcated into me from a very young age, and from both sides of my Chinese-Jewish heritage. It is something that caused me undue anxiety about a process that all comes down to a fairly random lottery. - Brielle, Columbia

I wish I had put less pressure on myself in getting into certain schools. I additionally wish I had not applied to schools that I am not personally interested in just because I felt like I should. Additionally, I wish I had been more open on writing about topics that I felt like were true to myself instead of letting people sway me into writing what sounds "right." - Talene, Cornell

I wish that I had listened to myself more and not leaned so heavily on my private college counselors or even my parents. The one application that I wrote without any guidance whatsoever (Dartmouth) was the one that ended up being successful! I wrote it without expecting much, just having fun with the prompt and being imaginative. I wish that I had this same approach for the rest of my essays, rather than being too strict with myself. - Love, Dartmouth

Though it's easy to say and harder to do, I wish I would have stressed less about everything. It was very much an emotional time for me, and I definitely was a little paralyzed by the fear of not getting into a top school, and wish I had just trusted the process a little more. - Christiane, Harvard

Spent less time on r/ApplyingToCollege, College Confidential, and other sites! My ChanceMe was bullshit and the neuroses of high-achieving anxious high schoolers is not a healthy environment. - Jade, MIT

Honestly, I don't know if I would have done anything differently. I know that isn't an interesting answer, but I feel like everything that I did was to get me exactly where I am today. I worked really hard and it paid off in the end. - Jessica, Rice

I did not give myself enough credit in high school. I wish I had more confidence in myself when applying to schools. - Shaun, Penn

Much of my touring was done while students were on breaks, since it best fit my schedule during junior year. I toured UChicago (and a few other midwestern schools) while no students were on campus, and I was astounded by the campus architecture and learning environment. I had no chance to engage with any students, and I think this detracted from my perspective of the social life. Also, I would have hugely benefited from more time spent reflecting on my personal preferences instead of being consumed by the allure of the elite college reputation. - Brian, U Chicago

From a college admissions perspective, nothing - things worked out incredibly for me. From a life perspective, I wish I started self-teaching computer science and writing in a nonacademic fashion in high school. A lot of things take a couple years to get good at, and I wish I started that process earlier! - Daavi, Vanderbilt

I wish I got more involved in groups I was interested in during high school. I could've become friends with a lot of cool people and learned a lot of new and interesting things if I simply took the time to show up to certain events. Lewis, Wash U

I think I should have ventured a bit outside my comfort zone in the choice of my extra-curricular activities. - Edward, Yale

How do you think that seniors should choose their college?

It is important to note that you will certainly change as a person while in college, and it is impossible to know what will be the best place for you four years down the line. So, don't overthink choosing the right college as things have a way of working themselves out. - Jake, Brown

If possible, try to get in contact with current college students to learn what their perspectives are. They'll be able to tell you about the social scene, the academics, and just the general campus feel. It's difficult to describe what makes a college feel like a "fit" for people, but if you have the resources to visit or get in contact with campus, you'll know the feeling. - Andrew, Cal Tech

High school seniors should choose their college based on price/financial implications, job/grad school/future prospects, overall fit, location, and how that school fits into their goals for undergrad.

Be honest with yourself about your preferences, and then see how they line up with more concrete measures such as job prospects and even prestige. In some cases, students may have to sacrifice fit for prestige and I don't judge anybody who has to make that choice. But when you are making that sacrifice, be honest with yourself about why you are making it, if it's necessary, and exactly how prepared you are for the ramifications of such a choice. - Love, Dartmouth

They should not just pick the best school possible. One thing that I've learned is that one should pick a school they can thrive at, not just the best possible school. I have a 3.4 ish at Duke but for what I want to do, law school, I could have gone to Miami, got a 4.0, done well on the LSAT, and still end up at the same law school I could have gotten into with a Duke degree. - Alex, Duke

The number one question I asked myself was can I see myself here: walking to class, making friends, doing whatever else? - Christiane, Harvard

For me, I prioritized culture foremost; if it was an environment I felt I could thrive in, I knew that I could shape my academic future to be successful. I've said that if MIT's student culture was at my state school and had none of the prestige, I would go there. - Jade, MIT

You absolutely need to choose your college based on fit. Take a stroll around campus; eat in the dining hall; go to a party. See what student life is actually like. - John, Notre Dame

Do your research on your options - watch YouTube videos, reach out to old high school alums or your friends' siblings, ask around to get to know the school in a truthful way and consider if it's a place you would like to be. - Miranda, Princeton

It's tempting to want to get to an Ivy League just because of its label, but you HAVE to put aside that urge and look deeply at each school for not just its academics, but also its social scene, its environment, and what they have that can offer you something you know will suit you. - Jessica, Rice

Choose a college that fits your needs, even if that means you have to do a bit of introspection to find out what your needs are. That is, figure out what's important to you (weather, neighborhood, urban/not urban, demography, etc.) and then find schools that match partially or totally with what you're looking for. Your needs and interests will change massively but honestly, going into college is a HUGE change and feeling safe (esp. for students of marginalized backgrounds and identities) is HUGE! Also, it's about what YOU want, not your parents! - Bernie, Stanford

I think you should choose based on (not in any particular order):

1. Whether or not your school offers a degree in what you want to study/in the areas you are interested if you don't know yet

2. Location, make sure you go somewhere where you don't mind the weather because honestly it can really affect your mental health

3. Size, make sure you pick a school that isn't too big or too small for you. If you are easily overwhelmed, go to a smaller school. If you want to branch out, go for a bigger school.

4. Look at the percentage of kids who actually graduate from that school out of those who enroll as freshmen. That gives you a good idea of whether or not people like the school/its difficulty level. - Danai, UCLA

It's pretty difficult to gauge fit especially because fit is dependent on so many factors besides just the school you go to - you might be a perfect "fit" at Duke, but if you show up and don't get along with your roommate or hallmates and have a tough first semester, you might hate it. Alternatively, you might go to a school that isn't a great fit on paper, but gel really well with your first-year floor and meet someone you start a business with, or marry.

With that being said - at the extremes, fit matters; if you have dyed hair, like having late-night conversations about philosophy, and are a hardcore leftist/activist, you'd probably prefer Brown or a small liberal arts college in the Northeast to Vandy[244], and if you're dead set on joining greek life or partying your ass off, you might like UCLA or Penn more than U Chicago. But for the 90% of kids that are in between those poles, you'll be able to succeed and find your people at any school, with the right attitude. - Daavi, Vanderbilt

Understanding your own habits and passions, whether they're academic, interpersonal, or hobbies, is crucial in recognizing the schools that best suit you. Also, college brochures are meant to bring in applicants, so visiting schools and asking questions of students is an integral part of seeing through any perceived grandeur. - Brian, U Chicago

Pick a school that has the social vibe you'd enjoy. - Madison, Vanderbilt

---

[244] Not to say those students don't/can't thrive at Vandy, they're just in much smaller numbers

Afterword

It is a lot easier to give advice than it is to take it.

Right now it's October of my last year of college, and I'm applying to jobs, studying for midterms, and putting the finishing touches on this book. And after writing and compiling hundreds of pages on detachment and outcome independence in uncertain processes, there are often moments when I am not detached.

It's easy to worry - about how I'll be perceived in a job interview, about how many copies my book will sell, about how well I'll do in my classes. But only so much of these processes is under my control.

In orienting my life after college, I think about my 17 and 18 year old self, sending out applications, curious and open to whatever the world would throw back at me. I had schools I was more excited about than others, but more than anything, I was excited for the unknown.

Now, in planning for my life after college, rigidity and worry can sap a lot of that excitement. Feeling like I have to make up for lost time or land the most prestigious opportunity makes me lose sight of the fact that my twenties and my life are going to be pretty awesome either way.

And so, in preparing for interviews and in throwing this creation out into the world, I remind myself of that happy, healthy mentality - of doing my best, and being cool with whatever comes of it.

Every chapter of our lives comes with it's own college process; applying to jobs, choosing a partner, trying to start a business, creating any kind of change in the world. And in all of these processes, all we can control is showing up as our authentic selves.

Right now, you've got the first of these many processes in front of you. I hope this book has prepared you well to tell your story effectively, to live high school in a way that is true to you, and to be happy and successful wherever you wind up for college.

Good luck.

Studies in Law and Politics

David A. Schultz
General Editor

Vol. 2

PETER LANG
New York • Washington, D.C./Baltimore • Boston
Bern • Frankfurt am Main • Berlin • Vienna • Paris

Along Racial Lines

David Michael Hudson

Along Racial Lines

Consequences of the 1965 Voting Rights Act

PETER LANG
New York • Washington, D.C./Baltimore • Boston
Bern • Frankfurt am Main • Berlin • Vienna • Paris

Library of Congress Cataloging-in-Publication Data

Hudson, David M.
Along racial lines: consequences of the 1965 Voting Rights Act /
David Michael Hudson.
p. m. — (Studies in law and politics; vol. 2)
Includes bibliographical references and index.
1. Minorities—Suffrage—United States—History. 2. Election law—
United States—History. 3. Election districts—United States—History.
4. Elections—Texas—Dallas. 5. Elections—Florida—Dade County. 6. Elections—
Arizona. I. Title. II. Series: Studies in law and politics (New York, N.Y.); vol. 2.
KF4891.H83   342.73'072—dc21   97-35696
ISBN 0-8204-3922-3
ISSN 1083-3366

Die Deutsche Bibliothek-CIP-Einheitsaufnahme

Hudson, David Michael:
Along racial lines: consequences of the 1965 voting rights act /
David Michael Hudson. –New York; Washington, D.C./Baltimore;
Boston; Bern; Frankfurt am Main; Berlin; Vienna; Paris: Lang.
(Studies in law and politics; Vol. 2)
ISBN 0-8204-3922-3

The paper in this book meets the guidelines for permanence and durability
of the Committee on Production Guidelines for Book Longevity
of the Council of Library Resources.

© 1998 Peter Lang Publishing, Inc., New York

All rights reserved.
Reprint or reproduction, even partially, in all forms such as microfilm,
xerography, microfiche, microcard, and offset strictly prohibited.

Printed in the United States of America.

With thanks to Leslie, Ben, and Hannah

who gave me the time I needed.

TABLE OF CONTENTS

List of Figures x
Introduction..1
Chapter 1: Voting Rights—The Issues...5
    Barriers to Registering and Voting..5
    Ability to Influence Elections 6
    Seeking a Candidate 7
    A History of Impediments 7
Chapter 2: Voting Rights and The Constitution..9
    Voting Rights in 18th-Century America...10
    Electing a President 11
    Electing Congress...11
    Rights Guaranteed to All 12
Chapter 3: History...15
    The Rise and Fall of Reconstruction 15
    The Courts Join In 19
    Added Legislation 21
    Dallas, Texas: a Blend of South and West 22
    Navajo Reservation: Dinétah...33
    Dade County, Florida: America's Youngest Metroplex..........................46
Chapter 4: Voting Rights Act of 1965...53
    Preparing for Legislation 53
    The Act 55
    The Arguments in Favor of the 1965 Act 59
    The Arguments Against the Voting Rights Act of 1965 62
    Results of the Initial Legislation 65
        Early Results and Challenges..65
        A Growing Government 70
        Early District Debates 72
    Dallas: Minority Progress and Pressure 73
    Navajo Reservation: Legislative Recalcitrance 75
    Dade County: Breeding Ground for Unrest...80
Chapter 5: The Amendments of 1970 81
    The Arguments in Favor of the 1970 Amendments 84
    The Arguments Against the 1970 Amendments 84
    Results of the Act After the Amendments of 1970 86
        Nixon's Dilemma 86
        Continued Expansion..87
        The Rise of Hispanic Rights 92
        The Start of Affirmative Action 93
    Dallas: The First Round of Litigation..96

    Navajo Reservation: The Beginnings of Franchise 101
    Dade County: Continued Cuban Growth... 107
Chapter 6: The Amendments of 1975 109
    The Arguments in Favor of the 1975 Amendments 111
    A Shot at Texas... 113
    The Arguments Against the 1975 Amendments 114
    Results of the Act After the 1975 Amendments 116
        Retrogression 116
        Growing Power of Preclearance 118
        Drawing District Lines 119
        Bail Out... 122
        Intent v. Effect.. 122
        Progress 124
    Dallas: At-large Districts and District Lines.. 125
    Navajo Reservation: The Rights of Indians 131
    Dade County: Fires and Flotillas... 132
Chapter 7: The Amendments of 1982 137
    The Arguments in Favor of the 1982 Amendments 141
    The Arguments Against the 1982 Amendments 143
    Results of the Act After the 1982 Amendments 145
        Affirmative Action—Looking for Results 145
        Court Drawn Plans 151
        Safe Districts... 151
        Other Developments... 154
        Changing Demographics.. 156
    Voting Rights Language Assistance Act of 1992 157
    Motor Voter Bill... 159
    Dallas: From White Control to Black Mayor 162
    Other Events Affecting Dallas Voters 180
    Navajo County: Enfranchised but Impoverished 186
    Dade County: Hispanicazation... 195
Chapter 8: The Unraveling?.. 211
Chapter 9: Conclusions... 221
    Immeasurable Goals are Unreachable Goals....................................... 221
    Social Redistribution: The Fallacy of Hispanic Needs........................ 222
    Racial Contention From "Fair Districts" 224
    U. S. Indian Policy 225
    The Future.. 227
        The Merits of Alternative Voting Systems 227
        Future Demographics 230

Table of Contents

The Solution	231
References	235
Case References	239
Notes	243
Index	269

LIST OF FIGURES

Figure 1: Blacks, in Former Confederate States, Elected to State and
    Federal Legislatures 17
Figure 2: Arizona County Map 45
Figure 3: Areas Affected by the Automatic Trigger (1965) 56
Figure 4: Registered Voters - 1968 69
Figure 5: Covered Jurisdictions after the 1970 Amendments 83
Figure 6: Black Registration—1965, 1967, 1972 96
Figure 7: Covered Jurisdictions After the 1975 Amendments 113
Figure 8: 20 Years of Black and White Registration 124
Figure 9: Blacks Elected in the South, 1970-1985 146
Figure 10: Registration in the South, 1970 and 1988 152
Figure 11: Gerrymandered Districts, Dallas Texas 178
Figure 12: Dallas Independent School District Demographics 181
Figure 13: Ethnic Composition of Dade County 198
Figure 14: Dade County Voter Data, 1991 199
Figure 15: Georgia's 11th District 217
Figure 16: Percentage of Voting-age Blacks Registered in All
    Eleven Southern States 222
Figure 17: Race Versus Income - 1991 223
Figure 18: Racial Populations Projections 230
Figure 19: Voting Participation in Presidential Elections 1964-1992 232

INTRODUCTION

In 1965, President Lyndon Johnson dedicated his administration to the creation of The Great Society. Despite the enactment of several civil rights acts, the civil rights era had just begun and the vision of that Great Society was still a blur. Blacks, especially in the Southern States, did not enjoy equal voting rights and opportunities. It was a time of marches and demonstrations over Viet Nam, civil rights, and nearly anything else that conflicted with the peace and tranquillity of the post-war era. Civil rights leaders spawned the March on Washington, the Student Non-violent Coordinating Committee's organization of the *Mississippi Freedom Summer*, and the historic voter registration march from Selma, Alabama.

After confrontation yielded bloodshed, Selma became an icon for Martin Luther King and the voting rights movement. Selma unearthed the nation's conscience; no longer would Americans tolerate the status quo. Moved by public sentiment, both parties of Congress overwhelmingly passed the powerful Voting Rights Act of 1965—an act aimed directly at the South, designed for the sole purpose of getting blacks into voting booths to let their preferences be felt in the political process.

After more than thirty years, the Voting Rights Act is still a timely topic. The "temporary" portions of the act that Congress designed to scrutinize, penalize, and reform the South, have been extended and re-extended to a current expiration date of 2007. The lofty goal of equal access to the polling place was achieved during the first five years as black registration in the South nearly doubled, from 29 percent to 56 percent. During the next ten years, with every conceivable impediment to registration removed, black registration increased only four percent. Mission accomplished or not, the mood was set and the time was right for civil rights leaders to exploit the momentum created by the act. They drove Congress to extend its life and amend its scope every few years and were aided by federal courts who interpreted the act and its constitutional underpinnings in the broadest, most encompassing ways.

Not even Dr. King's dream could have seen what was to come. The activists of the 1960s longed for a day when blacks could assimilate into the majority community and thus share equally, side-by-side with their white brothers. What loomed in the future had little of the brotherly image. Instead, the civil rights movement, led by the power of voting rights, separated Americans into carefully crafted enclaves. It set separate goals for minorities—goals that can only be measured in a segregated society. The separation was not only philosophical but also physical since civil rights leaders could best exploit the power of the act if minorities stayed in physically contiguous voting blocks. The Voting Rights Act evolved into an affirmative action program that contradicted the dream of assimilation.

With the passage of the act, Congress outlawed prerequisite tests, namely literacy tests, in most of the Southern States. The ban did not stem from a belief that literacy was an unimportant credential for voters; courts had long upheld the legitimacy of such testing. Rather, the ban derived from the conviction that such tests were unfairly administered in racially biased areas. Over the next 30 years, from the simple premise that some literacy tests were unfair, the law evolved to banning the need for English-literacy anywhere. Not stopping at the annihilation of a literacy requirement, momentum led to amendments that penalized states and municipalities, sometimes *ex post facto*, for failing to deal with each voter in his native tongue. The idea that America was a melting pot into which immigrants could assimilate, surrendered to the view that American society must adapt to the entrance of each immigrant.

The voting rights of oppressed minority groups expanded to include the political rights of immigrants. While many blacks and Native Americans suffered from restricted opportunity during America's history, most other minorities experienced no long-term discrimination. Still, the Great Society boarded all minority groups onto the same train of affirmative action. By the 1970s, civil rights advocates depicted all non-European immigrants as oppressed victims of bigotry. Hispanics were bound together only by a common language, but in the excitement over equal opportunity, all Hispanics were statistically lumped together. The usually-Republican Cubans were grouped with the usually-Democrat Mexicans. The economic successes of second-generation Hispanics were obscured by statistically averaging them with the economic struggles of new immigrants. Legislation singled out Hispanics for affirmative action although established Hispanics were assimilating well into the American mainstream. Activists kept the heat on, however, by portraying Hispanics as a single amalgam of downtrodden poverty.

The Voting Rights Act also modified the political infrastructure. Historically, states modeled themselves after the federal government, with one chamber representing discrete constituencies of equal population and the other representing counties or other physical regions. State by state, traditional institutions gave way to interpretations of voting laws. The whole bicameral system, adopted by most states, became a meaningless construct. Today, state senates must apportion themselves by population alone, thus making them nothing more than a second house of representatives—a second filter adding little meaning to the democratic process. Following the same logic, other institutions were outlawed because they diluted voting power. For example, New York's Board of Estimates, composed of a representative from each of the five boroughs, was banned because the boroughs did not represent equal populations. Other ideas that pummeled to near extinction include at-large-voting methods and requirements that candidates be elected by a majority, rather than a plurality of the electorate. Majority rule itself, a mainstay of American tradition, is often found illegal unless it has been carefully crafted to give adequate power to minority groups.

By the late 1970s, courts began to believe that equal opportunity to participate in a system of equally weighted votes was insufficient. The notion developed that the only true measure of equality of opportunity was the equality of result. The Supreme Court made some ambiguous decisions concerning equal results, prompting the Congress to amend the act in 1982, in practice, making equal results a statutory requirement. From that point on, the litmus test for fairness was the election of minority officials in equal proportion to the constituent population. Equal opportunity was to be found in quotas and to reach those quotas, the courts imposed, and sometimes designed, blatant racial gerrymandering. Even attempts to annex city property became a minority voting issue to the courts, and were frequently blocked where the annexed inhabitants might affect the racial balance of power.

A 1992 extension to voting rights provided for voter registration upon application for a driver's license. The registration is then non-cancelable for any reason short of relocation or a felony conviction. Minority voting has become so important to party politics that politicians who benefit from those votes can not leave registration to chance. Voting is no longer a right reserved for those who seek it. It is, instead, a chore to be thrust upon even the most disinterested.

Today, the act remains the most effective civil rights legislation ever passed. It has dramatically increased minority voting and the number of elected minority officials. It has given clout to minority issues on political agendas. Among civil rights advocates, however, each success has generated a greater need for reform rather than a lesser one. The need for greater minority influence and control has been insatiable and has led the nation into a political quagmire of racial contention and a mélange of invasive laws and procedures. Voting rights have emphasized polarity and separation rather than the original hope of integration and assimilation. Martin Luther King dreamed of a day when "little black boys and black girls will be able to join hands with little white boys and girls and walk together as sisters and brothers."[1] The voting system in America has not given life to King's dream. Blacks are more likely to go to the polls, but they are no more likely to walk with their white brothers and sisters, in part, because the system has encouraged segregation. Special districts created for the sole purpose of electing minorities justified the twisted notion that a segregated electorate is needed for an integrated Congress.

Even the majority of the Supreme Court has recognized the downsides to their previous tolerance of unrestrained gerrymandering designed to maximize minority representation. Recent decisions requiring non-racial explanations for voting district structures will begin a new era of litigation and bring a new texture to the voting-rights landscape.

The voting-rights journey since 1965 is the subject of this book. I have followed each step of the legislation, the debates, and the reshaping of statute by the federal courts. To explore further, I have plunged deeply into the history, society, and lives of three communities, one for each of three major American minority groups. The story of Dallas, Texas represents the struggle of blacks for representation in city government. The tale of Dade County, Florida depicts the assumption of power by Hispanic immigrants. Finally, the history of the Navajo Reservation in Arizona portrays changes in the political influence of the largest tribe of Native Americans.

The saga will continue past the checkpoint of this book. It will be played out on a bewildering field of many teams with many goals. The ultimate fate of America's democratic experiment will depend upon each group's willingness to coalesce its polarized special interests into a mutual American dream. America's continued greatness depends on it.

CHAPTER 1: VOTING RIGHTS—THE ISSUES

If liberty and equality, as thought by some, are chiefly to be founded in democracy, they will be best attained when all persons alike share in the government to the utmost.

—*Aristotle*

A republican democracy meets its goal of "representing the people" when all qualified citizens share in the selection of government officers and propositions. The ease with which people can vote or run for office defines the extent of democracy, but no society offers suffrage to all its constituents. Instead, governments whittle away at the electorate, usually beginning with children and aliens. Other exclusions may be criminals, illiterates, women and ethnic minorities. For federal elections, the U. S. Constitution initially enfranchised all persons who each state allowed to vote for the largest branch of that state's legislature. Generally, this translated into male citizens, over 21, who paid state taxes and owned property.

Equity in voting is determined not just through ballots, but also through the voting environment including: disseminating information, apportioning voting populations, drawing district boundaries, creating filing procedures, and a myriad of other activities. The voting potential of an individual can be viewed from three facets: the voter's ability to register, then go to the polling place, cast a vote, and have that vote tallied with everyone else's; the voter's ability to influence the outcome of an election; and the prospect of an individual's preferred candidate being among the choices on the ballot. Each of these areas merits elaboration essential to understanding the factors Congress addressed in 1965 when it created the most successful piece of social legislation since the Bill of Rights.

Barriers to Registering and Voting

Impediments to the simple ability to register to vote and to cast ballots permeate American politics and have been the target of civil rights and voting legislation. Although an endless number of devices can affect voter turnout, the most common have been: English literacy tests prerequisite to voter registration; poll tax requirements for voter registration; relocation of polling places; good character qualifications, such as references from other registered voters; Constitutional understanding tests; residency requirements; and frequency of voter re-registration.

Ability to Influence Elections

The second facet of voting potential, the individual's ability to have his vote influence the outcome of an election, can be affected by several factors. The most significant factor, the demographics of apportionment, takes several forms:

- District boundaries: The inherent difficulty in drawing voting-district lines is one of fairness. States, counties, and cities can be subdivided in hundreds of ways. Dividing lines can be placed along physical boundaries such as rivers or railroads, around traditional neighborhoods, or along racial lines. Gerrymandering[1] is a time-tested, political technique for influencing election outcomes. Whether designed to favor Democrats, Republicans, rich, poor, blacks or whites, district lines can tamper materially with election results.
- Equal apportionment: When cities, counties, and states create voting districts, they must comply with the legal requirement that each district contain nearly equal numbers of voters—the principle of *one-man, one-vote*.[2] This, however, may be difficult to guarantee because of rapid urban population shifts tracked by only once-a-decade recounting.
- Unusually large districts: Minority groups may become less significant as the district size increases.
- Multi-member districts: An at-large or multi-member district is one in which multiple representatives come from a single district or one in which a single representative covers more than one district. At-large districts generally represent the interests of the broadbased majority to the exclusion of smaller pockets of minorities.
- Annexations: Contention arises when annexation of additional city property changes its political or racial balance.

Voting rules and regulations also affect voter influence:

- Majority voting requirements: When more than two candidates receive votes, the candidate with the most votes may have a plurality. In jurisdictions with majority voting requirements, the top two candidates compete in a runoff. If the second and third place candidates have split the votes of the same constituency, the runoff may then give most of the third place candidate's votes to the second place candidate, thus defeating the plurality winner.

VOTING RIGHTS—THE ISSUES

- Single-shot versus full slate voting:[3] In some at-large voting systems, voters are required to select a "full slate" or cast as many votes as the number of at-large positions. In other locations, voters may cast votes "single-shot" or only for the candidates they wish to win. By forcing voters to cast ballots for candidates in whom they have no interest, those candidates may defeat the voters true choices.
- Named places: Used in at-large schemes, "named places" require that candidates run for a specific at-large seat. Although voting is still at-large, the race is broken down into single-district contests.

Seeking a Candidate

The third facet of voting potential is finding a candidate who represents the voters' preferences. Various factors block candidates:

- Change of elective office to appointed office, thus, removing the selection from the voters.
- Candidate registration fees and other prerequisites to running.
- Low pay for public offices: Poorer people are less likely to run for offices in which the salary amounts to an honorarium.

A History of Impediments

Each of these factors has played a role in the evolution of U. S. voting rights. Limitations on both the availability and effectiveness of suffrage have been applied in all parts of the nation—sometimes with malice, but often as accepted, common practice. Since the signing of the Constitution, the trend has been toward enfranchising more voters. The civil rights era greatly accelerated the availability of franchise and did much to level the influence of each voter. The remaining chapters describe the history of this expanded democracy.

CHAPTER 2: VOTING RIGHTS AND THE CONSTITUTION

The people are turbulent and changing; they seldom judge or determine right.[1]
—*Alexander Hamilton*

The next prerequisite to understanding modern voting rights legislation, is a brief review of the U. S. Constitution. The Constitution defines the structure and philosophy of government rather than being a set of statutes itself. John Marshall, Chief Justice from 1801 to 1835, said that the constitution was "intended to endure for ages to come, and, consequently, to be adapted to the various crises of human affairs. To have prescribed the means by which government should, in all future times, execute its powers, would have been to change entirely the character of the instrument, and give it the properties of legal code."[2] Article VI of the original Constitution distinguished between the Constitution and statute by stating, "This Constitution, and the Laws of the United States which shall be made in pursuance thereof . . . shall be the supreme law of the land . . ."[3] It is exactly this concept of laws made in pursuance of the Constitution that necessitates the passage of statutes such as the Voting Rights Act. Such laws are not intended to proscribe additional powers to the government, but serve to create mechanisms to carry out constitutional intentions.

Delegates to the Constitutional Convention in 1787 faced the task of designing a form of government that greatly differed from the monarchy that had ruled them from England. The crux of this task was to define power—how the federal government would share it with the states, and how the will of the people would be injected into the power structure. The result was a government of the people balanced by structures that kept the people's control indirect.

Delegates generally shared a belief in natural law which, among other convictions, espoused that government should limit the right to vote and hold office to those with a genuine stake in the society.[4] There was prolonged debate whether voters must own property and whether the citizenry was competent to vote at all. Roger Sherman of Connecticut said, "I am opposed to the election by the people. . . . The people should have as little to do as may be about the government. They lack in information and are constantly liable to be misled."[5] Elbridge Gerry of Massachusetts complained, "The evils we experience flow from the excess of democracy. The people do not lack virtue, but are the dupes of pretended patriots. . . ."[6] Edmund Randolph of Virginia expressed the thinking of many in his keynote speech when he asserted that any part of the government controlled by the people would swallow up all other branches. Hamilton's thinking was similar. He subsequently wrote, "The people are turbulent and changing; they seldom judge or determine right."[7]

Saving the franchise for common citizens, George Mason and James Madison, both of Virginia, championed the other side. Mason pictured the larger house of the legislature to be the ". . . grand repository of the democratic principle of government. . . . It ought to know and sympathize with every part of the community."[8] Madison insisted, "[P]opular election of one branch of the national legislature [is] essential to every plan of free government."[9] When the issue was put to a vote of the convention, suffragists carried the day.

State legislatures were given the power to select U. S. senators, partially out of a philosophical belief in what Madison called "refining popular appointments by successive filtrations."[10] It was also a concession to empower the state legislatures, thus easing their concerns about the new federal government.

Several methods of electing the president were debated, although direct election by the people was never a strong contender. The convention finally settled on the method of electors still in use today.

Patrick Henry, Thomas Jefferson, and Sam Adams, the democratic radicals of their day, were absent. These missing statesmen would have leaned more toward a populist structure, but compromised later by adding the Bill of Rights.

Voting Rights in 18th-Century America

The new government reserved the right to set the procedural rules for federal elections, but the Constitution gave the states general authority to set voter criteria for the election of state legislatures and the House of Representatives. A few examples depict the mentality of the day concerning state suffrage.

South Carolina franchised "Every free white man, of age of twenty-one years, being a citizen of this state, and having resided therein two years . . ., and who hath a freehold of fifty acres of land, or a town lot . . ., or not having such freehold or town lot, hath been a resident in the election district . . . six months before the said election, and hath paid a tax the preceding year . . ."[11] In Hew Hampshire, voters included "Every male inhabitant . . ., of twenty-one years of age and upward, excepting paupers, and persons excused of paying taxes at their own request . . ."[12] Delaware enfranchised "[E]very free, white male citizen of age twenty-two years or upwards, having resided in the state one year before the election, . . . and having within two years next before the election paid a county tax . . . [A]nd not idiot, or insane person, or pauper, or person convicted of a crime deemed by law felony."[13] Likewise, Pennsylvania voters included "[E]very white freeman of age of twenty-one years, having resided in the state one year, . . . and within two years paid a state or county tax . . ."[14]

Other constitutions were similar. The qualifications they contained—gender, competence, property ownership, term of residence, payment of taxes, and race—were generally accepted principles of the day. While radically discriminatory by today's standards, the nation was founded on these attitudes.

Electing a President

The presidential election process was a controversial issue at the convention. Nothing demonstrates the compromise between a lack of faith in the common citizen and the desire to confer ultimate trust upon him, better than the method of electing a president. Article II created a democratic process used to select electors who, in turn, selected a president and vice president. This permitted the influence of the people to be clearly felt while removing them from direct election.

In 1804, Amendment XII modified Article II. Although the process used by electors to select the president was changed, the people still would not directly elect the president. Through more than 200 years of subsequent history, an amendment has never been passed by Congress that would change the basic system even though it has three times failed to reflect the results of the popular vote.[15]

Electing Congress

The method chosen by the framers for electing a Congress, also reflects compromise between pure democracy and the more vague, represented will of the people. Article I of the Constitution provided for the people to directly select members of the House of Representatives and gave the state legislatures the duty of selecting the Senate. Specifically, Section 2 of Article I dictated that the people choosing members of the House of Representatives would have the same qualifications as the voters for the most numerous house of the state legislature. This provision was important in later debates because it clearly gave the states the right to set the qualifications of voters for the U. S. House.

Article I also gave the state legislatures the power to set the "times, places, and manner of holding elections for Senators and Representatives," but gave the federal government the right to pass laws at any time that could alter the manner of election. This reservation ultimately gave the Congress and courts heavy authority in dealing with the election process and is an essential underpinning of the Voting Rights Act.

Article I further provided that each house of Congress had the responsibility to "judge [its] elections, returns, and qualifications of its own members. . ." The clause referring to member qualifications could have given the majority in Congress power to keep the Congress a single race, single sex, or single philosophy. The power has not been greatly exercised, however. In 1969, when Congress debated the seating of black representative, Adam Clayton Powell, the Supreme Court ruled that "the Constitution leaves the House without authority to exclude any person, duly elected by his constituents, who meets all the requirements for membership expressly prescribed" in the Constitution.[16] This, along with subsequent decisions about the conduct of elections, has nullified the power that might have been given to the Congress by Article I.

The Seventeenth Amendment, adopted in 1913, finally conceded to a direct vote by the people for the election of Senators.

Rights Guaranteed to All

The "Reconstruction Amendments" passed after the close of the Civil War, affected greatly the rights and influence of individuals. The Fourteenth Amendment granted citizenship to all individuals born or naturalized in the United States and further protected all citizens by saying, "No state . . . shall abridge the privileges or immunities of citizens of the United States; nor shall any state deprive any person of life, liberty, or property, without due process of law; nor deny any person within its jurisdiction the equal protection of the laws."[17]

The courts have used this section of the Amendment in a myriad of civil-rights and individual-liberty litigation. The equal protection clause has been specifically used to reapportion voting districts. Equal protection requires that a state treat an individual in the same manner as others in similar conditions and circumstances. Equal protection does not intend to provide equality among individuals or races but only the equal application of the laws. Thus the result of a law is not relevant provided there is no discrimination in its application. This distinction is important; it forbids states from discriminating among individuals, but it does not address the discrimination of individuals against each other.

The second section of the Fourteenth Amendment caused apportionment in the House of Representatives would to be based on the count of the number of people in each state. However, the congressional representation of any state denying the vote to male citizens over twenty-one years old, would be scaled down by the same percentage as the percentage of twenty-one-year-old male citizens who were so denied.

The granting of citizenship to the newly freed blacks enfranchised most of them for the first time. Reconstruction constitutional architects dealt specifically with voting rights in the Fifteenth Amendment by saying that the "right of citizens of the United States to vote shall not be denied or abridged by the United States or any state as a result of race, color, or previous condition of servitude."[18] Thus voting rights were given to black, male citizens since all blacks born in the United States were granted citizenship by the Fourteenth Amendment.

Despite the enlargement of franchise, women were still left out. Susan B. Anthony was arrested for voting in 1872. Because women could not testify in federal court, her attorney spoke for her claiming that the Fourteenth Amendments gave all citizens the right to vote. The court claimed that the Constitution did not specifically protect women's right to vote and fined Ms. Anthony $100. Women's rights groups fought that decision for the next 48 years. Despite Grover Cleveland's 1905 opinion that sensible and responsible women did not want to vote, the Nineteenth Amendment was adopted in 1920 recognizing women as part of the electorate.

The Twenty-third Amendment, passed in 1961, extended the right to vote for President and Vice President to the citizens of Washington, D. C. In 1964, the Twenty-fourth Amendment outlawed any tax prerequisite to exercising the right to vote in any federal election. In 1971, after years of conflict in Vietnam had engaged hundreds of thousands of troops under 21 years old, the Twenty-sixth Amendment lowered the voting age for federal elections to 18 years.

In all, seven of the seventeen amendments passed since the Bill of Rights, deal directly with voting rights.

CHAPTER 3: HISTORY

The final prerequisite to understanding the Voting Rights Act is a grasp of the political and legislative background of black voting in the South.[1] Considered also are the histories of three communities: Dallas, Texas, a southern city that struggled with black rights; Dade County, a resort turned immigrant Mecca for Hispanics; and northeast Arizona, the location of a complex legal struggle for Native-American voting rights.

The Rise and Fall of Reconstruction

The Reconstruction Congress, hoping to eradicate the last vestige of slavery, not only initiated the passage of the Civil War Amendments, but also enacted a series of civil rights acts designed to give substance to these Amendments. Congress passed the Reconstruction Act of 1867, over President Johnson's veto, requiring all confederate states to call conventions to which blacks could be elected as delegates, and to write new state constitutions guaranteeing voting rights to black men. After the Fifteenth Amendment became effective in 1870, Congress passed the Enforcement Act of 1870 which "provided for criminal sanctions against those who interfered with the constitutionally guaranteed right to vote," and the Force Act of 1871 which "was to supplement the 1870 statute by supplying independent enforcement machinery . . . of federal officials to supervise the election process in each election district."[2]

The congressional effort was emphatic and prolonged. Black voter registration grew rapidly as did the success of black candidates. By 1867 there were 735,000 blacks and 635,000 whites on the voting rolls in the ten states of the Old South.[3] Blacks achieved political success holding a variety of public offices in each of the Southern States and occupying a majority of the seats in the lower house in South Carolina. Three states elected black lieutenant governors and the South sent twenty blacks to the U. S. House and two to the Senate.[4]

The extraordinary effort to reconstruct the South was met by violence, corruption, and determined litigation challenging the constitutionality of the civil rights acts. In two separate cases, both decided on March 27, 1876, the Supreme Court threw out indictments based on various provision of the Enforcement Act of 1870 and the Force Act of 1871, thereby nullifying important provisions of those acts. Among the Court's judgments was the holding that Congress could only protect voting rights in federal elections or other elections in which the right to vote was not free of racial discrimination.[5]

In that year's election, Republican Rutherford Hayes fought a close presidential battle with Democrat Samuel Tilden. Both parties apparently sent in falsified returns from the South leaving the election results in question. Finally Congress appointed an electoral commission, consisting of eight Republicans and seven Democrats, to recount the entire vote. When it became clear that the commission would decide for Hayes, the southern Democrats agreed to accept him if the Republicans would agree to withdraw Federal troops from the South and return self-government to these states. The Republicans agreed and the commission announced that Hayes had 185 electoral votes to Tilden's 184.[6]

The assault on Reconstruction continued. In the *1883 Civil Rights Cases*, the Supreme Court majority concluded that the Reconstruction Congress' attempts to control the actions of private citizens against recently freed blacks was unconstitutional.[7] The Court presented two conclusions. First, Congress had proactively passed laws that prohibited certain state actions before they were committed. The court reasoned that such laws were inappropriate and that federal law could only address a state that had taken some action to violate the 14th Amendment. Second, in many cases, the law did not deal with state actions at all, but rather with the conduct of individuals. The Court argued, "The wrongful act of an individual, unsupported by any such [state] authority, is simply a private wrong. . . . If not sanctioned in some way by the state, or not done under state authority, it is simply a crime of that individual."[8] Congress could only act when a state acted to interfere with a protected civil right.

Other decisions, especially the 1896 case of *Plessy v. Ferguson*, further slowed congressional momentum. In *Plessy*, the court affirmed "separate but equal" facilities in transportation. The court was able to reach its decision despite the equal protection clause of the Fourteenth Amendment. In an eight to one decision Justice Henry Brown wrote for the majority:

> The object of the [Fourteenth A]mendment was undoubtedly to enforce the absolute equality of the two races before the law, but in the nature of things it could not have been intended to abolish distinctions based upon color, or to enforce social, as distinguished from political equality, or a commingling of the two races upon terms unsatisfactory to either.[9]

Only Justice Harlan dissented:

> Our Constitution is color-blind, and neither knows nor tolerates classes among citizens. In respect of civil rights, all citizens are equal before the law. . . . In my

opinion, the judgment this day rendered will, in time, prove to be quite as pernicious as the decision made by this tribunal in the *Dred Scott* case.[10]

Harlan was right, but it would take until 1954, in *Brown v. Board of Education*, for the *Plessy* decision to be reversed.

Daunted by the Supreme Court and deflated by the general healing of the nation, northern surveillance diminished. Violence broke out against Republicans and blacks, election fixing became common, and structural discrimination through literacy tests and gerrymandering began. Blacks began to lose their newly gained franchise. Between 1896 and 1900, black registration in Louisiana alone declined from 130,334 to 5,320.[11] The effect of this disfranchisement showed itself in the ethnic makeup of officeholders.

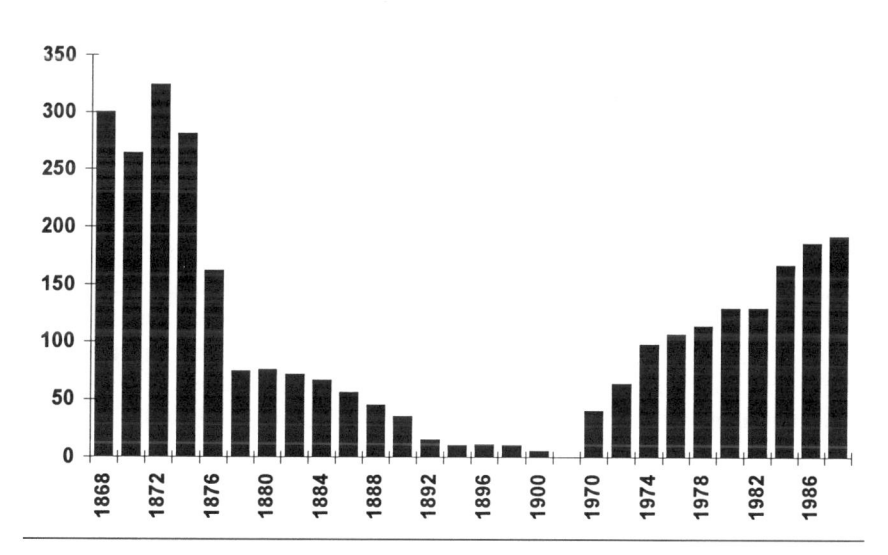

FIGURE 1: BLACKS, IN FORMER CONFEDERATE STATES, ELECTED TO STATE AND FEDERAL LEGISLATURES[12]

After reconstruction, the courts, recognizing strict principles of federalism—the separation of powers between the federal government and the states—left state districting and election politics to the discretion of each state. By the early 1940s, black voter registration in southern states remained near the level it had maintained since the first of the century. Best estimates set registered blacks at 2.4 percent of the black, voting-age population.

Alabama, Louisiana, and Mississippi boasted only two thousand black voters each.

States like Texas took their cue from the relative permissiveness of the judiciary. In 1905, the Texas legislature passed the Terrell Election Law which allowed Democratic party officials to determine who could vote in a primary election. It was assumed that the party would exclude blacks.[13] To add force, in 1923, the Texas legislature amended the law and resolved, "[I]n no event shall a Negro be eligible to participate in a Democratic primary election held in the state of Texas, and should a Negro vote in a Democratic primary election, such a ballot shall be void . . ."[14] In 1927, the Supreme Court declared the Texas Law unconstitutional.[15] Texas repealed the primary law but returned to the original Terrell Law leaving voter qualifications to party officials. In 1932, black suffrage won again when the Supreme Court outlawed the state's circumvention of the court's earlier decision.[16] Texas then allowed the Democratic Party to declare itself a "voluntary organization" with the power to choose its membership and voter qualifications. African Americans fought, but this time lost in a 1935 decision.[17] The courts were nearly silent until 1944 when the Supreme Court finally barred Texas' prohibition.[18] That ruling had an immediate influence on southern black registration promoting its expansion to about 9.5 percent by 1947.

Louisiana also showed determination to limit black suffrage. Louisiana blacks were enfranchised in 1867 and by 1898, 44 percent of the registered voters were black. That year, the Louisiana Constitution was modified to provide that no prerequisite tests to voting would apply to anyone registered before 1867 or to their sons or grandsons. This left only newly enfranchised blacks to be subjected to literacy tests. The provision was held unconstitutional in 1915, so, in 1921, Louisiana instituted a new constitution that replaced the "grandfather" clause with a constitutional interpretation test. From 1921 to 1944, blacks never comprised more than one percent of the registered voters. Louisiana also had an all-white primary law which was so effective, registrars rarely needed to resort to the interpretation test. After the 1944 Texas decision, Louisiana black registration began to slowly rise, reaching about 15 percent by 1956. To counteract this growth, the legislature created a legislative committee to reemphasize segregation. The committee required registrars to attend classes promoting white control. They challenged blacks on the rolls and purged thousands of names. Registrars of at least 21 parishes began using the interpretation test until its use was finally banned.[19]

Blacks had little defense against the half-century of abuse, but they did begin to organize. The embryonic beginnings of the civil rights movement commenced in 1905 when Harvard-educated historian and sociologist, W. E.

History

B. DuBois, brought together a group of black intellectuals to begin a movement of change for blacks, including black suffrage. The group formed the Niagara Movement which subsequently joined white reformers to produce the National Association for the Advancement of Colored People (NAACP).[20]

The Courts Join In

Despite the courts' occasional willingness to intercede on behalf of disfranchised blacks, justices continued to view state elections as a non-constitutional issue. In the 1946 trial of *Colegrove v. Green*, Illinois voters challenged the state's congressional apportionment as discriminatory on the grounds that some districts contained as much as eight times the population of other districts. The Supreme Court dismissed the case on the principle of federalism. Justice Felix Frankfurter wrote the majority opinion stating that courts cannot tell lawmakers how to settle political disputes.[21] Frankfurter drew strong dissent from Justice Hugo Black and others. Frankfurter and Black saw state powers differently. Frankfurter saw plenary state power to draw district lines. He claimed that the court could not intervene because "it is hostile to a democratic system to involve the judiciary in the politics of the people." Black contended that states could not exercise power at the expense of individual rights:[22]

> While the Constitution contains no express provision requiring that congressional election districts established by the states must contain approximately equal populations, the constitutionally guaranteed right to vote and the right to have one's vote counted clearly imply the policy that state election systems, no matter what their form, should be designed to give approximately equal weight to each vote cast.[23]

Nonetheless, black voter registration in the South continued rising from 12 percent in 1947 to 25 percent in 1956. This growth was broadbased except in Mississippi which remained near five percent.[24] Reaction to the increasing black registration varied. Mississippi instituted a literacy test to supplement its existing constitutional interpretation test. In some states, citizens' councils began persuading registered black voters to withdraw their names. By 1955, fifteen of Mississippi's rural counties had no black voters. Similar efforts in Louisiana, between 1956 and 1959, caused black registration to drop in forty-six of sixty-four parishes. Still, total southern registration continued to grow. By 1964, the black registration rate in the South was 43 percent.[25]

In 1959, blacks challenged the *Colegrove* decision which denied the courts' ability to enter the political thicket and set district lines. Newly drawn city lines around Tuskegee, Alabama excluded blacks from the city boundaries effectively limiting their participation in city politics. Blacks sued in *Gomillion v. Lightfoot*. This time Justice Frankfurter jumped to the other side ruling that the line would have to be redrawn. He argued that this was not a reversal of *Colegrove*. The court was not arguing the politics of which district a citizen votes in. Rather the court was defending the citizens right to vote at all. Of course, in or out of the city limits, the blacks still had the right to vote, but this crossed Frankfurter's threshold.[26]

Later that year, the *Colegrove* and *Gomillion* decisions were revisited in *Baker v. Carr*.[27] Charles Baker and other urban Tennessee voters sued the Tennessee Secretary of State claiming that the urban voters' franchise had been diluted because rural voters, one-third of the state's population, elected two-thirds of the state legislature. Violating its own state constitution, Tennessee had failed to reapportion the legislative districts since 1901. Dismissed by the lower courts, *Baker* worked its way to the Supreme Court in 1962 and secured a reversal of the *Colegrove* decision. The Court ruled that federal courts did indeed have the authority to decide reapportionment cases.

Baker sanctioned the federal courts to delve into state districting matters for the first time. It was this decision that created a basis for Congress to pass the Voting Rights Act with the expectation that the federal courts would act upon its enforcement. During oral arguments, the attorneys and justices considered the far-reaching effects the decision could have. As a friend-of-the-court, Archibald Cox testified for the United States:

> This is obviously an important case, one that will affect our representative institutions for a long time . . . The issue is not confined to Tennessee. It affects a number of states all over the country. Plainly it's also an important question for this Court in terms of the Court's place in our tripartite governmental system. . . . This court does not carry the whole burden of government, and for it to rush in to try and right political wrongs, instead of leaving them to the other branches . . . of the government, could impair its usefulness in our constitutional system. But I suggest to you that judicial inaction through excessive caution or through a fancied impotence, in the face of crying necessity and very serious wrongs, may also do damage to our constitutional system . . .[28]

Attorney Jack Wilson argued for Tennessee:

> The issue is with the legislature of Tennessee. . . . It's an issue with the sovereign state of Tennessee, one of the fifty states. . . . [W]e are interposing the plea of

sovereignty on behalf of the sovereign state of Tennessee; that it has not, in its constitution, by statute, or otherwise, given its consent to be sued in a federal district court on a reapportionment matter. [W]e come to another great constitutional principle, and that is the principle of separation of powers, and that is mentioned only incidentally by the appellants. I wonder why.[29]

After further debate of these arguments, Justice William Brennan delivered the opinion asserting that political issues were not the affair of the courts, but violations of the equal protection clause of the Fourteenth Amendment were. This case, he argued, was about violation of the Constitution and this finding made irrelevant the fact that the issue was political.[30]

Time proved that Justice Frankfurter's position in *Gomillion* was an aberration of his belief that the federal government should stay out of redistricting. Defending his *Colegrove* position of 15 years earlier, Justice Frankfurter vehemently dissented:

> However desirable and however desired by some among the great political thinkers and framers of our government, it [apportionment based exclusively on population] has never been practical, today or in the past. It was not the English system, it was not the colonial system, it was not the system chosen for the national government by the constitution, it was not the system exclusively or even predominantly practiced by the states at the time of the adoption of the Fourteenth Amendment, it is not predominantly practiced by the states today.[31]

Despite Justice Frankfurter's dissent, this decision launched the federal courts into a role as prime referee in apportionment cases and legitimatized the federal government's entanglement. Chief Justice Earl Warren called *Baker v. Carr*, "the most important case in my tenure on the court"[32]—a statement punctuated by the fact that Warren presided over *Brown v. Board of Education*.

Two years later, in *Reynolds v. Sims*, the Supreme Court further clarified its position. Writing about geographically-drawn district lines, Justice Warren stated, "Legislators represent people, not trees or acres."[33] Through that case, the Court established a principle subsequently known as *one-man, one-vote*, i.e., all election districts for any legislative body must contain roughly the same population.

Added Legislation

Not all of the work was done by the courts. The Civil Rights Act of 1957 gave the U. S. Attorney General the power to sue on behalf of the victims in cases of voting discrimination based on race or color. Additionally, it upgraded the Civil Rights Section to a full division of the Justice Department; it created a Commission on Civil Rights; and it gave the attorney general the power to prohibit threats and intimidation that deterred minority voting in federal elections. Despite the strong words of the act, civil rights proponents contended that the suits brought under its auspices were difficult to prosecute because the courts lacked the power to access voting registration records. They argued further that when minorities won a suit, the scope of relief was usually inadequate. Thus, in May 1960, Congress passed another civil rights act that granted the attorney general full power to inspect the voting documents held by local voting registrars and required that those records be preserved for 22 months. It also provided, in areas showing a pattern of discrimination, that any black whose application was rejected by local officials could apply to a federal court or federal voting referee to be certified.

Despite the legislative success, civil rights advocates remained dissatisfied with its effectiveness. Attorney General Robert Kennedy believed that the long term success of the civil rights movement depended more on gaining strength through elective power than through specific acts of desegregation. Ushering in the visible beginning of the civil rights era, Kennedy met with various civil rights groups in 1961 and pushed for greater voter registration work by holding out the promise of continued administration support and money from philanthropic organizations.[34]

As the civil rights focus on voting rights continued to gain strength, Congress passed yet another civil rights bill in 1964, this time expediting voting rights suits by providing for the appointment of three-judge federal district courts to hear cases. Appeals from those tribunals went directly to the Supreme Court. The 1964 Act also prohibited the use of voting qualifications, practices or standards different from those that had been applied in the past to other individuals; the denial of voter registration due to minor errors and omissions on application forms; and the use of literacy tests unless they were conducted wholly in writing. Furthermore, the law presumed literacy for anyone who had completed the sixth grade.

During this period of legislative and court activity on a national level, individual communities dealt with suffrage in the context of their own cultures. The following are the histories of three of those communities.

Dallas, Texas: a Blend of South and West

Dallas, Texas is a modern metropolis rising above the North Texas plains. Its population is a mix of origins, primarily European-American, African-

American, and Hispanic. While power is spread among these groups today, the struggle to reach this balance was a voting rights battle played out since the mid-1970s. A brief understanding of the city's history sets the stage for understanding this struggle.

Dallas' roots are split between the rugged, frontier spirit of the West and the agrarian, settled style of the South. The free, entrepreneurial spirit of America's westward expansion, seeded with a black population of southern slavery, set Dallas up for the racial power struggle that would occur 150 years after its founding.

In the 1700s, the site that is now Dallas was the roaming ground of Caddo Indians who lived in thatched huts along the Arkikosa River, now called the Trinity.[35] By the early 1800s, white settlers began populating North Texas. The region initially attracted the adventuresome who were willing to endure the droughts of the summers, the bitter northern, winter winds, and warfare with the Indians.[36]

In 1840, a Tennessee lawyer named John Neely Bryan, traveling with his Indian guide, established a camp along the river. Over the next three years, a small farming settlement began developing with a concentration northwest of today's Dallas. The early town looked more like the West than the South. The houses were built of logs and the men dressed in buckskin pants and moccasins. Settlers ate the vegetation they raised and enjoyed meat from the abundance of buffalo, deer, antelope, bears, and turkeys in the area.[37]

Bryan, clad in buckskin pants sporting strips of untanned deer hide up and down the legs, ran the new town. His home served as the courthouse, as well as a retail outlet for ammunition, tobacco, and whiskey. The fledgling town organized a vote in 1845 when the question of statehood was put to the people of the Texas Republic. Dallas had 32 qualified voters, 29 of whom favored statehood.[38] Settlements began to spring up around Dallas. Between 1845 and 1850 the new settlements of Hord's Ridge, now Oak Cliff, and Cedar Springs became so populous that they contended with Dallas to become the county seat.

Dallas' soil and climate were well suited for growing cotton, a resource that moved the city toward the look of the South. By the late 1800s, the surrounding soil produced one-sixth of the world's cotton.[39] Large scale cotton farming demanded slave labor, prompting the first slave to be sold in Dallas in 1845. Still, the number of slaves never became large within the city. At the outbreak of the Civil War, the county claimed 1080 slaves of which only 97 were in Dallas.[40]

By the early 1850s, Dallas had begun to develop the commerce and trade that would become its destiny. Retail stores began to open, hotels were built, and a new courthouse was constructed. Feeding the expansion, colonists arrived, including a utopian colony from France call *La Reunion*, that settled in Oak Cliff.

John Neely Bryan had set in motion a force that would develop into one of the country's most prosperous cities. To his misfortune, he gave away most of his own land, took to drinking, left Dallas, and wandered the new frontiers until he died in 1877 in the State Lunatic Asylum in Austin.

Despite the agrarian flavor of the South, Dallas remained a rugged frontier town. Law and order were managed western-style. In 1853, the first legal execution took place in which a slave woman, Jane Elkins, was hanged for murder. General lawlessness caused the people to incorporate Dallas in 1856 to provide better government and police protection.

Incidents took place throughout Dallas' history that pitted blacks and whites against one another. Memorable among these was an occurrence in July 1860, when fire broke out on the town square consuming all but the one brick building and destroying homes in all directions. Dallas citizens took the fire grimly. The emotions and prejudices of the developing strife between North and South were in the air. Looking for justice, the townspeople blamed the fire on a slave plot set up by two white abolitionist preachers from Iowa. The preachers were jailed, publicly whipped, and run out of town. A committee of 52 citizens was formed to find and bring justice to the blacks responsible. A black boy testified that a black man named Old Cato had prior knowledge of the fire. Old Cato, in turn, implicated two others and all three were executed while the town's remaining blacks were flogged. Soon after, the *Dallas Herald* editorialized, "Such a thing as an insolent, impertinent, or insubordinate Negro since the fire, is not known. . . . [They] have returned without a murmur into their normal condition of subordination to their masters."[41] It was never clear whether those executed had anything to do with the fire. The temperature that day was 112° and the trash pile that began the conflagration could have ignited spontaneously. Despite the fire damage, Dallas showed an irrepressible will to mend and grow. By the end of that year, new shops and hotels, more fireproof and substantial than before, replaced the damaged ruins.[42]

When Lincoln was elected in 1860, it became clear that the nation would fall apart. Texas, though not a true part of the South, was quick to join the southern nation. Editorials in the *Dallas Herald* echoed the independent, determined, even defiant attitude that exemplified Dallas' distrustful feelings about a far away government.[43]

In a state referendum in February 1861, Dallas voted 741 to 237 in favor of secession. After the war began, hundreds in Dallas joined the Confederate

Army. Dallas County authorized a gift of $5000 for the military to procure arms. Flour, cotton, munitions, and other supplies were shipped from North Texas to military depots across the South. Dallasites were short of necessities and, by the end of the war, many were broke and literally in rags.[44]

As Reconstruction began, citizens took the required oath of allegiance to the United States. Elections took place in 1868 with the registration board, under the reconstruction government, co-chaired by a black man named Melvin Wade. Wade refused to register white men who would not state that they favored "Negro suffrage." In the election that followed, more blacks than whites were able to vote in Dallas. The whites that did vote, passed between two lines of black troops.[45]

In 1870, Edmund J. Davis, became Texas' Reconstruction governor. Over the next three years, black influence in Texas government was greater than at any time until the 1980s, but the heavy influx of white settlers in the early 1870s tipped the balance of power. In 1872, the number of black lawmakers was reduced and the next year the governor was defeated. Reconstruction in Texas ended.[46]

Most of the county's newly-freed blacks remained rural, but some formed a settlement called Freedman's Town in the area later known as Deep Ellum. The new enclave created little problem for the Dallas establishment. Despite their new freedom, blacks, lacking education, job skills, and money, were little better off than before the war.

The war left Dallas less destroyed than most of the South and this relative prosperity attracted many more freed blacks as well as southern whites to the area.[47] Joining fleeing Southerners were Europeans from Germany, Switzerland, France, and Belgium who began arriving in large numbers when the railroads arrived in 1872 and 1873.[48] Business growth stemmed from this steady inflow. Much of this boom returned a wild west flavor to Dallas with a rapid growth in the number of saloons, shooting galleries, and gambling halls. Cowboys raced through town, yelling and firing their pistols to let off steam. During the 1870s, Dallas hosted such notorious outlaws as Belle Star and Sam Bass. Outward signs of prosperity included hotels of first class quality, previously unknown to the frontier town.

As Dallas grew and prospered, the headwind of Reconstruction passed, and the Ku Klux Klan appeared. Although put down by the press as not a part of regular community life, the Klan membership grew in the early 1870s. Their activities centered on frightening blacks and attempting to disrupt meetings of the Black Union League.[49]

Between 1870 and 1880, the Dallas population grew from roughly 3,000 to 10,000 residents. Even these numbers understate the growth because much of the population lived in the town of East Dallas, or in unincorporated areas of the county. The blend of immigrants and colonists that made up Dallas established a utilitarian attitude concerned with solid foundations, growth, and not too much flash. While not a beautiful or ornamental town, it had streetcars, and gas and water works. By 1883, electric lights lit the main streets and hotels. In 1884, the local paper described Dallas as "essentially a business town" with building in progress everywhere, "whether it be the half-finished mansion of some merchant prince, or the massive walls of a trade emporium."[50] In 1887, seven hundred buildings lined many paved streets. Growth continued outside the city limits as well. In 1886, Thomas L. Marsalis bought land and laid out the plat for the suburb of Oak Cliff, which voted to join Dallas in March of 1904. The Dallas quest for growth and expansion was exemplified in 1905 when J. H. Ardrey organized the *150,000 Club*, an organization whose goal was to expand the Dallas population to 150,000 by 1915.

As growth became the theme for the Dallas establishment, Dallas African Americans made their first attempts at organization and recognition. Inspired by a speech from Booker T. Washington, blacks organized and created the Colored Fair and Tri-Centennial Exposition in 1901. It included a long parade from the fairgrounds through downtown, headed by Dallas mounted police, and was seasoned with bands, exhibits of crafts and African art, and floats representing black businesses and professionals.[51]

After its incorporation in 1856, Dallas government operated using a ward system with a mayor, ten aldermen elected from single-member districts, and five aldermen elected at-large. Voters also elected key administrators such as the city attorney, tax collector, health officer, and various public works officials.[52] This system endured until 1907 when the level of corruption dictated a change. Voters instituted a commission-style government, composed of an elected mayor and elected commissioners for water, public works, police, and fire. This structure was more like a business with a president and vice-presidents—a structure amenable with Dallas' business-growth objective.

Henry Lindsley, President of Southwestern Life, took the lead in the new structure. Beginning Dallas' long-term tradition of business leadership, Lindsley selected heads of major businesses and formed an organization dedicated to municipal politics. He outlined a plan that would serve Dallas for decades. The city's most influential businessmen selected and supported candidates for the elected positions in city government. Lindsley was selected president of the new organization which took the name Citizens Association and was soon called "Cits." The organization's charter declared it to be non-partisan and open to everyone and, indeed, membership before the first election grew to 3,500 of the 7,800 eligible voters.[53] The Citizens Association nominated its slate and easily won every slot.

The strength of business leaders was crucial during this period. They took charge, not only of politics, but also of the community. In 1908, Dallas' greatest natural disaster occurred when floods caused the Trinity River to overflow its banks and destroy the "Long Wooden Bridge" between Cadiz and Oak Cliff. Several people lost their lives and 4,000 were left homeless. City business leaders, challenging one another in private meetings, raised the $50,000 necessary for the relief effort.[54]

After 1910, the population boomed again. Motorized vehicles took over the city's municipal fleet, and telephone service entered the mainstream. Herbert Marcus and his brother-in-law, Al Neiman, opened Neiman-Marcus which joined Sanger Bros. and A. Harris & Co. as major department stores. George E. Kessler prepared a plan for the future which, over the next two decades, took Dallas from a frontier town to a modern metropolis. The "Cits" established long term dominance in politics with overwhelming victories from 1909 to 1915. Although their membership was broad, power was concentrated in a hand full of business leaders who headed the organization.

Growth was accompanied by painful incidents. In 1911, a mob overpowered the sheriff and lynched Allen Brooks, a black who had allegedly assaulted a two-and-a-half-year-old white girl at her home where Brooks was employed. He was thrown from a second story window, roped at the neck and dragged up Main Street to an arch at the intersection of Main and Akard erected for the Elk's convention, and there hanged from a pole. The shame of the incident caused citizens to tear down the elaborate arch soon afterwards.

The city continued developing its foundations. In 1913, Dallas, with over 130,000 inhabitants, displayed its business and economic muscle by securing the Eleventh Federal Reserve District Bank. The Adolphus, a twenty-two story grand hotel was completed. In 1914, Ford opened the Dallas assembly plant where more than 5,000 cars a year would be produced. In 1915, Southern Methodist University opened. Neighborhoods grew, but were generally kept segregated with the help of a city charter prohibiting blacks from living in white neighborhoods. The post World War I period put the city back into boom and in 1919, tall modern office buildings shot up downtown. In the same year, Dallas voted for prohibition and, by a two-to-one majority, for women's suffrage.[55]

Henry Lindsley announced his own candidacy for Mayor in 1915. Although opposed by a growing force that disliked the concentration of city power in so few men, he easily carried the day. Growing opposition to the

Citizens Association led to his defeat in 1917 as all other Association candidates won. In 1919, the "Cits" snapped back, electing Lindsley's military underling, Frank Wozencraft.[56]

Fed by immigrants fleeing the 1910 Mexican Revolution, the Mexican population reached 3000 by the early 1920s. These impoverished newcomers settled in abandoned boxcars in the downtown railroad yard. Families soon settled in an area just north of downtown, a once-prosperous Jewish neighborhood that had degenerated to a red-light district. As police cleaned it up, the Mexicans moved in next to the remaining Jewish families. So concentrated were the Mexicans that the area was soon called "Little Mexico."[57]

The 1920s also marked an era of sophistication. The Dallas Little Theater was born, and the Majestic and Palace theaters were built. The Magnolia Building, at thirty stories, the tallest in the South, gave great pride to Dallasites. Ten years later the Magnolia Oil Company placed, atop the building, a rotating, "flying red horse" which later became an icon for the city. The era also ushered in a new resurgence of the Klan. It had nearly disappeared for fifty years, but it returned more strongly than ever before. On April 1, 1921, Klansmen flogged and branded a black named Alex Johnson. A year later, over 1000 Klansmen filed through the Dallas streets brandishing signs of white supremacy.

Klan membership was by no means just a way to join in the harassment of the black community. Its popularity stemmed from the concepts of law-and-order, maintenance of a moral, Christian community, womanhood, and Americanism. Members felt that a significant threat to these principles was the intermixing of the races. Many city officials including senior members of the police department were Klan members.[58] Although the Dallas press condemned the Klan, growth in membership continued with an initiation of more than five thousand new members before a crowd of spectators at Fair Park.

In 1921, the Citizens Association easily won again, but their remaining power was short-lived. Two years later, they opposed the *City Democrats* who were supported by the Klan. The Klan-supported candidates were all elected by landslides effectively killing the Citizens Association, but within a year, bad politics between the Klan founder and the Imperial Wizard began to diminish the Klan's influence.[59] By 1925, the membership in the Dallas Klan declined from 13,000 members to 1,200.[60]

Despite the city's growth and prosperity, housing for Dallas' blacks was poor. A survey in 1924 reported that 66 percent of black housing units had no water or accompanying sanitation. The situation for Hispanics in "Little

Mexico" was not much better. Housing remained segregated. Each city block was designated white or black when a black named Roby Williams moved into a house on Eighth Avenue. He was the only black on the block, although the neighboring block was all black. Supported by city ordinance, his white neighbors asked him to move. After Williams refused to move, charges were filed and a law suit ensued. Williams' attorney argued that a 1917 Supreme Court decision made the city ordinance unconstitutional. Although Williams lost his case, that Supreme Court decision ultimately struck down the Dallas ordinance.[61]

The city continued to grow. By 1930, the population was 260,475, representing a 64 percent growth for the decade of the twenties. Minorities accounted for nearly one-fourth of the population with 20 percent black and five percent Hispanic.[62] With this growth, the commissioner system became less workable. There was no central administration, no central personnel system, poor communications between departments, and a general incompatibility with a city whose commercial base demanded quick decisions, flexibility, and growth. In 1930, First National Bank Chairman, Nathan Adams, led opposition to the commission system by forming the Citizens Charter Association (CCA). The CCA was to set up a council-manager system in which a city manager answered to nine councilmen. Of these nine councilmen, six had to live in their own districts, three could live anywhere, and all were elected "at-large." The Council selected a mayor from within its ranks. The CCA selected the first slate of candidates, all businessmen, and all won the 1931 elections. This success launched the CCA into a long term role as the primary power broker in Dallas politics.

Like the earlier Citizens Association, the CCA closed its doors to select a slate of candidates. Its goal was also shared with its predecessor: place prominent businessmen into power to promote the reputation, growth, and prosperity of the city.

The CCA selected a City Manager named John Edy who became known for policies that haunted gamblers and bootleggers. He downgraded the rank of many police officers who profited from corruption, but many felt that such a puritanical stand would leave Dallas out of the running for the upcoming Texas Centennial.[63] Although Edy cleaned up city hall, there was a growing sense that the government was too far from the people. City council members, true to the council-manager system, did not intervene in city administration on behalf of their constituents. Edy's policies and an unpopular sewer tax that he enacted, left the CCA vulnerable in the 1935 elections. A group of discharged city employees, with the support of lower-income Dallasites, formed an opposition group called "The Organization." The group was so secretive that opponents accused them of living out-of-sight, in the mud—a portrayal that produced the nickname of Catfish Club. That April, the Catfish Club upset all nine of the CCA candidates.

In 1935, the city acted on its hope to attract the Texas Centennial of 1936. Through Robert Thornton, the archetype for strong mayors of Dallas, the city did attract the Centennial. Leaders like Thornton had growth and expansion on their minds. He formed a partnership with Nathan Adams and Fred Florence, chiefs of the two large Dallas banks, and captured the celebration for Dallas, a town that did not exist during the founding of Texas. The event had enormous impact on the city's prestige and attitude of Dallas. Seeing what this kind of coalition could provide, city leaders formed the Dallas Citizens Council in 1937. Its charter was "to study, confer and act upon any matter, civic or economic in character, which may be deemed to affect the welfare of the city of Dallas." The Citizens Council took on broad-scope issues and the CCA became its political arm.

In the mid-1930s, Dallas blacks began to organize their political strength. Although they were not permitted to vote in the Democratic primary (see Terrell Election Law), they were free to vote in state and local elections. However, the $1.75 poll tax was a barrier to most poor blacks. The Ministers Alliance and the Negro Chamber of Commerce encouraged black citizens to pay their poll tax as a step toward gaining a second black high school, jobs on the police and postal force, and better public works in black neighborhoods. The effort culminated in the formation of the Progressive Voters League (PVL) which registered nearly 7000 black voters for the 1937 elections. Blacks became one-sixth of the city electorate and wielded the balance of power by joining supporters of another faction, the Dallas Forward party, which captured five council seats including the mayor's. Promptly after the election, blacks were legally permitted to apply for employment on the police force at pay equal to whites and plans were announced to construct a new black high school in South Dallas.[64] Blacks had won a significant political victory demonstrating to all that the vote was power.

Despite the victory of the Dallas Forward party, the Citizens Council, through its affiliation with the CCA, began a long domination of city politics. The council was staffed with chairmen-of-the-board, leaders of industry, and regional executives of national corporations having significant Dallas payrolls. It grew from Thornton and the bankers to a group of about 250 men who cooperated "for the good of Dallas." Although this became the shadow government of Dallas, it failed to directly represent the poor, minorities, and working class. Nonetheless, its influence made Dallas grow and prosper. Decisions were not made for an individual's or a corporation's profit. The group believed that the trickle-down effect of a prosperous business climate would benefit all of Dallas' citizens. The Citizens Council could make bureaucracy disappear and attracted new businesses, one after another. Through the CCA, the Citizens Council selected city councilmen and financed their campaigns.

Prosperity did abound. National magazines described Dallas as a new kind of energetic city. They also credited Dallas women as being the best dressed in the nation. The average 1939 annual family income in Dallas was $3,600—more than ten times the average in Mississippi.[65]

Racial strife occasionally showed itself during this period. Slum areas, mostly black, had developed in West Dallas along the Trinity River. During the 1940s and 1950s, occasional race-oriented bombings disturbed the tranquillity. Racial restrictions on property deeds were still common. The city even engaged in buying homes from blacks and reselling them to whites. A housing shortage for blacks existed that both worsened conditions in the slum areas and drove blacks from the city. The black population dropped from 17 percent in 1940 to 13 percent in 1950.[66] Two elements were combining in the black community that would fuel the rise to real power in future decades: blacks had a glimpse of the power of the vote in 1937 and they were beginning to get frustrated at their lack of progress.

The Citizens Council and the CCA made decisions for Dallas for another 30 years. Its leadership was so overwhelming that no one bothered to oppose the CCA slate in 1943.[67] In 1949, proponents of popular election of the mayor took to the streets gathering signatures to demand a referendum. With the endorsement of ten percent of the voters, the matter was put to referendum and the charter was changed to popular election.[68] The events were a very early warning of later troubles for the CCA. Its leaders and the city council had publicly disagreed on policy while the citizenry demanded more influence in the decisions of government. In 1951, Jean Baptist Adoue, the man who led the drive for an elected mayor, was endorsed by the CCA and elected mayor. The endorsement was not without hesitation, and the Mayor's term was one of constant conflict with the council. Two years later, Adoue declined to run for medical reasons. For that matter, the entire sitting council decided not to run again. The CCA turned to seventy-two-year-old Robert Thornton who accepted the nomination. Thornton was elected and served with CCA sponsored councils until 1961. His style was businesslike, emphasizing that the city council serve as a board of directors rather than operators of government. Prior to each council meeting, members met in closed door session to discuss the day's issues.[69]

Growth and prosperity continued through the 1940s and 1950s under the strict leadership of the 25-member executive committee of the Citizens Council. The CCA's success spawned the creation of the Committee for Good Schools to select school board candidates. Besides electing candidates, the Citizen's Council acted on terms that were often altruistic, guaranteeing the success of many charitable efforts. In the early 1960s, its influence was so strong that it quietly integrated Dallas business. Realizing that an ugly confrontation over integration would hurt Dallas' businesses, the council demanded the cooperation of business and the police. Segregation in retail services instantly disappeared.

In 1961, Earle Cabell, founder of a chain of ice cream and convenience stores, took over from Thornton. His father and grandfather had both been Dallas mayors. In 1959, Cabell had run against Thornton in a bitter campaign during which Cabell blasted the CCA machine as arrogant and undemocratic. Although Thornton won, the close election shook the CCA. Seeing the need to change its image, it called for grass roots participation of every qualified citizen. The new openness of the CCA failed to lure Cabell into its camp and, running as an independent, he became the first non-CCA mayor since 1937.[70]

Also in 1961, the schools began desegregation with atypical calmness. Again, the business leaders simply would not tolerate the disruptions felt in other parts of the South. Dallas was one of the few large cities to traverse that tense period without racial incidents or riots.[71] President Kennedy praised the city's efforts. Dallas implemented a stair-step plan that began with integration of the first grade, then added another grade each year. Despite the smoothness of its inception, by 1964, only 131 black students attended "white" schools.[72]

By the mid 1960s, times were changing in the nation—a condition that was especially true of the South. The Citizens Council did not have the vision to carry Dallas forward. The council was all alike. These businessmen could see the danger of commercial segregation, but it did not see the unrest that could come from cultural or social segregation.

In 1963, a visit from Adlai Stevenson ended in riot and, a month later, an armed assassin took the life of President Kennedy. These chaotic events upset a heretofore peaceful, political landscape. Dallas had become a prosperous center of Texas business and trade. Its banking and financial institutions were second in Texas only to Houston, and its merchandising markets were first in the Southwest. The assassination and the start of the civil rights era ignited the kindling of unrest that started moderately, but would one day reorder the politics of Dallas.

A year before the passage of the Voting Rights Act, Robert Thornton died and his successor, Earl Cabell, left office to run for Congress. The majority of the city councilmen elected Erik Jonsson, a founder of Texas Instruments and President of the Dallas Citizens Council, to fill Cabell's unexpired term. The Citizens Council was so swift and powerful that some city council members were unaware of Jonsson's selection until they read it in the paper. Nonetheless, he was well accepted because he was the type of dynamic, growth-for-Dallas, leader that Dallas citizens expected. Jonsson began a program called *Goals for Dallas* which solicited thoughts and planning ideas from more than 100,000 Dallas citizens during its first five years. Despite the fact that Jonsson could list many worthwhile accomplishments while in office, he was destined to be the last CCA mayor.[73]

As Lyndon Johnson took office in his own elected term, Dallas was still upbeat and growing. It was home to Texas Instruments, EDS, Neiman-Marcus, Mary Kay Cosmetics, Dr. Pepper, 7-11, Frito Lay, and Blue Cross-Blue Shield. Dallas was business and its celebrities were businessmen.

The demographics of the city continued to be unquestionably white in 1964. South Dallas, almost entirely black by the 1990s was still almost entirely white. The wealthy Jews who had established the city's southern half were mostly gone, but the middle-class Jewish and Christian communities that replaced them were only beginning to move to the north. The main exodus was yet a few years off.[74]

Navajo Reservation: Dinétah

The study of Native-American voting rights presents a different challenge than the study of other major U. S. minorities. Since Indians were an impediment to white, westward expansion, much of government policy has dealt with moving and containing these native peoples. Unlike other minorities, the question of sovereignty stands prominent in any discussion of Indian rights. During George Washington's administration, Secretary of War Henry Knox recommended, and Congress adopted, a policy of negotiating with tribes as nations. Subsequent treaties generally traded vast areas of land for the promise that tribes could continue to govern themselves free of interference of local authorities.[75] This sovereignty question, still not completely answered, has clouded Indian pursuit of traditional civil rights. Looking for sovereignty and a life quite apart from the rest of America has precluded a sharp focus on the types of civil rights that blacks and others pursued. It is not easy to seek a place among equals and be separated by sovereignty at the same time.

Understanding today's Arizona Navajos requires a brief exploration into the history of the Navajo people, their culture, economics, and beliefs. Also necessary for a complete perspective is the legal and political history that affected all U. S. tribes.

Navajos call themselves *Diné*, meaning "the people" or "the only human beings in the world." Today about 200,000 Navajos live on a reservation that covers 4000 rugged square miles of New Mexico, Arizona, and Utah. They share with other American Indians a history of war with white settlers. This largest of American Indian tribes has been party to treaties, revisions, and one federal Indian policy after another. They have been given land and other special governmental treatment in an attempt to preserve their culture on the reservation.

Archeologists believe that two thousand years ago the Navajos were residents of Northwest Canada and Alaska. Over the next fifteen hundred years, they migrated to what is now the Southwest United States which became their *Dinétah*, or homeland.[76] There they learned from the other area tribes, notably the Pueblos and Hopi.

Since their arrival in New Mexico, Arizona, and Utah, the Navajos have been influenced by those who passed through. Missionaries brought religious teachings along with fruits and vegetables. The Spaniards brought the cattle, horses and sheep that became instrumental to transforming the tribe from hunters to ranchers.

Until the 20th century, the Navajos were never a cohesive tribe, but rather a group of communities with common heritage. They consisted of about sixty clans with names like Salt People and Bitter Water. Each clan believed it descended from a single relative. The children, products of parents from two clans, belonged to the mother's clan.[77] Families lived in clusters of hogans with doorways facing east toward the rising sun. The children were raised by the extended families in these housing clusters. The only cause for joining forces with other families and clans was common defense against other tribes or new world settlers. This lack of tribal cohesiveness allowed the early American settlers to encounter very little resistance from the Navajos. Ironically, the hardships that those settlers imposed on the Navajos slowly galvanized them into a single nation.

The long evolution of American perceptions that resulted in Indian relocations are not the subject of this book, however, some background is useful to the appreciation of Indian civil rights. In the 1830s, policy makers struggled with the Cherokee Tribe in Georgia. In the interest of white settlement, President Jackson proposed that the Cherokees be removed to an "ample district west of the Mississippi."[78] Congress and Georgia passed bills to effect the relocation, but the Cherokees sued Georgia in the Supreme Court. Plaintiffs contended they were members of a sovereign nation, thus, not subject to state laws. Chief Justice John Marshall denied the Cherokees petition, but he gave no further clarity to the law. He affirmed that Indian tribes were "a distinct political society, separated from others, capable of managing its own affairs and governing itself." However, he described the Cherokee status by stating, "Their relationship to the United States resembles that of a ward to his guardian."[79]

Two years later, two missionaries who were imprisoned for violating Georgia law by remaining on Cherokee land and encouraging the Indians in their struggle. The prisoners sued the state and ultimately Justice Marshall handed down a decision to free them. This time his words had greater force. He described the Cherokee Nation as "a distinct community . . . in which the laws of Georgia can have no force, and which the citizens of Georgia have no right to enter, but with the assent of the Cherokees themselves, or in conformity with treaties, and with acts of Congress."[80]

President Jackson wholly disagreed with the decision and provided no enforcement of the court's position. The Cherokees finally yielded and moved west. Law and reality frequently differed in the nation's dealings with native Americans.

Treaties were the typical way of reaching an understanding with Indian tribes until 1871 when Congress passed the Indian Appropriations Act. The act did not invalidate any previous treaties, but from that point forward, Congress could simply legislate without the need to negotiate.[81]

For almost all tribes, white settlement dictated a long history of change and hardship. In 1845, John O'Sullivan wrote in the *United States Magazine and Democratic Review*, "It is our manifest destiny to overspread the continent allotted by Providence for the free development of our yearly multiplying millions." *Manifest destiny* became the phrase that represented the expansionary view of the United States and with that expansion came the encampment of Indians.

The influx of Southwest settlers rose sharply after the 1848 Treaty of Guadeloupe Hidalgo ended the Mexican War. As settlements grew, the U. S. began to exert control over the region. In a treaty with the United States at Canyon de Chelly in Arizona, the Navajos made peace and acknowledged the rule of the United States, but conflict continued. In 1863, the Navajos were defeated by Colonel "Kit" Carson who attacked them, killing most of their sheep and starving them into submission. The Navajos were herded to encampments in eastern New Mexico and held for years until they were finally returned to their native land. Of the 12,000 detained at Fort Sumner, only 7,500 survived. The return to their land is known to the Navajos as the *Long Walk*. The tribe emerged from this experience not only greatly reduced in number, but destitute. Detainment and imprisonment became common and peaked around 1906 when as many as 28,000 were incarcerated.

Actions and people outside Dinétah also affected Navajo relations with white settlers. Driven by a conviction that all races were endowed with equal potential, teacher and temperance organizer, Amelia Stone Quinton organized the Women's National Indian Association and petitioned Congress in 1882 to establish programs to assimilate Indians through education, citizenship, and allotment of tribal lands to individual Indians. White America generally agreed with her position.[82] Policies designed to tame the Indians and give them the pride of individual land ownership were called *assimilation*.

These policies did not lead directly to voting rights, however. In April 1880, John Elk, an Indian who voluntarily separated himself from his tribal life to take up a "civilized" existence among whites in Omaha, Nebraska, presented himself to Charles Wilkins, the voting registrar, to have his name listed on the voting roles. Wilkins refused on the grounds that Elk was an Indian and therefore not a citizen. Four years later, the Supreme Court agreed saying that Indians, born as members of a recognized tribe who had not been naturalized or recognized by the United States or a state as a citizen, were not citizens within the meaning of the Fourteenth Amendment.[83] Blanket citizenship did not come to the native Americans for another forty years.

The dilemma of the Supreme Court decision and the sentiment of Quinton and her sympathizers drove Congress, through Senator Henry Dawes, to pass the General Allotment Act of 1887, often known as the Dawes Act. Under this act, Indians in many states could be granted land and given citizenship. The idea was that individual land owners would quickly succumb to white ideals and organization. In North and South Dakota, Indians were granted land and citizenship in a ritual developed by the Secretary of the Interior. Indians were told they had to live as white men. They used their Indian names for the last time, shot their last arrows, and placed their hands on a plow while being lectured about the importance of work. They finally took an oath while touching the stars and stripes.[84]

These cases and legislative activity reflected the attitude of most Americans, however most tribes, including the Navajos, had an existing political culture and society which did not embrace the idea of assimilation. Navajo voting rights were already liberal within the tribe. Each community selected a Headman or peacetime chief. According to Robert Young in his book, *The Political History of the Navajo Tribe*, "The People first carefully considered all available candidates, both male and female, weighing the strengths and weaknesses of one against those of another and finally selected a person in whom the majority had confidence. Women had an equal voice with men in the selection."[85] Once elected, the headman remained in office for life unless he was ejected by those who elected him.[86]

These headmen represented communities, but no one represented the tribe. Other than Indian wars, the greatest problem for the U. S. Government was finding an authorized party with whom to negotiate and make treaties. Time after time, U. S. officials had little success encouraging the establishment of tribal councils. A Navajo named Chee Dodge helped. He was the son of a Navajo mother and a Mexican father and was respected as an educated businessman, leader, and orator. Chee's mother had disappeared during the Kit Carson campaign and, as a young boy, a family found Chee wandering alone and took him to Fort Sumner. Later, living with an Aunt and her white husband, a clerk at Fort Defiance, Chee mastered English and became the translator for the fort.[87] His intelligence along with his understanding of the white man's business allowed him to amass considerable wealth. In 1884, the Department of Interior appointed Chee, Head Chief of the Navajo Tribe, however, the appointment carried considerably more weight with the government than with the Navajos.

Another legal problem that continually plagued Navajo relations with the settlers was land ownership. The Navajos had a much less formal concept of land ownership than the settlers. Natives believed they had rights to any land upon which they and their extended families had hogans. Furthermore, adjacent lands used for water, grazing, or hunting were not to be used by others without permission. The settlers drew stricter boundaries and did not honor "traditional use" kinds of claims. The growing sheep herds of the Navajos, along with a recovering population began to require more land. President Woodrow Wilson used executive orders to add small parcels for Navajo families. Tension with the settlers continued to mount until January 1918 when Wilson granted Navajos 94,000 acres in the Gray Mountain area. Members of the New Mexico delegation to Congress was so irritated at Wilson's actions that they managed to pass legislation giving Congress the exclusive power to grant land to the Indians.

The Tribal Council lead by Chee Dodge served adequately for many years but failed the leadership test in 1921 when the Midwest Refining Company took interest in an oil lease on Navajo land. Lacking a government to deal with, Midwest invited the adult citizens around the Shiprock area to negotiate an agreement. In August of that year, oil was discovered, ushering in a boom for the Shiprock area. The Bureau of Indian Affairs (BIA) believed that the

Navajo Nation as a whole should benefit from this boom, but the council lacked the influence to stand for any real Navajo Nation.[88]

The BIA attempted to rectify the problem, this time creating a business council for the entire reservation. Chee Dodge was a member of this three-man council, but, in the end, this approach failed because the council was not elected. Opponents challenged it based on the 1868 federal treaty providing that three-fourths of the adult Navajos needed to agree before any part of the reservation could be leased or sold.

In 1922, the BIA introduced the chapter system. Chapter officers were elected to represent small regions. This fit the Navajo culture and gave the BIA a reasonably small number of people with whom to deal. The next year, the BIA took another step by establishing rules for a tribal council. It was to be composed of 12 delegates with 12 alternates from the six reservation divisions that had been created in 1910. Although the Tribal Council did not originate with the Navajos, and most of the tribe were unaware of its existence, this was nonetheless an important step toward tribal unity. At the new council's first meeting, Chee Dodge was elected chairman and the federal government gave additional grazing land to the reservation. In exchange, the council gave the Secretary of the Interior the power to negotiate oil and gas treaties for the reservation. This agreement remained in effect for ten years, but it lost significance because the search for more oil and gas failed.

Other important government actions established the premise that all of the reservation was equally held by all Navajo people. These actions, while major steps toward the concept of a Navajo nation, were not intended as steps toward giving up federal control. The federal government still appointed a "Commissioner of the Tribe." The commissioner called meetings of the Tribal Council and the council could not meet without him. The Secretary of the Interior reserved the right to remove members from the council if he had cause. Lacking executive authority, the council was not truly a governing body.

As the fledging Navajo government continued to mature, Congress continued its efforts to grant citizenship and enfranchise the Navajo. Many Indians had been granted citizenship by the Veteran's Citizenship Bill which granted World War I veterans citizenship; by an 1888 act granting citizenship to Indian women who married white men; by the Dawes Act; and by actions of various states. In 1924, Congress passed the Indian Citizenship Act giving citizenship to all Indians to whom it had not previously been granted. Representative Homer Synder of New York introduced the legislation with the belief that the 125,000 Indians it affected would become responsible, good citizens.[89] Despite citizenship, it would take another 24 years before major obstacles to state and federal voting were removed. Many states still relied on an earlier Supreme Court case that concluded, "The Indians owe no allegiance to a state within which the reservations may be established, and the state gives them no protection."[90]

Three years later, John Hunter, a division councilman, introduced a new version of the chapter system in his own district. This gave those tribespeople greater control in local affairs and was popular enough that other divisions followed suit. Chapter meetings created an open forum for Indians to meet with the Public Health Service and the Indian Bureau.

At the council meeting in November 1928, Chee Dodge declined the nomination for Chairman. Deshna Chiscilly was elected and immediately faced a voting rights struggle. The southern district had sent two delegations, one elected the previous April and the other in September. Between the two elections, women gained the right to run, thus the latter delegation contained women. After considerable debate, the September delegation was seated.

As political unity slowly took shape, the economic structure began to unravel. A significant struggle brewed between the federal overseers and the tribe over grazing rights. The Navajos' sheep had so overgrazed the land that erosion was taking over. A compromise placed a limit on the number of livestock owned and levied a fine for any overage.

In 1928, the Rockefeller Foundation surveyed the status of American Indians. The report faulted the government for its approach to the Indians. It pointed out that government policy had been shaped around Indian lands rather than Indian welfare. Attempts to "Americanize" or "Christianize" Indian students in boarding schools had failed because the schools were poor and the Indians had little willingness to change their culture. Many of the schools became child labor camps where students spent half the day in classes and the remainder in vocational training doing laundry or heavy farm work. The report claimed that children slept in overcrowded attics and were frequently undernourished. Even where schools provided education, the cultural gulf between the Navajos and the BIA was enormous. The Navajos believed it was wrong to interact with non-Navajos. The families frequently performed squaw dances to cleanse the children from the cultural contamination of the schools.

English schooling problems were not unique to the Navajo. It is significant here because the schooling needed for English literacy was prerequisite to voting in U. S. elections. Indians across the nation have been the subjects of many educational experiments. In the early years of the Jamestown colony,

Indians attended white schools. In 1836, Harvard listed among its goals the education of Indians in knowledge and goodness. Later, the founder of Dartmouth College stated his plan to "cure the Natives of their Savage Temper" and to "purge all the Indian out" out of his Iroquois students. Most programs since have been designed to bring the Indian into western civilization. Such an approach was viewed as the only long-term solution to such vastly different cultures. Settlers generally considered the Indians to be amoral savages. Despite often genuine desires to improve the lot of the Indians, the message was most often the same. Whites expected Indians to culturally convert or face complete overrun. In 1819, The House Committee on Appropriations allocated $10,000 for a "Civilization Fund" for the education of Indians. The Committee stated, "Either that those sons of the forest should be moralized or exterminated."[91]

Arizona courts and Arizona law also played a role in Indian civil rights. A 1928 state Supreme Court decision denied Indians the right to vote on the ground that Indians living on the reservation are persons "under guardianship" and hence "wards of the national government" within the meaning of the Arizona Constitution. The opinion was emphatic.

> It is undisputed law. Laid down by the Supreme Court of the United States innumerable times, . . . that all Indians are wards of the federal government and as such are entitled to the care and protection due from a guardian to his ward.[92]

Only one justice dissented contending that Indians were now citizens and thus should be allowed to vote.[93] The decision was not appealed. It was construed by Arizona's Attorney General to apply not only to reservation Indians, but to all Indians, severance from tribal lands or affiliation notwithstanding. For twenty years the case went unchallenged.[94]

By the early 1930s, true tribal government began to emerge. Local chapter leaders began meeting to discuss regional matters. The Tribal Council was expanded to 24 members just by seating the alternates. In 1933, Thomas Dodge, Chee's son, aligned himself with the BIA, declaring that the council was out of date and that it should take greater control of Indian affairs. Agreeing, the council promptly rescinded the authority it had given the Secretary of Interior to negotiate oil leases.

The struggle for grazing land continued. Attempting to promote land stability, Congress passed the Indian Reorganization Act (IRA). It ended the unregulated sale of Indian land, set aside acreage for purchase by the Indians, and provided loans for economic development. Additional provisions gave the Interior Secretary power to control erosion by regulating land use and allowed the tribes to create their own constitutions. The act provided that individual tribes could reject it by popular vote. Most Navajos came to equate the IRA with livestock reduction and, by a narrow margin, the tribe rejected it.[95]

Chee Dodge very much wanted the Navajos to have a constitution, but he never got one. One draft constitution was drawn in 1936, but was rejected by Interior Secretary Harold Ickes because he disagreed with the government structure it would have created. The idea of a Navajo constitution generated controversy over fundamental questions. Some Washington officials questioned the right of Navajos, who had rejected the IRA, to construct a constitution. Some worried that the Navajo constitution could not be protected by Congress. Constitutions created under the IRA could only be abolished by the tribes themselves while the Navajo constitution could be abolished by a future Secretary of the Interior. Others recognized the conflicts between the federal government and the tribe and bemoaned the idea that the Navajos' constitutional power could negate federal programs. Still others contended that acceptance or rejection of the IRA was immaterial because tribes had "residual sovereignty" as ruled by the courts since the mid-1800s. This idea denied the ability of the federal government to take these powers from the tribes with or without a constitution.[96] These fundamental questions have never been fully resolved.

During the remainder of the 1930s, the Interior Department continued to fine tune the Tribal Council and control land use. The number of tribal delegates was increased to 74 to better represent a growing constituency. Chairman and Vice Chairman positions became elected. The previous six federal administrative districts became one located at Window Rock. The first agent of this new combined district carried out a soil erosion program by greatly reducing the number of flocks. Many Navajos, displaced from ranching, began seeking employment in nearby towns. Some found jobs with the railroad while others became waiters and maids. By the end of the decade, such employment was common.

In 1937, Navajos on the Utah side of the reservation were affected by the Utah Attorney General's contention that reservation Indians could not vote in Utah elections because they were not residents of the state. He maintained this despite Supreme Court decisions to the contrary.[97]

The BIA, part of the Interior Department, has always played a difficult role with respect to Indians. The Department has been protector, guardian, mentor, parent, and controller of the tribes. Despite arguments that the BIA has been overly bureaucratic and controlling, the Interior Department has generally championed Indian rights. In 1938, contrary to the Utah Attorney General, the Department's solicitor issued his opinion:

> I am of the opinion that the 15th amendment clearly prohibits any denial of the right to vote to Indians under circumstances in which non-Indians would be permitted to vote.

In 1940, Congress passed the Immigration and Nationality Act which naturalized any Indians who had somehow escaped all previous opportunities to become citizens.

World War II aided in further scattering the Navajos. Many went to war where some Navajos took on the unique job of Codetalkers, using the Navajo language and idioms to transmit secret codes. The number of American males in the military created a U. S. labor shortage which demanded Navajos for copper mines, shipyards, railroads and agriculture. Many of these Native Americans saw the world for the first time in a role other than as a ward of the government. This intermixing with the rest of America began to change the culture. For the first time, the English binomial system of naming people became popular. Such naming was practically a prerequisite to using U. S. administrative systems such as voter registration.

As the war ended, most of these workers were obliged to return to the reservation, creating new economic hardships for the tribe. The returning Navajos had a better understanding of possessions and the importance of education. The remaining effects of herd reduction and the discontinuity of the war left the reservation in cultural chaos. Peter MacDonald, subsequent leader of the Navajo Nation, described the reservation after his return from World War II:

> By the time I returned all . . . had changed. Suddenly drinking offered an escape from the sense of hopelessness. I saw alcohol openly consumed during squaw dances and other ceremonies. Navajo were becoming belligerent and depressed from drinking too much. They would sometimes disrupt sacred ceremonies, a shocking situation for someone like me who had not seen the slow decline of the people. Even worse was the alcohol consumption among the young. Teenagers of 15 and 16 were drinking openly.[98]

By 1946, less than one-third of the Navajo children were in schools. The government responded with programs to build schools in remote areas and bolster the boarding school programs, but illiteracy remained epidemic on the reservation.

A 1947 government report showed Navajos among the poorest people in the nation. Tribal chief Sam Ahkeah saw poverty and ignorance everywhere and believed that less federal wardship and greater Navajo self-determination was the answer. The report also determined that the land could support no more than half of the 70,000 Navajos on the reservation. It recognized that small businesses, such as garages, shops, tourist facilities, and mines for low grade coal, would open on the reservation. Finally, the report urged suffrage for the Indians.[99]

In 1948, disfranchising interpretations of the Arizona Constitution were declared unconstitutional by the Arizona Supreme Court. The Arizona Supreme Count narrowed the interpretation of the term "guardian" in the Arizona Constitution to mean only judicially established guardianships, thus the state was no longer a guardian to the Indians.[100] For the first time, Arizona Reservation Indians were then permitted to vote in state primaries.[101] Arizona was the one of the last states to grant Indian franchise; only New Mexico and Utah followed.[102]

Despite this empowering decision, the case had limited effect since the Arizona Constitution required that voters be able to "read the U. S. Constitution in the English Language."[103] This provision had been penned in 1912 to protect Arizona from dominance by Spanish speaking Americans.[104]

Nonetheless, this new power of voting prompted the Tribal Council to adopt, in September 1950, new election procedures which addressed many flaws of Navajo voting in earlier elections. They instituted voter registration; a provision that the chairman and vice-chairman run on the same ticket; a paper ballot containing photos of all the candidates; plurality victories; and absentee voting.[105]

By the late 1950s, the government instituted a program providing Navajo families one-way bus fare to major cities at which a BIA representative would meet the Navajo, help him find low rent housing, a job, and training if necessary. This minor integration of Navajos into the mainstream of American life inspired a new federal policy known as *termination*. This policy saw a gradual withdrawal of both federal funds and special protection for the reservation. It pushed more responsibility on the states and assumed that Indians would want to migrate into the white community, but most Navajos were not hoping to be treated like everyone else. Preserving, as best they could, their ancient ways, had not prepared them for mainstream life.

Continuing the policy of termination, Congress passed the Navajo-Hopi Rehabilitation Act of 1950. It encouraged the Navajos to take charge of their own economic affairs. The act granted $88 million over ten years for the development of schools and roads. School funding for the reservation was an issue in Arizona. Public schools were generally funded by the state, but residents of the reservation were exempt from state and local taxes. In 1953, the federal government agreed to fund the reservation school system.

Section 6 of the Navajo-Hopi Rehabilitation Act also allowed the Navajos to exercise their *residual powers*, that is, "any powers vested in the tribe or any organ thereof by existing law, together with such additional powers as the members of the Tribe may, with the approval of the Secretary of the Interior, deem proper to include therein." The Tribal Council interpreted the already vested powers to include all unrestricted authorities stemming from the residual sovereignty of the tribe. Federal officials, however, contended that this wording did not permit the tribe or the Secretary and the tribe to exclude the Navajos from any federal statutes generally applicable to Indians. They held that only Congress had the authority to make exceptions. The impasse of this debate effectively quelled another Navajo attempt at installing a constitution.[106]

In August 1953, Congress passed *House Concurrent Resolution 108* which declared its intention to "make the Indians within the territorial limits of the United States subject to the same laws and entitled to the same privileges and responsibilities as are applicable to other citizens of the United States, to end their status as wards of the United States, to grant them all the rights and prerogatives pertaining to American citizenship."[107] This continuing policy of termination did not lead to the demise of the reservation or any particular assimilation into white America, but the Navajos did begin taking more independent action. Rather than being a step toward tribal disappearance, it was a step toward sovereignty. Soon, Navajos were running their own courts and police departments. By 1960, they took over the irrigation system. As a result of an oil and gas find, the tribe was able to begin funding more of its own institutions.

In 1964, President Jonhson's War on Poverty created the Office of Navajo Equal Opportunity (ONEO) which provided legal aid against employment discrimination. The first head of the ONEO was Peter MacDonald, who later became leader of the Navajo Nation and a significant force in altering the reservation's role with the government.

Born in 1928 in the reservation community of Teec Nos Pos, MacDonald grew up learning traditional Navajo culture and lore. His grandmother was a bitter survivor of the *Long Walk* and told Peter stories of the early abuse by white settlers. He was the token child of the family, meaning he was given to the BIA boarding school system where he acquired his Anglo name. He repeatedly demonstrated his disinterest by escaping from the school. MacDonald's family was relatively prosperous until 1934 when the livestock reduction plan forced them to give up most of their sheep and cattle. He reflects that this reduction destroyed the possibility of maintaining a traditional Navajo lifestyle and robbed the tribespeople of any reward for hard work. He was a Codetalker in World War II and received a BS in electrical engineering in 1957 from Oklahoma University. He pursued an engineering career with Hughes Aircraft until 1963 when he returned to the reservation to work in tribal government. Later, MacDonald would play a pivotal role in building a more sovereign Navajo Nation.

FIGURE 2: ARIZONA COUNTY MAP

Arizona population is a product of the last half-century. After World War II, the population was only 700,000 compared with nearly 4,000,000 in 1995.[108] This rapid growth has brought the state into continuous creation and reallocation of voting districts.

Navajo and Apache Counties are located largely on the reservation, occupying about 21,000 square miles of Arizona. Their 1990 population was 139,276 of whom only 33,994 were old enough to vote. Together, the counties are 63 percent Native American, 31 percent white, and six percent Hispanic.[109]

As early as 1960, legal conflicts over Navajo voting power and representation began. In April, Gary P. Klahr sued the Governor of Arizona, claiming that the state districting laws were unconstitutional.[110] Arizona is unique in that over 80 percent of its land is owned by the federal government or the reservation. During the 1960s, the population shifted rapidly, obsoleting the data used for calculating district apportionment. Klahr alleged that both the state house and senate were apportioned on the basis of geography rather than population. A three judge federal court gave the legislature time to work out a new plan. In April of the next year, with no new plan having been drawn, the case was amended to include a claim that the U. S. congressional districts were also unfair. Arizona had three U. S. House districts containing 51, 34, and 15 percent of the population respectively. Reacting to the amended case, the Governor called a special session of the legislature and the court agreed to wait for the result of that session.

The special session produced Senate Bill 11 which attempted to deal with the state senate apportionment. Still, that bill created one senator for a county of 7,700 and another senator for a county of 55,000—numbers that diminished Navajo voter influence. The session took no action on reapportionment of the state house or U. S. congressional districts.

As President Johnson signed the Voting Rights Act in August 1965, the Klahr case was still in progress with no resolution in sight.

Dade County, Florida: America's Youngest Metroplex

Dade County history provides excellent insight into Hispanic voting rights in America. Today, more than 21 million Hispanics live in the United States, with a population increasing five times as fast as that of other inhabitants. Projecting into the future, one-third of the U. S. population could be Hispanic by the end of the 21st century.[111]

Dade County derived from Hispanic roots, but had no major Hispanic population until the mid-20th century. The county, whose largest city is Miami, is one of the most recently populated of America's metropolises. Despite this, Dade boosts one of the longest histories. Native Americans inhabited the area in 1513 when Juan de Ponce de Leon first sighted the Florida coast in search of the Fountain of Youth. In 1545, Hernando d' Escalante Fonteneda shipwrecked along the Dade County coast making him the first recorded white person to inhabit the area, albeit for 17 years as a captive of the local Indians. In the late 1560s, Spanish Jesuits tried to establish missions in the area, but the Spanish military could not defend fledging missions from Indian attack. Such were the early forays by explorers into south Florida.[112]

Nearly 200 years passed with little activity from the Spanish until 1743 when the Jesuits established the San Ignacio mission at what is now Coconut Grove. Natives not only threatened the missions, but the small tribes of south Florida, namely Timucua, Apalachee, and Calusa, also threatened one another.[113]

In the same year, following a seven-year struggle, Spain ceded Florida to Great Britain who dominated the territory through most of the American Revolution. Upon signing the Treaty of Paris in 1783, Spain regained Florida. By the end of the 18th century, colonization began in Dade County. Earlier activities centered on general exploration and Catholic conversion, but in 1796 The King of Spain issued the first land grant. Spain issued other land grants until 1819 when the United States bought Florida in the Adams-Onis Treaty.

South Florida still had few settlers. The first official census in 1830 counted only 517.[114] The threat of Indian attack thwarted development, so in 1832, the Seminoles, who along with the Creeks had absorbed most of the earlier tribes including Hispanic halfbreeds and runaway slaves from Georgia and Alabama,[115] were ordered to leave Florida for new lands in the West. Chief Osceola resisted in the second Seminole War (1835-1842), but the tribe succumbed and the survivors were moved to Oklahoma. One of the U. S. officers massacred in this war was Francis L. Dade for whom the county was later named.

The value of the south Florida port was recognized in 1834 when the military built a naval base on the Miami River. Two years later, the Florida territorial legislature established Dade County. Dade was larger than the county of today encompassing what is now Broward, Palm Beach, and part of Martin Counties. In 1915, those counties were carved out and Dade took on its present boundaries.

The heart of Dade's story is its unusual growth profile—lackluster at the start, followed by a rapid ramp-up in the 20th century. Despite government efforts to remove the Indians, in 1845 when Florida became a state, Dade had scarcely 150 white settlers, and a total population around 450. The count dropped to 159 in the 1850 census and dropped again to 83 in 1860.[116]

Florida entered the Union as a slave state. In 1861 it seceded and briefly became an independent republic which then fought alongside the South and was defeated with it.[117] After the War, Florida was left under military rule and was readmitted to the Union in 1868 only after adopting a state constitution that provided for black suffrage and the abolition of slavery.

Beginning in 1870, Dade made its first meager effort towards growth. The population was still less than 100, but William Brickell bought a section of land and opened a trading post on the south side of the Miami River.[118] The county elected its first commissioners in 1877 and by 1880 the population had grown to 257. Fifteen years after the end of the Civil War, the county opened its first hotel, the Peacock Inn.

In 1895, Miami hit a turning point when Henry Flagler took land for growing citrus in exchange for a promise to extend his railroad to Miami, install waterworks, and perform other public improvements. As the railroad approached, the Miami Hotel was begun and the county population reached 3,322. A year later Flagler's railroad reached Miami, spawning settlements along its path. Things were moving at last. Flagler began building the plush Royal Palm Hotel. Miami was connected by rail to Fort Lauderdale, new businesses opened, and the Miami city population reached 1000, most of whom had to live in tents. Mayor John Reilly, supported by seven councilmen, had yet to attract a fire department and a fire at Brady's Grocery Store burned down three city blocks of new businesses. Within months, Flagler's water system and a lighting system were inaugurated,[119] but soon the city center burned down again. This time a fire department was formed.

Preparing for Spanish-American War, Miami became an encampment for 7,500 troops—several times the local population—but the troops departed after an outbreak of yellow fever. As they left, Flagler's Royal Palm opened—six stories high with a swimming pool. This hotel was of such grandeur that it attracted celebrities like John D. Rockefeller, Vincent Astor, and Warren G. Harding.[120]

At the turn of the century, Dade County seemed to be on a roll at last. The population was nearly 5000, 1681 of whom were in Miami. Only five years later, Miami alone was nearly 5000. The fire had finally ignited, but visitors arrived only during a limited season. No one would visit between June and November and suffer the heat and mosquitoes. The Royal Palm, replete with European waiters, opened each January and closed with a lavish party on Washington's birthday.[121]

The seeds of tourism were planted as Miami continued to grow. By 1910, Dade had more than doubled since the turn of the century. Already 400 people had phones. Miami Beach had failed at efforts to raise coconuts and avocados, so John S. Collins, who owned most of the land, decided to sell lots to tourists. To make this possible, he sunk 100,000 1912-dollars into a bridge across Biscayne Bay only to run out of money one-half mile short. Carl Fisher, a self-made millionaire and builder of the Indianapolis Speedway, took over, completed the bridge, and began constructing golf courses, hotels, and mansions. He platted off the remainder into lots that could be auctioned off.[122]

Land within Miami was deeded in such a way that whites reserved all the bayfront property and land on both sides of the Miami River. Blacks were confined to the northwest corner beyond the railroad tracks in an area known as "colored town" or Overtown.[123]

By 1920 Dade was growing like topsy as World War I airmen who trained there returned with friends and families. Five years later the population had doubled again. The city had a skyline of high-rises in various stages of completion. There had been so little planning that, in 1923, Miami reorganized its street names by culling the duplicates and multi-named streets under threat that the post office would not deliver the mail. Land speculation in the 1920s became rampant and many lost their investment as their residential lots flooded.

Promoters like George Merrick, developer of Coral Gables, bought entire sections of the Miami newspaper, and filled them with illustrations of projected developments drawn by imaginative artists. He paid William Jennings Bryan, the "silver tongued orator," $100,000 per year to sell building lots. In 1925, the 115-acre Seminole Beach in Boward, for which developers paid $3,000,000, was sold in six hours for $4,645,000. Late that year, 400 acres of Miami shore waterfront lots were sold to near rioters for $34 million, but the buyers, unable to make quick profits, began defaulting. This damaged the boom, but the fatal shot came in 1926 when a hurricane caused massive destruction. Merrick went from assets of 100 million to those of a pauper.[124]

By 1930, Pam Am had started air service between Miami and Havana, the extravagant Royal Palm was condemned as unsafe, and the Dade County population reached 142,995.[125] Towns were rapidly being incorporated within Dade. The next decade would see many more incorporations and another doubling of population.

Economic hardship and corruption hit Miami with the depression of the 1930s. The city defaulted on its bonds. Policemen and public officials were involved in bribery and corruption. Big-time gambling and national gambling figures moved in spreading a network of crime. The Mayor and two councilmen were indicted on bribery charges, causing the court to demand recall elections. Although the officials were ultimately acquitted, they were removed from office.

In 1933, Guiseppi Zangara bought a pistol at a Miami hock shop and joined the crowds pouring into Bayfront Park seeking a glimpse of Franklin D. Roosevelt. Zangara shot at the president-elect, missed, and killed the President's friend, the Mayor of Chicago. Zangara was convicted shouting, "I kill presidents," and was later executed.[126]

Through the remainder of the 1930s, although Miami struggled with the depression, things began to boom. Jews arrived to pick up the slack as both brokers and buyers of property. The influx was so great that Yiddish, synagogues, delicatessens, and Hebrew academies became commonplace.[127] With this influx came the beginning of a tourist season for the city.

Toward the end of the decade the Ku Klux Klan became active, holding public parades and warning blacks not to vote in upcoming elections. Klan members burned crosses at one-block intervals. A dummy, hanging by a noose from a power pole bore a sign, "This Nigger voted."[128] Because blacks voted anyway, on May 10, 1939, the state legislature passed a law barring blacks from voting in primaries. Of Miami's 167,000 residents, about 30,000 were blacks including 5000 Bahama natives.[129] Blacks were limited to jobs as servants and laborers.

Dade County came out of the Depression into war. As tourists left, the permanent population growth slowed, but Miami became home to thousands of military personnel. Hotels were used as barracks and hospitals. South Florida was close to the war. A German submarine blew up a tanker 20 miles south of Cape Canaveral and another sub sank a Mexican tanker just off Miami.

Despite the war, the modern resort city was growing and the city's surrounding county became more important. Hotel row on Miami Beach had a good start by the early part of the 1940s, but hotels were still boarded up in the summertime. A succession of hurricanes during the decade caused widespread disasters. One in 1947 was so bad that it prompted a $208,000,000 Corps of Engineers project to build locks and levees. This drainage caused a housing boom, particularly in the less-expensive, unincorporated area of the county. Veterans could buy homes in these areas with their GI benefits. County services outside Miami were virtually non-existent. It frequently took over two years to get phone service. The gradual transformation of a city into a countywide system began. In the last half of the decade, 14 county school systems were consolidated into one and the airport along with the charity hospital were turned over to the county.

By 1950, Dade County contained nearly 300,000 people. Despite being the hurricane capitol of the world, people flocked there. The growth rate was even greater than the 1920s, although less riotously speculative. Until 1949, Florida laws allowed 25 or more persons of any town who were freeholders and registered voters to form an incorporated municipality by gaining concurrence of two-thirds of the affected residents. By doing so, they earned for themselves all the powers of taxation and regulation granted by the state to cities. In 1949 the laws became much stricter, but the damage was already done. Lax legislation had led to a checkerboard pattern of government across the county. Now with 26 cities in Dade County, there was a proliferation of local authorities, petty rivalries, and overlapping jurisdictions resulting in inefficient delivery of services. People moved into unincorporated areas to avoid city taxes altogether. Miami tried unsuccessfully to expand its boundaries into the unincorporated areas.[130] The momentum toward a countywide, metropolitan government was underway.

Tourism continued to prosper. The airline industry, boosted by war, now attracted commercial airlines. Travel agents created summertime packages between the hotels and airlines in hopes of keeping hotels open through cheap, off-season rates. Radio personality, Arthur Godfrey broadcast from the Kennilworth Hotel. Everyday, sunning himself by the pool, he promoted subtropical living to freezing Northerners.

Racial bias still had underpinnings in Miami. In 1951, dynamite blasts shook Carver Village in what many believed to be a protest against the opening of the apartments to blacks. In the same year, dynamite blasts hit a Hebrew School. On Christmas day, Harry T. Moore, the state coordinator for the NAACP, was murdered in an explosion that ripped through his residence. The next year, conservative Dade County began to deal with race problems. The Dade County Council of Community Relations began a process that began desegregation of the schools without trauma.

In 1954, a three year process began that would create the modern Dade County government. A study was published called *The Government of Metropolitan Miami* which took a comprehensive look at the problems of Dade County. The report found that the 650,000-person county lacked countywide administration, good financial procedures, common service levels, and reasonable organization. Among the changes recommended by the report was the addition of a countywide government. The report stated, "The metropolitan government should be constituted with an elective legislative body chosen at-large from specific representative districts of comparable population, plus representatives selected by the voters of local municipal units possessing at least eight percent of the population of the metropolitan area. Thus both the general public and the cities of suitable status would be represented in the metropolitan government."[131]

Over the next two years the issue of Dade County's government was debated as the county continued to grow. Most of the study recommendations won out. Florida voters approved a constitutional amendment that gave the county *home rule*. Counties had been constrained by state law to the limited authorities specifically delegated by the state. Home rule allowed self-government as long as it was not inconsistent with state or federal law. Given their new power, voters narrowly passed a new charter that created a county commission with 11 members, five elected at-large, five elected from and by districts, and one from Miami. This council was then the appointing body for the county manager.

By the late 1950s, the county was just shy of one million people. The commission expanded by two members, one representing Hialeah and one representing Miami Beach. School integration was materializing. Over 50 of Dade's 206 public schools were integrated with 5000 of the area's 38,000 blacks in formerly all-white schools.

On January 1, 1959, President Fulgencio Batista fled for his life leaving Cuba in the arms of Fidel Castro and communism.[132] Many Cubans who had left their homeland during the Batista regime, returned to Cuba. As Castro drifted further and further to the left, land owners and business people who could not negotiate with the new authorities, began to trickle back to Miami. Regular Havana-Miami airlifts continued to move escapees after the 1961 *Bay of Pigs* invasion, but ceased after the 1962 Cuban missile crisis. Immigration continued, however, and by 1963, registrants at the Cuban Refugee Center numbered 168,897. Two year later, the number reached 210,000. Despite these new residents, net growth had been kept down by white-flight to neighboring counties and the new Cuban Refugee program created by the Kennedy administration designed to resettle Cubans across the country.[133] Dade County, whose population had doubled in each of the last three decades, grew only 18 percent in the 1960s.

As the Voting Rights Act was constructed in Congress, Miami coped with this influx of Cubans. Dade County was a collection of newcomer Anglos and immigrants. It did not share the history and cotton culture of most of the South. Whites were as likely to carry a Boston accent as a Georgia one. Yet, as Cubans began trickling into the area in the early 1960s, they saw scenes of discrimination typical of southern cities. Blacks could not eat a white restaurants or swim at Miami's most famous beaches; they even paid taxes at a separate window in the Dade County courthouse.

Several Supreme Court decisions affected the Dade County Commissioners' apportionment.[134] New principles that called for districts of equal size could not be reconciled with the single-member districts in the current system. In 1963, Dade County split into warring factions over the best way to elect commissioners. Pushed by the Chamber of Commerce, Dade reapportioned itself into an all at-large commission.

CHAPTER 4: VOTING RIGHTS ACT OF 1965

Preparing for Legislation

Civil rights organizations stepped onto the front pages in 1964. The Student Non-violent Coordinating Committee (SNCC) led efforts to organize the "Mississippi Freedom Summer" in which black and white college students and volunteer lawyers joined local black workers to conduct door-to-door voter registration canvassing in Mississippi. That summer resulted in violence including bombed churches, injuries, beatings, and the deaths of civil rights workers. In the same year, Dr. Martin Luther King, Jr. noted, "Today, a shift in the Negro vote could upset the outcome of several state contests and affect the result of a Presidential election. Only with the growth of an enlightened electorate, white and Negro together, can we put a quick end to this century-old stranglehold of a minority [of whites] on the nation's legislative processes."[1]

The Southern Christian Leadership Conference (SCLC), led by Dr. King, chose to showcase its cause in Selma, Alabama because black registration was nearly impossible there and the local sheriff could be counted on to overreact to peaceful demonstrations. Dallas County, in which Selma is located, comprised 15,000 people, about half of whom were black. Only 156 blacks were registered to vote in the county—a number that had grown by only 14 in the previous ten years. King had gone to Selma two months before the demonstrations and announced that he would fight the town's voter registration policies. At the current rate of registration, he commented, "it would take about 103 years to register the adult Negroes."[2] Through Selma, he attempted to acquaint the nation with the issue of black disfranchisement in the South. King and the SCLC focused their vision on new voting rights legislation. They knew that white violence against peaceful blacks was their only short-term hope of energizing Congress. The Selma sheriff did his part. The demonstrations resulted in a bloody confrontation with state troopers producing many arrests, including, as planned, Dr. King's.[3] Federal officials became involved and on March 7, 1965, 4000 civil rights marchers, led by King and accompanied by federal troops, walked from Selma to Montgomery, Alabama.

Selma began a new era for media. Television brought scenes of ferocious, snarling police dogs into most American homes. Congress had no choice but to become energized. President Lyndon Johnson who had promised action in the voting rights area, personally supported the protest at Selma in a press conference:

> I should like to say that all Americans should be indignant when one American is denied the right to vote. The loss of that right to a single citizen undermines the freedom of every citizen. This is why all of us should be concerned with the efforts of our fellow Americans to register to vote in Alabama. . . . Nothing is more fundamental [than voting] to American citizenship and to our freedom as a nation and its people. I intend to see that that right is secured for all our citizens.[4]

Exploiting the energy produced by the Freedom Summer, a 1964 murder in Philadelphia, Mississippi, and the brutality of Selma, King met with the President and described what he thought new voting legislation needed:

> Such new legislation must provide machinery which is virtually automatic to eliminate the interposition of varying standards and crippling discretion on the part of hostile state officials. . . It must put to an end the use of literacy tests in those areas where Negroes have been disadvantaged by generations of inferior, segregated education. It must apply to all elections—federal, state, or even for sheriff, school board, etc. Enforcement of such legislation must be reposed in federal registrars appointed by and responsible to the President. They must be empowered to act swiftly and locally to insure the nondiscriminatory use of simplified federal machinery. Such legislation at the very minimum should be directed at the most oppressive regions as typified by Selma and other hard-core areas in the South.[5]

King had enormous influence in shaping the Voting Rights Act which was patterned directly from his request. Johnson asked Attorney General Nicholas Katzenbach to "write the god-damnest, toughest voting rights act you can devise."[6] A draft of the act was given to Johnson on March 5, 1965. Less than two weeks later, Reverend Reeb was beaten to death in Selma. The trauma was immediately felt in Washington and Congress began calling for passage of voting legislation.[7] Johnson trumpeted the cause by saying "we shall overcome" as he proposed the Voting Rights Act to a joint session of Congress. He added, "The vote is the most powerful instrument ever devised by man for breaking down injustice and destroying the terrible walls which imprison men because they are different from other men."

Legislators knew they were dancing on the edges of a constitutional issue, but they banked on the belief that the judiciary would back them up if they framed the legislation as a safeguard of the rights guaranteed by the 14th and 15th Amendments. In an 1880 case, the Supreme Court had committed to support "whatever legislation is appropriate, that is, adopted to carry out the objects the Amendments [13th, 14th, and 15th] have in view, whatever tend to enforce submission to the prohibitions they contain, and to secure to all persons the enjoyment of perfect equality of civil rights and equal protection of the laws against state denial or invasion, . . ."[8]

Pushed by outrage at the events in Selma, Congress passed the Voting Rights Act in the summer of 1965. The House passed the bill by a vote of 378 to 74, and the Senate by 79 to 18. Johnson, who signed the bill into law on August 6, 1965, would later claim that the signing of this act was his greatest accomplishment.[9]

Dr. King and the SCLC had triumphed. A perfectly planned and timed arrest in a stereotypical Alabama county seat had moved the nation to act against the political incumbents in the South. King prescribed the act that Congress passed, beginning a legal path that few of the drafters could have predicted.

The Act[10]

The Voting Rights Act, Chapter 20 of Title 42, Public Health and Welfare, is a set of legislation covering elective franchise or the right of citizens to vote. Congress designed this complex law to give the executive and judicial branches of government the ability to accelerate achievement of the guarantees of the 14th and 15th Amendments. Although earlier civil rights legislation contained all the necessary measures to protect the right of citizens to vote, the Voting Rights Act aided enforcement. Its provisions departed from earlier civil rights legislation by giving the attorney general and the courts broad new powers to grant relief whenever a court found violations of the 15th Amendment. Amendments to the act in 1970 and 1975 expanded its muscle and covered more minority groups, and amendments in 1982 gave it more sweeping powers that codified the increasingly liberal view of voting power that the courts developed during the 1970s.

It is necessary to understand some details of the act to analyze subsequent court actions. Broadly, the law did three things: It defined an enforcement mechanism to ensure the administration of a discrimination-free electoral process; it established extraordinary mechanisms or "special provisions" to monitor certain states and counties; and it created a triggering mechanism to bring most of the South under federal monitoring and the special provisions of enforcement. A few of the sections became so instrumental to plaintiff's claims that the section numbers became official jargon to describe aspects of the law itself. The 1965 Act was divided into fourteen sections. The most significant are presented here, out of order, to facilitate their understanding:

- Section 2: The act began with Section 2 stating, "No voting qualifications, prerequisite to voting, or standard, practice, or procedure shall be imposed or applied by any state or political subdivision to deny or abridge the right of any citizen of the United States to vote on account of race or color."
- Section 4(b): This section defined an "automatic trigger." A state or one of its political subdivisions came under "special provisions" of the act (described in subsequent sections) if, on November 1, 1964, it maintained any test or device that was a prerequisite to voter registration, and either the total number of registered voters was less than 50 percent of the voting age citizens or less than 50 percent of the voting age citizens voted in the 1964 presidential election. A test or device generally meant a literacy test (See Section 4(c)). If a state statistically qualified for the automatic trigger, all political subdivisions of the state were subject to its provisions. Thus, all counties and cities were at the mercy of every test used anywhere in the state during a statewide election. The states and counties affected in 1965 by this formula were Alabama, Alaska, Georgia, Louisiana, Mississippi, South Carolina, Virginia, Yuma County (Arizona), Honolulu County (Hawaii), and 39 counties of North Carolina.

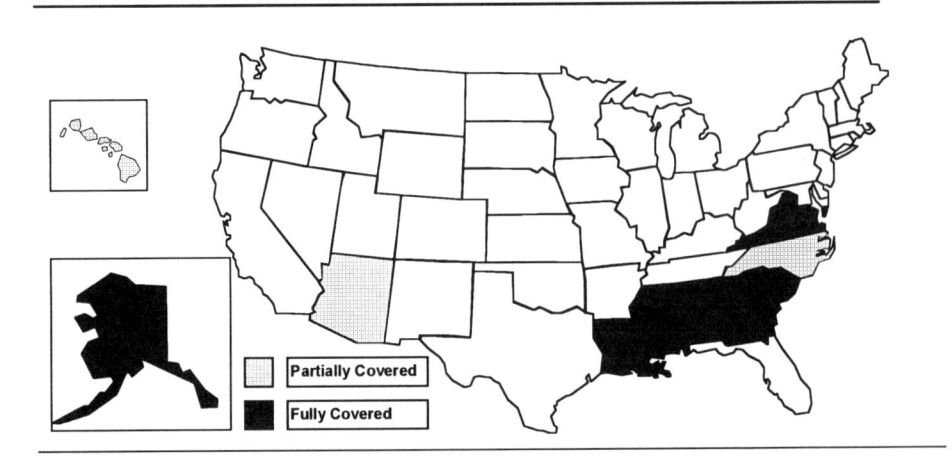

FIGURE 3: AREAS AFFECTED BY THE AUTOMATIC TRIGGER (1965)

- Section 4(c): This section defined the tests or devices, referenced in the automatic trigger mechanism (Section 4(b)), as any prerequisite to registration that demonstrated "the ability to read, write, understand, or interpret any matter," tests that demonstrated knowledge or achievement in any particular subject, anything used to establish "good moral character," or anything that proved voter "qualifications by the voucher of previously registered voters, or member of any other class."

- Section 4(a): This section defined the first "special provision" which was suspension of all tests or devices in any jurisdiction caught by the "automatic trigger" (Section 4(b)). The suspension was to remain in effect for five years. The authors assumed that the presence of a literacy test in districts with low voter participation was adequate proof that the test was materially responsible for the low participation. The section also defined a process called *bail-out* through which, a jurisdiction caught by the automatic trigger could file suit in the District Court of the District of Columbia and attempt to demonstrate that although a test had been used, it had not been used in a discriminatory manner for the previous five years. If the D. C. District Court vindicated the use of the test, no special provisions went into effect.
- Section 5: This section defined the second "special provision," a process called *preclearance*. In any jurisdiction subject to these provisions (see Section 4(b)), no "voting qualification or prerequisite to voting, or standard, practice, or procedure with respect to voting" could be changed without permission of the attorney general. Jurisdictions were to submit all proposed changes to the attorney general for preclearance, after which, the law gave the him sixty days to object. If he did object, the change could not be implemented. The only alternative to receiving permission from the attorney general was to file suit in the D. C. District Court and be granted permission through declaratory judgment. Preclearance assured the Congress that an election entity could not stay a few creative steps ahead of the courts by designing new election procedures that lessened the chance for minority participation. As plaintiffs and defendants shaped the application of the law over the next several years, Section 5 preclearance, became the mightiest provision in both use and abuse. But at its inception in 1965, Section 5 was viewed as simply the enforcement clause of Section 4. Unlike Section 2 which addressed existing voting procedures, Section 5 addressed potential changes to the procedures.
- Section 3(a): As the third "special provision," the attorney general could dispatch examiners to any covered area. Under the act, examiners could watch the registration process, cause voters to be registered, and ensure that they could vote.
- Section 4(e): Knowing that the act would face constitutional challenges, framers carefully perched it on the Fourteenth and Fifteenth Amendments, purporting only to give strength to the Constitution's enforcement. The

idea of abolishing all literacy tests was discussed but was abandoned for fear of failing a constitutional review. As recently as 1959, the Supreme Court upheld the state's interest in screening potential voters for their ability to read and write.[11] To avoid confronting the court on its previous decision, the Judiciary Committee proposed only to ban literacy tests in areas that were presumed guilty of Fifteenth Amendment violations, by virtue of voting statistics. This section also provided that anyone who had achieved a sixth grade education in an "American flag" school or any state accredited school in which the primary classroom language was not English, could not be required to read, write, or understand English.

- Section 6: This section extended the use of examiners. It gave the attorney general the right to appoint examiners whenever he received twenty meritorious complaints from voters of a jurisdiction alleging that they were denied the right to vote or whenever voter statistics caused him to believe that violations may be occurring.
- Section 10: This section outlawed the "poll tax" or any other requirement of payment as a prerequisite to voting. A constitutional amendment already banned the poll tax for federal elections and this provision extended that ban to local elections.
- Section 11: The act dealt with criminal actions by outlawing coercion at the ballot box; providing criminal penalties for creating false registrations or votes; providing criminal penalties for the untimely destruction of voting records; and giving the attorney general a number of powers to intervene where necessary in the election process.
- Section 14: This section contained miscellaneous terms and definitions. However, buried in Part 14(b) was a definition of *voting*: "The term 'vote' or 'voting' shall include all action necessary to make a vote effective . . ." The idea of making the vote effective later served as a springboard for the courts to carry the force of the act far past its design.

In summary, a jurisdiction could find itself subject to the "special provisions" of the act by either of two paths: it could fall under the statistical "automatic trigger" as described in Section 4(b), or it could be found guilty of violations of the 15th Amendment. Again, the three "special provisions" were:

- the suspension of all tests and devices that were prerequisites to voting;
- preclearance by the attorney general or the District Court of the District of Columbia for all changes to voting qualifications or prerequisites to voting, or standards, practices, or procedures affecting voting; and

- the potential appointment of federal examiners to assist in the registration of voters and to observe the elections.

Like most federal statutes, the Congress hammered out the law as succinctly as it dared then left to time and the courts the task of detailing the meaning and application of the law. As the voting rights saga unfolded, various District Courts interpreted the law in conflict with one another, but despite such inconsistencies, the trend from its 1965 inception was an increasingly liberal interpretation, that is, an interpretation that broadened the act's scope and power.

The Arguments in Favor of the 1965 Act[12]

The Democratic Congress of 1965 presented the bill. Drafters of the legislation recognized that this act was preceded by a long series of civil rights legislation designed to eradicate discrimination against minorities—primarily blacks. Since the provisions accumulated by earlier acts heavily overlapped with the proposed Voting Rights Act of 1965, proponents had to justify the need for additional legislation. They cited the enforcement experience of recent years which they believed demonstrated that the judicial process was far too slow to provide for the protection of individual rights. Seventy-one voting rights cases had been filed under the 1957, 1960, and 1964 Civil Rights Acts. Attorney General Nicholas Katzenbach testified to the Judiciary Committee:

> Three times in the last decade—in 1956, in 1960, and in 1964—those who oppose stronger federal legislation concerning the electoral process have asked Congress to be patient; and Congress has been three times since 1956, they have said that local officials, subject to judicial direction, will solve the voting problem. And each time Congress has left the problem largely to the courts and the local officials. Three times since 1956 they have told us that the prescription would provide the entire cure—this prescription aided by time and congress has followed that advice.[13]

After arguing that Congress had been patient beyond fairness, the attorney general went on to testify that voting rights in America were less than guaranteed because of the incredible time that was spent examining the voting records in each case. After considerable time was spent preparing for trial, the defendant would inevitably appeal. He also contended that even after a voting rights case gained victory in the courts, the result was often not realized because one method of discrimination was traded for another.

The argument supporting the 1965 Act was also based on statistical results achieved to date. Backers pointed to Alabama where the number of eligible blacks registered to vote was only 19.4 percent representing an increase of only 5.2 percent from 1958 to 1964. In Mississippi, only 6.4 percent of the voting age blacks were registered compared to 4.4 percent ten years earlier. In Louisiana, the black registration had increased only one-tenth percentage in nine years—31.8 percent of the eligible black voters were registered compared to 80.2 percent of the eligible white voters.[14]

In Dallas County, Alabama, which contains Selma, the voting age population in 1961 was 14,500 whites and 15,000 blacks. That year 64 percent of the whites and one percent of the blacks were registered. The Justice Department examined the voting records and, convinced that discriminatory practices caused this imbalance, filed suit on April 16, 1961. Thirteen months later the case came to trial. The attorney general proved discrimination against county registrars who were no longer in office, but the court also found that the registrars currently in office did not engage in such discriminatory practices and, thus, the court refused to issue an injunction. On September 30, 1963, the appeals court overturned the district court ruling and issued injunctions against some of the county procedures. The appeals court would not, however, demand that the voting prerequisites then in place be as lenient on registrants as those that had been employed during Dallas County's long practice of discrimination during which most white voters were registered. Since registration is life long in Alabama, the Justice Department argued that tightening of prerequisites, even if they were uniformly applied, discriminated against black voters who were unable to register before these new, higher hurdles were put into place. By October 1963, the processing of voting applications, most of which were for blacks, had slowed to one fourth the normal weekly average. Under new tests, adopted in 1964, applicants had to spell the words *emolument, impeachment, apportionment,* and *despotism.* They were also required to give an acceptable explanation of constitutional excerpts. In February 1965, the court finally eliminated the use of this literacy test and ordered a speed-up in the processing of applications. The entire process had taken nearly four years during which time only 383 of the 15,000 blacks were registered to vote.

Backers cited other examples. The Alabama literacy test was nothing short of a final exam for high school civics. It asked how much money could be appropriated for the armed services, who passes laws dealing with piracy, and who sets the time for adjournment of the Congress.[15] In Panola County, Mississippi, the registrar required blacks to interpret a provision of the state constitution that concerned the rate of interest on a certain school fund. In

Forrest County, Mississippi, the Registrar declared as illiterate, six blacks with baccalaureate degrees, three of whom had Masters. An anecdote told by southern blacks described a black man who went to the courthouse to register. The registrar quizzed him about the meaning of *habeas corpus*. After a few moments of pondering, the applicant replied, "*Habeas corpus*—that means this black man ain't gonna register today."[16]

These were the sorts of stories that fueled the fires of support. Sponsors contended from the beginning that literacy tests were an instrument that the South used to discriminate against blacks. They claimed that, prior to reconstruction, none of the Southern States required proof of literacy. Between 1895 and 1908, reading or writing tests were instituted in Mississippi, South Carolina, North Carolina, Virginia, Georgia, Alabama, and Louisiana;[17] requirements for a "perfectly" completed application form were introduced in Louisiana, Virginia, and Mississippi; oral constitutional "understanding" or "interpretation" tests were instituted in Mississippi, South Carolina, Louisiana, and Virginia; understanding the "obligation of citizenship" tests were instituted in Alabama, Georgia, Louisiana, and Mississippi; and good moral character requirements were added in Alabama, Georgia, Mississippi, and Louisiana.[18]

The argument supporting the act was simple: county-by-county litigation was burdensome and ineffective and such an approach was not producing the result guaranteed by the 15th Amendment. Knowing that concern would exist about the constitutionality of suspending tests without evidence of discrimination, backers turned to the Supreme Court decision in the *United States v. Louisiana*. In that case the court suspended a literacy test, without evidence that it was discriminatory, on the basis that previous tests had been used to discriminate.[19] Essentially, proponents argued, the Voting Rights Act would do the same thing.

Along with preclearance requirements and test suspensions, authors of the act believed that appointment of federal examiners having broad power to oversee and assist in the administration of an election was a reasonable approach. They cited examples such as a Louisiana case in which a three-judge federal district court stopped the use of certain literacy tests to which registrars responded by closing the registration process.

The provision that only the District Court of the District of Columbia could provide declaratory judgment approving a change in voting procedures was supported by the notion that greater consistency would result from a single court hearing all the cases. In reality, however, supporters of this provision mistrusted many of the southern federal district judges. Some of these judges, appointed for life, had roots in a deeply segregated South. One example was District Judge T. Whitfield Davidson, Jr.'s design for a segregation plan for Dallas, Texas public schools. Davidson provided a rambling, philosophical history of blacks in the South. The following excerpt exemplifies the tone of his writing:

> The Arab slave traders often brought him [the slave] to port . . . No one knew his name, and yet it was some generations before he had a family or a surname. To be freed from his recent captors and from the foul condition of the ship was for a moment a relief, no doubt, to this poor fellow when he was inducted into the wide open space of a southern plantation with open air, food, and kindness.[20]

Supporters felt that the avoidance of this sort of judge was necessary to the success of the preclearance provision.

The proponents recognized that Article 1 and the Seventeenth Amendment to the Constitution gave the states the right to set the qualifications for voters. However, the 15th Amendment guaranteed the right to vote without discrimination, thus, they argued, a state had no right to violate the basic tenants of constitutional freedom. Many states once had a statute dictating that voters be white—a qualification that had to yield to the Fifteenth Amendment. Justice Frankfurter, speaking for the Court said, "When a State exercises power wholly within the domain of State interest, it is insulated from Federal judicial review. But such insulation is not carried over when State power is used as an instrument for circumventing a federally protected right."[21]

The Arguments Against the Voting Rights Act of 1965[22]

Opposition to the act was heated. The Republicans offered an alternative act and several individual members of Congress offered amendments and modifications. Every dissenter publicly agreed that guaranteed suffrage for blacks and other minorities was an essential and correct objective. The opposition argued, though, that the act was hastily put together, was constitutionally unsound, and violated premises of basic fairness. They claimed, despite Katzenbach's claim to the contrary, Congress was not showing patience with existing legislation. The Civil Rights Act of 1964, which dealt with voters' rights, was only a year old. Even the former Assistant Attorney General in charge of civil rights had said that Mississippi as well as other states were making progress, and, since federally concentrated effort had just begun, it was simply too soon to judge.

The legislation, opponents claimed, did not allow for due process when a registrar raised a question of a voter's qualifications. They suggested that this be solved with some kind of method for provisional voting. The act gave federal examiners the right to list applicants on the register, count their votes, and certify the election result even though challenges to the listings could subsequently find that voters were actually not eligible. The Republicans acknowledged that allowing applicants to vote while their registrations were in dispute was probably necessary, but "to count such votes and certify the election of officials on the basis of such illegally cast votes was shocking."[23] They proposed instead that the votes be cast provisionally and not counted. When the non-provisional votes were counted, the examiner could determine whether the provisional votes could affect the election result. If they could, then the eligibility had to be finally determined for enough voters to determine the result.

The provision most offensive to the opposition was the automatic triggering mechanism. The law enjoined states, caught by the trigger, from using literacy tests, subjected them to federal preclearance, and allowed their elections to fall under intense federal scrutiny possibly involving federal examiners. This had an objectionable air of presumed guilt leaving the burden on the state or locality to prove its innocence.

This trigger was a "numbers game" that had nothing to do with factual evidence. Not only could a state be unfairly condemned, but the counties within that state were swept up with the same broom regardless of their individual scores in the statistical formula. The Republicans accused the Democrats of selecting the states they wanted to target, then devising a means of accomplishing the goal. The U. S. Attorney General had admitted that a large portion of the state of South Carolina was free from wrongdoing, yet the counties, cities, and school districts would all be uniformly regulated.

Opponents further argued that this law would allow any otherwise qualified citizen, white or black, to vote no matter how illiterate or even if the voter were a moron. An illiterate black citizen would have more rights in Alabama than in New York.

Objections also arose from the fact that the trigger was retroactive. If a state was named under the statistical trigger defined by the November 1964 election, and had subsequently enacted changes in their voting prerequisites or procedures that assured more fair and open elections, those new provisions would have to be rolled back under the act.

The alternate legislation proposed by the Republicans provided that dispatching federal examiners should be triggered by the receipt of meritorious complaints or 25 or more persons in any state or voting district. The attorney general would then send federal examiners to further evaluate the individual complaints. If they found that there was a pattern or practice of denial of voting rights based on race or color, examiners would have the authority to oversee the process and list qualified applicants.

As expected, opponents were inflamed that only the District Court of the District of Columbia could provide relief from the imposition of the automatic trigger. That court already had a backlog of more than 4000 cases and averaged more than two years between filing and final disposition. Clearly, the argument went, this provision could only be explained by the Congress' mistrust of southern judges. Congress was bypassing the government's own judicial system to achieve its goals. Congress disrupted the balance of power when it selected a court close to home to hear appeals against Justice Department actions.

The Republican alternative contained legislation for clean election provisions. Although the Democrats proposal might get voters registered and to the polling places, it did not encompass election problems, such as stuffed ballot boxes, tombstone voting, multiple voting, willful miscounting, and buying votes. Effective legislation, opponents asserted, must include these things.

As predicted by authors of the act, opponents raised the issue of the constitutional right of states to set voter qualifications. Not only did the Constitution reserve these rights for the states, but the Supreme Court had held that qualifications may include literacy tests, remarking that such tests can effectively determine an individual's competency to vote. Desirable or not, the act would eliminate literacy tests if a capricious statistical method declared that they were being used as a device against a race or color.

Republicans also took issue with Section 10 of the act which not only outlawed poll taxes, but also any other payment prerequisite to voting. They pointed out that in many political subdivisions the payment of property taxes was required before voting in referendums on changes in ad valorem tax rates or bond issuance. Again, they believed, the proposed act was hastily put together without adequate forethought of the consequences. Further, opponents doubted the constitutionality of the poll tax ban. Previous federal judicial hearings had upheld poll taxes. A constitutional amendment had been passed the year before outlawing poll taxes in federal elections. If such an abolition required a constitutional amendment for federal elections, then how could the tax be outlawed for local elections without another amendment?

John Lindsey, Republican from New York, added his view that the act was seriously lacking by not guaranteeing the candidates' rights to free speech in campaigning. Just because minorities could vote, they would not be able to participate in the political process unless their candidates ran without intimidation.

Edwin E. Willis from the Third District of Louisiana argued that 53 percent of the blacks in his district were registered, 73 percent of whom voted in the last election. Nonetheless, his district was entangled in the act's dragnet that captured the entire State of Louisiana. President Johnson had told a joint session of Congress, "Those who seek to avoid action by their national government in their home communities, . . . the answer is simple. Open your polling places to all of your people."[24] Willis insisted that his district's polling places were open, yet they were not exempted from the act's special provisions.

Results of the Initial Legislation

Early Results and Challenges

The effect of the act was seen immediately in the South. On the day President Johnson signed the law, Sumter County, Georgia dropped its opposition to a local black voter registration drive resulting in 300 new black voters registering on that day alone.[25] Three days later, the attorney general sent examiners to Alabama, Mississippi, and Louisiana to begin registering voters. Within 19 days, 27,385 blacks had registered.[26]

Excitement spread among civil rights proponents as barriers fell throughout the South. In November, the U. S. Commission on Civil Rights triumphantly announced, "In many area of the South, there is full compliance with the Voting Rights Act of 1965. In most areas, tests and devices which have been used in the past to deny Negroes the right to vote have been effectively suspended."[27]

During the first elections after passage of the act, 300 federal observers oversaw the polls in six black southern counties. Blacks, voting in the greatest numbers since reconstruction, sent black candidates into runoffs and helped defeat the most extreme white candidates. Jim Clark, sheriff of Selma, was cast out and replaced by a more moderate challenger. When Clark challenged the results in six, largely-black precincts, federal observers helped support his defeat.[28]

Johnson had done his best to negotiate with both civil rights and southern leaders. He minimized a show of federal force to give the Southern States a chance to adjust to the new realities. He believed the government had made a path down which minorities now had a responsibility to walk. He stated, "[The challenge presented by the act] cannot be met simply by protest and demonstrations. It means that dedicated leaders must work around the clock to teach people their responsibilities and to lead them to exercise those rights and to fulfill those responsibilities and those duties to their country."[29]

As in the congressional hearings, a general outcry arguing the constitutionality of this extraordinary legislation came from the Southern States. Their contentions relied on the arguments used successfully in the *1883 Civil Rights Cases*.[30] The landmark test of the constitutionality of the act was *South Carolina v. Katzenbach*. Attorney General Katzenbach successfully defended all the provisions of the act. The Supreme Court majority opinion stated that Congress ". . . had learned that substantial voting discrimination presently occurs in certain sections of the country, and it knew of no way of accurately forecasting whether the evil might spread elsewhere in the future. In acceptable legislative fashion, Congress chose to limit its attention to geographic areas where immediate action seemed necessary."[31] Justice Hugo Black, a Roosevelt appointee, dissented from the majority opinion on the constitutionality of Sections 4 and 5. Black had once been a member of the Ku Klux Klan but had evolved to become the judicial leader for minority rights and civil liberties.[32] Still his Alabama upbringing never allowed him to square with the act's punishments levied specifically on the South. Three years later he commented on the decision by saying that the preclearance mechanism was "reminiscent of old Reconstruction days when soldiers controlled the South and when those states were compelled to make reports to military commanders of what they did. . . . [I doubt] that any of the 13 colonies would have agreed to our Constitution if they had dreamed that the time might come when they would have to go to a United States Attorney General or a District of Columbia court with hat in hand begging for permission to change their laws."[33]

As the Viet Nam War raged, domestic protest of the 1960s peaked. President Johnson preached about the Great Society and Earl Warren liberally lead the Supreme Court. Justifying punitive measures against the South on the basis that southern evil might spread to other sections of the country fit the times but failed to be supported by any practical evidence. Nonetheless, the court judged that such regional legislation was within the authority of Congress to protect the Constitution. Chief Justice Warren summed up his overriding belief in the act:

Hopefully, millions of nonwhite Americans will now be able to participate for the first time on an equal basis in the government under which they live. We may finally look forward to the day when truly "[t]he right of citizens of the United States to vote shall not be denied or abridged by the United States or by any State on account of race, color or previous condition of servitude."[34]

Political subdivisions did not extensively use the bail-out provisions. Between passage of the act in 1965 and the introduction of amendments in 1969, the triggering mechanisms brought six states and various counties of other states under the special provisions. The D. C. District Court heard bail-out cases as jurisdictions attempted to show that tests or devices had not been used for discriminatory purposes for the previous five years. The Court released only the state of Alaska, along with a few counties in Arizona, Idaho, and North Carolina.

During the first four years, the attorney general assigned federal examiners to 64 counties and parishes to assist with voter registration. In addition, federal voting observers were assigned to elections in Alabama, Georgia, Louisiana, Mississippi, and South Carolina. Black voter registration in those five states had risen 29 percentage points to 52 percent. Correspondingly, an increasing number of nonwhite candidates successfully bid for public office.

Get-out-the-vote campaigns and registration drives were sponsored by civil rights groups all over the South; but groups like SNCC, NUL, and CORE did not have the financial resources to conduct drives in all underregistered areas. They turned toward Congress and the Justice Department to support registration drives as a part of the government's responsibility to disenfranchised blacks. Katzenbach defended the administration's policies as a matter of law. Congress has barred the administration from spending any of its money for the war on poverty on "any voting registration activity."[35] He stated, "The law contemplates that a federal examiner is to be put in any county where the state or local people are not performing their responsibilities. . . . I don't think I have the authority to go beyond that. And I don't intend to go beyond that."[36]

Southern states did attempt a few barricades. Shortly after the passage of the act, some state courts issued injunctions against the federal examiners sent by the attorney general. These injunctions contended that voter registration was a state matter as prescribed by the Constitution. Registrars, caught between orders from state courts and the federal government, were assisted in November 1965, when an Alabama federal court overruled the state orders.

As expected, states challenged the constitutionality of the poll tax ban. In a 1937 decision, the Supreme Court had unanimously upheld the right of Georgia to make payment of a poll tax a prerequisite to voting.[37] In 1951, the Supreme Court again upheld the poll tax, this time in Virginia.[38] By 1965, only five states still required payment of a poll tax to vote. Alabama, Mississippi, Texas, Virginia, and Vermont levied annual taxes between $1.50 and $2.00. While these payments appeared trivial, most blacks in the Southern States were poor. Some states required that unpaid, prior-years taxes be made up before the current year could be paid.[39] Virginia voters filed suit against the tax.[40] On appeal, the Supreme Court declared the Virginia poll tax unconstitutional on the basis of the equal protection clause of the Fourteenth Amendment. Justice Douglas, another Roosevelt appointee and an iron-willed proponent of individual liberty, especially free speech, wrote the opinion.[41] He was strongly opposed by Justice Black who contended that the earlier decisions allowing poll taxes were valid and that nothing had been changed in the Constitution since those cases. In 1966, the poll taxes in Alabama, Texas, and Vermont were stricken down.

In the same year, registered voters of New York City sued to challenge the constitutionality of Section 4(e) of the act. Because 4(e) outlawed any English literacy requirement for citizens educated in non-English, American-flag schools, the act enfranchised many Puerto Ricans in New York City. Senators Kennedy and Javits sponsored this provision to bring these Puerto Ricans into the electorate. Plaintiffs opposing the Puerto Rican vote, filed suit in the D. C. District Court where a three-judge court agreed with the plaintiffs by holding that Congress had overstepped its authority by usurping powers given to the states by the 10th Amendment. On appeal, Solicitor General Thurgood Marshall convinced the Supreme Court to overturn the district court on the basis that 4(e) was a valid way of enforcing the 14th Amendment.[42] The Court showed mixed convictions. Justice William Brennan, Jr., a consistent defender of individual rights, wrote the opinion. Although appointed by Eisenhower, Brennan was a moderate Democrat.[43] William Douglas, agreed with the judgment in the case, but, like Black, withheld an opinion of the constitutionality of either Section 4 or 5. Justices Harlan and Stewart dissented. They wrote that states had the right to administer literacy tests and that the New York literacy test was "reasonably designed to serve a legitimate state interest."[44] They went on to quote a 1959 decision in which the Supreme Court unanimously supported the states' right to establish literacy tests: "The ability to read and write . . . has some relation to standards designed to promote intelligent use of the ballot. . . . We do not sit in judgment of that policy [state literacy tests]. We cannot say, however, that it is not an allowable one measured by constitutional standards."[45]

Harlan further pointed out that the Federal Government required literacy in English as a prerequisite to naturalization, thus, "attesting to the national view of its importance as a prerequisite to full integration into the American political community." As the Warren Court became more activist, Harlan's dissents became sharper and more frequent. By the middle of 1968, registered voter demographics in the Southern States had changed markedly (Figure 4).

Rising registration rates led to success at the polls. By 1970, in Greene and Lowndes counties in Alabama, along with Hancock County, Georgia, blacks controlled the local governments. Holmes County, Mississippi elected the first black representative to the state legislature since reconstruction. In Fayette, Louisiana, Charles Evers triumphed as mayor.[46]

Despite these impressive results, in 1968 the Civil Rights Commission published another progress report, this time adding caution to their upbeat report of thirty months earlier. Conceding "significant progress in voter registration and political activity by Negro citizens," the report also detailed the remaining obstacles. The commission began to lay groundwork for the agenda that would form the future of the Voting Rights Act. "In areas where registration has increased, we have moved into a new phase of the problem."[47] Nine chapters then described problems with vote dilution, obstacles to black candidacy, discrimination in voting procedures, vote fraud, and voter harassment. The rapid and resounding success of the act led civil rights leaders to posture their movement for greater gains.

	Registered White Voters (%)	Registered Nonwhite Voters (%)	Pre 1965 Registered Nonwhite Voters (%)
Alabama	83	57	19
Georgia	85	56	27
Louisiana	88	59	32
Mississippi	92	59	7
North Carolina	79	55	47
South Carolina	66	51	37
Virginia	67	58	39

FIGURE 4: REGISTERED VOTERS - 1968[48]

A Growing Government

In 1967, in the Mississippi case of *Connor v. Johnson*, the federal district court dealt with several voting issues. Mississippi had reapportioned its house and senate in 1962, but was sued because neither the house nor senate districts followed the one-man, one-vote rule. At that time, many of the house and senate districts varied in population by more than ten percent. The court ordered the legislature to reapportion which it did in December 1966, but the result was only a small statistical improvement. To correct the situation, the court reluctantly took on the task of drawing a redistricting plan. It drew districts following county lines because population statistics were kept no lower than the county level and counties generally proceeded along natural boundaries such as rivers or highways. Even the court's plan produced some districts that varied from the average by more than ten percent. The court claimed that, despite one-man, one-vote, the Supreme Court had ruled that unequal apportionment was acceptable if explained by rational state policy. Explanations might include integrity of political subdivisions, the maintenance of compactness, or the recognition of natural or historical boundary lines. The plan even included some at-large districts to maintain county lines.[49] The court contended that it concerned itself only with population and remained blind to racial numbers.[50] The case broke new ground by permitting a federal court to draw boundary lines for a state election. The plan itself, however, would appear reactionary when compared to redistricting plans twenty years later.

Two new rules ultimately came from *Connor*. First, the Supreme Court agreed that single-member districts were preferable in court-fashioned apportionment plans. Second, court-fashioned plans were not subject to preclearance.

Although deviations in district size could be justified by legitimate state interest, the Supreme Court would not tolerate a rule-of-thumb, acceptable deviation percentages. In *Kirkpatrick v. Preisler*, the court insisted that absent such an interest, no significant deviation could be tolerated.[51]

In addition to court actions, the preclearance provisions were put to work. The attorney general was now able to pass judgment on any voting procedure or regulation changes in a "triggered" jurisdiction. As plaintiffs brought actions against election boards that failed to request preclearance, the courts rapidly defined exactly what constituted a change under the act. In 1969, in *Allen v. the State Board of Elections of Virginia*, the court enumerated examples of required preclearance, among which were structural issues such as changing the election of county supervisors from single-member districts to at-large. Less obvious items included any new method instituted for the casting of write-in ballots or Virginia's new rule that anyone who had voted in a primary could not run for office as an independent candidate. Chief Justice Warren instructed the lower courts that "[t]he Voting Rights Act was aimed at the subtle, as well as the obvious, state regulations that would have the effect of denying the citizens their right to vote because of race."[52]

In the same case, the court determined that the act gave broad interpretation to the meaning of the right to vote recognizing that voting includes all necessary actions to make a vote effective.[53] This notion came from the definition of voting found in Section 14. While it looked like legal boilerplate, it stands out as one of several examples of power given by the act, but outside of the original scope. The idea of making the minority votes effective expanded the scope of voting rights past the casting of ballots and entered the realm of voting power. Power encompassed the ability to have candidates of the voters' choice on the ballot and the ability to get them elected. No longer was the existence of a vote sufficient—now it had to have weight. This new realm formed a framework for dealing with at-large districts and ultimately the whole issue of apportionment.

Allen was a significant turning point in the force of the 1965 Act. In the three and one-half years between the passage of the act and the rendering of the *Allen* decision, the Justice Department had objected to only six changes submitted for preclearance. During the subsequent three years, there were 118 objections, most of which failed the attorney general's preclearance on the grounds of voting dilution rather than denial.[54] The decision in *Allen* separated the meanings of elective franchise in Section 4 and 5. Section 4 still guaranteed the right to register and cast ballots. Section 5, which to that point was the enforcement mechanism of Section 4, now concerned itself with the influence of the votes. Looking at the influence of each vote foreshadowed the later *results tests* that evaluated compliance by the race of the candidates elected. *Allen* was a substantial first step toward affirmative action. As Justice Harlan put it, *Allen* was a "revolutionary innovation in American government that [went] far beyond what was accomplished by Section 4."[55] The Warren Court had introduced a concept that had been carefully avoided in the debate in congressional chambers. This liberal influence prompted former President Eisenhower to call his appointment of Earl Warren "the biggest damn fool mistake I ever made."[56]

Other court cases between 1965 and 1970 demonstrated the courts' new strength in interpreting and enforcing voting rights and creating voting strength. In June 1969, the Supreme Court held in *Gaston County v. United*

States that Gaston County, North Carolina maintained a separate and inferior school system for blacks and thus could not reinstate a literacy test as a precondition for voting, holding that this would deny the right to vote based on race or color.[57] By the same logic, virtually no jurisdiction could exercise bail-out, because almost no southern jurisdiction could hope to convince the D. C. District Court that segregated school systems had always been equal. The South was thus locked into Section 5 preclearance as long as Congress choose to extend the special provisions of the act.

Early District Debates

The concept of voting effectiveness gave rise to the study of vote dilution. The victims of such an examination were multi-member voting schemes. Civil rights activists and the Supreme Court had a general mistrust for at-large districts, but never garnered sufficient cause to outlaw them. Since voting rights were based on equal opportunity, the at-large opposition was frustrated, trying to argue against the inherent statistical equality of such districts. In the year of the act's passage, the Supreme Court expressed its opinion by recognizing that at-large schemes were potentially discriminating. While not declaring them unconstitutional, the court said, "It might well be that, designedly or otherwise, a multi-member constituency apportionment scheme, under circumstances of a particular case, would operate to minimize or cancel out the voting strength of racial or political elements of the voting population." Plaintiffs claimed that multi-member districts violated the equal protection clause of the constitution since voters in single-member districts were allowed to "select their own [state] senators" while voters in multi-member districts were not.[58] The Supreme Court disagreed, contending that senators in multi-member counties were representatives of the whole county and not of an individual district, thus the voters were indeed selecting their own senators. While this whole challenge would appear conservative seventeen years later, it represented an early attempt to infringe upon the states' historical ability to apportion their own entities.

The next year, the crack slightly widened when the Supreme Court restated its bias about at-large voting districts. The Court said it would rule against multi-member schemes if "they would operate to minimize or cancel out minority voting strength."[59] It did not matter to the court whether the districting was designed to dilute voting strength or it just happened by circumstance.

Congress joined the at-large debate in 1967 by passing a requirement that U. S. congressional districts be single-member.[60] Throughout American history, Congress had vacillated on this point, first requiring single-member districts in 1842, then dropping the requirement in 1852, restoring it in 1862 and dropping it again in 1929. Congress' intent in 1967 was to protect the interests of racial minorities in the South.[61]

The issues surrounding at-large districts were exacerbated when annexation was involved. In 1967, the Supreme Court heard a suit brought against the districting plan for Virginia Beach.[62] The city of Virginia Beach had recently merged with Princess Anne County and created a borough form of government. The government comprised seven boroughs, one being the original city of Virginia Beach and six being the magisterial districts of Princess Anne County. An 11 member government was elected at-large. Five members could reside anywhere while the remaining seven resided one in each borough. Plaintiffs argued that this residency requirement was unconstitutional because the boroughs were not of equal population. The court supported the at-large plan by again pointing out that the plan made no distinction based on race, creed, economic location, or location. The court argued that all councilmen were representatives of the entire electorate, not only their individual borough, thus, the representative would be attentive to the needs of all boroughs. For the next 25 years, this would stand as one of the last conservative decisions of the Supreme Court regarding voting rights and redistricting.

Dallas: Minority Progress and Pressure

The years immediately following the passage of the Voting Rights Act marked the start of real progress for Dallas minorities. Political and legal events laid the groundwork for the political struggles to follow.

Despite official desegregation in 1961, the Dallas Independent School District (DISD) could boast little real progress in its stair-step, one-grade-a-year integration program. A federal court, dissatisfied with the results, ordered junior high schools desegregated in 1965 followed by senior high schools in 1967.[63]

Dallas' minorities reached other milestones. Black attorney Joseph Lockridge won election from Dallas County to the state legislature. He died two years later and was replaced by another black, Rev. Zan W. Holmes, a graduate of SMU's Perkins School of Theology. In 1967, C. A. Galloway, a black man whose house had been bombed in the 1950s, was appointed to the city council for two weeks.[64] In the same year, the first black was appointed to the school board. New opportunities had arrived for Dallas' African Americans, but the power was still unequally shared. The next goal became evident—the restructuring of the election system.

In 1967, Dallas was 25 percent black and eight percent Mexican American.[65] The era's push for voter registration gave new influence to blacks. The CCA, seeking support from black leaders, agreed to push for expansion of the city council from nine to eleven members and provide support for two minority candidates.[66]

In April 1967, Max Goldblatt, a white, hardware-store owner from the middle-class Pleasant Grove section of Dallas, lost in his bid for city council. Goldblatt carried a majority of his home district but was defeated in the citywide, at-large totals. He filed suit in federal district court claiming that the powerful millionaires in the CCA controlled the city elections, thus, the at-large system denied equal protection to independent candidates who could not compete with the money of the CCA on a citywide basis. Goldblatt lost the suit and appealed to the 5th Circuit Court.[67]

Two years later, the 5th Circuit Court rebutted him again saying, "The appellant is complaining because the citizens of Dallas either from apathy or design have not exercised the power of the ballot to rid themselves of what the appellant regards as an evil political machine. . . . The wrong of public apathy cannot be righted by judicial compulsion."[68]

In 1968, the CCA made good on its promise to expand the council. Under the new scheme, three members, including the mayor, could reside anywhere in the city. The remaining eight needed to live in specific districts, although all seats were elected at-large. Other changes to the city charter removed a segregation clause through which the city manager could specify sections of Dallas for blacks, whites, and Latinos.

In the 1969 elections, the first under the eleven-member council, the CCA backed two minority candidates, one black and one Hispanic. George Allen, the black candidate, received 71 percent of the vote in his bid against a black opponent.[69] Without CCA backing, Allen had unsuccessfully bid for the council twice before. He was aligned with the NAACP and had successfully sued the University of Texas Law School for denying him access to a law school seminar. Allen was also no stranger to city politics having served as the first black on the city's Plan Commission and the Board of Adjustment.[70] Joining Allen on the council was Hispanic Anita Martinez.

Other signs of racial pressure evidenced the changing atmosphere. In 1968, the Student Non-Violent Coordinating Committee organized an aggressive boycott against the white-owned *OK Supermarkets* in South

Dallas. When the controversy was over, *OK* sold the ten stores to black businessmen.[71]

As the initial term of the Voting Rights Act neared completion, the tensions over race and opportunity in Dallas were still in their early days. The nascent steps of exodus from downtown to the suburbs was not yet of much impact. Dallas still shone above the rest as *Look* magazine named it the *All-American City* in 1970.[72]

Navajo Reservation: Legislative Recalcitrance

In October 1965, the pretrial hearing began in the *Klahr* case. Attorneys for Klahr argued that the most recent voter registration figures should be used to reapportion the state house, senate, and U. S. congressional districts. Defendants wanted to impose less trauma on the system and simply use the 1960 census data to realign U. S. congressional Districts 1 and 3 to balance their population with District 2.

Both sides did recognize that electing two state senators from each of the fourteen Arizona counties was unacceptable to the one-man, one-vote concept. They also agreed that there was no chance to settle and that the court would have to do the reapportionment for them.[73]

The trial began in November and by February, the District Court reached its conclusions. The Court favored the defendants by leaving U. S. District 2 alone and redrawing the line between Districts 1 and 3, thus balancing the population of all three. Population figures were based on the aging 1960 census because testimony showed that newer registration predictions were unreliable.

For State Legislature reapportionment, the court declared "unconstitutional and invidious," Senate Bill 11, the legislature's attempt to deal with redistricting. The court sculpted an exotic plan requiring ninety seats in the legislature rather than the state constitutional limit of eighty. Sixty of the seats were to be in the House and thirty in the Senate. Judges designed the House with six districts, some of which had subdistricts. The Navajo-Apache-Greenlee district was to have four representatives and two senators.

The court relied on *Reynolds v. Sims* to reject the idea that there was any basis other than total population for reapportionment count. Oddly, the court felt that registration data, rather than total population data, was adequate for apportioning subdistricts within counties. "But because it cannot be assumed that within a single county there are widely variant ratios between voter registration and population, it is clear that this subdistricting can be done on the basis of the 1964 voter registration figures."[74] The court's negative assumption was somehow twisted into a positive conclusion.

Judge Mathes, the Senior District Judge, shook his head at the whole proceeding. "So I must assume, although I am unable to comprehend how, an 'unconstitutional' state legislature can possess the power to enact a constitutional scheme of apportionment; failing which a federal court has the power to 'enact' a reapportionment plan of its own, and by some legal legerdemain convert that plan into positive State Law."[75] Nonetheless, the court enjoined the enforcement of Senate Bill 11. Although given ample time, the legislature had failed to create a plan, thus the court implemented its plan as "temporary and provisional" for the 1966 election.

In February 1966, Apache, Navajo, and Coconino Counties joined the state of Arizona in suing for bailout from the special provisions of the Voting Rights Act. As prescribed by the act, the trial took place in the D. C. District Court. The plaintiffs' goal to reinstate the literacy test, required the first court action of its kind. Arizona law stated that "[E]very resident of the state is qualified to become an elector and may register to vote at all elections authorized by law if he . . . [i]s able to read the Constitution of the United States in the English language . . . [and] is able to write his name . . ."[76] Twenty-one members of the Navajo Tribal Council intervened urging the court to dismiss the requested action. The literacy test had been suspended in Apache County only one day after the Voting Rights Act was signed and in Navajo and Coconino Counties three months later.[77] Unsure of the liability presented by the new law, the Apache County recorder gave the order that any election official giving a literacy test would be fired. She did not want any liability and reasoned that illiterate Indians would not vote anyway.[78]

Evidence presented in the bailout proceedings included affidavits and letters of voting officials in the three plaintiff counties, stating that they had not applied a literacy test resulting in discrimination. Attorneys followed the lead from *South Carolina v. Katzenbach* which said, "an area need do no more than to submit affidavits from voting officials, asserting that they have not been guilty of racial discrimination through the use of tests and devices during the past 5 years, and then to refute whatever evidence to the contrary may be adduced by the Federal Government."[79] The federal government spent 16 days investigating in the three counties. They turned up only one incident. An Apache County official went to the polls and there challenged registered voters on their ability to read and write English. The legislature responded by making challenges at the polls illegal. In July, the D. C. District Court, drawing words from statute, declared that "the incidents had been few in number," were "corrected by state or local action," and "there was no reasonable probability of their recurrence in the future." Judgment was granted for the three Arizona Counties and the literacy tests were again legal.[80] Despite successful bail-out, Apache County did not resume literacy tests.[81] The counties were victorious, but the American system was still turned upside-down. The presumption of innocence did not exist. The roles of plaintiff and defendant were reversed and the burden of proof misplaced.

Despite the ongoing suffrage debate, the 1966 elections gave the legislature its first Navajo, a 40-year-old Northern Arizona University graduate and the social security director for the tribe.[82] After the elections, the state legislature made another pass a reapportioning. In June 1967, they enacted *Chapter 1, House Bill 1, 28th Legislature*[83] which was challenged in the courts less than a month later. Sufficient signatures were filed with the Arizona Secretary of State to trigger an Arizona law prohibiting a bill from becoming law without its endorsement from a public referendum. The court deferred action on the challenge until after the referendum. Bureaucratic wheels turned very slowly. The referendum for the new apportionment plan passed in November 1968, and the Governor signed it into law in January 1969. The hearing then recommenced on the original challenges. In April, the U. S. Supreme Court heard *Kirkpatrick v. Preisler* and concluded that states could not establish a tolerance limit for district deviations.[84] Arizona's plan allowed 40 percent population deviations until 1971 and 16 percent thereafter. The Arizona legislature targeted a 16 percent deviation, believing it was acceptable to the courts. In July 1969, the court declared the plan illegal because the districts were not as evenly populated as possible and the deviations could not be explained by any legitimate state interest. The court ordered that the 1966 plan remain in effect until a new plan was devised.[85]

In January 1970, the legislature enacted *Chapter 1, 29th Legislature*.[86] Plaintiffs challenged and the court heard testimony in April. Plaintiff-intervenor Herbert Ely, Chairman of the Arizona Democratic Party, complained that legislative redistricting was not properly based on the current population distribution in Arizona. He contended that the mathematics were done on the erroneous assumption that actual population could be calculated from voter registration data. He proposed another plan using projections from Arizona's 1960 and 1965 census data and based it on census tract rather than existing precinct boundaries. The court generally liked his plan, but it failed to provide legal descriptions of the boundaries and would have caused nearly every district to be redrawn. On the other hand, the co-plaintiff, Gary Klahr, conceded that the apportionment of the state legislature was adequate, but contended that the three U. S. congressional districts could have been more evenly apportioned. He suggested that the three congressmen be elected at-large.

In the mean time, the validity of the 1966 plan was eroding. Voter registration estimates suggested that deviations of 47 percent existed between districts. The legislature's plan ostensibly had only 1.8 percent deviations, but those deviations were based on admittedly poor data. Based on extrapolating registration data into total population data, the computer was programmed to create districts as equal in population as possible. The computer was further constrained to put one incumbent senator and two incumbent representatives in each district and make the districts as homogeneous as possible as to political party. Somehow this was all to be done creating relative compactness. This numerical hocus-pocus may have served little more than perpetuating the existing politicians.

Pandemonium continued during 1970. The election was close at hand. Once again, there was not time to devise a new plan. The court even considered electing the entire legislature at-large, but reason prevailed before voters were each presented with candidates for ninety offices. The court denied Klahr's proposal for at-large U. S. representatives.[87] Both the new plan and the 1966 plan were defective. Since the next election could use 1970 census data, the 1970 solution would be temporary. The court chose the legislative plan as the "lesser of two evils."[88] In June, plaintiffs appealed to have the plan enjoined. Adding to the confusion, the state required a complete re-registration of all voters.[89]

During this half-decade of voting history, the Navajos took little stand on voting issues. They did, however, make some institutional moves. In July 1968, the Navajo Community College opened and was the first college run by Indians; it even employed a medicine man to teach traditional Indian ceremonies. The next year the Tribal Council resolved to enhance the Navajo identity by calling themselves the *Navajo Nation*.

Raymond Nakai remained tribal chief of the Navajos, although the contest for Navajo leadership between Nakai and MacDonald was on. In a conflict over joint land use with the Hopi's, the Navajos were defeated in the courts. This circumstance cast doubt on the effectiveness of the Nakai administration leaving MacDonald in a position of strength.

The activism and social change that was the 1960s was aimed primarily toward black rights, but its effect also ushered in concepts to replace the traditional assimilation strategy for Indians. The idea of greater tribal sovereignty fit the trends toward participative democracy and cultural pluralism. Early change was enhanced by funding from the new Office of Economic Opportunity (OEO). The OEO was able to bypass the BIA along with Republican controlled state and local governments by working directly with tribal leaders and funding Indian responsibility for managing local reservation institutions. So widespread was the administration's interest in empowering the Native Americans that more than a dozen government agencies were directly involved by the end of the Johnson presidency.[90]

The Navajo Reservation was on the vanguard of this movement. In 1966, the small community of Rough Rock, just off one of the loneliest paved roads in Arizona, contracted its Community School to DINE, a Navajo corporation formed to gain control of the school. This experiment received favorable publicity and four years later the OEO provided funds for contracting the Ramah school, also on the reservation. As other schools followed, the BIA became critical of the education standards in the new schools. The BIA was reluctant to relinquish control and was able to gain concurrence from many tribal leaders.[91]

As the Navajo and other tribes began to drift toward independence and sovereignty, concern arose that semi-sovereign tribal councils could deny civil rights of reservation inhabitants. Addressing that concern, Congress passed the Indian Civil Rights Act of 1968. The act established Bill-of-Rights-type protection. It said that tribal councils could not "deny to any person within its jurisdiction the equal protection of its laws or deprive any person of liberty or property without due process of law."[92] Later the courts, including the Supreme Court, would deal with the complexities and contradictions of policies giving tribes sovereign rights while simultaneously limiting that sovereignty by guaranteeing rights to the constituents of these sovereign governments.

A month before the original 1965 act was scheduled to expire, President Richard Nixon set out new Indian policy that continues in force today. Nixon stated, "Both as a matter of social justice and as a matter of enlightened social policy, we must begin to act on the basis of what the Indians themselves have long been telling us. . . . The time has come to decisively break with the past and to create the conditions for a new era in which the Indian future is determined by Indian acts and Indian decisions." He stated that Indian policy must strengthen the Indians' sense of autonomy without threatening their sense of community. We must assure the Indian that he can assume control of his own life without being separated involuntarily from the tribal group. And we must make it clear that Indians can become independent of federal control without being cut off from . . . federal support."[93] These words led to a frenzy of congressional and policy activities favoring Indian control and sovereignty. House Concurrent Resolution 108, the policy of termination, was repudiated and repealed.[94]

Dade County: Breeding Ground for Unrest

Minorities in Dade County did not begin a visible struggle for voting equality until the 1980s. The 1960s and 1970s were the decades that Dade built its minority population, replete with the emergence of racial strife. On arriving in Miami in April 1966, Martin Luther King consulted with the SCLC and announced that they had found "hostility and alienation of the city."[95] Six months later, three white youths were stabbed while "looking around" a black neighborhood. This and other incidents increased the city's awareness of a growing crime problem. In December 1967, Police Chief Headley who had had enough of crime and violence, stepped up patrols and began to use police dogs and shotguns to check crime. The NAACP demanded his resignation. The ACLU announced they would seek a federal injunction, but Headley defended himself and gained the support of the city commission. According to police a month later, the violent crime rate had dropped 60 percent.

Tension continued to grow. In February 1968, two policemen stripped a black youth and dangled him from a highway overpass. In May, 14 blacks were arrested when they refused to vacate the President's office at Miami University after pressing for more "blackness" on campus. In August, Republicans held their convention in Miami Beach. Protesting conservative policies, violence flared in the black Liberty City district with fires, looting, and injuries. The violence led to a shoot-out with police resulting in the slaying of three blacks.

Things were not going well for the black community economically either. Even the newly immigrated Cuban minorities enjoyed income 20 percent higher that that of blacks.[96]

As early results of the Voting Rights Act played out across the South, Dade County waited for immigrant voting rights to come to the forefront a decade later.

Chapter 5: The Amendments of 1970[1]

By 1969, most voters still believed in minority causes, although enthusiasm had dwindled as fear and resentment grew from the riots that occurred in the early part of the decade. Minority leaders had split, seeking goals in two directions: The National Association for the Advancement of Colored People (NAACP) and the National Urban League (NUL) remained committed to desegregation, black voting rights, and a partnership with liberal whites; the Student Non-violent Coordinating Committee (SNCC) and the Congress for Racial Equality (CORE) had drifted toward racial nationalism and a growing advocacy for violent retaliation. Stokley Carmichael headed SNCC in 1966 and passed the leadership to H. Rap Brown a year later. As many whites looked on with horror at the black, urban riots that ignited in the North, they blamed the rhetoric of these black leaders. After a riot in Cleveland, Carmichael remarked, "When you talk about black power, you talk about building a movement that will smash everything Western civilization has created."[2] At a rally in Cambridge, Maryland, Brown shouted, "If America don't come around, we're going to burn it down, brother."[3]

Despite disillusionment with the movement and a growing belief by whites that the major goals of civil rights had been met, few believed that black citizens should be denied access to franchise. Politicians had little enthusiasm for standing against those who wished to strengthen the Voting Rights Act.

In January 1969, former Attorney General Ramsey Clark submitted legislation to the House extending all the provisions of the Voting Rights Act of 1965 for an additional five years. Without this further legislation, jurisdictions caught by the automatic trigger in 1965 could all meet the bailout requirement beginning in 1970. Those jurisdictions could then reinstitute literacy tests and join the twelve states outside the South still requiring some showing of literacy.

President Nixon was "determined to ensure that the young liberal lawyers in the Civil Rights Division of the Department of Justice would be prevented from running wild through the South enforcing compliance with extreme or punitive requirements that they had formulated in Washington, D. C."[4] Thus in June 1969, the administration proposed legislation that would have weakened the act considerably.[5]

The South had supported Nixon and was viewed by Republicans as vital to their political future. While southern congressmen would have liked to see the act lapse altogether, they especially objected to Section 5 preclearance and the regional nature of the legislation. It was obvious from the Gaston[6] decision, no southern jurisdiction could prove that it historically offered blacks equal education; thus, no jurisdiction was likely to succeed with the act's bail-out provisions. The Voting Rights Act would remain a stigma on the South. Representing the administration, Assistant Attorney General Jerris Leonard supported the South by promoting a nationwide ban on literacy tests. He insisted that the current situation discriminated against poorly educated blacks who had migrated to the North and could not pass literacy tests there.[7] The administration's proposal would have not only banned literacy tests, but would also have eliminated Section 5 preclearance, and shifted the burden of voting discrimination proof to federal prosecutors.

When Attorney General John Mitchell unveiled the plan to Congress, he defended it contending, ". . . voting rights is not a regional issue. It is a national concern for every American which must be tested on a nationwide basis."[8] The proposal drew fire from the press and civil rights advocacy groups. Even Northern liberals objected to the suspension of literacy tests in places such as New York, claiming that New York did not have a racial problem that needed solving. Northern states defended their own literacy tests as non-discriminatory, in contrast to those in the South, but this argument failed with southern Congressmen since their literacy tests had been banned without any examination of fairness.

The Mitchell proposal went to the Judiciary Committees in both Houses. The House Committee, controlled by civil rights supporters, rejected it and recommended an extension of the act with no amendments. The reception was warmer in the Senate. Sam Irwin of North Carolina, who headed the Judiciary Subcommittee, lauded the proposal because, ". . . it does eliminate the unjust and repressive aspects which are so objectionable."[9] After conducting hearings, the Senate suspended deliberations until the House ruled on the bill.

In the House, a coalition of Republicans and southern Democrats seriously challenged the liberals. Every lawmaker representing districts in the jurisdictions covered under the 1965 statute backed the administration's measure. Through skillful maneuvering and a somewhat disorganized opposition, the Mitchell proposal passed the House.

A Senate, bipartisan coalition which included the Republican Majority leader and the Minority Whip, bent on saving the Voting Rights Act, decided to accept the nationwide ban on literacy tests. They insisted, however, that the other provisions remain intact. Congress then added the national right of 18-year-olds to vote, creating another conflict with the President who realized that such an extension would favor Democrats in the next election. Ultimately, supporters of 18-year-old suffrage outmaneuvered presidential supporters. Thus, the final legislation imposed a temporary ban on all literacy tests, extended the special provisions until 1975, and offered 18-year-olds the vote. To ensure the constitutionality of the 18-year-old-voter provision, Congress and the states enacted the Twenty-sixth Amendment, extending suffrage protections to citizens between 18 and 21 years of age. Since another presidential election had occurred since the original legislation, the amendment also provided that new voting entities would be captured by the trigger if they had literacy tests or other devices in effect during the 1968 election, and their registration rate or voting rate was less than 50 percent.

Miscellaneous provisions limited to 30 days any residence requirement for voters in presidential elections and established a nationwide, uniform standard for absentee balloting in presidential elections. The amendments also gave any citizen denied the right to vote, the ability to initiate, in the name of the United States, an action in a U. S. District Court after which there would be direct appeal to the Supreme Court. Additionally, the new law provided fines and imprisonment for persons violating the act.

The areas newly covered by the special provisions were Bronx, King, and New York Counties, New York; Campbell County, Wyoming; Monterey and Yuba Counties, California; Apache, Coconino, Cochise, Mojave, Pima, Pinal, and Santa Cruz Counties, Arizona; Elmore County, Idaho; Election Districts 8, 11, 12, and 13 in Alaska; and towns in Connecticut, New Hampshire, Maine, and Massachusetts.

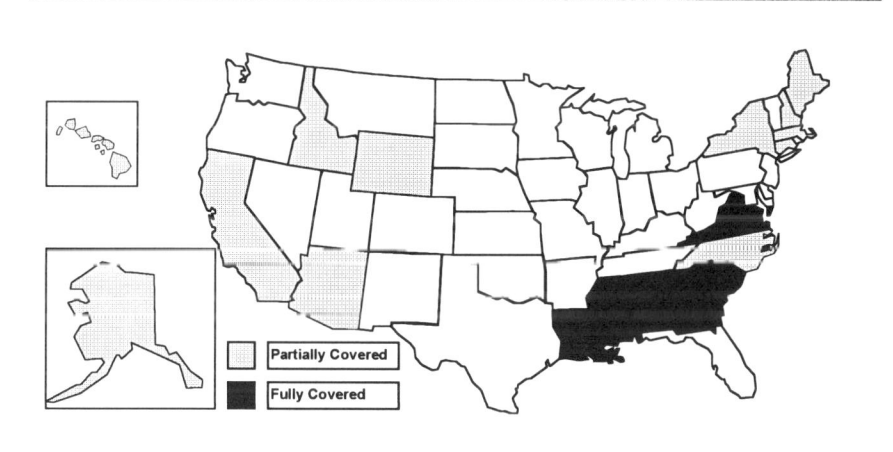

FIGURE 5: COVERED JURISDICTIONS AFTER THE 1970 AMENDMENTS

The Arguments in Favor of the 1970 Amendments

Proponents of the amendment noted that although there were considerable improvements in the southern statewide averages, many counties still had low voter registrations. Across Alabama, Georgia, Mississippi, and South Carolina, about one third of the counties still registered less than 50 percent of the minority voters; about 10 percent registered less than 35 percent.

The argument in favor of extending the act revolved around the notion that the progress made should not be lost. To the contrary, more progress was required, thus the act should not become less demanding. If minorities had to rely once again on traditional litigation, the South would return to the quagmire that brought about the original need for the act.

The argument continued that evidence existed showing that the elective franchise for minorities was still being propped up in some areas by the federal government's strength derived from the special provisions of the act. Efforts at continued divisiveness abounded; the U. S. Commission on Civil Rights noted the emergence of techniques such as switching to at-large elections; *packing*, to concentrate black voting strength in particular districts; increasing filing fees where black candidates were running; abolishing positions being sought by black candidates or making them appointive; extending the term of office for incumbent whites; and withholding, from blacks, information about qualifying for office. Supporters postulated that the basic frame of mind in the Southern States had not yet changed enough for the federal government to trust them. The Supreme Court said in *Allen v. State Board of Elections*, "The achievement of the act's laudable goal could be severely hampered, however, if each citizen were required to depend solely on litigation."[10]

The Arguments Against the 1970 Amendments

The Nixon administration provided some opposition to the extension of the temporary features of the act calling them "regional" legislation. Senator Sam Erwin of North Carolina tried unsuccessfully to introduce many mollifying amendments.

Richard H. Poff of Virginia filed the dissenting view. He presented an argument on behalf of the State of Virginia proposing that it was unwise to extend the expiring provisions of the law for another five years since it was a law "which raises a legal presumption of voter discrimination against a state at large because its voter turnout is lower than other states. . ." He contended that, "The law also bases its presumption on election returns five years old and ignores the progress made since then [which is] more of a penalty than a reward."[11]

When *South Carolina v. Katzenbach* confirmed the constitutionality of the 1965 Act, Justice Black had dissented from the majority opinion. Justice Black wrote:

> [The Voting Rights Act], by providing that some of the States cannot pass State laws or adopt state constitutional amendments without first being compelled to beg federal authorities to approve their policies, so distorts the constitutional structure of government as to render any distinction drawn in the Constitution between state and federal powers almost meaningless. One of the most basic premises upon which our structure of government was founded was that the Federal Government was to have certain specific and limited powers and no others, and all other power was to be reserved either to the States respectively, or to the people. Certainly, . . . at least the States have the power to pass laws and amend their constitutions without first sending their officials hundreds of miles away to beg Federal authorities to approve them. . . . I cannot help but believe that the inevitable effect of any such law that forces any one of the States to entreat Federal authorities in far away places for approval of local laws before they can become effective is to create the impression that the State or States treated this way are little more than conquered provinces.[12]

Justice Black added that he saw similarities between preclearance and the English Crown's treatment of the American Colonies. The Declaration of Independence protested that the King "has called together legislative bodies at places unusual, uncomfortable, and distant from the depository of their public records, for the sole purpose of fatiguing them into compliance with his measures. . . "

Mr. Poff dealt with the question of why a state that was free of voting discrimination would have any reason to worry about a five year extension of the act's provisions. He articulated, "[I]t is offensive to Virginians to think that Virginia, where the first democratic legislature in the New World was convened, whose sons contributed so much to the deeds and documents of independence and union, should be foreclosed from amending their own Constitution and laws without prior permission of a federal official or a federal court."[13]

The final argument against extending the provisions of the act was simply that the job was done. Gone were the institutional barriers that had long prevented black registration in the South. The act was designed to give blacks the right to vote and parity between black and white registration was at hand. Even the Civil Rights Division considered the task essentially complete "both by means of federal registration effort and by the impetus that federal registration had given to local registrars to go ahead and register people."[14]

Results of the Act After the Amendments of 1970

Nixon's Dilemma[15]

The Nixon administration, unsuccessful in passing its own version of the 1970 Voting Rights Act amendments, was in no mood to show leadership in enforcing Section 5. In April 1970, the Mississippi State Legislature passed an open primary law which abolished all party primaries and required all candidates to run in the general elections. If no candidate received a majority, the top two candidates would compete in a runoff. The previous system had allowed plurality candidates victory, but white politicians feared that black, bloc voting could produce black plurality successes. Under Section 5, the change was submitted on July 23. At the end of the 60-day period, Assistant Attorney General Jerris Leonard informed Mississippi that he could not conclude that black rights had been violated, therefore, he would not object.

Suffragists immediately objected, led by Howard Glickstein, the Staff Director of the Commission of Civil Rights. Glickstein asserted that Mitchell did not understand his responsibilities under the Voting Rights Act. He claimed that the law placed the burden of racial proof on the states and that the Justice Department, unconvinced of a proposal's racial neutrality, was bound to object.

Mitchell's staff stood its ground. In October, Leonard refused to object to a redistricting plan for Copiah County, Mississippi on the basis that the plan was too complex for Civil Rights Division attorneys to analyze in sixty days. He stated that Congress did not intend for the Justice Department to object unless there was convincing evidence of racial effect or intent.

In March 1971, Jacob Javits of New York, along with Senators Philip Hart and Hugh Scott visited David Norman who had succeeded Jerris Leonard. The coalition began to pressure Norman for a Justice Department policy for rejection of unresolved Section 5 requests. Soon Congressmen, civil rights lawyers, and activists began sending letters to Mitchell demanding a stronger stance. In April, a federal district court panel in Mississippi said that Mitchell had erred in not giving a negative or positive response to the open-primary litigants or, at least, quietly waiting out the 60 days. Instead, Leonard had said he was unable to make a determination. The same ruling suggested that Section 5 preclearance requests bore the same positive burden of proof that a submission to the D. C. District Court required.[16]

Don Edwards, Chairman of the House Judiciary Subcommittee on Civil Rights, announced a probe into the attorney general's actions. The day before the probe began, the Justice Department caved in and wrote into its procedures, "If evidence as to the purpose or effect of a change is conflicting, and [the attorney general] is unable to resolve the conflict within the 60-day period, he shall . . . enter an objection."

Continued Expansion

The era from 1970 to 1975 continued the government's expanding interpretation of the Voting Rights Act. Impediments to minority influence were assaulted from all sides. Through the courts, minorities made progress in the mechanisms of voting and in the more-leveraging area of apportionment.

Court decisions after the 1970 Amendments continued to support Congress' desire that the federal government be involved in even the most minor alterations in voting practices. This invasive attention began to spot even the most subtle discrimination, real or perceived. North Carolina extended the prohibition against electioneering near a polling place from 50 feet to 500 feet. This, a federal judge concluded, was a change requiring preclearance. The next year, a Mississippi district court ruled that a change in polling places required preclearance under the law. The courts further interpreted the law to extend past the realm of official state or local election entities. In 1972, Alabama plaintiffs challenged the ability of the Democratic and Republican Parties to make rules for the selection of convention delegates without preclearance under Section 5. Political party officials argued that Section 5 of the act was clear when it began, "Whenever a State or political subdivision . . ." The court concluded, however, that Alabama could not avoid the act by empowering other bodies—in this case, political parties—to regulate the electoral process, thus, changes in convention rules were subject to preclearance.[17]

Although the constitutionality of preclearance was already confirmed seven years earlier in *South Carolina v. Katzenbach*, in 1973 federal authority was again challenged in *Georgia v. United States*. The state of Georgia had reapportioned its legislature. During the preclearance process, the attorney general objected to the reapportionment plan because he was unable to conclude that the plan did not have discriminatory purpose or effect. Litigants argued that the Attorney General had to find the plan discriminatory to reject it. However, the Supreme Court, in its opinion written by Justice Potter Stewart, upheld the attorney general's objection, concluding that he had no obligation to find fault with a plan; he needed only to be unconvinced by the submitter's case. The opinion stated that preclearance was offered by the act as a fast alternative to suing in the D. C. District Court. The district court, Justice Stewart contended, would need to bear the much higher burden of finding fault with the submitter's proof. Justice Byron White wrote a dissenting opinion. He reasoned, "[A]ny objection whatsoever filed by [the attorney general] will suffice to foreclose the effectiveness of the new legislation . . . I cannot believe, however, that the Congress intended to visit upon the States the consequences of such uncontrolled discretion of the attorney general. . . . Why," he wrote, "should the State be forced to shoulder that burden where its proposed change is so colorless that the country's highest legal officer professes his inability to make up his mind as to its legality?"[18] Nonetheless, the court decided that a determined attorney general could deny preclearance by stating only that he was unconvinced.

The number of requests for preclearance had grown each year since 1965. Confusion abounded concerning the exact requirements and likely outcome of a Section 5 submission. White southern conservatives, radical activists, and the Supreme Court all wanted the Justice Department to publish guidelines.[19] In September 1971, the Civil Rights Section published a list of procedures. Included in the list were examples of changes requiring preclearance. The list demonstrated how comprehensive the Act's preclearance authority had become:

- Any change in qualifications or eligibility for voting;
- Any change in procedures concerning registration, balloting, or informing or assisting citizens to register and vote;
- Any change in the constituency or boundaries of a voting unit (e.g. through redistricting, annexation, or reapportionment), the location of a polling place, change to at-large elections from district elections or to district from at-large;
- Any alteration affecting the eligibility of persons to become or remain candidates;
- Any change in the eligibility for independent candidates;
- Any action extending or shortening the term of an official or changing the method of selecting an official;
- Any change in the method of counting votes.[20]

Efforts to locate polling places to serve the black community began in the early 1970s. Civil rights leaders contended that many locations in the Southern States were hostile to blacks and that although blacks were allowed to vote, they might be too frightened. For example, when Leflore County,

Mississippi, redistricted in 1973, county officials changed the polling places. When minorities sued, the court found all the Board's changes to be reasonable except the selection of the VFW Club. The court said, "The VFW Club . . . has a membership of Whites only; and black citizens who constitute the voter majority in Southeast Greenwood may likely be inhibited or embarrassed in free access to vote at that location."[21]

Civil rights activists took issue with filing fees that were prerequisite to running for office. In 1970, a federal district court declared filing fees unconstitutional for candidates to the Mobile, Alabama City Commission. The court's position was that the $360 fee was excessive when compared to a commissioner's salary of $18,000 per year.[22]

Courts began to delve more deeply into the details of apportionment plans. Again in Leflore County, a redistricting plan was challenged, in part, because the resulting districts did not contain the same land area or number of miles of county maintained roads. The 5th Circuit Court of Appeals considered this significant because the county allotted equal dollars for road maintenance to each district.[23] The 5th Circuit somehow found a relationship between the Voting Rights Act and county road maintenance budgets.

The Supreme Court in 1971 had stated that the Voting Rights Act legitimately concerned itself with annexation.[24] Liberal justices interpreted annexation as a change in voting rules or procedures on the basis that it could influence the effectiveness of a vote. In 1968, the Crusade for Voters, a black civic organization, ran successful candidates for three of Richmond, Virginia's nine city council seats. These victories, in the city's at-large voting plan, were the result of a 52 percent black majority. The next year, the city annexed 23 acres of an adjacent county. The annexed property was 97 percent white which reduced the black portion of the city population to 42 percent. In the 1970 elections Richmond enfranchised the new population without having secured preclearance from the attorney general. Two years later, the Supreme Court stopped the elections in an attempt to give the lower court time to find a just solution. After another two years, the court found that the annexation was discriminatory in both purpose and result. The city ultimately proposed, coincident with the annexation, to change its at-large, election system to a nine-ward system. The District Court still refused the plan but was overruled by the Supreme Court which held, "As long as the ward system fairly reflects the strength of the Negro community as it exists after annexation, we cannot hold . . . that the annexation is . . . barred by Section 5.[25] Had the election scheme not changed, the court would most certainly have reversed the annexation. This exemplified new found power of the act and the type of negotiated exchange that election entities began to make with the courts and plaintiffs.

Petersburg, Virginia provided a similar case. In 1966, the city council approved an annexation of primarily white neighborhoods, reducing the city's minority population from 56 to 47 percent. Ironically, the annexation was introduced by a black councilman and was unanimously approved. In 1972, the city submitted its plan to the attorney general who objected because the annexation would adversely affect minorities in light of the city's at-large election scheme. Not accepting the attorney general's position, the city tried the case in the D. C. District Court. The court faced a dilemma: the minorities in the city government had favored the annexation, but the plan could dilute their voting strength. The court stepped out onto new ground by approving the annexation, then ordering the city to institute a system of single-member districts. This was not a compromise worked out among the parties, but was an order of the court on an issue that was not on trial. Although the courts had consistently held that at-large elections were not unconstitutional *per se*, the court could now declare one illegal without testing its constitutionality. On appeal, the Supreme Court affirmed the decision of the district court.[26]

Many other cases strengthened the courts' influence over annexation. A Mississippi Federal District Court ruled that any annexation that resulted in a change in the number of eligible voters required federal preclearance. This step was necessary, the court argued, to give the attorney general a chance to understand and potentially disapprove any demographic changes caused by annexation.[27] From 1971 through 1974, one-fourth of the preclearance requests made of the Department of Justice involved annexation. All other types of redistricting accounted for only half as many requests.

During this period of the act's history, the courts began dismantling at-large voting districts. The Nacogdoches, Texas city charter provided for at-large city elections that included provisions to give victory to the plurality candidate. In 1972, a black candidate won a plurality of votes. In the following June, the city commission changed the city charter to require a majority vote for election to each at-large seat. The next year another black candidate ran and gained a plurality, but was defeated in the run-off election. In 1975, a federal district court judge instituted single-member districts for Nacogdoches on the grounds that the at-large systems, with a majority-vote requirement, abridged the voting rights of blacks.[28] This type of judgment made it very difficult for municipalities to predict the outcome of a voting rights strategy. Neither at-large districting nor majority-voting requirements were illegal, but under these particular circumstances, and in this particular court, the combination of the two was illegal. The court was looking for results, and in this case, the principal of majority-rule did not produce those results.

In 1971, a Louisiana federal district court created a reapportionment plan for the state legislature. Objectors to this plan proposed several alternatives, but the court enforced its own plan which met all the constitutional requirements while the other proposals did not. The court decision stated, "Single-member districts have been used exclusively in the court-approved plan because they better protect the constitutional rights of Louisiana citizens." The order went on to say, "Single-member districts . . . result in less deviation from the one-man, one-vote requirement than do multi-member districts."[29] The courts logic was faulty since at-large voting perfectly supports the one-man, one-vote principle; by its very definition, all at-large districts all have precisely the same number of voters.

The use of "historical" and "natural" boundaries for voting districts usually aided the courts in setting a reapportionment plan, but many suits attacked their use. In 1971, a Louisiana court stated, "The historical boundaries of voting districts in Louisiana reflect a history of racial discrimination. . . . Historical boundaries . . . must give way to federally guaranteed constitutional rights."[30] In another Louisiana case in 1972, the Supreme Court held that a court-imposed plan that violated traditional boundaries was preferable to the state plan that left boundaries intact.[31]

Since the Amendments of 1970 had suspended all literacy tests, English-illiterate citizens could vote anywhere in the country. This provision was challenged in late 1970 in *Oregon v. Mitchell*. The Supreme Court concluded that the ban was valid under the enforcement clauses of the Fourteenth and Fifteenth Amendments. Although that appeared to be a reversal of earlier cases permitting literacy tests, Justice Douglas explained that those cases simply asked whether states could perform such tests under the constitution. In *Oregon*, the Justice contended, the question was quite different—could the Congress constitutionally pass a law to ban such tests? Congress, they determined, has the constitutional right to remedy the civil rights abuse often derived from literacy tests.

> [Congress] can rely on the fact that most states do not have literacy tests; that tests have been used at times as a discriminatory weapon against minorities, not only Negroes but Americans of Mexican ancestry, and American Indians; that radio and television have made it possible for a person to be well informed even though he may not be able to read and write.[32]

In 1975, five years into the suspension of all literacy tests, the Civil Rights Commission published its assessment of the first ten years under the Voting Rights Act. In that work, Commissioner Frankie M. Freeman took a strong stand for the permanent abolition of literacy tests. He based his thesis on the premise that literacy tests could not guarantee intelligent or informed voting:

> Literacy tests guarantee only that a class of citizens, many of whom are victims of unconstitutional discrimination in education, may not participate in their own self-government. . . . The illiterate, like the blind person, may be well informed concerning public affairs through the broadcast media, public meetings, and conversation with family, friends, and coworkers. . . . That a citizen who has been unconstitutionally deprived of equal education opportunity by one state may then be deprived of the right to vote by another state is contrary to the spirit of a free society.[33]

The commission Vice Chairman, Stephen Horn, recognized the need for some extension of the ban on literacy tests, but believed that any ban should be short-lived. He argued, "I do not believe that the more illiterates who vote, the better. Neither do I believe that only those with a high school or college education should vote. I do believe, however, that there is a certain minimum level of literacy which a polity that prides itself on effective citizenship has a right to expect."[34]

The debate went on to legal issues. Clearly, the ban danced at the edges of the states-rights guarantees of the 17th Amendment. Still, the five year experiment banning literacy and other prequalifying tests, had proved to be an important success factor in registering new voters. The evidence was clear that many of these tests discriminated. Had the tests ever been allowed reinstitution, an ongoing, divisive, public debate would have followed. The need for literacy, its definition, and its fair determination would surely have continued to elude consensus.

With literacy off the slate, the new initiative of civil rights groups was *assistance*. States now had to step up to the chore of providing assistance to illiterates. Courts decided that states had to provide the same quality of assistance to illiterates as they would for physically disabled or blind voters.[35] The courts left latitude to the local administrators to determine the exact nature of the assistance despite civil rights leaders' insistence that blacks be available to help blacks, or that family members be allowed in the polling booth.

The Rise of Hispanic Rights

The voting rights of non-English speaking citizens emerged as an issue in the early 1970s. The Voting Rights Act, as passed in 1965, had protected only non-English speakers who were educated at "American flag schools."

Civil rights leaders insisted on bilingual voting material and assistance at the polls. In 1974, only California had laws requiring the posting of bilingual materials and ballots.[36] In that year, a New York City case resulted in a court order for the city to provide the same.[37] Unrelated to voting rights, but an important indicator of the times, was the Supreme Court's decision in *Lau v. Nichols*. In 1974, Kinney Lau, a Chinese student unable to speak English, sued the San Francisco school system for not providing him special help.[38] The court sided with Lau declaring that non-English speaking children had a constitutional right to special language programs.[39] This conclusion became a basis for the voting rights of non-English speaking citizens.

Based on simple numbers, Hispanics posed the greatest non-English issue. To gain special language rights for Hispanics, civil rights leaders had to present them as victims, just as blacks and Native Americans were victims. Traditional immigrants, such as Irish, Germans, Jews, Italians, Greeks and Poles, assimilated quickly into American mainstream. They had not been conquered or enslaved. They may have experienced initial prejudice and discrimination, but they made no claim on the American conscience. To some extent, Mexican Americans were a conquered group, but at the end of the Mexican-American War, Mexicans comprised only four percent of the Southwest U. S. population. As pointed out by author Peter Skerry, "[V]ery few Mexican Americans today can trace their lineage back to that conquest. The vast majority are either immigrants themselves or the descendants of immigrants who arrived here in one of the various waves that have swept across the border since the turn of the century."[40] Actually, Mexican Americans had been successful in joining the American economic mainstream. Early demonstrations to persuade the public that Hispanics were victims were seen during the 1967 congressional hearings on bilingual education. Texas Senator Ralph Yarborough, principal sponsor of the Bilingual Education Act, argued that "bilingual programs were appropriate for Mexican Americans because, unlike other non-English speaking groups in the United States, they had not come here voluntarily but had been conquered and had our culture imposed on them."[41] Such perspectives, though widespread, clashed with the realities of voluntary immigration.

The Start of Affirmative Action

Language and literacy were important issues, but were ultimately replaced by *results*, the most extensive new concept of the 1970s. Results meant viewing the fairness of an election process by counting the minorities who got elected. In 1971, in *Whitcomb v. Chavis*, black voters challenged a redistricting plan in Indianapolis, Indiana, that provided for the election of eight state senators and fifteen assemblymen from a single, countywide district. The District Court ruled for the plaintiffs because black representation had been historically disproportionately low. The Supreme Court disagreed. The overruling decision stated, "The fact that the number of ghetto residents who were legislators was not in proportion to ghetto population [does not] satisfactorily prove invidious discrimination, absent evidence and findings that ghetto residents had less opportunity than did other residents to participate in the political process and elect legislators of their choice." The court contended that the dilution of voting strength of black Democrats in a largely Republican county was "a mere euphemism for defeat."[42]

Not to be discouraged by a single defeat, civil rights lawyers began to fight for a stronger tie to results. Only two years later, the 1973 decision in *White v. Regester* showed that the court would indeed consider results in areas of historical racial discrimination. Plaintiffs in Dallas and Bexar (San Antonio) Counties in Texas convinced the district court that the small number of minorities elected to the legislature from these counties was the result of discrimination. The Supreme Court, by a unanimous decision, agreed. The court did not require that there be discriminatory intent in the election systems. Instead they found the "totality of circumstances," including the fact that Hispanics had not been elected in proportion to their population, sufficient to find for the plaintiffs. The court explained that the differing decisions came from differing circumstances in *White* and *Whitcomb*. Indiana, they said, did not have a long history of discrimination still lingering in the mechanics of the present system as did Texas.

In his opinion, Justice White did not contend that Mexican-Americans lacked access to the election machinery—the goal of the act only eight years earlier. This idea of "totality of circumstances" became a significant tool in striking down multi-member districts. In *White v. Regester*, Dallas and Bexar Counties were ordered to use only single-member districts. When *White* was sent back to the district court for handling, that court outlawed at-large voting schemes in seven other Texas counties as well. To do this, the district court not only had the strength of the Supreme Court's confirmation, but the court also had guidelines from another landmark case, *Zimmer v. McKeithen*.

The decision in *Zimmer* struck down the at-large voting scheme in East Carroll Parish, Louisiana. The court prescribed several tests to be used in establishing the *totality of circumstances* in multi-member district cases. Courts were instructed to look for elements of vote dilution:

> ... where minorities can demonstrate a lack of access to the process of slating candidates, the unresponsiveness of legislators to their particularized interests, a tenuous policy underlying the preference for multi-member or at-large districting, or that the existence of past discrimination, in general, precludes the effective participation in the election system. Such proof is enhanced by a showing of the existence of large districts, majority-vote requirements, anti-single-shot voting provisions, and the lack of provision for at-large candidates running from particular geographical subdistricts.[43]

The Fifth Circuit Court judged that these factors could be used in combination to show vote dilution, that all the factors need not be present, and that no single factor was sufficient evidence by itself. These points became known as the Zimmer factors and provided a checklist in many subsequent cases.

On remand in *White*, the court noted only two instances in which at-large apportionment would be favored. First, multi-member districts should be used where "a district court determines that significant interests would be advanced by the use of multi-member districts and the use of single-member district would jeopardize constitutional requirements." Second, multi-member districts would be appropriate when they "afford minorities a greater opportunity for participation in the political process than do single-member districts." Thus the courts' general dislike for at-large apportionment would be overridden by demonstrating a benefit to minorities. This suggested that whites might not be entitled to the same defense as other groups or, at least, left open the question of who could be considered a minority.

By 1975, the option of first seeking judgment from the D. C. District Court rather than seeking approval of the attorney general had been used only once.[44] In contrast, thousands of changes had been sent to the attorney general. Federal examiners had been sent to only 60 counties but had registered about 15 percent of the one million new black voters that had registered since 1965.[45] More than 6,500 federal election observers had been sent to the Southern States.

Black registration, although up markedly since 1965, had notably leveled after the first 3 years of the act. Reliable data on actual voter turnout by race is scarce, but studies by the Bureau of the Census and others find that most of the disparity between black and white voting by the mid-1970s was socioeconomic based. No longer were the gaps accounted for by the lingering effects of disenfranchise techniques.[46]

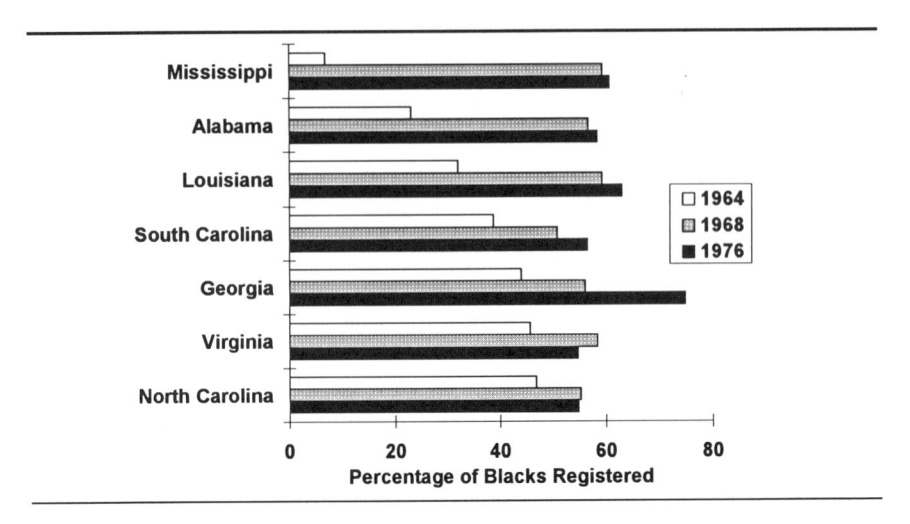

FIGURE 6: BLACK REGISTRATION—1965, 1967, 1972

Before 1965, there were probably fewer than 100 black elected officials in the seven Southern States. By 1975, the count had risen to more than one thousand including one member of Congress, 68 state legislators, and the remainder in county and municipal offices.[47] In January 1975, fifteen blacks became members of the Alabama State Legislature in the same building upon which blacks had marched ten years earlier.[48] Still, no black held a statewide office in a Southern State nor had one come close to being elected. The period from the Amendments of 1970 to the additional amendments that would be passed in 1975, marked an ever increasing reach of the law and an ever increasing level of arbitration and direction from the courts.

Dallas: The First Round of Litigation

In the fall of 1970, as Erik Jonsson's final mayoral term neared completion, the CCA was indecisive about a replacement. Wes Wise, a former sportscaster with good name recognition, announced his candidacy, along with black activist Al Lipscomb. Lipscomb, who would become a major player in Dallas politics, graduated from Dallas' Lincoln High School in 1942. After serving in the Army in World War II, he spent ten months on a work farm for selling drugs. He returned to Dallas in 1950 to work as a waiter in the Adolphus Hotel Dining Room and the First National Bank Executive Dining Room. In 1966 he began working in the War on Poverty and the Block Partnership program sponsored by the Greater Dallas Council of Churches.[49]

CCA president John Schoelkoph finally selected Avery Mays, a traditional CCA businessman, for the Mayor's post. Accused of lacking diversity, the CCA defended its choice by pointing out that the ticket contained three men in their thirties, along with one black and one Hispanic. On election day, Mays received a plurality of votes forcing a run-off in which Wise garnered most of Lipscomb's votes and defeated Mays. Nine of the ten remaining seats were filled by CCA candidates. Burned by the mayoral defeat, the CCA hired consultants to assess its image in the community. Their report said that the group needed to broaden its base, that there were too many different interests in Dallas for the business-only emphasis of the CCA. The coalition further unraveled as the new council was seated and CCA-sponsored, black councilman George Allen openly sought the position of Mayor Pro Tem. Rebuffing him, the council selected Tim Holland, causing Allen to rip off his lapel button for the *All American City* and declare that his failure to win was an act of "absolute racism."[50]

The anti-war youth of the 1960s had led the way for the more general social activism of the early 1970s. These forces influenced city council meetings which drifted far from the business discussions of the past. It became routine for activists to grab the podium and shout about the way business was conducted.[51]

On March 10, 1971, the CCA's terminal challenge began as eighteen plaintiffs filed suit against the city of Dallas. Al Lipscomb, the candidate defeated by Wise, was the lead plaintiff, but he was joined by a *who's who* of Dallas' racial activists. The essence of the suit, according to Lipscomb, was to no longer "continue to let some people downtown decide what black candidates should run for office."[52] The suit went to the court of U. S. District Judge Joe Estes, the same judge who had ruled against Max Goldblatt four years earlier.

The complaint lodged by the suit covered two areas. First, the plaintiffs contended that the city violated its own charter by not redrawing the residence districts for more than two years. Not only were the districts outdated, but they contained greatly unequal populations, thus violating the one-man, one-vote principle. Second, they claimed, "under the current system . . . [voters in] the ghetto voting area have virtually no political force or control over members of the city council because the effect of their vote is canceled out by other, well-established and hostile interest groups in other areas of the city of Dallas." They claimed that the at-large scheme had "the invidious effect of diluting the vote of the ghetto residents" in violation of the Equal Protection Clause of the 14th Amendment.[53]

Seventeen days later, Judge Estes dismissed the suit. He said the suit failed to make any claim upon which the court could grant relief. An at-large system counted all votes equally, he contended. Residency districts may have been unequal, but all voting districts were the whole city, thus, all districts were equal. Furthermore, the Supreme Court had upheld the validity of at-large plans. Judge Estes said he saw no invidious dilution of voting strength and "further, it is clear that the plaintiffs cannot present facts necessary to support such a claim."[54]

Lipscomb and the other plaintiffs did not give up. They appealed and in April 1972, the 5th Circuit Court of Appeals ruled that it was possible that the plaintiffs could present a case "proving that the Dallas City Council election plan is a purposeful attempt by the white majority . . . to force Ghetto area residents out of the city council."[55] The court was able to rely on a new Supreme Court decision, *Whitcomb v. Chavis*,[56] in which the success of minority candidates was validated as a relevant factor for the court's consideration.

The case stalled for the next two years, during which CCA President Schoelkoph sought again to modernize the Association. He created an "open door" policy in which candidates from all walks of life were encouraged to seek CCA endorsement.[57] Nonetheless, CCA control continued to wane as evidenced in the 1973 election when the CCA did not even run a mayoral candidate against the popular Wes Wise. They did, however, add to the slate another black, Lucy Patterson, and a new Hispanic, Pedro Aguirre to replace Anita Martinez. Against their policy to discourage the creation of professional politicians, they endorsed George Allen for a third term. Nine of the CCA candidates won the 1973 election, but the slate was nothing like the white, business establishment of the past. There was a liberal, a Jewish woman, two blacks, and one Hispanic. Schoelkoph said, "The establishment is dead and we can't pull it together again."[58]

In July 1974, testimony began in the retrial of Al Lipscomb's case. Judge Mahon was assigned to the case.[59] In December, the trial got off to a rocky start when the judge refused to let the Mexican Americans be plaintiffs or intervenors. Judge Mahon reasoned that Mexican Americans, representing eight percent of the population, were spread all over town and, therefore, would not contribute to resolving the at-large question the court wanted to settle.[60]

During the testimony heard by Judge Mahon, George Allen asserted that he could not win an at-large election without CCA backing.[61] On January 17, 1975, Mahon ruled that the all-at-large system was unconstitutional because it diluted the voting strength of African Americans. The judge explained his decision by pointing to evidence of a long-term lack of minority influence. Ninety-three percent of Dallas' blacks lived in one contiguous area which was itself ninety percent black. The inner-city area had lower per capita income, lower property values, less education, and higher unemployment than the rest of the city. The voting was generally polarized, black-for-black and white-for-white. Among the black candidates who had run since 1959, most had received a majority of the black vote but lost in the citywide count. Judge Mahon stressed the *Zimmer* factors: Minorities lacked access to the slating process; the Council's preference for at-large districts was based on a tenuous policy; and past discrimination had precluded effective minority participation in the elective process.[62]

He gave the city twenty days to come up with a new plan, but the city responded in just three days with a plan calling for eight single-member and three at-large districts. Various plaintiffs offered other eleven-member plans. George Allen drew up an 8-3 plan with three majority-black districts, while the city's plan contained only two, one 74 percent and the other 87 percent black. A third district in the city's plan was 26 percent black and 20 percent Hispanic. The remaining five districts were less than six percent black.[63]

Within a month, Judge Mahon accepted Dallas' 8-3 plan. He said, "I'm not saying it's the best plan. It's not even the plan the court would have drawn. But the court's not in the plan drawing business."[64] He did note improving circumstances since the filing of the lawsuit in that the CCA had supported the election of two black candidates. Further, he noted, "The court stresses that in the case of the city of Dallas that there has been no evidence of any design or purposeful intent to dilute the vote of any of its minority citizens. Rather, it is in the operation of the exclusive at-large election plan in combination with the existence of a historical pattern of discrimination which supports the finding of dilution."[65]

Mahon allowed the Hispanics to be intervenors in the remedy portion of the case. He pointed out that it would take the creation of 20 single-member districts in Dallas to create one safe for Hispanics. Unlike blacks, Hispanics had not been relegated to one part of town. Their cohabitation with the white community limited their chances of gaining group power. The judge favored 8-3 over 10-1 or 11-0 because three at-large seats gave Hispanics some chance of being slated and winning citywide. He also believed that some at-large seats were appropriate to construct a council with a citywide view.

Plaintiffs argued that the high minority percentages in the two black minority districts constituted packing that diluted minority votes. The judge concluded, "In this case, however, evidence is clear that racial gerrymandering was not the purpose or intent of the district lines formulated in 1972 and readopted by the city as a result of this litigation. I find that the eight districts in the city's plan follow natural and rational boundaries and that no gerrymandering is present. Generally the boundaries of each district are major thoroughfares, rivers, creeks, or city limits. . . . [A]lthough the percentage of black voters in Districts 6 and 8 is somewhat high, the concentration, in and of itself, does not amount to dilution of the black vote."[66] Because Judge Mahon thought the city had acted responsibly, he did not grant attorney's fees to the plaintiffs.

The CCA had from February to April to prepare for elections. The group's slate continued to erode from the do-everything-business-image of the past. Their mayoral candidate was John Schoelkoph, a former reporter with little business experience. Aside from two blacks and one Hispanic on the slate, the non-political CCA endorsed two operatives of the Republican Party. In April 1975, Wes Wise thoroughly tromped Schoelkoph and the CCA held just six of the eleven seats. Their 6-5 majority was reversed when George Allen quit to become a Justice of the Peace and seventy-three-year-old Julia Craft took over. Craft had been active in the NAACP since 1935, leading protests, registering voters, organizing pickets to desegregate the State Fair, and helping to establish the 180 Texas branches of the NAACP.[67]

Signs of unrest and change continued: Federal courts ordered the institution of single-member districts in San Antonio; white flight to the suburbs left the DISD less than 50 percent white;[68] and a downtown riot occurred after a Dallas policeman killed a 12-year-old Hispanic boy upon whom they played Russian Roulette to extract a theft confession.[69] The riot grew out of a demonstration which drew 1500 Mexican Americans and the local chapter of the Brown Berets. Tension remained when the police officer was convicted and given only five years in jail.[70]

During the early 1970s, the Committee for Good Schools (CGS) struggled to regain control of the school board from the League for Educational Advancement (LEAD), a liberal group of educators who had taken over the board in 1968. A press report claimed that reading comprehension skills among Dallas students had dramatically dropped since LEAD took control. The accuracy of the report was debated, but the exposure, along with rising school taxes, led to a CGS victory. The conservative rush was quickly slowed however, when federal Judge Taylor ordered busing for 15,000 students—an order he later modified to 7000 students. The Dallas Independent School

District was already 30 percent black while schools in the nearby suburbs were 93 percent white.[71] The judge further set up a Tri-ethnic Committee of whites, blacks, and Hispanics to oversee the desegregation process.[72]

As Congress prepared for the enactment of the Voting Rights Act Amendments of 1975, the 5th Circuit Court ruled that Dallas schools were still not integrated. Judge Taylor raised the busing requirement to 17,000 students. While whites and Hispanics were satisfied with the plan, blacks believed it still left too many all black schools. Ultimately the NAACP influenced the 5th Circuit to accelerate the busing in a case that went on to the Supreme Court in 1979.

Navajo Reservation: The Beginnings of Franchise

Peter MacDonald won the 1970 tribal election against Nakai by a landslide. He was the first college graduate to lead the tribe and was the first to be elected without the support of the non-Indians working on the reservation or the townspeople of Gallup, Winslow, and Flagstaff. MacDonald inspired the tribe: He advocated replacing BIA and other non-Navajo, reservation employees with Navajos; he encouraged educated Navajos to return to the reservation to assume positions of leadership; and he pledged not to barter away the Indians' birthright for quick profits. The election was a great success for MacDonald and the voter registration drives that helped elect him caused non-Indian Arizonans to take note.[73]

Although Navajos voted in the tribal elections, only five percent of the Indians on the Arizona portion of the reservation were registered to vote in U. S. elections. This was far behind the general population or Indian country as a whole. Fourteen years earlier a count of reservation Indians nationwide showed 39 percent registered and 17 percent actually voting.[74] Reservation Navajos were generally unaccustomed to general elections and they still harbored a hatred of the white man and his politics which diminished their interest in white elections.

In 1970, literacy test were still given in several Arizona counties. Only 41 percent of the reservation Navajo adults had attended more than five years of formal schooling.[75] After passage of the amendments, Gary K. Nelson, the Arizona Attorney General, advised the county recorders to continue literacy tests until the amendments were declared constitutional by a federal court.[76] However, literacy tests may not have been a factor in the low registration rates. Apache County had discontinued its literacy tests in 1965, but registration rates there were no higher than Navajo and Coconino Counties.[77]

Because raising sheep and cattle was a common form of livelihood on the vast, sprawling reservation, voters were often far from the polling places. A 1970 act of the Arizona legislature allowed absentee voting for anyone living more than fifteen miles from a polling place.[78]

During the same 1970 elections, the Arizona House and Senate were elected under the Arizona House's new plan. In June 1971, *Ely v. Klahr* was argued before the Supreme Court. Still discontent with the 1966 plan, Ely contended that the court should construct a constitutionally valid plan for the state legislature and should displace that plan only if the legislature created its own valid plan by November 1971, the date that the district court had mandated for a new legislative plan based on 1970 census data. The Supreme Court decided that the district court had done the right thing in allowing the legislature until November 1971. The plaintiffs were concerned that no valid plan was forthcoming and, once again, that there would be no time to fix it before the 1972 elections. The Supreme Court Justices disagreed, arguing that the plaintiff could have his own plan ready in November, far in advance of the June 1972 startup of campaign activities.[79]

Remember that the state's *Chapter 1, House Bill 1* protected incumbents. It appeared that there were plenty of Indians on the reservation in Northeast Arizona to justify a safe Navajo district. However, the incumbency rule did the Indians in. Near the reservation, two white senators lived only ten miles from one another. Protecting these senators split the reservation into two districts. Justice Douglas commented, "A valid apportionment plan will seemingly mean the defeat of several incumbents."[80]

In October 1971, just before the court-imposed deadline, the legislature passed a new apportionment plan, creating four U. S. congressional districts, up one from the 1960 census. It also created 30 legislative districts with one senator and two at-large representatives in each.

Again Klahr and Ely challenged the new plan, but this time they were joined by Peter MacDonald. By the time the legislative plan was enacted, at the insistence of house members that resided in the district, the reservation was divided among three districts. A three-judge district court concluded deliberations in March 1972. The justices held that the reapportionment plan operated to destroy the possibility that the Navajos might successfully elect representatives and they ordered the districts combined.[81]

Plaintiffs wanted also to require a census, not only at the start of each decade, but also at years three and seven. They based this request on Arizona's rapid growth. The court denied the request, quoting *Reynolds v. Sims*: "[C]ompliance with such an approach [a decennial census] would clearly meet the minimal requirements for maintaining a reasonably current scheme of legislative representation."[82]

Peter MacDonald also claimed that the logic that caused legislative districts 2, 3, and 4 to be combined on the reservation, should be applied to the U. S. congressional districts, putting the reservation in one district. The court disagreed, stating there was no evidence that any single district had ever been contemplated as it had with the legislature. The court was looking for intent. Since the legislative districts were first introduced with the reservation intact, the court had examined the motives for changing it. By contrast, the congressional boundaries were split along county lines from the beginning.

According to a government report, there was a serious shortage of polling places on the Navajo Reservation in Apache and Coconino Counties. In Apache County, only 10 polling places served the extensive reservation area; during heavy turnout, Navajos waited several hours in bad weather to vote. At Chinle, in the northern part of the county, voters waited 2½ hours to cast their ballots. According to the Apache County manager, "Many did not have the stamina for the long wait; others had to return to work." After much haggling, the reservation portion of the county obtained new polling places, raising the total number to 21. The same thing happened in Coconino County where four polling places were added.[83]

Despite alleged problems with the 1972 elections, the first Navajo member of the Apache County Board of Supervisors was elected. Unfortunately it took the action of the Supreme Court to place him into office. Thomas Minyard, having received 1105 votes, unsuccessfully sued Tom Shirley who received 3169 votes. Minyard argued that Shirley, a Navajo, should not be seated because he was immune from civil process while on the reservation and did not own any taxable property.[84] The court disagreed.

Courts became generally supportive of Indian claims. In the northern part of the reservation, in Bluff, Utah, Ben Yanito and Seth Bigman sought office as the commissioners of San Juan County. The hopeful candidates were directed to Clytie Barber, the county clerk. As instructed by Mrs. Barber, Yanito and Bigman filled out the required forms and paid the appropriate filing fee. The clerk failed to mention that there was an additional requirement—a petition signed by 50 electors of the district. Learning of the situation, the county attorney called the candidates and informed them of the additional requirements. They both obtained the signatures and submitted them five days late only to find that the signatures needed to be notarized. At that point they brought suit. Because the clerk knew of the additional requirement and did not offer that information and in light of the fact that she did offer some information and accepted the filing fees, the court ruled that the Navajos were subjects of discrimination and ordered that their names be placed on the ballot. While there may be debate about how much help a county clerk is expected to provide a would-be candidate, the court ruled that help cannot be doled out on a discriminatory basis.[85]

When he was elected, MacDonald had promised the Indians a "new era of self determination." He began the process of persuading the BIA to turn over the authority of some agencies to the Navajos. He garnered government funding to build roads, sewers, and houses on the reservation. He even had some success at promoting industrial growth by persuading General Dynamics to make missile parts on the reservation, finding new markets for the tribal lumber industry, entering the computer software market, and starting a venture to grow Shiitake mushrooms.

Court cases continued and in 1973, the Arizona Supreme Court ruled that status as an Indian, whether on the reservation or off, whether paying taxes or not, cannot be used to deny the right to hold public office.[86]

In October 1973, the U. S. Commission on Civil Rights held hearings at the Navajo headquarters in Window Rock, Arizona. Testimony was given on the gamut of tribal issues including economic development, private employment, education, and healthcare. Notably absent from the presentations was any discussion of voting rights or political power within the state. The subject of voting only came up twice. First, in reference to unemployment in the southern portion of the reservation, an advocate from legal services alleged that employment would improve if the school district lines were redrawn to include more Navajos on the board.[87] Second, in the open sessions, Acting Chairman Stephen Horn asked Lena Tsiosdia, Youth Director of the Gallup Indian Community Center, her opinion on Navajo voting.

> *Acting Chairman Horn:* Is it difficult for some people on the reservation, regardless of age, to vote because there aren't sufficient voting booth areas available? Do you know anything about that?
> *Ms. Tsiosdia:* I think that the participation in voting is due to the fact that the community people are not well informed on it.
> *Acting Chairman Horn:* Well, do you know, offhand, about the physical location of voting booths at all?
> *Ms. Tsiosdia:* The physical location?
> *Acting Chairman Horn:* Yes. Where the . . .
> *Ms: Tsiosdia:* The chapter communities, at the chapter houses.
> *Acting Chairman Horn:* Where they permit people to vote. Is it in the chapter houses?
> *Ms. Tsiosdia:* Right.[88]

That was the entire conversation, but two years later, in its report on the first 10 years of the Voting Rights Act, the same commission would paint a desperate picture of Navajo voting rights even though the subject did not bear discussion at the Window Rock meetings.

In 1974, Congress passed the *Relocation Act*,[89] calling for land that had been contentiously shared by the Navajos and Hopis for 100 years to be reallocated strictly to the Hopis, an action that forced the movement of 10,000 Navajos. Although the use of this land had been contentious in the past, agreements had been worked out that restricted Hopi movement and Navajo building. The result of the Relocation Act was disaster. Old people, farmers, and ranchers were moved off the reservation to nearby towns where cultural and language barriers prevented assimilation. Some believed Congress was set up by a mineral rights lobby that believed the Hopi would be easier to deal with. True or not, a conflict began between Barry Goldwater and the Navajos. To fight the Relocation Act, MacDonald organized a lobby and attracted the interest of George McGovern, Ted Kennedy, and Walter Mondale. He also met with AFL-CIO leaders who took an interest in opposing Goldwater. Many on the reservation believed, however, that MacDonald had not taken a strong enough position and that his efforts were too late.

Republicans have traditionally ruled Arizona. Arizona is the only state to support the Republican presidential nominee in every election between 1948 and 1996.[90] In 1974, Democrat Raul Castro became governor. Nine thousand Navajos voted for Castro in a statewide election which he won by barely 4000 votes. For the first time, Goldwater lost Navajo and Apache counties. Although evidence was not produced in a subsequent Justice Department investigation, Goldwater claimed that AFL-CIO gave coupons for free beer and travel pay to Navajo voters.[91]

In Tuba City, during the November 1974 elections, there were ten propositions on the ballot and there were 13 polling booths. The English language problems of the Navajo were apparent. One-third of the tribe— 40,000 Navajos—were illiterate in English. According to a government report, the presence of only one interpreter caused the line to grow to a three hour wait. As in the 1972 elections, many voters gave up and left.[92]

In the same election, MacDonald won by a comfortable margin. His popularity began to slide, however, because things had not really changed that much for the Navajo people. The per capita income on the reservation was about $1000, one-third of the national average.[93] Of the total labor force, 35 percent were unemployed. Add to that the number that were on temporary, seasonal, or occasional jobs, the underemployment rate was 56 percent.[94] At the same time, progress could be claimed in voting rights. Four Arizona counties had faced the scrutiny of the special provisions of the Voting Rights Act. Native-American voter registration had grown markedly over the previous five years. By the 1974 general election, 82 percent of the eligible voters on the reservation were registered.[95] Native Americans now sat on the school board and despite language problems at the polls, the state senator and both representatives from the reservation were Navajos.

The policy of Indian self-determination espoused by Richard Nixon in 1970 had considerable effect during this half decade. A steady flow of new laws increased spending for Indian schools and established federal responsibility for the protection of traditional religious practices. In 1972, the Nixon administration began converting the BIA to an organization staffed largely by Indians, at all levels. With policies markedly favoring Indian hiring, the administration created the first openly discriminatory hiring policy. However, despite administration support and changes in personnel, the BIA field organization proved to have considerable tenacity and prevented much real handover of power to the tribes.

Congress passed the Indian Self Determination and Educational Assistance Act of 1975 declaring that "Indian people will never surrender their desire to control their relationships both among themselves and with non-Indian governments."[96] The legislation took another important step toward removing the BIA from tribal contracting. The BIA's role moved from contract administrator to auditor.[97] Although tribes were slow to take full advantage of these provisions, the act led to Indian control of grants and assistance for the Indian-run reservation projects improving facilities for tribal government and health care.

In 1975, suit was brought against Apache County in federal district court. The county had three supervisors, each elected from single-member districts. About 75 percent of the county's residents were Navajos living on the reservation, however, the reservation residents were packed into one district. Once again the county's justification for this malapportionment was the contention that Navajos on the reservation were not U. S. citizens, should not be allowed to vote, and should not be counted for apportionment. The contention was again based on the fact that Native-American residents of the reservation were immune to certain kinds of taxation and, to some extent, immune from the judicial process. The case, *Goodluck v. Apache County*,[98] was in progress when the Voting Rights Act came up for renewal in 1975.

Dade County: Continued Cuban Growth

The period between 1970 and 1975 was relatively quiet for Dade County politics. The Cuban population continued its steady growth and began to break political ethnic barriers.

In 1971, a back-room, shadow government was created for the betterment of Miami. Alvah H. Chapman, Jr., President of the Miami Herald, and Harry Hood Bassett hand picked a group of businessmen which called itself the "Non-Group." Like the Dallas CCA, the Non-Group applied its collective clout to a wide variety of problems and projects.[99]

Of the half-million Dade County Hispanics, 300,000 were Cuban refugees. Of these, only 80,000 were voting-age citizens, about half of whom were not registered. In preparation for the 1972 elections, Cuban Americans staged a massive voter registration drive. The election resulted in a Puerto Rican, Maurice A. Ferré, being elected mayor of Miami and the election of the first Cuban member of the Miami City Commission.[100]

A survey done in 1973 indicated that already 27 percent of the Cubans whom the government had relocated to other parts of the country, had returned to Miami. By 1975, 52 percent of Miami's inner city was Cuban.[101]

Chapter 6: The Amendments of 1975[1]

In January 1975, as the special provisions of the act again neared expiration, the Civil Rights Commission issued its report evaluating the Act's impact, especially in the South. While the report conceded progress, it argued that the job was just begun. Civil Rights Commissioner, Robert S. Rankin believed that another ten years was necessary, but he expressed hope that extensions beyond that would be unnecessary. Of the commission's report he said, "This point [improved voting rights], to my mind, should have received greater emphasis. . . . I would draw attention to the rapidly decreasing number of complaints that are filed with the commission that concern the alleged deprivation of voting rights. Ten years ago these complaints were numerous. Today the complaints concern employment, housing, and other matters while claims of the deprivation of voting rights are the least numerous of all."[2]

Indeed, progress for southern blacks was real. Looking at Selma, the icon of the civil rights movement, Sheriff Jim Clark was no longer there with his cattleprods for peaceful demonstrators; seventy percent of Selma's black population had registered to vote; and half of the town council was black. At a ten-year reunion of the 1965 march, celebrants encountered friendly police, some of whom were black. Public restrooms were open to all and the word "nigger" was an expletive rarely used on black citizens.[3]

Gerald Ford, in office only a few months, wanted to avoid a showdown with black advocacy groups and liberals in Congress. On Martin Luther King's birthday in 1975, he announced his support for another five year renewal of the act without suggesting any major changes. Black civil rights groups were content with the proposal, but the Mexican-American Legal Defense and Education Fund (MALDEF) insisted on new protection for Chicanos. Conflict brewed between the black advocacy groups and the Mexican Americans because the simple extension of the act was meeting very little resistance. Blacks feared that major new provisions could cause conservatives to reach a state of "enough is enough" and mobilize to soften the act or oppose its extension.[4]

The Ford administration struggled with Congress to gain some concessions for the southern legislators upon whom Ford would rely in the next election. While the president was not successful in gaining a simple extension, he did rebuff a strong momentum for a ten-year renewal.

Ultimately, Mexican-American interests prevailed, but not to the detriment of blacks. On August 6, the Congress passed new language provisions, extended the special provisions of the Voting Rights Act for another seven years, and made permanent the 1970 temporary ban on literacy tests. Like the temporary ban of 1970, this applied to all jurisdictions, whether or not they were already subject to the special provisions of the act. The final House vote reflected the progress blacks had made among southern Democratic legislators, 52 of whom supported the bill against 26 who opposed it. Southern Republicans, on the other hand, who were newly recruited southern whites, opposed the bill 17 to 10.[5]

The seven-year extension was a compromise. Conservatives believed that ten years was too long while liberals were afraid to let the special provisions run out before the redistricting that would result from the 1980 census. Thus an entity under the special provisions of the act—requiring preclearance by the Department of Justice for any election changes, and allowing the appointment of federal examiners—would remain under scrutiny. The language was also updated to include additional political entities in those special provisions if, during the presidential election of 1972, a test or device was in place, and either less than 50 percent of the potential voters were registered or less than 50 percent voted.

Since literacy tests had been banned from 1970 to 1975, it would seem that no new jurisdiction could fall under the Act's cover. However, with MALDEF influence, jurisdictions now became subject to new provisions protecting language minorities. The first decade of the act had focused on the voting rights of blacks. New provisions in the language extensions brought in the era of Chicano rights. Under the amendments, if five percent of the voting population in a political subdivision were members of a single language minority, then printed voting materials needed to be produced and distributed in both English and the minority language. Recognized language minorities were restricted to American Indians, Asian Americans, Alaskan Natives, and citizens of Spanish Heritage. The new language provisions of the act were to remain in effect until 1985.

The greatest power of the amendments lay in some carefully crafted definitions. The bill defined English-only-voting materials as a test or device when used in a jurisdiction having at least five percent of the voting age population from a single-language minority. The act then outlawed the use of such a test or device. Under the existing provisions of the act, this new definition of "test or device" was to be used to bring under the special provisions of the act any election entity which had a single-language-minority population of at least five percent; did not provide for a "multi-lingual" election in 1972; and had a voter registration or voter turnout of less than 50 percent in the 1972 presidential election. In other words, many areas having significant minority language populations that held English-only elections would be deemed to have imposed a literacy test. Then, the 10-year-old trigger provisions that combined the presence of a literacy test with a low voter registration or turnout, could bring a state or subdivision under the special provisions.

Congress had trapped a whole new slate of targets. The new law was arguably unlike the 1965 Act. In both cases the laws imposed penalties on jurisdictions giving them no grace period to comply, but the 1965 Act followed the logic that literacy tests were designed to discriminate. Calling the lack of foreign-language voting materials a discriminatory test or device was insupportable. There was no history to suggest that English voting materials were created as a response to Hispanic or Asian voting. There had been no actions to eliminate people from the electorate. In truth, the idea of providing multi-language voting material was liberal enough, but radical was the notion that jurisdictions should be punished for not anticipating the future aspirations of Congress. The law reached back to 1972 even though the first litigation determining the need for such material was not tried until 1974. The bill dealt harshly with any jurisdiction newly covered by the bilingual trigger by providing that each was to freeze its election laws as of November 1972. Any subsequent changes, albeit in place for as long as three years, required preclearance. The amendments also added a provision allowing the court, in any case concerning the 14th or 15th Amendment, to grant recovery of attorney's fees to the prevailing party. The success of the act had provided so many opportunities to sue that Congress had to provide a method of funding.

In 1972, Timothy O'Rourke, writing for the Brookings Institution, commented:

> The paradox of the Voting Rights Act, then, is that success has bred a seemingly greater need, not a lesser one, for action against discrimination in voting. The scope of the law, the volume of voting rights litigation, and the level of Justice Department activity have expanded dramatically, even though, virtually all commentators agree that the status of voting rights in America has manifestly improved since 1965.[6]

Framers of the amendments anticipated that the new areas covered by the language trigger of the bill would be parts of Arizona, California, Florida, Colorado, New Mexico, Oklahoma, New York, North Carolina, South Dakota, Utah, Virginia, Hawaii, and the entire states of Texas and Alaska. (See Figure 7.)

The Arguments in Favor of the 1975 Amendments

As in 1970, the Congress faced the chore of determining whether the act had done its job. If so, the special provisions could be allowed to lapse. The permanent portions of the act still allowed parties deprived of their right to vote, to sue and obtain remedies. Lacking any new legislation, "bail-out" would have dropped the requirement for federal preclearance of election rule changes along with liberal allowances for the appointment of federal examiners and observers.

The arguments presented favoring another extension of the special provisions were similar to those offered in 1970. Although considerable progress had been made, it was not enough and relaxing the terms of the law would stop the forward movement as well as allow some jurisdictions to revert to their previous status. Despite the impressive changes after passage of the 1965 Act, a gap between white and black registration still existed.

Supporters conceded the some progress had been made in the election of black officials, but they argued that most of the elected blacks held relatively minor offices in small jurisdictions of overwhelmingly black population. In the seven southern states totally or partially covered by the special provisions of the act, none had a statewide, black, elected official. Furthermore, in Mississippi, 0.6 percent of the state legislative seats were held by blacks against a state black population of 36.8 percent. In South Carolina, only 7.6 percent of the state legislators were black in a state with a 30.7 percent black population.

Amendment supporters argued that preclearance accounted for the most progress thus far. Letting the provisions run out would eliminate this powerful tool. By 1975, the Justice Department received about 1000 changes annually. Denial of preclearance had been used to defend minorities against polling place changes, majority vote requirements, staggered terms, increased candidate filing fees, redistricting, switches from elective to appointed offices, at-large districts, and annexations.

Proponents also presented the merits of permanently banning all literacy tests. Since the 1970 temporary removal of literacy tests had helped minorities in the South to register, they reasoned that removal nationwide also had to positively affect minority franchise. They believed that lower minority literacy was the result of long-established discrimination in the education system. By 1975, only 21 years had passed since the Supreme Court had ruled on *Brown v. Board of Education*. Although disparities still existed for the education of blacks in the South, the disparity between older black and white citizens was even more dramatic.

The argument against English-only election material, in areas having large language minority populations, went hand-in-hand with the debate on literacy tests. Supporters argued that a person literate only in Spanish was, in effect, handed an English-literacy test if all the election materials were presented in

English. Proponents claimed that the Census Bureau figures proved language discrimination. In 1972, only 44 percent of the Hispanic population was registered to vote and only 23 percent voted—a rate about half that of Anglos.

Besides, backers argued, if a political jurisdiction had not used English-only elections for discriminatory purpose or effect, it could bail-out by simply demonstrating that fact. Jurisdictions that had been able to bail-out of the earlier provisions of the act included: Alaska; Wake County, North Carolina; Elmore County, Idaho; and Apache, Navajo, and Coconino Counties, Arizona.

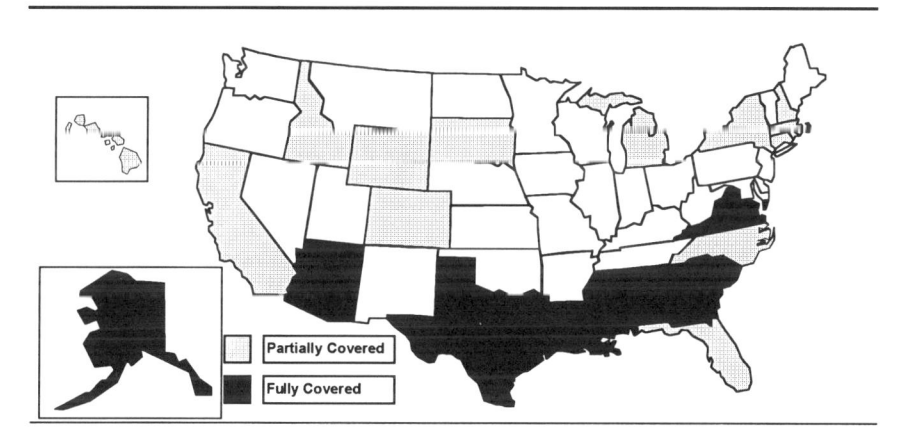

FIGURE 7: COVERED JURISDICTIONS AFTER THE 1975 AMENDMENTS[7]

A Shot at Texas

The report from the Senate Judiciary Committee, supporting the Amendments of 1975, went out of its way to make a special attack on Texas the real target of the language provisions. The Committee had heard testimony that Texas' substantial Mexican-American and black populations had long been victims of discrimination. Turnout in the presidential elections had been consistently below 50 percent of the voting-age population. Texas had escaped special coverage of the Voting Rights Act because it had never used literacy tests, but the Senate reported that Texas had used other restrictive devices.

In 1966, the attorney general sued Texas to give up its poll tax. This was two years after the constitutional amendment banning its use and one year after the Voting Rights Act outlawed it. In 1972, in the case of *Graves v. Barnes*, a federal district court found that, subsequent to eliminating the poll tax, Texas had enacted the most restrictive voting procedures in the nation. Contrary to that finding, evidence showed that Texas blacks registered in greater percentages than whites. According to Voter Education Project data, in 1972, 68 percent of blacks were registered compared to 57 percent of whites.[8] On the other hand, registration rates among Hispanics was low. In 1975, Mexican Americans comprised 16.4 percent of the Texas population, yet they held only 2.5[9] percent of the elective positions. Texas defenders contended that a lower percentage was reasonable since 25 percent of the Hispanics living in Texas were aliens and 40 percent were under the legal voting age.

Texas, the Senate report claimed, made a widespread use of at-large voting schemes to dilute the strength of minority voters. The courts had challenged and stricken down many of these schemes. Also noted was a habit of annexing white areas adjacent to existing cities while failing to annex minority areas.

Finally, the Senate Committee dwelled on its belief that Texas had not provided anywhere near equal education for Mexican Americans and thus the higher rate of illiteracy among these Hispanics was not a result of choice or happenstance. The report dwelt on this despite its recognition that Texas did not use literacy tests and thus the allegation had no relevance to voting.

In 1973, *Graves v. Barnes* was appealed to the Supreme Court. The court upheld the earlier conclusion that the Hispanic population in Texas had "historically suffered from, and continues to suffer from, the result and effects of invidious discrimination and treatment in the fields of education, employment, economics, health, politics, and others."[10]

The bilingual provisions of the amendments brought Texas under the automatic trigger for the first time. These provisions were aggressively sponsored by black Texas representative Barbara Jordan. She was opposed not only by the governor, but also by liberal, Hispanic Representative Henry B. Gonzalez. Gonzalez contended that the provisions were unnecessary and did not want to see Texas brought under them.[11]

The Arguments Against the 1975 Amendments[12]

Senator Roman L. Hruska filed one of the minority views. He argued, "When the act was passed in 1965 it was done so with the thought that it was a temporary measure designed to apply unusual remedies to a few states . . . where voting discrimination seemed prevalent." The Senator believed that the act meddled into matters reserved for the states, but that the abuses in 1965 warranted such meddling. Ten years later, however, there had been a tremendous rise in minority registration and voting, thus the original purpose of the act was accomplished. Letting the special provisions of the act lapse would not lessen anyone's rights or the power of the courts to defend voting rights. Removing these provisions would simply put this legislation on par with other laws in which an injured party could sue to recover his rights and all of his costs. Continuing the special provisions simply failed to recognize the progress that had been made. Senators Eastland (MS), McClellan (AR), Thurmond (SC), and Scott (VA), representing their southern states, expressed similar views.

Even the Commission on Civil Rights and the Justice Department questioned the need for special coverage for Hispanics. The Assistant Attorney General for Civil Rights testified, "The Department of Justice has concluded that the evidence does not require expansion based on the record before us. In other words, that record is not compelling." The Civil Rights Commission noted that Hispanic voting statistics "do not paint the shocking picture that . . . 1965 statistics on Mississippi did."[13]

Critics advanced philosophical arguments about English as the language of the land and whether to alter it for the sake of the few who refused to learn it. What would happen, asked critics, if non-English speaking candidates were elected to office? How would these officeholders communicate with the public majority? Days of congressional hearing produced very little evidence that Hispanics had been prevented from voting by the language barrier.

The hearings had not promoted debate. No one argued that English-language ballots were in any way related to the southern literacy tests that were created for the purpose of excluding blacks from voting. Testimony was presented that 40 percent of Hispanics who were not registered were also not U. S. citizens, still members of Congress insisted on using total population percentages to prove that Hispanics were the victims of underrepresentation.[14] Studying citizen-only data would have painted a far milder picture.

One other fact eluded the Committee. To vote, one must be a U. S. citizen, and to be naturalized, one must demonstrate a knowledge of English. The only exceptions are 20-year residents over 50 years-of-age or 15-year residents over 55.[15] If English was required for citizenship and citizenship was required for voting, why was English not a logical prerequisite to voting?

Opponents of the language provisions believed in the model of U. S. immigration. For the entire history of the nation, immigrants had struggled to learn English as a first step toward becoming *American*. Now the government was interested in reversing that tradition for success in America. They contended that Hispanic leaders were wrong to lump their constituents in with blacks. Most American-born Hispanics were doing well by easily surpassing the economic progress of blacks. It was only the recent immigrants that were doing poorly, and those should be given a chance to assimilate.

The retroactive nature of the provisions also alarmed opponents. There had not been federal law requiring that election and voting materials be prepared in multiple languages. Now, in 1975, the Congress proposed that states with large minority populations be placed under the "punitive" surveillance of the federal government for the monolingual voting materials used during the presidential election three years earlier. These states had no way of knowing in 1972 that Congress would reverse a 200 year tradition of English and there was no possibility to atone for what Congress now perceived as misconduct.

Opponents viewed bail-out as an impractical alternative since the act itself assumed low voter registration in language minority communities to be the result of discrimination. A state or other jurisdiction would have to prove that all the failures to register resulted from some other cause.

Barriers in Texas did not justify these remedies. Mexican Americans held many elective seats including two congressional seats—an unthinkable accomplishment for southern blacks.[16] Abigail M. Thernstrom, in her authoritative work, *Whose Votes Count?*, claims that English voting material was a thin veil. "No one actually believed that the primary problem in the Southwest was the disenfranchising effect of English-language election materials. Rather, the new formula was devised as a means of combating districting plans and other aspects of the electoral environment that the Mexican-American groups believed to be discriminatory."[17]

Results of the Act After the 1975 Amendments

Segregation is dead. It's outlawed and it won't be again.

—George Wallace, Former Alabama Governor

Retrogression

A 1976 landmark case, *Beer v. United States*, tested a principle called retrogression. This principle held that any plan could be precleared whenever the new plan was less discriminatory than the plan it replaced. After the 1970 census, New Orleans tried to realign its seven-member city council which consisted of five wards and two at-large seats. Although the new plan improved the voting strength of blacks by giving them a slight minority in two wards, it did not provide much realistic hope of their electing candidates. Both the attorney general and the D. C. District Court denied preclearance because the plan diluted black voting strength. The Supreme Court disagreed, ruling in favor of clearing the plan on finding it was not retrogressive to blacks. It merited approval provided it lacked discriminatory intent.[18] The court further held that the act required preclearance only of changes, that is, only those things that were different between the old and the new plan. Thus, the law did not intend that existing, unchanged provisions of a voting regime be subject to preclearance. The court went on to say:

> . . . Congress desired to prevent states from "undoing or defeating the rights recently won" by Negroes. . . . Section 5 was intended "to insure that the gains thus far achieved in minority political participation shall not be destroyed through new, discriminatory procedures and techniques". . . . Congress explicitly stated that "the standard [under Section 5] can only be fully satisfied by determining . . . whether the ability of minority groups to participate in the political process and to elect their choices to office is augmented, diminished, or not affected." . . . It is apparent that a legislative reapportionment that enhances the position of racial minorities with respect to their effective exercise of the electoral franchise can hardly have the "effect" of diluting or abridging the right to vote on account of race within the meaning of Section 5.[19]

Justice Byron White, usually a centrist on the court, dissented believing that preclearance should not be granted unless blacks were entitled to elect representatives roughly equal in number to their proportion of the population. Justice Thurgood Marshall, the Court's first black member, took issue with the idea that the court did not view the at-large seats as part of the preclearance litigation simply because those districts had not been changed. Marshall, who had headed the NAACP Legal Defense Fund and been U. S. Solicitor General, believed that the fairness of the whole districting plan was subject to preclearance review.[20] Justice Brennan concurred with Marshall. Supporters of this retrogression test argued that jurisdictions would not make any positive changes at all if each change subjected the whole system to review.

The *Beer* decision marked an important point in the evolution of the enforcement of the Voting Rights Act. Although it was never reversed, it was often ignored. The attorney general and the lower courts continued to rule on entire voting schemes rather than applying a retrogression test to the proposed changes. However, retrogression did have some place in the courts. In 1975,

Rome, Georgia sought preclearance of a number of voting changes made since 1966. The net result of the changes was an increase in the number of votes needed to elect a city commissioner. Both the old and the new system called for at-large elections, thus the city's 20 percent black voting population had no chance of electing candidates without help from white voters. Under the new system, they needed slightly more help than under the old system. Evidence established, however, that despite the absence of black elected officials, Rome's black citizens were effective participants in the political process. Blacks frequently determined the election of white candidates and elected officials were generally responsive to the needs of the black community. Under the interpretation of Section 2 at that time, blacks did not have a valid voting rights claim. The courts ruled against the city, however, because the change was retrogressive to blacks. This case showed that retrogression would not be permitted, no matter how effectively the minority group was participating in the political process. The Supreme Court effectively ruled that Section 5 had powers independent and beyond Section 2's right to cast an effective vote.[21]

Growing Power of Preclearance

The strengths and limitations on the power of preclearance were etched out over years by the Justice Department and the courts. In 1977, the attorney general sued the Hale County, Alabama Commission for changing its method of election from single-member wards to at-large. The court held that any election held under the new rules was unlawful because Hale County had not received preclearance. Whether the change violated a provision of the Voting Rights Act was not material. The absence of pre-clearance alone was sufficient to void the elections.[22]

Even changes that had nothing *per se* to do with the election process became subject to the act. In 1978, the Dougherty County, the Georgia Board of Elections passed a rule that employees must take an unpaid leave of absence while campaigning for political office. The Board enacted this regulation less than a month after the first Dougherty County black in recent years sought election to the Georgia State Assembly. The district court determined, under the auspices of the Voting Rights Act, that the county's action imposed a substantial economic disincentive to blacks and thus had sufficient potential for discrimination to require preclearance.[23] The Supreme Court affirmed this judgment.

The need for federal preclearance was generously applied, whether the proposed change added to or subtracted from the voting power of the

The Amendments of 1975

electorate. In 1978, South Carolina had enacted a change which would have required a previously appointed governing body to be chosen by popular election. A federal district court ruled that this change, albeit an empowerment of the voters, also required preclearance.[24]

By the end of the decade, preclearance had become a regular institution. In 16 years, 32,000 requests had been submitted, 26,000 of which occurred after 1975. More than half of the submissions since 1975 came from Texas. The most popular reason for submissions—over 8000—was a change in polling places. Nearly 7000 were annexations while only 1000 were redistricting. The fact that less than one percent of the post-1975 submissions were turned down supported the notion that preclearance created excessive bureaucratic overhead.[25]

The power of the attorney general in granting or denying preclearance was bolstered in 1977 when the Supreme Court ruled that preclearance decisions by the attorney general were not subject to judicial review. Thus, if litigants were not satisfied with the attorney general's judgment, they could not appeal the decision or file suit against him.[26] Of course, plaintiffs could still file for preclearance with the D. C. District Court.

Drawing District Lines

At-large-district suits continued, but the courts were mixed in their decisions. Numerous cases eliminated at-large schemes. Courts required evidence that the system diluted or canceled black voting strength, but they struggled with the required magnitude of this evidence. In 1976, a Louisiana federal district court invalidated the at-large system for electing Shreveport city commissioners. The court contended that although at-large elections mathematically met the one-person, one-vote requirement, minority votes were not equal in a racially biased system.[27] In 1980, in a Texas case, the Supreme Court ruled that the 14th Amendment authorized Congress to amend the Voting Rights Act to eliminate purposeful discriminatory maintenance of vote-diluting, at-large districting schemes.[28] In the same year in Alabama, the court decided that the at-large districts did not abridge the rights of blacks in Mobile since they were allowed to vote without restriction.[29] Also in 1980, in a case in Vinton, Louisiana, the judge decided that minority groups had the burden to prove that at-large electoral schemes unconstitutionally diluted their votes. Finally, in the same year, an Alabama federal court ruled that the 1965 Alabama law establishing at-large elections for members of the County Commission of Hale County had the purpose and effect of abridging the minority right to vote.[30]

Another at-large case alleged that Burke County, Georgia, with a 54 percent black population, had never elected a black to the five member county commission because the at-large system discriminated against blacks. The district and appeals courts agreed and noted that the county had allowed "some blacks to be educated in largely segregated and clearly inferior schools, . . . [failed] to hire more than a token number of blacks to county jobs, . . . [paid] those blacks hired lower salaries than their white counterparts, . . .[and contributed] public funds to the operation of a private school established to circumvent the requirement of integration."[31] This decision represented the inclination of the courts to consider the history of a jurisdiction before judging the acceptability of an apportionment scheme. This was the "totality of circumstances" described in *White v. Regester*.

Redistricting single-member districts proved as difficult for the courts as at-large apportionment. In 1976 the court ruled that the Hinds County, Mississippi redistricting plan must not divide along racial lines, either geographical or proportional, but must be prepared honestly on non-racial and rational criteria. Furthermore, the plan must provide every group equal access to the political process and a full chance to realize its full voting potential.[32] The court struggled to believe that a rational, well thought out plan could be without racial input. The notion ignored race in the development of a plan but somehow used race as a test of its validity.

Determining who could claim vote dilution was another redistricting issue. The Supreme Court spoke on this issue in 1977 in *United Jewish Organizations of Williamsburgh, Inc. v. Carey*. In 1974, New York had submitted a reapportionment plan which redrew the Kings County district lines to provide 65 percent non-white majorities in an area also inhabited by a white, Hasidic Jewish Community. To accomplish this, New York divided the Hasidic community between two senatorial districts. The Hasidic Jews sued on the basis that their voting power had been diluted. The district court dismissed the complaint asserting that the Hasidic Jews had no constitutional right in reapportionment to separate community recognition. The appeals court and the Supreme Court agreed. Justice White, speaking for the court, contended that the Constitution permitted the state to draw lines in such a way that "the percentage of districts with a non-white majority roughly approximates the percentage of non-whites in the county." Further, he wrote, "[A]s long as Kings County whites, as a group, were provided with fair representation, there was no cognizable discrimination against whites." The decision was based on the emerging idea that careful setting of racial

THE AMENDMENTS OF 1975
121

percentages on a voting-district-by-voting-district basis could tend to guarantee the overall election results.

By the mid-1970s, the Supreme Court was a mixture of liberal and conservative justices who produced decisions all over the political spectrum. By 1975, the only Democratic appointees were Thurgood Marshall and Byron White. During the late 1970s the court had ruled on both sides of the death penalty and affirmative action.[33] This mixed record contrasted with the more liberal court of the mid-1960s when Democratic appointees outnumbered Republican appointees and the court was the vanguard of individual rights.[34]

Exhibiting the new, conservative side of the court was Chief Justice Warren Burger. Appointed by President Nixon, Burger tried to lead the court away from the liberal expansion of the Earl Warren court.[35] Considering the plight of the Hasidic Jews, he contended that the 1960 case of *Gomillion v. Lightfoot* held against drawing political lines for the sole purpose of reaching a racial goal. He pointed to testimony that New York could have kept the Hasidic community together by providing non-whites a 63.4 percent majority, but that New York officials believed that the attorney general would accept no less than 65 percent. Burger also pointed out that there was nothing close knit about the white or non-white communities in Kings County. "The 'whites' category consists of a veritable galaxy of national origins, ethnic backgrounds, and religious denominations. . . [N]on-whites include, in addition to Negroes, a substantial portion of Puerto Ricans. . . The Puerto Rican population . . . has expressly disavowed any identity with the interest of the Negroes."

Burger closed his argument by expressing the conservative view of what was evolving from the Voting Rights Act: "The result reached by the court today in the name of the Voting Rights Act is ironic. The use of mathematical formula tends to sustain the existence of ghettos by promoting the notion that political clout is to be gained or maintained by marshaling particular racial, ethnic, or religious groups in enclaves. It suggests to the voter that only a candidate of the same race, religion, or ethnic origin can properly represent the voter's interests, and that such candidates can be elected only from a district with a sufficient minority concentration."[36]

Denial of annexation continued to be a tool used to enforce the act after the 1975 amendments. In 1979, the city of Rome, Georgia wanted to annex property. The D. C. District Court denied the change, but said that it would allow the motion to be resubmitted and would grant clearance if the city would eliminate the residency requirement for voting.

Bail Out

As the provisions of the act were more liberally interpreted, the desire for bail-out grew. In 1980 again in the *City of Rome, Georgia v. United States*, the Supreme Court determined that Rome could not bail-out because Georgia was still under the special provisions. In a dissenting opinion, Justice Powell argued that the constitutionality of preclearance depended on the ability to bail-out. It was his view that the court was acting unconstitutionally denying Rome bail-out after 15 years of non-discriminatory practices. The resulting debate gave rise to changes to these provisions in 1982.

Intent v. Effect

By the end of the 1970s, the court's requirement for evidence from the plaintiffs had become less clear. Court decisions had generally recognized that any voting laws or procedures resulting in a discriminatory *effect* were in violation of the Voting Rights Act. While this position had become dominant, the more conservative view established that a violation existed only if the laws or procedures had been set up with discriminatory *intent*. The benchmark case used as the precedent for this prevailing viewpoint was the 1975 conclusion from *White v. Regester* in which the Supreme Court upheld the District Court's decision to invalidate the multi-member districts in Dallas and Bexar counties in Texas on the basis that they were discriminatory against Mexican Americans and blacks. The court reached this decision based on the result rather than the intent of the system. The court, however, denied that a minority group having disproportionately low representation was the only criteria. Along with this "result," the plaintiffs were obliged to show that the political process was not equally open to them. Nonetheless, the result could be part of the plaintiff's evidence, irrespective of the intent of the system or the specific cause of the poor result.

In contrast, the Fifth Circuit Court of Appeals in New Orleans required a demonstration of intent in its March 1978 decision in *Nevett v. Sides*. The court created exhaustive logic to conclude that intent of discrimination was a requirement for invoking the equal protection clause of the constitution in a voting rights case. In this case, the small city of Fairfield, Alabama had apportioned itself into six wards with twelve aldermen, two residing in each ward. All aldermen were elected at-large. The city, composed of roughly 50 percent blacks, had elected six of the seven black candidates seeking office in 1968. In 1972, after the new apportionment, none of the eight black candidates was elected. The lower court had held that these disparate results could be attributed to racially polarized voting "by an electorate in close and changing racial balance." Blacks, although comprising a slight majority of the registered voters, claimed that "such absolute control of the city government by one race" in an at-large arrangement was a violation of their constitutional rights. The court conceded that vote dilution could be found by weighing the Zimmer factors, with or without proof of discriminatory intent. However, if the *Zimmer* factors were insufficient, as they were in this case, intent was required to show discrimination.

The court upheld the at-large system because blacks could not show that the at-large system was designed to discriminate. In order to prove discriminatory intent, the court claimed, plaintiffs would need to show at least one of three factors:[37] The scheme was implemented for the purpose of diluting the voting strength of blacks; the intent of the voting scheme was neutral, but it built upon and enhanced practices or laws that were designed to be racially discriminating; or the factors that had changed since the design of the at-large system were a result of discriminatory intent.

In 1980, the Supreme Court hearing in *Mobile v. Bolden* dealt a blow to *White v. Regester's* "totality of circumstances." Plaintiffs challenged the city of Mobile, Alabama for its at-large system of electing its city commissioners. The appeals court concluded that the system was discriminatory and asked the parties to the suit to submit alternate plans, after which the court replaced the three-commissioner system with a single-member-district, council-mayor system. Finally the Supreme Court heard the *Bolden* case. A plurality of justices reached the verdict in a deeply split court. The opinion stated, "Racially discriminatory motivation is a necessary ingredient of a Fifteenth Amendment violation." Furthermore, since the Voting Rights Act is simply the legislative vehicle for enforcing the Fifteenth Amendment, actions alleging violation of the Voting Rights Act also require discriminatory intent.[38] Justice Potter Stewart, a centrist and Eisenhower appointee, wrote the opinion in which he was joined by Justices Burger, Powell, and Rehnquist. Justice Blackmun and Stevens concurred in the decision but thought the court had become too consumed with at-large districts while failing to look at the overall districting plan as the issue. Justices Brennan, White, and Marshall dissented.

Adding to the confusion, on the same day as the *Bolden* decision, the Supreme Court, in *The City of Rome, Georgia v. United States*, explicitly upheld Congress' authority to provide for rejection of a voting provision either on the grounds of discriminatory purpose or discriminatory effect. A few months later in *Fullilove v. Klutznick*, Justice Burger, writing for the Court, reiterated that protection of voting rights does not require proof of intent.

Progress

During the 1970s, blacks made considerable progress in electing officials although the success rate still dragged considerably behind blacks' proportional population. In Georgia, Alabama, Mississippi, and North Carolina, blacks held more than 11 percent of the state house seats. Southern states with single-member districts in metropolitan areas elected blacks to 8 to 12 percent of their lower-house seats. Those with multimember districts elected only 2 to 4 percent.[39] Blacks also faired well in county governments and school boards. They made only about half as much progress in the state senates and city governments and had little success in the U. S. House and Senate.[40] There were 80 black mayors in cities including the former white strongholds of Atlanta, New Orleans, and Birmingham. Blacks comprised over twenty percent of the population, but still held only five percent of the elected offices.[41] Nonetheless, the officeholder profile in 1980 was an unthinkable dream in 1965.

More than just holding office, the election of blacks raised their standard of living. Gains included upgraded parks, streets, sanitation services, and health facilities. Fear of police justifiably diminished as black police were hired and abusive sheriffs were ousted at the polls. The courts also became more friendly in their judgment of blacks as more black jurors were selected from the voter registration rolls which now contained a significant number of blacks.[42]

	1964 Registration Black	White	1982 Registration Black	White
Alabama	23	68	58	79
Georgia	44	66	52	67
Louisiana	32	80	69	72
Mississippi	7	70	76	91
North Carolina	47	93	44	66
South Carolina	39	79	53	55
Virginia	31	72	54	58

FIGURE 8: 20 YEARS OF BLACK AND WHITE REGISTRATION[43]

The election of blacks also created jobs as black officials appointed blacks to county and municipal projects. White politicians had changed as well. Staunch segregationists were now few in number; blacks and whites worked together in the state houses without significant incidents. Even George Wallace, best known for saying, "segregation forever," had changed his mantra and had announced, "Segregation is dead. It's outlawed and it won't be again."[44] Registration had also changed dramatically. Figure 8 shows the progress made in 18 years.

In 1982, the 1975 extensions to the special provisions neared termination. Amazing progress had been realized in 17 years. Martin Luther King, Jr.'s prediction, that black votes would sway a presidential election, had come true in 1976. Jimmy Carter was elected by a minority of whites and an overwhelming majority of blacks. Despite successes, civil rights leaders were faced with a problem. The results test, or "totality of circumstances" described in *White v. Regester* was the desired benchmark for civil rights activists, yet the Supreme Court had dealt it a disabling blow in *Bolden*. With Ronald Reagan's overwhelming election, civil rights leaders began to worry about their ability to pass a strong amendment. In addition, the Senate had a Republican majority for the first time in 30 years. Strom Thurmond of South Carolina had become the chairman of the Senate Judiciary Committee and Orrin Hatch of Utah chaired the Senate Subcommittee on the Constitution. The House posed no problem for a strong amendment, but the chances of getting a strong bill through the Senate appeared poor.[45]

Dallas: At-large Districts and District Lines

The period between 1975 and 1982 marked another significant phase in the minority struggles in the Dallas school district and the city council. In 1977, the school district dropped at-large elections in favor of single-member districts, ending the reign of the Committee for Good Schools.[46] Busing had not been very successful and even many blacks were disillusioned with it. After hearing the DISD and the NAACP arguments about more busing, the Supreme Court turned the problem back to the 5th Circuit Court. Judge Taylor, who had been tied to the case for ten years, withdrew among accusations that he was too close to downtown business interests. Judge Barefoot Sanders took over.[47] Since white flight had reduced whites to only 32 percent of the student body by 1980, Judge Sanders did not order more busing.[48]

In 1976, Wes Wise resigned as mayor and ran for Congress. Dallas papers called what ensued the "million dollar mayoral campaign" between wealthy land developer Robert Folsom and equally-wealthy Gary Webber. Folsom was the traditional Dallas mayor and won by taking the northern, mostly-white half of the city.[49]

The 1976 election included a City Charter referendum in which voters approved the court-endorsed eight single-member, three at-large plan under which the elections were held. This approval was the final bullet that sealed the fate of the Citizens Charter Association. By the end of the year, the association's president announced that the CCA would no longer endorse candidates.[50]

The next year, even in the absence of a CCA, the city council elections produced the same racial results as 1975. Two blacks and no Hispanics were elected. Black physician Emerson Emory made a run against Mayor Folsom and received 62 percent of the black vote but only 17 percent city wide.

Plaintiffs appealed Judge Mahon's approval of the 8-3 system to the 5th Circuit. Blacks still objected to the existence of the three at-large districts as well as the positioning of the lines for the eight single-member districts. They claimed that the districts clustered black votes into an impermissibly small number of districts. Mexican-American plaintiffs claimed the case had not dealt with the vote dilution of Hispanics at all.

The 5th Circuit Court rendered an opinion in May 1977. Circuit Judge Tuttle recognized that even if all eleven council positions were single-member districts, it would be impossible to create a safe Hispanic district. The court had no authority to create more districts and Hispanics could not prove that the at-large positions of the current system discriminated against them, thus Hispanics could be offered no remedy.

However, the Judge continued his logic by referring to *East Caroll Parish School Board v. Marshall*,[51] in which the Supreme Court advised that whenever district courts are required to create districting plans, "single-member districts are preferred absent unusual circumstances." Judge Tuttle thus reasoned that Judge Mahon's agreement to support three at-large districts partially to protect Mexican-Americans was moot because Mexican Americans had no valid claim that needed protecting. In other words, there was no special circumstance supporting the at-large districts, and absent any such circumstance, the Supreme Court required institution of single-member districts. Tuttle ordered that the city divide itself into the appropriate number of single-member districts or he would do it for them.[52]

The 5th Circuit's logic was fatally flawed because the 8-3 plan was not a court devised plan, and therefore the Supreme Court's advice did not apply. The case remained on appeal for nearly a year before it was heard by the Supreme Court. In June 1978, the Court reversed Judge Tuttle for his incorrect interpretation of whether or not this was a court-designed plan. Thurgood Marshall dissented, arguing that the plan was court-ordered because the Dallas City Charter gave the city council no authority to reapportion without voter approval which it did not have at the time. Had Marshall's logic prevailed, the city, on its own, could never have settled any redistricting suit. Justices Brennan and Stevens joined Marshall in dissent.[53]

This judgment had another repercussion. Since the 8-3 plan was an action of the city and not the court, it required preclearance which had never been requested. Dallas decided to address the D. C. District Court rather than the Justice Department. The essence of the city's argument was that the three at-large districts did not need preclearance because they were at-large before the new plan; they did not constitute a change. The court denied that motion, substantiating the theory that any change in a districting scheme required a judicial review of the whole plan, not just the changes.[54]

In February 1979, Elsie Faye Heggins filed a law suit against the city in an attempt to stop the April elections until the matter of preclearance was settled. Heggins had been an activist around Dallas for a decade. She got into politics through her membership in the Fair Park homeowners group. After whites fled the Fair Park area leaving mostly blacks behind, the city used eminent domain to buy homes around the park to construct parking lots. Protesting the city's action, she was involved in a threat to block the Cotton Bowl parade. She worked with the War on Poverty and fought long battles for the creation of an MLK community center. She was one of the plaintiffs in the Al Lipscomb lawsuit and was part of the Frederick Douglas Voting Council that had accepted the 8-3 plan. When she took a city council seat in 1980, she was the first truly independent black on the council, having no ties to the white community.[55]

The case went back to the 5th Circuit who returned it to a three-judge district court in North Texas. The District Court granted Heggins' motion and enjoined the city from holding the April elections. One judge, Robert Hill, dissented, pointing out that the Supreme Court gave no indication that the plan was unconstitutional. Elections had been held under the plan in 1975 and 1977. If the plan were found illegal, he argued, a newly elected council would be no less legal than the last.[56]

Unable to resolve the redistricting case in the D. C. District Court, the city submitted the plan to the attorney general for preclearance. In November, Assistant Attorney General Drew Days III approved the plan saying he found no evidence that the plan was devised with discriminatory intent. He also noted that the 8-3 plan was better for minorities than the all at-large elections, thus, the plan was valid under the non regression rule from *Beer*.[57]

When the delayed 1979 election took place in January 1980, the two majority-black districts elected two blacks, Elsie Faye Heggins and Fred Blair. The mixed-minority district elected an Hispanic, Ricardo Medrano who had become a significant Hispanic leader from Dallas' *Little Mexico*. His father, Pancho, could remember an earlier Dallas. He had grown up near Pike Park that carried a *No Mexicans* sign. Under pressure from the Mexican community, the city allowed Hispanics to swim in the park pool from 7:00 A.M. to 8:15 A.M. after which the pool was drained and refilled for white swimmers. Pancho was an skillful politician, supported by the *Progressive Voters League*, an organization with clout among blacks.[58]

When the 1980 census was taken, Dallas was 29 percent black and 12 percent Hispanic. The three minority districts had become even more minority. District 6 had gone from 83 to 94 percent; District 8 from 72 to 91 percent; and District 2 from 69 to 77 percent.[59]

By April 1981, the Frederick Douglas Voting Council, with members like Heggins, expressed dissatisfaction with the district lines in the current plan. The three at-large positions had not brought in minority councilmen. North Dallas white males had won the seats, so demands arose for all eleven seats to be single-member districts, or at least ten single-member districts with an at-large mayor. When it was brought to the city council, Heggins threatened another law suit if a third black district were not created. Several council members, including Max Goldblatt, objected to dealing with the issue again, so it was temporarily tabled.

The affirmative action portion of the civil rights era was taking firm hold. Although not yet endorsed by courts or law, the shift from equal opportunity to equal results had already taken place in the civil rights community. The circuit court and the Justice Department had approved the three at-large districts. The Supreme Court had let them stand, yet they were not producing the results desired by activists, so the lawsuits continued.

Folsom completed his final term as mayor in 1981, then gave his support to Jack Evans, head of a major grocery chain. Even without the CCA, businessmen kept securing the top job. Evans had humble beginnings growing up in Dallas and attending Woodrow Wilson High School. He made his first money boxing behind the Ford Plant on East Grand for the nickels and dimes that workers would throw into the ring. In 1978, after he became president of the grocery chain, he was kidnapped and held at an *8 Days Inn* for ransom. His son scraped together $84,000 that was never recovered. It took him several years to get over this incident, but Evans had a dream to become Mayor of Dallas. He sought the job of bond chairman in 1978 for a number of propositions that voters had defeated the previous June. Working 15 to 18 hours a day, he got all of the propositions passed. This was the way Evans tested the waters and began to accumulate political support. By the time of his election, he had quietly rung the doorbells of Dallas' most influential, leading him to be a shoe-in for the mayor's office.[60]

Elsie Faye Heggins continued her efforts by working for months to get the city council to study the feasibility of a third black district. In October, the city staff returned eleven alternate plans. Seven of these plans created the district that Heggins requested, but several undermined Medrano's Hispanic district in the South. Surrounding the existing two black districts was Medrano's district, along with a white, albeit dwindling, district in Oak Cliff, and a white district represented by Max Goldblatt in the Pleasant Grove area.

None of the representatives of the neighboring districts intended to see their constituency carved up. Goldblatt was the most colorful and vocal. He said, "We're not going to cross any rivers, we're not going to cross any railroads, we're going to use natural boundaries, and we're going to use contiguous territory. We're not going to jut out into different directions like an octopus. We're going to disturb the city as little as we can." History would find his words anything but prophetic.

Medrano said he was looking to add only people who could identify socially with people in his current district. Don Hicks, the Oak Cliff councilman, threatened that the remaining whites would leave Oak Cliff if all the southern Dallas representatives were black. All the adjacent districts, with a large, black constituency, were standing firm. The 1980 census also showed that the Medrano and Heggins districts had lost population and were each needing 30,000 more people to be of equal size with other districts.[61]

Amid the uproar of the weekly city council meetings in which Heggins would lose all decorum to make her points, several minority organizations threatened to file suits. In January 1982, Mayor Jack Evans said, "I think it is a well planned and organized performance, but I still have reservations whether we have heard from the total black community."[62] The Mayor said he had talked to a number of black leaders who said they were not in favor of carving out black districts.

The intensity increased. John Wiley Price, who would become Dallas' chief black activist, said he would set up pickets at the Tom Thumb grocery stores of which Evans was the President. Black Councilman Fred Blair voiced his complaints. Heggins continued to push her plan by trying to lure Medrano with the fact that his district would become more Hispanic. Medrano balked, knowing that her plan, although giving him more Hispanics, removed many blacks that had supported him. The resultant district would be an "unsafe" 53 percent minority.

The council meetings neared a political circus. Black activist J. B. Jackson, a debate team member with Dr. Martin Luther King, accompanied

Elsie Heggins and advised her on every move. Mayor Evans, aggravated by this teaming, asked why she needed counsel. Jackson responded that President Reagan had advisors, so why not Elsie. One veteran journalist said, "[W]e'd like to see Mrs. Heggins talk while J. B. Jackson drank a glass of water - the old ventriloquist trick." Still Jackson said of Heggins, "The only reason we are getting anything done is because of this woman here. She doesn't mind them kicking her, treating her like a dog; she hangs on like a snapping turtle, and she gets things done."[63]

Ex-mayor Wes Wise, who was back as an at-large council member, objected to the notion that he could not represent blacks. Don Hicks talked about the resegregation of Oak Cliff. Max Goldblatt said he would see anyone in Hell who said a council member had to be a certain race to represent a district. Fred Blair objected to the idea that whites would vote for blacks saying, "Let's deal with the facts at hand. People don't want to go to school with us. How can they vote for us?" Ricardo Medrano yelled at Ms. Heggins for her tirades and walked out of the room. Such were the council meetings.[64]

On March 15, 1982, 150 people organized a march from South Dallas to City Hall. Heggins and Blair led the procession shouting their demands for a third black district. The crowd was small for such a protest, but it stood out in a city that was not used to such demonstrations. It was juxtaposed to an atmosphere of hyper-prosperity in which half of the large cranes west of the Mississippi, constructing millions of new square feet of office space, decorated the Dallas skyline.

The council struggled with three plans, labeled A-4, B-1, and C-3. Plan A-4 maintained the three minority districts and was supported by seven of the eight white members of the council. Three days after the march, the majority vote prevailed and received approval of the city attorney.[65] The tempers of black activists were raised. Paul Rivers said, "I hope you have enough fire trucks. We're going to burn that . . . city down." The city attorney was asked to file charges against Rivers, black attorneys threatened to file law suits, and councilman Lee Simpson said he would push for a city Charter amendment that would increase the council from 11 to 13 members.[66] The lines for a fight were drawn, but the Congress and the courts would soon change the rules.

Navajo Reservation: The Rights of Indians

Goodluck v. Apache County continued into September 1975. The county still contended that Navajos on the reservation were not U. S. citizens, should not be allowed to vote, and should not be counted for apportionment. Recall that the contention was based on the fact that Native-American residents on the reservation were immune to certain kinds of taxation. Attorneys for Apache County argued that the *Immigration and Nationality Act* that had granted Indians' citizenship was unconstitutional. Their defense rested on an 1884 case in which the Supreme Court looked at the 14th Amendment and concluded that a reservation Indian was not a citizen.[67] The 14th Amendment reads, "Representatives shall be apportioned among the several states according to their respective numbers, counting the whole number of persons in each state, excluding Indians not taxed."

Indians, living on the reservation are generally exempt from state taxes, but the district court concluded that the phrase "not taxed" was an historical anomaly of no relevance today. Justices believed that the granting of citizenship by the *Immigration and Nationality Act* recognized that the Indian is now subject to many federal taxes. "It is much too strict a reading of the Constitution to require subjection to state taxes before citizenship can be granted."[68]

In 1976, the tribal leader, Peter MacDonald, was tied to a scandal at the Navajo Housing Authority. Barry Goldwater, his old enemy, called for a federal audit. MacDonald was indicted by a grand jury and hired F. Lee Bailey to defend him. The jury was unable to find him guilty on any of the eight federal charges.[69] Despite his brush with the courts, MacDonald was again elected in 1978.

The struggle over Indian policy continued at the federal level. Recall that the Indian Civil Rights Act of 1968 guaranteed reservation Indians civil rights, including due process and equal protection. The Santa Clara Pueblo, near Santa Fe, New Mexico, barred from tribal membership offspring of female members who married outside the tribe. The pueblo law did not apply to children of male members under the same circumstance. Thus, the children of female members, even those born on the reservation, were denied the right to vote in tribal elections or hold tribal office.

Julia Martinez, a tribal member who married a Navajo non-member, sued the pueblo on the basis that it discriminated against her daughter and denied her daughter due process of law. The pueblo argued that membership rules were at the very core of its culture and that control of these rules was basic to its sovereignty. The district court agreed. In 1978, the Supreme Court upheld the district court in *Santa Clara Pueblo v. Martinez*. Thurgood Marshall wrote the opinion and argued that the promotion of Indian self-determination was more important than "providing in wholesale fashion for the extension of constitutional requirements of tribal governments."[70] Justice White disagreed stating that he could not believe that Congress intended by passage of the Indian Civil Rights Act to leave enforcement of those rights up to the tribal powers from whom the act was trying to protect the Indians. He pointed out that "the extension of constitutional rights to individual citizens is indeed to intrude upon the authority of government."[71]

In the same year, the Supreme Court declared that tribes "still possess those aspects of sovereignty not withdrawn by treaty or statute."[72] Three years later, the court considered the authority that tribes had over the conduct of non-Indians on non-Indian land within the reservation. It concluded that the tribes could regulate their conduct "when that conduct threatens or has some direct effect on the political integrity, the economic security, or the health or welfare of the tribe."[73] The next year, the court dealt with tribes that were trying to exercise sovereign rights that they had not exercised or claimed during their entire reservation history. The Supreme Court claimed that "sovereign power, even when unexercised, is an enduring presence."[74]

During this era of voting rights, Arizona Indian participation in federal elections continued to grow. Less than half of Arizona's voting-age Indians were registered. Of those registered, however, 80 percent voted in the 1976 election. In Navajo and Apache Counties, where the Navajo populations are highest, 84 percent of the registered Indians turned up at the polls.[75]

Dade County: Fires and Flotillas

The Amendments of 1975 were especially significant to south Florida because of the protection provided to those of Spanish language heritage. Dade County was not caught by the automatic trigger, but five other south Florida counties were, including Monroe County which shared a congressional district with Dade. Any election involving the covered counties was subject to preclearance, thus any statewide redistricting required preclearance.[76]

The Cuban population continued to grow in Dade County. By 1976, it reached 400,000, up one-third since 1970. By the late 1970s, Dade had over half a million Cubans. Families crowded into abandoned buildings, often one family per room. Zoning laws were broken, but officials looked the other way. Cubans, traditionally sequestered in downtown Miami, began to move to adjacent business areas and neighborhoods.[77]

Before the end of the decade, hundreds of Sandinista guerrillas, muddied and toughened from town-to-town combat, closed in on and captured

Managua.[78] The events in Nicaragua signaled another immigration storm brewing for south Florida.

Throughout the decade, migration had sewn the seeds of racial unrest and on December 17, 1979, Miami race relations prepared for riot. Arthur McDuffie, a black insurance agent, was chased on his motorcycle by Dade County police officers who claimed he had run a red light. McDuffie was stopped and beaten in a melee involving at least six white officers. He died four days later. The senior officer at the Liberty Station reviewed the *Use of Force Report* and declared he was not satisfied with police actions.

A week later, reports of inconsistency began to appear in the newspaper. The day after Christmas, the Police Chief suspended four of the officers involved in the slaying. The next day five more officers were suspended. Janet Reno, attorney for Dade County, filed manslaughter and tampering with evidence charges against the four officers and accessory-after-the-fact against another. On January 1, prosecutors announced that two officers would be granted immunity in trade for their testimony. Demonstrators soon appeared in front of the Criminal Justice Building. On February 1, Reno escalated the charges by filing second degree murder charges against Alex Marrero. She added charges of aggravated battery against three others. Marrero went to jail as he and seven others were fired from the force.

Defense attorneys, fearful of a trial in Miami, secured a change of venue to Tampa. The trial began on the last day of March and six weeks later the case went to the all-white jury who returned not-guilty verdicts for the remaining defendants.

News of the verdict spread through Miami. About 5 P.M. that Saturday, the first rocks were thrown near African Square Park. By 6 P.M., police pulled back, and full-scale violence broke out in Liberty City. A rally protesting the verdict was quickly organized in front of the Metro Justice complex. By 8 P.M., the 3000 people present erupted into a major riot. Several police cars were destroyed and the Municipal Building was set ablaze. By 11 P.M., small fires and looting broke out in black areas all over Dade County. By the next night, five people were dead and three more who would soon die lay in area hospitals.

Looting spread as the Governor mobilized 1100 National Guardsmen, 170 Florida Highway Patrolmen, 75 state wildlife officers, and 50 Florida Marine Patrol officers. Nine more people soon died from police actions and drive-by shootings. By Sunday evening, 270 people had been treated in Dade hospitals and hundreds of businesses had been burned, looted, or otherwise destroyed. On Monday morning, amid sporadic violence, schools were closed and busses were shut down. By evening, calm returned to the streets and a riot which caused 19 deaths and $100 million in damage, ended.[79]

The McDuffie riot was not the only problem facing Miami in those chaotic days of 1980. In April, the month before the riot, Jose Antonio Rodriguez Gallegos rammed his minibus through the gates of the Peruvian embassy in Havana in an effort to gain political asylum. Castro showed his anger by withdrawing police protection from the embassy. The unprotected political free-ground drew 10,000 Cubans seeking asylum. The public demonstration of people's desire to leave Cuba embarrassed Castro, so he opened the port of Mariel declaring that anyone who wanted to leave could. He invited Cuban exiles in the U. S. to come pick up their relatives.[80]

On April 20, two lobster boats carrying about forty Cubans arrived at Key West, beginning the freedom flotilla. Castro declared in his Mayday speech, "Those leaving the country for Miami are the scum of the country—anti-socials, homosexuals, drug addicts, and gamblers, who are welcome to leave Cuba if any country will have them."

Mariel was unique because the immigrants were not brought in by the government nor did they come on their own. They were brought in by earlier immigrants. Boats went back and forth manned by Miami Cubans who spent millions on the lift. Many newspaper reports and other media painted the immigrants as criminals, but later studies showed that the number of criminals was a small percentage. During the next six months, 125,000 Cubans were released. The bad press stigmatized the reputations of the Miami Cubans and affected Miami's allure as a tourist attraction.[81]

The federal government seemed to be paralyzed. Editorials in the Miami Herald accused President Carter of being afraid to anger the Cuban-Americans by demanding an end to the influx and at the same time, not wanting to legitimize it by mobilizing federal assistance.[82] Miami was on its own. The administration was further paralyzed by Carter's initial reaction. The first boats did pick up relatives for emotional reunions with their families. Carter gave his blessing "with open heart and open arms." As the exodus progressed, Castro opened the prisons and released what fit his "anti-social scum" description. After the exodus, Miami experienced a crime wave that won it the unenviable title of crime and cocaine capital of the world.[83]

As the Cubans flowed in, so did the Haitians. These were poor peasants huddled shirtless on makeshift boats. They had been immigrating since 1977, but their numbers peaked during the Mariel influx. Their immigration was very different from that of the Cubans. The Cuban influx was sponsored by Cuban Americans; many had families they could join. The Haitians had no sponsors and no network in Miami to support them.[84]

In Washington, the exiles were an important symbol in the fight for Cuba and Latin America. Everyone in Miami felt betrayed by Washington: the Cuban exiles for Kennedy's failure to follow through on the Bay of Pigs and subsequent administration efforts to prevent a raid on Cuba by exiles; and the Anglos for the administration's failure to save Miami from Cubans.

Despite the influx, Miami residents probably believed that nothing much had really changed. Immigrants would eventually learn English and life would go on as usual. But fundamentals were changing. The first decade of post-Castro Cuban arrivals did not see themselves as long-term residents. Before the lift, only a handful of Cubans held office and those who did played down their nationality. But by the 1970s, Cuban Americans began to involve themselves in political parties. As freedom flights brought in another 250,000, Cubans began to put the future of Miami in their own hands rather than view themselves as temporary. This led to a significantly growing naturalization rate by 1970.[85] Cubans began to create non-Anglo civic and political organizations.

In June 1980, President Carter granted a special six-month immigration status for those who arrived before that date. County residents took legal action to keep immigrants out of Dade schools as property values began collapsing all over town. Three months later, Castro closed the boat lift. Reacting to the new world of Dade, the *Citizens of Dade United*, a grass roots Anglo organization, put on the ballot an ordinance that prohibited "the expenditure of any county funds for any purpose of utilizing any language other than English or any culture other than that of the United States."[86] The ordinance passed, setting up a legal stalemate with the Voting Rights Act.

The Reagan administration took a more active stance. It ordered Coast Guard cutters to patrol the Haitian waters so that Miami-bound boats could be intercepted at sea and not reach the U. S. Policies for Cubans and Haitians differed because the U. S. considered Cubans as political refugees and the Haitians as economic refugees. With pressure from some congressmen, including the black caucus, the government relented and the Haitians gained reprieves from deportation. Many Anglo residents felt they could not win. Their efforts to stop Cubans failed in the face of Cuban exile influence with conservatives in Washington. Efforts to stop the Haitians were stemmed by liberal activists. A popular bumper sticker read, "Will the last American leaving Miami, please take the flag."[87]

As the Voting Rights Act came up for renewal in 1982, Dade County boasted a population of 1.6 million, up from 43 thousand in 1920. Median family income had risen to $26,000 for non-Hispanic whites, but Hispanics and blacks lagged behind with family incomes of $20,000 and $17,000 respectively. Dade residents were now only 46 percent non-Hispanic white, 36 percent Hispanic, and 17 percent non-Hispanic black.

CHAPTER 7: THE AMENDMENTS OF 1982[1]

Supreme Court Justice Kennedy: "Have we said in our cases that people have group rights? I though the whole underpinning of our constitution is that people are treated as individuals."
Plaintiffs' Attorney Joel Klein: "It is, but it's not the underpinning of the Voting Rights Act."[2]

Congress viewed the Amendments of 1982 as necessary for two reasons: The 1975 extensions of the special provisions were about to expire and the Supreme Court had left a dilemma for the lower courts with *Bolden v. Mobile*. Proponents in Congress believed the voting rights cause would meet serious trouble if discriminatory intent had to be shown along with discriminatory effect. Citing numerous decisions denying the need to show intent, they contended that the meaning of the court in *Bolden* was unclear—perhaps the decision was an aberration. Still, this uncertainty made backers of the amendments nervous.

Congress dealt with the threat of expiration with more force than ever by extending the special provisions for 25 years. Thus any jurisdiction that could not bail out would be subject to preclearance until 2007. The bilingual requirements that were added in 1975 were extended to 1992.

The 1982 Amendments cleared up the controversy between *White* and *Bolden* by taking critical wording directly from the *White* decision. The amendment read, in part, as follows:

> A violation of subsection (a) [that voting discrimination by race or color is illegal] of this section is established if, based on the totality of circumstances, it is shown that the political processes leading to nomination or election in the state or political subdivision are not equally open to participation by members of a class of citizens protected by subsection (a) of this section in that its members have less opportunity than other members of the electorate to participate in the political process and to elect representatives of their choice. The extent to which members of a protected class have been elected to office in a state or political subdivision is one circumstance that may be considered. Provided, nothing in this section establishes the right to have members of a protected class elected in numbers equal to their proportion in the population.[3]

This established a *results test* to help determine compliance with the act. "[L]ess opportunity than other members . . . to elect representatives of their choice . . ." meant quotas. Senator Robert Dole insisted on the last sentence which technically denied the right to quotas, but the law allowed failure to achieve a quota to become evidence of violation of the act. The difficulty that the plaintiffs had in *Bolden* was the court's contention that the Fourteenth Amendment had not been violated. With this new wording in the act, the Fourteenth Amendment would no longer be the test. Instead, violating Section 2 would be an adequate claim without relying on the Constitution. Although the *Bolden* decision seemed to threaten the continued strength of the act, it actually served to galvanize believers in a results test. Without *Bolden*, the results test might have been lost in congressional debate.

The potential impact of the results test was enormous. Since opponents to the amendments were quiet, civil rights leaders downplayed the importance of the change. They passed off the amendment language as a clarification of the original intent of the act. Henry Hyde, the leading Republican on the House Subcommittee on Civil and Constitutional Rights, unwittingly endorsed the Section 2 changes. He consumed his political influence trying to lessen the power of Section 5 while being willing to support Section 2. He proposed that the existing jurisdictions, held under the special provisions of the act, be released. He suggested instead that any jurisdiction found guilty in a voting rights case be placed under the special provisions for four years. The ensuing debate turned the focus from the strengthening of Section 2 to the undermining of Section 5. Civil rights leaders skillfully ran with the debate, painting a picture of all gains lost without the continued Section 5 enforcement.[4] Suffragists dominated the House committee hearings and Hyde's proposal was swept away, leaving Section 5 intact and the rewritten Section 2, unchallenged.

After passage by the House, the Senate took up debate on Section 2. In an effort to recover the ground lost by Hyde, conservative Orrin Hatch of Utah conceded that the special provisions should be extended, but he argued that Section 2 should be maintained without revision.[5] Hatch, however, lacked the support of any organized group. Even the Reagan White House had sent no one to testify in the House hearings. The act had become so complex by 1982, that few people grasped that Hatch was arguing about racial quotas rather than voting rights. The League of Women Voters had announced that the cause was too clear cut to debate.[6] Lacking sufficient support, Hatch was eclipsed by Senator Dole. Dole proposed the final wording of Section 2, slightly softening the "results" wording that the House had passed. The administration backed Dole and Hatch was defeated.

The resulting Senate report made clear the factors that should be considered in a Section 2 vote-dilution case. They were a combination of the *Zimmer* factors and the wording in *White*:

The Amendments of 1982

- the extent of any history of official voting discrimination;
- the extent to which voting is racially polarized;
- the extent to which a state or political subdivision has used unusually large election districts, majority vote requirements, anti-single-shot provisions, or other voting practices or procedures that may enhance the opportunity for discrimination against a minority group;
- in jurisdictions with a candidate-slating process, the extent to which the members of the minority group have been denied access to it;
- the extent to which members of the minority group bear the effects of discrimination in such areas as education, employment and health;
- whether political campaigns have been characterized by overt or subtle racial appeals; and
- the extent to which members of the minority group have been elected to public office in the jurisdiction.[7]

Hyde did succeed in slightly modifying the bailout provisions. Congress realized that some counties, cities, and school boards, while still covered by the special provisions of the act, had been in compliance with the law for 17 years. Until this time, a political entity within a state could not bail out until the state itself was able to bail out. The Amendments of 1982 provided for bail-out irrespective of the status of the state, but required that a jurisdiction show the District Court of the District of Columbia a ten year record of full compliance with the act and positive steps to achieve full minority access to the political process. Ten year compliance meant the jurisdiction had not: used a discriminatory test or device; failed to obtain preclearance before implementing covered changes in the law; enacted changes that were discriminatory and therefore objected to under Section 5 (preclearance); been found in violation in a court proceeding; nor required the assignment of federal examiners.

Further provisions of the Amendments were designed to deal with others who would have difficulty in voting. The bill allowed blind, disabled, or English-illiterate persons to bring another person of their choice to the voting booth to assist them.

Linda Chavez, former head of US English and member of the Civil Rights Commission, recounted an episode in the hearings which she claims typified the nature of the bilingual debate:

> ... Hispanic witnesses claimed that the bilingual ballot provisions had enhanced the participation of Hispanic voters. One witness summarized the changes brought by bilingual ballots, quoting from a newspaper article from McAllen, Texas:

"Dominga Sausedo was nervous as she walked from the cramped house to the neighborhood school a few blocks away. For the first time in forty-eight years since she was born here in Texas, Mrs. Sausedo was on her way to vote. Like thousands of American citizens, Mrs. Sausedo speaks no English. The language and information barriers that existed until recently were enough to keep her away from the voting booth."

Only Congressman Henry Hyde . . . sounded a sour note during the hearings. "Is it common that someone would be born in America and live 48 years here and not be able to speak English or to understand it?" Hyde asked. "It is. It sure is," the witness responded, but offered no evidence to back the claim.[8]

Ms. Chavez claims that the overwhelming majority of Mexican-American adults speak English. She points out that most of the non-English speakers are recent immigrants.[9]

The final change offered by the Amendments was the replacement of the word *legislators* with *representatives*, potentially opening more positions to the purview of the act. The results test could then be applied to both elective and non-elective positions. This had the enormous possibility of applying the Voting Rights Act to positions that were not even a matter of voting.

The Amendments passed the House 385 to 24. The Senate passed the bill with revisions by a vote of 85 to 8 and the House ultimately concurred. The concern of civil rights groups about a Republican President and Senate had been ill-founded. The fact was that 17 years of the Voting Rights Act had been more successful than anyone realized. If indeed the act was designed to give blacks in the South their share of political influence, here was the evidence: eighteen of 22 southern Senators supported the legislation. This overwhelming majority resulted from a pragmatic recognition that blacks in the South were a new political force that could easily swing the balance of a senatorial election.

Statistics in the House were similar. In 1965, only 32 percent of the House southerners supported the Voting Rights Act. By 1970, the number dropped to 28 percent, but the 1960s massive buildup of black voters bore results in the 1970s. By 1975, 63 percent of the House southerners supported the Voting Rights Act Amendments and in 1982, it became 82 percent. All members of Congress with districts containing more than 40 percent blacks, voted for the 1982 Amendments.

Outside the South, simple politics played a forceful role in the congressional vote. Most members of Congress felt these amendments had little effect on their constituents. Representatives pick their fights, and a fight against any civil rights legislation, no matter what the principle underlying the opposition, looks like a fight against civil rights. The Congress presented the veto-proof bill which President Reagan signed on June 29, 1982.

The Arguments in Favor of the 1982 Amendments[10]

Senator Mathis presented the majority views. The general premise supporting the amendments echoed that of the previous two amendments, namely, that all progress could be lost if the special enforcement provisions did not remain in effect. If the Congress took no action, most jurisdictions could bail out. While supporters admitted that considerable progress had been made to reduce the direct impediments to voting, they argued that keeping jurisdictions under these provisions should be unobjectionable since they would have no effect on jurisdictions that proposed changes with good intent. Good intent was not universal, however, since many proposed changes were still rejected by the attorney general. Without the special provisions, only the arduous process of litigation could deal with objectionable changes. The main reasons that the Justice Department denied preclearance were the failure to choose unobjectionable alternatives; the absence of innocent explanations for the changes; or departure from past practices as minority voting strength reached new levels.

The supporting presentations cited examples of things that the attorney general had recently rejected in preclearance. They illustrated the types of changes that might be implemented unchecked if the bondage of the special provisions were to lapse:

- Holly Springs, Mississippi, a majority black city, redrew its lines into four districts packing most of the black residents into two overpopulated (thus underrepresented) districts, leaving most of the whites in the two other districts.
- The Burleson County, Texas Hospital District eliminated 12 of 13 polling places, the remaining one of which was 19 miles from the black voter concentration and 30 miles from the Mexican-American population
- In De Kalb County, Georgia, the Board of Registration no longer approved requests for voter registration drives even though only 24 percent of the black voters were registered.

These were the blatant cases where intent was obvious. In addition, the attorney general rejected many instances of district line drawing because they diluted the voting strength of minorities. Some covered jurisdictions overtly ignored the preclearance requirement. Examples of this included:

- Seven Georgia counties changed from single-member to at-large systems and had to be sued before preclearance was sought.
- Haneyville, Alabama incorporated itself into a gerrymandered shape in order to create an 85 percent white city in a 77 percent black county. The city was forced to submit the change for preclearance ten years after its implementation.

Backers of the amendments contended that the attorney general's preclearance process was still frequently needed. Since the 1980 census, considering only statewide election plans, the Attorney General had rejected plans in Virginia, Arizona, North Carolina, South Carolina, Georgia, Alabama, Mississippi, and Texas. In some cases, plans had been resubmitted and successively rejected.

Proponents also argued the need to reverse *Bolden*. One case, they pointed out, had been successfully defended because the challenged election system was established early in the century at a time when blacks were not allowed to vote. Thus, there could have been no discriminatory intent in the election method since it was designed when discrimination was already achieved by law.

Defenders of the bill knew that opponents would attack "totality of circumstances" as vague, but they believed that these words allowed the court to consider the *Zimmer* factors. The very phrase, "totality of circumstances," they argued, should put to rest any concern that the bill was an institution of racial quotas. Backers pointed out that most of the courts had already used this results test, and there had been no widespread institution of quotas.

In the language-minority area, the emphasis of the legislation was on an increasingly bilingual America. The Mexican-American population, once existing only in large pockets near the Mexican border, was beginning to move into the cities. The non-English speaking portion of the American Indian population, while not rapidly increasing, had been given the right to vote in the 1960s. The Senate report stated, "Because of their need for assistance, members of these groups are more susceptible than the ordinary voter to having their vote unduly influenced or manipulated. As a result, members of such groups run the risk that they will be discriminated against at the polls and that their right to vote in state and federal elections will not be protected. . . It is only natural that many such voters may feel apprehensive about casting a ballot in the presence of, or may be misled by, someone other than a person of their own choice."[11] Thus the bill read that any blind, disabled or English-illiterate may bring a person of his choice to the voting booth.

The Amendments of 1982

Advocates of the new bill contended that the first condition toward bail-out, a ten year record of compliance with the law, sought out and identified jurisdictions with good records. In theory, jurisdictions would be newly motivated to comply with the law since they could now bail out regardless of the conduct of the whole state. It would also be no burden on a "clean" jurisdiction to demonstrate that it had lost no voting rights litigation and had none pending. They conceded that assignment of examiners was up to the whim of the attorney general, but they argued that he followed strict standards and had not exhibited any record of abuse. The Justice Department, they claimed, only assigned examiners when there were meritorious complaints.

Knowing that covered jurisdictions were antagonized by the presence of federal examiners, backers countered with these statistics: There were 533 counties covered by the act as passed in 1965; black registration was less then 50 percent in 243 of them; of these, only 63 counties had ever received examiners to list or register voters.[12] Most sensitive was Mississippi which had received half of the 12,000 examiners dispatched by the Justice Department since 1965.[13]

The Arguments Against the 1982 Amendments

The Senate argument against the 1982 Amendments was spearheaded by Senators Strom Thurmond, Jesse A. Helms, and John P. East.[14] They recognized that election entities that had long been under the jurisdiction of the act probably felt some hope from the new bail-out provisions. For the first time, there was some way to request declaratory judgment from the court. Nonetheless, Senator Thurmond spoke for many when he expressed objection and worry about the harshness of the new bailout procedures: "The bail-out contained in [these amendments], for the most part, inserts new criteria into bail-out. New concepts and schemes, never before faced by covered jurisdictions for bail-out purposes, have been introduced by this legislation."

The new bail-out procedure, while somewhat alluring to opponents of the amendments, was not satisfactory. There had been a dearth of evidence given to the House and Senate hearings that any qualifying jurisdictions existed. They argued that having everything precleared is almost impossible: "A student of Section 5 can always find nits to pick." For example, a polling place might have been moved because it burned down the night before the election, or preclearance might technically be required if a registrar moves from one floor to another. Besides, opponents contended, the appointment of federal examiners is done by the Justice Department with no appeal or other due process of law. The jurisdiction could only hope that an unjust complaint did not catch the ear of the attorney general. The matter of inventing new requirements for bail-out was serious to affected jurisdictions. Since the bill would extend the special provisions for 25 years, covered jurisdictions had no hope of extricating themselves other than through bail-out. Opponents thus believed that the Amendments codified into law special provisions that were left completely to the impulse of the attorney general, and that an impossible burden of proof was placed on the jurisdiction seeking bail-out.

The argument went on to allege that it was unclear what constituted constructive efforts. It was difficult "for this subcommittee to believe that this term is intended to be employed as anything other than a vehicle to promote 'affirmative action' principles of civil rights to the voting process."[15] Orrin G. Hatch of Utah wrote, "The objective of these amendments are vastly different than those of the original act. In place of the traditional focus upon equal access to registration and the ballot, the amendments would focus on equal outcome in the electoral process."

Statistics seemed to show that the law had been very effective since 1965 in getting minorities registered and voting. Now, having accomplished the goal, Congress protected its agenda by raising the hurdle for bail-out.

As expected, opponents pointed out, as they had with the previous amendments, that the 1965 special provisions were supposed to have been temporary. The original period of five years had already aggregated to 17 years. By comparing the 1960 and 1980 data, it was clear that the job of the emergency provisions was complete. Certainly, they argued, the law needed to remain in effect, and the individual's right to sue should remain the plaintiff's weapon, but the statistics no longer portrayed an arguable emergency. It was time to let the special provisions die and return the justice system to one of presumed innocence.

Opponents also argued that "totality of circumstances" was vague and did not help define the meaning of the law. They contended that one needs a "core value" to determine results and that there was no core value in a results test except for the outcome of the election. Furthermore, they believed, a results test could only lead to proportional representation or a quota system. While the amendment said that the courts must consider the totality of circumstances, the only result to which it specifically alluded was the electoral success of a protected class. The sought after consequence of the results test was the statistical reflection of the racial makeup of the constituency in the elected body, but such a result was an outcome that the amendment specifically did not guarantee. Oxymoron or not, court decisions would soon leverage the act to create racial quotas in voting districts.

Opponents also believed that the emphasis on race would produce long term detriment to racial causes. The city attorney for Rome, Georgia summed up their view:

> While the proposed amendment to Section 2 may be perceived as an effort to achieve proportional representation aimed at aiding a group's participation in the political processes, in reality it may very well frustrate the group's potentially successful efforts at coalition building across racial lines. The requirement of a quota for racial political success would tend strongly to stigmatize minorities, departmentalize the electorate, reinforce any arguable bloc voting syndrome, and prevent minority members from exercising influence on the political system beyond the bounds of their quota.[16]

John P. East believed that the liberal members of the committee had simply twisted constitutional law to meet their agenda without regard to history or the actual intent of the Constitution. The defeated Senator Hatch asked, "Are individuals elected to office to represent individual citizens or are they elected to office to represent ethnic and racial blocks of voters?"[17]

Results of the Act After the 1982 Amendments

Affirmative Action—Looking for Results

After the passage of the amendments, the Supreme Court essentially overturned *Bolden* in *Rogers v. Lodge*. The decision set a new standard allowing circumstantial evidence to be indicative of the intent to discriminate. The court said, "[D]iscriminatory intent need not be proved by direct evidence. . . . [A]n invidious discriminatory purpose may often be inferred from the totality of the relevant facts. . . ."[18] With the institution of the results test, the number of cases reaching the federal courts each year jumped from about 150 to 225.[19]

Blacks in the South continued to improve their electoral success as demonstrated in Figure 9.

As with the original act, cases were brought to the courts challenging the constitutionality of the 1982 amendments. In 1984 in *U. S. v. Marengo County [Alabama] Commission*, the court decided that nothing in the Constitution either explicitly or implicitly prohibited a results standard in determining voting rights violations. Thus, it concluded, the amendment was constitutional. The court did not conclude that the Constitution guaranteed the results sought by the amendments. It only ruled that the amendment did not violate the Constitution. Thus the results test could be used to judge future cases despite the fact that no such guarantee was made in the Constitution.[20]

The courts danced on both sides of the racial quota issue. In 1985, in *Seastrunk v. Burns*, the appeals court pointed out that the act does not purport to guarantee proportional minority representation. Many other cases made the same point. In 1984, in *Jordon v. Winter*, the Mississippi District Court reiterated the no guarantee clause. In 1988 in Louisiana, the East Jefferson Coalition for Leadership and Development faced the same conclusion in its suit against Jefferson Parish.

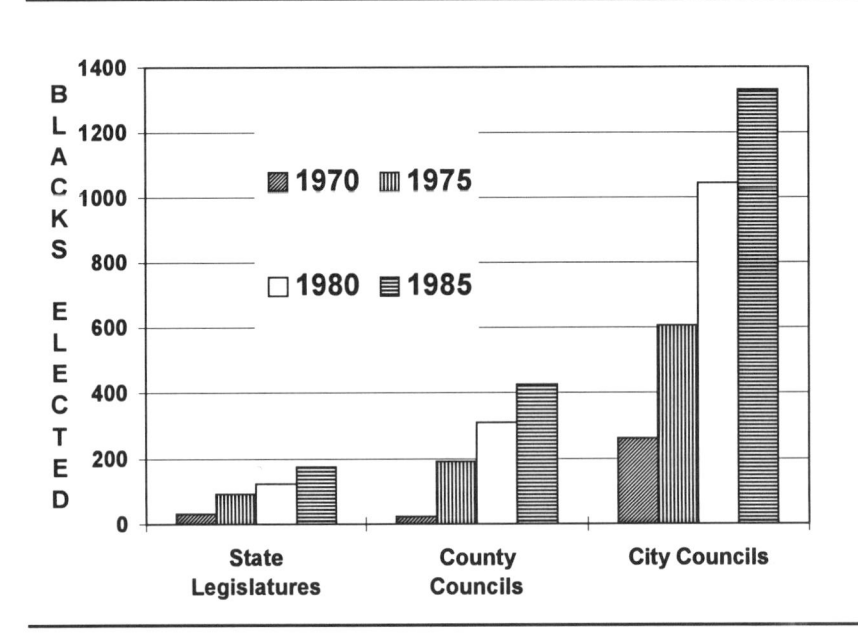

FIGURE 9: BLACKS ELECTED IN THE SOUTH, 1970-1985[21]

Despite the fact that results, *per se*, were not guaranteed by the act, the Justice Department and the courts began looking for evidence of results. Voting schemes that were previously precleared began to be successfully challenged. In 1987, the Justice Department changed the requirements for submitting preclearance requests by requiring that the request include data relating to the "totality of circumstances" section. This included results thus far achieved, history of discrimination, and positive steps and programs employed to eradicate discrimination.

Minority groups began to successfully challenge districting schemes—especially at-large schemes. The 1986 case of *Thornburg v. Gingles* became the landmark case for vote dilution. Justice Brennan, writing for the majority, described three conditions required to evidence voting dilution:

1. The minority group significantly bloc votes;

2. The majority bloc votes against the candidates chosen by the minority; and

3. There exists a large enough, reasonably-compact or, at least, contiguous minority, to form an election district.

These three factors became known as the Gingles three-prong test. Plaintiffs claiming a Section 2 violation by virtue of not achieving proportional representation, were expected to prove that the three *Gingles* factors existed. Although proof that the election plan was designed to discriminate would help persuade a court, it was no longer required after the 1982 amendments.

The court was not precise in any defining compactness. The best reference is probably the lower court's opinion in *Gingles*: "There obviously must be some size (as well as dispersion) on those aggregation of voters to whom the concept [vote dilution] can properly be applied."[22] Equally unspecific was the meaning of significant bloc voting. The generally accepted definition is an overwhelming majority—only slightly more precise.

Thornburg reinforced the premise that at-large districting was not illegal but it lowered the hurdle for claims of vote dilution. The easier it became to demonstrate vote dilution, the easier the attack on at-large districts. Words from the *Thornburg* opinion gave insight that the court would be lenient in reviewing evidence of bloc voting: "In a district where elections are shown usually to be polarized, the fact that racially polarized voting is not present in one election or a few elections does not necessarily negate the conclusion that the district experiences legally-significant bloc voting. Furthermore, the success of a minority candidate in a particular election does not necessarily prove that the district did not experience polarized voting in that election."[23]

The court also maintained that racial bloc voting could stand as the necessary prerequisite in a vote dilution case even if the bloc voting could be traced back to non-racial causes:

Insofar as statistical evidence of divergent racial voting patterns is admitted solely to establish that the minority group is politically cohesive and to assess its prospects for electoral success, such a showing cannot be rebutted by evidence that the divergent voting patterns may be explained by causes other than race.[24]

Although the majority of the court agreed with the verdict, several opinions stated the differing circumstances under which they concurred. Justice O'Connor, however, vehemently dissented believing that the three-prong test went far beyond Congress' intent in Section 2. She argued that the decision had guaranteed a right to proportional representation by race—a notion that the 1982 Amendments specifically denied. She claimed that the court defined undiluted voting strength as the "maximum feasible minority voting strength." The Court calculated the maximum number of districts in which the minority group could possibly constitute a majority in the most favorable single-member district plan. Any result falling short of this ideal was fair game for a vote-dilution challenge. Justice O'Connor argued that such an arrangement considered only the minorities ability to elect candidates and ignored all other avenues of participation in the political process.[25]

As significant as the *Gingles* factors became, they did not supplant the *Zimmer* factors or the restatement of *Zimmer* which generally became know as the *1982 Senate Report Factors*. Plaintiffs still use these factors. Even the Supreme Court reviewed each of these factors when considering *Gingles*. In practice, the three-prong *Gingles* test establishes the existence of a claim, and the *Zimmer* factors determine the extent of relief.[26]

The *Gingles* factors have remained a fundamental tool in establishing vote dilution. Several examples point out their use:

- In the 1987 case of *Houston v. Haley*, the city employed an election scheme whereby four aldermen were elected in single-member districts and a fifth was elected at-large. The court ruled that a violation of the Voting Rights Act did not exist even though no black alderman had been elected under the plan. Challenges to the at-large position failed because the black voters were not politically cohesive and whites did not vote in enough of a bloc to defeat black candidates.
- In Gretna, Louisiana, the appeals court ruled that Gretna's at-large scheme was illegal. Black voters challenging the at-large system had to demonstrate that racial block voting existed. Whites claimed that blacks did not bloc vote as proved by the fact that two white candidates received more black votes than did the black candidate. The courts determined, since all candidates were elected at-large and only one black candidate

ran, blacks had to vote for white candidates which disguised the black bloc voting.[27]
- In Woodville, Mississippi, even though there was a strong racial bloc voting by blacks, there had also been a significant degree of black crossover to the white candidate in the last election. Further evidencing the lack of minority cohesiveness was the fact that the 60 percent of the city population that was black had failed to put candidates into local offices. Because minority bloc voting was not proved, the court held in favor of the at-large system.[28]
- In Baytown, Texas, the city defended its at-large system stating that the minority population was not compact. The appeals court ruled against the city because minorities would be compact and populous enough if blacks and Hispanics were combined to create a single district.[29]
- In 1984, the Texas District Court determined that there was no possible district configuration that would allow Hispanics to have their own district and that to have equal participation in the political process, the Hispanics would need to form coalitions with other minority groups.[30] The *Gingles* compactness was not demonstrated and the plaintiff's claim failed.
- In 1989 in *Gunn v. Chickasaw County, Mississippi*, the court ruled that taking a county with a 36 percent black minority and distributing them in order to preclude any black district, was in violation of the Voting Rights Act. Evidence showed that there was extreme racial bias in voting and black candidates had nearly totally failed to gain office.

And so it went, in case after case across the South. *Gingles* gave definition to vote dilution, a prerequisite to seeking relief.

Some decisions brought into question the meaning of majority; the Supreme Court never defined the term. Plaintiffs frequently used a total-population base rather than voting-age statistics because they could more easily show the potential for a minority single-member district. The advantage of using total population stems from minorities groups having a high percentage of underage citizens. On the other hand, if minorities could easily demonstrate the possibility of a majority-minority district, they may choose to use voting-age statistics as a base in order to sufficiently pack the district with voters to ensure minority electoral success. Court decisions generally upheld the latter definition. In 1988, the Seventh Circuit Court wrote that the requirement from *Gingles* "roughly measures voters' potential to elect candidates of their choice. Because only minorities of voting age can affect this potential, it is logical to assume that the Court intended the majority requirement to mean voting-age majority."[31] In 1989, the 5th Circuit Court said, "[T]he need for voting-age population data, as opposed to total population data, in making the *Thornburg* analysis should be obvious."³² Obvious or not, in 1990 the California Appeals Court in *Garza v. the City of Los Angeles* stated that the total population, rather than the voting-age population needed to be the measure used. The city tried to point out that many Hispanics in the district were not citizens and should not count. The court ruled that counting only voters would deny aliens and minors their rights under the Constitution, and would amount to a denial of equal valued heritage.

By the end of the 1980s, immigration, continued white-flight, and higher minority birth rates began to make whites a minority in some major American cities. In *Whitfield v. Arkansas Democratic Party*, the appeals court declared that race or color as used in the Voting Rights Act applied only to traditionally disadvantaged groups. This sort of precept was necessary in order to avoid a virtual collapse of the effect of the act whenever the traditional minorities become the numerical majorities in a political entity. The appeals court recognized the act as a tool of affirmative action rather than merely a guarantee of rights.

The Supreme Court's suspicion about annexation surfaced again in 1982 in *Port Arthur v. U. S.* In order to annex property, Port Arthur, Texas had traded an all at-large system for a system of eight councilmen and a mayor wherein six councilmen were elected from wards while two councilmen and the mayor were elected citywide. Of the city's voting-age population, 35 percent were black while the city council was 44 percent black. Despite the success achieved by blacks under the new system, the court ruled that the majority vote requirement of the two at-large districts unlawfully discriminated against black candidates.³³

At-large systems became easier and easier to attack. In 1989, a Florida District Court stated that determining whether or not an at-large system diluted minority voting strength could be simply based on the fact that Starke, Florida was 31 percent black, but a black candidate had never been elected to city office.³⁴

In some cases even apparently successful results were examined to ensure that they really represented minority progress. In 1983, Hispanic plaintiffs in Corpus Christi, Texas successfully challenged a slating process that had resulted in the election of Hispanic candidates. The challenge contended that even though Hispanics were slated and elected, the slating process was Anglo controlled and the winning Hispanics were defeating other Hispanic candidates who were actually the choice of the minority community.³⁵ In a 1988 trial, although the number of black appellate court judges roughly reflected that percentage of black voters, black voters successfully launched a vote dilution suit contending that the current black judges were not the choices of black voters.[36]

Court Drawn Plans

During the 1980s, the courts were more aggressive than in the 1970s. They were much less likely to wait for redistricting resolutions from the next regular legislative session or to let an illegal election proceed. As plaintiffs successfully proved violations of the Voting Rights Act, the courts took swift and broad action. They declared elections illegal and called for special elections. In cases of vote dilution, they demanded redistricting plans or drafted their own.

Still, the courts did not usurp complete control. While courts could draft and enforce their own plans, they generally gave the election entity an opportunity to create a lawful plan. A court could not substitute what it considered an objectively superior plan for a constitutionally valid plan that the state proposed.[37] Thus the courts limited themselves in their ability to modify a legal government plan, albeit a suboptimal plan for minorities. Furthermore, if minority voters were not sufficiently numerous to constitute a majority in any voting district, the district court could not increase the number of districts in order to decrease the district size, but was limited to the number of seats and districts under the challenged plan.[38] However, any voting changes in areas having too few districts would be unlikely to pass preclearance by the Justice Department.

Safe Districts

Courts struggled with the careful packing of minority districts. Although disclaiming any rule-of-law, courts generally accepted a 65 percent supermajority. The number 65 came from a Mississippi case in 1977 in which the district court determined that 65 percent should be the supermajority number given the data for a particular Mississippi county.[39] The number consisted of a 50+ percent majority plus five points for the younger than average age of the minority population, five points for lower registration numbers, and five points for lower voter turnout.[40] Never was this number statistically supportable for the general case. Through misinterpretations of earlier cases, the 65 percent rule became enshrined in court wisdom and was espoused by some expert witnesses.[41] Both internal documentation and written correspondence from the Department of Justice referred to the 65 percent "rule-of-thumb." The idea that minority voters could not be depended upon to show up at the polls in the same numbers as whites was compensated for in the preclearance procedures. It became routine for the Section 5 procedure to fail to recognize a minority district without a 65 percent majority. Jurisdictions showing historically high minority turnout made little difference; the 65-percent-rule was still applied.

Supporting the need for a supermajority, some gap still existed between black and white registration in the South. Black registration had grown tremendously between 1965 and 1970. After 1970, despite the absence of any significant barriers to registration, progress was slow. Still, the gaps were small, as they had been for ten years. By 1988, Louisiana black registration actually outstripped whites.

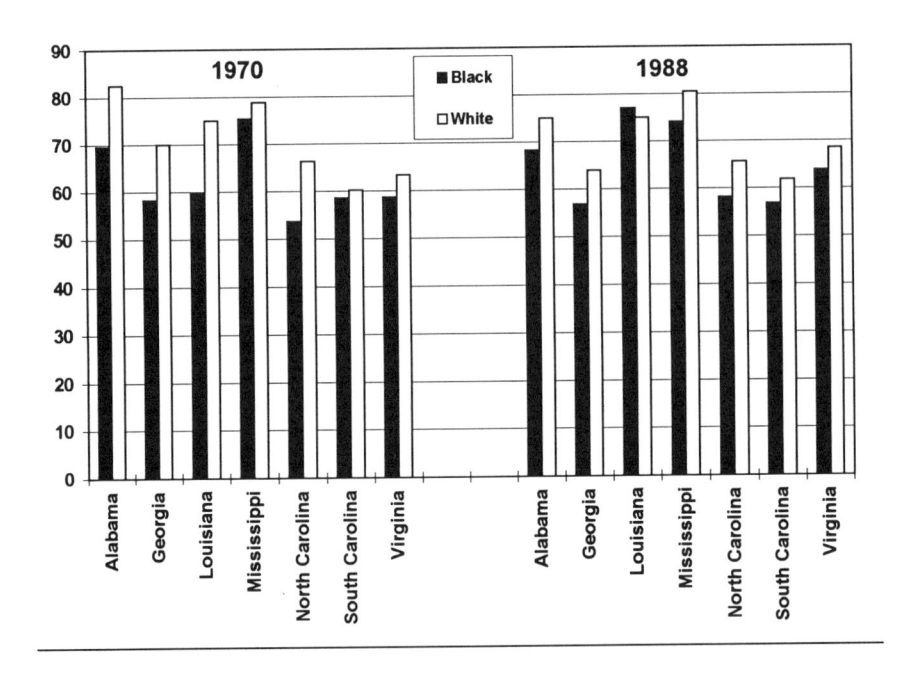

FIGURE 10: REGISTRATION IN THE SOUTH, 1970 AND 1988[42]

However, the case was different for Hispanics. By the 1988 election, Hispanics were turning out in lower proportions than in 1976. This was a result of a larger percentage of non-citizen Hispanics caused by high immigration and low naturalization. Hispanic leaders claimed that low turnout rates were the result of discrimination. The alleged discrimination was then used to justify the creation of safe districts. Legislative seats are apportioned by a count of the entire population, citizen or non-citizen. Hispanic areas, because of their high alien rate, were given more legislative seats, then were compensated with safe districts in order to gain control of those districts.[43] Courts then supported the "equal value of all citizens" espoused in *Garza* while stacking the deck with carefully packed districts.[44] The Supreme Court refused to hear cases that challenged using the gross population for determining equal districts dictated by the one-man, one-vote rule.

Again supporting the "safe" district concept, in 1988 an Arkansas District Court approved a plan that divided a two member state legislative district into two single-member districts. One of these districts had a 65 percent black population while the other had 16 percent. There was no convincing evidence in these districts of low voter registration or low participation.[45] Nonetheless, the court accepted the plan pursuant to the well-documented national pattern of lower minority registration and voter turnout. Affirmative action rather then the realities of the case, guided the court.

It is a fine line between the percentages that make a district *safe* and the percentages that bring on the accusation of *packing*, that is, clustering the minority vote so that it will have minimum impact on the remaining election districts. In case after case, the attorney general denied preclearance where the minority percentage rose much above 65 percent. When high percentages were permitted, the courts did so specifically to recognize minority interests. For example, in 1986 the Massachusetts Appeals Court determined that the 82 percent majority figure in a district was not "packing" because it could reflect the lessened degree to which minority voters had similar voting preferences or the lessened degree to which they voted as a bloc.[46] Loosely applying the *Gingles* factors, the judge adopted an affirmative action position Stretching the "safe" level to accommodate varying levels of voting polarity represents one of the greatest racial injustices dealt by the courts. The logic of such a judgment argues that minorities who do not vote in stereotypical patterns, cannot be counted as true minorities. They are, in essence, packed with whites into districts with 65 percent stereotypical minority voters.

There were other exceptions to the 65 percent rule of thumb. A 1988 judgment coming from a Louisiana District Court stated that remedying prior vote dilution with a "safe" district containing a supermajority was not warranted nor was the establishment of a single member district with a majority of black voters.[47] Similarly, in 1987 the appeals court in Louisiana allowed a redistricting plan with three black-majority districts, three white-majority districts, and one roughly equal district having 52 percent white and 48 percent black voters. Although it could have been worked statistically, the plaintiffs had failed to convince the court that the seventh district should be a "safe" district.[48]

Other Developments

In the 1982 Indiana legislative elections, Democrats gained only 43 percent of the seats despite garnering 52 percent of the votes. They claimed their failure to gain more seats was caused by the districting plan that included a mixture of single-member and multi-member districts. Their suit resulted in a district court order to redraw the district lines. The Supreme Court did not support the district court decision, but instead shattered new ground by declaring, for the first time, that political parties can have justiciable claims under the Equal Protection Clause. Justice White stated that a claim submitted by a political group rather than a racial group does not distinguish it in terms of justiciability. Justices Sandra Day O'Connor, Warren Burger, and William Rehnquist dissented questioning what standard could be applied to groups making such claims. Justice O'Connor claimed there was a great difference between racial groups with "immutable characteristics" and political groups whose members can vote for both parties or can change from one party to another.[49]

The next year, the Supreme Court heard *Karcher v. Daggett* in which a New Jersey legislative plan created 14 districts which varied in population, from the largest to the smallest, by only .7 percent. The district was challenged on the grounds that the state had no legitimate interest that justified even that small deviation. The state argued that such a small deviation was irrelevant and was in fact smaller than the estimated undercount of the 1980 census. The court ruled for the plaintiffs stating that "districts be apportioned to achieve population equality as nearly as practicable" and that such a standard was "inconsistent with adoption of fixed numerical standards which excuse population variances with regard to the circumstances in each particular case."[50] This decision was consistent with *Kirkpatrick v. Preisler* (1969), but applied the deviation standards even more rigorously.

The authority of the act over the election of judges long perplexed the courts. In 1988, black voters in Georgia claimed that the judicial-election mechanism was discriminatory, pointing out that only five of 135 justices were black. A federal district court agreed that the system discriminated through the use of at-large elections with majority voting requirements and named places.[51] In Texas, black and Hispanic voters challenged the at-large judicial system employed in many of Texas' metropolitan areas. There too, the federal district court agreed that the elections were governed by the Voting Rights Act. The Fifth Circuit Court, however, held by a slim margin that judicial elections were not covered because judges "do not represent people, they serve the people," and the act only guarantees equal opportunity to elect representatives. The issue escalated to the Supreme Court, who, without even hearing the arguments, affirmed that the act covered judicial elections.[52] In another case, *Chisom v. Roemer*, the Supreme Court held that the results test of Section 2 applied to judicial elections. Justice Stevens wrote the majority opinion stating that Congress would have explicitly excluded justices from the act if that were its intent. Justices Rehnquist, Kennedy, and Scalia disagreed arguing, "There were an endless number of things that Congress did not exclude in the act, but to conclude that those things were therefore included was insupportable logic."[53]

Although not new with the 1982 Amendments, the one-man, one vote concept was applied ever more broadly. In 1989, the Supreme Court, in *Board of Estimate of City of New York v. Morris*, declared unconstitutional the electoral makeup of the New York Board of Estimate. The board consisted of three members elected citywide plus the presidents of the city's five boroughs. The residents of Brooklyn, the city's most populous borough, brought suit because their votes carried less weight than the votes of residents of smaller boroughs. Even though the city had legitimate interests—"that the board is essential to the successful government of New York City, is effective, and accommodates natural and political boundaries as well as local interests"—those interests were insufficient to permit large to small district population deviations of 78 percent. The city claimed that borough presidents were not elected to this board and that the board was not legislative, thus not subject to the one-man, one-vote rule. The court disagreed pointing out that the board assisted in the construction of the city budget, the control of land use, contracting, and franchising and were therefore representatives of the voters. Thus, New York was no longer allowed to use boroughs as the basis of board representation.

The legality of state registration procedures was tested in 1991. A Maryland statute required that voters who had not voted for the previous five years would be removed from the rolls. The plaintiffs pursued logic contending that their right to vote included their right not to vote. They claimed that they were victims of discrimination because they were canceled from the voting roles just because they had exercised their right not to vote. The judge dismissed their claim asserting that they could easily exercise their right not to vote whether they were registered or not. He further held that there was a legitimate state interest to employ reasonable administrative procedures to protect against voter fraud.[54]

Although authors of the 1982 Amendments expected an onslaught of bail-out requests, only Alaska filed for relief and that attempt never came to trial.[55] No other attempts came during the ten years after the passage of the new bail-out provisions. Jurisdictions that might have qualified viewed the costs and risks higher than the benefits.

In February 1991, the Supreme Count let stand a circuit court ruling that the Voting Rights Act does not prohibit runoff elections in a county where a minority of the registered voters are black. Plaintiff included two black Arkansas residents who each gained the most votes in a primary election, then were defeated by whites in a runoff. Part of the state's defense was that the runoff rule could not have been designed to discriminate because it was passed in 1938 before blacks were allowed to vote in the Arkansas primary. Arkansas remained one of eight states with a runoff requirement for primaries.[56]

In June 1992, the Supreme Court ruled on a state's right to prohibit write-in votes. The court voted 6-3 to support Hawaii, Nevada, Oklahoma, and South Dakota prohibitions. Justice Byron White, writing for the court majority, said Hawaii's ban was a "very limited" intrusion on voting rights. This limited burden is outweighed by the state's interest in averting write-in campaigns for people who lost in primaries, failed to file in time or never intended to run. Moreover, he contended, a state cannot be required to count protest votes for Donald Duck or some other non-candidate.

In hopes of expanding franchise, even homeless people were the subject of legislation. In December 1992, Republican Governor Jim Edgar of Illinois signed legislation removing the requirement for a permanent residence address for voters. The legislation permitted the voter to list a shelter, soup kitchen, or drop-in program as a residence.[57]

Changing Demographics

A brief review of the changing demographics of the United States illustrates the growing importance of racial and ethnic data. In 1977 the

Office of Management and Budget issued *Directive No. 15* which established minimum standards for reporting race and ethnicity information. It recognized only four races and two ethnic groups. The races were American Indian or Alaskan Native, Asian or Pacific Islander, black, and white. The ethnic groups were simply Hispanic and non-Hispanic.[58] The 1990 census showed a considerable increase in minorities compared to 1980. By race, the population comprised 80 percent whites, 12 percent blacks, three percent Asians, and one percent Indians. By ethnicity, the population was nine percent Hispanic and 91 percent non-Hispanic. Of the Hispanics, 60 percent were of Mexican origin, 12 percent Puerto Rican, five percent Cuban, and 23 percent all others. Interestingly, the black population percentages actually decreased in every southern state except Texas between 1960 and the late 1980s.[59]

Between 1980 and 1990 the Asian and Pacific Islander population had increased by 105 percent, whereas Hispanics increased by 53 percent, and American Indians, Eskimos and Aleuts grew by 38 percent. In contrast, blacks grew 13 percent and whites only 6 percent. The white population, some of whom were Hispanic, dipped to the lowest percentage since the first population census taken in 1790. Census data leads to the prediction that Hispanics will outnumber blacks sometime between 2010 and 2020.[60] Projections indicate that by the year 2050, America will be home to 392 million people—almost evenly divided between non-Hispanic whites and minorities.

Voting Rights Language Assistance Act of 1992[61]

In 1992 the language assistance provisions of the Voting Rights Act were scheduled to expire. These provision provided that political subdivisions must provide multilingual voting material in areas where five percent or more of the voting age population derived from a recognized language minority.[62] The 1982 Amendments made it more difficult for minority language communities to qualify because of an added provision requiring the community be generally unable to speak English. This additional qualification cut to nearly half the number of counties that qualified for language assistance. To determine a community's English proficiency, the Census Bureau sent 17 percent of the residents the "long form" which allowed them to categorize their ability to speak English as "Very Well," "Well," "Not Well," or "Not at All." Assuming that people overrated their English skills, the Census Bureau deemed any response other than "Very Well" to be English-illiterate. Thus, counties that lost their language assistance status only did so because most of the minorities claimed to speak English "Very Well." Democrats held the presidency and controlled the Congress. Immigrants generally favored Democrats, so Congress drafted the 1992 Language Assistance Act to do two things: it extended the language provisions for an additional 15 years and it added additional language minorities to the coverage. The 15-year extension brought the language provisions into parallel timing with the other special provisions. This legislation changed the five percent rule for mandatory coverage to a numerical count of 10,000 people. The additional coverage provided was more complex because it attempted to target specific city and regional problems. The bill also introduced a new, politically-correct term—*limited-English proficient* or LEP.

The new benchmark brought 38 new communities under the coverage of the act. This rule not only increased the number of covered Hispanics and Native Americans, it also added new language groups to the coverage. For example, under the new legislation Los Angeles had to provide assistance in Hispanic, Chinese, Filipinos, Japanese, and Vietnamese. Sixty-two election districts began receiving Chinese ballots in New York City alone.

Other provisions involved Native Americans. Many reservations do not follow state or county lines, thus they do not align with political subdivisions when applying the five percent test. Framers of this legislation wanted Native Americans covered, so the amendment provided coverage to residents of a reservation if five percent of the voting-age residents on that reservation were LEP. The whole reservation was included in the calculation, no matter how small a portion was included in the political subdivision conducting the election. The bill even redefined the term reservation to include certain areas of Indian and Native Alaskan population despite the fact that they were not on a reservation.

The familiar argument asserting that the job was not yet complete spearheaded the passage of the amendments. Much of the argument presented by the House Subcommittee on Civil and Constitutional Rights concerned itself with the allegedly poor education that language minorities receive in the United States. Because the English education was inadequate, the need to provide assistance existed.

The arguments against the amendments were presented by Henry Hyde and seven other Congressmen. Their argument centered on constitutional law. They claimed that the Congress had no right to expand federal intervention into a state election process without a constitutional interest to protect. Further, even if there were a constitutional interest to protect, the Congress' actions must reasonably be expected to solve the problem.

Opponents argued that there was no evidence "of widespread discrimination in voting [or] unremitting attempts by state and local officials to frustrate citizens in their equal enjoyment of the right to vote." Assistant Attorney General Dunne reported that his department had heard no widespread complaints of voting discrimination in areas to which the bill would be expanded.

Hyde went on to argue that even the current legislation was ineffective and should not be extended or expanded. He suggested that the 1982 Amendments had not increased voter registration or voter participation. In fact, the gap between white and Hispanic voting had actually widened slightly. Given that the problem had not significantly expanded and that the solution was ineffective, opponents believed that the legislation was unconstitutional.

The committee argument ended in a lengthy plea against fostering a multi-language society. They quoted Arthur M. Schlesinger, Jr.

> Nonetheless, a common language is a necessary band of national cohesion in so heterogeneous a nation as America. Institutionalized bilingualism remains another source of the fragmentation of America, another threat against the dream of *one people*.[63]

Such was the conservative argument. Both sides had presented what had become hallmark of their defense. Conservative Republicans argued to preserve the America that had become the strongest nation on earth. They longed for an America in which the entrants adapted to the nation rather than one in which the nation adapts, little by little, to the new entrants. Liberal Democrats, on the other hand, forged forward on general principals of goodness, addressing the perceived needs of the poor and oppressed.

The bill passed the House in July and the Senate in early August, in time to provide continuous coverage.

Democrats quickly recognized that non-English-speaking immigrants generally vote Democrat. English skills, a requirement for naturalization since 1906, are now ignored. The year after passage of the Language Assistance Act, the Clinton administration conducted the first citizenship ceremony conducted in a language other than English. They boasted that there would be more such ceremonies until a congressional protest forced them to back down.[64]

Motor Voter Bill

In the early 1980s, activists Richard Cloward and Frances Fox Piven began work to counter President Reagan's attack on the welfare state.

Recognizing that nearly 40 percent of the voting age population was not registered, they believed that universal registration would likely contribute many more votes to liberal causes than conservative ones. Their initial strategy was to employ the energies of the nation's social workers to warn clients about social program cuts and distribute voter registration forms. They reasoned that social workers would be motivated because their jobs hinged on the funding of these programs. Cloward and Piven formed *Human SERVE* to promote their program.

Their movement never materialized because of the sheer size of the welfare program and the incalculable number of agencies that needed to participate. Human SERVE then began to shift its emphasis from mobilization of the social sector to advocating universal voter registration. They assisted governors and mayors in creating voter registration assistance programs tied to the doling out of government services. Among these were liberal Democrats like Mario Cuomo in New York and Richard Celeste in Ohio, who had won office in 1982 as a result of a surge in voter participation among the poor.[65]

"Motor Voter" was a concept that came from the Michigan Secretary of State who combined the voter registration and drivers license applications functions. Human SERVE latched onto the move, recognizing that 90 percent of America's voting age citizens had drivers licenses.

In January 1993, Bill Clinton assumed the presidency by garnering only 43 percent of the popular vote. He captured nearly all of the black votes making Martin Luther King's prediction again come true: blacks had swung the election. Congress rapidly pushed new voting legislation through committees and presented the *National Voter Registration Act of 1993* to the President on May 18. Better known as Motor Voter, the act required states to institute additional voting procedures for federal elections. These procedures required the state welfare and driver's license applications and renewal forms to double as voter registration applications. Further, it required all states to accept a mail-in registration form designed by the Federal Elections Commission. States were forbidden to ask for notarization or any other formal authentication of the voter's identify or eligibility to vote.[66]

With Cloward and Piven standing behind him, the President signed the measure on May 20 on the south lawn of the White House after playing a tape of Lyndon Johnson's 1965 remarks on signing the Voting Rights Act. Clinton said, "Voting should be about discerning the will of the majority, not about testing the administrative capacity of a citizen." It seemed as though this were a triumph, but Clinton failed to acknowledge that the triumph occurred years earlier as prerequisites disappeared, as literacy tests were abolished, as registration drives began to take place in shopping malls. Nor did he note that the 35 percent of the voting age public who failed to register had little interest in voting as demonstrated by their lack of commitment to the system. In every state, the initial acquisition of a driver's license is a far greater administrative burden than voter registration, usually involving written and physical-skills tests. Clinton closed his remarks thanking Congress and supporting organizations, then he specifically noted the contribution of the "young people, the activists [and] MTV."[67]

The bill made its registration procedure mandatory on the states by January 1, 1995. As of that date, California, Illinois, Michigan, Pennsylvania, and South Carolina had not implemented procedures. California and South Carolina openly defied the federal government's right to impose such legislation on the states without adequate federal funds to implement it. Attorney General Janet Reno filed suit against these states[68] as did the ACLU, the League of Women Voters and others.[69] In July, the Ninth Circuit Court ruled that California had to move forward to implement the law.[70]

Many issues are raised by Motor Voter. On the plus side for democracy is the notion that easier registration produces more voters on election day. Human SERVE claims that the new procedures registered 20% of the previously unregistered voters during the bill's first year.[71] However, considerable registration occurs each year as people move from place to place. New registrants, who previously used the voting registrars to sign up, my have found the motor vehicle department or other agency more convenient. It is unknown whether these new processes are responsible for a large number of new registrants, or whether much of the registration would have occurred anyway. Furthermore, significant nationwide increases in voting have not appeared since 1992, so there is only anecdotal evidence that the bill will have a great affect on democracy. Nonetheless, the potential for expanded democracy might justify this law if there were no negatives to outweigh this benefit.

There are, however, detracting issues. It does indeed add cost to each state budget to administer yet another set of voter registration procedures. Also, there is fraud. Clearly Motor Voter was not enacted to ease the burden on the voting public. It was promoted and enacted on behalf of groups that were under-registered, namely, the poor and ethnic minorities. Although the potential for voter fraud often appears as a scapegoat behind which to hide class and racial concern, fraud does, nonetheless, exist. There are some genuine reasons for concern about the integrity of the voting system and any new fraud opportunities brought about by Motor Voter. Absentee, mail-in ballots have been the vehicle used in fraud cases in Philadelphia,

Pennsylvania; Venice, California; Laredo, Texas; and elsewhere. Campaign workers have taken ballots into low income, low-turnout areas and convinced voters to vote absentee while influencing their electoral selection. False registrations are a problem in California where lax registration laws have allowed mail-in registration with no ID or proof of citizenship. Motor Voter opens the door to this type of fraud.[72]

Dallas: From White Control to Black Mayor

It depends on whether you like Rembrandt or Picasso. Don't try to understand it, just live with it.

—— *Bob Greer, the federal court's expert on redistricting describing Dallas district lines.*[73]

The early years following the 1982 Amendments saw continued economic boom for Dallas. Not since Neiman and Marcus built their first store had development been more apparent. In 1983 and 1984, 29.3 million square feet of new office space were erected—an amount equivalent to all of the office space in Miami.[74]

Blacks continued to break racial barriers. Larry Baraka became the first black state district judge. John Wiley Price became a Dallas County Commissioner, and Diane Ragsdale and Al Lipscomb were elected to the city council. The council appointed a black city manager—a move impossible a few years earlier.

With its new emphasis on city politics rather than city business, the nature of the council began to change. Members were no longer part time advisors concerned with city investment and prosperity. They now worked long hours, had staffs, and debated police-citizen relations, investments in South Africa, redistricting plans, and opportunities for minorities.[75] Contrasting the upbeat economic climate, racial strife appeared daily in Dallas politics. Mayor Starke Taylor expelled activist Roy Williams—soon to become the cardinal player in districting reform—from the city council chambers after Williams accused Taylor of creating a racial climate. Council meetings became shouting matches. Newspaper columnist Henry Tatum described the mood created by Councilwoman Elsie Faye Heggins:

"Never in the history of municipal government have so many racial connotations been attached to so many city issues. If a consultant needed to be hired to review a serious city problem, she [Heggins] wanted to know how many minorities were on its staff. If Dallas officers shot and killed a black suspect, she publicly aired rumors that the shootings were unjustified, that officers were 'trigger happy' and more willing to shoot blacks."[76]

In July 1986, a highly diverse group of Hispanics met in an SMU auditorium to discuss their frustration over the unelectability of Hispanic candidates. Only three Hispanics had ever been elected to the Dallas City Council. The group sowed the seed for a lawsuit seeking new electoral districts. René Martinez, executive of a large Dallas department store and an officer of MALDEF, a likely sponsor of any litigation, suggested converting the two at-large seats to single-member-district seats. Such action would have reduced the district size from 118,000 to 94,000 giving Hispanics a better shot at a majority-minority district. With only 150,000 Mexican-Americans living in Dallas, it had been impossible to create a safe district for them. Hispanics had been successful in integrating into Dallas communities rather than being driven into ghettos as had blacks, but this social success played against their group political power. Strength was also eroded by the fact that only one-third of Hispanics were registered to vote and a small fraction of these actually went to the polls. Furthermore, many Hispanics were ineligible to vote, averaging age 20 in contrast to age 28 for the city as a whole.[77]

Dallas' Hispanics struggle to discover power was part of a nationwide phenomenon which suffered from a lack of understanding of who was even Hispanic. In Miami, it usually meant Cuban descendants. Other than language, Cubans and Mexicans had little in common. Hispanics widely disliked the word *Latinos*, the term used by the EEOC. Oliver A. Ferres, Consul General of Mexico, said it included everyone, even Italians. He preferred *Hispanics* which made René Martinez cringe. "That's a word the U. S. census bureau made up to include everyone who speaks Spanish. We are Mexican or Chicanos." Others viewed the word *Chicano* as derogatory slang.[78] And so it went.

As the districting controversy brewed, white-flight continued from Dallas Schools. More than half of the 1987 student population was black with the remainder split between whites and Hispanics. Despite the demographics, federal supervision of school desegregation continued. When white trustees joined one Hispanic trustee in asking the court to end the 15-year-old lawsuit, new accusations of racism appeared.

Amidst the turmoil, black leaders came together and selected Marvin Robinson as an at-large candidate for the city council. Robinson was a well-educated, successful, black business executive and was active in civic and community affairs. Supporters tried to raise the $150,000 that would be required for the campaign, but Robinson raised only $15,000 and borrowed another $15,000. He lost to white candidate Jerry Rucker who had raised the $150,000.[79]

By 1987, the pressure against the city council structure intensified. Activists on the council, like Diane Ragsdale and Al Lipscomb, missed few opportunities to talk about inequality. They complained that council members still made $50 a meeting and shared a staff with the city manager. Ragsdale, a nurse who had been involved in civil rights since childhood, hired aids to draft legislation advocating a system that paid a decent wage. She said, "The system serves the wealthy few very well because it excludes the working class from running for public office." Ragsdale claimed her mother had to help her because of her modest salaries from nursing and the city council.[80]

The council had diverse opinions about the remaining at-large districts. The Mayor, Annette Strauss, was a white female who had won the mayors seat in a runoff election by garnering nearly all of the black vote. Still, she was concerned about the idea of having fewer at-large seats. She was willing, however, to support an opinion referendum on the subject.[81] Ragsdale and Lipscomb pushed for all single-member districts while others on the council vacillated. Minorities might have been better off with all at-large positions. During the next decade, it was certain that Dallas would be a majority-minority city, in which case, single-member districts might lessen minority power. Besides, at-large council positions were not unusual. Many cities, including New York, San Diego, Boston, Phoenix, San Francisco, Seattle, Pittsburgh, El Paso, Fort Worth, Austin, Miami, and Tucson, still had all at-large districting.[82]

On May 18, 1988, Roy Williams and Marvin Crenshaw filed suit against the City of Dallas asserting that the current election system was unfair and needed to be replaced by a single-member, eleven-district system. Judge Jerry Buchmeyer was chosen by lottery to hear the case. The suit claimed that the city used its eight single-member districts to pack and cluster black votes into two areas—the Fair Park area represented by Diane Ragsdale and the South Oak Cliff area represented by Al Lipscomb.

Roy Williams, a six-foot-six, forty-seven-year-old black, was a self-employed Dallas businessman who had run for city council but had been defeated by a white candidate in an at-large race. He had been found guilty of driving while intoxicated three times, but later claimed to have had a spiritual awakening which led him into counseling others for substance abuse. He lived in a north Dallas condominium, ate at the French bakery near SMU, and toted a book bag filled with books on spiritualism and philosophy. Williams described himself as a spiritualist who meditated five hours a day, and claimed he had begun fasting to focus his attention on the trial. "This is a pinnacle in my life. My life will never be the same. This is a landmark decision."

Marvin Crenshaw was a sometimes private investigator and an unsuccessful candidate for mayor. He mowed lawns, but said his real occupation was "lobbyist for justice." Crenshaw lived in South Oak Cliff with his parents. In the 1970s be became heavily involved in gambling and, in 1973, he joined the Black Panthers and was an activist helping form several black interest groups. Two years earlier, Mayor Strauss had paid his tuition at UTD where he studied history.

Both Crenshaw and Williams had called city council members racists. Security guards had escorted them to their seats for overrunning allotted speaking time. After repeated badgering, they forced a council resolution denying city business to South African companies.[83]

Judge Buchmeyer had a history of liberal decisions and had already presided over several racial cases in Dallas, most notably a suit over discrimination by the Dallas Housing Authority. That suit had been settled in 1981, but, five years later, Buchmeyer would reopen it. Although everyone believed that he would remove the federal court from supervision of the case, he ruled that blacks were still victims of discrimination despite the fact that 88 percent of the residents admitted to public housing since 1987 were black.[84] In the same year, Buchmeyer would declare unconstitutional the teen curfew passed by the city council despite the city's attempts to address the issues that had led to such ordinances being unconstitutional in other cities. The Supreme Court ultimately overruled him.

Already facing a lawsuit from blacks, the establishment tried to avoid Hispanic litigation by making another attempt to deal with their concerns. The business community backed Al Gonzalez for city council. Although he admitted that his presence on the council was doing something for the Hispanic community, Gonzalez specifically said he was not running on an Hispanic platform. His presence did do something; newly recruited Hispanics were now as committed as blacks. They aligned their efforts in The Ledbetter Homeowners Association and filed a motion with Judge Buchmeyer to join Williams and Crenshaw in the suit. The group was financed by the Houston based Texas Rural Legal Foundation and San Antonio's Southwest Voter Registration Education Project.[85] In August, Buchmeyer granted them status as intervenors.

With the citizenry polarized in three directions—the mostly white establishment, blacks and Hispanics—economic fortunes of Dallas turned upside-down. What had been a downtown of cranes and new construction, was now a metropolis of empty buildings and a declining tax base. All of the major department store chains except Neiman-Marcus left downtown. Not a single movie theater remained. Homeless people wandered the streets using the public library as their headquarters.[86]

Racial incidents tightened tensions. In 1988 two white policemen were shot. In response to racial stress, Mayor Strauss created the *Dallas Together Commission*. The commission gleaned testimony from eight members of the council including the mayor. Six said the 8-3 system was fair or equitable. *Dallas Together*, however, concluded that the system was unfair. They said it was urgent to appoint a Charter Review Committee to review the need for redistricting.[87] The mayor responded by appointing a 14-member Charter Review Commission (CRC) headed by Ray Hutcheson.

The CRC had quite a time of it. Hutcheson favored a 10-4-1 system comprised of 10 single-member districts, four superdistricts dividing the city into quadrants, and a mayoral position elected at-large. The CRC held 26 public meetings. Pettis Norman, a black, Oak Cliff resident, and former member of the Dallas Cowboys, co-chaired the committee. He tried to speed things along by calling a separate meeting of minority leaders. That meeting generally favored a 12-1 plan although Norman preferred a 12-2-1 plan. Hutcheson took great exception to Norman's independent actions and created such friction that Norman asked for a ten-day cooling off period.[88]

Three weeks later, Hutcheson called another meeting which ended in disaster. Lipscomb and Ragsdale called Norman an Uncle Tom and suggested to the only Asian on the commission that Asians did not have the courage to stay home and fight communism. Only four members, including Lipscomb and Ragsdale, refused to support the 10-4-1 compromise, a plan that guaranteed three safe black districts and one safe black quadrant.

Bernice Washington, a black north Dallas civic leader appeared before the council and sang "We shall overcome." Twenty-four men and women swayed and joined hands singing as the council voted 7 to 4 to put 10-4-1 before the citizens on the August ballot. Brochures said that 10-4-1 would increase minority representation, allow the citizens to choose their form of government, protect the neighborhoods of Oak Cliff and Pleasant Grove and allow more citizens to participate in government.[89]

Testimony in the *Williams* trial exposed Judge Buchmeyer's general sympathy with the plaintiffs. Plaintiff's experts testified that there was racial bloc voting in the city. The city's expert, Professor Delbert Taebel, said the case was not conclusive. He cited the fact that many blacks had sided with Annette Strauss rather than Marvin Crenshaw during the last two mayoral elections. Buchmeyer amazingly concluded that blacks would have voted for

Crenshaw if he had had the money to run a credible campaign. From that speculation, he dismissed the city's expert's testimony. The city argued that the four regional members in a 10-4-1 system would have a broader perspective than single-member-district representatives and that each citizen would have two council members to call on rather than one. Buchmeyer wrote that that argument "should not be tossed away lightly; it should be thrown away with great force."[90]

In August 1989, voters approved 10-4-1. It was overwhelmingly approved by whites and generally disapproved by minorities. The vote divided rather than united the electorate. One hundred people showed up for a civil disobedience workshop led by civil rights leaders from Atlanta. The SCLC in Atlanta called for major civil disobedience in Dallas and it was not just because of 10-4-1. The SCLC campaign reflected frustration with a series of police shootings, the defeat of a ballot proposal for a stronger Citizens Police Review Board, and the perceived lack of economic opportunities for blacks and Hispanics.[91]

The hearing ended in September 1989, but Buchmeyer needed a few months to rule on the case. The next month the Justice Department refused to clear the 10-4-1 plan because it had not been submitted with the district lines drawn. The city could have tried the case in the D. C. District Court. Instead the council chose to wait for Buchmeyer's decision since he had the power to declare the plan constitutional.[92]

In March 1990, Buchmeyer produced 248 pages of text in his decision. He concluded the following:

> Under the system (8-3), African Americans and Hispanics are denied access to the three at-large seats because they cannot raise from their communities the amount of money required for an effective citywide campaign; moreover, under the system, blacks have been unfairly prohibited from electing more than two single-district council members by the *packing* of African-Americans into two districts with 75 to 87 percent [voting] concentration and 85 to 91 percent total minority population and by *cracking* the remaining African-American population in Dallas between two districts to prevent the creation of a third black district. . . . [M]any of the at-large members of the council—almost all of whom were from North Dallas—had not provided any citywide view. Instead, they simply ignored the minority areas of the city and represented the interests of North Dallas that contributed the money for the at-large races.[93]

The Judge filled more than 100 pages trying to apply the *Gingles* test and most of the *Zimmer* factors. Because Buchmeyer had also been the judge in the Dallas housing case, he went into great depth on housing issues. He gave many quotes to support his findings without crediting his sources. Buchmeyer ruled that the existing 8-3 plan was illegal. Since the trial was not about the 10-4-1 plan, he could not say that it was illegal unless it was offered as a settlement.

With the judgment in, debate ceased and pure city politics took over. Unless the city created a new plan within 30 days, Buchmeyer threatened to make his own. Most council members believed enough was enough and thought they should comply. Council members Glen Box, Jerry Bartos, and Harriet Miers would not rule out an appeal. Box and Bartos believed that no redistricting should take place until the compilation of the 1990 census was complete in 1991. By March, Box and Bartos had convinced the majority of the council to appeal. Buchmeyer replied to the request to wait for the 1990 census data by saying, "In no way will this court tell the African Americans and Hispanics that they must wait any longer for their new voting rights."

Glenn Box became the beacon for 10-4-1. Box was 32 and still fresh in his legal career. At age nine, he had nailed up signs for Republican Congressman Jim Collins. His mother, Alma Box, was president of the Dallas County Council of Republican Women.[94] Box had strong opinions about the power of the Judiciary and specifically the power of Buchmeyer. "A judge ought to apply the law and not make the law. I have a real problems with judges that see statutes and the Constitution as malleable documents which they can use to achieve their own particular political ends."[95]

Lipscomb led the opposition to the city's appeal of Buchmeyer's decision. He complained, "The unmitigated arrogance. [Buchmeyer] was nice enough to give us thirty days to fix our house. For someone to have the unprecedented gall to try to impede or circumvent this man's ruling just won't work."[96]

Still, Dallas leaders were faced with the dilemma that the majority of voters supported 10-4-1. Buchmeyer had not ruled on 10-4-1, but stated that it appeared inadequate to him. Council members were torn between their own beliefs, their pragmatic view of alternatives, and their obligation to uphold the city charter. The city council agreed that there was virtue in being prepared and instructed city attorneys to draw up a 14-1 plan.

In late April, the council finally agreed on a 12-1 plan. Although there was considerable dissension among the ranks, the majority realized that 12-1 would probably pass federal scrutiny, would increase minority representation, and would keep major Dallas neighborhoods intact. Because the plan did not create a safe Hispanic district, a lawyer for Hispanics, Domingo Garcia, responded, "It's unfortunate we once again have to ask a federal judge to tell the city council to follow the Voting Rights Act, to follow the Constitution, to

THE AMENDMENTS OF 1982   169

follow the law. Seems like this thing never ends."[97] Garcia and his co-counsel Bill Garrett wanted voters to believe that the Voting Rights Act guaranteed each minority a seat on the council.

Councilmen from the southern half of the city, where most of the racial gerrymandering would occur, were unhappy. Councilman Charles Tandy said, "The plan just adds to the long held adage that it's okay to do what's necessary as long as you can do it in the southern half of the town—and not to those who are privileged to live in the north." Councilman Jim Buerger said, "it's a non-plan that alienated half of the city." Even the plaintiff, Roy Williams, was not satisfied. "Their choice of 12-1 shows that they continue to make decisions that hurt minorities."[98] The debate about waiting for the 1990 census continued until Buchmeyer ordered the city to set a plan for elections by May 25, 1990. Council members who wanted to use the 1990 census, did not expect census data to be available before April 1991.

Ignoring Buchmeyer's order, on May 25 Dallas submitted its 12-1 plan to the Justice Department along with a planned election date of January 1991. Documentation included 3,500 pages bound in 14 volumes. Within a month, however, Justice asked for more information. The city attorney said it was one of the most extensive requests that she had ever seen.[99] Among other documentation, the attorney general asked the city to provide notes, tapes or transcripts of all meeting or hearings, whether formal or informal, public or non-public, relative to redistricting; describe all of the redistricting plans that the city reviewed, how each plan originated and why each alternative was rejected; and submit copies of all articles, editorials, advertisements, and other publicity by print and broadcast media that address or describe the proposed changes and describe how the city publicized the proposed changes, including the steps taken by the city to ensure that the minority communities were made aware of the matter in which the proposed plan would distribute minority population among the districts.[100] Effectively, the Justice Department rebuffed the city's efforts by constructing a bureaucratic mountain. Ultimately, the city attorney responded.

During the summer of 1990, the council went around and around debating 12-1, 14-1, and 10-4-1. The debate jumped from protecting neighborhoods, to Hispanic rights, to the integrity of the citizens' 10-4-1 vote, to the need to have the lawsuit settled. Late that summer, the council negotiated with plaintiffs over a referendum to ask voters to approve a 14-1 plan. This seemingly simple idea was nit-picked. When would the elections be? What would members' salaries be? Would the city pay attorney's fees? How many terms could councilmen serve? Could the black incumbents start their term count over again? Where would the lines be drawn? How much would the city spend promoting 14-1?

Another seemingly endless debate ensued over staffing a committee to draw district lines. Heated arguments centered on whether or not the plaintiffs could be represented on the committee. Finally, it was agreed that the mayor would consult with the plaintiffs on two of the 15 seats. She would find one appointee acceptable to Hispanics and one acceptable to blacks.[101]

Many residents of the Oak Cliff community in southern Dallas had become disgruntled and frustrated at the political games that were taking place to divide their community into multiple districts. Oak Cliff was already ethnically divided, mostly between whites and blacks, but had managed to maintain a sense of community and pride of belonging. Reports compiled by Oak Cliff committees maintained that the southern half of Dallas had been disadvantaged in capital improvements since 1962. A report from the city government confirmed this finding. By the end of the summer of 1990, 21 committees of the Oak Cliff Chamber of Commerce were studying de-annexation.[102]

Ultimately, the council agreed to a referendum proposing the use of the 1990 census, a 14-1 districting plan, a November 1991 election, payment of attorney's fees, and a raise in councilmen's pay. The agreement also defined the 14 districts, five of which were at least 60 percent black and another 60 percent Hispanic. Voters were to be asked for their approval in December 1990.

The next battle in the ceaseless string of quibbling was over the formation of the committee charged to promote the 14-1 plan. Williams and Crenshaw wanted to pick their own co-chairman and have the city earmark $250,000 for the campaign. Instead, Mayor Strauss appointed former council member Al Gonzalez to chair the 14-1 committee.[103] Plaintiffs were skeptical and formed their own committee to press for votes in the southern half of the city.

In October, Glenn Box and his mother Alma Box hosted a dinner at which an anti-14-1 committee, *Just Say No to 14-1*, was formed.[104] The battle lines for public opinion were drawn.

Marvin Crenshaw appeared on a community forum radio talk show in October and indicated that there had been fighting within the black camp. He accused Al Lipscomb of offering him a $10,000 bribe not to file the lawsuit. The same day, the *Dallas Morning News* reported that Williams and Crenshaw accused Diane Ragsdale and Al Lipscomb of generally blocking settlement of the lawsuit.[105] When Crenshaw was asked about the $10,000 by the press, he said, "I really don't have any comment on it. The only comment

THE AMENDMENTS OF 1982   171

I have is that it's a family matter and we'll handle it inside the family. We'll resolve it that way." Asked what he meant by "family matter," he said, "I'm talking about the African-American community." Nonetheless, according to Williams, Lipscomb was so put off, he refused to voluntarily testify and had to be subpoenaed. Williams said, "All I can figure is that he wanted to file the suit, to be the one to go down in history as having his name on the suit that finally dismantled the 8-3 system."[106] Lipscomb could have filed the suit. Since his loss in the mayoral race of 1971, he had unsuccessfully launched low-budget campaigns for the commissioners court in 1972, the DISD board in 1974, and city council in 1973, 1975, and 1983.[107]

Dallas became a bouillabaisse of political campaigns. Some opposed and some supported 14-1. Some wanted Oak Cliff to secede, others did not. A committee for every possible position was quoted daily in the press. Roy Williams gathered a crowd of 100 people at Flips Wine Bar and Trattoria and belted out a rap tune:

> *14-1 government is our plan*
> *Representative government, yes we can*
> *Red, brown, black, yellow, white*
> *We have the ability, we have the right*[108]

Business leaders and Chambers of Commerce began endorsing 14-1. They mostly wanted the matter closed and life to go on. Religious leaders from all parts of town began to do the same.

Racial division was never higher in Dallas. John Wiley Price, a Dallas County Commissioner, staged a demonstration demanding the resignation of a Dallas police officer who jogged past Price's home and allegedly called out "Nigger." Price then struck the officer. Price admitted to having a pellet gun, but the officer accused him of holding an Uzi to his head. Earlier, Price had said that if the Police Chief was not hired from outside the city, he would urge constituents to shoot bothersome police officers. He later apologized.[109]

On November 17, more than 1000 people showed up at City Hall to support Price's actions. Later Williams said, "We saw a lot of pent-up frustration manifest itself in the demonstration for Commissioner John Wiley Price at City Hall this week. In the words of Malcolm X, it is the ballot or the bullet for Dallas. I'm hoping for the ballot."[110]

As the referendum neared, a public debate took place between Al Gonzalez, head of the 14-1 committee, and Tom Pauken, head of *Just Say No to 14-1*. Emotions were high as Gonzalez shouted, "How many times do you ever drive on the other side of the Trinity? [To South Dallas and Oak Cliff]

Do you think that North Dallas isn't any better off than South Dallas? Do you really think that in your heart? Do you really think it's fair? That's what this is about." Pauken responded, "The question is whether the 10-4-1 election was legal, and if it was, then why are we being asked to throw out the democratic process? This is not democracy."[111]

On November 30, Mayor Strauss cautioned voters that the Judge would impose his own plan if voters rejected 14-1. Opponents of the plan protested asking how she knew this. Had she had private discussions with Buchmeyer? If so, they would be illegal discussions. Strauss dismissed the matter saying that her statement was just a common assumption.[112] If it was a common assumption, it reflected what had become of the voters' power. They had two choices—vote with the Judge or be overruled by him.

On December 8, voters went to the polls to decide the fate of 14-1. They were asked to endorse one Hispanic and five black districts based on the 1990 census which no one had yet seen. Voters defeated the proposition by less than 400 votes. Ninety percent of blacks supported 14-1 while 71 percent of whites opposed it. Only 20 percent of the minorities voted. In a separate item, voters overwhelmingly rejected a salary increase for council members.

Roy Williams was expectedly bitter over the vote. He said that the vote indicated that "institutionalized racism is still alive and well in Dallas. It was designed to fail. They [city officials] really didn't have their hearts behind 14-1 and their lack of visibility in the minority community showed it."[113]

The city council had no choice but to again debate the merits of the 10-4-1 plan. No matter how slight the margin, the voters had spoken twice. Attention went back to the idea of four superdistricts. If Buchmeyer set the boundaries himself, the plan would be court-constructed and would not require preclearance, although the order could be appealed.[114]

After debating legal strategies, the city council decided to submit to Buchmeyer a 10-4-1 plan with elections in November 1991 based on 1990 census data. Members also instructed lawyers to withdraw the 12-1 plan from the attorney general.[115] The council then set out to draw district lines based on the 1980 census data. This was not a serious effort but was preemptive so that Buchmeyer could not draw his own plan based on the absence of data from the council. Serious or not, line-drawing became divisive enough for Ragsdale and Lipscomb to walk out. In reality, the council members began to realize how difficult it was going to be to draw a 10-4-1 map that would appease the plaintiffs or garner judicial approval. The council was unable to agree on a plan.

Tom Pauken, head of *Just Say No to 14-1*, and Councilman Jerry Bartos joined the Dallas City Charter Defense Committee and the Grass Roots for

Dallas to ask Buchmeyer to let them be intervenors in the suit. Since the city was unable to submit a 10-4-1 plan, they reasoned the judge should grant them status as intervenors to properly represent the voters of Dallas who had passed 10-4-1. Pauken subpoenaed eight council members to testify that the council no longer represented 10-4-1. Buchmeyer refused to allow the group intervenor status. He would not even allow the testimony of the subpoenaed Councilmen.

Mayor Strauss had appointed James Oberwetter as head of a new redistricting task force. Buchmeyer told him, "You need to advise the city council they are required by law to hold an election on May 4, 1991. . . . If you don't, you leave me no alternative; I have to order a single-member-district election plan." In an exchange with Oberwetter, Buchmeyer showed his frustration and developing bias. To the open court, he read letters he had received that made sexual and racial epithets against him. He read one that expressed the writers desire to see his whole family run over by the end of the year. The judge said he read the letter because several witnesses presented by the city said that they believed that race played no major role in the 10-4-1 election or the 14-1 election. Expressing his disdain for the letter writers, Buchmeyer stated, "I have no doubt that those were people who voted against 14-1 because they didn't want another Al [Lipscomb] or Diane [Ragsdale] on the council."[116]

In February 1991, Buchmeyer directed Dallas to hold an election under 14-1. He reserved the right to modify any district lines that were given to him. He pointed out that the law required him to use all single-member districts. He ordered a May 4 election and supplied a redistricting expert to join Oberwetter's committee.[117] Even if 10-4-1 could pass preclearance in Washington, it would still fall back on Buchmeyer to see if the plan would settle the suit and he had already stated his bias that such a plan was unfair to Hispanics.[118]

Two days later the council decided to appeal to the 5th Circuit Court and asked for a stay of the May 4 election. Buchmeyer then put things into full speed. He set February 14 as the last day to submit plans and February 20 for the council to present a plan using the 1990 census. Candidates for office could file between February 28 and March 20.[119]

In another attempt to promote the 10-4-1 plan, the council instructed the city attorney to ask Buchmeyer to remove the Hispanic intervenors. Hispanics were enraged and confusion ensued. Two council members claimed they could not even remember giving the city attorneys those instructions.[120] The president of Barrios Unidos said, "You will see a lot of civil disobedience."[121] The SCLC held a noontime rally and threatened to boycott the city if it maintained its 14-1 appeal. The SCLC speaker said, "Michael Jackson is not going to come here and sing to white children." Noting other voting rights clashes, the Rev. Randal T. Osburn, national administrator for the SCLC, said, "Dallas has to be the new Miami. Dallas has to be the new Arizona." [122]

Activity emanated from all sides. Tom Pauken and the Washington Legal Foundation filed a complaint of judicial misconduct against Buchmeyer. The complaint alleged the judge was biased as demonstrated by the clandestine disclosures to Mayor Strauss and his reading of crank letters at the hearings.

The city filed for a stay of the election until November and asked the Appeals Court to rule before February 26, the date when Buchmeyer demanded the district lines be submitted. The motion for stay said that Buchmeyer "refused even to consider the city's legislative policy choices, contrary to the law articulated by the Supreme Court." Because the judge would not consider 10-4-1, the city motion said, "The issues raised here are most grave—and the harm most acute—because the election orders go to the core of democratic society: the way it governs itself." [123]

On February 23, the council finally approved, ten to five, a very gerrymandered 14-1 plan. A white district remained in Pleasant Grove, but Oak Cliff was torn apart. Ronald Weber, a political science professor from the University of Wisconsin testified that at least eight of the fourteen council districts were gerrymandered, i.e., defied natural geographic boundaries and split voting precincts and census tracts.[124] Royce Hanson, redistricting expert and professor at the University of Texas at Dallas, said, "The council districts created by the commission may be one of the worst cases of gerrymandering in American history."[125] Two days later, Buchmeyer accepted the city's 14-1 proposal. Meanwhile, the city resubmitted a request for a stay of the election, along with a 10-4-1 plan, to the Justice Department under Section 5.

Political mischief influenced the 14-1 map. Redistricting struggles go through two phases. In the first, the battle is for equality or representation. By the final phase, the petty, me-first of politicians takes over. The game is power and the power accrues to people, not races. Council hopeful Sharon Boyd saw her home carefully gerrymandered out of the district in which she planned to run. The gerrymander was a blatant notch in the district just to avoid her block. She said she would move back into the district, but would give no one her address until the lines were final.[126] There was also a mystery of three district lines that changed with no one's apparent knowledge. Jerry Bartos said, "District K, which I will be a candidate in, has changed twice without a meeting of the commission, and without the commission member I appointed knowing about it."

THE AMENDMENTS OF 1982   175

Seeing the city's actions as delay tactics, the SCLC kept up its pressure. It threatened boycotts and civil disobedience. Peter Johnson, head of the local chapter, said, "We will be doing the kinds of things we do best. There will probably be arrests. There will probably be some famous people in jail here next week."[127] The SCLC had a repertoire of threats and performances for such occasions.

The majority of the council voted to continue a legal blitz to block the May vote. They asked the appeals court for a speedy ruling on 8-3 appeal leading to even louder rhetoric from the SCLC who claimed that thousands were poised to march on Dallas and "fill the jails" if Dallas did not stop trying to block the May 4 election. Peter Johnson said, "We may bring people from all over America to Dallas. This is a national organization and not to be played with."[128]

Bob Greer, the expert appointed to the redistricting commission by Buchmeyer commented on the odd-shaped districts, "It depends on whether you like Rembrandt or Picasso. Don't try to understand it, just live with it." Greer told James Ragland, staff writer of the *Dallas Morning News*, "True gerrymandering is a deliberate contortion of district lines with the intent and effect of diluting minority voting strength." Ragland asked, "Now when you turn it around and do just the opposite, when you twist and contort to enhance minority representation, is that gerrymandering?" "I don't know," said Greer.[129] This was the expert Judge Buchmeyer had foisted upon the commission. A matter as grave as voting rights was boiled down to, "Don't try to understand it, just live with it."

The Justice Department refused to stay the election, but the 5th Circuit Court gave the city and the plaintiffs each thirty minutes to argue 10-4-1 verses 14-1. On March 16, the court stayed the May election to give the city time to gain approval of 10-4-1 from the Justice Department. The Chief Judge said of 10-4-1, "Just looking at it on its face, it looks like a fair plan."[130]

The SCLC, though angered by the court's decision, decided to withhold its boycott until the Justice Department had ruled. Peter Johnson said, "We would prefer that the Justice Department confirm a plan that conforms with the Voting Rights Act. If it doesn't, we're going to wreck their convention business."[131] To press its case, the SCLC arranged one-half hour with John Dunne, head of the Civil Rights Division of the Justice Department.

The 5th Circuit Court still had to deal with Tom Pauken's impropriety charges against Buchmeyer. The Chief Judge ordered Buchmeyer to respond in writing to charges. Buchmeyer admitted to telling Strauss that if voters rejected 14-1, he would order a 14-1 election anyway. He claimed that he had talked to all the attorneys first and all had given their permission. Strauss admitted she had lied. The Dallas city attorney said no one had talked to her. Buchmeyer said he had talked to Mike McCool, one of the city's private attorneys, but McCool later denied it.[132] Judge Clark took no action against Buchmeyer.[133]

The city council continued to work on a 10-4-1 plan. Planners tried to make a stronger Hispanic district, but ended up with a 16 percent variation among district populations.[134] Supporters of 14-1 kept insisting that the city drop 10-4-1 or at least promise to support 14-1 if 10-4-1 were rejected by the attorney general. On May 6, Civil Rights Section head John Dunne rejected 10-4-1. He claimed, "Regional districts are, in many respects, the functional equivalent of the at-large council positions that have been found to be racially discriminatory . . ."[135] The city had submitted two sets of district lines with the plan. The Voting Rights Section did not believe that either set sufficiently favored minorities. Despite Dunne's rejection of the plan, he did not wholly reject the concept of 10-4-1, only the specific district lines submitted. The rejection nearly closed the door on 10-4-1, however, by saying, "Concerns have been raised, however, that under the proposed 10-4-1 system, it is not possible to devise a plan in which minority voters will be afforded the same opportunity as white voters to elect their preferred candidates to the city council."[136] The Justice Department did not even consider the principle of retrogression—a test 10-4-1 would surely have passed.

The remaining holdouts on the council began to throw in the towel. Glen Box stood alone saying, "It's the height of irresponsibility not to go back and revise the map."[137] Mayor Strauss said she was relieved that 10-4-1 was rejected. Councilman Jerry Bartos said, "The whole process was corrupt. We hired an attorney and spent $1,000,000 plus to fight a case we didn't want to win."[138]

The pure politics of line drawing began again. Many 14-1 plans were put together to save this neighborhood or that politician. Attempts continued to discredit Buchmeyer for claiming to have talked to attorneys, but the 5th Circuit finally declared the whole event as ill-advised, but not indicative of bias. The council approved plan 14T which created only four black districts rather than the five expected by plaintiffs. At that point, Al Lipscomb threw down his chair and left the meeting. The council sent the new plan to the Justice Department for preclearance.

The council meetings continued in chaos. At a typical meeting, arrows flew from all directions. Al Lipscomb began by saying, "Apparently . . . some white people will do anything in this city under the guise of the city of excellence, the all-American city, the can-do city, the together city, to deny people of color their right at this horseshoe [city council desk]." Councilman John Evans argued, "It [the map] destroyed basically the single representation of a community that's been a community since eighteen hundred thirty-eight when the Elams came there, before John Neely Bryan built his log cabin. I think those people deserve better than that." Glenn Box contended that 400 people at a town hall meeting were "concerned about the hurt and anger and disbelief that they feel seeing the map that destroyed that southeast Dallas community. I couldn't in good conscience, hearing those concerns and those complaints, vote for a map that did not . . . try to preserve that southeast Dallas neighborhood." Mayor Strauss added, "If we had five African-American districts, we would have to dismantle either Oak Cliff or Pleasant Grove. As you know, from the beginning, I had been committed to fair representation, but if at all possible, to try to have it without doing that." Strauss said that she thought that within a very few years a minority would be elected mayor, based on qualifications rather than color. Black Councilwoman Diane Ragsdale replied, "Were you based on qualifications? Give me a break."[139]

Reality set in on the council. Lawyers warned them that rejection of the submitted 14-1 plan would lead to a court-drawn plan. Faced with John Dunne and Jerry Buchmeyer, Councilman Max Wells said, "We get to draw the districts or the judge gets to draw the districts. Either way, it's going to be five African-American districts. It seem to me it's better for the council to draw the plan rather than any judge."[140]

On June 26, Glen Box cast the deciding vote to splinter Pleasant Grove among four black districts in order to leave his East Dallas district intact. The plan had five, safe black districts, two Hispanic districts and one swing white district in Oak Cliff that would likely become Hispanic during the decade.[141]

Figure 11 shows the 14 districts that the commission created. Although few of the districts pretend to be compact, note particularly the shapes of Districts 2, 3, 4, 5, 6, and 8. To further show the effect of racial gerrymandering, District 2 is detailed to show the effort that was needed to create a 60 percent Hispanic district.

On August 2, John Dunne approved a November election date and a four-year term for mayor. Black plaintiffs objected to the attorney general's ruling on the mayoral term. They reasoned that since it was likely that the mayor would be white, a four-year term would give whites an unfair political advantage. "It's just there to maintain white domination in that particular position," argued Crenshaw.[147] Once again, the issue was affirmative action, well beyond equality.

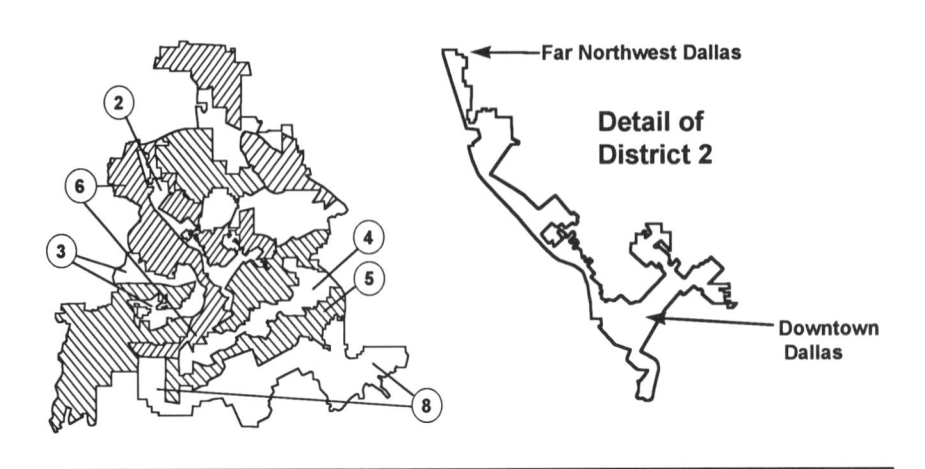

FIGURE 11: GERRYMANDERED DISTRICTS, DALLAS TEXAS[143]

In September, the 5th Circuit ruled on the request of several Dallasites to intervene in the suit because the city had abandoned 10-4-1. Circuit judges decided that Jerry Buchmeyer's court should make the determination.[144] This ended the request.

In the November election, thirty-six percent of the electorate turned out, the highest for a municipal election in the 22 years that city records had been kept. Marvin Crenshaw got 32 percent of the votes in his district, forcing him into a runoff.[145] Black incumbent and advocate Diane Ragsdale was also forced into a runoff. In the runoff, both Ragsdale and Crenshaw were defeated. Crenshaw lost to a white candidate in his safe, black district. Ragsdale was defeated by another black woman who was strongly supported by white voters. The new council had gone from two minorities to six, one short of the vision of the plan designers.[146]

There was one unfinished piece of business in the city council 14-1 debate—the voters had never approved it. Under the state law, such approval was necessary.[147] A referendum on 14-1 was, of course, no more democratic than placing a single candidate on a Soviet ballot. Whether or not the plan was approved, the 14-1 system would remain. The dominion of voters had long since been taken away by the federal judiciary. The City Attorney ordered a special election costing the city more than $400,000.

THE AMENDMENTS OF 1982 179

As the city began to adjust to the new city council, racial discord and economic slump continued. Outside the Cotton Bowl game at Fair Park, County Commissioner John Wiley Price shouted over a microphone, "Welcome to Dallas. This is just like Johannesburg" and "Dallas is the most racist city in the country."[148] A parade celebrating the Dallas Cowboy's Superbowl victory ended in looting and violence along the downtown parade route. Dallas never really recovered from the recession of the mid-1980s. Ten years of lack-luster economy, racial strife, white-flight, and increasing crime had taken its toll. The building vacancy in downtown was the highest in the nation at 34 percent. Gangs formed and businesses relocated to the suburbs. In the mid-1960s, 70,000 people had lived within two miles of city hall. By the early 1990s that number had dwindled to 30,000.[149]

Despite continuing clamor to the contrary, Dallas minorities had made great progress. Two of the city managers had been black. In 1988, 72 percent of the police recruits were black and seven percent were Hispanic. By late 1993, 30 percent of police were minorities and over half of the members recruited since 1990 were minorities. The majority of school administrators, five of nine DISD trustees, the school board president, and the school superintendent were black. The city attorney and the director of public housing were black. Most of the city and county employees were minorities. Still, most of this was cloaked by the high level of protest.[150]

Marvin Crenshaw continued as an activist. In May 1994, he was banned from city council meetings for two months after guards twice had to subdue him for violence when the council refused to change the name of Illinois Avenue to Malcolm X Boulevard.[151]

Redistricting lawsuits seem to never die completely. In October 1994, Crenshaw was still at it as his lawyer appeared before the 5th Circuit demanding that the Mayor's term be reduced to two years and that a plurality vote be adequate to elect the mayor.[152] Crenshaw's logic was shortsighted considering the demographics of Dallas. The Hispanic population was rising rapidly and whites tended to bloc vote. Plurality candidates are advantaged only when opposing a large electoral bloc whose vote is split. Within the next two or three elections, plurality victories were more likely to benefit Hispanics and whites than blacks.

In May 1995, a black, an Hispanic, and a white candidate ran for mayor in a peaceful, low-key race. Ron Kirk, the black candidate, swept the election with a 62 percent majority, much of which came from white North Dallas. Kirk's candidacy prompted a record black turnout of 25 percent while the white turnout was 21 percent and Hispanic was 15 percent. Historically, in

Dallas elections, whites accounted for 70 percent of the vote, but in this election, whites accounted for only 51 percent.[153]

As Kirk took office, the suburbs flourished, but downtown was a shadow of its glory days. What had been the largest department stores of the Southwest were now junior colleges, office buildings, or boarded up. The skyscrapers that had housed the banking empires of Fred Florence and Robert Thornton stood empty and nameless, awaiting the wrecking ball.

Other Events Affecting Dallas Voters

As the long, city council dispute began to settle, a raft of other voting rights issues took the stage. While most of the fundamental changes in U. S. voting rights occurred in the 1970s and 1980s, the early 1990s was the period of peak activity. The 1992 elections were the first to use new census figures since the 1982 Amendments. Dallas citizens were numbed by the montage of voting rights issues. To avoid the confusion of describing these events in their interwoven chronology, the following accounts abandon chronology to more clearly present each issue.

The first piece of this montage was the continuing battle in the Dallas school system. By late November 1991, the redistricting of the Dallas Independent School District (DISD) Board became a hot issue with Hispanics. The 1990 census showed 25 percent of the city to be Hispanic. Although the school board had two Hispanic members, only one came from a "safe" Hispanic district. Hispanic leaders argued in public meetings that the proposed DISD plan needed safe Hispanic districts, and if the Board failed to make those changes, the school systems would warm the same court benches the council had just vacated.[154]

The school board passed a new plan without a second Hispanic district. Oddly, the two Hispanics on the Board supported the plan while the three blacks opposed it. The Justice Department precleared the plan.[155]

Two years later, 25 years of federal supervision of the DISD ended. Whether the problem of desegregation was solved or simply pushed to non-existence is philosophical. The white participation in the district had diminished to the point that it could hardly have been an issue (see Figure 12).

In 1991 the Texas legislature began a year-long struggle to set new boundaries based on the 1990 census. Texas had a Democratic governor and legislature, but like much of the South, was becoming more Republican all the time. Simple party politics obstructed the redistricting process. Just before Christmas, a three-judge federal court drew its own lines, contending that all

THE AMENDMENTS OF 1982 181

of the legislature's proposals discriminated against minorities. Ironically, to empower minorities, their traditional supporters, Democrats were forced to yield seats to the Republicans. Governor Ann Richards called a special session to draw a plan more favorable to Democrats.[156]

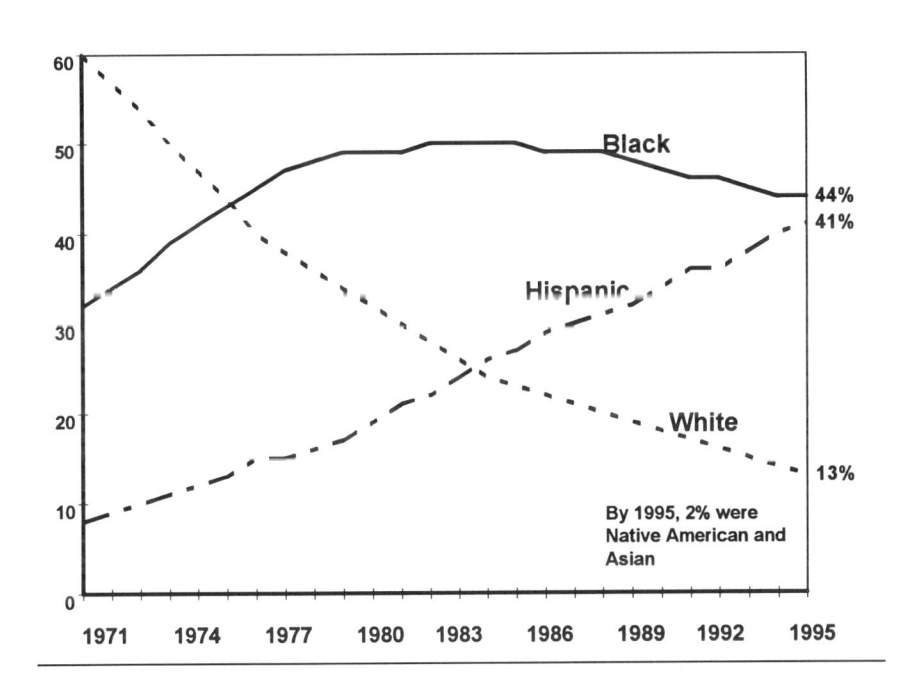

FIGURE 12: DALLAS INDEPENDENT SCHOOL DISTRICT DEMOGRAPHICS[157]

The special session dusted off one of their earlier plans that had already been precleared by the Justice Department. The three-judge court threw it out saying that the court drawn plan would stand for the March 1992 primaries.[158] Democrats denounced the order as "blatantly partisan" and an unprecedented "power grab" by Republican federal judges. The Justice Department then actually withdrew its preclearance saying it needed to compare the legislative proposal to the court-ordered plan. The Texas Attorney General took the matter to the U. S. Supreme Court. Appellate matters such as stays of orders are referred for immediate decision to an individual judge assigned to matters originating in a particular area of the country. In this case, that judge was

Antonin Scalia, a conservative Republican appointed by President Reagan. Justice Scalia had consistently espoused a "states' rights" philosophy that decried judicial activism.[159] He denied state officials' efforts to block the court-ordered Texas house and senate districts for the March primaries.

Jim Harrington, lawyer for the plaintiffs said, "The Voting Rights Act is becoming the Republican gerrymandering statute." Democratic Lt. Gov. Bob Bullock said, "What the Republican Party failed to accomplish at the ballot box they've engineered from behind the bench, cloaked in the black robes of Republican judges."[160]

The Texas Attorney General appealed to the Supreme Court again in February. This new appeal was based on the fact that a Republican legislator had helped the district judges draw the state senate map. One of the District Judges drew so much flack over the accusation, that he withdrew from the case. At the same time, the state gained approval of the D. C. District Court for the legislature's plan. The Texas Secretary of State announced in August that the general election would take place under the legislature's plan rather than the court-constructed plan that had been used in the primaries. In Dallas County, this caused two-thirds of the voters to change Senate districts from the districts used in the primaries.[161] Republicans quickly filed suit and obtained a reversal of the Secretary's actions.[162] The Republican victory was short-lived, however. In April 1993, the debate flip-flopped yet again. A three-judge federal court found that the legislature-drawn plan did not contain biased gerrymandering, thus they imposed the legislative plan over the court-drawn plan.[163]

While the legislative redistricting bounced through the courts, yet another redistricting battle for Dallas County surfaced. A case over the legality of at-large judicial districts had been in the courts for four years, but had gained momentum after the Supreme Court ruled that judicial elections fell under the auspices of the Voting Rights Act. In the 1992 elections, Appeals Judge Kevin Wiggins, a black, lost his bid for election to a state judgeship. Minorities then complained that they could not win in a countywide, at-large election system. Nowhere in the complaints did they address the fact that the current system had elected Judge Wiggins in the first place. The League of United Latin American Citizens (LULAC) was the plaintiff. Bill Garrett, the same lawyer who represented Hispanics in the *Williams* case, represented the minorities.[164]

The following January, a three-judge panel of the 5th Circuit Court of Appeals agreed with LULAC and declared the judicial election system unconstitutional for eight of the state's most populous counties, including

Dallas County. It gave the legislature six months to produce a plan for electing judges from single-member, rather than countywide, districts.[165]

Black and Hispanic plaintiffs were jubilant about the court's decision, but the case was as much about party politics as race. Democrats would gain judgeships which left Democratic Attorney General, Dan Morales, with the sticky political choice of defending the Texas Constitution or the minorities and the Democratic Party. The Democratic Governor, Ann Richards, and her Lieutenant Governor, met with Morales and prevailed upon him to abandon the lawsuit and propose a settlement.[166] Morales secured top Democratic support of a proposed settlement that would institute single-member districts in the eight metropolitan counties.[167] He and other supporters tried to create a crisis atmosphere by warning that racial unrest would result if the legislature failed to pass the proposal. State Senator Rodney Ellis who worked with Morales on the settlement said, "If we don't do a better job of addressing some of the concerns of our minority citizens, one of our cities will blow up. I'm convinced of that."[168] In May, the legislature voted, along party lines, to support Morales' settlement plan.

The proposed settlement was scheduled for review by the Appeals Court in New Orleans. Dallas County Commissioner John Wiley Price conducted a rally supporting the settlement and encouraging black voters to go to New Orleans to apply pressure to the judges. He sparked the crowd by saying, "Every semblance of rights you have you got through the courts," and holding a sign reading, "Judicial seats are held by 'good-ole-boys' who convict INNOCENT black citizens," and chanting "No justice, no peace" and "Single-member districts."[169] The NAACP also organized rallies in major Texas cities.

In New Orleans, the settlement plan got a cool reception from the bench. Judge Edith H. Jones of Houston characterized the Morales plan as an attempt to "change the Texas Constitution by fiat." Judge E. Grady Jolly said the attorney general and LULAC seemed to be usurping power by trying to change the judicial selection method by neither voter approval nor a final appeals court ruling. "You can decide the law? The lawyers in the case can decide the law?" another judge demanded of the state solicitor.[170]

The 5th Circuit upheld the countywide, at-large method of electing judges. So upset was the plaintiff's attorney that he said, "These judges were selected because of their hostility towards minority rights."[171] LULAC, with state support, appealed to the Supreme Court[172] and in January 1994, the Court refused to hear that appeal.[173] The Texas State Constitution, endorsed by the voters of the state, provided for countywide judicial elections. The 5th Circuit Court upheld the system, and the Supreme Court refused to tamper with the

5th Circuit's opinion. Still, the attorney general contended the system was discriminatory. The power of preclearance was given to the Justice Department to expedite cases rather than bog down the judicial system, but the Justice Department decided to use its power to prevent creation of any new judicial districts. The state was held hostage.[174] No matter how desperate the need to add a judge in a particular county, the Justice Department would deny preclearance until it could achieve its philosophic goals.

Even the Justice of the Peace Courts plagued Dallas County officials. In 1990, plaintiffs sued the county because minorities did not have sufficient opportunity to elect justices and constables. A settlement was reached with the county commission. Participants were the now type-cast characters of Jerry Buchmeyer as judge and Bill Garrett as the plaintiffs' attorney.[175] The agreement created, for the first time, an Hispanic J. P. district, along with two majority black districts.

U. S. House districts laid one last gerrymandered jigsaw puzzle over Dallas County. The state legislature's congressional redistricting committee, chaired by Eddie Bernice Johnson, created a badly distorted District 30 in the southern part of the county. The district lines were the result of politics and misuse of the Voting Rights Act. Johnson had created a district in which a black was nearly sure to win, while protecting her fellow Democrats. Without shame, Ms. Johnson said her primary objective was to ensure the election of an African-American while protecting some of the black voter base of Democratic representatives Martin Frost and John Bryant, whose districts surround the 30th. "It was necessary for them [Frost and Bryant] to share in some of that base and at the same time comply with the Justice Department."[176]

Encouraged by the *Shaw v. Reno* (see Chapter 8) decision in North Carolina, plaintiffs, calling themselves the Coalition for a Color Blind Texas, sued to have the U. S. Congressional districts redrawn prior to the congressional primaries. They claimed that the current Texas map "represents an unconstitutional effort to segregate the races for purposes of voting."[177]

In late June 1994, trial began over Dallas District 30 and two similar districts in Houston. Eddie Bernice Johnson again defended her district by pointing out that state lawmakers had a computer database that resulted in equal numbers of people in each district. "I am willing to go on any witness stand and defend these districts." The Justice Department joined Johnson as intervenors in the suit. When asked why they did so, the assistant Texas Attorney General said, "They are in the case to protect the voting rights of minorities under the Voting Rights Act. They see this whole attack as an attack on the meaning of the Voting Rights Act.[178]

Indeed, that was what it had come to. Somehow influences such as compactness, community, and geography had become meaningless benchmarks for civil-rights redistricting advocates. Compare this to the 1967 *Connor v. Johnson* case in which the Supreme Court approved a plan with population variances of more than 10 percent in order to preserve the state's interest in compact districts drawn along natural boundaries.[179] Government intervenors had lost sight that the 1982 amendments allowed consideration of results in the context of the totality of circumstances, but the amendments did not provide for super-gerrymandering to produce those results.

In August 1994, a three-judge federal panel ruled against District 30. Despite the defense's position that the gerrymandering was pure party politics and thus not subject to the Voting Rights Act, the court found the district lines to be racially drawn. The decision said, "If these districts—torturously constructed block by block and from one side of the street to another across entire counties to satisfy the desired racial goal—are constitutional, then the state could more easily hand each voter a racial identity card and allow him to participate in racially separate elections."[180]

After continued litigation, the federal panel finally decided that the November elections could proceed with the existing District 30. The legislature was given until early 1995 to redraw the districts. In December the Supreme Court agreed to hear Louisiana and Georgia cases that would clarify how extreme racial gerrymandering could be. These decisions could then serve as guidance for the several pending appeals including Texas District 30. Antonin Scalia granted the state a stay in redrawing district lines until the Supreme Court could consider the Louisiana and Georgia cases.[181]

In June 1996, the Supreme Court sealed the fate of District 30 by a plurality vote. Justice Sandra Day O'Connor delivered the opinion that the Dallas district was an unconstitutional racial gerrymander based on *Shaw* and *Miller*. While noting that party politics was an important factor, the court ruled that race was indeed the major impetus for drawing district lines. The judgment pointed out once again that "strict scrutiny" did not apply simply because redistricting was performed with race consciousness; nor did it apply simply because the state attempted to draw a majority-minority district. It restated from earlier cases that strict scrutiny applies where a district ". . . is so extremely irregular on its face that it rationally can be viewed only as an effort to segregate the races for purposes of voting, without regard for traditional districting principles"[182] or, where "race for its own sake, and not other redistricting principles, [is] the legislature's dominant and controlling rationale in drawing district lines."[183]

This case was snagged by the race-for-its-own-sake principle. O'Connor pointed out that districts cannot be labeled unconstitutionally bizarre in shape in Texas because Texas has never used traditional districting principles such as geographical boundaries, compactness, or conformity to political subdivisions. Three important facts faced the court proving primary racial intent. First, Eddie Bernice Johnson had previously submitted a more compact plan which presumably met her political agenda. Her plan differed from the final plan in its number of blacks and the district lines required to encompass these additional voters. Second, the computer program used to draw the lines contained racial data at a block-by-block level. Finally, the state's own Section 5 submittal explained the rejection of Johnson's original plan in exclusively racial terms.[184]

Navajo County: Enfranchised but Impoverished

During the early 1980s, federal policy toward Indians changed very little, although the Reagan administration's commitment to supporting state governments conflicted with tribal support.[185] This conflict appeared in water rights and some funding issues, but the directions already set for Indian self-determination and sovereignty remained intact.

Also in the early 1980s, the courts began dealing with totality-of-circumstances in Indian Country redistricting. Indians lagged behind blacks in achieving the legal sophistication required to try redistricting suits. In 1985 in South Dakota, the 8th Circuit Court of Appeals thoroughly castigated a lower court for not considering *Thornberg* and other cases when considering Indian rights in the drawing of district lines.[186] The next year, in Montana, the district court found in favor of the Crow and Northern Cheyenne of Big Horn County by ordering the at-large commissioner and school board elections to be changed to single-member districts. Judge Rafeedie described the unique difficulties of dealing with Indian civil rights cases:

> The dual status of Indians as both United States citizens and as members of sovereign tribes that are self-governed and not subject to full control by state and local government has long presented conflicts over land, mineral and fishing rights, taxation, and the authority of tribal, state, and federal courts. To further complicate the situation, the citizens of Big Horn County, white and Indian alike, are victims of shifting court decisions and federal policies over the last one hundred years concerning the unique status of American Indians in the United States and their relationship to the non-Indian residents of the counties and states where their reservation are located. . . . It must be remembered that this one

decision under the Voting Rights Act does not answer any of the difficult questions raised by the issues just mentioned.[187]

By 1982, MacDonald's popularity had waned so much that he was defeated by Zah. Although MacDonald had fought hard to build a sovereign nation, the tribe was suffering from unemployment, alcoholism, and loss of the best of its youth to jobs outside the reservation. The tribal leader had been harsh with corporations on the reservation and had run off some major employers. MacDonald took a job as a sales manager for power plant equipment in Phoenix from which he emerged a strong proponent of capitalism. With new resolve and a pro-business spirit, MacDonald fought back and re-emerged as the tribal leader in the 1986 elections.[188]

Meanwhile, the U. S. Attorney General pressed for Navajo voting strength. In 1984 he enjoined Navajo County from having a Board of Supervisors election because only one Indian district was created out of five in a county that was forty percent Navajo. The election proceeded when a second district was created.

In June 1987, the Civil Rights Commission set up shop again in Window Rock to investigate possible violations of the 1968 Indian Civil Rights Act by Navajo tribes. The commission's investigation covered several questions: Did the closure of the *Navajo Times Today* newspaper by the tribal government demonstrate a lack of freedom of the press? Since *Santa Clara Pueblo v. Martinez* dictated that Indian civil rights cases could only be tried in Indian courts, how did the tribe's sovereignty affect the rights of tribal members who might have a grievance against the tribe? Did the lack of separation of power among the three branches of Navajo government affect the civil rights of tribal members?[189] Although the Indian Civil Rights Act guaranteed certain rights, it provided no enforcement mechanism. Indians could not take their cases to federal courts if they failed to get redress in the tribal courts.

The Navajo Attorney General, Michael Upshaw, along with many of the Navajo justices, were critical of the investigation stating that he doubted that the commission had any legal right to investigate. Former Tribal Chairman, Peterson Zah, believed that the Indian Civil Rights Act did not apply to Navajos because they had their own bill of rights. Navajos contended that their bill of rights covered everything in the civil rights act and, in many cases, added more.

One reason the commission gave particular concern to the Navajos was Chairman MacDonald's 1978 creation of a supreme judicial council that had the power to reverse tribal court decisions. Even though Zah dissolved the council in 1983, questions lingered about the independence of the judiciary.[190]

During the hearings, witnesses claimed that Navajo civil rights had never been lower and implored the tribe to adopt a constitution establishing federal-style separation of powers. Although Navajo leaders claimed that the *Navajo Times Today* went broke, witnesses testified that five armed policemen entered the newspaper office the day it was closed and gave employees a very short time to remove their possessions. Some witnesses maintained that Navajo citizens did not even understand civil rights. One attorney described a case in which he spent an hour and a half just trying to convince a defendant that he did not have to plead guilty to a crime.[191]

Showing insolent autonomy, the night before the hearings, Peter MacDonald led the tribal council to pass a resolution ordering tribal leaders not to testify before the commission. The commission chairman, Clarence Pendleton Jr., swore he would subpoena every witness on the list. Navajo leaders argued that the Navajo Chief Justice had ruled in 1984 that the civil rights act is "not an explicit authorization allowing suit against the Navajo Nation." When asked if the Indian tribes in the nation were enforcing civil rights, Pendleton said, "No, definitely not. The tribal councils are the only ones who have civil rights."[192]

The hearings were part of a two-year effort by the commission to understand Indian civil rights across the nation. The hearings closed, but reopened the next summer. Clarence Pendleton had died during the preceding year, so William Allen headed the commission. This time, Allen did issue subpoenas to tribal officials. Navajo Attorney General Upshaw challenged the subpoenas and said he would take the matter to federal court. He stated that the commissions actions defied President Reagan's promise that he would treat tribes as "equal partners."[193] "We are willing to cooperate with the Civil Rights Commission on a government-to-government basis."[194]

The hearings were concluded without any Navajo testimony. On July 28, the issue was raised in the U. S. Senate by Senator Daniel Inouye of Hawaii who amended a commission funding bill with a rider that would prohibit the investigations unless permission were given by the U. S. Comptroller General.[195] The rider passed the Senate, but, undeterred, the commission reissued its subpoenas a month later. This time three of the judges, including the Navajo Chief Justice, agreed to testify. Ultimately, the testimony yielded little. The justices read prepared statements and refused to discuss the allegations that had been brought before the commission.

Language issues surfaced again in 1987. In July, the Justice Department told Apache County to change its election system to bring it into conformance with the Voting Rights Act. James P. Turner, Acting Assistant Attorney General, accused the county of not providing even basic election information in the Navajo language. The Justice Department claimed that of the 56,000 county residents, 42,000 were Navajos, 23,000 of whom did not speak English well enough to effectively participate in the election process. Election material was distributed in English which the Department called "wholly ineffective." The county manager said he was "flabbergasted" by the accusation. "All of our poll workers speak Navajo. We think Apache County is far and above any other county as a place where Navajos can vote effectively."[196]

In December 1987, Arizona's attempt to clean up its registration rolls drew additional fire from the Department of Justice. The state had passed a bill that would purge anyone who failed to vote in the 1986 election. The proposal would have affected half of the state's voters or about 1.5 million people.[197] The ACLU pointed out that minorities traditionally have a lower voter turnout and would thus be disproportionately affected. The attorney general barred the plan's implementation to protect voters with traditionally lackluster participation. In this case the action was based solely on historical stereotype. Navajos actually had very high registration rates, and there was no reason to believe they would not re-register if necessary.

In March 1988, the Justice Department again threatened to sue Apache and Navajo counties for not doing enough to educate voters in their native tongue. Since Navajo was not historically a written language, the counties proposed TV advertising, audio-video tapes, and individual visits to homes. The Hopi tribal chairman said he had no problem with the current system. The Navajo County supervisor, himself a Navajo, said they already go "more than the extra step. They go to the homes of the infirmed, take them an absentee ballot, and take the ballot to the polls."[198] The Arizona Secretary of State said enough was being done. Even Peter MacDonald said enough was being done.[199] The Assistant Arizona Attorney General called the suit irresponsible. "Those counties had used radio to transmit information not only on issues, but on polling places, candidates, and other information. They've also had interpreters at the polls.[200] None of this was enough to appease the attorney general.

Later that year the Justice Department insisted on oral translations of Navajo referendums, absentee voting requirements, candidate requirements, and election procedures to audio tape for distribution on the reservation and to local Navajo radio stations. Officials estimated the cost of these requests at $500,000 for Navajo County.

The Justice Department kept up its pursuit of Northern Arizona. Prior to the 1988 elections, the Holbrook Unified School District in Navajo County settled a lawsuit by agreeing to abandon it at-large voting scheme and create two predominately Navajo wards for the 1990 elections. This action violated Arizona state law which proscribed at-large elections.[201]

In the 1988 election, voters had the opportunity to vote on Proposition 106 which made English the official language of the state. The bill would be abolished by the courts seven years later,[202] but as the bill passed handily, the Justice Department focused on the 1990 election. Of the 301 election observers that the federal government sent out nationwide, 38 were assigned to Navajo County and 47 to Apache County.[203]

The Justice Department was still not content. In December the federal government sued Apache and Navajo Counties to force elections in both English and Navajo. U. S. Attorneys claimed, "A majority of the Navajo residents of the two counties are unable to participate effectively in the electoral process when conducted in the English language."[204] Navajos made up 75 percent of Apache County and 48 percent of Navajo County. The claim was extravagant because two-thirds of the Navajos were functionally literate in English. In May 1989, a consent decree was reached to provide audio and video translations of voting procedures in the Navajo language and to require deputy registrars to explain election procedures in Navajo.[205]

MacDonald's troubles returned in 1989. He was accused of profiteering on a land deal in which he made $850,000 plus a BMW on a quick transaction. He was further accused of receiving kickbacks from contractors. After nearly 25 years in office, on-and-over-the-edge deal making had become McDonald's style. He accepted kickbacks, expense-paid trips, and Christmas shopping expenses. He spent $650,000 renovating his private office.[206]

MacDonald admitted to taking the money, but asserted that he was just being polite. He didn't want to insult the gift givers. Protesters signed petitions and gathered outside council chambers demanding MacDonald's resignation. Pro-MacDonald protesters warned that MacDonald's ouster would lead to a BIA takeover of the tribe. MacDonald himself tried to raise the fear level claiming that actions by his opposition would destroy the tribal government and would support the tribe's enemies including the FBI, the BIA, and the Senate. He also claimed that corporations and creditors would abandon the tribe if they viewed the government as unstable.

The council had never before been asked to remove a sitting chairman. There was still no constitution and no clear governmental separation of powers.

That summer, MacDonald was stripped of all of his power and put on paid leave. The Tribal Council appointed Leonard Haskie to fill out the term, but MacDonald did not depart without a fight. His supporters forcibly took back the tribal offices after which he signed orders installing his own judges who reinstated him as chairman. Two protesters were fatally shot by tribal police, one of them after wounding an officer. Two other demonstrators were injured and a tribal administration building was ransacked. Ultimately, the Navajo Supreme Court ruled that MacDonald's removal would stand. Subsequently, the shoot-out at Window Rock led to MacDonald's conviction on conspiracy charges.

In 1990, the final chapter was written for MacDonald. He was brought to trial in Navajo Nation Courts, found guilty on forty-two charges and sentenced to nearly seven years in jail. Facing state and federal charges, MacDonald's lawyer son, Peter MacDonald Jr., filed suit on behalf of himself and his father claiming that the case should be thrown out because it was not filed in a Navajo court. The Maricopa County Superior Court Judge rejected their assertion.[207] Two years later, MacDonald was convicted on sixteen federal charges and sentenced to fourteen and a half years in prison.[208] The appeal process would take four years, but in the end, the Ninth Circuit Court of Appeals ruled that the federal courts had jurisdiction even though this was a crime on the reservation.[209] This debate over tribal sovereignty casts legal doubt on the ability of the U. S. to guarantee voting rights to reservation residents.

The relationship of tribal governments to Washington was still confused and that confusion was troubling. In 1991, President Bush described Indian tribes as "quasi-sovereign domestic dependent nations . . . [whose] government-to-government relationship is the result of sovereign and independent tribal governments being incorporated into the fabric of our nation."[210]

A case tried in the Arizona Supreme Court in 1991 gave some insight into the struggle involved in determining jurisdiction between the Navajo and state courts. The case was *Tracy v. the Navajo Nation*. K. Tom Tracy was named during testimony before a senate subcommittee as one of those involved in the Big Boquillas transaction, the transaction that brought down Peter MacDonald. Complaints were filed in Navajo District Court against MacDonald, but not against Tracy because the tribal courts have no jurisdiction over non-Indians, even for crimes committed in Indian country. Needing Tracy for testimony, the Navajo prosecutor recommended to the tribal council the enactment of a law common to many states called the *Uniform Act to Secure Attendance of Witnesses from Without a State in Criminal Proceedings*. That was done and a Navajo Judge issued a certificate to compel Tracy to testify. In August 1990, an Arizona Superior Court Judge signed orders for Tracy to testify. The court held that the Navajo reservation was a territory as defined by the similar Arizona act. Tracy went to the appeals court seeking a new decision and was rejected. Finally the Arizona Supreme Court considered the case. Tracy based his case on several questions. Among them, he asked whether the Navajo Nation could be considered a state or territory within the act. He also claimed that his testimony was an undue hardship because the Navajo courts would not recognize the same level of fifth-amendment, non-incrimination rights as the U. S. courts. Thus, his failure to testify against himself could land him in a Navajo jail, and giving full testimony might cause him to say things that Arizona and federal authorities could use against him. Either way, his right to withhold self-incriminating testimony was in danger.

The court considered, at length, the meaning of the word "territory" in various statutes and previous cases. They finally decided that there was no fixed definition. An argument that the 1937 legislature that passed the act could not possibly have anticipated the Navajo reservation as becoming so sovereign as to be considered a territory did not hold up. The justices finally determined that the laws had to be flexible enough to deal with new environments. The court was able to agree with some past courts and disagree with others, but through some legerdemain the justices reconciled the incompatibilities enough to declare the reservation a territory of the United States. Whether their logic was good or not, Indian law today is an invention of new interpretations to deal with the "sovereign" nature of the tribes. Decisions are reached today that could not have been reached 30 years ago even though no new laws are supporting these decisions.

In dealing with Tracy's fifth amendment rights, the court went back to an 1896 case in which the U. S. Supreme Court did not uphold an Indian defendant's right to the fifth amendment.[211] The same court, however, recognized that Congress has plenary authority over tribes to limit, modify, or eliminate powers of self-government. Exercising that authority, Congress passed the Indian Civil Rights Act. That act protects Indians and non-Indians alike while testifying on the reservation. Thus, since Tracy should be protected by the Indian Civil Rights Act, he was compelled to testify. Two justices dissented on the basis that the 1937 legislature had no intention of including the reservation in the definition of a state or territory and that any speculation about what the same legislature might say today was "beside the point, because the legislature is the only proper body to consider and adopt amendments to its statutes."[212] Thus, they contended that the current legislature needed to rule.

In 1992, after the 1990 census was complete, havoc broke loose in Arizona politics. Data showed that the Navajo Nation had grown to

200,000—nearly double the 1960 number. New district lines were drawn for the state legislature, many of which were designed simply to keep incumbents in office. Two new minority districts were added to the four that previously existed. The Hispanic community announced in February that they were displeased with the plan and would draw their own plan with the help of the San Antonio based Southwest Voter Research Institute. They proposed dismantling the at-large house positions and creating sixty separate districts.

The new legislative plan took its toll. Many cities were split up to meet the needs of minorities and incumbents. In April 1991 the city council of Chandler, Arizona, just south of Phoenix, passed a resolution asking that their city not be split in redistricting. They petitioned the legislature and were assured by their own representative, a key author of the plan, that there would be no problem. When the plan came out, one of the maps divided Chandler among Districts 6, 7, and 30. District 7's proposed lines snaked from the south through downtown to include city hall, the Chamber of Commerce, and Chandler High School, biting off minority neighborhoods along the way. Holbrook in Navajo County, Casa Grande south of Phoenix, and Nogales, near the Mexican border, suffered the same fate. The irony of this botched political surgery was that the mayor of Chandler was the only black mayor in Arizona.

In 1992, the Justice Department sent a record 100 federal observers from the Office of Personnel Management to cover the primaries in Navajo, Apache, and Yuma Counties. The observers were to determine whether or not the Navajo and Apache Counties were in compliance with the consent decree over Navajo language voting materials.[213]

The 1990 census yielded an additional U. S. congressional seat for Arizona. The Navajos made moves to join the Hopis in a more compact congressional district, but the Hopis were reluctant for fear of being swallowed up by the Navajos.[214] The debate continued until February 1994 at which time the Justice Department finally approved a plan that had been on the drawing board since 1989. That plan created District 6, encompassing nearly the entire eastern half of the state including Navajo and Apache counties, but carefully excluding the Hopi reservation. Indians comprised 22 percent of the population. Despite continuing increases in Arizona representation in Congress, Navajo strength diminished. During the last half century, the Navajo population had doubled while the overall state population had increased nearly six fold.[215]

In 1995, efforts to protect and enhance Native-American voting power continued. Despite population growth that had packed Arizona court dockets, the Justice Department refused to preclear the addition of elected judges in

Navajo County even though it had precleared new judgeships in other parts of the state. The attorney general insisted that adding judges constituted a voting change although the judges would be added to the countywide count that had been elected at-large for 80 years. With 51 percent Navajos, the county had no Navajo judges, a prima facia case of vote dilution to the attorney general. He overlooked, however, that there were no more that a handful of Navajo lawyers with the legal prerequisite of five years of county residence. He further ignored the fact that no Navajo had ever run for office and that Navajos had made no effort to challenge the system.[216]

As this chapter of political empowerment for the Navajos closes, the *Diné* are faring less well than most Americans. They have made little progress in melding into the broader society and, encapsulated on the reservation, near-poverty is the rule. Of the ten major American-Indian tribes, Navajos rank last in income and education. The median family income is $13,940 compared to $27,025 for the Iroquois and $35,225 for the U. S. overall. Navajos graduate 51 percent of their youth from high school, compared to 73 percent for the Creeks and 75 percent for the entire nation.[217]

Despite the lack of progress for the Navajos so far, the concept of tribal sovereignty continues to grow. Ada Deer, the first woman to head the Bureau of Indian Affairs, addressed the Senate Select Committee on Indian Affairs at her confirmation hearings saying, "There is no reason for me or for any of you not to support the permanency of tribal sovereignty any more than we would be reluctant to support the permanency of federal or state sovereignty. . . . The role of the federal government should be to support and to implement tribally inspired solutions to tribally defined problems. The days of federal paternalism are over."[218]

Apparently Deer saw no need for a government-father, but she still saw the requirement for a deep-pockets Uncle Sam to "support" tribally-inspired ideas. Another concept imbedded in her words and prevalent among today's polemic thinkers is the notion that tribal sovereignty does not create a constitutional crisis. The role of the federal government is defined in the Constitution with all other rights left to the states or the people. There is no fourth level of sovereignty accommodated by the Constitution.

In May 1995 Albert Hale, the new tribal leader for the Nation, took the lead in convincing the tribal council to pardon Peter MacDonald for all of the charges leveled by the Navajo courts. Hale said, "I am willing to step forward and say, 'I forgive.' It is remembering we are Navajo. It is remembering our relationship. It is remembering forgiveness is one of the principles we have been taught."[219] MacDonald continues, however to serve his fourteen-year federal sentence in a Bradford, Pennsylvania federal prison.

In January 1996, President Hale told the 88-member tribal council that he opposed efforts underway to make the Navajo Nation the 51st state. He admonished the council, "The Navajo Nation currently enjoys the status of semi-sovereign nation. In spite of all the limitations on our sovereign status, a semi-sovereign nation status is a step higher than a state sovereign status."[220]

Today, no national organization coordinates a united Indian voting rights effort. There is no VEP or SVREP (Southwest Voter Registration Education Project) for Native Americans, but there are individuals and small groups that support both Indian and non-Indian candidates who support Indian causes. Indians have been, and remain, the subjects of more legislative actions than any other minority group.[221]

Dade County: Hispanicazation

Within 10 years there will not be a word of English spoken [in Miami] . . . one day residents will have to learn Spanish or leave.

—*Miami Mayor Maurice Ferré* [222]

The decade following the 1982 Amendments redefined minority power in Dade County. The major battleground was the fight for minority representation on the Dade County Commission. By 1982, the Mariel flotilla was over but its impact on Hispanic influence was permanent.

The Non-Group still influenced Dade County. Once all non-Hispanic whites, the body doubled in size in 1980 and added two blacks, two Cubans, and a woman to its rolls. Miami Mayor Ferré, who himself was a member in the early 1970s, said, "The Non-Group is the shadow government of metropolitan Dade County. The system of government we have creates a vacuum that's filled by this group. This is the central power in Miami. This is where things are decided." Over the years, their concerns ranged from rapid transit to riot torn Liberty City to a symphony orchestra. Steve Clark, Dade's mayor of 13 years, said he had never been invited to a Non-Group meeting. Like the Dallas CCA, most of its members were men with the financial resources to back their chosen causes, with the status to gain the ear of politicians from the governor on down, and with the leadership positions to influence some of Miami's most important civic institutions.[223]

Racial tension raised by the McDuffie incident continued. Miami's Overtown section exploded in rioting after a white policeman shot and killed a black youth in what witnesses claimed was an unprovoked incident.[224]

The school district had generally the same experience as Dallas. White-flight began in 1970 when the Dade school system adopted a court-ordered integration plan. Within two years, non-Hispanic whites dropped below 50 percent of the total students. Their enrollment steadily decreased until 1982 when they comprised only 28 percent, while Hispanics accounted for 39 percent and blacks, 32 percent.[225]

Cuban leaders sought to gain political clout. Unlike many Hispanic groups, Cuban immigrants were generally conservatives. Between 1982 and 1984, Hispanic voters grew five percent, increasing Dade Republicans by ten percent.[226]

In 1984, a bipartisan effort in Dade County launched HAVE, Hispanic-American Voter Education. The group's goal was to naturalize and then register immigrants. Hispanic registration had grown 30 percent nationwide between the 1976 and 1980 elections. By 1984, nearly four million Hispanic Americans were registered. During 1984, the monthly number of applicants for citizenship processed by the Dade County INS went from 1,200 to 2,400; the backlog of unprocessed applications went from 9,500 to 27,000.[227]

U. S. immigration policy fueled this growth by allowing new immigrants the right to bring in spouses and minor children.[228] The *Cuban Adjustment Act of 1966* facilitated Cuban citizenship by allowing any Cuban who lived in the United States one full year to become a citizen.[229]

As a heterogeneous mix of new Hispanic citizens filled the city, federal policies continued to treat race and ethnicity as a simple black, white, and Hispanic problem. As of 1986, blacks constituted 19 percent of the county, but comprised black Americans, Haitians, and other Caribbeans. Haitians did not relate to American blacks; they did not even speak the same language. Dade's Hispanic community was culturally diverse, including middle-class, conservative Cubans and poor, liberal Nicaraguans. Further, the consensus of the Jewish community, mostly Anglos, was not the same as other Anglos.[230] A 1988 Dade County estimate listed 60,000 Nicaraguans, 48,000 Puerto Ricans, 40,000 Colombians, 16,000 Mexicans, 500,000 Cubans, and 105,000 Other Hispanics.[231] Ironically, voting rights case law repeatedly allowed blacks and Hispanics to join forces against non-Hispanic whites while recognizing that they had little in common. Justices continually allowed minorities to join during the hearing phase, then separated their unique interests during the remedy phase.

By 1987, Miami boasted more Hispanics than any metropolitan area in the U. S. outside of New York and Los Angles. The only city in the world with more Cubans than Miami was Havana. The population of Dade had doubled since 1960, but there were actually fewer non-Hispanic whites.[232]

In the last half of the 1980s, Nicaraguans displaced Cubans as the fastest growing group of Hispanics in Miami. They crammed together in small apartments and worked for low wages. In 1987, Attorney General Edwin Meese directed the Immigration and Naturalization Service to halt deportation of virtually all Nicaraguans from the United States, to "encourage and expedite Nicaraguan applications for work authorizations," and to "encourage Nicaraguans, whose claims for asylum or withholding of deportation have been denied, to reapply."[233]

In the same month, Jorge Valdes, the only Cuban-American on the Dade Commission, sponsored a referendum to remove the 1980 law that barred the county from spending money on anything that was not in English or about American culture. Hispanic leaders pressured Valdes to abandon his plan, fearing a bloody ethnic war over language.[234] The issue of language was paramount to county residents. By 1988, *US English* was busily at work in Florida. Their leaders hoped to adopt an English-only provision in enough state constitutions to persuade Congress to draft a federal amendment. Their efforts had already passed an amendment in California.[235] They collected 500,000 signatures statewide and in November, Florida voters passed the amendment by an 84 percent majority.

In 1989, racial tensions opened the new year with an Overtown riot preceding the Superbowl game.[236] The new year also saw a continuing flood of immigrants from Central and South America. They were even poorer than previous immigrants. The Contra War had wound down and Nicaraguan refugees poured across the Texas border, then went to Miami on specially assigned Greyhound busses.[237]

That April the Non-Group again expanded with new members including one Cuban and one black. The 52-member group now counted four blacks, six Cuban-Americans, and two women.[238] Despite its attempts to diversify, the Non-Group's power base was eroding. It had hung on past the demise of the Dallas CCA, but such a group of business leaders was anachronistic in a politically correct society. Its leadership was suspect in a society that looks more toward equal results for all and is quick to suspect corporate greed and malice.

Any discussion of ethnicity in Dade County requires a higher degree of precision than in most parts of the country. Because the Hispanic population was so significant, careful distinctions are made between Hispanic and non-Hispanic whites. Whites are further divided between Jewish and non-Jewish. A study completed by the Cuban-American National Council in 1990 analyzed the County's demographics. (See Figure 13.)

In 1990, fifty-four percent of all Cuban Americans lived in Dade County. This percentage was higher than in any of the past three decades. A phenomenal 45 percent of Dade County residents were foreign born and about 70 percent of all Cuban Americans were born in Cuba. Data suggested that 68 percent of Cuban Americans, although immigrants, spoke English well or very well even though most spoke Spanish at home. Considering their recent immigration along with the fact that Miami housed large Hispanic barrios, this percentage was very high.

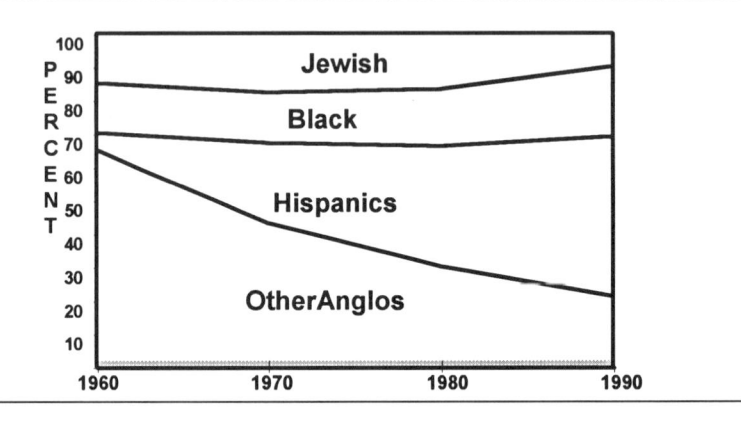

FIGURE 13: ETHNIC COMPOSITION OF DADE COUNTY[239]

In the early 1990s, Dade hosted registration campaigns to recover voter participation lost since 1982, a period during which the rest of the state showed major gains. Less than half of Dade County residents were registered despite the fact that registration was easy. Voters needed only to register at any of the elections offices around the county and swear that they were at least 18, a resident of the county, and an American citizen. The county required no documents of proof.[240] Election supervisor David Leahy, who took some of the heat for the no-documentation policy, commented, "It's a third-degree felony if you tell a lie, . . . A good percentage of those who register to vote do so at shopping malls, at registration drives conducted at supermarkets . . . places where people are not likely to be carrying their birth certificates or naturalization papers. . . . [requiring documentation] would severely cut down on those types of registration activities."[241] Dorothy Joyce, the Tallahassee Division of Elections director, wrote, "If proof of citizenship is required for every person when registering to vote, our state could encounter problems which other states might not, as we have a sizable elderly population, some of whom do not have birth certificates."[242] Unquestionably, Dade's policies were not designed to prevent minority registration.

Statistics after the 1990 census showed Cubans were more likely to register than any other Hispanic group, however, all Hispanic groups fell behind non-Hispanics.[243]

	% of Total Population	% of Registered Voters
Non-Hispanic Whites and Others	30	52
Black	21	20
Hispanic	49	28

FIGURE 14: DADE COUNTY VOTER DATA, 1991[244]

The towering levels of immigration during the 1980s led to increases in integration. A 1991 study of Dade County showed 33 percent of the blacks were racially isolated, that is lived in neighborhoods more than 90 percent black. This number was down from 46 percent a decade earlier. Forty-nine percent of whites were racially isolated compared to 75 percent ten years earlier. This integration level was far ahead of the national average.[245]

As another sign of the times, a second elite group, similar to the Non-group, formed, this time with Hispanic leaders of industry. The group, called La Mesa Redonda, consisted of 15 Cuban-American men, one Nicaraguan American, and one Cuban-American woman. La Mesa Redonda inducted leaders of banks, newspapers, and broadcast stations,[246] while the Non-Group followed the same futile gestures of the Dallas CCA by inducting 21 new members, six blacks and nine Hispanics.[247]

Against this backdrop of rising ethnicity, Dade began its struggle to share power in the county commission. In 1984, the commission was made up of nine members. Each commissioner was elected for four years with staggered terms such that four commissioners were replaced in one election and five were replaced two years later. The mayor could live anywhere in the county, but the other eight had to live in specific districts. All commissioners were elected at-large.[248]

In May 1986, the Citizens Charter Review Committee, established by the County, asked the county commissioners to put on the November ballot proposals for a strong mayor to replace the County Manager, for the expansion of the commission from nine to seventeen members, and for the election of eleven of those members from specific districts. The commission unanimously rejected putting any of these proposals on the ballot.[249] Former state representative Bill Sadowski, who was pushing for reforms, said he would begin the expensive process of collecting 100,000 signatures on a petition to put the items on the ballot. This was the first salvo in a six-year war over the commission structure.

In August, State Senator Carrie Meek filed a suit against Dade County's at-large election system. Joining Meek in the suit were former Miami mayor, Maurice Ferré, current Miami mayor Xavier Suarez, and eight other plaintiffs. A young lawyer named Steven Cody, an associate of Sadowski's, led the group. Meanwhile, the petition drive headed by Sadowski's committee fizzled.[250]

Eleven days after the filing of the lawsuit, the County Commissioners put their own proposal on the ballot. The proposal added four members and raised commissioner's salaries from $6,000 to $41,000 per year.[251] The four new members were to be elected from single-member districts, leaving the original nine at-large. Two days after announcing its proposals, the commission withdrew them from the November 4 ballot.[252]

In 1988, Carrie Meek's suit appeared in court. Minorities asked Federal District Judge Kenneth Ryskamp to skip a trial and require Dade County Commissioners to be elected by single-member districts. Genie L. Stowers, a professor of political science at the University of Alabama, did a statistical analysis for the plaintiffs. She claimed that a technique call "ecological regression" led her to the conclusion that racial bloc voting prevented minorities from being elected to the commission. On the other side, the county attorney confidently asked the judge to dismiss the case.[253]

The judge held a hearing in which he expressed reservations about district elections in a county so ethnically splintered as Dade. With Democratic Puerto Ricans and Republican Cubans, he questioned whether Dade Hispanics could be considered a cohesive minority that votes as a bloc. Ryskamp said, "Your case would be stronger if you brought it [only] on behalf of blacks [because] the black minority is cohesive, geographically insular and votes as a unit."[254] Still, he disappointed the county by refusing to dismiss the case. Instead, he asked attorneys to prepare arguments and submit them in twenty days.

Political analyst John Lasserville agreed with Ryskamp's central point. Latin influence continued to increase in Dade, but Cuban growth had slowed to a trickle while growth from South America increased sharply. Lasserville pointed out that voting patterns varied considerably. "The Cuban pattern and the Puerto Rican pattern are as different as comparing the Anglo pattern with the Jewish pattern."[255]

Elections occurred on September 6 as voters wiped out one-third of the incumbents. Exactly one month later, Judge Ryskamp announced that he found no violation of the Voting Rights Act. "The plaintiffs have failed to prove the existence of a non-Latin white bloc majority that usually defeats the election of the minority's preferred candidates." Ryskamp said that the plaintiffs confused "losing" with "diluted votes."

Steven Cody and his plaintiffs appealed to the 11th Circuit Court in Atlanta. The appeal might have been unnecessary since the new commission had more supporters of single-member districts than not, but the commissioners placed the matter into study by one committee after another. In September 1989, to everyone's surprise, commissioners brought forth a proposal to expand the commission to eleven members, seven of whom would be elected from single-member districts. Discussions degenerated and soon the commission was awash with varying proposals and entangled in arguments. They killed all of the proposals and sent the matter to yet another committee.[256]

By February 1990, each county commission meeting turned into a debate over charter changes. At one meeting some commissioners would be absent; at others, some would walk out. The County Mayor, Steve Clark, said "The status quo is perfect. I don't know why you want to change horses in the middle of the stream."[257]

Finally they agreed to place a charter amendment on the ballot that called for seven members of an expanded commission to be elected from single-member districts. They once again lumped into the proposal a raise in commissioner's salaries from $6,000 per year to $51,000 along with a change in the county name to Metro-Miami-Dade County. Proponents of single-member districts feared that lumping all of these changes together would jeopardize the redistricting portion.[258] Indeed, in the May election, voters overwhelmingly defeated the proposal.

In August, the 11th Circuit dealt a blow to Ryskamp's decision. A three-judge panel said Ryskamp had erroneously concluded Anglos could not block the election of black candidates because Ryskamp overlooked the hostility between blacks and Hispanics in Miami, and the tendency of Hispanics to side with Anglos in voting against blacks. They also said that he erroneously determined that minorities would be unable to elect more representatives under a single-member district plan.[259] The last point stemmed from a difference in assumptions. Ryskamp had calculated the potential for minority success based on single-member districts that were drawn along the same lines as the current commissioners districts. The appeals court believed that new districts could be drawn that would lead to greater minority success.

During the 1990 election campaign, redistricting was the top issue. All of the candidates had an opinion, most believing that there should be some mix of at-large and single-member districts. Commissioner Charles Dusseau instructed county attorneys to begin settlement talks with Steven Cody and the plaintiffs since the majority of the commission seemed to favor structural reform.[260]

The 1990 elections produced only one Hispanic and one black commissioner. Ironically, these two, Arthur Teele and Alex Penales both lost in their respective districts, but won countywide. Betty Ferguson, a black, who joined the lawsuit, gained a majority in her district but lost the countywide election.[261]

In December, Judge Ryskamp encouraged the county to find some settlement with the plaintiffs to avoid a trial. Armed with the election results and the judge's prompting, seven commissioners agreed to put the issue back on a ballot, this time separating the pay increase from an eight-ward, five-at-large-district proposal.[262] Stephen Cody and the plaintiffs sought 21 single-member districts.

In February 1991, Judge Ryskamp announced that he could not begin the retrial in March because of a full docket of criminal trials. If he delayed the criminal trials, the Speedy Trials Act would cause dismissal of the cases. The county supported the delay, hoping that it could be postponed until after the public referendum in September. Ryskamp denied such a long delay and ordered both sides to submit evidence within 50 days.[263] Steven Cody commented, "I saw previous commissions put redistricting on the ballot on Tuesday and pull it off two days later, so my willingness to grant them a measure of good faith has been diminished over the years."[264]

District Judge Kenneth Ryskamp was lined up to fill a vacancy on the 11th U. S. Circuit Court of Appeals. He was a conservative judge appointed by Reagan in 1986. At that time he claimed to be no political activist, but rather a strict interpreter of the Constitution and past case law. His supporters claimed that Ryskamp had many successes from the bench that were openly praised by Miami citizenry and the newspapers. He was deemed well qualified by the American Bar Association and no one complained until the promotion came up.

On the other side, his potential promotion attracted the attack of civil-rights groups. Thomas Poole, head of the Florida NAACP, said, "He's not ranting and raving and calling you racial names. It is more subtle. You have to read between the lines of what he's saying to discover that he has a plantation mentality—he's the old guard, elitist, separationist type of fellow."[265] The idea of subtlety had become the rallying cry of some activists by 1990. When no clear, demonstrable evidence of discrimination could be produced, they simply declared it present but too subtle to clearly identify.

In truth, of the 1,915 cases Judge Ryskamp had had on his docket since coming to the Southern District bench, losing parties had appealed 345 of those decisions. The 11th U. S. Circuit Court of Appeals had overturned his decisions only 15 of those times—an enviable record for any judge.[266]

During his confirmation hearings for appointment to the Court of Appeals, Ryskamp drew heavy fire from liberal members of the Senate for his treatment of minorities in the courtroom. Opposition centered on Ryskamp's alleged insensitivity to blacks and Hispanics, including his comment in a civil rights case brought by three black men bitten by police dogs in West Palm Beach. Two of the men were admitted thieves. Senate Democrats were dumbfounded that Ryskamp wouldn't apologize for remarking, "It might not be inappropriate to carry around a few scars to remind you of your wrongdoing in the past."[267] Ryskamp became the first Bush appointee to be denied promotion to the appeals court. He said he found statements of Senate Democrats "repugnant to all that I stand for."[268] Even Steven Cody said he did not believe that Ryskamp showed bias. Ryskamp then removed himself from the voting rights case because he had discussed the case extensively with the Senate Judiciary Committee. The case was turned over to Judge James Lawrence King.

In May 1991, The Metro Commission unanimously endorsed a plan for 13 districts, nine of which were to be single-member and four were to be superdistricts. They also agreed to present a second referendum to greatly increase the power of the mayor and raise everyone's salary to $52,600 per year. The strong mayor would lose his right to vote but could veto legislation, set the annual budget, and with the commission's approval, hire the county manager.[269] The referendums were set for September 3.

The rhetoric heated up during the remainder of the summer. Black activists who expected blacks to get three seats said even that wasn't enough. Anglos could still out-vote blacks. A white commissioner responded that such logic was un-American. Don Paul, drafter of the single-member-district system that existed from 1957 to 1963 said, "We've already tried [single-member districts] and it didn't work. It will divide Dade County instead of uniting it."[270] Proposed district lines were irregular, protecting incumbents and catering to race. Lloyd Miller, activist and fruit grower said, "It's ridiculous. They've split the agricultural area and included it with the condo canyons. The only vegetables they've ever seen up there are corn, green beans, and sauerkraut."[271] Commissioner Penales, who designed the plan, became its vocal champion. He gave 70 speeches and appeared on television and radio talk shows across the county. This was the freshman Commissioner's political unveiling. His 27 page plan mentioned his name 65 times.

That September voters defeated the charter changes. Non-Hispanic whites most often rejected the plan while blacks and Hispanics mostly supported it. Interestingly, voters had recently approved a referendum for single-member districts for Dade School Board.[272]

By October the Meek case was transferred again, this time to Judge Donald Graham, a registered Democrat. In December, he said he would decide the case before the 1992 elections.

The coalition between black and Hispanics plaintiffs began to falter. Black representative Jim Burke quit the plaintiff group to join a group representing only blacks. He said, "It was more important for me to try to represent the interests of the African-American community that nourished me than to be politically correct." Blacks were asking the question of whether Hispanics who represented more than half of Dade County could still be considered a minority in the Voting Rights Act. Joining Meek in the case was civic activist Ralph Packingham who was also black. Fourteen months earlier, Billy Ferguson, unsuccessful black candidate for the commission, petitioned the court to join the lawsuit. She hired her own law firm rather than join the coalition. Now Burke and Packingham told Steven Cody they were pulling out of the coalition to join Ferguson. They predicted that Meek would follow.[273] Within weeks, however, plaintiffs agreed to continue the suit together, although multiple law firms now represented them.

Ironically, voting rights case law repeatedly allowed blacks and Hispanics to join forces against non-Hispanic whites while recognizing that they had little in common. Justices continually allowed minorities to join during the hearing phase, then separated their unique desires for political power during the remedy phase. Judge Graham agreed with Ryskamp's conclusion that Hispanics had proven two of the three Gingles factors necessary for vote dilution. They were populous enough to comprise a voting district and they were politically cohesive. They had yet to prove whether non-Latin white voters kept them from office. Randy Duvall, Assistant City Attorney handling the case, said the Hispanic community "is not suffering from a legacy of past,

[or] purposeful discrimination at the hands of Dade County officialdom. You show me an immigrant community that has amassed political, economic, and social power more quickly than the Cuban community in Dade County."[274]

In June, as the trial began, H. T. Smith, spokesman of the black convention boycott, and Betty Ferguson testified that the county's at-large electoral system inhibited black voters from electing the candidates they wanted.[275] Miami's former mayor Maurice Ferré commented, "The current system is an anachronism. The result is that blacks and Hispanics can't get elected." When he first ran for Florida State Legislature in the mid-1960s—when Dade was still predominantly white—Ferré said he was continually tagged by the press as "a Puerto Rican-born industrialist." He said he got elected by playing down his ethnicity. He agreed that things had improved some since then, but not enough. He said minorities were so demoralized they stayed away from the polls altogether. "People feel that there is an unspoken, unwritten rule that there is one black seat and one Hispanic seat. There is no use running for that seat because they are not going to win."[276]

Miami's activist thinking was influenced by the liberal interpretation of the Voting Rights Act which peaked nationwide in 1992. This attitude was reflected in a Cuban-American publication which stated, "Federal law requires that minorities be given maximum opportunity to elect candidates of their choice."[277] These words were not from an extreme publication, in fact, the courts frequently used similar verbiage. Nonetheless, there was no such verbiage in the Voting Rights Act. Representative Meek stated that "Blacks have been excluded from the political process. The current system does not provide one-person, one-vote."[278] She, like many others, misunderstood the meaning of one-person, one-vote.

Statistics in the case were complex. Meek pointed out that in 1990 Ferguson carried a large majority of the black vote in her race against Collins, but Collins won by getting the white and Hispanic vote. In 1990, incumbent Barbara Carey captured the majority of the black vote, but was defeated by Arthur Teele, a black Republican who got the white and Hispanic vote. The same year, Commissioner Jorge Valdez won the majority of the Hispanic vote, but Alex Penales won the white vote and won the election. David Lipman, a voting rights attorney said, "I am not sure whether it would be in the interest of black voters to have a majority of single-member districts held by Hispanics. I'm not sure their political agendas really coincide."[279] Testimony ended on June 13.

On August 15, Judge Graham wiped away the Dade County election system. He canceled the September elections and gave the Metro Commission 20 days to come up with a plan. He stated that the case met all of the *Gingles* criteria.[280] His findings were an interesting conclusion to the six-year-old case. He cited extreme racial polarity exemplified by "keen hostility" between blacks and Hispanics. This hostility, he concluded, had caused each group to form coalitions with non-Hispanic whites to defeat candidates from the other group. As a result, whites were often left in charge.[281] His conclusion showed extraordinary logic. Because minority groups voted for the same candidates as whites, whites were too powerful.

Controversy followed immediately. Commissioner Mary Collins, the strongest opponent of single-member districts, said, "With single-member districts, everyone will have their own agenda. Where would you put the jails, the hospitals, the garbage dumps? The system won't work." By contrast, there was jubilation in the Hispanic community. Hispanic talk shows heralded the decision and vehemently opposed any thoughts of the county appealing. A week later, Mayor Steve Clark announced the county would not appeal.[282]

County elections took place in September without the mayor or commissioners' races. Hurricane Andrew obliterated 200 polling places. Of the election proceedings that did occur, many were in Army tents. Later that month, the commission endorsed a two-tiered election plan. Like Dallas' 10-4-1 proposal, the plan created four regional representatives, nine single-member districts, and an at-large mayor's position. The nine districts were expected to produce five Hispanic, two white, and two black commissioners while the regional representatives were expected to be two Hispanics, one black, and one white. Despite complete surrender of the white power structure, Steven Cody immediately responded that the plan was unacceptable.[283]

Two weeks later, Dade County voters endorsed a strong-mayor plan. Heavy rains kept the turnout to 13 percent. Under the plan, the mayor elected in 1996 would have veto power over any vote of the commission. That veto could withstand anything less than a two-thirds override by the commission. Although the mayor would have veto power, he would not have a normal vote. Commissioners Penales and Teele believed that this kind of non-voting executive position did not fall under the purview of the Voting Rights Act.[284]

On December 3, 1992 various citizens groups gained a hearing at the Appeals Court whom they asked to restore the old system on the basis that Judge Graham was wrong about racial hostility in Dade.[285] Justice Edward Carnes said he was skeptical that Hispanics needed relief since they comprised a majority of the population. "I guess I have a problem with math," he said, "I just don't understand."[286] The debate was extensive for the tribunal; a judgment would not arrive for three months. In the meantime candidates waged tentative campaigns.

On December 10, Judge Graham said he could go along with the nine districts, but he contended the four super-districts would perpetuate historical unfairness. He also commented that an at-large mayor who voted on the council was unacceptable. At-large anything was unacceptable to Judge Graham.[287] Since the new, executive mayor would not come into being until 1996, Graham temporarily abolished the position of mayor altogether on the basis that minorities could not elect a mayor of their choice. If minorities could not elect their own in a county that was 70 percent minority, the judge believed the office should simply be abolished. He conceded that the commission could internally elect a mayor to carry out normal ceremonial duties.[288] He told the commission to start drawing an all-single-member-district plan.

Bedlam followed as incumbents began trying to save themselves. Competition became fierce as white commissioners jockeyed for what might be as few as two non-Hispanic white seats. Minorities began lining up for the new positions. Many commissioners actually moved their households to improve their reelection chances.

On December 18, commissioners came up with a 13-single-member-district plan. Thirteen gave a bit more room for incumbents to be reelected. Commissioners also reinstalled the mayor's seat and sent the plan to plaintiffs seeking their approval. The 13-member plan had seven Hispanic districts, but the drawing of lines brought reality home. A least two of the districts could not be counted on to deliver a Hispanic commissioner. Miami Beach, for example, was 66 percent Hispanic, but many were not citizens and many citizens were not registered.[289]

Judge Graham was given three plans. Hispanic plaintiffs could not reach agreement with the county and therefore submitted their own plan. The second plan was the 13-member plan drawn by the county and the third was a nine-member plan drawn by the court expert. The Hispanic plan was "safer" for Hispanics, but blacks claimed it diluted one black district. Two days later, Penales filed papers for a nine-member plan of his own. He asked the judge to postpone the election again because there was inadequate time to campaign. Just before Christmas, the judge approved the commission's 13-member plan, with no mayor, saying that it satisfied the Voting Rights Act. The districts in that plan included seven Hispanic, three black, two white, and one plurality white.[290]

Mayor Clark, who had held that office since 1971, threw up his hands and decided to retire. He left an entirely different county than he had first been elected to lead. The landscape was permanently altered by Mariel, McDuffie, and Meek.

By the time the filing deadline arrived on January 27, 1993, ninety-one candidates vied for the thirteen offices. The *Miami Herald* described the entourage:

> The final list includes three ministers, two people named Mary Collins, eight former state representatives and one member of the Socialist Workers Party. One candidate who declared himself 'the choice of Mohammed, Moses and Jesus Christ' led a troupe of homeless men into the clerk's office.[291]

Dade voters were bewildered. Many were unaware of the current election date, who was running, who was not running, and what election district they lived in. The appeals court still had not ruled on the citizens petition to restore the old system, so many candidates were conserving their money because they believed the election date would slip again.[292]

On February 27, the news finally came from the appeals court. Despite the conservative leaning of the three-judge panel, the justices voted unanimously to endorse Judge Graham's decision.[293] The election was scarcely two weeks away and candidates began to empty their coffers for a final blitz.

The Justice Department joined the confusion less than a week before the election by filing suit against the county for not providing multilingual voting leaflets. The county had distributed 400,000 leaflets printed in English in accordance with county ordinance. The government demanded that 400,000 Spanish leaflets be delivered to homes before the election. Time did not allow compliance. A district judge ordered thousands of leaflets to be available at polling places.[294]

The election was now about race rather than county business. Arthur Teele was accused of not being black enough and was accused of using the term "field Niggers" to describe some constituents. A Miami Beach candidate ran on being an Argentine who did not like Cubans. Mary Collin's supporters urged her to drop out of a Latin district. One candidate bragged of his Italian roots and his Jewish wife. One ran as the only non-Cuban Hispanic. Maurice Ferré, a Puerto Rican, played up his Cuban grandfather while in front of Cuban constituents and his Puerto Rican ancestry while in the Puerto Rican neighborhoods. The rhetoric heard during the campaign would have lured the wrath of civil libertarians during any normal campaign, but this race was about race.

Election day came and 21 of the 91 candidates either won or, at least, stayed in the running. All but two of the winners were veteran politicians.[295] Ultimately, six Hispanics, four blacks, and three whites made the commission. The election reflected highly polarized voting patterns. The racial appeals had worked.

The suit was over and the plaintiffs and Steven Cody had won. Cody was the hero of the saga. Over the six year trial, plaintiffs had raised only $8,000 to pay him. He spent $32,000 more than that in fees to experts. He went into the trial with one child and emerged at the end with three. He spent his savings and borrowed his dad's car. On April 20, he received a check for $640,000 as part of the settlement and went on to fight the Dade School Board.[296]

The new county commission unanimously repealed the county's English-only ordinance. The born-again commission then went on to try to spread reform by instructing county attorneys to intervene in a federal lawsuit attempting to force the Dade County School Board into single-member districts. As the new commission rounded out its first year, commission staff had doubled and gasoline taxes were increased. Many civic projects were begun. Most importantly, the tri-ethnic free-for-all that many had feared never materialized.

Today on Flagler Street in Miami stands the *Vanguard—Miami's Forerunners of Human Progress*, a museum commemorating the passage of 1965 Voting Rights Act. Also in Miami is the U. S. congressional district of Carrie Meek, the granddaughter of a slave and plaintiff against Dade County's commissioner-election system. Her district begins on the north side of Miami in the Dade County suburbs, but carefully carved out are the mostly white high-rise condominiums on the shores of Biscayne Bay and heavily Cuban Hialeah. Her district extends south taking in a narrow corridor and expanding periodically to take in heavily black areas.[297] The museum and her district epitomize the legacy of the Voting Rights Act.

Like Dallasites, Dade County voters were besieged by other voting issues while they dealt with the county commission. During the years that Dade County worked its way to a minority-run commission, a statewide racial-redistricting conflict played out with Dade County as one of its battlezones. Before the 1982 election, redistricting took place for U. S. congressional and state legislative districts. State districts were changed from at-large to single-member districts. Dade grew from three to four U. S. House seats, to which voters elected white, male Democrats. Before the 1982 reapportionment, there was only one Hispanic state representative and no Hispanic state senators from the county. Following reapportionment, single-member districts produced seven Hispanic representatives and three Hispanic senators in the state house.[298]

The system endured until 1992 when Miguel DeGrandy filed suit. His complaint was against the Speaker of the Florida house, alleging that the districts for the state legislature and state senate were malapportioned since they did not reflect demographic changes that had occurred since their creation in 1982.[299]

In April of that year, the state legislature adopted a redistricting plan that created 40 single-member districts for the senate and 120 single-member districts for the house. DeGrandy and the NAACP amended their complaint to say that the new districts diluted minority voting strength. They pointed out areas of the state where additional, reasonably-compact Hispanic districts could have been drawn. The Justice Department filed a similar complaint saying that Hispanic votes were diluted in an area largely covered by Dade County.[300]

On July 1, a judge ruled that the state's plan was a violation of Section 2 because more than Dade's nine Hispanic districts could have been created without casting a negative effect on black voters. The judge went past equal results to seek maximum representation. The court imposed a remedial plan, proposed by DeGrandy, creating 11 majority-Hispanic districts.[301]

The case ultimately worked its way to the Supreme Court which heard it in October 1993. Joel Klein represented Florida. In an exchange between Klein and Justice Kennedy, Klein said, "We are an immigrant population, so we tend to come into a nucleus and disperse evenly from there. If you're telling us that in a statewide plan that we cannot just prove dilution in one area and apply it proportionately statewide, then we will always be under-represented."

Kennedy replied, "Have we said in our cases that people have group rights? I though the whole underpinning of our constitution is that people are treated as individuals."

Klein responded, "It is, but it's not the underpinning of the Voting Rights Act."[302]

In June 1994, the Supreme Court announced its decision. Perhaps most important was a clear statement that the Voting Rights Act does not require the creation of the maximum number of majority-minority districts. The Court concluded that the three *Gingles* factors were met but that the totality of circumstances was not. This was a statewide redistricting plan and Hispanics could be expected to elect representatives roughly in proportion to their numbers. There was no requirement that the representation be proportional county-by-county.[303] Justice Thomas, joined by Justice Scalia, even contended that the case should be dismissed because apportionment is not a cognizable claim under Section 2 because it is not a "standard practice or procedure".[304]

CHAPTER 8: THE UNRAVELING?

With majority rule and a racially organized majority, 'we don't count' is the 'way it works' for minorities. In a racially divided society, majority rule is not a reliable instrument of democracy....[1]

—*Lani Guinier, President Clinton's nominee to head the Civil Rights Division of the Department of Justice*

In August 1992, Ed Brown, the head of the Voter Education Project, turned out the lights of his organization. Private funding had dried up. For three decades, the VEP had been the most influential organization supporting efforts to get out the black vote. Blacks were now registered at roughly the same rate as whites—between 55 and 65 percent. Despite the untapped political potential of unregistered black voters, funding sources for the project believed the job was done and the crisis was over.[2]

This perceived lack of need was supported by the factual results of redistricting that had occurred since the 1982 Amendments. The 103rd Congress featured record numbers of women, African-Americans and Hispanics, as well as the first American Indian elected to the Senate in more than 50 years. Voters sent 28 new women members to Congress—including the first black woman ever elected to the Senate. They increased the overall number of blacks in the House to 39 by electing 17 new African-American members. The new House also included 20 Hispanics, a net gain of six.[3]

The very influential Southwest Voter Registration Education Project (SVREP) also recognized its role was changing, although it did not fall apart. With SVREP help, more than two million Hispanic voters were registered in California and 1.3 million were registered in Texas. Hispanic office holders in Texas alone had increased 259 percent to 2,030 and, nationwide, to over 4000.[4] As Andy Hernandez, the organization's president, left his post to join the Democratic National Committee, he said, "The last 20 years were a struggle for social and political power. We were telling Latinos, 'You have to get into the system to gain what you need.' The struggle over the next 20 years will be for accountability. The point of political power is to use it. We now have to hold those elected to vote the way they said they would, to hold both parties accountable." Antonio Gonzalez, the organization's acting director acknowledged that Hispanics now had power. "The question is now, what do we do with it? . . . We are going to do a lot more work on governance, on keeping elected officials accountable, and we're going to be doing more work on policy studies, such as the North American Development Bank." The Bank was a provision of the North American Free Trade Agreement for which SVREP lobbied hard.[5] This kind of effort stands as a sharp contrast to the *we shall overcome, get out the vote* beginnings of the 1960s and 1970s. The politically oppressed had joined the ranks of the political power brokers.

During the month following the 1993 passage of Motor Voter, President Clinton issued a statement to the press on his support of the Voting Rights Act. He made an interesting comment about the passage of the 1982 Amendments:

> As more subtle forms of disenfranchisement came to be employed, the Congress, with bipartisan agreement, strengthened and extended the Voting Rights Act in 1982.[6]

Recall that the 1982 amendments strengthened Section 2 which began looking for equal results. Section 5 was designed to prevent new ways to disenfranchise people, and Section 5 was nearly unchanged in 1982. In truth, the 1982 Amendments were passed because the liberal agenda was simply not complete. The desired results had not yet been achieved, because legislation until that time simply could not achieve it.

In August 1993, blacks won control of the Selma, Alabama City Council. After the 1990 census, the threat of a 58 percent black majority caused the white-dominated city council to approve a redistricting plan which allowed them to retain a 5 to 4 majority. Blacks sued and won, reversing the tables in the next election as blacks gained a majority. Ironically, the mayor remained Joe Smitherman who had been in office for 28 years—back to the Martin Luther King marches.[7]

In 1993, the Supreme Court conservatives slightly loosened-up on the decisions of the mid-1970s. In *Presley v. Etowah County Commission*, Alabama voters sued the commission for changing its method of allocation of monetary authority to each commissioner. After the 1987 election of a black commissioner, the white-majority commission ruled that all funding decisions would be made by the commission at-large rather than allocating funds for the discretionary use of each commissioner. The majority opinion written by Justice Kennedy ruled that the commission's action did not require Justice Department preclearance because the action was not governed by the Voting Rights Act. The court reiterated that the Act's jurisdiction only covered issues of a change in the manner of voting, changes in candidacy requirements, composition of the electorate, or changes in affecting the creation or abolition of elective office. Kennedy said that the suit was about changes in "governance" and not about changes "with respect to voting".[8] Justices Stevens, White, and Blackmun dissented.

In the same year, the Court further demonstrated its new leanings in *Voinovich v. Quilter*. Ohio law required that the legislature reapportion itself every ten years. The reapportionment board of three Republicans and two Democrats, enacting a redistricting plan, voted along party lines. The new plan created eight safe majority-minority districts. Plaintiffs, headed by Barney Quilter, Speaker Pro Tempore of the House, believed that minority influence could have been increased by spreading out the minority votes and counting on white-crossover votes to elect minority candidates. They accused the Republicans of packing the eight districts to minimize minority influence. The district court held for the plaintiffs, causing Governor George Voinovich to appeal. The Supreme Court overruled the lower court because the plaintiffs had no claim under Section 2 unless they could show that voting rights had been abridged. The court pointed out that the federal courts could not mandate districts except as a remedy for a violation of the law. However, states could voluntarily pass any plan they wanted provided Section 2 was not violated. Further, the district court had forgotten the three-part test of *Gingles* which required evidence of white bloc voting. This case, by contrast, actually depended on white crossover voting.[9]

In the same case, Democrats maintained that the plan was illegal because districts deviated in population by more than 10 percent. The Republicans maintained that they were only following Ohio's constitutional policy favoring districts that follow county lines. The Supreme Court acknowledged that a legitimate state interest would override a strict application of one-man, one-vote and asked the District Court to reconsider whether Ohio had any such state interest.

In June 1993, the Supreme Court, in a narrow 5 to 4 vote, decided that racial gerrymandering could become so blatant that it could not be constitutionally defended. The case was *Shaw v. Reno* in which North Carolina submitted a congressional redistricting plan to the attorney general who refused to preclear it. The attorney general contended that North Carolina could have drawn two black-majority districts rather than only one as in the submitted plan. The North Carolina General Assembly then passed legislation creating a second black-majority district. Five white citizens sued the state and the attorney general on the grounds that the revised plan contained dramatically irregular borders which constituted an unconstitutional racial gerrymander. A three-judge District court dismissed the charges against the state contending that the rights of white citizens had not been violated because whites were proportionately represented on a statewide basis. The

District Court believed it did not have jurisdiction to dismiss the charges against the attorney general, so it deferred the case to the Supreme Court. Sandra Day O'Connor delivered the courts surprising decision which returned the case to the district court advising that the white citizens' had a valid claim. The court described the contested district:

> The second majority-black district, . . . is approximately 160 miles long and, for much of its length, no wider than the I-85 corridor. It winds in snake-like fashion through tobacco country, financial centers, and manufacturing areas "until it gobbles in enough enclaves of black neighborhoods."

The district had been compared to a "Rorschach ink-blot test" and "a bug splattered on a windshield." The Washington Post of April 20, 1993 quoted a North Carolina legislator as saying, "If you drove down the interstate with both car doors open, you'd kill most of the people in the district."

The court's words were harsh concerning districts that are drawn on no basis other than race:

> Classifications of citizens based solely on race are by their nature odious to a free people whose institutions are founded upon the doctrine of equality, because they threaten to stigmatize persons by reason of their membership in a racial group and to incite racial hostility. . . . By perpetuating stereotypical notions about members of the same racial group—that they think alike, share the same political interests, and prefer the same candidates—a racial gerrymander may exacerbate the very patterns of racial bloc voting that majority-minority districting is sometimes said to counteract. It also sends to elected representatives the message that their primary obligation is to represent only that group's members, rather than their constituency as a whole.

This decision was not meant to overturn past decisions nor did the suit contend that white votes were diluted. Further, the Court agreed that race-conscious decision making is permissible in some circumstances. The court only ruled that this particular district was so irregular that it could not be defended.

Reaction to the decision was strong among the minority leadership. Rep. Kweisi Mfume, Maryland Democrat and Chairman of the Congressional Black Caucus, joined black and Hispanic members of Congress challenging the North Carolina decision. Vice President Gore said it was a bad decision. The stake for minorities was potentially tremendous. A year prior to the decision, 26 new majority-minority districts were created with the approval of the Bush administration.[10] After the 1994 elections, of the 38 black representatives in the U. S. House, all but four were elected from majority-minority districts.

Continuing an active year, the Supreme Court decided *Holder v. Hall* in October. Black voters and the NAACP of Beckley County, Georgia, argued against the single-commissioner system in which the county vested all legislative and executive authority in one person. Since its creation in 1912, Beckley County had had a single commissioner even though, in 1985, the state legislature authorized county referendums that could establish five-member commissions. The referendum failed although the Beckley County voters had previously authorized a five-member school board and most other Georgia counties approved a five-member commission. The single-commissioner system was supported by the district court, reversed by the court of appeals, and then supported again by the Supreme Court.

Since no black had ever run or been elected commissioner, plaintiffs argued that the system was discriminatory when compared to a theoretical five-member system. They convinced the courts that a compact majority-minority district could be drawn in a five-member system. Wrestling with the problem, Justice Kennedy wrote for the majority: "With respect to challenges to the size of a governing authority, respondents fail to explain where the search for reasonable alternative benchmarks should begin and end and they provide no acceptable principles for deciding future cases. The wide range of possibilities makes the choice inherently standardless."[11]

The court then decided against the plaintiffs, but was highly fragmented. Although five justices agreed with the conclusion, no majority agreed on all of the reasons for the conclusion. Justice Blackmun wrote a dissent in which he was joined by Justices Souter, Stevens, and Ginsburg. They argued, in essence, that the commission's size would be a valid issue in a Section 5 case were the size being altered. In arguing that Section 2 must be at least as broadly interpreted as Section 5, they concluded that size must certainly be a valid Section 2 claim. Blackmun stated, "Nearly 30 years after the passage of this landmark civil-rights legislation, its goals remain unfulfilled."

Justice Thomas, however, wrote a very lengthy concurring opinion. He took the conservative position of believing that the Voting Rights Act and the Constitution did not apply in this case, and, furthermore, many of the earlier decisions of the court dealt with "questions of political philosophy, not questions of law. . . . [I]n a majoritarian system, numerical minorities lose elections." He argued that the courts were in an ineffective, inappropriate pursuit.

> [W]e have immersed the federal courts in a hopeless project of weighing questions of political theory. . . . Worse, in pursuing the ideal measure of voting strength, we have devised a remedial mechanism that encourages the federal courts to segregate voters into racially designated district to ensure minority electoral success.

In December 1993, a three-judge federal court, armed with the North Carolina *Shaw* decision, declared Louisiana's congressional districts unconstitutional because they were drawn only to guarantee the election of two black representatives.[12] The opinion read, "We find the plan in general, and Louisiana's Congressional District 4 in particular, are the product of racial gerrymandering and are not narrowly tailored to further any compelling government interest."[13] In Georgia, white voters in the Eleventh Congressional District filed suit against the legislature's redistricting plan that created a black-majority district stretching from Savannah to the black neighborhoods of Atlanta, 260 miles away. Similar suits were filed in Texas and California. In December 1994, the Supreme Court decided to hear the Louisiana and Georgia cases as benchmarks for the others.[14] The Justice Department, determined not to see its authority eroded, joined the litigation in the Georgia case and filed friend-of-the-court briefs in Texas and Louisiana. Kweisi Mfume and Jesse Jackson warned that the lawsuits threatening political gains of blacks were similar to the challenges that eliminated the post-Civil War gains of blacks in the South.[15]

The increasingly conservative nature of the federal court system was being felt. By the end of the Bush presidency, more than two-thirds of the judges on the federal district and appellate courts were appointees of Bush and Reagan.[16] The alarm felt by civil rights activists at the potential weakening of the results test was expressed by President Clinton in July 1994:

> [I]t is increasingly clear that a direct attack is being mounted on electoral districts that contain African-American or Hispanic population majorities. . . . [I]f necessary, I will work with Attorney General Reno and members of Congress to enact legislation to clarify and reinforce the protections of the Voting Rights Act.[17]

Radically different voting schemes became headline material as President Clinton promoted Lani Guinier as his choice to head the Civil Rights Division of the Department of Justice. The President immediately took heat from conservatives and many moderates—enough heat to cause him to withdraw the nomination before confirmation hearings.[18] Her near appointment would have passed as trivial history except that her philosophies constituted another major step forward in liberal voting theory. She recognized that the current election systems were winner-take-all by 50.1 percent of the electorate. Since many communities have polarized majorities and minorities, and these groups may be fixed for years, she reasoned that minorities would always be losers and effectively have no power at all.

She envisioned the follow-on to one-man, one-vote to be *one-vote, one-value*. To achieve such a value, she favored appropriate use of supermajority voting or minority vetoing. She also advocated, under specific circumstances, the use of cumulative voting, a system in which each voter gets several votes which he may apply to several candidates or use all for a single candidate. This legalized "stuffing the ballot box" would give minorities power in areas in which the minorities were evenly spread among the majority population. She believed the political process required more give and take, more compromise, than winner-take-all.

Guinier did not invent the process; cumulative voting has been used several times, usually to balance the power of political parties. Chilton County, Alabama increased black power by implementing cumulative voting rather than expanding the size of the seven-member county commission.[19] In April 1994, a Maryland court ordered cumulative voting because it was a less drastic remedy than grossly gerrymandered districts.[20] While such schemes may have upsides, they are difficult to reconcile with democracy.

In June 1995, the Supreme Court rendered decisions in the Louisiana and Georgia redistricting cases. The Louisiana case was dismissed on a technicality over whether the plaintiffs, living outside the district, could claim that they were harmed. In the Georgia case, however, the Court held that the gerrymandered Eleventh Congressional District was illegal because it was drawn predominantly for racial reasons. White plaintiffs successfully argued that they were denied the equal protection of the Fourteenth Amendment.

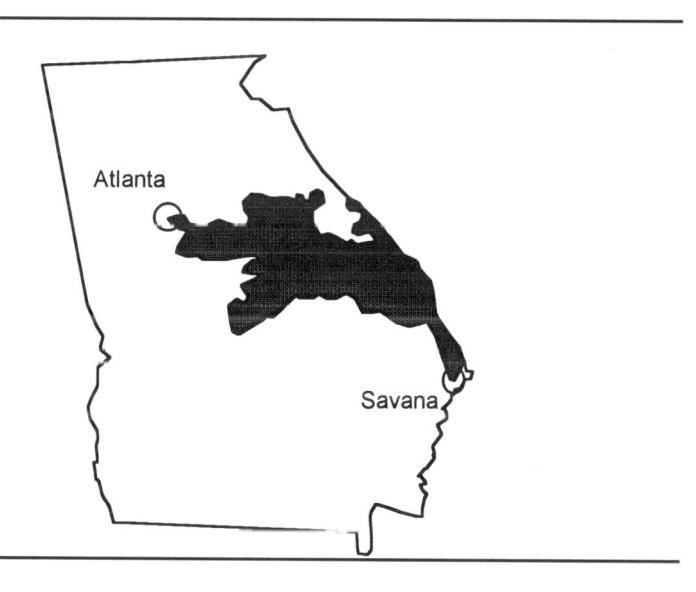

FIGURE 15: GEORGIA'S 11TH DISTRICT

In an attempt to redistrict after the 1990 census, Georgia twice submitted, to the Justice Department, a congressional redistricting plan that created two predominantly-black districts. Each time, the attorney general rejected the plan because a third black district could be derived from Georgia's black population. Between the submissions, the ACLU designed a three-black-district plan for the Georgia General Assembly's black caucus. That plan, known as "max black" was specifically used by the attorney general as a reason why the state's two-black-district plan was rejected. The General Assembly responded with a three-black-district plan that included the Eleventh District which grouped voters in Savannah with the black sections of Atlanta, 260 miles away. Between the two ends, the district split eight counties and five municipalities. Opponents called the district *Sherman's March*. The Justice Department approved the plan. Eleventh-District, white plaintiffs successfully opposed the district in federal district court. The state appealed to the Supreme Court which upheld the ruling of the district court.

Justice Kennedy delivered the opinion in a five-to-four ruling. He claimed that "the social, political, and economic makeup of the Eleventh District tells a tale of disparity, not community."[21] The critical question left from *Shaw* was how bizarre the shape of the district needed to be before the court would declare it a racial gerrymander. Kennedy wrote, "Shape is relevant, not because bizarreness is a necessary element of a constitutional wrong or the threshold requirement of proof, but because it is persuasive circumstantial evidence that race for its own sake, and not other districting principles, were the legislature's dominant and controlling rationale in drawing its district lines."[22] The opinion dealt a long overdue blow to the Justice Department and said that states cannot hide behind Section 5 rejections; states cannot claim that there is any compelling state interest in satisfying the attorney general. The court revived the principle of retrogression established in *Beer v. United States*. Prior to any redistricting, Georgia had one black district, thus the two-black-district plans that the attorney general rejected could not possibly violate Section 5 because they were not retrogressive.

The decision was even more conservative than most interpretations of *Shaw*. The court's new standard, the *Miller Test*, says strict scrutiny will take place not only when traditional districting practices are abandoned, but also when those factors are given less weight than race.

Justices Ginsburg, Stevens, Breyer, and Souter dissented. These dissenters hung onto a turnabout in logic. For thirty years, the liberal contingent of the court had put its hands into state districting processes and for thirty years, the court upheld the power of the attorney general under Section 5. Now Justice Ginsburg's dissent reminded the court that the Constitution leaves these matters to the state. If a state voluntarily draws a race-conscious plan, it is not up to the courts to object. Justice Stevens objected on the basis that the plaintiffs were not harmed. The plaintiffs failed, he wrote, to demonstrate that the elected representatives ignored their needs as was speculated would happen in *Shaw*.

The Georgia legislature and the courts spent over a year trying to design new districts. Ultimately, the job had to be left to a three-judge federal panel whose two-black-district plan withstood the scrutiny of the Supreme Court.

The Georgia decision quickly lead to other litigation in grossly gerrymandered districts. Among these was Eddie Bernice Johnson's District 30 in southern Dallas County. In December 1995, that case went to the Supreme Court. The essence of the defense was that the primary reason for the bizarre shape of the district was simple politics. The gerrymandering was done simply to protect the neighboring incumbents and the black majority-minority District 30 was a serendipitous result.[23] Politicians were willing to expose their petty, protectionist deal making rather than give up a district. Earlier that year, the Supreme Court ruled in a Tennessee case on the requirement for majority-minority districts. A district court had ordered the addition of one black-majority district in the Memphis area, while the state and plaintiffs had requested two black districts. The Supreme Court voted 8-1 to not hear the case, thus upholding the lower court. The brief ruled that states with large minority populations need not always create majority-minority districts. It even suggested that creating several districts, each of 25 percent minority could afford minorities greater influence.[24]

On June 13, 1996, the Supreme Court ruled on Dallas' District 30 along with two Houston districts. Using the logic of *Shaw* and *Miller*, the court declared the districts unconstitutional racial gerrymanders. A plurality of justices could not accept Texas' argument that politics was the primary motive for the district's bizarre configuration (see the Dallas portion of Chapter 7).[25] Attempting to add clarity to her thoughts, Sandra Day O'Connor wrote a concurring opinion even though she also wrote the court's opinion. Her thoughts are especially important because she is considered the swing vote on this issue. She noted that, although the Supreme Court has never validated the constitutionality of Section 2, numerous lower courts have and that states should behave consistently with the assumption that Section 2, with the 1982 amendments, is constitutional. She reiterated that states may intentionally create majority-minority districts as long as race does not dominate over traditional districting criteria. She encouraged areas that have strong evidence of the presence of all the *Gingles* factors to create majority-minority districts.[26]

The minority reaction was one of dismay. "Only the shell [of the Voting Rights Act] still stands," stated Theodore Shaw of the NAACP Legal Defense and Education Fund.[27]

CHAPTER 9: CONCLUSIONS

What should one learn from the history of the Voting Rights Act and the tales of Dallas, Dade and Arizona? Are the results of the act not desirable in a society that so loves to vaunt its democracy? Do the ends justify the means? Undoubtedly the path would have been steeper, the climb perhaps unmanageable, had the act not cleared the way.

The 1965 Act was fully justified. America simply could not square its principles with the denial of voting rights in some regions of the nation. While there may have been other, less-confrontational approaches, extraordinary effort from the Congress was justified. Despite its virtue and early effectiveness, however, the act and its subsequent amendments were flawed, both in their social intent and in their legal construction. Several aspects have ensured long-term social failure:

- The act lacked any measurable goals, thus allowing it to run far afield of its original intent.
- The act's inclusion of language minorities turned it from an equal opportunity act to a social reallocation program.
- Rather than overcoming the long-term effects of race, the Act's 1982 *results test* maximized racial contention through inequitable voting schemes.

Ultimately, these flaws have diminished the value of the act for both the majority and minorities. Unique among those minorities, however, are Native Americans and their complex relationship with federal policy. A long history of failed U. S. Indian policy has eclipsed any real benefits that Native Americans have gained from new-found voting rights.

Immeasurable Goals are Unreachable Goals

The act's first flaw was its failure to define success—a defect that created the vacuum in which other problems could develop. The 1965 Act contained no measure to declare the task complete, no safeguard to keep its noble intent from running afoul to ignoble ends. Congress believed that certain tests, prerequisite to voting, were evil attempts to deny franchise, yet Congress did not define the job complete when all such tests were eradicated. Framers of the legislation believed that the low registration rate of blacks was the measure that identified discriminatory regions, but they suggested no percentage that would allay that belief. The law had temporary, extraordinary enforcement provisions, yet gave the courts and states no clue of what benchmark would obviate their need. Congress provided a single criteria for termination—the passage of five years, then five more, then seven, then twenty-five—forty-two years of *temporary* provisions. How could Congress continually extend the special provisions? Without a goal, the job was never quite done.

The goal of the 1965 Act was to get minorities registered so that they could participate in political life. In this regard, the act's total effectiveness to date was completed during the first five years. The following chart illustrates:

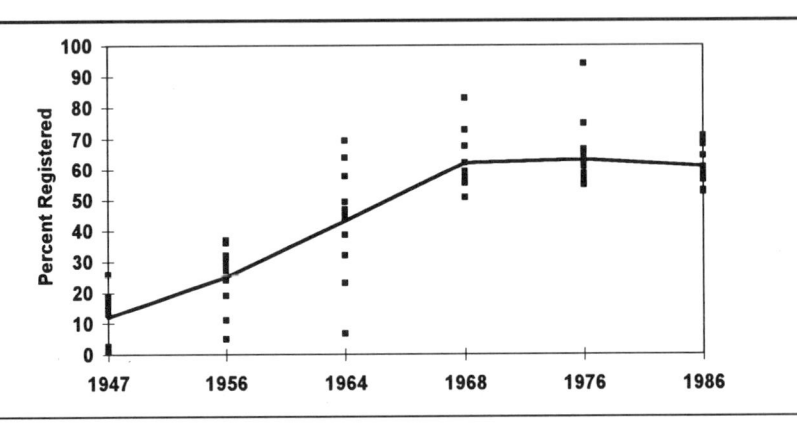

FIGURE 16: PERCENTAGE OF VOTING-AGE BLACKS REGISTERED IN ALL ELEVEN SOUTHERN STATES[1]

The plotted points are individual state numbers;[2] the solid line is the average for all of the Southern States. The process of registering black voters was well underway before 1965. Court cases and civil rights acts were making their mark, but the Voting Rights Act moved the *holdout* states. Mississippi had maintained a seven percent black registration rate until the Voting Rights Act catapulted it to fifty percent.

The South never improved on its 1968 black registration numbers, thus civil rights leaders had to find other ways to exploit the act. This ultimately lead Congress into the political thicket of affirmative-action democracy.

Social Redistribution: The Fallacy of Hispanic Needs

The second great flaw in the Voting Rights Act was the assumption from 1975 forward that the plight of all racial minorities in America was the same as the plight of blacks. The largest identified group was Hispanic—a set of American subgroups with no relational, cultural, or original commonality. The case for extreme measures supporting Hispanic voting stemmed from the Hispanic voters' failure to perform. No general argument supported the idea that they had been denied the right to vote as had blacks. Liberals claimed Hispanics were oppressed as evidenced by their high level of joblessness and poverty, but U. S. immigration policy was the main driver. While Cubans may have once been well off in Cuba, they entered the U. S. without assets. Other large rushes of Hispanics fled revolutions in Haiti and Nicaragua arriving penniless on American shores. Mexicans mostly entered for low paying jobs that raised their standard of living. Second generation Hispanics have fared well in America, both in economic gain and assimilation into the society.

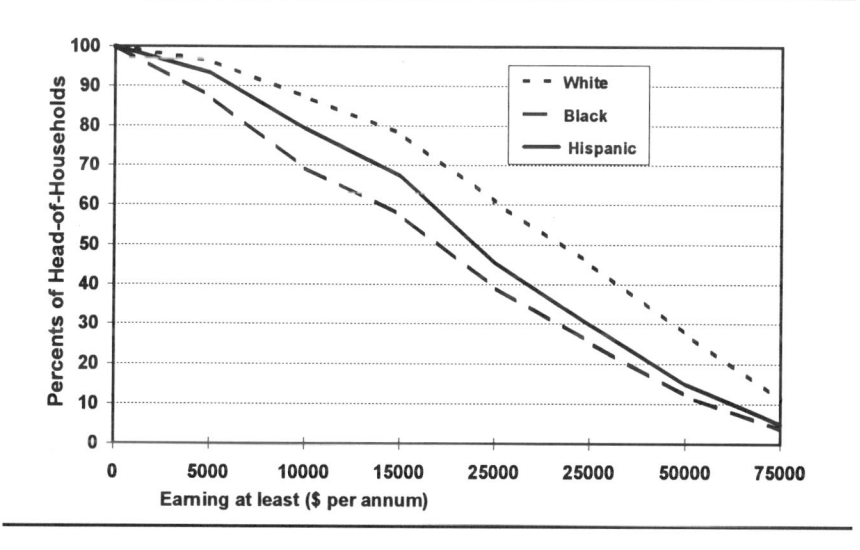

FIGURE 17: RACE VERSUS INCOME - 1991[3]

The Hispanic population grew from 14 million in 1980 to 26 million in 1995. Of the twelve million new Hispanics, nearly eight million were immigrants. Despite the continuing economic drag of poor immigrants joining the ranks, Hispanics overall have faired considerably better than blacks in income.[4] Half the adult Hispanic population in the U. S. today is foreign-born. Statistically lumping all of these people together inadequately depicts the true success of Hispanic Americans. Widescale prejudice is not evident. Six

Hispanic governors have been elected in three states that do not have anything near a majority-Hispanic electorate.

If assimilation is a goal, as it was for earlier immigrants, Hispanics have done well. One measure of assimilation is the intermarriage rate between Hispanics and whites. Of the 26 million Hispanics in the United States in 1995, more than 1.2 million are married to non-Hispanic spouses.[5] This number is high considering that most of the 26 million are too young to marry and many of the adults were married before entering the U. S.

The idea that Hispanics must be nurtured through affirmative action creates a permanent underclass. Spanish voting materials do nothing to further their cause. Non-citizens have nothing to gain from the material and most Hispanic citizens could get along adequately with English. Almost no one will become economically or politically powerful in the United States without a good grasp of English. Putting off the day that Hispanics must learn English only forestalls the possibility of individual success. More importantly, such programs assume that today's immigrants are not the hardy stock that built America in the last century. Linda Chavez, former member of the U. S. Civil Rights Commissions, argues this point:

> Previous immigrants had been eager to become 'American,' to learn the language, to fit in. But the entitlements of the civil rights era encouraged Hispanics to maintain their language and culture, their separate identity, in return for the reward of being members of an officially recognized minority group. Assimilation gave way to affirmative action.[6]

Like redistricting, obsessive insistence on multilingual ballots has segmented rather than united the nation. It has helped build the barriers to assimilation. The civil rights era has removed the responsibility placed upon immigrants to walk themselves through the door into a room where all can share the American dream. Instead it has moved the boundaries of the room so that no one is outside and in doing so it has chipped away at that dream. The value of membership in an organization always declines when the entrance requirements are lowered and that decline in value applies not only to the establishment, but to the new entrants as well.

Racial Contention From "Fair Districts"

I do not discount the achievements of the Voting Rights Act. It opened the polls to blacks in the South. As blacks gained political clout, some whites attempted to diminish their power by "cracking and packing" in various redistricting schemes. While such practices flouted democracy, voting-rights advocates began to believe that full turnaround was justified. American traditions and color-blind ideals absolutely demanded drawing districts lines on bases other than color, but the courts and Congress carved a color line. To counteract black vote dilution, they advocated maximizing black strength. If blacks were to be winners, whites would be losers, thus racial lines were drawn.

The courts were established to judge matters of law, not philosophy. The Constitution espouses the rights of the individual. These rights are constitutionally assured by specifying the protections that each individual has against the government. Where race has been mentioned in law, it was only designed to clarify that the rights of individuals supersede race. Never did the Constitution or its amendments give rights to a race of people.

Lacking a goal, Congress refused to terminate the special provisions even though the polls were open to blacks. The act moved from voting rights to voting results, from equal opportunity to affirmative action. Along with other social legislation, the act began to further polarize ethnic groups. With affirmative action, there are only winners and losers and a winner-or-loser mentality can only lead to polarization.

Beginning in the 1970s, bizarre districts were drawn to maximize voting strength. Political redistricting, aided by the power of modern computers, allowed politicians to select their constituents rather than voters selecting their representatives. This increased polarization and diminished the possibility of compromise since politicians could construct districts in which they could safely take hard-line positions and never compromise.

Supreme Court Justice Clarence Thomas commented, "As a practical matter, our drive to segregate political districts by race can only serve to deepen racial divisions by destroying any need for voters or candidates to build bridges between racial groups or to form voting coalitions."[7]

The lack of political bridges and coalitions yields polarization. Drawing racial voting lines forces minorities and whites into power-grabbing contention across those district lines.

U. S. Indian Policy

Of the three stories presented, Native Americans seemed to have gained the least, at least in terms of their empowerment from the Voting Rights Act. In contrast to the other stories, the Justice Department did most of the fighting in Arizona. Indians, living on reservations, do not fit into the general constituency of their states because they are governed by tribal and federal laws more than by state laws. Voting rights give power to individuals seeking independence and responsibility. Within the artificial walls of a reservation, the citizens remain somewhere between wards of the government and members of independent sovereign nations; these issues transcend and obscure voting rights.

The current system of reservations, while perhaps showing some respect for an overrun people, is a hopeless trap for most inhabitants. Native Americans are twice as likely as other Americans to be murdered or to commit suicide. High rates of alcoholism make Indians five times as likely to die of cirrhosis of the liver. Fifty percent of the reservation youth drop out of high school and college graduation rates are half that of the rest of the nation.[8]

Poverty and ignorance abound on the Navajo Reservation and will remain there as long as Navajos are not forced to join the rest of America. It is more from guilt than compassion that the system survives.

The Navajo culture was changed once as settlers brought sheep and cattle to a people who were previously hunters. There is no reason to suspect that the Navajo culture would be lost with the demise of the reservation. Look in Boston to see if the Irish or Italian cultures are lost. Look in San Francisco to see if the Asian cultures are lost. The culture could be maintained without the brutality of an economic system that depends on ranching on America's roughest land or one that has the lure of running bingo parlors and lotteries in conflict with state laws. The enduring culture of the Indians, one of rugged independence, is not enhanced by government handouts, living in HUD houses, being on energy assistance, or being unemployed. What has already been lost is a culture of proud, independent, self-sufficient people.

Is there any realistic hope? Yes, some tribes stand in sharp contrast to the Navajo. The Choctaws in Mississippi shared the Navajo plight of poverty until the early 1970s. In the succeeding years, the reservation has been transformed into an industrial success now bringing in more than $100 million annually. Today the Choctaws assemble sophisticated electronics, telephones, and speakers for high-end technology firms. They manufacture 83 million hand-finished greeting cards each year and they run one of the largest printing plants for direct-mail advertising. The unemployment rate of 80 percent on the reservation has been transformed into full-employment. In fact, the plants now employ blacks and whites from the neighboring impoverished Mississippi countryside. Salaries have increased seven-fold, health care facilities are the envy of the area, and the reservation schools employ the top teachers. During the transformation, the role of and need for the BIA was nearly extinguished. These changes came from determination, leadership, and tenacity which carried the tribe through the early failures. Choctaw leadership recognized that the tribe's competition was the third world of Asia where many countries had the will to succeed. Choctaws also had the will to succeed and are now in a position of independence from which tribal members can aspire to any height they wish. The Choctaws have not assimilated so much as individuals, but they have assimilated as a tribe. In this regard, they can serve as a model to Navajos and others.

The final problem of U. S. Indian policy—perhaps the biggest for the future—is the growing recognition and acceptance of tribal sovereignty. The concept completely contradicts to the U. S. Constitution. Current policy supports the dichotomous objectives of protecting and enhancing Indian voting rights while expanding Indian sovereignty to the point that individual voting rights within the reservation are no longer guaranteed by the federal government.

The Future

We must continue to divide this nation up into voting jurisdictions. How do we, then, draw district lines? Do we ignore lines by moving important issues to statewide or nationwide referendum? Perhaps, but there are still local officials and local issues. Liberal thinkers have begun looking toward alternative voting systems which create logical or virtual rather than physical districts. These should be considered, but any method must be capable of changing with the dynamics of population.

The Merits of Alternative Voting Systems

Social scientists have created many alternative voting methods designed to cope with multi-member and many-candidate districts. These methods avoid the need to carve regional councils and boards into single-member districts. Some of the most talked about methods are cumulative voting, the Hare system of single transferable vote, the Borda count, and approval voting.

For 30 years, the remedy for discriminatory voting schemes has been the institution of single-member districts where minority candidates could be assured of proportional success. Since there seemed to be no limit on how grossly gerrymandered the districts became, civil rights activists had only the mildest interest in other remedies such as alternative voting methods. After the 1992 *Shaw v. Reno* decision, activists began to panic about the legitimacy of the most bizarre districts, thus their interest in alternative schemes grew. Robert D. Ritchie, national director of the Washington-based Center for

Voting and Democracy, says, "Single-member districts are inherently unfair to large numbers of people."[9] These are the same words used in the 1970s and 1980s to describe multi-member districts. If neither multi-member nor single-member districts are fair, then logic suggests that only schemes that carve out minorities, voter-by-voter are fair. This institutionalizes the concept that race must always be the controlling factor in district construction.

The need for any alternative method is based on faulty logic. The mathematical inability to carve out racially homogeneous districts results from integration. A jurisdiction so integrated as to defy the creation of a "safe" minority district is not subject to the evils that justices generally require to show vote dilution. Besides, true dilution is not evidenced by the skin color of electoral success. It is evidenced by the failure of a particular group to receive a fair share of government services and it would be nearly impossible to create discriminatory service levels based on race in a fully integrated community. Alternate methods each introduce their own new problems.

Cumulative voting, discussed in an earlier chapter, is based on poor logic. It is a reversion to a contorted form of at-large representation which could help minorities be proportionately represented in multi-member political bodies. If cumulative voting systems were installed nationwide, the losers would soon complain because cumulative voting contains a fatal flaw. Voters must gamble to maximize their voting strength. Each voter in the polling booth must decide not only how many votes to give his favorite candidate, but also how many votes that candidate needs. Suppose the favorite candidate of a minority group received twice as many cumulative votes as necessary to win. Suppose further, as a result of the voters' spendthrift attention to the winning candidate, two other minority-choice candidates lost by narrow margins. The next morning's news would contain a quote from someone, "Cumulative voting is inherently unfair to large numbers of people."

The Hare system[10] of single transferable vote was first proposed by Thomas Hare in England and Carl George Andrae in Denmark in the 1850s. It is used for some elections in Massachusetts and New York and in several foreign countries. In this system, voters express their preferences by ranking all or some of the candidates. As part of a complex mathematical formula, votes not needed for the election of the most preferred candidate are passed on to the next most preferred. The advantage to this systems is that minorities can elect candidates in an at-large race in rough proportion to their numbers in the electorate. The disadvantages stem from the system's complexity. The mathematics are complicated enough to prove enigmatic to most voters. Many voters would mistrust a system they did not understand. Because all candidates can be ranked, each voter not only expresses his positive feeling about candidates, but also his negative feelings. Thus, such a system not only relies on candidate support, but also voter contempt—a concept not found in traditional democratic methods. Finally, the complexity can lead to some mathematical aberrations wherein raising a candidate in one's preference order can actually hurt that candidate.

The Borda Count[11], proposed over 200 years ago, is used by many private organizations today. Like the single transferable vote, Borda asks voters to rank candidates with a zero going to the lowest-ranked candidate, a one to the next, and so on. The points for each candidate are then added and the candidate with the largest sum wins. This has the advantage over Hare in that it is explicable to the voters. It suffers serious problems, however, because it can be easily manipulated by the voters. Like Hare, voters can support their candidates by giving them the highest number while voting against other candidates by giving them zeros. This system is also very sensitive to candidates with no hope of winning entering the race. Since such a candidate will still fall somewhere in the rankings for each voter, the losing non-viable candidate can still seriously affect and even reverse the outcome.

Approval voting[12] proposed in the 1970s, is a system in which each voter selects all of the candidates he considers viable for a position. This system has been proposed for use in some state legislatures, has been used in Democratic Party straw polls, and is used in some elections in the Soviet Union. With approval voting, each viable candidate receives one vote and the candidate(s) with the largest sum wins. Voters can vote for a single candidate, thus showing a strong preference, or vote for multiple candidates. Thus the voters have more flexible options. The candidate with the strongest support wins. Voters express support for their second choice if their first choice is unsuccessful. Also, voters would not have to vote against their favorite candidate just because that candidate had no hope of winning. Such voters could vote for their favorite candidate along with their most pragmatic pick.

Approval voting avoids many of the drawbacks of the other systems and, while bizarre by traditional standards, it does avoid run-off elections as well as giving the voters a sense of greater power and expression. Even so, it does not ensure success of minority candidates and does not force voters to make the tough, one-answer choices that are ultimately the result of the election process.

There is not a perfect election system. Simple-majority elections with run-offs ensure that most of the voters agreed at a moment in time. Ultimately, elections are winner-take-all no matter how great the variety of choice for the voter. New systems should continue to be examined, but a useful one must be simple and always reflect the voice of the voters.

Future Demographics

The majority-minority districts result in minority power too greatly based on demographics. If minorities move around and enclaves disappear, black, Hispanic, or Indian representation could be lost; the current system relies on segregation. Furthermore, blacks cannot expect to retain even their current strength under the present system. Government estimates predict that Hispanic population will catch up to black population around 2020. Asian populations will become nearly as great as blacks by 2050.

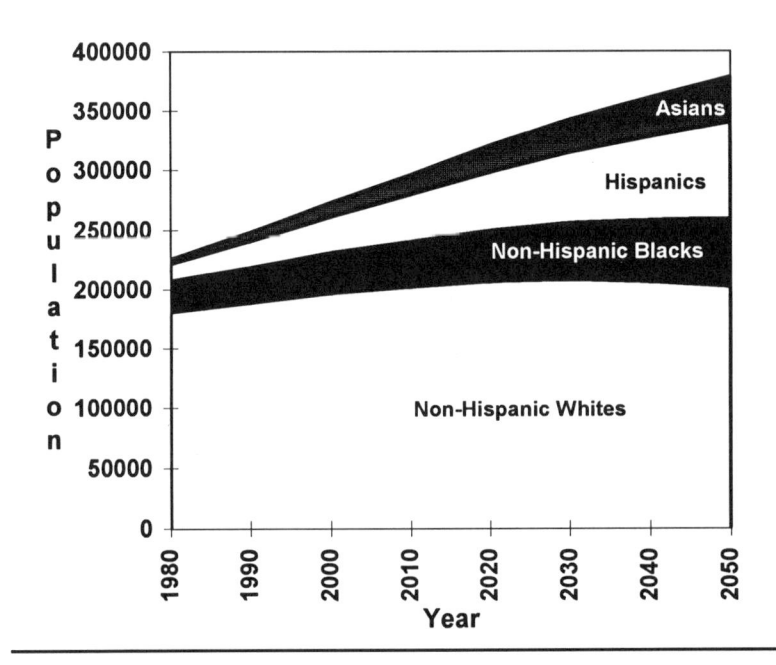

FIGURE 18: RACIAL POPULATIONS PROJECTIONS[13]

Even these projections give an oversimplified picture of race in America. Interracial marriages are increasingly common, especially between Hispanics and non-Hispanic whites. The ethnicity of the children of these marriages cannot be slotted into a single category. In Dade County, under pressure from mixed-race families, the Dade school district added "Multicultural" to its list of racial choices.[14] Minority districts and guaranteed minority results barely work in a two-race system and most certainly will fail in four-race apportionment. Not only would results be difficult to guarantee, but the system would serve as a limit on ethnic success just as surely as it would serve as a guarantee.

The Solution

Was the NAACP's Theodore Shaw correct that only the shell of the Voting Rights Act still exists? Absolutely not. Gone are the literacy tests that denied southern blacks political power; gone is the poll tax; gone are the deep South rural counties with practically no black voters; and virtually gone are the sheriffs that left blacks unwilling to vote. After 30 years, increases in minority voters and elected minority officials have put more minority issues on political agendas. Minorities appointed to commissions and boards, the heightened use of minority contractors, and the number of minority oriented programs evidence the persistent influence of the act.

The footprint of the act can be seen everywhere, but have recent Supreme Court decisions weakened the voting rights of minority Americans? Will an easing of the law return us to 1965? Nothing could return us to 1965. Blacks now vote; they hold office; they have political strength. They are powerful. By 1990, 24 blacks and ten Hispanics sat in Congress, 417 blacks and 124 Hispanics were in state legislators, and six of the ten largest U. S. cities had elected black mayors. Although the decision in Georgia's 11th District may temporarily reduce the number of minorities in Congress, most majority-minority districts are compact enough to pass the *Miller* test. If the court had supported race based districting, there would be very few additional opportunities for blacks to create majority-minority districts. Possibilities for a total of four additional congressional districts exist in Philadelphia, New York, and Mississippi. Beyond that, blacks could only make progress by forming coalitions with non-black communities. If blacks want to make progress in Congress, gerrymandering is not the way.

If minorities want to continue strengthening their influence in politics, they must learn to vote. This book has looked at the marked improvements in black voting and black opportunity in the South, but the countrywide data draw a different picture. Apathy is the greatest deterrent to minority strength and democratic theory in general. In 1992, total U. S. voting barely topped 55 percent of the voting age population. Countries such as Japan, Canada, Israel, Germany, Britain, Denmark, and even South Africa outpaced the U. S. Australia, with mandatory voting laws, topped 96 percent. Americans participated at rates similar to Russia, Mexico and India[15] (see Figure 19).

232   CONCLUSIONS

These data suggest that the greatest advantage minorities could garner requires going back to the get-out-the-vote campaigns of the 1960s. Forty-six percent of blacks and even more Hispanics remain silent on election day.

The most important reason that gerrymandering will not serve any segment of America in the long run is this: representation of races, cohesive philosophies, and social strata are not centered on a core value but on a desired result. Such methods must yield to representation of towns and neighborhoods where people live. America simply must evolve to race-blind, neighborhood-based districting. Race-blind no longer means minorities lose. In such a system, equal rights are carefully protected. While districts cannot be drawn for the sole purpose of maximizing minority strength, they cannot be designed to dilute that strength either. Minorities would face losses only in areas in which they represented a very small portion of the population or where they were well integrated into an otherwise white community. I have already argued that strong integration prevents discrimination in government services. Where races live together, they must work to form coalitions and compromises.

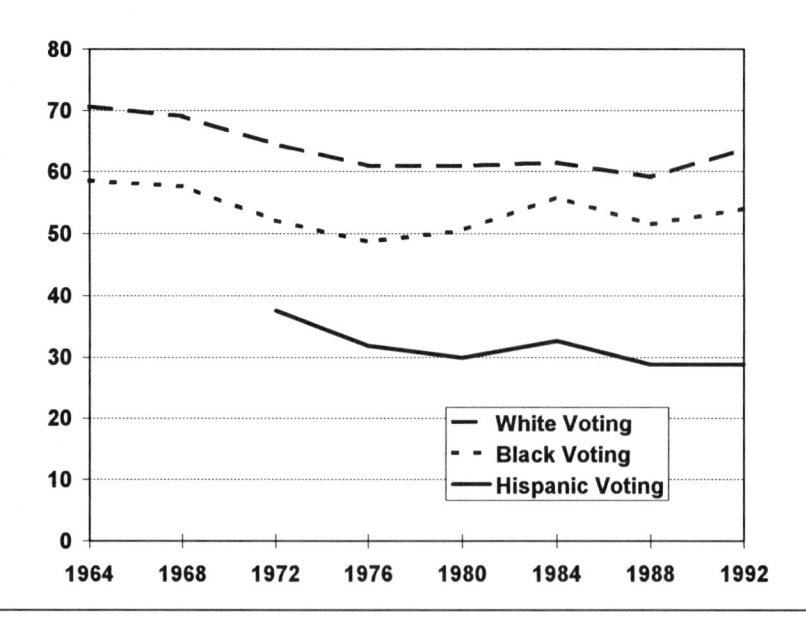

FIGURE 19: VOTING PARTICIPATION IN PRESIDENTIAL ELECTIONS 1964-1992[16]

CONCLUSIONS 233

Neighborhood coalitions and compromises are the only hope for rescue from the long-term decay of many of America's cities. Contention and self-interest are the hallmarks of the current system. Neighbors need to live together through some give-and-take. They must deal with the real issues of security, services, aesthetics, and plans. This process is key to the life-quality of the vicinity and its ability to change and lobby for government services. Dividing people by race and ethnicity only emphasizes the very element that divides neighborhoods.

The segregation of voters produced by a majority-minority system has an adverse effect on minorities. Blacks have been removed from white districts to form safe districts leaving behind districts that are whiter than before. Representatives in these new districts are less inclined than before to spend time on minority needs because their reelections are less dependent on the few minorities remaining in their districts. State sponsored minority quotas in Congress can actually lessen minority influence.

Attitude and demographic changes already in motion cannot be reversed. Suffering the adverse effects of a propped-up system is no longer justified. Minorities are on a roll. They must seriously consider the consequences of affirmative action. It serves as a ceiling to their potential strength and influence.

REFERENCES

Ball, Howard, Dale Krane, and Thomas P. Lauth, *Compromised Compliance: Implementation of the Voting Rights Act*. Westport, Connecticut: Greenwood Press, 1982.

Barone, Michael, and Grant Ujifusa, *The Almanac of American Politics 1996*. Washington, D. C.: National Journal, 1966.

Black, Earl, and Merle Black, *Politics and Society in the South*. Cambridge, Massachusetts: Harvard University Press, 1987.

Bordewich, Fergus M., *Killing the White Man's Indian: Reinventing Native Americans at the End of the Twentieth Century*. New York: Doubleday, 1996.

Buchanan, James E., *Miami - A Chronological and Documentary History*. New York: Oceana Publications, Inc., 1978.

Bucko, Richard Lewis, *Voting Participation of the Arizona Navajos in State and National Elections*. Thesis in Social Science. Flagstaff, Arizona: University of Northern Arizona, September 14, 1970.

Bullock, Charles S. III, and Charles M. Lamb, *Implementation of Civil Rights Policy*. Monterey, California: Brooks/Cole Publishing, 1984.

Chavez, Linda, *Out of the Barrio*. New York: Basic Books, 1991.

Davidson, Chandler, and Bernard Grofman, Editors, *Quiet Revolution in the South: The Impact of the Voting Rights Act 1965-1990*. Princeton: Princeton University Press, 1994.

Davis, Mary B., Editor, *Native America in the Twentieth Century: An Encyclopedia*. New York: Garland Publishing, Inc., 1994.

Deloria, Vine Jr., Editor, *American Indian Policy in the Twentieth Century*. Norman Oklahoma: University of Oklahoma Press, 1985.

Diaz, Guarione M., Editor, *Law and Politics in Florida's Redistricting*. Miami: Cuban American Policy Center, 1992.

Flemming, Arthur S., *The Voting Rights Act: Unfulfilled Goals, A Report of the United States Commission on Civil Rights*. Washington, D. C.: United States Commission on Civil Rights.

———, *The Voting Rights: Act 10 Years After*. Washington D. C.: United States Commission on Civil Rights, 1975.

Foster, Lorn S., Editor, *The Voting Rights Act, Consequences and Implications*. New York: Praeger, 1975.

Garrow, David J., *Protest at Selma*. New Haven: Yale University Press, 1975.

Green, A.C., *Dallas USA*, Texas Monthly Press, 1984.

Grofman, Bernard, Lisa Handley, and Richard G. Niemi, *Minority Representation and the Quest for Voting Equality*. Cambridge, Massachusetts: Cambridge University Press, 1992.

———, and Chandler Davidson, Editors, *Controversies in Minority Voting*. Washington, D. C.: Brookings Institution, 1992.

Hazel, Michael V., Editor, *Dallas Reconsidered: Essays in Local History*. Dallas, Texas: Three Forks Press, 1995.

Holmes: Maxine, and Gerald Saxon, Editors, *The WPA Dallas Guide and History*. Denton, Texas: University of North Texas Press, 1992.

Irons, Peter, and Stephanie Guitton, *May it please the Court*. New York: The New Press, 1993.

Iverson, Peter, *The Navajos*. New York: Chelsea House Publishers, 1990.

King, Martin Luther Jr., *Why We Can't Wait*. New American Library, 1991.

Lawson, Steven F., *Black Ballots: Voting Rights in the South 1944-1969*. New York: Columbia University Press, 1976.

———, *In Pursuit of Power: Southern Blacks and Electoral Politics, 1965-1982*. New York: Columbia University Press, 1985.

Locke, Raymond Friday, *The Book of the Navajo*. Mankind Publishing, 1992.

Lotz, Aileen R., *Metropolitan Dade County: Two-tier Government in Action*. Boston: Allyn and Bacon, 1984.

Lyden, Fremont J., and Lyman H. Legters, Editors, *Native Americans and Public Policy*. Pittsburgh: University of Pittsburgh Press, 1992.

MacDonald, Peter, with Ted Schwarz, *The Last Warrior*. The Library of the American Indian, 1993.

Maisel, L. Sandy, Editor, *Political Parties and Elections in the United States: An Encyclopedia*, Vol. 1., New York: Garland, 1991.

Nixon, Richard M., *RN: The Memoirs of Richard Nixon*. Easton Press, 1988.

O'Brien, David M., *Supreme Court Watch, 1993*. New York: W. W. Norton and Company, 1993.

Payne, Darwin, *Big D: Triumphs and Troubles of an American Supercity in the 20th Century*. Dallas: Three Forks Press, 1993.

———, Editor, *Sketches of a Growing Town*. Dallas: Southern Methodist University Press, 1991.

Peters, William, *A More Perfect Union: The Making of the United States Constitution*. New York: Crown Publishers, 1987.

Portes, Alexandro, and Alex Stepick, *City on the Edge: The Transformation of Miami*. Berkeley: University of California Press, 1993.

Rush, Mark E., *Does Redistricting Make a Difference?*. Baltimore: Johns Hopkins University Press, 1993.

REFERENCES

Schutze, Jim, *The Accommodation: The Politics of an American City*. New Jersey: Citadel Press, 1986.

Smiley, Nixon, *Miami Herald Front Pages 1903-1983*. N. H. Abrams, 1983.

Thernstrom, Abigail M., *Whose Votes Count?*. Cambridge, Massachusetts: Harvard University Press, 1987.

Trevor, Ellen Lloyd, Editor, *Arizona: A Chronology and Documentary Handbook*. New York: Oceana Publications Inc., 1972.

Wagman, Robert J., *The Supreme Court, A Citizens Guide*. New York: Pharos Books, 1993.

Williams, Roy H., and Kevin J. Shay, *Time Change*. Dallas: To Be Publishing Co., 1991.

Young, Robert W., *The Political History of the Navajo Tribe*, Tsaile, Arizona: Navajo Community College Press, 1978.

CASE REFERENCES

Allen v. the State Board of Elections, 393 US 544 (1969).
Alonzo v. Jones, C-81-227, S. D. Texas (1983).
Apache County v. United States, 256 F.Supp 903 (1966).
Baker v. Carr, 369 US 186 (1962).
Beer v. United States, 425 US 130 (1975).
Board of Estimate of City of New York v. Morris, 489 US 688 (1989).
Bolden v. the City of Mobile, Alabama, 542 F.Supp. 1050 (1982).
Blacks United for Lasting Leadership v. City of Shreveport, Louisiana, 71 F.R.D. 623 (1976).
Breedlove v. Suttles, 302 US 277 (1937).
Brewer v. Ham, 876 F.2d 448 (1989).
Brooks v. Georgia State Board of Elections, 90-272 (1990).
Brown v. Thomson, 462 US 835 (1983).
Buchanan v. Warely, 245 US 60 (1917).
Buckanaga v. Sisseton Independent School District, 804 F.2d 469 (1986).
Burns v. Richardson, 384 US 73 (1966).
Bush v. Vera, S. Ct. 94-805 (1996).
Bussie v. Governor of Louisiana, 333 F.Supp. 452 (1971), 457 F.2d 796 (1971).
Butler v. Thompson, 341 US 937 (1951).
Campos v. Baytown, Texas, 840 F.2d 1240 (1988).
Chisom v. Roemer, S. Ct. 2354 (1991).
Citizens for a Better Gretna v. City of Gretna, La, 834 F.2d 496. (1987), Certiorari denied 492 US 905 (1989).
City of Dallas v. United States, 482 F.Supp 183 (1980).
City of Mobile v. Bolden, 446 US 55 (1980).
City of Petersburg, Virginia v. United States, 354 F.Supp 1021 (1972), 410 US 962 (1973).
City of Richmond v. U. S., 376 F.Supp 1344 (1974), 422 US 358 (1975).
City of Rome, Georgia v. United States, 472 F.Supp. 221 (1979), 466 US 156 (1980).
Clark v. Marengo County, 469 F.Supp. 1130 (1985), 731 F.2d 1546 (1984).
Clayton v. North Carolina State Board of Elections, 317 F.Supp. 915, (1970).
Colegrove v. Green, 328 US 549 (1946).
Connor v. Johnson, 265 F.Supp. 492, (1967), 402 US 690 (1971).
Davis v. Bandemer, 478 US 109 (1986).
DeGrandy v. Johnson, 512 US 997 (1994).

Dougherty County, Georgia v. White, 431 F.Supp. 919 (1977), 439 US 32 (1978).
Dusch v. Davis, 387 US 112 (1967).
East Caroll Parish School Board v. Marshall, 424 US 636 (1976).
East Jefferson Coalition for Leadership and Development v. Jefferson Parish, 691 F.Supp. 991 (1988).
Elk v. Wilkins, 112 US 94 (1884).
Ely v. Klahr, 403 US 108 (1971).
Ex Parte Virginia, 100 US 339 (1880).
Evers v. State Board of Election Commissioners, 327 F.Supp. 640 (1971).
Fortson v. Dorsey, 379 US 433 (1965).
Garza v. the City of Los Angeles, 918 F.2d 763 (1990), Certiorari denied 498 US 1028 (1991).
Gaston County v. United States, 395 US 285 (1969).
Georgia v. United States, 411 US 526 (1973).
Georgia State Board of Elections v. Brooks, 775 F.Supp. 1470 (1989).
Gomillion v. Lightfoot, 364 US 339 (1960).
Goodluck v. Apache, 417 F.Supp. 13 (1976).
Graves v. Barnes, 378 F.Supp 640 (1973).
Grovy v. Townsend, 295 US 45 (1935).
Gunn v. Chickasaw County, Mississippi, 705 F.Supp. 315 (1989).
Hale County v. U. S., 496 F.Supp. 1206 (1980).
Harper v. Virginia Board of Elections, 383 US 663 (1966).
Harrison v. Laveen, 67 AZ Reports 337 (1948).
Hays v. Louisiana, 839 F.Supp. 1188 (1993).
Heggins v. City of Dallas, Texas, 469 F.Supp. 739 (1979).
Hoffman v. Maryland, 928 F.2d 646, CA 4 (1991).
Holder v. Hall, 512 US 874 (1994).
Horry County v. U. S., 449 F.Supp. 990 (1978).
Houston v. Haley, 663 F.Supp. 346 (1987).
Jordon v. Winter, 604 F.Supp. 807 (1984).
Karcher v. Daggett, 462 US 725 (1983).
Katzenbach v. Morgan, 384 US 641 (1966).
Kirkpatrick v. Preisler, 394 US 526 (1969).
Kirksey v. Board of Supervisors, 528 F.2d 536 (1976).
Klahr v. Goddard, 250 F.Supp 537 (1964).
Klahr v. Williams, 303 F.Supp 224 (1969).
Klahr v. Williams, 313 F.Supp 148 (1970).
Lassiter v. Northampton Election Board, 360 US 51 (1959).
Latino Political Action Committee v. Boston, 784 F.2d 409 (1986).

CASE REFERENCES

Lau v. Nichols, 414 US 563 (1974).
Lipscomb v. Jonsson, 459 F.2d 335 (1972).
Lipscomb v. Wise, 399 F.Supp 782 (1975).
Lipscomb v. Wise, 551 F.2d 1043 (1977).
Lipscomb v. Wise, 583 F.2d 212 (1978).
Lodge v. Buxton, 639 F.2d 1376 (1981).
MacGuire v. Amos, 343 F.Supp. 119 (1972).
McDaniels v. Mehfoud, 702 F.Supp. 754 (1988).
McGhee v. Granville County, North Carolina, 860 F.2d 110 (1988).
Merrion v. Jicarilla Apache Tribe, 455 US 130 (1982).
Miller v. Johnson, 515 US 900 (1995).
Mississippi State Chapter, Operation PUSH v. Mabus, 717 F.Supp. 1189 (1989), 932 F.2d 400 (1991).
Monroe v. City of Woodville, Mississippi, 897 F.2d 763 (1990), Certiorari denied 498 US 822 (1990).
Montana v. United States, 450 US 544 (1981).
Moore v. Leflore County Board of Election Commissioners, 361 F.Supp. 609 (1973), 502 F.2d 621 (1974).
NAACP v. City of Starke, 712 F.Supp. 1523 (1989).
Nevett v. Sides, 571 F.2d 209 (1978).
Nixon v. Condon, 286 US 73 (1932).
Nixon v. Herndon, 273 US 536 (1927).
Oregon v. Mitchell, 400 US 112 (1970).
Perkins v. Matthews, 400 US 379 (1971).
Plessy v. Ferguson, 163 US 537 (1896).
Port Arthur v. U. S., 459 US 159 (1982).
Porter v. Hall, 34 ARIZ 308 (1928).
Powell v. McCormack, 395 US 486 (1969).
Presley v. Etowah County Commission, 112 S. Ct. 820 (1992).
Reynolds v. Sims, 377 US 533 (1964).
Rogers v. Lodge, 458 US 613 (1982).
Romero v. City of Pomona, 883 F.2d 1418 (1989).
Santa Clara Pueblo v. Martinez, 463 US 49 (1978).
Seastrunk v. Burns, 772 F.2d 143 (1985).
Shaw v. Reno, 509 US 630, (1993).
Shirley v. Superior Court, 513 P.2d 939, Arizona (1973).
Skorepa v. City of Chula Vista, 723 F.Supp 1384 (1989).
Smith v. Allwright, 347 US 483 (1944).
Smith v. Clinton, 687 F.Supp. 1361 (1988), 488 US 988 (1988).
South Carolina v. Katzenbach, 383 US 301 (1966).

Talton v. Mayes, 163 US 376 (1986).
Taylor v. McKeithen, 407 US 191 (1972).
Terrazas v. Clements, 581 F.Supp. 1329 (1984).
Thomas v. Mims, S. D. Alabama, 317 F.Supp. 179 (1970).
Thornburg v. Gingles, 478 US 30 (1986).
Torres v. Sachs, 381 F.Supp. 309 (1974).
Tracy v. Navajo Nation, AZ Supreme Ct., No.CV-90-0407-SA (1991).
United Jewish Organizations of Williamsburgh, Inc. v. Carey, 430 US 144 (1977).
U. S. v. Uvalde Consolidated School District, 101 S. Ct. 2341.
U. S. v. County Commission, Hale County, Alabama, 425 F.Supp. 433 (1976).
U. S. v. Dallas County Commission, 739 F.2d 1529 (1984).
U. S. v. Kagama, 118 US 375 (1886).
U. S. v. Louisiana, 265 F.Supp 703, 386 US 270 (1967).
U. S. v. Marengo County [Alabama] Commission, 731 F.2d 1546 (1984).
U. S. v. McBratney, 104 US 621 (1981).
U. S. v. Mississippi, 256 F.Supp 344 (1966).
U. S. v. Mississippi, 444 US 1050 (1980).
U. S. v. Reese, 92 US 214 (1875).
U. S. v. Wheeler, 435 US 322 (1978).
Uvalde Consolidated School District v. U. S., 451 US 1002 (1981).
Voinovich v. Quilter, 507 US ___, 113 S Ct 1149 (1993).
Washington v. Tensas Parish School Board, 819 F.2d 609 (1987).
Whitfield v. Arkansas Democratic Party, 890 F.2d 1423 (1989).
Whitfield v. Clinton, 90-383.
White v. Regester, 412 US 755 (1973).
Windy Boy v. County of Big Horn, 647 F.Supp 1002 (1986).
Williams v. City of Dallas, Texas, 734 F.Supp 1317 (1990).
Williams v. State Board of Elections, 696 F.Supp. 1563 (1988).
Wise v. Lipscomb, 437 US 535 (1978).
Whitcomb v. Chavis, 403 US 124 (1971).
Worcester v. Georgia, 31 US 515 (1832).
Yanito v. Barber, 348 F.Supp. 587 (1972).
Zimmer v. McKeithen, 485 F.2d 1297 (1973).

NOTES

NOTES FROM INTRODUCTION

1. From a speech by Dr. Martin Luther King delivered on the steps at the Lincoln Memorial in Washington D. C. on August 28, 1963.

NOTES FROM CHAPTER 1: VOTING RIGHTS -- THE ISSUES

1. The word, gerrymander, was coined in 1812 after the Massachusetts Legislature established an odd looking district in Essex County to favor the party of Gov. Elbridge Gerry. Critics said the district looked like a giant salamander. Someone called it a gerrymander and the name stuck.
2. In 1901, Congress said legislative districts should be about equal in population. The legislation had little effect until the Supreme Court ruled in *Reynolds v. Sims*.
3. The effect of single-shot and majority vote provisions are discussed by Frankie M. Freeman in United States Commission on Civil Rights, *The Voting Rights Act: Ten Years After*. Washington D. C.: Government Printing Office, 1975.

NOTES FROM CHAPTER 2: VOTING RIGHTS AND THE CONSTITUTION

1. *Debates of the Federal Convention (May 14-September 17, 1787)*, June 18, 1987.
2. *McCulloch v. Maryland*, 4 Weaton 316, 415.
3. United States Constitution, Article VI.
4. Peters, William, *A More Perfect Union: The Making of the United States Constitution*. New York: Crown Publishers, 1987, pp. 35-36.
5. Ibid., p. 43.
6. Ibid., p. 43.
7. *Debates of the Federal Convention (May 14-September 17, 1787)*.
8. Peters, p. 44.
9. Ibid., p. 45.
10. Ibid., p. 45.
11. South Carolina Constitution, Article 1:4.
12. New Hampshire Constitution, Paragraph 12.
13. Delaware Constitution, Article 4:1.
14. Pennsylvania Constitution, Article 3:1.
15. The candidate with the most votes was not elected president in 1824, 1876, or 1888. League of Women Voters of California Education Fund, *Choosing the President - 1992*. New York: Lyons and Burford, 1992, pp. 91-97.
16. *Powell v. McCormack*, 395 US 486 (1969).
17. United States Constitution, Amendment 14.
18. United States Constitution, Amendment 15.

NOTES FROM CHAPTER 3: HISTORY

1. The South, unless noted, refers to Alabama, Georgia, Louisiana, Mississippi, North Carolina, South Carolina, and Virginia.
2. Grofman, Bernard, Lisa Handley, and Richard G. Niemi, *Minority Representation and the Quest for Voting Equality*. Cambridge, Massachusetts: Cambridge University Press, 1992, p. 5
3. American Civil Liberties Union, *Briefing Paper 11*. New York: ACLU, 132 W 43rd St., New York, N. Y. 10036.
4. Grofman, *Minority Representation and the Quest for Voting Equality*, p. 5.
5. See *United States v. Reese*, 92 US 214 (1876) and *United States v. Cruikshank*, 92 US 542 (1876).
6. Compton's Interactive Encyclopedia, Compton's NewMedia, Inc., 1994.
7. Ball, Howard, Dale Krane, and Thomas P. Lauth, *Compromised Compliance: Implementation of the Voting Rights Act*. Westport, Connecticut: Greenwood Press, 1982, pp. 36-37.
8. *Civil Rights Cases*, 109 US 3 (1883).
9. *Plessy v. Ferguson*, 163 US 537 (1896).
10. Ibid.
11. American Civil Liberties Union, *Briefing Paper 11*.
12. J. Morgan Kousser, "The Voting Rights Act and the Two Reconstructions," in Grofman, Bernard and Chandler Davidson, Editors, *Controversies in Minority Voting*. Washington, D. C.: Brookings Institution, p. 140. Statistics include Alabama, Arkansas, Florida, Georgia, Louisiana, Mississippi, North Carolina, South Carolina, Tennessee, Texas, and Virginia. 1992 figures from U. S. Department of Commerce, *Statistical Abstract of the United States, 1993, 113th Edition*. Washington D. C.: Government Printing Office, Table No. 449.
13. W. Marvin Dulaney, "The Progressive Voters League: A Political Voice for African Americans," in Hazel, Michael V., Editor, *Dallas Reconsidered: Essays in Local History*. Dallas, Texas: Three Forks Press, 1995, p. 169.
14. Lawson, Steven F., *Black Ballots: Voting Rights in the South 1944-1969*. New York: Columbia University Press, 1976, p. 25.
15. *Nixon v. Herndon*, 273 US 536 (1927).
16. *Nixon v. Condon*, 286 US 73 (1932).
17. *Grovy v. Townsend*, 295 US 45 (1935).
18. *Smith v. Allwright*, 347 US 483 (1944).
19. *Louisiana v. U. S.*, cited in Congressional House Committee on the Judiciary, *Leading Court Decisions Pertinent to Proposed Voting Rights Act of 1965*. Washington D. C.: U. S. Government Printing Office, March 25, 1965.
20. American Civil Liberties Union, *Briefing Paper 11: Social Justice*.
21. *Colegrove v. Green*, 328 US 459 (1946).
22. Rush, Mark E., *Does Redistricting Make a Difference?* Baltimore: Johns Hopkins University Press, 1993, pp. 16-17.
23. *Colegrove v. Green*, 328 US 459 (1946).

NOTES

24. Davidson, Chandler, and Bernard Grofman, Editors, *Quiet Revolution in the South: The Impact of the Voting Rights Act 1965-1990.* Princeton: Princeton University Press, 1994, p. 374.
25. Ibid.
26. Rush, pp. 18-19.
27. *Baker v. Carr*, 369 US 186 (1962).
28. Irons, Peter, and Stephanie Guitton, *May it please the Court.* New York: The New Press, 1993, pp. 11-12.
29. Ibid., p. 12.
30. Ibid., pp. 7-20.
31. *Baker v. Carr*, 369 US 186.
32. Irons, p. 15.
33. *Reynolds v. Sims*, 377 US 533 (1964).
34. Thernstrom, Abigail M., *Whose Votes Count?* Cambridge, Massachusetts: Harvard University Press, 1987, p. 13.
35. Holmes, Maxine, and Gerald Saxon, Editors, *The WPA Dallas Guide and History.* Denton, Texas: University of North Texas Press, 1992, p. 36.
36. Ibid., p. 37.
37. Ibid., pp. 39-41.
38. Ibid., pp. 44-46.
39. Payne, Darwin, *Big D: Triumphs and Troubles of an American Supercity in the 20th Century.* Dallas: Three Forks Press, 1993, p. 5.
40. Holmes, p. 48.
41. Thomas H. Smith, "African Americans in Dallas: From Slavery to Freedom," in Hazel, p. 129.
42. Holmes, pp. 53-55.
43. Ibid., p. 55.
44. Ibid., pp. 55-56.
45. Ibid., p. 59.
46. Davidson, *Quiet Revolution in the South*, p. 234.
47. Holmes, p. 58.
48. Michael V. Hazel, "From Distant Shores: German and Swiss Immigrants in Dallas," in Hazel, p. 109.
49. Ibid., p. 59.
50. Ibid., p. 74.
51. Thomas H. Smith, "'Cast Down Your Buckets:' A Black Experiment In Dallas," in Hazel, p. 145.
52. Payne, *Big D*, pp. 8-9.
53. Ibid., pp. 11-13.
54. Ibid., pp. 20-25.
55. Holmes, pp. 87-91.
56. Payne, *Big D*, pp. 55-64.
57. Gwendolyn Rice, "Little Mexico and the Barrios of Dallas," in Hazel, p. 158.
58. Payne, *Big D*, 73-76.
59. Holmes, pp. 91-95.
60. Payne, *Big D*, p. 96.

61. See *Buchanan v. Warely* (1917).
62. Payne, *Big D*, pp. 140-141.
63. Holmes, p. 137. Edy's police personnel polices downgraded the captain of plain clothes detectives to ordinary detective and many detectives to patrolmen.
64. Payne, *Big D*, pp. 182-185 and W. Martin Dulaney, "The Progressive Voters League: A progressive Voice for African Americans," in Hazel, p. 175.
65. Hazel, p. 172.
66. Schutze, Jim, *The Accommodation: The Politics of an American City*. New Jersey: Citadel Press, 1986, pp. 9-10.
67. Payne, *Big D*, p. 207.
68. Ibid., pp. 244-246.
69. Ibid., p. 265.
70. Ibid., pp. 289-293.
71. Schutze, p. 134.
72. Payne, *Big D*, p. 302.
73. Ibid., p. 327.
74. Schutze, p. 6.
75. Senators Dennis DeConcini and John McCain, "Removing barriers to Indian opportunity," *Arizona Republic*, March 5, 1989, p. 1C.
76. Iverson, Peter, *The Navajos*. New York: Chelsea House Publishers, 1990, p. 18.
77. Locke, p. 16.
78. Bordewich, Fergus M., *Killing the White Man's Indian: Reinventing Native Americans at the End of the Twentieth Century*. New York: Doubleday, 1996, p. 44.
79. Ibid., p. 45. The author is quoting from *Cherokee Nation v. Georgia*, 30 US 1 (1831).
80. Ibid., p. 46. The author is quoting form *Worcester v. Georgia*, 31 US 515.
81. 16 US Stat. 544.
82. Davis, Mary B., editor, *Native America in the Twentieth Century: An Encyclopedia*. New York: Garland Publishing, Inc., 1994, p. 116.
83. *Elk v. Wilkins*, 112 US 94 (1884).
84. Davis, p. 117.
85. Young, Robert W., *The Political History of the Navajo Tribe*. Tsaile, Arizona: Navajo Community College Press, 1978, p. 25.
86. Ibid., p. 15.
87. Ibid., pp. 43-44.
88. Ibid., pp. 56-57.
89. Davis, P. 117.
90. *U. S. v. Kagama*, 118 US 375 (1886).
91. Bordewich, pp. 280-281.
92. *Porter v. Hall*, 34 ARIZ 308 (1928).
93. Ibid.
94. Daniel McCool, "Indian Voting," in Deloria, Vine, Jr., Editor, *American Indian Policy in the Twentieth Century*. Norman Oklahoma: University of Oklahoma Press, 1985, p. 110.
95. Young, p. 86.

Notes

96. Ibid., p. 109.
97. For a discussion of reservation status within a state, see *U. S. v. McBratney*, 104 US 621 (1981).
98. MacDonald, Peter with Ted Schwarz, *The Last Warrior*. New York: Orion Books, 1993, p. 72.
99. Trevor, Ellen Lloyd, Editor, *Arizona: A Chronology and Documentary Handbook*. New York: Oceana Publications Inc., 1972, p. 31.
100. McCool, "Indian Voting," in Deloria, pp. 110-111.
101. Ibid., p. 31. Also see *Harrison v. Laveen*, 67 AZ Reports 337 (1948).
102. Bucko, Richard Lewis, *Voting Participation of the Arizona Navajos in State and National Elections, Thesis in Social Science*. Flagstaff Arizona: University of Northern Arizona Press, 1970, p. 12. McCool, "Indian Voting," in Deloria, p. 108.
103. *Arizona Revised Statues*, Sec. 16-101, 1933.
104. Bucko. p. 14.
105. Young, p. 135.
106. Ibid., pp. 141-142.
107. *House Concurrent Resolution 108*, 1953.
108. Barone, Michael and Grant Ujifusa, *The Almanac of American Politics 1996*. Washington, D. C.: National Journal, 1966, p. 37.
109. *The Software Toolworks, US Atlas®*.
110. *Klahr v. Goddard*, 250 F.Supp. 537 (1964).
111. Chavez, Linda, *Out of the Barrio*. New York: Basic Books, 1991, p. 2.
112. Buchanan, James E., *Miami - A Chronological and Documentary History*. Dobbs Ferry, N. Y. : Oceana Publications, Inc., 1978, p. 1.
113. *Encarta*, Microsoft Corporation, 1995.
114. Buchanan, pp. 1-2.
115. Portes, Alexandro and Alex Stepick, *City on the Edge: The Transformation of Miami*. Berkeley, California: University of California Press, 1993, p. 67.
116. Buchanan, pp. 2-3.
117. Portes, p. 70.
118. Buchanan, p. 3.
119. Ibid., p. 5.
120. Ibid., p. 6.
121. Nixon Smiley, *Miami Herald Front Pages 1903-1983*. New York: N. H. Abrams, 1983, p. 17.
122. Portes, p. 73.
123. Ibid., p. 76.
124. Smiley, p. 75.
125. Lotz, Aileen R., *Metropolitan Dade County: Two-tier Government in Action*. Boston: Allyn and Bacon, 1984, p. 11.
126. "Resilient Miami Has Long Coped With Trouble," *Miami Herald*, December 9, 1990.
127. Portes, p. 84.
128. Ibid., p. 78.
129. Buchanan, p. 35.
130. Portes, pp. 80-81.

131. Dade County Archive report entitled, "The Government of Metropolitan Miami," 1954.
132. Smiley, p. 143.
133. Portes, pp. 102-103.
134. See *Baker v. Carr* and *Reynolds v. Sims* which establish the principle of *One-man, one-vote*.

NOTES ON CHAPTER 4: VOTING RIGHTS ACT OF 1965

1. Martin Luther King Jr., *Why We Can't Wait*. New York: Harper and Row, 1964.
2. Lawson, *Black Ballots*, p. 308.
3. See Garrow, David J., *Protest at Selma*. New Haven: Yale University Press, 1975, for a discussion of the SCLC strategy for Selma.
4. Garrow, pp. 51-52.
5. Ibid., p. 57.
6. Johnson, Lyndon Baines, *Vantage Point: Perspectives of the Presidency, 1963-1969*. New York: Holt, Rinehart, and Winston, 1971, p. 161.
7. Ball, p. 47.
8. *Ex Parte Virginia*, 100 US 339 at 345-6 (1880).
9. Garrow, p. 132.
10. See Public Law 89-110, August 6, 1965 and *1965 U. S. Code Congressional and Administrative News*, p. 2473.
11. *Lassiter v. Northampton Election Board*, 360 US 51 (1959).
12. Some of the material in this Section was taken from *1965 U. S. Code, Congressional and Administrative News*, beginning p. 2437; See "Voting rights hearings before Subcommittee No. 5 of the House Committee on the Judiciary" 89th Congress, 1st Session, Serial No. 2.
13. Flemming, Arthus S., *The Voting Rights Act: Unfulfilled Goals, A Report of the United States Commission on Civil Rights*. Washington, D. C.: Government Printing Office, p. 6.
14. Registration numbers used throughout this book vary slightly depending on source. Some numbers are estimates of Congress, some are the result of referenced research, and others come from the *U. S. Statistical Abstract*. None of the discrepancies undermines the point for which the author has used the statistic.
15. Ball, pp. 238-242.
16. Lawson, *Black Ballots*, p. 86.
17. Davidson, *Quiet Revolution in the South*, p. 374.
18. *Report from the Committee on the Judiciary to Accompany H.R. 6400*, 89th Congress 1st Session, Report No. 439.
19. *U. S. v. Louisiana*, 265 F.Supp 703, 380 US 145 (1965).
20. Schutze, p. 122.
21. *Gomillion v. Lightfoot*, 364 US 339 (1960).
22. Some of the material in this Section was taken from *1965 U. S. Code, Congressional and Administrative News*, beginning p 2437.
23. *1965 U. S. Code, Congressional and Administrative News*, p. 2437.

24. See Public Law 89-110, August 6, 1965 and *1965 U. S. Code Congressional and Administrative News*, p. 2487.
25. Garrow, p. xi.
26. Chandler Davidson, "The Voting Rights Act: A Brief History," in Grofman, *Controversies in Minority Voting*, p. 21.
27. U. S. Commission on Civil Rights, *The Voting Rights Act . . . The First Months*. Washington, D. C.: Government Printing Office, 1965, p. 3.
28. Lawson, Steven F., *In Pursuit of Power: Southern Blacks and Electoral Politics, 1965-1982*. New York: Columbia University Press, 1985, p. 35.
29. *Public Papers of the Presidents, Lyndon Johnson, 1965*, II, 843, quoted from Lawson, *Black Ballots*, p. 332.
30. Ball, p. 52.
31. *South Carolina v. Katzenbach*, 383 US 301 (1966).
32. Wagman, Robert J., *The Supreme Court, A Citizens Guide*. New York: Pharos Books, 1993, p. 244.
33. *Allen v. State Board of Elections*, 393 US 544 (1969).
34. *South Carolina v. Katzenbach*, 383 US 301 (1966).
35. Lawson, *In Pursuit of Power*, p. 26.
36. Ibid.
37. *Breedlove v. Suttles*, 302 US 277 (1937).
38. *Butler v. Thompson*, 341 US 937 (1951).
39. Lawson, *Black Ballots*, p. 56.
40. *Harper v. Virginia Board of Elections*, 383 US 663 (1966).
41. Wagman, p. 246.
42. *Katzenbach v. Morgan*, 384 US 641 (1966).
43. Wagman, p. 254.
44. *Katzenbach v. Morgan*, 384 US 641.
45. *Lassiter v. Northampton Election Board*, 360 US 51 (1959).
46. Lawson, *In Pursuit of Power*, p. 129.
47. U. S. Commission of Civil Rights, *Political Participation: A Study of the Participation by Negros in the Electoral and Political Processes in 10 Southern States Since the passage of the Voting Rights Act of May 1965*, Washington, D. C.: Government Printing Office, May 1968.
48. U. S. Department of Commerce, *Statistical Abstract of the United States, 113th Edition*, Washington, D. C.: Government Printing Office, 1969.
49. *Connor v. Johnson*, 265 F.Supp. 492 (1967), 402 US 690 (1971).
50. Ibid.
51. *Kirkpatrick v. Preisler*, 394 US 526 (1969).
52. *Allen v. State Board of Elections*, 393 U. S. at 565 (1969).
53. Ibid.
54. Chandler Davidson, "The Voting Rights Act: A Brief History" in Grofman, *Controversies in Minority Voting*, p. 28.
55. *Allen v. State Board of Elections*, 393 U. S. 544 (1969).
56. Wagman, p. 253.
57. *Gaston County v. United States*, 395 US 285 (1969).
58. *Fortson v. Dorsey*, 379 US 433 (1965).

59. *Burns v. Richardson*, 384 US 73 (1966).
60. 2 USCS 2c, n2.
61. The Center for Voting and Democracy, 6905 Fifth Street NW, Suite 200, Washington, D. C. 20012.
62. *Dusch v. Davis*, 387 US 112 (1967).
63. Payne, *Big D*, p. 341.
64. Ibid., p. 336.
65. *Williams v. City of Dallas, Texas*, 734 F.Supp 1317 (1990).
66. *Lipscomb v. Wise*, 399 F.Supp 782 (1975).
67. *Max Goldblatt v. City of Dallas*, 414 F.2nd 774 (1969).
68. Ibid.
69. *Lipscomb v. Wise*, 399 F.Supp 782 (1975).
70. Payne, *Big D*, p. 338.
71. Ibid., p. 343.
72. Ibid., p. 331.
73. Klahr v. Goddard, 250 F.Supp 537 (1965).
74. Ibid.
75. Ibid.
76. *Arizona Revised Statutes*, Section 16-101.
77. *Apache County v. United States*, 256 F.Supp 903 (1966).
78. Bucko, p. 15.
79. *South Carolina v. Katzenbach*, 383 US 301 (1966).
80. *Apache County v. United States*, 256 F.Supp 903 (1966).
81. Bucko, p. 19.
82. Trover, p. 32, Bucko p. 34.
83. Chapter 1, House Bill 1, 28th Arizona Legislature.
84. *Kirkpatrick v. Preisler*, 394 US 526 (1969).
85. *Klahr v. Williams*, 303 F.Supp 224 (1969).
86. Chapter 1, 29th Legislature, State of Arizona, Special Session.
87. *Klahr v. Williams*, 313 F.Supp 148 (1970).
88. *Ely v. Klahr*, 403 US 108 (1971).
89. United States Commission on Civil Rights, *The Voting Rights: Act 10 Years After* Washington, D. C.: Government Printing Office, 1975, pp. 93 and 331.
90. Duane Champagne, "Organizational Change and Conflict: A Case study of the Bureau of Indian Affairs," in Lyden, Fremont J. and Lyman H. Legters, Editors, *Native Americans and Public Policy*, Pittsburgh: University of Pittsburgh Press, 1992, pp. 42-43.
91. Ibid., p. 46.
92. Bordewich, p. 86.
93. Bordewich, p. 83, quoting a speech by Richard Nixon to Congress, July 8, 1970.
94. Senators Dennis DeConcini and John McCain, "Removing barriers to Indian opportunity," *Arizona Republic*, March 5, 1989, p. 1C.
95. Buchanan, p. 57.
96. Ibid., p. 60.

NOTES ON CHAPTER 5: THE AMENDMENTS OF 1970

1. See Public Law 91-285, June 22, 1970.
2. Quoted in Lawson, *In Pursuit of Power*, p. 5.
3. Ibid., p. 6.
4. Richard M. Nixon, *RN: The Memoirs of Richard Nixon*, Groset and Dunlap, 1978, p. 440.
5. Chandler Davidson, "The Voting Rights Act: A Brief History," in Grofman, *Controversies in Minority Voting*, p. 29.
6. *Gaston County v. United States*, 395 US 285 (1969).
7. Quoted in Lawson, *In Pursuit of Power*, p. 133.
8. Ibid., p. 136.
9. Ibid., p. 140.
10. *Allen v. State Board of Elections*, 393 US 544 (1969).
11. *1970 U. S. Code, Congressional and Administrative News*, p. 3288.
12. *South Carolina v. Katzenbach*, 383 US 301 (1966).
13. *1970 U. S. Code, Congressional and Administrative News*, p. 3290.
14. Taken from an interview with Gerald Jones, Chief, Voting Rights Section, Civil Rights Division, Department of Justice, September 2, 1977, Washington, D. C., in Ball, p. 62.
15. See Lawson, *In Pursuit of Power*, pp. 163-173.
16. *Charles Evers et al v. State Board of Election Commissioners*, 327 F.Supp. 640 (1971).
17. *MacGuire v. Amos*, 343 F.Supp. 119 (1972).
18. *Georgia v. United States*, 411 US 526 (1973).
19. *Allen v. State Board of Elections*, 393 US 544 (1969).
20. *Procedures for the Administration of Section 5 of the Voting Rights Act of 1965*, 28 C. F. R. Section 51.4.
21. *Moore v. Leflore County Board of Election Commissioners*, 361 F.Supp. 609, (1973), 502 F.2d 621 (1974).
22. *Thomas v. Mimes*, 317 F.Supp. 179 (1970).
23. *Moore v. Leflore County Board of Elections Commission*, 502 F.2nd 621 (1974).
24. *Perkins v. Matthews*, 400 US 379 (1971).
25. See *The City of Richmond v. U. S.*, 376 F.Supp 1344 (1974), 422 US 358 (1975).
26. *City of Petersburg, Virginia v. United States*, 354 F.Supp 1021 (1972), 410 US 962 (1973).
27. *Perkins v. Matthews*, 400 US 379 (1971).
28. *Weaver v. Muckleroy*.
29. *Bussie v. Governor of Louisiana*, 333 F.Supp. 452 (1971), 457 F.2d 796 (1971).
30. Ibid.
31. *Taylor v. McKeithen*, 407 US 191 (1972).
32. *Oregon v. Mitchell*, 400 US 112 (1970).
33. Flemming, *The Voting Rights: Act 10 Years After*, pp. 357-358.
34. Ibid., quoting Stephen Horn.
35. *U. S. v. Mississippi*, 256 F.Supp 344 (1966), and *U. S. v. Louisiana*, 265 F.Supp 703 (1966), 386 US 270 (1967).

36. Flemming, *The Voting Rights: Act 10 Years After*, p 118.
37. *Torres v. Sachs*, 381 F.Supp. 309 (1974).
38. *Lau v. Nichols*, 414 US 563 (1974).
39. Chavez, p. 14.
40. Peter Skerry, "The Ambivalent Minority: Mexican Americans and the Voting Rights Act," *Journal of Policy History*, Vol. 6, No. 1 1994, p. 73.
41. Ibid., p. 76.
42. *Whitcomb v. Chavis*, 403 US 124 (1971).
43. *Zimmer v. McKeithen*, 485 F.2d 1297 (1973).
44. Flemming, *The Voting Rights: Act 10 Years After*, p 29.
45. Ibid., p 33.
46. Bullock, Charles S. III and Charles M. Lamb, *Implementation of Civil Rights Policy*. Monterey, California: Brooks/Cole Publishing, 1984, pp. 43-44.
47. Ibid., pp. 49, 62.
48. Ibid., p 1.
49. Williams, Roy H. and Kevin J. Shay, *Time Change*, Dallas: To Be Publishing Co., 1991, p. 7.
50. Payne, *Big D*, pp. 351-355.
51. Ibid., p. 344.
52. Williams, p. 103.
53. *Lipscomb v. Jonsson*, 459 F.2d 335 (1972).
54. Ibid.
55. Ibid.
56. *Whitcomb v. Chavis*, 403 US 124 (1971).
57. Payne, *Big D*, p. 356.
58. Ibid., p. 357.
59. *Lipscomb v. Wise*, 399 F.Supp. 782 (1975).
60. Ibid.
61. Williams, p. 109.
62. *Lipscomb v. Wise*, 399 F.Supp. 782 (1975).
63. Williams, p. 109.
64. Ibid., p. 110.
65. *Lipscomb v. Wise*, 399 F.Supp. 782 (1975).
66. Ibid.
67. Payne, *Big D*, pp. 358-359.
68. Ibid., p. 342.
69. Ibid., pp. 363-364.
70. Gwendolyn Rice, "Little Mexico and the Barrios," in Hazel, p. 165.
71. Payne, *Big D*, p. 341.
72. Ibid., pp. 340-342.
73. Locke, Raymond Friday, *The Book of the Navajo*, Mankind Publishing, 1992, pp. 459-460.
74. Bucko, p. 1.
75. Ibid., p. 45.
76. Ibid., p. 21.
77. Ibid., p. 42.

NOTES 253

78. Arizona Legislature, House Bill IV, Section 79E, 1970.
79. *Ely v. Klahr*, 403 US 108 (1971).
80. Ibid.
81. *Klahr v. Williams*, 339 F.Supp. 922 (1972).
82. *Reynolds v. Sims*, 377 US 533 (1964).
83. Flemming, *The Voting Rights: Act 10 Years After*, p. 109-111.
84. *Shirley v. Superior Court*, 415 US 917 (1974).
85. *Yanito v. Barber*, 348 F.Supp. 587 (1972).
86. *Shirley v. Superior Court*, 109 ARIZ 110 (1973).
87. United States Commission on Civil Rights, *Hearing before the Commission on Civil Rights, Hearing held in Window Rock, Arizona, October 22-24, 1973*, p. 249.
88. Ibid., p. 428.
89. See Public Law 93-531.
90. Barone, p. 38.
91. Peter MacDonald, p. 195.
92. Flemming, *The Voting Rights: Act 10 Years After*, p. 117.
93. Locke, p. 458.
94. Hearing before the Commission on Civil Rights, Hearing held in Window Rock, Arizona, October 22-24, 1973.
95. Flemming, *The Voting Rights: Act 10 Years After*, p 58.
96. Bordewich, p. 84.
97. C. Patrick Morris, "Termination by Accountants: The Reagan Indian Policy," Lyden, p. 51.
98. *Goodluck v. Apache*, 417 F.Supp. 13 (1976).
99. "Barriers crumble as civic elite pass leadership," *Miami Herald*, April 13, 1994.
100. Buchanan, p. 62.
101. Ibid., p. 63.

NOTES ON CHAPTER 6: THE AMENDMENTS OF 1975

1. See Public Law 94-73, August 6, 1975 and *1975 U. S. Congressional and Administrative News*, p. 774.
2. Flemming, *The Voting Rights: Act 10 Years After*, p. 363.
3. Lawson, *In Pursuit of Power*, pp. 224-225.
4. Thernstrom, p. 50.
5. Lawson, *In Pursuit of Power*, p. 252.
6. Timothy O'Rourke, "The 1982 Amendments and the Voting Rights Paradox," in Grofman, *Controversies in Minority Voting*, p. 88.
7. Flemming, *The Voting Rights Act: Unfulfilled Goals*, p. 5.
8. Bullock, p. 42.
9. Abigail M. Thernstrom contends in *Whose Vote Counts?* that other research shows that this percentage is 6.7.
10. *Graves v. Barnes*, 378 F.Supp 640 (1973).
11. Chandler Davidson, "The Voting Rights Act: A Brief History," in Grofman, *Controversies in Minority Voting*, p. 36.

12. See *1975 U. S. Code, Congressional and Administrative News*, beginning p. 774.
13. U. S. Commission on Civil Rights, Staff Memorandum, *Expansion of the coverage of the Voting Rights Act*, June 5, 1975, p. 47.
14. Chavez, p. 46.
15. Immigration and Nationality Act, 8 U. S. C. 1423, Section 312.
16. Ibid., p. 43.
17. Thernstrom, p. 60.
18. *Beer v. United States*, 425 US 130 (1975).
19. Ibid.
20. Wagman, p. 258.
21. Katherine I. Butler, "Denial or Abridgment of the Right to Vote: What Does It Mean?," in Foster, Lorn S., Editor, *The Voting Rights Act, Consequences and Implications*. New York: Praeger, 1975, pp. 49-50. Katherine I. Butler is Associate Professor of Law at University of South Carolina and former trial attorney in the Civil Rights Division of the Department of Justice.
22. *U. S. v. County Commission, Hale County, Alabama*, 425 F.Supp. 433 (1977).
23. *Dougherty County, Georgia v. White*, 431 F.Supp. 919, 439 US 32, 1978 (1977).
24. *Horry County, South Carolina v. U. S.*, 449 F.Supp 990 (1978).
25. Ball, pp. 244-249 quoting the U. S. Department of Justice, Civil Rights Section, September 1980.
26. *Morris v. Gressette*, 432 US 493 (1977).
27. *Blacks United for Lasting Leadership v. City of Shreveport, Louisiana*, 71 F.R.D. 623 (1976).
28. *Uvalde Consolidated School District v. U. S.*, 451 US 1002 (1981).
29. *Bolden v. the City of Mobile, Alabama*, 542 F.Supp. 1050 (1982).
30. *Hale County v. U. S.*, 496 F.Supp. 1206 (1980).
31. *Lodge v. Buxton*, 639 F.2d 1376 (1981).
32. *Kirksey v. Board of Supervisors*, 528 F.2d 536 (1976).
33. In *Gregg v. Georgia*, 428 US 153 (1976), the court determined that the death penalty was not cruel and unusual punishment although it struck down mandatory death sentences. In *Coker v. Georgia*, 433 US 584 (1977), the court reversed a death penalty for rape ruling that it was cruel and unusual punishment. In *Regents of the University of California v. Bakke*, 438 US 265 (1978), the court ruled that race-based admissions policies were not justified. In *United Steelworkers v. Weber*, 443 US 193 (1979), the court allowed voluntary race-based policies in industry.
34. Examples include: *Griswold v. Connecticut*, 381 US 479 (1965), in which the court struck down anti-contraceptive laws; *Miranda v. Arizona*, 384 US 436 (1966), in which the court suppressed a confession given before the defendant knew his legal rights; *Tinker v. Des Moines School Independent Community School District*, 393 US 503 (1969), which supported school children's First Amendment Rights; *Brandenberg v. Ohio*, 395 US 444, in which the court stuck down the Smith Act which forbade teaching the overthrow of the government; and *Benton v. Maryland*, 395 US 784 (1969), in which the court extended the meaning of double jeopardy.
35. Wagman, p. 259.
36. *United Jewish Organizations v. Carey*, 430 US 144 (1977).

37. *Nevett v. Sides*, 571 F.2d 209 (1978).
38. *Mobile v. Bolden*, 446 US 55 (1980).
39. Black, Earl and Merle Black, *Politics and Society in the South*. Cambridge, Massachusetts: Harvard University Press, 1987, p. 147.
40. Flemming, *The Voting Rights Act: Unfulfilled Goals*, p. 15.
41. Lawson, *In Pursuit of Power*, p. 264.
42. Ibid., p. 268. The Civil Rights Act of 1968 required juries to be selected from updated voter registration rolls.
43. 1964 Data from Watters, Pat and Reese Cleghorn, *Climbing Jacob's Ladder*. New York: Harcourt, Brace and World, pp. 376-77; 1982 data from Joint Center for Political Studies, *Focus*, June 1983, 11:8 for black figures and U. S. Department of Commerce, Bureau of Census, *Statistical Abstract of the United States, 1982-1983*. Washington, D. C.: Government Printing Office, p. 448 for white figures. Both references were reported in Lawson, p. 291.
44. Ibid., p. 270.
45. Lorn S. Foster, *Political Symbols and he Enactment of the 1982 Voting Rights Act*, in Foster, pp. 95-96, Lorn S. Senior is a Fellow, Joint Center for Political Studies, Washington, D. C.
46. Ibid., p. 341.
47. Payne, *Big D*, p. 367.
48. Ibid., p. 374.
49. Ibid., pp. 360-361.
50. Ibid., p. 361.
51. *East Caroll Parish School Board v. Marshall*, 424 US 636 (1976).
52. *Lipscomb v. Wise*, 551 F.2d 1043, (1977).
53. *Wise v. Lipscomb*, 437 US 535 (1978).
54. *Heggins v. City of Dallas, Texas*, 469 F.Supp. 739 (1979).
55. Schutze, p. 164.
56. *Heggins v. City of Dallas, Texas*, 469 F.Supp. 739 (1979).
57. *Beer v. United States*, 425 US 130 (1975) as referenced in *City of Dallas v. United States*, 482 F.Supp 183 (1980).
58. Rowland Stiteler, "Lords of Little Mexico," *D Magazine*, May 1980, p. 116.
59. Williams, p. 115.
60. Beth Ellyn Rosenthal, "The Mayor Nobody Knows," *D Magazine*, May 1981, p. 94.
61. *Dallas Morning News*, October 14, 1981.
62. *Dallas Morning News*, January 23, 1982.
63. Rowland Stiteler, "The voice of Elsie Faye," *D Magazine*, February 1984, p. 113.
64. Michael Berryhill, "Something unusual is going on at city Hall: Politics," *D Magazine*, April 1982, p. 95.
65. Williams, p. 120.
66. *Dallas Morning News*, March 15, 1982.
67. See *Elk v. Wilkins*, 112 US 94 (1884).
68. *Goodluck v. Apache County*, 417 F.Supp. 13 (1975).
69. See Iverson.
70. *Santa Clara Pueblo v. Martinez*, 436 US 49 (1978).

71. Ibid.
72. *United States v. Wheeler*, 435 US 313 (1978).
73. *Montana v. United States*, 450 US 544 (1981).
74. *Merrion v. Jicarilla Apache Tribe*, 455 US 130 (1982).
75. Bureau of the Census, *Current Population Reports*, Series P-23, No. 74, September 1978 as reported in McCool, "Indian Voting," in Deloria, Editor, *American Indian Policy in the Twentieth Century*, p. 126.
76. Guarione M Diaz, Editor, *Law and Politics in Florida's Redistricting*, Cuban American Policy Center, 1992, p. 11.
77. Smiley, p. 255.
78. "Nicaraguan exile community forges new life in S. Florida," *Miami Herald*, July 16, 1989.
79. The history of the McDuffie riot came from "McDuffie riot chronology," *Miami Herald*, May 13, 1990.
80. Portes, p. 18.
81. Ibid., pp. 20-22.
82. Ibid., p. 24.
83. Smiley, pp. 255-256.
84. Portes, p. 51.
85. *Ethnic Block Voting and Polarization in Miami*, Cuban American Policy Center, Summer 1991.
86. Portes, p. 161.
87. Portes, pp. 54-55.

Notes on Chapter 7: The Amendments of 1982

1. See Public Law 97-205, June 29, 1982 and *1982 U. S. Congressional and Administrative News*, p. 177.
2. National Public Radio, *All Things Considered*, October 4, 1993 discussing *Shaw v. Reno*, 509 US ____ (1993).
3. Public Law 97-205, June 29, 1982.
4. Thernstrom, pp. 83-84.
5. Ibid., p. 108.
6. Ibid., p. 118.
7. United States Senate, *Senate Report No. 97-417*, 1982, reprinted in the *US Congressional Code and Administrative News 1982*, pp. 177, 206-207.
8. Chavez, p. 51.
9. Ibid., p. 51.
10. Some of the material in this and the next Section was found in *1982 U. S. Code, Congressional and Administrative News*, beginning p. 177.
11. Ibid.
12. Mach H. Jones, "The Voting Rights Act as an Intervention Strategy for Social Change: Symbolism or Substance," Foster, pp. 63-84, Mach H. Jones is Chairman of the Political Science Department at Atlanta University and a member of the Georgia ACLU.

13. Bullock, p. 33.
14. Chandler Davidson, "The Voting Rights Act: A Brief History," in Grofman, *Controversies in Minority Voting*, p. 39.
15. *1982 U. S. Code, Congressional and Administrative News*, beginning p. 177.
16. Senate Hearings, February 11, 1982, Robert Brison, City Attorney, Rome, Georgia as reported in *1982 U. S. Code, Congressional and Administrative News*, p. 322.
17. Ibid.
18. *Rogers v. Lodge*, 458 US 613 (1982).
19. Laughlin McDonald, "The 1982 Amendments of Section 2 and Minority Representation," in Grofman, *Controversies in Minority Voting*, p 71. Mr. McDonald is the head of the ACLU's Voting Rights Project.
20. *U. S. v. Marengo County*, 731 F.2d 1546 (1984).
21. *National Roster of Black Elected Officials*, Joint Center for Political Studies.
22. C. Robert Heath, "*Thornburg v. Gingles*: Unresolved Issues," *National Civic Review*, January 1, 1990, p. 50, describing *Thornburg v. Gingles*, 478 US 30 (1986).
23. Ibid.
24. Ibid.
25. Grofman, *Minority Representation and the Quest for Voting Equality*, p. 53.
26. C. Robert Heath, *Thornburg v. Gingles: Unresolved Issues*, National Civic Review, January 1, 1990, p 64
27. *Citizens for a Better Gretna v. City of Gretna, La*, 834 F.2d 496 (1987), Certiorari denied 492 US 905 (1989).
28. *Monroe v. City of Woodville, Mississippi*, 897 F.2d 763 (1990), Certiorari denied 498 US 822 (1990).
29. *Campos v. Baytown, Texas*, 840 F.2d 1240 (1988).
30. *Terrazas v. Clements*, 581 F.Supp. 1329 (1984).
31. Grofman, *Minority Representation and the Quest for Voting Equality*, p. 62, describing *McNeil v. Springfield Park District*, 851 F.2nd 937 (1988).
32. *Brewer v. Ham*, 876 F.2d 448 (1989).
33. *Port Arthur v. U. S.*, 459 US 159 (1982).
34. *NAACP v. City of Starke, Florida*, 712 F.Supp 1583 (1989).
35. *Alonzo v. Jones*, C-81-277. S. D. Texas (1983).
36. *Williams v. State Board of Elections*, 696 F.Supp 1563 (1983).
37. *Mississippi State Chapter, Operation PUSH v. Mabus*, 717 F.Supp. 1189 (1991), 932 F.2d 400 (1989).
38. *Skorepa v. City of Chula Vista*, 723 F.Supp. 1384 (1989).
39. *Kirksey v. Board of Supervisors of Hinds County*, 544 F.2nd 139 (1977).
40. Diaz, p. 18.
41. Grofman, *Minority Representation and the Quest for Voting Equality*, p. 120.
42. Sources: 1970: *Statistical Abstract of the United States* (1974, Tables 701, 705); 1988 U. S. Department of Commerce, Bureau of the Census, (1989, Table 4).
43. Chavez, p. 33.
44. *Garza v. the City of Los Angeles*, 918 F.2d 763 (1990).
45. *Smith v. Clinton*, 687 F.Supp. 1361 (1988), 488 US 988 (1988).

46. *Latino Political Action Committee v. City of Boston*, 784 F.2d 409 (1986).
47. *East Jefferson Coalition for Leadership and Development v. Jefferson Parish*, E. D. La., 691 F.Supp. 991 (1988).
48. *Washington v. Tensas Parish School Board*, 819 F.2d 609 (1987).
49. *Davis v. Bandemer*, 478 US 109 (1986).
50. *Karcher v. Daggett*, 462 US 725 (1983).
51. *Brooks v. Georgia State Board of Elections*, 90-272 (1990).
52. *Georgia State Board of Elections v. Brooks*, 775 F.Supp. 1470 (1989).
53. *Chisom v. Roemer*, 111 S Ct 2354 (1991). Also see O'Brien, David M., *Supreme Court Watch, 1993*. New York: W. W. Norton and Company, 1993, p. 75.
54. *Hoffman v. Maryland*, 928 F.2d 646 (1991).
55. Timothy G. O'Rourke, "The 1982 Amendments and the Voting Rights Paradox," in Grofman, *Controversies in Minority Voting*, p. 98.
56. Greg Henderson, UPI Newswire, February 25, 1991, concerning *Whitfield v. Clinton*, 90-383 (1990).
57. "Edgar signs voter's rights legislation," *AP Wire Service*, December 23, 1992.
58. *Recommendations for the United States Government Measurements of Race and Ethnicity*, Miami Florida: Cuban American National Council, Issue Brief No. 1, August 1994, p. 1.
59. Black, p. 127.
60. Ibid., p. 2.
61. Voting Rights Language Assistance Act of 1992, Public Law 102-344.
62. In 1975, Section 207 (3) of the Voting Rights Act defines: "The term 'language minorities' or 'language minority group' means persons who are American Indian, Asian American, Alaskan Natives, or of Spanish heritage."
63. Arthur M. Schlesinger, Jr., *The Disuniting of America, Reflections on a Multicultural Society*, W. W. Norton and Company, 1992. pp. 108-110.
64. Jim Boulet, *Dallas Morning News*, May 19, 1996, p. J1.
65. Jordan Moss, "Motor Voter: From Movement to Legislation," *Social Policy*, Winter 1993, pp. 20-31.
66. *Citizen's Guide to the National Voter Registration Act of 1993*, League of Women Voters Education Fund.
67. White House press release, May 20, 1993.
68. "Reno may sue 5 states over voter law." *Dallas Morning News*, January 12, 1995.
69. Press release, American Civil Liberties Union, January 25, 1995.
70. Press release, American Civil Liberties Union, July 24, 1995.
71. Human Serve Internet Server, www.essential.org/human_serve/ratios.html, September 19, 1996.
72. Rich Lowry, "Vote Fraud in America," *National Review*, June 17, 1966.
73. James Ragland, *Dallas Morning News*, March 11, 1991.
74. Payne, *Big D*, p. 370.
75. Ibid. pp. 374-375.
76. Henry Tatum, columnist, *Dallas Morning News*, February 10, 1984.
77. Dennis Holder, "The Forgotten Minority," *D Magazine*, September 1986.
78. Ibid.
79. *Williams v. City of Dallas, Texas*, 734 F.Supp 1317 (1990).

80. Chris Kelley, "Stronger Council suggested," *Dallas Morning News*, February 22, 1987, p. 29A.
81. Chris Kelley, "Hopefuls split on districts," *Dallas Morning News*, April 8, 1987, p. 1A.
82. Rena Penderson, Column, *Dallas Morning News*, April 15, 1987.
83. "Once seen as gadflies, pair gain legitimacy with suit," *Dallas Morning News*, September 4 1989.
84. "Housing Suit: Reopening case makes little sense," *Dallas Morning News*, January 16, 1992, p. 28A.
85. "Hispanics call for new council election system," *Dallas Morning News*, August 3, 1988.
86. Payne, *Big D*, p. 388.
87. *Williams v. City of Dallas, Texas*, 734 F.Supp 1317, 1990.
88. Williams, p. 148.
89. Ibid. p. 149.
90. Ibid., p. 156.
91. "Dallasites to study protesting," *Dallas Morning News*, August 20, 1989.
92. "US refuses to approve 10-4-1 plan," *Dallas Morning News*, October 17, 1989.
93. *Williams v. City of Dallas, Texas*, 734 F.Supp 1317, 1990.
94. Lori Stahl, "Redistricting battle frustrating Box," *Dallas Morning News*, May 7, 1991.
95. Ibid.
96. Richard R. Aguirre, "City leans toward test of ruling," *Dallas Morning News*, March 30, 1990, p. 1A.
97. *Dallas Morning News*, April 26, 1990.
98. Lauren Robinson, "12-1 plan hits court; rift grows," *Dallas Times Herald*, April 27, 1990, p. 1A.
99. James Ragland, "City wants to settle voting suit," *Dallas Morning News*, June 28, 1990, p. 1A.
100. Ibid.
101. Steve Scott, "Oak Cliff city plan still alive," *Dallas Morning News*, August 11, 1990.
102. Ibid.
103. William A. Scott, "Mayor wants Gonzalez to lead 14-1 campaign," *Dallas Times Herald*, August 30, 1990, p. 15A.
104. William A. Scott, "14-1 opponents decried as racist," *Dallas Times Herald*, October 11, 1990, p. 1A.
105. Lauren Robinson, "All's quiet after 14-1 bribe charge," *Dallas Times Herald*, October 18, 1990.
106. Ibid.
107. Payne, *Big D*, p. 378.
108. Stacey Freedenthal, "Benefit supports 14-1 plan," *Dallas Morning News*, October 29, 1990.
109. William A. Scott, "Price Furor spurs 14-1 foes," *Dallas Times Herald*, November 16, 1990, p. 1A.

110. Lawrence E. Young, "Seeking a minority voice," *Dallas Morning News*, November 18, 1990.
111. Quoted during a debate at Fritz Park by Lawrence E. Young, "North Dallas residents hear opposing sides of 14-1 debate," *Dallas Morning News*, November 29, 1990.
112. David Jackson, "Strauss sounds 14-1 alert," *Dallas Morning News*, November 30, 1990, p. 1A.
113. *Dallas Morning News*, December 10, 1990.
114. Richard R. Aguirre, "City has three options," *Dallas Times Herald*, December 13, 1990.
115. William A. Scott, "Action could take 5 years, $1.5 million," *Dallas Times Herald*, December 20, 1990, p. 1A.
116. James Ragland, "Judge: City warned on vote," *Dallas Morning News*, February 1, 1991, p. 23A.
117. James Ragland, "Judge set May 4 vote under 14-1," *Dallas Morning News*, February 2, 1991, p. 1A.
118. Lauren Robinson, "Dallas must hold May 4 election," *Dallas Times Herald*, February 2, 1991, p. 1A.
119. James Ragland, "Judge wants 14-1 plan by Feb. 20," *Dallas Morning News*, February 6, 1991, p. 23A.
120. William A. Scott, "City's 14-1 appeal shocks minorities," *Dallas Times Herald*, February 13, 1991, p. 1A.
121. Craig Flournoy, "Hispanics assail city's lawsuit plan," *Dallas Morning News*, February 14, 1991.
122. Jeffrey Weiss, "Boycott urged if Dallas maintains its 14-1 appeal." *Dallas Morning News*, February 14, 1991, p. 1A.
123. James Ragland, "Districting goal eludes city panel," *Dallas Morning News*, February 19, 1991, p. 15A.
124. James Ragland, "14-1 lines gerrymandered, witness says," *Dallas Morning News*, February 27, 1991, p. 25A.
125. Royce Hanson, "Dallas needs election system that facilitates racial politics," *Dallas Morning News*, March 10, 1991.
126. William A. Scott, "Bartos wants judge to probe," *Dallas Times Herald*, March 6, 1991, p. 1A.
127. Jeffrey Weiss, "SCLC targeting city council," *Dallas Morning News*, February 28, 1991, p. 25A.
128. Lauren Robinson, "Boycott imminent, city warned," *Dallas Times Herald*, March 8, 1991.
129. James Ragland, *Dallas Morning News*, March 11, 1991.
130. James Ragland, "Future of Dallas government in limbo after appeals ruling," *Dallas Morning News*, March 16, 1991, p. 1A.
131. Lauren Robinson, "Ink readied as weapon in 10-4-1," *Dallas Morning News*, March 20, 1991, p. 15A.
132. Lauren Robinson, "Attorney hints judge's claim false," *Dallas Times Herald*, April 11, 1991, p. 13A.

133. David Jackson, "Strauss admits to lying," *Dallas Morning News*, April 3, 1991, p. 1A.
134. David Jackson, "New 14-1 proposal touted," *Dallas Morning News*, May 1, 1991.
135. John Dunne, Assistant U. S. Attorney General, in a letter to Analeslie Muncy, May 6, 1991.
136. David Jackson, "Justice Department rejects 10-4-1," *Dallas Morning News*, May 7, 1991, p. 1A.
137. David Jackson, "Council to seek 14-1 settlement," *Dallas Morning News*, May 8, 1991, p. 1A.
138. David Jackson, "Council tells lawyers to settle lawsuit," *Dallas Morning News*, May 9, 1991, p. 1A.
139. David Jackson, "Council's divisions echo those of city," *Dallas Morning News*, May 25, 1991, p. 33A. Article references the May 20 council meeting.
140. David Jackson, "5 black districts favored," *Dallas Morning News*, June 20, 1991, p. 1A.
141. David Jackson, "Dallas adopts new 14-1 map," *Dallas Morning News*, June 27, 1991, p. 1A.
142. "Black plaintiffs dislike U. S. agency's approval of four-year mayor's term," *Dallas Morning News*, August 4, 1991, p. 40A.
143. League of Women Voters, *Dallas Morning News*, April 16, 1995, Special Supplement.
144. David Jackson, "Court rules on 10-4-1 intervenors," *Dallas Morning News*, September 25, 1991, p. 26A.
145. Ed Housewright, "Duncan to face Crenshaw in runoff for District 4 position," *Dallas Morning News*, November 6, 1991, p. 27A.
146. Lori Stahl, "Mayes ousts Ragsdale after bitter race," *Dallas Morning News*, November 20, 1991, p. 1A.
147. Lori Stahl, "Need for 14-1 vote stuns city officials," *Dallas Morning News*, September 16, 1992, p. 27A.
148. Payne, *Big D*, p. 395.
149. Ibid., p. 399.
150. Ibid., pp. 396-397.
151. Ibid., p. 412.
152. "Election rules unfair to blacks, court told," *Dallas Morning News*, October 4, 1994.
153. "Ron Kirk's dominance," *Dallas Morning News*, May 8, 1995, p. 11A.
154. Joseph Garcia, "Trustees to hear Hispanic demands," *Dallas Morning News*, November 26, 1991, p. 22A.
155. Melanie Lewis, "Dallas school board adopts remap plan," *Dallas Morning News*, December 17, 1991, p. 31A.
156. Wayne Slater, "Judges uphold congressional remap plan," *Dallas Morning News*, December 25, 1991, p. 1A.
157. "Changing Demographics," *Dallas Morning News*, March 4, 1995, p. 40A.
158. Sam Attlesey, "Judges void state remap boundaries," *Dallas Morning News*, January 11, 1992, p. 1A.

159. Gregg Cooke, "GOP's judicial activists," *Dallas Morning News*, January 15, 1992, p. 19A.
160. Sam Attlesey, "Remap plan upheld," *Dallas Morning News*, January 17, 1992, p. 1A.
161. "Redistricting mess," *Dallas Morning News*, August 10, 1992, p. 12A.
162. Terrence Stutz, "Federal judges restore GOP-backed remap," *Dallas Morning News*, August 22, 1992, p. 1A.
163. Sam Attlesey, "U. S. judicial panel upholds Democrats' remap of senate," *Dallas Morning News*, April 6, 1993, p. 1A.
164. Anne Belli, "Black judge's defeat fuels debate on vote's fairness," *Dallas Morning News*, November 5, 1992, p. 20A.
165. Sylvia Moreno, "State urged not to appeal judicial election ruling," *Dallas Morning News*, January 29, 1993, p. 36A.
166. Christy Hoppe, "Settlement of judicial suit urged," *Dallas Morning News*, February 12, 1993, p. 29A.
167. Christy Hoppe, "State leaders sign pact on election of judges," *Dallas Morning News*, March 26, 1993, p. 1A.
168. Christy Hoppe, "Morales, senators warn that racial unrest is possible," *Dallas Morning News*, April 2, 1993, p. 34A.
169. Todd J. Gillman, "Price rallies for judicial reform proposal," *Dallas Morning News*, May 20, 1993, p. 30A.
170. Todd J. Gillman, "5th Circuit questions judicial election plan," *Dallas Morning News*, May 25, 1993, p. 21A.
171. Christy Hoppe, "Appeals court upholds election system," *Dallas Morning News*, August 25, 1993, p. 1A.
172. "State to appeal U. S. court rejection of plan to increase minority judges," *Dallas Morning News*, August 26, 1993, p. 34A.
173. Anne Marie Kilday, "High court leaves election system for judges intact," *Dallas Morning News*, January 19, 1994, p. 25A.
174. Christy Hoppe, "Justice bars new courts," *Dallas Morning News*, November 18, 1994, p. 1A.
175. Tracy Everbach, "County OKs new districts in bid for more minority JPs, constables," *Dallas Morning News*, December 15, 1993, p. 29A.
176. Catalina Camia, "District's design is issue in race," *Dallas Morning News*, October 19, 1992, p. 19A.
177. "Suit seek congressional primary delay," *Dallas Morning News*, January 28, 1994, p. 27A.
178. Anne Marie Kilday, "Texas redistricting suit bound for trial this month," *Dallas Morning News*, June 5, 1994, p. 10A.
179. *Connor v. Johnson*, 265 F.Supp. 492 (1967), 402 US 690 (1971).
180. Sam Attesey, "Judges: Dallas-area district racially gerrymandered," *Dallas Morning News*, August 18, 1994, p. 1A.
181. "Deadline lifted for redrawing 3 congressional districts," *Dallas Morning News*, November 24, 1994, p. 21A.
182. *Shaw v. Reno* (Shaw I), 509 US 630 (1993).
183. *Miller v. Johnson*, 515 US 900 (1995).

184. *Bush v. Vera*, S. C. 94-805 (1996).
185. C. Patrick Morris, "Termination by Accountants: The Reagan Indian Policy," Lyden, p. 70.
186. *Buckanaga v. Sisseton Independent School District*, 804 F.2d 469 (1986).
187. *Windy Boy v. County of Big Horn*, 647 F.Supp. 1002 at 1007 (1986).
188. David Poppe, "Convert to capitalism," *Arizona Republic*, November 30, 1987, p. 1.
189. "U. S. panel investigates tribal rights," *Arizona Republic*, June 10, 1987, p. 1B.
190. Mark Shaffer, "Hearing will examine Navajo civil rights," *Arizona Republic*, August 13, 1987, p. 4B.
191. Mark Shaffer, "Navajos urged to adopt constitution," *Arizona Republic*, August 14, 1987, p. 1B.
192. Mark Shaffer, "Rights official threatens to subpoena tribal leaders," *Arizona Republic*, August 15, 1987, p. 1B.
193. "Navajos challenging subpoenas." *Arizona Republic*, July 19, 1988, p. 1B.
194. Bill Donovan, "Tribal lawyer to explain boycott," *Arizona Republic*, July 20, 1988, p. 7B.
195. Bill Donovan, "Senate rider backs tribe in rights-panel dispute," *Arizona Republic*, July 19, 1988, p. 4C.
196. Mark Shaffer, "Apache County told to start bolstering voting by Navajos," *Arizona Republic*, July 29, 1987, p. 5B.
197. Steve Yozwiak, "Statewide purge of voting roster delayed," *Arizona Republic*, December 19, 1987, p. 1B.
198. Mark Shaffer, "Indian voting rights still a battle royal," *Arizona Republic*, September 6, 1988, p. 1A.
199. Victoria Harker, "US threatens lawsuit on Indian voting rights," *Arizona Republic*, March 2, 1988, p. 1A.
200. Randy Collier, "U. S. sues state, 2 counties to bolster Indian voting," *Arizona Republic*, December 9, 1988, p. 1F.
201. Mark Shaffer, "Pact to give Navajo panel seats," *Arizona Republic*, November 4, 1988, p. B1
202. Guarione Diaz, editor, "Arizona appeals court upholds English-only law reversal," *The Council Letter: Cuban American National Council, Inc.*, Miami, Florida, December 1995, p. 2.
203. Carle Hodge, "Rush fizzled, began again, few problems," *Arizona Republic*, November 9, 1988, p. A11.
204. "Justice Department sues counties on English issue," *Arizona Republic*, December 9, 1988, p. E2.
205. John Winters, "Translation of voting data for Navajos mandated," *Arizona Republic*, May 23, 1989, p. A1.
206. Bordewich, p. 316.
207. Anthony Sommer, "MacDonald loses court argument," *Phoenix Gazette*, January 26, 1990, p. 7B.
208. Ibid., p. 319.
209. "Convictions upheld in '89 Navajo riot," *Phoenix Gazette*, November 8, 1994, p. 14B.

210. Policy speech by President Bush, June 14, 1991 as reported by Bordewich, p. 112.
211. See *Talton v. Mayes*, 163 US 376 (1986).
212. *Tracy v. Navajo Nation*, AZ Supreme Ct., No. CV-90-0407-SA, 1991, quoted from *Arizona Business Gazette*, May 10, 1991, p. 21.
213. *Phoenix Gazette*, September 5, 1992, p. 4B.
214. Steve Yozwiak, "Incumbents gain in legislature's redistricting plan." *Arizona Republic*, February 14, 1992, p. A1.
215. Barone, pp. 37, 57.
216. John Kolbe, "A crusade for Indian judges polarized," *Phoenix Gazette*, June 16, 1995, p. B5.
217. Michael Haederle, "Navajo students straddle 2 cultures," *Dallas Morning News*, April 16, 1995, p. 39A.
218. "Standing Ovation for Deer," *Indian Country Today*, July 21, 1993, quoted from Bordewich, p. 313.
219. Tim Giago, "No tribe is an island," *Phoenix Gazette*, May 22, 1995, p. 5B.
220. Brenda Norrell, "Navajo president against proposed statehood, urges passage of interior budget," *Indian Country Today*, January 27, 1996.
221. Davis, p. 117.
222. November 2, 1982 said by Miami Mayor Maurice Ferre.
223. "The 38 people who secretly guide Dade," *Miami Herald*, September 1, 1985.
224. Smiley, pp. 255-256.
225. "Schools believe white-flight is over," *Miami Herald*, November 10, 1983.
226. "Cuban-Americans hope to ride Reagan sweep into office," *Miami Herald*, September 2, 1984.
227. "Hispanic go for clout in voter registration," *Miami Herald*, April 27, 1984.
228. "Expected Cuban influx triggers old fears," *Miami Herald*, December 9, 1984.
229. "County Cubans leap at chance for citizenship," *Miami Herald*, February 4, 1985.
230. Cuban-American Policy Center, *Miami Mosaic: Ethnic Relations in Dade County*, Miami, 1986.
231. "Region more Latin but less Cuban," *Miami Herald*, September 12, 1988.
232. New exiles flocking to Dade," *Miami Herald*, April 11, 1987.
233. "U. S. offers work permits for Nicaraguan refugees," *Miami Herald*, July 9. 1987.
234. "Push begins to repeal anti-bilingual law," *Miami Herald*, July 3, 1987.
235. "Supporters of English target polls," *Miami Herald*, March 6, 1988.
236. Portes, p. 163.
237. Ibid., pp. 150-151.
238. "Civic power group breaking the mold with new members," *Miami Herald*, May 14, 1989.
239. The Cuban American Policy Center, *The Cubanization and Hispanicazation of Metropolitan Miami*, Miami, 1994.
240. ". . . With government and community leaders," *Miami Herald*, September 7, 1990.
241. "INS: Non-citizens voted in 1989 election," *Miami Herald*, March 9, 1991.
242. Ibid.
243. *Ethnic Block Voting and Polarization in Miami*, Cuban American Policy Center, Summer 1991.

NOTES 265

244. Ibid. p. 10.
245. "Neighborhoods show small gains in integration," *Miami Herald*, April 9, 1991.
246. "City's new elite addressing issues of community," *Miami Herald*, April 29, 1992.
247. "New members of Non-Group add diversity to leadership ranks," *Miami Herald*, December 19, 1992.
248. Lotz, p. 36.
249. "Charter proposals rebuffed metro tells group to get petition," *Miami Herald*, May 7, 1986.
250. "Suit claims racial bias in elections," *Miami Herald*, August 23, 1986.
251. "Metro proposes four district seats on commission," *Miami Herald*, September 3, 1986.
252. "Metro rescinds district plan," *Miami Herald*, September 5, 1986.
253. "Minorities seek district elections," *Miami Herald*, March 14, 1988.
254. "Judge cool to metro district elections," *Miami Herald*, March 30, 1988.
255. Ibid.
256. "Metro tables charter changes," *Miami Herald*, September 6, 1989.
257. "Debate over changing Dade's charter pits old guard against new," *Miami Herald*, February 11, 1990.
258. "Backers rip 1-shot vote on charter," *Miami Herald*, February 23, 1990.
259. "Court sends voting bias case back for review," *Miami Herald*, August 18, 1990.
260. "Dade seeks agreement on district elections," *Miami Herald*, October 22, 1990.
261. "Judge delays voting trial," *Miami Herald*, February 14, 1991.
262. "Metro again sets stage for vote on districts," *Miami Herald*, December 8, 1990.
263. "Judge delays voting trial," *Miami Herald*, February 14, 1991.
264. "Census data sets stage for redistricting," *Miami Herald*, April 1, 1991.
265. "Judge's rights record sparks debate," *Miami Herald*, May 6, 1990.
266. Ibid.
267. "Ryskamp furor comes up again in Senate," *Miami Herald*, July 1, 1991.
268. "Ryskamp won't hear two rights cases," *Miami Herald*, April 19, 1991.
269. "Plan broadens Dade Mayor's power," *Miami Herald*, May 24, 1991.
270. "At stake blueprint for Metro," *Miami Herald*, September 1, 1991.
271. Ibid.
272. "Vote on racial line thwarted districts," *Miami Herald*, September 4, 1991.
273. "Breakup of minority coalition . . .," *Miami Herald*, February 29, 1992.
274. "Metro may lose voting bias suit," *Miami Herald*, March 5, 1992.
275. "Activists blast electoral system," *Miami Herald*, June 4, 1992.
276. "Dade's at-large system an anachronism says ex-mayor," *Miami Herald*, June 13, 1992.
277. Diaz, p. 17.
278. "Suit may change face of Metro," *Miami Herald*, June 3, 1992.
279. Ibid.
280. "The old order passeth," *Miami Herald*, August 15, 1992.
281. "Judge scraps Metro election system," *Miami Herald*, August 15, 1992.
282. "Metro may not fight voting-rights ruling," *Miami Herald*, August 21, 1992.
283. "Metro offers three-part election plan," *Miami Herald*, September 19, 1992.
284. "Dade strong mayor wins easily on 3rd try," *Miami Herald*, October 2, 1992.

285. "Appeals court urged to restore Metro election system," *Miami Herald*, December 3, 1992.
286. Ibid.
287. "Your plan or mine?" *Miami Herald*, December 11, 1992.
288. "Mayor's seat tossed," *Miami Herald*, December 11, 1992.
289. "Metro districting proposal stirs up ethnic tensions," *Miami Herald*, December 19, 1992.
290. "Judge OKs 13-member Metro plan," *Miami Herald*, December 24, 1992.
291. "Rush is on," *Miami Herald*, January 27, 1993.
292. "Dade voters bewildered as election nears," *Miami Herald*, February 24, 1993.
293. "Judge clears way for election," *Miami Herald*, February 27, 1993.
294. "US sues to force bilingual election," *Miami Herald*, March 12, 1993.
295. "Metro's new faces not unfamiliar," *Miami Herald*, March 18, 1993.
296. "He fought for right and change," *Miami Herald*, April 26, 1993.
297. Barone, p. 333.
298. Diaz, p. 8-9.
299. *DeGrandy v. Johnson*, 512 US 997 (1994).
300. Ibid.
301. Ibid.
302. National Public Radio, *All Things Considered,* October 4, 1993.
303. *DeGrandy v. Johnson*, 512 US 997 (1994).
304. Ibid.

NOTES ON CHAPTER 8: THE UNRAVELING?

1. Lani Guinier, *The Tyranny of the Majority: Fundamental Fairness in Representative Democracy*. New York: The Free Press, 1994.
2. Melanie Lewis, "Demise of voter project leaves void in Mississippi," *Dallas Morning News*, August 3, 1992, p. 1A.
3. Richard Whittle, "New Congress to show racial, gender diversity," *Dallas Morning News*, November 5, 1992, p. 19A.
4. David McLemore, "Hispanic voter group, leader parting paths to chart new goals," *Dallas Morning News*, May 22, 1994, p. 45A.
5. Mercedes Olivera, "Voter education project doesn't plan to rest on laurels," *Dallas Morning News*, June 5, 1994, p. 36A.
6. White House press release, June 17, 1993.
7. "Blacks win control of Selma City Council," *The Washington Times*, August 27, 1993, p. A6.
8. *Presley v. Etowah County Commission*, 502 US 491 (1992).
9. *Voinovich v. Quilter*, 1993, 507 US ___ (1993).
10. O'Brien, p. 77.
11. *Holder v. Hall*, 512 US 874 (1994).
12. *Hays v. Louisiana*, 839 F.Supp. 1188 (1993).
13. "Shaw v. Reno Reaction," *The Washington Times*, July 15, 1993.
14. Steve McGonigle, "Supreme Court to Hear Louisiana Voting Rights Case," *Dallas Morning News*, December 10, 1994, p. 12A

NOTES 267

15. "Justice Department jumps to defense of pro-minority districts," *Washington Times*, February 23, 1995, p. A5.
16. Tracy Everbach, "GOP appointments seen as transforming federal courts," *Dallas Morning News*, October 22, 1992, p. 8A.
17. White House Press Release, July 27, 1994.
18. "Pressure against nominee grows," *Dallas Morning News*, June 2, 1993, p. 4A.
19. "Voting plans Guinier backed are used with little controversy," *Dallas Morning News*, June 6, 1993, p. 11A.
20. "Worcester County, Maryland," *Christian Science Monitor*, April 7, 1994, and "Worcester County, Maryland," *The Washington Star*, April 6, 1994.
21. *Miller v. Johnson*, 515 US 900 (1995).
22. Ibid.
23. David Jackson, "High court hears remapping case," *Dallas Morning News*, December 6, 1995, p. 4A.
24. "Black challenge to Tennessee districting fails," *Miami Herald*, October 3, 1995, p. 8B.
25. David Jackson, "Justices reject Texas congressional map," *Dallas Morning News*, June 14, 1996, p. 1.
26. *Bush v. Vera*, S. C. 94-805 (1996), Sandra Day O'Connor, concurring.
27. Ellis Cose, "Voting Rights Act, R.I.P.," *Newsweek*, Vol. 127, Issue 26, June 24, 1996, p. 36.

NOTES ON CHAPTER 9: OBSERVATIONS

1. Davidson, *Quiet Revolution in the South*, p. 374.
2. The 11 states reported are Alabama, Arkansas, Florida, Georgia, Louisiana, Mississippi, North Carolina, South Carolina, Tennessee, Texas, and Virginia.
3. *Statistical Abstract of the United States, 1993*, Table 713.
4. Ibid., Table 8.
5. "Latino/Non-Latino intermarriages increase," *The Council Letter*, Cuban American National Council, Inc., April 1995, p. 1, quoting Lucy Hood, "Latino intermarriages boom, produce 1.5 million children," *Hispanic Link Weekly Report*, Vol. 13, No. 10, March 6, 1995, pp. 1-2.
6. Chavez, p. 5.
7. *Holder v. Hall*, 512 US 874 (1994).
8. Bordewich, p.16.
9. Dave Kaplan, "Alternative Election Methods: A Fix for a Besieged System?" *Congressional Quarterly*, April 2, 1994, pp. 812-813.
10. Steven J. Brams and Peter C. Fishburn in Maisel, L. Sandy, Editor, *Political Parties and Elections in the United States: An Encyclopedia, Vol. 1*. New York: Garland, 1991, pp. 23-31.
11. Ibid.
12. Ibid.
13. *Statistical Abstract of the United States*, 1993, Tables 19 and 20.
14. National Public Radio, *All Things Considered*, August 29, 1995.

15. "Different Votes," *Time Magazine*, May 23, 1994, Vol. 143, Issue 21, p. 18.
16. Source: U. S. Bureau of the Census, Current Population Reports, Series P20, Nos. 453, 466.

INDEX

1883 Civil Rights Cases, 16, 66
Adoue, Jean Baptist, 31
AFL-CIO, 105
Aguirre, Pedro, 98
Ahkeah, Sam, 42
Allen v. State Board of Elections, 66, 70, 71, 84
Allen, George, 74, 97, 98, 99, 100
Alonzo v. Jones, 150, 257
annexation, 6, 88, 89, 90, 114, 121
Apache County v. United States, 76, 77
Astor, Vincent, 48
bail-out, 57, 67, 112, 113, 116, 122, 139, 143, 144, 156
Baker v. Carr, 20, 21
Baraka, Larry, 162
Bartos, Jerry, 168, 172, 174, 176
Batista, Fulgencio, 52
Beer v. United States, 116, 117, 127, 218
Blackmun, Harry, 123, 213, 215
Blacks United for Lasting Leadership v. City of Shreveport, Louisiana, 119
Blair, Fred, 127, 129
Board of Estimate of City of New York v. Morris, 155
Bolden v. Mobile, 119, 125, 137, 142
Breedlove v. Suttles, 68
Brewer v. Ham, 130
Breyer, Stephen, 218
Brickell, William, 47
Brooks, Allen, 27
Brown v. Board of Education, 21, 112
Bryan, John Neely, 23, 24
Bryan, William Jennings, 49
Bryant, John, 184
Buchmeyer, Jerry, 164, 165, 166, 167, 168, 173, 174, 175, 176, 184
Buckanaga v. Sisseton ISD, 186

Buerger, Jim, 169
Bureau of Indian Affairs, 37, 38, 39, 43, 44, 104
Burger, Warren, 121, 123
Burke County, 120
Burke, Jim, 204
Burns v. Richardson, 72
Bush v. Vera, 186, 219
Bush, George, 203, 214, 216
Bussie v. Governor of Louisiana, 91
Butler v. Thompson, 68
Cabell, Earl, 32, 33
Campos v. Baytown, Texas, 149
Carson, Kit, 35, 37
Castro, Fidel, 52, 134, 135
Castro, Raul, 105
Catfish Club, 30
CGS, 100
Charter Review Commission, 166
Cherokee Nation v. Georgia, 35
Chiscilly, Deshna, 39
Chisom v. Roemer, 155
Citizens Association, 26, 27, 28, 29
Citizens for a Better Gretna v. City of Gretna, 148
Cits. See Citizens Association
City of Petersburg, Virginia v. United States, 90
City of Rome, Georgia v. United States, 122
Clinton, Bill, 160, 211, 212, 216
Cloward, Richard, 159, 160
Codetalker, 42, 45
Cody, Steven, 200, 201, 202, 203, 204, 206, 209
Colegrove v. Green, 19, 20
Collins, Jim, 168
Collins, John S., 48
Collins, Mary, 205, 206, 208

Connor v. Johnson, 70, 185
CRC. See Charter Review Commission
Creeks, 47
Crenshaw, Marvin, 164, 165, 166, 170, 177, 179
cumulative voting, 217
Cuomo, Mario, 160
Dallas Citizens Council, 30, 33
Davis v. Bandemer, 154
DeGrandy v. Johnson, 210
Dinétah, 34
Dodge, Chee, 37, 38, 39, 41
Dodge, Thomas, 40
Dougherty County, Georgia v. White, 118
Dunne, John, 159, 175, 176, 177
Dusch v. Davis, 73
Dusseau, Charles, 202
Duvall, Randy, 204
East Caroll Parish School Borad v. Marshall, 126
East Jefferson Coalition for Leadership and Development v. Jefferson Parish, 154
East, John, 143, 145
Edy, John, 29
Eisenhower, Dwight, 68, 71, 123
Elk v. Wilkins, 36, 131
Elkins, Jane, 24
Ellis, Rodney, 183
Ely v. Klahr, 102
Emory, Emerson, 126
equal protection clause, 12
Erwin, Sam, 84
Estes, Joe, 97
Evans, Jack, 128, 129
Evans, John, 177
Evers v. State Board of Commissioners, 87
Ex Parte Virginia, 55
Ferguson, Betty, 202, 205

Ferguson, Billy, 204
Ferré, Maurice, 107, 195, 200, 205, 208
Fillilove v. Klutznick, 123
Flagler Street, 209
Flagler, Henry, 48
Folsom, Robert, 125, 128
Fonteneda, Hernando, 46
Forrest County, 61
Fortson v. Dorsey, 72
Galloway, C. A., 73
Garcia, Domingo, 168
Garza v. the City of Los Angeles, 150, 153
Gaston County v. United States, 72, 81
Georgia State Board of Elections v. Brooks, 155
Georgia v. United States, 87, 88
Ginsburg, Ruth, 215, 218
Godfry, Arthur, 51
Goldblatt v. City of Dallas, 74
Goldblatt, Max, 74, 97, 128, 130
Gomillion v. Lightfoot, 20, 62, 121
Goodluck v. Apache County, 106, 130, 131
Graham, Donald, 204, 205, 206, 207
Graves v. Barnes, 114
Greer, Bob, 162, 175
Grovy v. Townsend, 18
Gunn v. Chickasaw County, Mississippi, 149
Hale County v. U. S., 119
Hamilton, Alexander, 9, 116
Hanson, Royce, 174
Harding, Warren G., 48
Harlan, John, 68, 69, 71
Harper v. Virginia Board of Elections, 68
Harrington, Jim, 182
Harrison v. Laveen, 43
Haskie, Leonard, 190
Hays v. Louisiana, 216

INDEX

Heggins v. City of Dallas, Texas, 127
Heggins, Elsie, 127, 128, 129, 130, 162
Helms, Jesse, 143
Hoffman v. Maryland, 155
Holbrook, 193
Holbrook Unified School District, 189
Holder v. Hall, 215, 225
Holmes, Zan, 73
Horry County, South Carolina v. U. S., 119
Houston v. Haley, 148
Hruska, Roman, 114
Hutcheson, Ray, 166
Hyde, Henry, 138, 139, 140, 158
Ickes, Harold, 41
Indian Reorganization Act, 40
Johnson, Eddie Bernice, 184
Johnson, Lyndon, 46, 53, 54, 55, 65, 66, 160
Johnson, Peter, 175
Jonsson, Erik, 33, 96
Jordon v. Winter, 146
Karcher v. Daggett, 154
Katzenbach v. Morgan, 68
Katzenbach, Nicholas, 54, 59, 62, 66
Kennedy, Anthony, 137, 155, 210, 212, 215, 218
Kennedy, John, 32, 52, 135
Kennedy, Robert, 22
Kennedy, Ted, 68, 105
Kessler, George, 27
Kirkpatrick v. Preisler, 77, 154
Kirksey v. Board of Supervisors, 120, 151
Klahr v. Goddard, 46, 75
Klahr v. Williams, 77, 102
Klahr, Gary, 45, 46, 75, 77, 78, 102
Ku Klux Klan, 25, 28, 50, 66
Lassiter v. Northampton Election Board, 58, 69
Latino Political Action v. Boston 153

Lau v. Nichols, 93
Lau, Kinney, 93
LEAD, 100
Leahy, David, 198
Ledbetter Homeowners Association, 165
LEP, 158
Lindsley, Henry, 26, 27
Lipman, David, 205
Lipscomb v. Jonsson, 98
Lipscomb v. Wise, 98, 99
Lipscomb, Al, 96, 97, 98, 127, 162, 164, 166, 168, 170, 171, 172, 173, 176
literacy test, 19, 22, 54, 60, 61, 63, 64, 68, 72, 83, 91, 92, 110, 111, 112, 113
Lockridge, Joseph, 73
Lodge v. Buxton, 120
Long Walk, 36, 44
Louisiana v. U. S., 18
LULAC, 182, 183
MacDonald, Peter, 42, 44, 78, 101, 102, 104, 105, 131, 187, 189, 190
MacGuire v. Amos, 87
Mahon, Judge, 98, 99, 126
MALDEF, 109, 110, 163
manifest destiny, 35
Mariel, 134, 195, 207
Marshall, John, 9
Martinez, Anita, 74, 98
Martinez, Rene, 163
McCool, Mike, 176
McCulloch v. Maryland, 9
McDuffie Riot, 134, 195, 207
McDuffie, Arthur, 133
McGovern, George, 105
Medrano, Recardo, 129
Medrano, Ricardo, 127, 129
Meek, Carrie, 200, 204, 205, 207
Merrion v. Jicarilla Apache Tribe, 132
Mfume, Kweisi, 214, 216
Miller v. Johnson, 218
Minyard, Thomas, 103

Mississippi State Chapter, Operation PUSH v. Mabus, 151
Mobile v. Bolden, 123
Mondale, Walter, 105
Monroe County, 132
Monroe v. City of Woodville, Mississippi, 149
Montana v. United States, 132
Moore v. Leflore County Board of Elections Commissioners, 89
Moore, Harry, 51
Morales, Dan, 183
Morris v. Gressette, 119
Muncy, Analeslie, 176
NAACP, 19, 51, 80, 101, 117, 125, 183, 203, 210, 215
NAACP v. City of Starke, Florida, 150
Nevett v. Sides, 122
Nixon v. Condon, 18
Nixon v. Herndon, 18
Nixon, Richard, 81, 84
O'Connor, Sandra, 148, 214
Oberwetter, James, 173
one-man, one-vote, 6, 21, 70, 75, 91, 97, 153, 155, 213, 216
ONEO, 44
Oregon v. Mitchell, 91
Organization, The, 29
Osburn, Randal, 174
Osceola, Chief, 47
Packingham, Ralph, 204
Panola County, 60
Patterson, Lucy, 98
Pauken, Tom, 171, 172, 174
Penales, Alex, 202, 204
Perkins v. Matthews, 89
Piven, Frances, 159, 160
Plessy v. Ferguson, 16
Poff, Richard, 84, 85
poll tax, 5, 58, 64, 68
Port Arthur v. U.S., 150

Porter v. Hall, 40
Powell v. McCormack, 12
Powell, Adam Clayton, 12
Powell, Lewis, 122, 123
Presley v. Etowah County Commission, 212
Price, John Wiley, 129, 162, 171, 179, 183
Ragsdale, Diane, 162, 164, 166, 170, 172, 173, 177, 178
Rankin, Robert, 109
Reagan, Ronald, 125, 130, 135, 138, 141, 159, 182, 202, 216
Reconstruction, 13, 15, 16, 17, 25, 61, 66
Reconstruction Amendments, 12
Reeb, Reverend, 54
Rehnquist, William, 123, 155
Reilly, John, 48
Relocation Act, 105
results test, 71, 125, 137, 138, 144, 145
retrogression, 116, 117, 176, 218
Reynolds v. Sims, 6, 21, 75, 102
Richards, Ann, 181, 183
Robinson, Marvin, 163, 164
Rogers v. Lodge, 145
Rucker, Jerry, 164
Rutherford Hayes, 16
Ryskamp, Kenneth, 200, 201, 202, 203, 204
Sadowski, Bill, 200
Sandinista, 132
Santa Clara Pueblo v. Martinez, 131, 187
Sausedo, Dominga, 140
Scalia, Antonin, 155, 182, 185, 210
Schoelkoph, John, 97, 98, 100
SCLC, 53, 55, 80, 167, 173, 174, 175
Seastrunk v. Burns, 146
Selma, Alabama, 1, 53, 54, 55, 60, 212
Seminoles, 47

INDEX

Shaw v. Reno, 184, 185, 213, 216, 227
Shirley v. Superior Court, 103
Shirley, Tom, 103
Simpson, Lee, 130
Single-shot voting, 7, 95, 139
Skorepa v. City of Chula Vista, 151
Smith v. Allwright, 18
Smith v. Clinton, 153
Smitherman, Joe, 212
Souter, David, 215, 218
South Carolina v. Katzenbach, 66, 76, 85, 87
Stevens, John, 123, 127, 155, 213, 215, 218
Stevenson, Adlai, 32
Stewart, Potter, 68, 87, 88, 123
Strauss, Annette, 164, 165, 166, 170, 172, 174, 175, 176
Student Non-violent Coordinating Committee, 53
Susan B. Anthony, 13
SVREP, 211
Tandy, Charles, 169
Taylor v. McKeithen, 91
Teele, Arthur, 202, 205, 206, 208
termination, 43
Terrazas v. Clements, 149
Terrell Election Law, 18, 30
The City of Richmond v. U. S., 89
The City of Rome, Georgia v. U. S., 123
Thomas v. Mimes, 89
Thornburg v. Gingles, 147, 148, 153, 213
Thornton, Robert, 30, 31, 32, 33
Thurmond, Strom, 115, 125, 143
Torres v. Sachs, 93
Tracy v. Navajo Nation, 191, 192
Tuttle, Judge, 126
U. S. v. Hale County, Alabama, 118
U. S. v. Cruikshank, 16
U. S. v. Louisiana, 61, 92

U. S. v. Marengo County [Alabama] Commission, 145
U. S. v. McBratney, 41
U. S. v. Mississippi, 92
U. S. v. Reese, 16
U. S. v. Uvalde Consolidated School District, 119
U. S. v. Wheeler, 132
United Jewish Organizations of Williamsburgh, Inc. v. Carey, 120, 121
Valdes, Jorge, 197
VEP, 211
Voinovich v. Quilter, 213
Voter Education Project. See VEP
Washington v. Tensas Parish School Board, 154
Weaver v. Muckleroy, 90
Webber, Gary, 125
Whitcomb v. Chavis, 94, 98
White v. Regester, 94, 120, 122, 125, 137, 139
White, Byron, 88, 117, 120, 123, 156, 213
Whitfield v. Arkansas Democratic Party, 150
Whitfield v. Clinton, 156
Wiggins, Kevin, 182
Williams v. State Board of Elections, 151, 257
Williams, Roby, 29
Williams, Roy, 162, 164, 165, 169, 170, 171, 172
Windy Boy v. County of Big Horn, 187
Worcester v. Georgia, 35
Yanito v. Barber, 103
Yarborough, Ralph, 93
Zah, 187
Zangara, Guiseppi, 49
Zimmer factors, 95, 99, 123, 142
Zimmer v. McKeithen, 94, 138, 148

About the Author

DAVID MICHAEL HUDSON is a senior manager and computer technologist for a major United States corporation. Politically active during Dallas's redistricting and voting rights struggles, he became personally engrossed in the study of United States voting law. *Along Racial Lines* is the product of four years of intensive research conducted in law libraries, newspaper archives, and on location at some of the nation's greatest modern voting rights struggles. David Hudson received a degree in Statistics from the University of Texas and studied Business Administration at Southern Methodist University's graduate school.

About the Author

DAVID MICHAEL HUDSON is a senior manager and computer technologist for a major United States corporation. Politically active during Dallas's redistricting and voting rights struggles, he became personally engrossed in the study of United States voting law. *Along Racial Lines* is the product of four years of intensive research conducted in law libraries, newspaper archives, and on location at some of the nation's greatest modern voting rights struggles. David Hudson received a degree in Statistics from the University of Texas and studied Business Administration at Southern Methodist University's graduate school.

STUDIES IN LAW AND POLITICS

The new series Studies in Law and Politics is devoted to texts and monographs that explore the multidimensional and multidisciplinary areas of law and politics. Subject matters to be addressed in this series include, but will not be limited to: constitutional law; civil rights and liberties issues; law, race, gender, and gender orientation studies; law and ethics; women and the law; judicial behavior and decision-making; legal theory; sociology of law; comparative legal systems; criminal justice; courts and the political process; and other topics on the law and the political process that would be of interest to law and politics scholars. Submission of single-author and collaborative studies, as well as collections of essays are invited.

David A. Schultz, *General Editor*
1120 St. Clair Avenue
St. Paul, MN 55105